Managing Quality

Fourth Edition

EDITED BY BARRIE G. DALE

Blackwell
Publishing

© 1999, 2003 by Blackwell Publishing Ltd
except for editorial material and organization © 1999, 2003 by Barrie G. Dale

350 Main Street, Malden, MA 02148-5018, USA
108 Cowley Road, Oxford OX4 1JF, UK
550 Swanston Street, Carlton South, Melbourne, Victoria 3053, Australia
Kurfürstendamm 57, 10707 Berlin, Germany

The right of Barrie G. Dale to be identified as the Author of the
Editorial Material in this Work has been asserted in accordance with the
UK Copyright, Designs, and Patents Act 1988.

First edition published 1990 by Philip Allan
Second edition published 1994 by Prentice Hall Europe
Third edition published 1999 by Blackwell Publishers Ltd
Reprinted 2000 (twice), 2001, 2002

Library of Congress Cataloging-in-Publication Data
Managing quality / edited by Barrie G. Dale. – 4th ed.
    p. cm.
Includes bibliographical references and index.
ISBN 0–631–23614–7 (pbk : alk. paper)
1. Engineering management. 2. Total quality management. I. Dale, B. G.

TA190 .M38 2003
658.5′62–dc21

2002151835

A catalogue record for this title is available from the British Library.

Set in 10/11^{1}/$_{2}$pt Galliard
by Graphicraft Limited, Hong Kong
Printed and bound in the United Kingdom
by MPG Books Ltd, Bodmin, Cornwall

For further information on
Blackwell Publishing, visit our website:
http://www.blackwellpublishing.com

Contents

Figures

Tables and boxes

Tables

Boxes

Standards

The standards listed here are referred to within this book. Copies of the standards can be obtained from BSI, London or ISO, Geneva.

British Standards

BS EN 12973 (2000), *Value Management*. London: British Standards Institution.

BS EN ISO9000 (2000), *Quality Management Systems: Fundamentals and Vocabulary*. London: British Standards Institution.

BS EN ISO9001 (2000), *Quality Management Systems*. London: British Standards Institution.

BS EN ISO9001 (2000), *Quality Management Systems: Requirements*. London: British Standards Institution.

BS EN ISO9004 (2000), *Quality Management Systems: Guidance for Performance Improvements*. London: British Standards Institution.

BS4778 (1991), *Quality Vocabulary*, part 2: *Quality Concepts and Related Definitions*. London: British Standards Institution.

BS5760 (1991), *Reliability of Systems, Equipment and Components*, Part 5: *Guide to Failure Modes, Effects and Criticality Analysis (FMEA) and FMECA*. London: British Standards Institution.

BS600 (1935), *The Application of Statistical Methods to Industrial Standardisation and Quality Control*. London: British Standards Institution.

BS600R (1942), *Quality Control Charts*. London: British Standards Institution.

BS6143 (1990), *Guide to the Economics of Quality*, part 2: *Prevention Appraisal and Failure Model*. London: British Standards Institution.

BS6143 (1992), *Guide to the Economics of Quality*, part 1: *Process Cost Model*. London: British Standards Institution.

BS7000 (1989), *Design Management Systems*, Part 1: *Guide to Managing Product Design*. London: British Standards Institution.

BS7782 (1994), *Control Charts: General Guide and Introduction (ISO7870: 1993)*. London: British Standards Institution.

BS7785 (1994), *Shewhart Control Charts (ISO8258: 1991)*. London: British Standards Institution.

BS8600 (1999), *Complaints Management Systems: Design and Implementation*. London: British Standards Institution.

BS8800 (1996), *Guide to Occupational Health and Safety Management Systems*. London: British Standards Institution.

BSI-OHSAS 18001 (1999), *Occupational Health and Safety Series Specification*. London: British Standards Institution.

International Standards

Note that the ISO series is designated BS EN ISO in the UK and Europe.

ISO10011-1 (1990), *Guidelines for Auditing Quality Systems*, Part 1: *Auditing*. Geneva: International Organization for Standardization.

ISO10011-2 (1991), *Guidelines for Auditing Quality Systems*, Part 2: *Qualification Criteria for Quality Systems Auditors*. Geneva: International Organization for Standardization.

ISO10011-3 (1991), *Guidelines for Auditing Quality Systems*, Part 3: *Management of Audit Programmes*. Geneva: International Organization for Standardization.

ISO10013 (1995), *Guidelines for Developing Quality Manuals*. Geneva: International Organization for Standardization.

ISO14001 (1996), *Environmental Management Systems: Specification with Guidance for Use*. Geneva: International Organization for Standardization.

ISO19011 (2001), *Guidelines on Quality and Environmental Auditing*. Geneva: International Organization for Standardization.

ISO9001 (1994), *Quality Systems: Model for Quality Assurance in Design, Development, Production, Installation and Servicing*. Geneva: International Organization for Standardization.

ISO9001 (2000), *Quality Management Systems: Requirements*. Geneva: International Organization for Standardization.

ISO9004 (2000), *Quality Management Systems: Guidelines for Performance Improvements*. Geneva: International Organization for Standardization.

Abbreviations

ABC	Activity-Based Costing	CIPD	Chartered Institute of Personnel and Development
APQP	Advanced Product Quality Planning		
AQ+	Aeroquip Quality Plus	CPA	Critical Path Analysis
AQA	Australian Quality Award	Cpk	Process Capability Index
AQAP	Allied Quality Assurance Publications	CQAD	Corporate Quality Assurance Department
AQL	Acceptable Quality Level	CRIP	Catch, Reflect, Improve, Pass
ASI	American Supplier Institute	CRISP	Catch-Reflect-Improve-Scrutinize-Pass
ASQC	American Society for Quality Control (now the American Society for Quality)	CWQC	Company-Wide Quality Control
		DOE	Design of Experiments
B2B	Business-to-Business	DPA	Departmental Purpose Analysis
BPM	Business Process Management	DPU	Defects Per Unit
BPR	Business Process Re-engineering	DTI	Department of Trade and Industry
BSI	British Standards Institution	EC	European Commission
BSS	British Standards Society	EDI	Electronic Data Interchange
BU	Business Unit	EFQM	European Foundation for Quality Management
CAD	Computer-Aided Design		
CAM	Computer-Aided Manufacture	EMAS	Eco-Management and Audit System
CANDO	Cleanliness, Arrangement, Neatness, Discipline and Orderliness	EMS	Environmental Management System
		EOQ	European Organization for Quality
CAPD	Check-Act-Plan-Do	EPSRC	Engineering and Physical Sciences Research Council
CEDAC	Cause-and-Effect Diagrams with Addition of Cards		
		EQA	European Quality Award
CEN	European Committee for Standardization	ERP	Enterprise Resources Planning
		EVA	Economic Value Added
CENELEC	European Committee for Electrotechnical Standardization	FMEA	Failure Mode and Effects Analysis
		FPL	Florida Power and Light Company
CEO	Chief Executive Officer	FTA	Fault Tree Analysis

GAO	General Accounts Office	PDPC	Process Decision Program Chart
GE	General Electric	PDSA	Plan-Do-Study-Act
GM	General Manager	PERA	Production Engineering Research
HR	Human Resources		Association
HRM	Human Resources Management	PERT	Programme Evaluation and Review
IMS	Integrated Management Systems		Technique
IQA	Institute of Quality Assurance	PIMS	Profit Impact of Market Strategy
ISO	International Organization for	PKI	Public Key Infrastructure
	Standardization	POC	Price of Conformance
IT	Information Technology	PONC	Price of Non-Conformance
JIT	Just-In-Time	P*pk*	Preliminary Process Capability Index
JUSE	Japanese Union of Scientists and	PPM	Parts Per Million
	Engineers	PR	Public Relations
KJ	Kawakita Jiro	QCD	Quality Cost and Delivery
KPI	Key Performance Indicator	QCs	Quality Circles
LSL	Lower Specification Limit	QFD	Quality Function Deployment
MBNQA	Malcolm Baldrige National Quality	QM	Quality Management
	Award	Q-MAP	Quality Management Activity
MBO	Management by Objectives		Planning
MITI	Ministry of International Trade and	QSATs	Quality Service Action Teams
	Industry	QSG	Quality Steering Group
MOD	Ministry of Defence	QUENSH	Quality Environment Safety Health
MRO	Maintenance, Repair and	R&D	Research and Development
	Operating	RPN	Risk Priority Number
MRP II	Manufacturing Resources Planning	RPQ	Relative Perceived Quality
NACCB	National Accreditation Council for	SABAC	Society of British Aerospace
	Certification Bodies		Companies
NAMAS	National Measurement	SDT	Supplier Development Team
	Accreditation Service	SLA	Service-Level Agreement
NATLAS	National Testing Laboratory	SMED	Single Minute Exchange of Die
	Accreditation Service	SMMT	Society of Motor Manufacturers
NATO	North Atlantic Treaty Organization		and Traders
NIST	National Institute of Technology	SMS	Safety Management Systems
np	Number Defective Charts	S/N	Signal-to-Noise
NWW	North West Water	S&P	Standard and Poor
OEM	Original Equipment Manufacturer	SPC	Statistical Process Control
OH	Occupational Health	SQA	Supplier Quality Assurance
OHSAS	Occupational Health and Safety	STA	Success Tree Analysis
	Series	SWOT	Strength, Weakness, Opportunities
OH&SMS	Occupational Health and Safety		and Threats
	Management Systems	TARP	Technical Assistance Research
O&M	Organization and Method		Programs
p charts	Proportion/percentage charts	TOPS	Team-Orientated Problem-Solving
PAF	Prevention-Appraisal-Failure	TOR	Terms of Reference
PAL	Pooling, Allying and Linking Across	TPM	Total Productive Maintenance
	Organizations	TQ	Total Quality
PAT	Project Action Team	TQC	Total Quality Control
PDCA	Plan-Do-Check-Act	TQM	Total Quality Management

TQMSAT	Total Quality Management Sustaining Audit Tool	UMIST	University of Manchester Institute of Science and Technology
TQSG	Total Quality Steering Group	USL	Upper Specification Limits
UK	United Kingdom	VFO	Vital Few Objectives
UKAS	United Kingdom Accreditation Service	XML	Extensible Mark-up Language
		YIT	Yield Improvement Teams

Contributors

John Aldridge is Quality Manager with Siemens Standard Drives, Congleton.

Allan Brown is Professor of Human Resources Management, Edith Cowan University, Australia.

Bernard Burnes is Senior Lecturer in Operations Management, Manchester School of Management, UMIST.

Ian Ferguson is Managing Director of Ferguson Associates, Birmingham.

David Lascelles is Managing Director of David Lascelles Associates, Carrington Business Park, Manchester.

Roy Lee is Squadron Leader, Support Management Group, Royal Air Force, Wyton.

Barbara Lewis is Professor of Marketing, Manchester School of Management, UMIST.

Rory Love is Quality Engineer, Alexanders Ltd., Falkirk.

John Macdonald is Managing Director of John Macdonald Associates, Surrey.

Peter Shaw was TQM Project Officer, Manchester School of Management, UMIST.

Rolf Visser is Chair of investment company, AAA, Amsterdam, Holland.

Adrian Wilkinson is Professor of Human Resource Management, University of Loughborough.

George Wilkinson was Operations Manager, British Telecom, Manchester.

Roger Williams is Professor of Business and Management, Erasmus University, Rotterdam, Holland.

Preface

The first edition of *Managing Quality* sold well and the second and third editions sold even more copies which, according to the publisher, is unusual for a book of this type. The fourth edition builds on the success of these previous editions.

In the book the term total quality management (TQM) is used to describe the process of transformation by which all parts of the organization have a focus on quality with the ultimate objective of customer satisfaction and delight. Some people argue that the term TQM has fallen out of use, with directors and managers regarding it as a fallen star and a jaded concept. They have then moved on to what they perceive to be newer, more fashionable concepts (for example, excellence, benchmarking, business process re-engineering and customer focus). Other companies are persevering in their attempts to make progress on their TQM journey but struggling to ensure that the initiative survives and that benefits are still being derived. Another set of companies has carried on operating to the principles of TQM, sometimes unknowing, under the umbrella of what are perceived to be more fashionable themes such as excellence and organizational performance improvement. However, irrespective of what an organization terms an initiative, quality as a competitive reality in the global marketplace remains as powerful as it was when the first edition was launched. There is little doubt that in a number of companies and industries the issue of improvement in the quality of products and services remain urgent. Therefore in this book I am sticking to the term TQM.

In the spirit of continuous improvement a complete revision of the book has been undertaken with some chapters having undergone extensive revision and additional chapters introduced to reflect developments in the field; for example, new material has been introduced on: the received wisdom on TQM; business-to-business, old-economy businesses and the quality function; and integrated management systems. In addition, there has been some reordering and reconfiguration of material and changes to terminology, and two chapters have been dropped.

The book is a very comprehensive TQM text and has developed a track record and following amongst students, academics and practitioners. Its purpose is to provide the reader with an appreciation of the concepts and principles of TQM. It has proved to be a wide-ranging source of reference for the many tools, techniques and systems which are associated with the concept. The feedback indicates that the book has been useful to industrialists, management consultants, academics, and undergraduate and postgraduate students from a variety of disciplines; TQM is not the special province of one group of people or one discipline. People studying for professional examinations which involve considerations of quality have also benefited from use of the book.

In a book of this size and format it is not easy to decide the depth and detail of the text, what is to be put in and what is to be left out, and who should contribute. The comments from reviews and users of the previous editions and the views of colleagues at UMIST and elsewhere have assisted in this task. I have tried to achieve a balance between the number of contributions from practitioners and those from the academic community; the views and ideas expressed by both parties are supportive of each other. I believe this mixture of approaches under one cover adds to the value of the book.

I hope readers will read the whole book to gain an understanding of the breadth and depth of TQM. However, most of the chapters do stand alone and readers may choose to dip into the book in order to learn more about a particular subject.

The subject of TQM is vast. There are many issues and interfaces to consider, and there are a considerable number of tools, techniques and systems which an organization can use to assist it in the introduction and development of the concept. An attempt has been made in the text to cover the main aspects and functions of TQM, from identifying customer needs and requirements through to quality planning, supply and subcontract, human resources, and production/operations. While there is nothing particularly radical in the text, the book does cover the main concepts and issues currently being debated and considered by business leaders throughout the world. The academic contributors have also outlined some of their recent research findings. I do hope that readers will find some new ideas and angles on subjects which have been brought to their attention.

The brief given to the contributors was to keep the level of technical detail to a minimum and to write in non-specialist language. This is much easier in some subjects than others, but I believe that this objective has been achieved, and hope the reader will find that the structure of the book is logical and the content is clear and free from confusing jargon.

For the purposes of presentation, the text is conveniently arranged into four main groups: the development, introduction and sustaining of TQM; the business context of TQM; quality management systems, tools and techniques; and TQM through continuous improvement. The initiative for editing and contributing to the first edition of this book arose from the UMIST TQM research and education and training activities. These activities have remained at a very high level during the intervening period with the award of a number of major research contracts. Supported by the responses and comments with respect to the early editions, I believe the need for the book has become even stronger. It is to be hoped that, through study of the text, readers will be encouraged to take up the challenge of strengthening their commitment and dedication to TQM and continuous improvement.

In my role as editor I have attempted to ensure that each topic is adequately covered in breadth and depth and is presented simply and clearly. Subject to these constraints I have tried not to interfere with contributors' styles because I believe an author's style is an integral part of getting his or her message across to the reader. I should add too that apart from the chapters bearing my name, the views and opinions expressed in individual contributions are those of the authors and not myself.

Finally, I wish to thank all the contributors for making this book possible. I have learned much from them. I hope the readers will too.

Barrie Dale
United Utilities Professor of Quality Management
Head of the Manchester School of Management
UMIST
Manchester
UK

part one

The Development, Introduction and Sustaining of Total Quality Management (TQM)

The purpose of part 1 is to introduce the reader to some of the fundamentals of TQM. It deals with how to introduce TQM into an organization and its subsequent development. Sustaining TQM is far from easy, and the final chapter examines issues to which attention needs to be given. It contains the following seven chapters:

Chapter 1 – TQM: An Overview
Chapter 2 – The Role of Management in TQM
Chapter 3 – The Received Wisdom on TQM
Chapter 4 – The Introduction of TQM
Chapter 5 – A Framework for the Introduction of TQM
Chapter 6 – Levels of TQM Adoption
Chapter 7 – Sustaining TQM

Chapter 1 examines the evolution of *quality management* ('co-ordinated activities to direct and control an organization with regard to quality') from *inspection* ('conformity evaluation by observation and adjustment accompanied as appropriate by measurement, testing or gauging') to *quality control* ('part of quality management focused on fulfilling quality requirements') to *quality assurance* ('part of quality management focused on providing confidence that quality requirements will be fulfilled' (BSEN ISO 9000 (2000)) and finally to *Total Quality Management* (TQM). In describing this evolution a comparative analysis is made of the essential difference between detection- and prevention-based approaches. The key elements of TQM are also discussed. TQM is not defined in BSEN ISO 9000 (2000) but, put simply, it is the mutual co-operation of everyone in an organization and associated business processes to produce products and services which meet and, hopefully, exceed the needs and expectations of customers. In describing this evolution a comparative analysis is made of the essential differences between detection- and prevention-based approaches. The key elements of TQM are also discussed.

Chapter 2 outlines the main reasons why senior management should become personally involved in TQM. It examines what they need to know about TQM and what they need to do in terms of actions. The role of middle and first-line management is also key to putting in place the principles of TQM, and the activities which they need to get involved with are outlined and examined.

Chapter 3 deals with the received wisdom on TQM. Quality management experts such as Crosby, Deming, Feigenbaum and Juran have had a considerable influence on the development of TQM throughout the world and their views and teachings are summarized in this chapter. The Japanese have had a profound influence on the understanding and development of TQM. Therefore, no book on TQM would be complete without some discussion of the way in which Japanese companies develop and manage the concept. The views of four influential Japanese experts (Imai, Ishikawa, Shingo and Taguchi) are explored and a summary is provided of Japanese-style Total Quality.

Chapter 4 deals with the introduction of TQM. It sets out by examining change and continuous improvement and deals with how the improvement process is triggered, which is usually in combination: the Chief Executive, competition, demanding customers and fresh-start situations. Following this, the chapter goes on to examine a range of approaches which can be followed in the introduction of TQM.

Chapter 5 presents a framework to assist with the introduction of TQM. The material draws together a number of issues which need to be considered in its introduction and development. The structure of the framework consists of four main sections: organizing, using systems and techniques, measurement and feedback, and changing the culture. The framework has been used by a number of organizations in both the public and private sectors and in manufacturing and service industries to introduce the basic elements and practices of TQM.

Companies adopt and commit themselves to TQM in a variety of ways. Chapter 6 examines six different characteristics and behaviours which have been found to be typically demonstrated by organizations across the world. These six levels of TQM adoption can be used as an internal measure by which organizations can compare their standing and which help them review their performance.

Most organizations will encounter problems and obstacles in the introduction and development of TQM. If they are aware of what these are, they can agree actions to steer around or minimize them. Chapter 7 explores some of the typical problems in sustaining TQM. Also presented is an Audit Tool by which organizations can assess if they are experiencing the factors which can have a negative impact on the sustainment of TQM.

Reference

BS EN ISO9000 (2000), *Quality Management Systems: Fundamentals and Vocabulary*. London: British Standards Institution.

chapter one

TQM: An Overview

B. G. Dale

Introduction

In today's global competitive marketplace the demands of customers are for ever increasing as they require improved quality of products and services. Also, in some markets there is an increasing supply of competitively priced products and services from low labour cost countries such as those in the Far East, the former Eastern bloc, China, Vietnam and India. Continuous improvement in total business activities with a focus on the customer throughout the entire organization and an emphasis on flexibility and quality is one of the main means by which companies face up to these competitive threats. This is why quality and its management and the associated continuous improvement are looked upon by many organizations as the means by which they can survive in increasingly aggressive markets and maintain a competitive edge over their rivals. The companies that do not manage this change will fail. As a result of the efforts made by organizations to respond to these marketplace demands the quality of products, services and processes has increased considerably during the last two decades. Feigenbaum and Feigenbaum (1999) point out that:

> Total Quality is a major factor in the business quality revolution that has proven itself to be one of the 20th century's most powerful creators of sales and revenue growth, genuinely good new jobs, and soundly based and sustainable business expansion.

Having said this, it should be pointed out that in many markets today quality, narrowly defined as the reliability of product and service quality, is not the competitive weapon it once was. It is now expected as a given requirement and is considered an entry-level characteristic to the marketplace.

These days the most progressive organizations are embarking on a journey of transformation towards total quality management (TQM) and this is coupled with its spread, from the manufacturing to the service sector and on to public services. Total quality management is an ever-evolving practice of doing business in a bid to develop methods and processes which cannot be imitated by competitors. What is TQM? In simple terms, it is the mutual co-operation in an organization and associated business processes to produce value-for-money products and services which meet and hopefully exceed the needs and expectations of customers.

This chapter provides an overview of TQM and introduces the reader to the subject. Many of the themes outlined are explored later in the book. It opens by examining the different interpretations which are placed on the term 'quality'. It then examines why quality has grown in importance during the last decade. The evolution of quality management ('Co-ordinated activities to direct and control an organization with regard to quality': BS EN ISO9000 (2000)) is described through the stages of inspection, quality control, quality assurance and onwards to TQM. In presenting the details of this evolution the drawbacks of a detection-based approach to quality are compared to the recommended approach of prevention. Having described these stages the chapter examines the key elements of TQM – commitment and leadership of the chief executive officer (CEO), planning and organization, using tools and techniques, education and training, employee involvement, teamwork, measurement and feedback, and culture change.

The chapter ends by presenting a summary of the points which organizations need to keep in mind when developing and advancing TQM. This is done under the broad groupings of organizing, systems and techniques, measurement and feedback, and changing the culture.

What is Quality?

'Quality' is now a familiar word. However, it has a variety of interpretations and uses, and there are many definitions. Today and in a variety of situations it is perhaps an over-used word. For example, when a case is being made for extra funding and resources, to prevent a reduction in funding, or to keep a unit in operation and in trying to emphasize excellence, just count the number of times the word 'quality' is used in the argument or presentation.

Many people say they know what is meant by quality, they typically claim 'I know it when I see it' (i.e. by feel, taste, instinct and/or smell). This simple statement and the interpretations of quality made by lay people mask the need to define quality and its attributes in an operational manner. In fact, quality as a concept is quite difficult for many people to grasp and understand, and much confusion and myth surround it.

In a linguistic sense, quality originates from the Latin word 'qualis' which means 'such as the thing really is'. There is an international definition of quality, the 'degree to which a set of inherent characteristics fulfils requirements' (BS EN ISO9000 (2000)).

In today's business world there is no single accepted definition of quality. However, irrespective of the context in which it is used, it is usually meant to distinguish one organization, event, product, service, process, person, result, action, or communication from another. For the word to have the desired effect as intended by the user and to prevent any form of misunderstanding in the communication, the following points need to be considered:

- The person using the word must have a clear and full understanding of its meaning.
- The people/audience to whom the communication is directed should have a similar understanding of quality to the person making the communication.

- Within an organization, to prevent confusion and ensure that everyone in each department and function is focused on the same objectives, there should be an agreed definition of quality. For example, Betz Dearborn Ltd. define quality as: 'That which gives complete customer satisfaction', and Rank Xerox (UK) as 'Providing our customers, internal and external, with products and services that fully satisfy their negotiated requirements'. North-West Water Ltd. use the term 'business quality' and define this as:

> Understanding and then satisfying customer requirements in order to improve our business results.
> Continuously improving our behaviour and attitudes as well as our processes, products and services.
> Ensuring that a customer focus is visible in all that we do.

There are a number of ways or senses in which quality may be defined, some being broader than others but they all can be boiled down to either meeting requirements and specifications or satisfying and delighting the customer. These different definitions are now examined.

Qualitative

When used in this way, it is usually in a non-technical situation. BS EN ISO9000 (2000) says that 'the term "quality" can be used with adjectives such as poor, good or excellent'. The following are some examples of this:

- In advertising slogans to assist in building an image and persuade buyers that its production and services are the best: Esso – Quality at Work; Hayfield Textiles – Committed to Quality; Kenco – Superior Quality; Philips Whirlpool – Brings Quality to Life; Thompson Tour Operations – Thompson Quality Makes the World of Difference.
- By television and radio commentators (a quality player, a quality goal, a quality try).
- By directors and managers (quality performance, quality of communications).
- By people, in general (quality product, top quality, high quality, original quality, quality time, quality of communications, quality person, loss of quality, German quality, 100 per cent quality).

It is frequently found that in such cases of 'quality speak' the context in which the word quality is used is highly subjective and in its strictest sense is being misused. For example, there is more than one high street shop which trades under the name of 'Quality Seconds', and there is even a shop which advertises under the banner of 'Top Quality Seconds'. A van was recently spotted with the advertising slogan 'Quality Part-Worn Tyres' on its side.

Quantitative

The traditional quantitative term which is still used in some situations is acceptable quality level (AQL). This is defined in BS4778 (1991) as: 'When a continuing series of lots is considered, a quality level which for the purposes of sampling inspection is the limit of a satisfactory process'. This is when quality is paradoxically defined in terms of non-conforming parts per hundred (i.e. some defined degree of imperfection).

An AQL is often imposed by a customer on its supplier in relation to a particular contract. In this type of situation the customer will inspect the incoming batch according to the appropriate sampling scheme. If more than the allowed number of defects are found in the sample the entire batch is returned to the supplier or the supplier can, at the request of the customer, sort out the conforming from non-conforming product on the customer's site. The employment of an AQL is also used by some companies under the mistaken belief that trying to eliminate all defects is too costly.

The setting of an AQL by a company can work against a 'right first time' mentality in its people as it appears to condone the production and delivery of non-conforming parts or services, suggesting that errors are acceptable to the organization. It is tantamount to planning for failure. For example, take a final product which is made up of 3,000 parts: if the standard set is a 1 per cent AQL, this would mean that the product is planned to contain 30 non-conforming parts. In all reality there are likely to be many more because of the vagaries of the sampling used in the plan or scheme, whereby acceptance or rejection of the batch of product is decided.

Another example of a quantitative measure is to measure processes using sigmas (a sigma is a statistical indication of variation) and parts per million defects. A sigma is essentially a measuring device that is an indication of how good a product or service is. The higher the sigma value the lower the number of defects. For example, 3 sigma equals 66,807 defects per million opportunities, while 6 sigma equals 3.4 (these values assume a normal distribution with a process shift of 1.5 sigma). The sigma level is a means of calibrating performance in relation to customer needs.

The concept of 6 sigma (a quality improvement framework) has developed from its origins in Motorola in the 1980s as an approach to improving productivity and quality and reducing costs. Six sigma is the pursuit of perfection and represents a complete way of tackling process improvement, involving many of the concepts, systems, tools and techniques described in this book. The 6 sigma concept is currently very popular as a business improvement approach. It is a quantitative approach to quality improvement. The key features include a significant training commitment in statistics and statistical tools, problem-solving methodology and framework, project management, a team-based project environment, people who can successfully carry out improvement projects (these are usually known as black belts and green belts), leaders and project champions.

Yet another example of a quantitative measure of quality are levels of service performance requirements; see the data in table 1.1.

Uniformity of the product characteristics or delivery of a service around a nominal or target value

If a product or service dimensions are within the design specification or tolerance limits they are considered acceptable; conversely, if they are outside the specification they are not acceptable (see figure 1.1). The difference between what is considered to be just inside or just outside the specification is marginal. It may also be questioned whether this step change between pass and fail has any scientific basis and validity.

Table 1.1 Levels of service performance requirements

Comparative measure	Grade	Billing queries: % answered within 5 days	Written complaints: % answered within 10 days	Billing metred customers: % read minus % unread
Well above average	A	>95	>98	>99.4
Above average	B	92–95	96–98	98.5–99.4
Average	C	89–92	94–96	96.0–98.4
Below average	D	86–89	92–94	93.0–95.9
Well below average	E	<86	<92	<93.0

Source: OFWAT (1995/6)

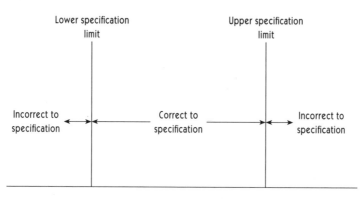

Figure 1.1 The inside/outside specification dilemma

Designers often establish specification limits without sufficient knowledge of the process by which the product and/or service is to be produced/delivered and its capability. It is often the case that designers cannot agree amongst themselves about the tolerances/specification to be allocated, and it is not uncommon to find outdated reasoning being used. They also tend to define and establish a tighter tolerance than is justified to provide safeguards and protect themselves. In many situations there is inadequate communication on this matter between the design and operation functions. Fortunately, this is changing with the increasing use of simultaneous or concurrent engineering.

The problem with working to the specification limits in a manufacturing situation is that it frequently leads to tolerance stack-up and parts not fitting together correctly at the assembly stage. This is especially the case when one part which is just inside the lower specification limit is assembled to one which is just inside the upper specification. If the process is controlled such that a part is produced around the nominal or a target dimension (see figure 1.2), this problem does not occur and the correctness of fit and smooth operation of the final assembly and/or end product are enhanced.

The idea of reducing the variation of part characteristics and process parameters so that they are centred around a target value can be attributed to Taguchi (1986). He writes that the quality of a product is the (minimum) loss imparted by the product to the society from the time the product is shipped. This is defined by a

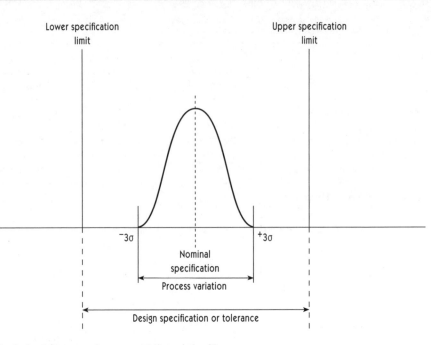

Lower specification
limit

Upper specification
limit

$^-3\sigma$

$^+3\sigma$

Nominal
specification

Process variation

Design specification or tolerance

Figure 1.2   Design tolerance and process variation relationship

quadratic loss curve. Among the losses he includes time and money spent by customers, consumers' dissatisfaction, warranty costs, repair costs, wasted natural resources, loss of reputation and, ultimately, loss of market share.

The relationship of design specification and variation of the process can be quantified by a capability index, for example, Cp which is a process potential capability index:

$$Cp = \frac{\text{Total specification width}}{\text{Process variation width}}$$

Conformance to agreed and fully understood requirements

This definition is attributed to Crosby (1979). He believes that quality is not comparative and there is no such thing as high quality or low quality, or quality in terms of goodness, feel, excellence and luxury. A product or service either conforms to requirements or it does not. In other words, quality is an attribute (a characteristic which, by comparison to a standard or reference point, is judged to be correct or incorrect) not a variable (a characteristic which is measurable). Crosby makes the point that the requirements are all the actions required to produce a product and/or deliver a service that meets the customer's expectations, and that it is management's responsibility to ensure that adequate requirements are created and specified within the organization.

This is a useful definition to use in the development of service-level agreements (SLAs) in an internal customer–supplier relationship. For example, the purpose and scope of the SLA between the Regional Engineering Managers and Distribution Finance of Norweb Distribution is detailed below:

This agreement specifies the services to be provided by Distribution Finance to Regional Engineering Managers for the period 1st July, 1995 to 30th June, 1996.
The agreement covers the following services:

- Management accounts
- Revenue and capital forecasting, commentary, budgeting and monitoring
- Business modelling
- Auditing
- Capital appraisal
- Administration of financial aspects of capital projects
- Overtime monitoring
- Financial aspects of strategic and business planning
- Ad hoc professional financial advice and investigations
- Control account reconciliation
- Capital and revenue costing
- Financial policy
- Corporate financial and taxation returns
- Cashiering services
- Rechargeable billing, disputed accounts and sales ledger facilities
- Retention of records
- Administration of financial aspects of fault projects

Some products and services are highly sophisticated in terms of their design but are poor in terms of conformance to requirements. On the other hand, some are simple in terms of their design but exhibit high levels of conformance to requirements. The 'quality of design' (the degree to which the design of the product and/or service achieves its purpose) can be confused with the 'quality of conformance' (how well the product and/or service conforms to the design). Stemming from this confusion about design and conformance there can be a tendency to believe that 'better' quality means higher costs. This view results from the confusion between quality and grade. Grade represents the addition of features and characteristics to satisfy the additional needs of customers and this clearly requires extra monies, but grade is different to quality.

Fitness for purpose/use

This is a standard definition of quality first used by Juran (1988). Juran classifies 'fitness for purpose/use' into the categories of: quality of design, quality of conformance, abilities and field service. Focusing on fitness for use helps to prevent the over-specification of products and services. Over-specification can add greatly to costs and tends to militate against a right-first-time performance. How fit a product or service is for use obviously has to be judged by the purchaser, customer or user.

Satisfying customer expectations and understanding their needs and future requirements

A typical definition which reflects this aim is: 'The attributes of a product and/or service which, as perceived by the customer, makes the product/service attractive to them and gives them satisfaction.' The focus of the definition is adding value to the product and/or service.

Satisfying customers and creating customer enthusiasm through understanding their needs and future requirements is the crux of TQM, and all organizations are dependent on having satisfied customers. TQM is all about customer orientation and many company missions are based entirely on satisfying customer perceptions. Customer requirements for quality are becoming stricter and more numerous, and there are increasing levels of intolerance of poor-quality goods and services and low levels of customer service and care. The customer is the major reason for an organization's existence and customer loyalty and retention is perhaps the only measure of organizational success. In most situations customers have a choice: they need not place future orders with a supplier who does not perform as they expected or who they feel has deceived them. They will certainly not jeopardize their own business interest out of loyalty to a supplier whose products and service fail to perform properly, and will simply go to a competitor. In the public sector the customer may not have the choice to go elsewhere; however, they can go to litigation, write letters of complaint, cause disruption, and use elections to vote officials out of office. The aim of superior-performing companies is to become the supplier of choice to their customers and to 'lock' themselves into their customers' mode of operation by becoming their sole supplier, and by adding value to their customers' businesses by process improvement and cost-down activities. A number of countries (e.g. America and Sweden) have now developed a customer satisfaction index. The American index, for example, indicates satisfaction with the quality of goods and services in the following areas:

- Retail and finance
- Insurance
- Transportation
- Communication
- Utilities and services
- Manufacturing durables and non-durables

The superior-performing organizations go beyond satisfying their customers: they emphasize the need to delight them by giving them more than what is required in the contract; they also now talk about winning customers and becoming infatuated with their customers. The wisdom of this can be clearly understood when we consider the situation where a supplier has given more than the customer expected (e.g. an extra glass of wine on an aircraft; a sales assistant going out of their way to be courteous and helpful and providing very detailed information) and the warm feelings generated by this type of action.

A customer-focused organization also puts considerable effort into anticipating the future expectations of its customers (i.e. surprising quality), and, by working with them in long-term relationships, helps them to define their future needs and expectations. They listen very closely to their customers and 'real' users of the product or service, in order to gain a clearer perspective on customer experiences. They aim to build quality into the product, service, system and/or process as upstream as is practicable. Excitement and loyalty are the words used to describe this situation.

Those companies intent on satisfying customer needs and expectations will have in place a mechanism for facilitating a continuous two-way flow of information between themselves and their customers. There are a variety of means available to companies for them to assess issues such as:

- How well they are meeting customer expectations
- How well the brand is respected
- What are customers' chief causes of concern
- What are the main complaints
- What suggestions customers might have for improvements
- How they might add value to the product and/or service
- How well they act on what the customer says
- The best means of differentiating themselves in the marketplace

The trend is for increasing the level of contact with the customer. These 'moments of truth' (Carlzon 1987) occur far more frequently in commerce, public organizations, the Civil Service and service-type situations than in manufacturing organizations. The means include:

- Customer workshops
- Panels and clinics
- Using 'test' consumers and mystery shoppers
- Focus groups
- Customer interviews
- Market research
- Dealer information
- Questionnaire surveys
- Product reports
- Trailing the service and/or product
- Trade shows

Customer complaints are one indication of customer satisfaction, and many organizations have a number of metrics measuring such complaints. BS8600 (1999) provides guidance on how to develop an effective complaints management system in order to analyse and use complaints effectively. The rationale is that managing complaints in a positive manner can enhance customer perceptions of an organization, increase lifetime sales and values and provide valuable market intelligence.

Having listened to 'customer voices' an organization should put in place appropriate strategy and actions for making the necessary changes and improvements. It is also important to clarify and identify the elements and characteristics of the product and service which the customer finds attractive. The SERVQUAL questionnaire developed by Parasuraman et al. (1988) may be used to track these kinds of issues. This customer-required quality (i.e. their wants) should be translated into the language of internal needs and driven back through all levels in the organizational hierarchy. It is important that the requirements are put into terms that are measurable, realistic and achievable; the use of quality function deployment (QFD) is useful in this respect. Customer needs and requirements are for ever changing, and organizations have to live up to their customers' expectations; they are never satisfied, even though the supplying organization may think they are.

Why is Quality Important?

To answer this question just consider the unsatisfactory examples of product and/or quality service that you, the reader, have experienced, the bad feelings it gave, the resulting actions taken and the people you told about the experience and the outcome. Goodman et al. (2000), based on a range of studies carried out by TARP (Technical Assistance Research Programs), outline two arguments that are effective in selling quality to senior management.

First, quality and service improvements can be directly and logically linked to enhanced revenue within one's own company; and secondly, higher quality allows companies to obtain higher margins.

The following extracts some quantitative evidence in relation to these arguments:

- 'Problems decrease customer loyalty by 15 per cent to 30 per cent'
- '50 per cent of individual consumers and 25 per cent of business customers who have problems never complain to anyone at the company'
- 'If the call center can resolve a customer's problem using quality service, thus changing a dissatisfied customer to a satisfied one, the company usually gets an increase in loyalty of 50 percentage points'
- 'One potential customer will be lost for every 50 who hear someone complain about a product or service'
- 'Market leaders can change between 5 per cent and 10 per cent premiums for outstanding quality and service'

The customer service information in Box 1.1 provides additional quantitative facts about this. These data emphasize the importance of customer acquisition and retention.

The following are examples of survey data which have focused on the perceived importance of product and service quality.

Public perceptions of product and service quality

In 1988 the American Society for Quality (ASQ) commissioned the Gallup organization to survey public perceptions on a variety of quality-related issues. This survey was the fourth in a series which began in 1985; the 1985 and 1988 surveys focused on US consumers and the 1986 and 1987 studies surveyed attitudes of company executives. The 1988 study was done by conducting telephone interviews with 1,005 adults in the United States during the summer of 1988. A selection of results, as reported by Ryan (1988) and Hutchens (1989), is outlined below:

- The following is a ranking of factors that people consider important when they purchase a product:
    - Performance
    - Durability
    - Ease of repair, service availability, warranty, and ease of use (these four factors were ranked about the same)
    - Price
    - Appearance
    - Brand name
- People will pay a premium to get what they perceive to be higher quality.

BOX 1.1 CUSTOMER SERVICE FACTS

Customer Service Facts: Did You Know That* . . .

1 If 20 customers are dissatisfied with your service, 19 won't tell you. 14 of the 20 will take their business elsewhere.
2 Dissatisfied customers tell an average of 10 other people about their bad experience; 12 per cent tell up to 20 people.
3 Satisfied customers will tell an average of 5 people about their positive experience.
4 It costs five times more money to attract a new customer than to keep an existing one.
5 Up to 90 per cent of dissatisfied customers will not buy from you again, and they won't tell you why.
6 In many industries, quality of service is one of the few variables that can distinguish a business from its competition.
7 Providing high quality service can save your business money. The same skills that lead to increased customer satisfaction also lead to increased employee productivity.
8 Customers are willing to pay more to receive better service.
9 95 per cent of dissatisfied customers will become loyal customers again if their complaints are handled well and quickly.

* *Statistics compiled by Mattson & Associates from service sector companies in the USA.*

Source: CMC Partnership Ltd. (1991)

- Consumers are willing to pay substantially more for better intrinsic quality in a product.
- According to the respondents, the following are the factors what make for 'higher' quality in services:
  - Courtesy
  - Promptness
  - A basic sense that one's needs are being satisfied
  - Attitudes of the service provider
- When consumers do experience a problem with the product, they appear reluctant to take positive action with the manufacturer. The 1987 survey revealed that executives regard customer complaints, suggestions and enquiries as key indicators of product and service quality.

An ASQ/Gallup survey (ASQ/Gallup 1991) was conducted to survey the attitudes and opinions of consumers in Japan, West Germany and the United States in relation to questions such as: 'What does quality really mean to them? How do they define it and does it influence their buying behaviour? What is their perception of the quality from other parts of the world? and What are the dynamics underlying a consumer's reasons for buying or not buying something produced in a foreign country?' On a number of issues, this survey updates American attitudes expressed in the 1988 survey. Over 1,000 people in each country were questioned. A selection of summary highlights from the report are outlined below:

- 'Consumers in the US, Japan and West Germany in many respects are alike in terms of the attributes they consider important in determining the quality of the products they buy. For example, approximately one in five look to the brand name of a product. Durability is also important to at least 10 per cent of the consumers in each of the countries surveyed.'
- 'Asked what factors are most important in influencing their decision to buy a product, price is the leading response in West Germany (64 per cent) and in the US (31 per cent). Performance (40 per cent) is most important among Japanese consumers, followed by price (36 per cent).'
- 'A majority (61 per cent) of US consumers believe it is very important to US workers to produce high quality products or service.'
- 'Price and quality are the reasons given most frequently by American consumers for buying a product made in Japan or Germany.'

Views and roles of senior management

1 In 1992 ASQ commissioned the Gallup organization to study the nature of leadership for quality within American business organizations by surveying opinions of senior management in both large and small organizations. The objective was to explore their views concerning quality improvement and the role of directors with regard to quality. Some 684 executives were interviewed. The following is a summary of the main findings extracted from ASQ/Gallup (1992).

   - 'At least six in ten executives report that they have a great deal of personal leadership impact on customer focus and satisfaction, strategic quality planning, quality and operational results and financial results.'
   - 'Most executives believe management plays a greater role than the board in determining quality policy within their company.'
   - 'More than four in ten (45 per cent) report their board does discuss quality frequently.'
   - 'Four in ten (43 per cent) executives report their board reports on consumer satisfaction frequently, and almost as many (38 per cent) report the board reviews reports on customer retention or loyalty frequently.'

2 The European Foundation for Quality Management (EFQM) contracted McKinsey and Company to survey the CEOs of the top 500 west European corporations in relation to quality performance and the management of quality; 150 CEOs responded to the survey. The following are some of the main findings as reported by McKinsey and Company (1989).

   - Over 90 per cent of CEOs consider quality performance to be 'critical' for their corporation.
   - 60 per cent of CEOs said that quality performance had become a lot more important than before (late 1970s).

- The four main reasons why quality is perceived to be important are:

  - Primary buying argument for the ultimate customer
  - Major means of reducing costs
  - Major means for improving flexibility/responsiveness
  - Major means for reducing throughput time.

- The feasible improvement in gross margin on sales through improved quality performance was rated at an average of 17 per cent.
- More than 85 per cent of the leading CEOs in Europe consider the management of quality to be one of the top priorities for their corporations.

3 Lascelles and Dale (1990), reporting on a survey they carried out of 74 UK CEOs, say that 'Almost all the respondents believe that product and service quality is an important factor in international competitiveness. More than half have come to this conclusion within the past four years.'

Quality is not negotiable

An order, contract or customer which is lost on the grounds of non-conforming product and/or service quality is much harder to regain than one lost on price or delivery terms. In a number of cases the customer could be lost for ever; in simple terms the organization has been outsold by the competition.

If you have any doubt about the truth of this statement just consider the number of organizations who have gone out of business or lost a significant share of a market, and consider the reported reasons for them getting into that position. Quality is one of the factors which is not negotiable and in today's business world the penalties for unsatisfactory product quality and poor service are likely to be punitive.

Quality is all-pervasive

There are a number of single-focus business initiatives which an organization may deploy to increase profit. However, with the improvements made by companies of their mode of operation, reduction in monopolies, government legislation, deregulation, changes in market share, mergers, takeovers, collaborative joint ventures, there is less distinction between companies than there was some years ago. TQM is a much broader concept than previous initiatives, encompassing not only product, service and process improvements but those relating to costs and productivity and to people involvement and development. It also has the added advantage that it is totally focused on satisfying customer needs.

A related issue is that organizations are often willing to pay more for what they perceive as a quality product; see the results of the ASQ/Gallup survey of 1992, as outlined in table 1.2.

Quality increases productivity

Cost, productivity and quality improvements are complementary and not alternative objectives. Managers sometimes say that they do not have the time and resources to

Table 1.2   Customers willing to pay for quality

Industry type	Number of customers willing to pay more for a quality product	Number of customers unwilling to pay extra for better quality
Clothing/textiles	135	5
Furniture	74	4
TV/audio	66	6
Home	55	4
Automotive	36	10

Source: ASQ/Gallup (1992)

ensure that product and/or service quality is done right the first time. They go on to argue that if their people concentrate on planning for quality then they will be losing valuable operational time, and as a consequence output will be lost and costs will rise. Despite this argument, management and their staff will make the time to rework the product and service a second or even a third time, and spend considerable time and organizational resources on corrective action and placating customers who have been affected by the non-conformances.

Remember 'Murphy's Law' – 'There is never time to do it right but always time to do it once more.'

Quality leads to better performance in the marketplace

The Profit Impact of Market Strategy (PIMS), conducted under the Strategic Planning Institute in Cambridge, Massachusetts, have a database which contains over 3,000 records of detailed business performance. The Institute is a co-operative run by its members. The database allows a detailed analysis of the parameters which influence business performance. A key PIMS concept is relative perceived quality (RPQ); this is the product and service offering as perceived by the customer. PIMS data is often used to model options before adapting a change initiative and to assess how improvements translate into improved profits and enhanced customer loyalty. It has been established that the factors having most leverage on return on investment are RPQ and relative market share, and that companies with large market shares are those whose quality is relatively high, whereas companies with small market shares are those whose quality is relatively low (see Buzzell and Gale 1987). Another key finding is that businesses who know and understand customers' priorities for quality improvements can achieve a threefold increase in profitability (Roberts 1996).

Quality means improved business performance

Kano et al. (1983) carried out an examination of 26 companies which won the Deming Application Prize (this is a prize awarded to companies for their effective implementation of company-wide quality control; for details see chapter 24). Between 1961 and 1980 they found that the financial performance of these companies in terms of earning rate, productivity, growth rate, liquidity, and net worth was above the average for their industries.

A report published by the US General Accounting Office (GAO) (1991) focused on the top 20 scorers of the Malcolm Baldrige National Quality Award (MBNQA) in the period 1988–9. Its purpose was to determine the importance of TQM practices on the performance of US companies. Using a combination of questionnaire and interview methods, the companies were asked to provide information on four broad classes of 20 performance measures – employee-related indicators, operating indicators, customer satisfaction indicators and business performance indicators. Improvements were claimed in all these indicators (e.g. market share, sales per employee, return on assets, and return on sales). Useful information on financial performance was obtained from 15 of the 20 companies who experienced the following annual average increases:

- Market share: 13.7 per cent
- Sales per employee: 8.6 per cent
- Return on assets: 1.3 per cent
- Return on sales: 0.4 per cent

Larry (1993) reports on a study carried out on the winners of the MBNQA and found that they 'Yielded a cumulative 89 per cent gain, whereas the same investment in the Standard and Poor (S&P) 500 – Stock Index delivered only 33.1 per cent.' Wisner and Eakins (1994) also carried out an operation and financial review of the MBNQA winners from 1988 to 1993. One of the conclusions reached was that the winners appear to be performing financially as well as or better than their competitors.

As reported by Bergquist and Ramsing (1999), Bergquist carried out a study in 1996, entitled 'An Assessment of the Operational and Financial Impact on Companies of Quality Awards in the United States', which used the same approach as the 1991 GAO study, expanding to 40 the original 20 performance measures. The focus of the study was a questionnaire survey of winners and applicants of MBNQA and State Quality Awards, between the years 1990 and 1995. They conclude:

> 89 per cent of the winners and 77 per cent of the applicants who responded to the mail survey believed that using award criteria did have a positive impact on company performance, a link appears to exist between award criteria and perceived company performance.

The Bradford study (Letza et al. 1997), carried out at the University of Bradford Management Centre, identified 29 companies within the UK which display characteristics associated with TQM. Following the US GAO work the study was first carried out over the period 1987 to 1991 and has been repeated for the period 1991 to 1995. Nine measures have been used by the study team to compare company performance with the median for the particular industry. The second study reveals the following:

- 81 per cent of companies are above the industry median for turnover per employee.
- 81 per cent of the companies provide a higher salary to turnover ratio than their peers.
- 74 per cent of the organizations remunerate their employees above the median for the industry.

- 65 per cent of the organizations produce above-median profit per employee for their industry.
- 62 per cent of the organizations have a higher net asset turnover than their peer group.

The authors also go on to say that 'Four of the nine measures are marginally below the median for their industry but this is to be expected as quality becomes institutionalised and more widespread.'

Easton and Jarrell (1998) have undertaken an extremely thorough study which has examined the impact of TQM on financial performance for a sample of 108 firms. The impact of TQM has been assessed by examining the unexpected changes in financial performance for a five-year period following the introduction of TQM. Easton and Jarrell (1998) conclude that 'The findings indicate that performance, measured by both accounting variables and stock returns, is improved for the firms adopting TQM. The improvement is consistently stronger for firms with more advanced TQM.'

Another very thorough study is that undertaken by Hendricks and Singhal (1996) in America, which began in 1991. They have measured the effects of TQM on long-term business performance. The study sample comprised nearly 600 award-winners (e.g. MBNQA, State Quality Awards and Supplier Awards) and compared their performance with that of similar companies that had not won such an award. The study found that it required a long time period to establish the link between TQM and financial performance because of its evolutionary nature. For the implementation period which started six years before a company won an award, they found no difference between award-winners and non-award-winners. The following are some of the key results from the post-implementation period:

- Winners experienced a 91 per cent increase in operating income compared with their respective controls (43 per cent).
- Winners gained a 69 per cent increase in sales compared with their controls (32 per cent) and attained a 79 per cent increase in total assets compared with the respective controls (37 per cent).
- Winners increased their employees by 23 per cent compared with their the respective controls (7 per cent).
- Over the five-year study period the award-winners outperformed the S&P 500 index by 34 per cent.

In the X factor report (1999) the award submissions from 14 European and UK quality/business excellence award-winning companies were analysed regarding financial performance. The results were examined for (1) three-year trends and sustained good performance; (2) five-year trends and sustained excellent performance; and (3) favourable comparisons with set targets. Strong positive trends and/or sustained excellent performance over three years were demonstrated by over 70 per cent of the companies using three main financial measures:

- Revenue growth
- Operating profit
- Return on assets

Other financial measures against which these role-model companies performed well over three and five years and against targets/benchmarks, included:

- Cashflow
- Liquidity
- Debtor days
- Shareholder funds

George (2002) reports on the Q-100 index, which was established in 1998. This is based on investments in American-based organizations which are using TQM. The search for such companies is undertaken by the Malcolm Baldrige National Quality Award criteria. The Q-100 consists of approximately 100 of the 500 S&P companies, which are weighted and diversified to align them with the weightings and sectors in the S&P 500. Among the findings reported by George (2002) are:

> From September 30th, 1998 to December 31st, 2001 the Q-100 returned 26.97 per cent compared with the S and P 500 return of 17.59 per cent.
>
> A $10,000 investment in both indices on September 30th, 1998 would have grown to $12,697 for the Q-100 on the last day of 2001, compared with $11,759 for the S and P 500.

Perhaps the best-known quality/financial metric is the 'Baldrige Index'. This is a fictitious stock fund made up of publicly traded US companies that have received the MBNQA during the years 1991 to 2000. The US Commerce Department's National Institute of Technology (NIST) invested a hypothetical $1,000 in each of the two whole company winners and the parent companies of 18 subsidiary winners. They also made the same investment in the S&P 500 at the same time. The investments have been tracked from the first business day of the month following the announcement of the award receipts through to 3 December 2001. NIST (2002) reported that the two company winners outperformed the S&P 500 by more than 4.5 to 1, achieving a 512 per cent return on investment. The group of whole-company award-winners plus the parent companies of the subsidiary winners outperformed the S&P 500 by 3 to 1, a 323 per cent return on investment compared to a 110 per cent return for the S&P 500.

The cost of non-quality is high

Based on a variety of companies, industries and situations, the cost of quality (or to be more precise the cost of not getting it right the first time) ranges from 5 to 25 per cent of an organization's annual sales turnover in manufacturing or annual operating costs in service-type situations; see chapter 9 and Dale and Plunkett (1999) for details. An organization should compare its profit-to-sales turnover ratio to that of its quality costs-to-sales turnover ratio in order to gain an indication of the importance of product and service quality to corporate profitability.

A related cost issue is that of product liability, which is concerned with the legal liability of a manufacturer or supplier of goods for personal injuries or damage to property suffered as a result of a product which is defective and unsafe; see European Commission Directive (1985). A powerful example of the cost and implications of the failure to get a product right is provided by Wilks (1999):

In July this year General Motors was fined a record $4.9 billion following a crash in 1993 which seriously burned six people involved in a rear end car collision. The severity of their injuries – some suffered 60 per cent burns – was put down to design fault in placing the petrol tank too close to the rear bumper. The victims' lawyers discovered that an internal GM study had highlighted this danger and that the manufacturer had known 'for years' that this model was potentially unsafe. To alter the design would have cost the company $8.59 per car.

Customer is king

In today's markets, customer requirements are becoming increasingly more rigorous and their expectations of the product and/or service in terms of conformance, reliability, dependability, durability, interchangeability, performance, features, appearance, serviceability, user-friendliness, safety, and environmental friendliness is also increasing. These days many superior-performing companies talk in terms of being 'customer-obsessed'. At the same time, it is likely that the competition will also be improving and, in addition, new and low-cost competitors may emerge in the marketplace. Consequently there is a need for continuous improvement in all operations of a business, involving everyone in the company. The organization which claims that it has achieved TQM will be overtaken by the competition. Once the process of continuous improvement has been halted, under the mistaken belief that TQM has been achieved, it is much harder to restart and gain the initiative on the competition, (see figure 1.3). This is why TQM should always be referred to as a process and not a programme.

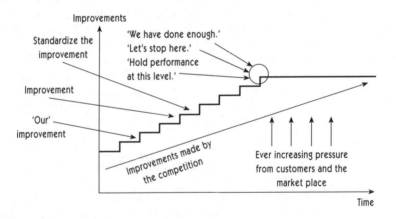

Figure 1.3   Quality improvement: a continuous process

Quality is a way of life

Quality is a way of organizational and everyday life. It is a way of doing business, living and conducting one's personal affairs. In whatever each one person does, and in whatever situation, the task(s) must be undertaken in a quality conscious way. Quality is driven by a person's own internal mechanisms – 'heart and soul', 'personal beliefs'. Belief in it can be likened to that of people who follow a religious faith.

An organization committed to quality needs quality of working life of its people in terms of participation, involvement and development and quality of its systems, processes and products.

The Evolution of Quality Management

Systems for improving and managing quality have evolved rapidly in recent years. During the last two decades or so simple inspection activities have been replaced or supplemented by quality control, quality assurance has been developed and refined, and now many companies, using a process of continuous and company-wide improvement, are working towards TQM. In this progression, four fairly discrete stages can be identified: inspection, quality control, quality assurance and total quality management; it should be noted that the terms are used here to indicate levels in a hierarchical progression of quality management (figure 1.4). British and International Standards definitions of these terms are given to provide the reader with some understanding, but the discussion and examination are not restricted by these definitions.

Inspection

Conformity evaluation by observation and judgement accompanied as appropriate by measurement, testing or gauging. (BS EN ISO9000 (2000))

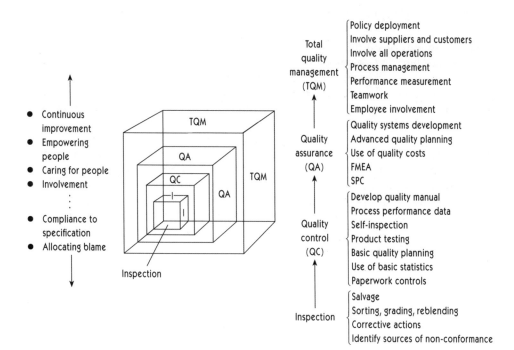

Figure 1.4 The four levels in the evolution of TQM

At one time inspection was thought to be the only way of ensuring quality, the 'degree to which a set of inherent characteristics fulfils requirements' (BS EN ISO9000 (2000)). Under a simple inspection-based system, one or more characteristics of a product, service or activity are examined, measured, tested, or assessed and compared with specified requirements to assess conformity with a specification or performance standard. In a manufacturing environment the system is applied to incoming goods and materials, manufactured components and assemblies at appropriate points in the process and before finished goods are passed into the warehouse. In service, commercial and public service-type situations the system is also applied at key points, sometimes called appraisal points, in the production and delivery processes. The inspection activity is, in the main, carried out by dedicated staff employed specifically for the purpose, or by self-inspection of those responsible for a process. Materials, components, paperwork, forms, products and goods which do not conform to specification may be scrapped, reworked, modified or passed on concession. In some cases inspection is used to grade the finished product as, for example, in the production of cultured pearls. The system is an after-the-event screening process with no prevention content other than, perhaps, identification of suppliers, operations, or workers, who are producing non-conforming products/services. There is an emphasis on reactive quick-fix corrective actions and the thinking is department-based. Simple inspection-based systems are usually wholly in-house and do not directly involve suppliers or customers in any integrated way.

Quality control

Part of quality management focused on fulfilling quality requirements. (BS EN ISO9000 (2000))

Under a system of quality control one might expect, for example, to find in place detailed product and performance specifications, a paperwork and procedures control system, raw material and intermediate-stage product-testing and reporting activities, logging of elementary process performance data, and feedback of process information to appropriate personnel and suppliers. With quality control there will have been some development from the basic inspection activity in terms of sophistication of methods and systems, self-inspection by approved operators, use of information and the tools and techniques which are employed. While the main mechanism for preventing off-specification products and services from being delivered to customers is screening inspection, quality control measures lead to greater process control and a lower incidence of non-conformance.

Those organizations whose approach to the management of quality is based on inspection and quality control are operating in a detection-type mode (i.e. finding and fixing mistakes).

What is detection?

In a detection or 'firefighting' environment, the emphasis is on the product, procedures and/or service deliverables and the downstream producing and delivery processes; it is about getting rid of the bad things after they have taken place. Considerable effort is expended on after-the-event inspecting, troubleshooting, checking, and testing of the product and/or service and providing reactive 'quick fixes' in a bid to ensure that only conforming products and services are delivered to the customer. In this approach, there is a lack of creative and systematic work activity, with planning and improvements being neglected and defects being identified late in the process, with all the financial implications of this in terms of the working capital employed. Detection will not improve quality but only highlight when it is not present, and sometimes it does not even manage to do this. Problems in the process are not removed but contained, and are likely to come back. Inspection is the primary means of control in a 'policeman' or 'goalkeeper'-type role and thereby a 'producing' versus 'checking' situation is encouraged, leading to confusion over people's responsibilities for quality – 'Can I, the producer, get my deliverables past the checker?' It also leads to the belief that non-conformances are due to the product/service not being inspected enough and also that operators, not the system, are the sole cause of the problem.

A question which organizations operating in this mode must answer is: does the checking of work by inspectors affect an operator's pride in the job? The production–inspection relationship is vividly described by McKenzie (1989).

With a detection approach to quality, non-conforming 'products' (products are considered in their widest sense) are culled, sorted and graded, and decisions made on concessions, rework, reblending, repair, downgrading, scrap, and disposal. It is not unusual to find products going through this cycle more than once. While a detection-type system may prevent non-conforming product, services and paperwork from being delivered to the customer (internal or external), it does not prevent them being made. Indeed, it is questionable whether such a system does in fact find and remove all non-conforming products and services. Physical and mental fatigue decreases the efficiency of inspection and it is commonly claimed that, at best, 100 per cent inspection is only 80 per cent effective. It is often found that with a detection approach the customer also inspects the incoming product/ service; thus the customer becomes a part of the organization's quality control system.

In this type of approach a non-conforming product must be made and a service delivered before the process can be adjusted; this is inherently inefficient in that it creates waste in all its various forms: all the action is 'after-the-event' and backward-looking. The emphasis is on 'today's events', with little attempt to learn from the lessons of the current problem or crisis. It should not be forgotten that the scrap, rework, retesting, reblending, etc. are extra efforts, and represent costs over and above what has been budgeted and which ultimately will result in a reduction of bottom-line profit. Figure 1.5, taken from the Ford Motor Company three-day statistical process control (SPC) course notes (1985), is a schematic illustration of a detection-type system.

An environment in which the emphasis is on making good non-conformance rather than preventing it from arising in the first place is not ideal for engendering team spirit, co-operation and a good climate for work. The focus tends to be on switching the blame to others, people making themselves 'fireproof', not being prepared to accept responsibility and ownership and taking disciplinary action against people who make mistakes. In general, this behaviour and attitude emanates from middle management and quickly spreads downwards through all levels of the organizational hierarchy.

Organizations operating in a detection manner are often preoccupied with the survival of their business and little concerned with making improvements.

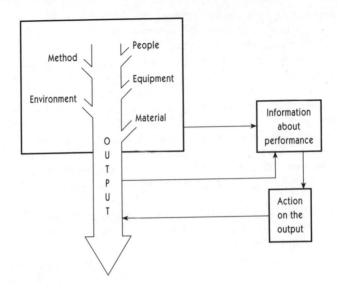

Figure 1.5   A detection-based quality system
Source: Ford Motor Company (1985)

Quality assurance

Finding and solving a problem after a non-conformance has been created is not an effective route towards eliminating the root cause of a problem. A lasting and continuous improvement in quality can only be achieved by directing organizational efforts towards planning and preventing problems from occurring at source. This concept leads to the third stage of quality management development, which is quality assurance:

> Part of quality management focused on providing confidence that quality requirements will be fulfilled. (BS EN ISO9000 (2000))

Examples of additional features acquired when progressing from quality control to quality assurance are, for example, a comprehensive quality management system to increase uniformity and conformity, use of the seven quality control tools (histogram, check sheet, Pareto analysis, cause-and-effect diagram, graphs, control chart and scatter diagram), statistical process control, failure mode and effects analysis (FMEA), and the gathering and use of quality costs. The quality systems and practices are likely to have met, as a minimum, the requirements of the BS EN ISO9001 (2000). Above all one would expect to see a shift in emphasis from mere detection towards prevention of non-conformances. In short, more emphasis is placed on advanced quality planning, training, critical problem-solving tasks, improving the design of the product, process and services, improving control over the process and involving and motivating people.

What is prevention?

Quality assurance is a prevention-based system which improves product and service quality, and increases productivity by placing the emphasis on product, service and

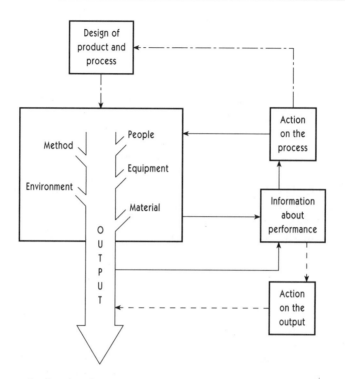

Figure 1.6 A prevention-based quality system
Source: Ford Motor Company (1985)

process design. By concentrating on source activities and integrating quality into the planning and design stage, it stops non-conforming product being produced or non-conforming services being delivered in the first place; even when defects occur they are identified early in the process. This is a proactive approach compared with detection, which is reactive. There is a clear change of emphasis from downstream to the upstream processes and from product to process (see figure 1.6); 'product out' to 'customer in'. This change of emphasis can also be considered in terms of the plan, do, check, act (PDCA) cycle. In the detection approach the 'act' part of the cycle is limited, resulting in an incomplete cycle, whereas, with prevention, act is an essential part of individuals and teams striving for continuous improvement as part of their everyday work activities. With prevention there is a clearly defined feedback loop with both negative and positive feedback into the process, product, and service development system.

Quality is created in the design stage and not at the later control stage; the majority of quality-related problems are caused by poor or unsuitable designs of products and processes. In the prevention approach, there is a recognition of the process as defined by its input of people, machines, materials, method, management and environment. It also brings a clearer and deeper sense of responsibility for quality and eliminates the root cause of waste and non-value-adding activity to those actually producing and delivering the product and/or service.

Changing from detection to prevention requires not just the use of a set of tools and techniques, but the development of a new operating philosophy and approach which requires a change in management style and way of thinking. It requires the various departments and functions to work and act together in cross-functional teams to discover the root cause of problems and pursue their elimination. Quality planning and continuous improvement truly begin when top management includes prevention as opposed to detection in its organizational policy and objectives and starts to integrate the improvement efforts of various departments. This leads to the next level, that of total quality management.

Total quality management

The fourth and highest level – TQM – involves the application of quality management principles to all aspects of the organization, including customers and suppliers, and their integration with the key business processes.

Total quality management requires that the principles of quality management should be applied in every branch and at every level in the organization with an emphasis on integration into business practices and a balance between technical, managerial and people issues. It is a company-wide approach to quality, with improvements undertaken on a continuous basis by everyone in the organization. Individual systems, procedures and requirements may be no higher than for a quality assurance level of quality management, but they will pervade every person, activity and function of the organization. It will, however, require a broadening of outlook and skills and an increase in creative activities from those required at the quality assurance level. The spread of the TQM philosophy would also be expected to be accompanied by greater sophistication in the application of tools and techniques, increased emphasis on people (the so-called soft aspects of TQM), process management, improved training and personal development and greater efforts to eliminate wastage and non-value-adding activities. The process will also extend beyond the organization to include partnerships with suppliers and customers and all stakeholders of the business. Activities will be reoriented to focus on the customer, internal and external with the aim to build partnerships and go beyond satisfying the customer to delighting them. The need to self-assess progress towards business excellence is also a key issue.

There are many interpretations and definitions of TQM. Put simply, TQM is the mutual co-operation of everyone in an organization and associated business processes to produce value-for-money products and services which meet and hopefully exceed the needs and expectations of customers. TQM is both a philosophy and a set of guiding principles for managing an organization to the benefit of all stakeholders. The eight quality management principles are defined in BS EN ISO9000 (2000) as:

- *Customer focus.* Organizations depend on their customers and therefore should understand current and future customer needs, meet customer requirements and strive to exceed customer expectations.
- *Leadership.* Leaders establish unity of purpose and direction of the organization. They should create and maintain the internal environment in which people can become fully involved in achieving the organization's objectives.
- *Involvement of people.* People at all levels are the essence of an organization and their full involvement enables their abilities to be used for the organization's benefit.
- *Process approach.* A desired result is achieved more efficiently when activities and related resources are managed as a process.

- *System approach to management.* Identifying, understanding and managing interrelated processes as a system contributes to the organization's effectiveness and efficiency in achieving its objective.
- *Continual improvement.* Continual improvement of the organization's overall performance should be a permanent objective of the organization.
- *Factual approach to decision-making.* Effective decisions are based on the analysis of data and information.
- *Mutually beneficial supplier relationships.* An organization and its suppliers are interdependent and a mutually beneficial relationship enhances the ability of both to create value.

The Key Elements of TQM

Despite the divergence of views on what constitutes TQM, there are a number of key elements in the various definitions which are now summarized. Other chapters will provide more detail of these elements.

Commitment and leadership of the chief executive officer

Without the total demonstrated commitment of the chief executive officer and his or her immediate executives and other senior managers, nothing much will happen and anything that does will not be permanent. They have to take charge personally, lead the process, provide direction, and exercise forceful leadership, including dealing with those employees who block improvement and impetus. However, while some specific actions are required to give TQM a focus, as quickly as possible it must be seen as the style of management and the natural way of operating a business.

Planning and organization

Planning and organization feature in a number of facets of the improvement process, including:

- Developing a clear long-term strategy for TQM which is integrated with other strategies such as information technology, production/operations and human resources and also with the business plans of the organization.
- Deployment of the policies through all stages of the organizational hierarchy with objectives, targets, projects and resources agreed with those responsible for ensuring that the policies are turned from words into actions (see chapter 8).
- Building product and service quality into designs and processes.
- Developing prevention-based activities (e.g. mistake-proofing devices).
- Putting quality assurance procedures into place which facilitate closed-loop corrective action.
- Planning the approach to be taken to the effective use of quality systems, procedures and tools and techniques, in the context of the overall strategy.
- Developing the organization and infrastructure to support the improvement activities. This includes allocating the necessary resources to support them. While it is recommended that some form of steering activity should be set up to provide direction and support and make people responsible for co-ordinating

and facilitating improvement, the infrastructure should not be seen as separate from the management structure.

● Pursuing standardization, systematization and simplification of work instructions, procedures and systems.

Using tools and techniques

To support and develop a process of continuous improvement an organization will need to use a selection of tools and techniques within a problem-solving approach. Without the effective employment and mix of tools and techniques it will be difficult to solve problems. The tools and techniques should be used to facilitate improvement and be integrated into the routine operation of the business. The organization should develop a route map for the tools and techniques which it intends to apply. The use of tools and techniques as the means will help to get the process of improvement started: employees using them feel involved and that they are making a contribution, quality awareness is enhanced, behaviour and attitude change starts to happen, and projects are brought to a satisfactory conclusion.

Education and training

Employees, from top to bottom of an organization, should be provided with the right level and standard of education and training to ensure that their general awareness and understanding of quality management concepts, skills, competencies, and attitudes are appropriate and suited to the continuous improvement philosophy; it also provides a common language throughout the business. A formal programme of education and training needs to be planned and provided on a timely and regular basis to enable people to cope with increasingly complex problems. It should suit the operational conditions of the business: is training done in a cascade mode (everyone is given the same basic training within a set time-frame) or is an infusion mode (training provided as a gradual progression to functions and departments on a need-to-know basis) more suitable? This programme should be viewed as an investment in developing the ability and knowledge of people and helping them realize their potential. Without training it is difficult to solve problems, and, without education, behaviour and attitude change will not take place. The training programme must also focus on helping managers think through what improvements are achievable in their areas of responsibility. It also has to be recognized that not all employees will have received and acquired adequate levels of education. The structure of the training programme may incorporate some updating of basic educational skills in numeracy and literacy, but it must promote continuing education and self-development. In this way, the latent potential of many employees will be released and the best use of every person's ability achieved.

Involvement

There must be a commitment and structure to the development of employees, with recognition that they are an asset which appreciates over time. All available means, from suggestion schemes to various forms of teamwork, must be considered for achieving broad employee interest, participation and contribution in the improvement process; management must be prepared to share information and some of their powers and responsibilities and loosen the reins. This also involves seeking and listening carefully to the views of employees and acting upon their suggestions. Part of the approach to TQM is to ensure that everyone has a clear understanding of what is required of them, how their processes relate to the business as a whole and how their internal customers are dependent upon them. The more people who understand the business and what is going on around them, the greater the role they can play in the improvement process. People have got to be encouraged to control, manage and improve the processes which are within their sphere of responsibility.

Teamwork

Teamwork needs to be practised in a number of forms. Consideration needs to be given to the operating characteristics of the teams employed, how they fit into the organizational structure and the roles of member, team leader, sponsor and facilitator. Teamwork is one of the key features of involvement, and without it difficulty will be found in gaining the commitment and participation of people throughout the organization. It is also a means of maximizing the output and value of individuals.

There is also a need to recognize positive performance and achievement and celebrate and reward success. People must see the results of their activities and that the improvements they have made really do count. This needs to be constantly encouraged through active and open communication. If TQM is to be successful it is essential that communication must be effective and widespread. Sometimes managers are good talkers but poor communicators.

Measurement and feedback

Measurement, from a baseline, needs to be made continually against a series of key results indicators – internal and external – in order to provide encouragement that things are getting better (i.e. fact rather than opinion). External indicators are the most important as they relate to customer perceptions of product and/or service improvement. The indicators should be developed from existing business measures, external, competitive and functional generic and internal benchmarking, as well as customer surveys and other means of external input. This enables progress and feedback to be clearly assessed against a roadmap or checkpoints. From these measurements, action plans must be developed to meet objectives and bridge gaps.

Ensuring that the culture is conducive to continuous improvement activity

It is necessary to create an organizational culture which is conducive to continuous improvement and in which everyone can participate. Quality assurance also needs to be integrated into all an organization's processes and functions. This requires changing people's behaviour, attitudes and working practices in a number of ways. For example:

- Everyone in the organization must recognize that whatever they do can be improved. They must be involved in 'improving' the processes under their control on a continuous basis and take personal responsibility for their own quality assurance.
- Employees must be encouraged to identify wastage in all its various forms to take out cost and get more value into a product or service.
- Employees can stop a process without reference to management if they consider it to be not functioning correctly.
- Employees must be inspecting their own work.
- Defects must not be passed, in whatever form, on to the next process. The internal customer–supplier relationship (everyone for whom you perform a task or service or to whom you provide information is a customer) must be recognized.
- Each person must be committed to satisfying their customers, both internal and external.
- External suppliers and customers must be integrated into the improvement process.
- Mistakes must be viewed as an improvement opportunity. In the words of the Japanese, every mistake is a pearl to be cherished.
- Honesty, sincerity and care must be an integral part of daily business life.

Changing people's behaviour and attitudes is one of the most difficult tasks facing management, requiring considerable powers and skills of motivation and persuasion; considerable thought needs to be given to facilitating and managing culture change. In the words of a government chief engineer in the Hong Kong civil engineering department, 'Getting the quality system registered to ISO9001 is the easy bit, it is changing people's attitudes and getting them committed to continuous improvement what is presenting the greatest challenge.'

Summary: Developing TQM

In concluding this chapter a list of points is offered which organizations should keep in mind when developing TQM. Many of them are expanded upon in the chapters that follow:

Organizing

- There is no ideal way of assuring the quality of an organization's products or services. What matters is that improvement does occur, that it is cost-effective, and that it is never-ending.
- There is no one best way of starting a process of continuous improvement which suits all organizations and cultures.
- Senior management's commitment is vital in order to gain credibility, assure continuity and establish longevity of the process. They need to think deeply

about the subject and commit to it the necessary resources. Managers must also place more emphasis on leadership and create an environment in which people can develop and apply, to full potential, all their skills.

- Planning should have a 10-year horizon in order to ensure that the principles of TQM are firmly rooted in the culture of the organization. Patience and tenacity are key virtues.
- Quality objectives and strategies must be developed and deployed down through the organizational hierarchy, along with agreeing goals for improvement.
- The improvement process needs to be integrated with other organizational improvement initiatives and business strategies.
- A multi-disciplinary TQM steering committee chaired by the chief executive must be established and appropriate infrastructure established to support the improvement process. It is important that this infrastructure is integrated into the existing structure.
- At the outset the main quality problems must be identified and tackled by the senior management team – 'lead by example'.

Systems and techniques

- The quality management system must be well documented, provide direction and feedback and be audited internally on a regular and effective basis.
- The day-to-day control and assurance activity must be separated from the improvement process.
- There must be a dedication to removing basic causes of errors and wastage.
- At the design stage all potential non-conformances must be identified and eliminated.
- A system by which all staff can raise those problems which prevent them turning in an error-free performance should be in place.
- It should be recognized that tools, techniques, systems, and packages are used at different stages in different organizations in their development of TQM.
- The timing of the introduction of a particular tool, technique, system or package is crucial to its success.
- Mistake-proofing of operations should be investigated.
- Statistical methods should be used.

Measurement and feedback

- It should be recognized that customer satisfaction is a business issue and that all processes should work towards satisfying the customer.
- All available means must be used to determine customer requirements and develop systems and procedures to assess conformance.
- It should be easy for the internal and external customer to complain. Ensure that all customer complaints are picked up and analysed, and that there is appropriate feedback.
- The attitude that 'the next process/person is the customer' must be encouraged.
- Measures of customer satisfaction and quality indicators for all internal departments must be developed.

- Regular self-assessment of the progress being made with quality improvement against the criteria of the Malcolm Baldrige National Quality Award for Performance Excellence (1999) and the EFQM excellence model (1999), or a similar model should be carried out. This will assist in making the quality improvement efforts more efficient and cost effective.

Changing the culture

- All aspects of customer and supplier relationships should be developed, improved and assessed on a regular basis.
- Teamwork must be practised at all levels.
- People must be involved at all stages of the improvement process, and not simply in those aspects which directly affect their role.
- Education and training should be continuous and widespread, in order to foster changes in attitudes and behaviour and to improve the skills base of the organization.
- Recognize that change is continuous and must be embedded in the culture of the organization.

References

ASQ/Gallup (1991), *An International Survey of Consumers' Perceptions of Product and Service Quality*. Milwaukee: ASQ.

ASQ/Gallup (1992), *An ASQ/Gallup Survey on Quality Leadership Roles of Corporate Executives and Directors*. Milwaukee: ASQ.

Bergquist, T. M. and Ramsing, K. D. (1999), Measuring performance after meeting award criteria. *Quality Progress*, September, 66–72.

British Quality Foundation (1999), *The X Factor Executive Report*. London: British Quality Foundation.

BS EN ISO9000 (2000), *Quality Management Systems: Fundamentals and Vocabulary*. London: British Standard Institution.

BS EN ISO9001 (2000), *Quality Management Systems: Requirements*. London: British Standards Institution.

BS EN ISO9004 (2000), *Quality Management Systems: Guidance for Performance Improvements*. London: British Standards Institution.

BS4778 (1991), *Quality Vocabulary*, part 2: *Quality Concepts and Related Definitions*. London: British Standards Institution.

BS8600 (1999), *Complaints Management Systems: Design and Implementation*. London: British Standards Institution.

Buzzell, R. D. and Gale, B. T. (1987), *The Profit Impact of Marketing Strategy: Linking Strategy to Performance*. New York: The Free Press.

Carlzon, J. (1987), *The Moments of Trust*. Cambridge, Mass.: Ballinger.

CMC Partnership Ltd. (1991), *Attitudes Within British Business to Quality Management Systems*. Buckingham: The CMC Partnership.

Crosby, P. B. (1979), *Quality is Free*. New York: McGraw Hill.

Dale, B. G. and Plunkett, J. J. (1999), *Quality Costing*, 3rd edn. Aldershot, Hants.: Gower Press.

Easton, G. S. and Jarrell, S. L. (1998), The effect of total quality management on corporate performance: an empirical investigation. *Journal of Business*, 71(2), 253–307.

EFQM (2001), *The EFQM Excellence Model*. Brussels: EFQM.

European Commission Directive (1985), *Liability for Defective Products* (85/375/EEC). Brussels.

Feigenbaum, A. V. and Feigenbaum, D. S. (1999), New quality for the 21st century: developments are the fundamental drivers of business. *Quality Progress*, December, 27–31.

Ford Motor Company (1985), *Three-Day Statistical Process Control Course Notes*. Brentwood, Essex: Ford Motor Company.

George, S. (2002), Bull or bear: the Q-100 index proves that if you have quality, you'll beat the market. *Quality Progress*, April, 32–7.

Goodman, J., O'Brien, P. and Segal, E. (2000), Turning CEOs into quality champions. *Quality Progress*, March, 47–54.

Hendricks, K. B. and Singhal, V. R. (1996), Quality awards and the market value of the firm: an empirical investigation. *Management Sciences*, 42(2), 415–36.

Hutchens, S. (1989), What customers want: results of ASQ/Gallup survey. *Quality Progress*, February, 33–6.

Juran, J. M. (editor-in-chief) (1988), *Quality Control Handbook*. New York: McGraw Hill.

Juran, J. M. and Godrey, B. (1999), *Quality Control Handbook*, 5th edn. New York: McGraw Hill.

Kano, N., Tanaka, H. and Yamaga, Y. (1983), *The TQC Activity of Deming Prize Recipients and its Economic Impact*. Tokyo: Union of Japanese Scientists and Engineers.

Larry, L. (1993), Betting to win on the Baldrige winners. *Business Week*, 18 October, 16–17.

Lascelles, D. M. and Dale, B. G. (1990), Quality management: the chief executive's perception and role. *European Management Journal*, 8(1), 67–75.

Letza, S. R., Zairi, M. and Whymark, J. (1997), *TQM – Fad or Tool for Sustainable Competitive Advantage? An Empirical Study of the Impact of TQM on Bottom Line Business Results*. Bradford: University of Bradford Management Centre.

McKenzie, R. M. (1989), *The Production–Inspection Relationship*. Edinburgh and London: Scottish Academic Press.

McKinsey and Company (1989), Management of quality: the single most important challenge for Europe. European Quality Management Forum, 19 October, Montreux, Switzerland.

NIST (2002), Baldrige Award Winners Beat the S and P 500 for the Eighth Year. <http://www/nist.gov/public affairs/stockstudy.htm>, 7 March.

OFWAT (1995/6), *Levels of Service Report*. London: HMSO.

Parasuraman, A., Zeithamal, V. A. and Berry, L. L. (1988), SERVQUAL: a multiple item scale for measuring consumer perceptions of service quality. *Journal of Retailing*, 64(1), 14–40.

Roberts, K. (1996), Viewpoint: customer value and market-driven quality management. *Strategic Insights into Quality*, 4(2), 3.

Ryan, J. (1988), Consumers see little change in product quality. *Quality Progress*, December, 16–20.

Taguchi, G. (1986), *Introduction to Quality Engineering*. New York: Asian Productivity Organization.

US Department of Commerce (2001), *Baldrige National Quality Program 2001 Criteria for Performance Excellence*. Gaithersburg: US Department of Commerce National Institute of Standards and Technology.

US General Accounting Office (1991), *Management Practices: US Companies Improve Performance Through Quality Efforts*. Washington: United States General Accounting Office.

Wilks, N. (1999), A damages limitation exercise. *Professional Engineer*, 11 August, 35.

Wisner, J. D. and Eakins, S. G. (1994), Competitive assessment of the Baldrige winners. *International Journal of Quality and Reliability Management*, 11(2), 8–25.

chapter two

The Role of Management in TQM

B. G. Dale

Introduction

It is the responsibility of the senior management team to create the strategic dialogue, organizational environment, atmosphere, values and behaviour in which TQM can achieve its potential. This has been well articulated by the international authorities on quality management (e.g. Crosby, Deming, Feigenbaum and Juran) who typically point out that the leadership provided in these matters is the key to the success or failure of the initiatives. This requires changing, through a deliberate, structured and systematic process, the behaviour and attitudes of people at all levels in the organization hierarchy. People who, because of the respective cultures of the organizations in which they have worked, lack of TQM education and training, lack of opportunity, neglect, mistreatment, etc. have, in manufacturing industry, regarded quality as a means of sorting conforming from non-conforming product and reworking product to prevent non-conforming goods being passed to customers and, in service situations and public services, have sometimes adopted a 'take it or leave it' attitude to the consumer and the public.

It is not an easy task to create an organizational culture in which each person in every department is fully committed to improving their own performance and is dedicated to satisfying their internal customers' needs and future expectations. This takes many years and requires senior managers to take a long-term view, and is compounded by the evolving nature of business. Along the TQM journey it is easy for people, especially when under pressure, to slip back into the old traditional fire-fighting way of doing things. It should be expected that a number of employees will tend to be cynical and expect TQM to go the way of all new initiatives and eventually fizzle out. So it is not surprising that organizations do encounter a wide range of obstacles in pursuing a process of continuous and company-wide improvement.

This chapter outlines the main reasons why it is important that senior managers should become personally involved in TQM. Total quality management is the prime responsibility of senior management and they need to become immersed in it; without this commitment and focus nothing of significance will happen. The chapter examines what they need to know about TQM and what they should do in terms of actions. Middle management and first-line management also have a key role to play in putting the principles of TQM in place at the sharp end of the business, and the activities which they need to get involved are also outlined.

The Need for Senior Managers to Get Involved in TQM

The decision to introduce TQM can only be taken by the chief executive officer (CEO) in conjunction with the senior management team. Senior management have got to devote time to learning about the subject, including attending suitable training courses and conferences. Developing and deploying organizational vision, mission, philosophy, values, strategies, objectives and plans, and communicating the reasons behind them together with the underlying logic is the province of senior management. This is why senior management have to become personally involved in the introduction and development of TQM and demonstrate visible commitment and confidence to it by leading this way of thinking and managing the business. This not only requires their personal commitment but a significant investment of time. To ensure that senior management focus their attention on issues of continuous improvement there is emerging evidence that a proportion of their remuneration (e.g. bonus or performance related pay) is related to metrics such as customer satisfaction and employee satisfaction figures and scores achieved against the EFQM excellence model (see chapter 24).

TQM requires the commitment, confidence and conviction of the senior management team. If this is achieved it avoids false starts and helps to ensure longevity. They have to encourage a total corporate commitment to continually improve every aspect of the business. Everyone in the organization has a role to play in continuous improvement, but this effort is likely to be disjointed and spasmodic if senior managers have not made the organizational requirements clear. If they fail to get involved, it is likely that the improvement process will stagnate and disillusionment will set in amongst employees. Quality is an integral part of the management of an organization and its business processes and is too important an issue to delegate to technical and quality specialists.

The ultimate aim is to have people taking ownership of the quality assurance of their processes and to have a mindset of continuous improvement. This state of affairs is not a natural phenomenon and does not happen overnight, and senior managers must be prepared to spend time coaching people along this path and providing the necessary influences. Once people have seen senior managers leading the TQM initiative and respect has been earned, then this will start to happen and will encourage the emergence of followers in the form of quality leaders and champions from various parts and levels of the business.

Senior managers should be sensitive to the fact that some employees will resist the change to TQM. The usual reasons for this are that they are uncertain of the nature and impact of TQM and their ability to cope: the change may lessen their authority over decisions and allocation of resources, and it threatens their prestige and reputation. If senior managers are personally involved in the change process it can help to breakdown these barriers.

There is a very strong relationship between the business achievements of an organization and senior managers' understanding of and commitment to TQM. The cost of non-conformance or mismanaging quality is likely to be 5 to 25 per cent of an organization's annual sales turnover or operating costs in not-for-profit organizations (see chapter 9). If these figures are compared to profit as a percentage of sales turnover or expenditure in not-for-profit organizations, the key questions are: 'Can the CEO afford not to get involved in TQM?', 'How much will it cost the organization not to put in place a process of continuous improvement?', and 'Is investment in TQM and continuous improvement worthwhile?'

McKinsey and Company (1989), reporting on a survey of CEOs in the top 500 European corporations in relation to the key requirements for success in TQM, found the following:

- Top management attention   95 per cent agreement
- People development   85 per cent agreement
- Corporate team spirit   82 per cent agreement
- Quality performance information   73 per cent agreement
- Top management capability-building   70 per cent agreement
- Sense of urgency   60 per cent agreement

These findings support the point made earlier that the role of senior management is critical to success. Lascelles and Dale (1990), reporting on their research, also say: 'the CEO is the primary internal change agent for quality improvement'. They point out that in this capacity he or she has two key roles: 'shaping organizational values, and establishing a managerial infrastructure to actually bring about change'.

The CEO must have faith in the long-term plans for TQM and not expect immediate financial benefits. However, there will be achievable benefits in the short term, providing that the introduction of TQM is soundly based. Senior managers need to create and promote an environment in which, for example:

- People can work together as a team and teamwork becomes an integral part of business activities.
- People co-operate with their peers and teams work with teams.
- Mistakes are freely admitted without recriminations and are perceived as an opportunity for improvement (i.e. a 'blame-free' culture).
- People are involved in the business through decision-making.
- People genuinely own the process.
- People improve on a continuous basis the processes under their control (i.e. the continuous improvement and passion for doing things better mindset).
- People direct their attention to identifying, satisfying, delighting and winning over customers, whether they be internal or external.
- Ideas are actively sought from everyone.
- Development of people is a priority.
- Employee involvement in the business is worked at continually.
- Permanent solutions are found to problems.
- Departmental boundaries between functions are non-existent.
- Effective two-way communication is in place.
- Recognition is given for improvement activities.
- Status symbols are removed.

Change is not something that any department or individual takes to easily, and administering changes in organizational practices has to be considered with care. In the majority of Western organizations, people have witnessed the latest fads, fashions and 'flavours of the month' which have come and gone. They have become accustomed to senior managers talking a lot about a topic or issue, but failing to demonstrate visible commitment to what they are saying. Typical of the comments made by employees are: 'He's at it again, let's humour him/her'; 'TQM will go the way of all other fads and fancies'; 'Let's keep our heads down and things will revert to normal'; and 'They're all talk and don't really believe what they say'. It is only senior managers who can break down this cynicism, influence the indifference and persuade people that the organization is serious about TQM. It is they who have got to communicate in person to their people why the organization needs continuous improvement and demonstrate that they really care about quality. This can be done by getting involved in activities such as:

- Setting up and chairing a TQM steering committee or quality council.
- Identifying the major quality issues facing the organization and becoming personally involved in investigating them, ideally as a leader, member, sponsor or foster-parent to an improvement team, problem-elimination team or the like.
- Getting involved in quality planning, audit, improvement meetings and organizational housekeeping.
- Leading and/or attending quality training courses.
- Chairing individual sessions with operatives about the importance of following and adhering to procedures and working instructions.
- Organizing and chairing defect review and customer return committees.
- Instigating and carrying out regular audits, self-assessment and diagnosis of the state of the art of TQM and continuous improvement.
- Dealing with customer complaints, and visiting customers and suppliers.
- Leading customer workshops, panels and focus groups.
- Visiting, on a regular basis, all areas and functions of the business, and discussing improvement issues.
- Developing, communicating and then following a personal improvement action plan.
- Communicating as never before on TQM. For example, carrying out team briefs, preparing personal thankyou notes to both teams and individuals and writing articles for the company newsletter.
- Practising the internal customer–supplier concept (see figure 2.1). (With this approach, a supplier identifies his or her customers and determines their requirements. In some cases the supplying process may have to be developed to meet the stated requirements. The supplier then undertakes the task and carries out self-inspection and control before the work is passed to the internal customer. Taking responsibility for following processes is part of this approach.)

In ways such as this, senior managers lead and teach by example and employees can develop a sense of purpose about continuous improvement. Once commitment and leadership have been demonstrated ideas, innovations and improvements will start to feed through from the lower levels of the organizational hierarchy. At this stage in the development of TQM senior managers must also be aware that some employees will be complying through fear and have no real commitment or belief in the concept; it takes time to change attitudes and culture.

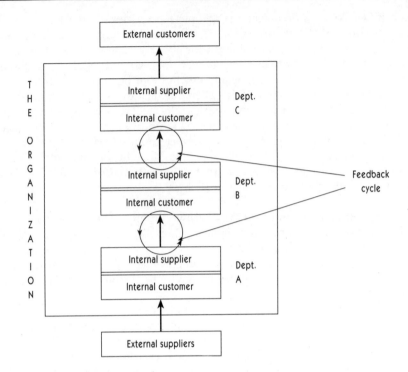

Figure 2.1   The customer–supplier network

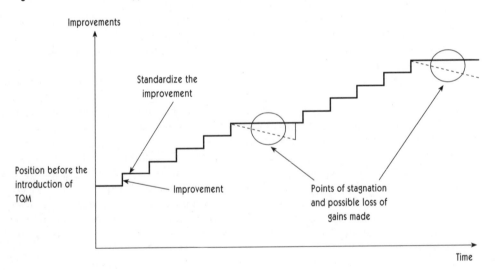

Figure 2.2   The quality improvement process

The improvement process is a roller-coaster of troughs and peaks (see figure 2.2). At certain points in the process, the situation will arise that while a considerable amount of organizational resources are being devoted to improvement activities, little progress appears to be being made. In the first three or so years of launching a process of continuous improvement, and when the process is at one of these low points, it is not uncommon for some middle and first-line managers and functional specialists to claim that TQM is not working and start to raise issues such as: 'Why are we doing this?'; 'Are we seeing real improvements?'; 'What are the benefits?'; 'Have we the time to spend on these "outside our function" activities?'; 'Improvement teams are a waste of time'; and 'Such-and-such a concept would be a better bet.' Consequently, they will perhaps wish to switch their attention to what they claim are other more pressing matters. If the CEO is personally involved in TQM and perceived to be so, people are much less likely to express this type of view. The CEO and senior managers have a key role to play in helping to get people through this crisis of confidence in TQM. There are a number of mechanisms which can assist with this. For example, the managing director of a speciality chemicals company introduced the concept of 'Quality Action Days' to give all employees the opportunity to meet him and express their views and concerns on the company's progress with TQM and what could be done to speed up the process of employee involvement.

In most Western organizations, a few key people are vital to the advancement of the improvement process, and if such a person leaves it can result in a major gap in the management team. In the case of leadership and organizational changes, the CEO plays a major role in developing the understanding and diffusing beliefs with respect to TQM to new managers and technical and business specialists. In this way, the effects of any organizational changes are minimized. When key people leave and the improvement process continues without interruption and improvement teams continue to meet and make a contribution, this is an indication that an environment which is conducive to TQM is firmly in place. These types of issues are explored in detail by Bunney and Dale (1996) as part of a longitudinal study in a speciality chemical manufacturer.

Organizations are not usually experienced in maintaining the gains made in TQM. In addition to leadership and organizational changes, factors such as take-overs, human resources and industrial relations problems, short-time working, redundancies, cost-cutting, streamlining, no salary increases, growth of the business, and pursuit of policies which conflict with TQM in terms of resources, etc. can all have an adverse effect on the gains made and damage the perception of TQM. People will be looking to senior managers to provide continuity and leadership in such circumstances.

What Senior Managers Need to Know about TQM

The first thing senior managers must realize from the outset is that TQM is a long-term and not a short-term intervention and that it is an arduous process. They must also realize that TQM is not the responsibility of the quality function. There are no:

- Quick fixes
- Easy solutions
- Universal panaceas
- Tools, techniques and/or systems which will provide all the answers
- Ready-made packages which can be plugged in and guarantee success

What is being talked about here is a long-term culture change. The planning horizon to put the basic TQM principles into place is between eight and 10 years. The Japanese manufacturing companies typically work on 16 years made up of four

four-year cycles – introduction, promotion into non-manufacturing areas, development/expansion, and fostering advancement and maintenance. Consequently, senior managers have got to practise and communicate the message of patience, tolerance and tenacity. It is highly likely that there will be some middle-management resistance to TQM, in particular from those managers with long service, who are concerned with the new style of managing, more than from staff and operatives.

In spite of the claims made by some writers, consultants and 'experts', senior managers must recognize there is no single or best way of introducing and developing TQM. There are, however, common strands and principles which apply in all organizations. Organizations are different in terms of their people, culture, history, customs, prejudices, structure, products, services, technology, processes and operating environment.

What works successfully in one organization and/or situation will not necessarily work in another. A good example of this is TQM awareness training. As mentioned in chapter 1, there are two main approaches: (1) cascade ('sheep-dipping'), in which training is given to everyone over a relatively short time-frame, and (2) infusion, where people are trained on a need-to-know basis. In some organizations 'sheep-dipping' has been successful and in others it has been a dismal failure. The same two-way argument holds for the infusion approach. With respect to training it is important that senior managers have a clear idea of the strategic direction of the improvement activities after the training has been given.

In the long run what really matters is that senior managers demonstrate long-term commitment and leadership to the process of continuous improvement. They must be prepared to think through the issues for themselves and test out ideas and thoughts, modify them and adapt, as appropriate to the operating environment of the business. The key point is to learn from experience. Employees are usually forgiving of management if mistakes are openly admitted rather than covered up, and explanations given.

Senior managers need to commit time in order to develop their own personal and group understanding of the subject; cohesion in the senior management team, which comes from understanding, is important in making the changes which are necessary with TQM. They need to read books, attend conferences and courses, visit the best practices in terms of TQM and talk to as many people as possible. The self-assessment criteria of the MBNQA and EFQM performance and excellence models (as outlined in chapter 24) can assist in developing this overall understanding. It is also important that improvement ideas are for ever circulating in the minds of senior managers along the lines of the PDCA cycle. In this way they will avoid the false trails laid down by their own staff, consultants and 'experts'.

This understanding of TQM will also assist the CEO in deciding, together with other senior managers and key staff, how the organization is going to introduce TQM. For example,

- What method and format of training are required?
- How many and what type of teams will be introduced?
- How many teams can be effectively supported?
- Is a TQM steering committee necessary and, if so, what form should it take?
- Which tools and techniques should be used?
- What is the role of a quality management system?
- How will TQM contribute to reducing warranty claims?

To start and then develop a process of continuous improvement, an infrastructure is required to support the associated tasks and departments and people need to be able to devote time to quality planning, and to prevention and improvement activities. Cook and Dale (1995) point out that management do not give sufficient care in reviewing the effectiveness of their organizational improvement infrastructure to ensure that the momentum of the improvement process is being maintained. Their research evidence indicates that the initial infrastructure is sometimes removed too quickly before the process has become embedded.

People have got to be encouraged to take part in improvement activities, and to do this they need to be released from their day-to-day work routines. The employment of a full-time quality co-ordinator and/or facilitator(s) relieved of day-to-day work pressures, can help to integrate individual improvement activities under a common umbrella, in addition to providing advice and guidance on matters of improvement. The issue of getting started is not an easy one. Prior to embarking on TQM most organizations will already have undertaken a number of improvement initiatives, and a key issue is how to bring together those initiatives and build on them. A number of elements of TQM, such as empowerment, are nebulous and senior managers sometimes have difficulty in seeing how they might operate in their organization. It is important that the more nebulous elements are combined with the readily understood aspects such as quality systems, procedures and practices, teamwork, and tools and techniques. As part of getting started senior managers must diagnose the organization's strengths and opportunities for improvement in relation to the management of quality. This typically takes the form of an internal assessment of employees' views and perceptions (internal and group assessments, and questionnaire surveys), a systems audit, a cost of quality analysis, and obtaining the views of customers (including those accounts which have been lost) and suppliers about the organization's performance in terms of product, service, people, administration, innovation, strengths and weaknesses, etc. This type of internal and external assessment of perspectives should be carried out on a regular basis to gauge the progress being made towards TQM and help decide the next steps. This is the benefit of self-assessment against a recognized model for business excellence. Once senior management have realized the need for TQM they need to translate this awareness into effective action.

Their dilemma is often compounded not just by a lack of knowledge of TQM and the process of continuous improvement but also by a lack of experience in managing organizational change. The overwhelming quantity and variety of available advice, which is often conflicting, sometimes biased and sometimes incorrect, simply adds to the confusion and chaos.

In terms of the quality management structure it should be understood that day-to-day control and assurance of quality should be separated from improvement and TQM promotion activities. If this is not done, quality assurance staff will quite naturally focus their efforts on daily, short-term-type activities and activities related to the quality management system, and commit little time to long-term planning and improvements. It is a fact of business life that people will give more priority to the day-to-day activities for which they are responsible. These tasks are more easily recognized, assessed and rewarded than are those related to improvement, especially those involving some form of teamwork. In particular, this applies when assessment and appraisal of individual performance takes no account of improvement achievements.

The CEO and senior managers may need to develop a company vision and mission statement; this should include developing an organizational definition of quality. However, the vision and mission have to be supported by organized changes rather than by stand-alone statements of objectives.

As a final point senior managers should be sufficiently knowledgeable about TQM to know what type of questions to ask their people in relation to the improvement mechanisms. They should also be able to query results and the process by which they were obtained, and have some indication of what non-conforming products and/or services are costing their organization.

What Senior Managers Need to Do about TQM

This section is opened by reviewing the leadership criteria of the EFQM excellence model (EFQM 2001; see chapter 24 below). The criteria detail the behaviour of all managers in driving the company towards business excellence. They concern how the executives and all other managers inspire and drive excellence as an organization's fundamental process for continuous improvement. The leadership criteria are divided into the following four parts:

- Leaders develop the mission, vision and values and are role models of a culture of excellence.
- Leaders are personally involved in ensuring the organization's management system is developed, implemented and continually improved.
- Leaders are involved with customers, partners and representatives of society.
- Leaders motivate, support and recognize the organization's people.

Senior managers need to decide the actions they are going to take to ensure that quality becomes the number one priority for the organization. They need to allocate time and commitment to:

- Communicate in an effective manner their views on TQM, recognizing the difference between the art and medium of communication. Executives should take every opportunity to talk and act in a manner consistent with the principles of TQM.
- Decide how the company will approach the introduction and advancement of TQM.
- Lead education and training sessions, including the review of courses.
- Assess the improvements made.
- Get personally involved in improvement activities.
- Determine if the main principles of TQM are being absorbed into the day-to-day operations of the business.
- Understand how key competitors are using TQM.
- Become involved in benchmarking as this will enable them to see, for example, what the superior-performing organizations have achieved and the discrepancies with or gaps in their organization's performance.
- Lead and encourage the use of self-assessment methods and principles.

Senior managers should consider how they are going to demonstrate to people from all levels of the organization their commitment to TQM. They need to visit every area to see what is happening in relation to TQM, ask about results and problems, give advice, and create good practice through leadership. In relation to this latter point senior managers should take the lead in organizational housekeeping with the objective of seeing that the operating and office areas are a model of cleanliness and tidiness.

Senior managers should work as a team to develop improvement objectives and plans, and identify the means by which they can measure organizational improvement (i.e. self-assessment). They are responsible for pinpointing opportunities, prioritizing projects and steering the improvement efforts.

Teamwork is an essential element of TQM, providing an opportunity for co-operative action in pursuit of continuous improvement. The CEO and senior managers need to give more thought to the means by which teamwork may be facilitated and how the achievement of effective team members can be recognized. The use of teams is a way of involving everyone in a continuous improvement initiative (see chapter 23). They:

- Aid the commitment of people to the principles of TQM.
- Provide an additional means of communicating between individuals, management and their direct reports, across functions, and with customers and suppliers.
- Provide the means and opportunities for people to participate in decision-making about how the business operates.
- Improve relationships, develop trust and facilitate co-operative activities.
- Help to develop people and encourage leadership traits.
- Build collective responsibility.
- Aid personal development and build confidence.
- Develop problem-solving skills.
- Facilitate awareness of improvement potential, leading to behaviour and attitude change.
- Help to facilitate a change in management style.
- Solve problems.
- Improve morale.
- Improve operating effectiveness as people work in a common direction.

There are considerable demands on senior managers' time and a vast number of projects and matters seeking their attention. A CEO of a complex high-technology printed circuit board manufacturer uses the term 'spinning like a top' to describe this situation. However, if TQM is to be successfully introduced it has got to take precedence over all other activities. The CEO should plan his or her diary to ensure that they devote some time each week to TQM activities.

It is the responsibility of senior managers to ensure that everyone in the organization knows why the organization is adopting TQM and that people are aware of its potential in their area, department, function and/or process. Their commitment must filter down through all levels of the organization. It is important that all employees feel they can demonstrate initiative and have the responsibility to put into place changes in their own area of work. This involves the establishment of owners for each business process. Consideration needs to be given to how this should be addressed.

A company-wide education and training programme needs to be planned and undertaken to facilitate the right type and degree of change. The aim of this programme should be to promote a common TQM language and awareness and understanding of concepts and principles, ensure that there are no knowledge gaps at any level in the organization, and provide the skills to assist people with improvement activities; this should include team leadership, counselling and coaching skills. A planned programme of training is required in order to provide employees with tools and techniques on a timely basis. In most organizations it is frequently found that there is a good deal of variation in relation to understanding what the process of continuous improvement actually involves. Executives also need to consider the best way of making an input to leading some of the quality-related training.

The senior management team needs to commit resources to TQM, for example releasing people for improvement activities and ensuring that key decision-makers are available to spend time on TQM issues. The CEO needs to delegate responsibility for continuous improvement to people within the organization. Some organizations appoint a facilitator/manager/co-ordinator to act as a catalyst or change agent. However, if this is to be effective the CEO must have a good understanding of TQM and the continuous improvement process. The CEO needs to develop an infrastructure to support the improvement activities in terms of:

- Monitoring and reporting the results (there is nothing like success to convert cynics and counter indifference).
- Providing a focus and the people to make it happen.
- Developing and deploying improvement objectives and targets.
- Involving people from non-manufacturing areas.

It is helpful to establish a TQM steering committee or quality council type of activity to oversee and manage the improvement process. The typical role of such a group is to:

- Agree plans, goals, provide and manage resources.
- Monitor progress.
- Determine actions.
- Create an environment which is conductive to continuous improvement.
- Concur on issues of continuous improvement.
- Facilitate teamwork.
- Ensure that firm foundations are laid down.
- Identify impediments to progress.

From the vision and mission statements a long-term plan needs to be drawn up which sets out the direction of the company in terms of its development and management targets. This plan should be based on the corporate philosophy, sales forecast, current status, and previous achievements against plan and improvement objectives. From this long-term plan an annual policy should be compiled, and plans, policies, actions, and improvement objectives established for each factory, division, department and section. These plans and objectives typically focus on areas affecting quality, cost, delivery, safety and the environment. Middle managers and first-line supervisors should, at the appropriate point, participate in the formulation of these plans, targets and improvement objectives. This ensures that the policies and objectives initiated by the CEO and senior management team are cascaded

POLICY DEPLOYMENT

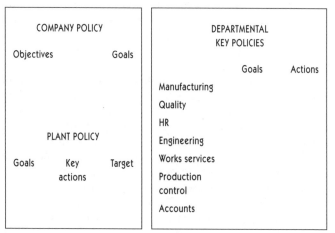

POLICY DEPLOYMENT

MANUFACTURING DEPARTMENT

Figure 2.3 A typical framework for policy deployment

down through the organizational hierarchy so that all employees in each function of the business can carry out their activities within their own area of influence with the aim of achieving common goals and improvement targets. A typical framework for policy deployment is shown in figure 2.3 and details of policy deployment are given by Dale (1990) and Akao (1991), and also in chapter 8.

The process of policy deployment ensures that the quality policies, targets and improvement objectives are aligned with the organization's business goals. The ideal situation in policy deployment is for the senior person at each level of the organizational hierarchy to make a presentation to their staff on the plan, targets and improvements. This ensures the penetration and communication of policies, objectives and continuous improvements throughout the organization, with general objectives being converted into specific objectives and improvement targets. In some organizations, as part of this policy deployment, a plan is formulated every year which focuses on a different improvement theme. One of the key aspects of policy deployment is its high visibility, with company and departmental policies, targets, themes and projects being displayed in each section of the organization.

There must also be some form of audit at each level to check whether or not targets and improvement objectives are being achieved, and the progress being made with specific improvement projects. This commitment to quality and the targets and improvements made should be communicated to customers and suppliers. Some organizations use seminars to explain these policies and strategies. The respective reporting and control systems must be designed and operated in a manner which will ensure that all managers co-operate in continuous improvement activities. They also need to ensure that the tasks delegated to staff with respect to TQM are being carried out in the manner ascribed.

The CEO must ensure that his or her organization really listens to what its customers are saying and is sensitive to what they truly need and to their concerns. This is more easily said than done; none of us likes criticism and we have a tendency to think we know best. This customer information is the starting point of the improvement-planning process. In many organizations information is collected directly by computer links to and from customers' processes, particularly in process industries.

Executives must ensure that they don't disguise things from the customer; honesty is the byword in TQM. Senior managers should ensure their organization takes every opportunity to join the customers and suppliers improvement processes; mutual improvement activities can strengthen existing partnerships and build good working relationships. For example, a major blue-chip packaging manufacturer works with its customers to ensure that the packaging it produces is suited to the customers' packaging equipment. Senior managers must ensure that corrective action procedures and defect analysis are pursued vigorously and a closed-loop system operated to prevent repetition of mistakes.

It is important that the CEO ensures that the organization has positive quantifiable measures of quality as seen by its customers. This enables an outward focus to be kept on the market in terms of customer needs and future expectations. These typical performance measures include:

- Field failure statistics
- Reliability performance statistics
- Customer returns
- Customer complaints
- 'Things gone wrong' data
- Adverse customer quality communications
- Customer surveys
- Lost business

- Non-accepted tenders
- Prospect to customer conversion rate

They also need to develop internal performance measures on metrics such as:

- Non-conformance levels
- Quality audit results
- Yield results
- Quality costs
- Employee satisfaction
- Employee involvement
- Service level agreements
- Score achieved against the EFQM or MBNQA models
- Percentage of employees satisfied that the organization is customer-focused and is a quality company

It is usually necessary to evaluate the current internal and external performance measures to assess their value to the business.

A measurement system to monitor the progress of the continuous improvement process is a key necessity; without it improvement will be more difficult. In the words of Scharp (former president and CEO of A B Electrolux), 'What gets measured gets done' (Scharp 1989). Consequently people will focus on those actions necessary to achieve the targeted improvements. All the evidence from the Japanese companies (Dale 1993) indicates that improvement targets and objectives act as key motivators. However, these need to be carefully set and monitored. It is possible to improve indicators without improving real performance, especially if targets are unrealistic or not seen as controlled by the individuals responsible for them, who fear they will be blamed and may consequently focus on indicators, not performance.

Senior managers should never overlook the fact that people will want to be informed on how the improvement process is progressing. They need to put into place a two-way process of communication for ongoing feedback and dialogue: this helps to close the loop. Communications, up, down and across the organization, are one of the most important features of the relationship between directors, managers and staff. Regular feedback needs to be made about any concerns raised by employees; this will help to stimulate further involvement and improve communication. This also enables them to pinpoint any impediments to the process of continuous improvement.

Senior managers should be prepared to learn about statistical methods, use them in their decision-making processes, and demonstrate an active interest and involvement in techniques such as SPC and Design of Experiments. This ensures that knowledge and decisions are based on fact not opinion. For example, when passing through manufacturing and office areas they should get into the habit of looking at the control charts which are on display and direct questions to the people responsible for charting and analysing the data. They can also learn, from the data portrayed on the charts, of any problem which the 'operator' is experiencing with the process. The control chart is a communication to senior management on the condition of the process – it is a 'window' on the operating world of processes. Ignoring the message will only cause frustration amongst those involved with SPC and will hinder the process of continuous improvement. It should also not be forgotten that SPC teaches people to ask questions about the process.

Continuous improvement can be facilitated by the rapid diffusion of information to all parts of the organization. A visible management system and a storyboard-style presentation in which a variety of information is collected and displayed is a very useful means of aiding this diffusion. The CEO needs to consider seriously this form of transparent system.

The CEO and senior managers must never become satisfied and complacent with the progress the organization has made in TQM. They must strive continually to achieve improvements in the product, service and associated processes. They need to adopt the philosophy and mindset that there is no ideal situation and that the current state can always be improved upon. Areas of organizational waste and uselessness need to be identified and attacked in a ruthless manner.

The Role of Middle Managers

Middle managers have a vital part to play in the introduction and development of TQM. They will only be effective, however, if they are committed to it as a concept. Senior managers should not lose sight of the fact that middle and first-line management have been victims of previous 'flavour of the month' management. There is also a fear from middle management that they will be bypassed as a result of improvement activities. A number of middle managers shine as troubleshooters (this is how they have achieved promotion) and do not know anything else. They commonly express the concern that, if there is no firefighting, they have nothing else to do, and naturally fear for their jobs, especially in the current climate of developing flatter organization structures.

The middle manager's role typically involves:

- Developing specific improvement plans for the departments and processes for which they are responsible.
- Ensuring that the objectives, values, policies and improvement initiatives of their departments are aligned with the company's business goals, TQM strategy, and quality management system.
- Communicating the company's approach to TQM in commonsense and jargon-free language to first-line managers and other employees.
- Acting as TQM coach and counsellor to the employees for whom they are responsible.
- Ensuring that first-line managers are individually trained in the use of tools and techniques and that these are used effectively.
- Acting as a 'guardian, or sponsor or mentor' to improvement teams and securing the means to reward employees.
- Providing top management with considered views on how to manage the continuing implementation and development of TQM, taking into account feedback from first-line managers and employees on potential difficulties or obstacles.

The Role of First-Line Managers

First-line managers and supervisors are at the forefront of TQM. They have the key role of encouraging its implementation in the workplace, and are especially important because of the numbers of people they influence and lead. If first-line managers lack commitment, training, appropriate resources and a supportive management system and culture then the TQM cascade will fail at its most critical level. They are directly responsible for:

- Analysing the individual procedures and processes for which they are responsible in order to identify areas where improvements might be initiated and made.
- Encouraging individual employees and operators to contribute improvement ideas, and ensuring that good ideas and efforts are acknowledged and rewarded by middle and top management.
- Ensuring that any quality concerns reported by employees are analysed and resolved through permanent long-term corrective action.
- Participating in improvement teams in their own and related work areas.
- Providing workplace training in the use of specific techniques and tools to capture improvement data.
- Communicating the results of improvement activities and initiatives effectively to middle managers.
- Providing the data and responses required by the company's formal quality management system, including where applicable the requirements of the appropriate part of the ISO9000 series.
- Providing the data for the self-assessment process.
- Representing the people and processes they supervise in management discussions about TQM resources and strategies.

Summary

This chapter has examined the role which senior managers need to take and the visionary leadership they need to display if TQM is to be successful. They will often ask what they need to do to demonstrate their commitment to TQM. The chapter has outlined some of the things they need to get involved with, including chairing the TQM steering committee, organizing and chairing Defect Review Boards, leading self-assessment of progress against a model for business excellence, developing and then following a personal improvement action plan and sponsoring improvement teams. The chapter has summarized what senior management need to know about TQM and what they need to do to ensure TQM is successful and treated as part of normal business activities.

It is also pointed out that middle managers and first-line managers have a vital role in putting the principles of TQM in place and they must have unified thinking with senior management. Typical activities they should get involved with have been outlined.

References

Akao, Y. (ed.) (1991), *Hoshin Kanri: Policy Deployment for Successful TQM*. Massachusetts: Productivity Press.

Bunney, H. S. and Dale, B. G. (1996), The effect of organizational change on sustaining a process of continuous improvement. *Quality Engineering*, 8(4), 649–57.

Cook, E. and Dale, B. G. (1995), Organizing for continuous improvement: an examination. *The TQM Magazine*, 7(1), 7–13.

Dale, B. G. (1990), Policy deployment. *The TQM Magazine*, 2(6), 125–8.

Dale, B. G. (1993), The key features of Japanese Total Quality Control. *Quality and Reliability Engineering International*, 9(3), 169–78.

EFQM (2001), *The EFQM Excellence Model*. Brussels: EFQM.

Lascelles, D. M. and Dale, B. G. (1990), Quality management: the Chief Executive's perception and role. *European Management Journal*, 8(1), 67–75.

McKinsey and Company (1989), Management of quality: the single major important challenge for Europe. European Quality Management Forum, 19 October, Montreux, Switzerland.

Scharp, A. (1989), What gets measured gets done: the Electrolux way to improve quality. European Quality Management Forum, 19 October, Montreux, Switzerland.

chapter three

The Received Wisdom on TQM

B. G. Dale

Introduction

The purpose of this chapter is to introduce the reader to what the leading exponents of TQM have to say on the subject and explore, in brief, their teachings and advice.

In the Western world the four best-known quality management experts are all Americans – Crosby (1979), Deming (1982), Feigenbaum (1983) and Juran (1988). These four men have had a considerable influence on the development of TQM in organizations throughout the world. In addition to the approaches and philosophies of these four experts the Japanese quality management culture is also widely publicized. In recent times the work and ideas of a number of Japanese quality experts have been published in English. They include Imai (1986), Ishikawa (1985), Mizuno (1988), Nemoto (1987), Ozeki and Asaka (1990), Shingo (1986) and Taguchi (1986). The ideas of these Japanese experts are all being applied in the West, but perhaps the work of Imai, Ishikawa, Shingo and Taguchi is the best known. It is for this reason that it is briefly reviewed here before considering some of the familiar concepts associated with how Japanese companies manage a process of continuous and company-wide improvement.

Crosby

Philip Crosby's audience is primarily top management: he sells his approach to them and stresses increasing profitability through quality improvement. His argument is that higher quality reduces costs and raises profits. He defines quality as conformance to requirements not as goodness. Crosby's programme has 14 steps (Crosby 1979) that focus on how to change the organization and tend to be a specific action plan for implementation (see box 3.1).

Crosby's approach is based on four absolutes of quality management, summarized as:

- Quality is defined as conformance to requirements.
- The system for achieving quality is prevention not appraisal.
- The only performance standard is zero defects.
- The measurement of quality is the cost of quality.

BOX 3.1   CROSBY'S 14-STEP QUALITY IMPROVEMENT PROGRAMME

1   Management commitment
2   Quality improvement team
3   Quality measurement
4   Cost of quality evaluation
5   Quality awareness
6   Corrective action
7   Establish an ad hoc committee for the zero defects programme
8   Supervisor training
9   Zero defects day
10 Goal-setting
11 Error cause removal
12 Recognition
13 Quality councils
14 Do it over again

Crosby has also produced a 'quality vaccine' comprising 21 areas divided into the five categories of integrity, systems, communications, operations and policies, which he treats as preventative medicine for poor quality. He argues that a business can be vaccinated against non-conformance to quality requirements.

He does not accept the optimal quality level concept because he believes that higher quality always reduces costs and raises profits. Cost of quality is used as a tool to help achieve that goal. With respect to the cost of quality he produced the first serious alternative to the prevention, appraisal, failure (PAF) categorization with the price of conformance (POC) – doing things right – and price of non-conformance (PONC) – doing things wrong – model. In terms of employee roles, Crosby allocates a moderate amount of responsibility to the quality professional. Top management has an important role, and the hourly workforce has a role which is limited to reporting problems to management. One way that Crosby measures quality achievement is with a matrix, the quality management maturity grid, that charts the stages that management goes through from ignorance to enlightenment.

In summary, Crosby is acknowledged as a great motivator of senior management in helping them to understand how to get the improvement process started. His approach is generally regarded as simple and easy to follow. His critics often claim he lacks substance in giving detailed guidance on how to apply quality management principles, tools, techniques and systems. However, on the other hand, it can be argued that he simply wishes to avoid being prescriptive.

Deming

W. Edwards Deming's argument is that quality, through a reduction in statistical variation, improves productivity and competitive position. His early thinking was influenced by Shewhart, who is considered as the father of statistical quality control. Shewhart became Deming's teacher and mentor and Deming subsequently became the evangelist for the statistical method. He defines quality in terms of quality of design, quality of conformance, and quality of the sales and service function. Deming's main argument is that by improving quality it is possible to increase productivity and this will improve organizational competitiveness. He does not accept the trade-off shown in the 'economic cost of quality' models and says there is no way to calculate the cost of delivering defective products to customers, which he believes is the major quality cost.

Deming advocates the measurement of quality by direct statistical measures of manufacturing performance against specification. While all production processes exhibit variation, the goal is to reduce variation. Deming's approach is highly statistical and he believes that every employee should be trained in statistical quality techniques. A 14-point approach (Deming 1986) summarizes his management philosophy for improving quality and changing the organization's culture (see box 3.2).

Deming's view is that quality management and improvement are the responsibility of all the firm's employees: top management must adopt the 'new religion' of quality, lead the drive for improvement and be involved in all stages of the process. Hourly workers should be trained and encouraged to prevent defects and improve quality, and be given challenging and rewarding jobs. Quality professionals should educate other managers in statistical techniques and concentrate on improving the methods of defect prevention. Finally, statisticians should consult with all areas of the company.

Deming's other contributions include the PDCA (plan, do, check, act) or the PDSA (plan, do, study, act) cycle of continuous improvement, which Deming termed the Shewhart cycle, and the pinpointing of the seven 'deadly diseases' (lack of consistency of purpose; emphasis on short-term profits; evaluation of performance, merit rating, or annual review; mobility of management; running a company on visible figures alone; excessive medical costs; and excessive cost of liability), which he used to criticize Western management and organizational practices.

In summary, Deming expects managers to change – to develop a partnership with those at the operating level of the business and to manage quality with direct statistical measures without cost-of-quality measures. Deming's approach, particularly his insistence on the need for management to change the organizational culture, is closely aligned with Japanese practice. This is not surprising in view of the assistance he gave to the Japanese after the Second World War. Late in his life Deming defined his approach to management as a system of profound knowledge.

A number of Deming user groups and associations have been formed which are dedicated to facilitating awareness and understanding of his work and helping companies introduce his ideas. Also a number of authors (e.g. Aguayo 1990; Howard and Gitlow 1987; Kilian 1992; Scherkenbach 1991; Yoshida 1995) have produced books explaining Deming's approach and ideas.

BOX 3.2   DEMING'S 14 POINTS FOR MANAGEMENT

1	Create constancy of purpose towards improvement of product and service, with the aim to become competitive, stay in business, and to provide jobs.
2	Adopt the new philosophy – we are in a new economic age. Western management must awaken to the challenge, learn their responsibilities and take on leadership for future change.
3	Cease dependence on inspection to achieve quality. Eliminate the need for inspection on a mass basis by building quality into the product in the first place.
4	End the practice of awarding business on the basis of price tag. Instead, minimize total cost. Move towards a single supplier for any one item on a long-term relationship of loyalty and trust.
5	Improve constantly and for ever the system of production and service, to improve quality and productivity, and thus constantly decrease costs.
6	Institute training on the job.
7	Institute leadership (see point 12): the aim of supervision should be to help people, machines and gadgets to do a better job. Supervision of management, as well as supervision of production workers, is in need of overhaul.
8	Drive out fear, so that everyone may work effectively for the company.
9	Break down barriers between departments. People in research, design, sales and production must work as a team, to foresee problems of production and problems in use that may be encountered with the product or service.
10	Eliminate slogans, exhortations and targets for the workforce that ask for zero defects and new levels of productivity. Such exhortations only create adversarial relationships, as the bulk of the causes of low quality and low productivity belong to the system and thus lie beyond the power of the workforce.
11a	Eliminate work standards (quotas) on the factory floor; substitute leadership instead.
11b	Eliminate management by objectives, by numbers and by numerical goals; substitute leadership instead.
12a	Remove barriers that rob the hourly worker of his or her right to pride of workmanship. The responsibility of supervisors must be changed from sheer numbers to quality.
12b	Remove barriers that rob people in management and in engineering of their right to pride of workmanship. This means, inter alia, abolishment of the annual or merit rating, and of management by objectives.
13	Institute a vigorous programme of education and self-improvement.
14	Put everybody in the company to work to accomplish the transformation. The transformation is everybody's job.

Feigenbaum

Armand V. Feigenbaum was General Electric's world-wide chief of manufacturing operations for a decade until the late 1960s. He is now president of an engineering consultancy firm, General Systems Co., that designs and installs operational systems in corporations around the world. Feigenbaum was the originator of the term 'total quality control', defined in 1961 in his first edition of *Total Quality Control* as:

> an effective system for integrating the quality-development, quality-maintenance, and quality-improvement efforts of the various groups in an organization so as to enable marketing, engineering, production, and service at the most economical levels which allow for full customer satisfaction.

Feigenbaum doesn't try so much to create managerial awareness of quality as to help a plant or company design its own system. To him, quality is a way of managing a business organization and is the responsibility of everyone. (At the time this was a major contribution to the quality debate.) Significant quality improvement can only be achieved in a company through the participation of everyone in the workforce, who must, therefore, have a good understanding of what management is trying to do. Firefighting quality problems has to be replaced with a very clear, customer-oriented quality management process that people can understand and commit themselves to.

Senior management's understanding of the issues surrounding quality improvement and commitment to incorporating quality into their management practice is crucial to the successful installation of Feigenbaum's total quality system. They must abandon short-term motivational programmes that yield no long-lasting improvement. Management must also realize that quality doesn't mean only that customer problems have to be fixed faster. Quality leadership is essential to a company's success in the marketplace.

Feigenbaum takes a very serious financial approach to the management of quality. He believes that the effective installation and management of a quality improvement process represents the best return-on-investment opportunity for many companies in today's competitive environment.

Feigenbaum's major contribution to the subject of the cost of quality was the recognition that quality costs must be categorized if they are to be managed. He identified three major categories: appraisal costs, prevention costs and failure costs (Feigenbaum 1956). Total quality cost is the sum of these costs. He was also the first of the international experts to identify the folly of regarding quality professionals as being solely responsible for an organization's quality activities.

According to Feigenbaum the goal of quality improvement is to reduce the total cost of quality from the often quoted 25 to 30 per cent of annual sales or cost of operations to as low a percentage as possible. Therefore, developing cost-of-quality data and tracking it on an ongoing basis is an integral part of the process.

Feigenbaum says that management must commit themselves to:

- Strengthening the quality improvement process itself.
- Making sure that quality improvement becomes a habit.
- Managing quality and cost as complementary objectives.

In summary, though he does not espouse 14 points or steps like Deming or Crosby, it is obvious his approach is not significantly different: it simply boils down to

BOX 3.3   FEIGENBAUM'S 10 BENCHMARKS FOR TOTAL QUALITY SUCCESS

1   Quality is a company-wide process
2   Quality is what the customer says it is
3   Quality and cost are a sum, not a difference
4   Quality requires both individual and team zealotry
5   Quality is a way of managing
6   Quality and innovation are mutually dependent
7   Quality is an ethic
8   Quality requires continuous improvement
9   Quality is the most cost-effective, least capital-intensive route to productivity
10 Quality is implemented with a total system connected with customers and suppliers

managerial know-how. He does, however, identify 10 benchmarks for success with TQM (see box 3.3).

Juran

Joseph Juran has made perhaps a greater contribution to the quality management literature than any other quality professional. Like Deming he has had an influence in the development of quality management in Japanese companies and also worked with Shewhart at the Hawthorn plant. While Deming provided advice on statistical methods to technical specialists from the late 1940s onwards, Juran in the mid-1950s focused on the role of senior people in quality management. Juran was the first to broaden the thinking in quality control by emphasizing the importance of management and the need for a supportive infrastructure. The focus of his series of lectures was that quality control must be an integral part of the management function and practised throughout the organization. It can be argued that the teachings of Juran provided the catalyst which resulted in the involvement of first-line supervisors and operators in the improvement process (Juran and Godfrey 1999).

Part of his argument is that companies must reduce the cost of quality. This is dramatically different from Deming. Deming ignores the cost of quality while Juran, like Crosby and Feigenbaum, claim that reducing it is a key objective of any business. A 10-point plan summarizes his approach (see box 3.4).

Juran defines quality as 'fitness for use', which he breaks down into quality of design, quality of conformance, availability, and field service. The goals of Juran's approach to quality improvement are increased conformance and decreased cost of quality, and yearly goals are set in the objective-setting phase of the programme. He developed a quality trilogy comprising quality planning, quality control and quality improvement. Basically, his approach focuses on three segments: a programme to attack sporadic problems, one to attack chronic problems, and an annual quality programme, in which top management participates, to develop or refine policies. Juran defines two major kinds of quality management – breakthrough (encouraging

BOX 3.4   THE JURAN METHOD

```
 1   Build awareness of the need and opportunity for improvement.
 2   Set goals for improvement.
 3   Organize to reach the goals.
 4   Provide training.
 5   Carry out projects to solve problems.
 6   Report progress.
 7   Give recognition.
 8   Communicate results.
 9   Keep the score.
10   Maintain momentum by making annual improvement part of the regular
     system and processes of the company.
```

the occurrence of good things), that attacks chronic problems, and control (preventing the occurrence of bad things), that attacks sporadic problems. He views the improvement process as taking two journeys – from symptom to cause (diagnosis) and cause to remedy (diagnosis to solution).

Juran also allocates responsibility among the workforce differently from Deming. He puts the primary responsibility onto quality professionals (who serve as consultants to top management and employees). The quality professionals design and develop the programme, and do most of the work. While granting the importance of top management support, Juran places more of the quality leadership responsibility on middle management and quality professionals. The role of the workforce is mainly to be involved in quality improvement teams.

In summary, Juran emphasizes the cost of quality, because the language of top management is money, and he recommends cost of quality for identifying quality improvement projects and opportunities and developing a quality cost scoreboard to measure quality costs. Juran's approach is more consistent with American management practices – he takes the existing management culture as a starting point and builds a quality improvement process from that baseline. In contrast to Deming he considers that if the energy generated by fear is harnessed and focused in a positive direction it can be a positive rather than a negative factor.

Are the Approaches of these Gurus Different?

Advocates of each guru are apt to claim that 'their man's' approach is the only one likely to work. This is an arrogant and myopic stance to adopt; each approach has its strengths and weaknesses and they are all proven packages. None of the experts has all the answers to the problems facing an organization, despite each guru and, in particular, their supporters stressing the exclusivity of their approaches and methods. It is also worth remembering that all four of these experts are consultants (not forgetting that Crosby and Deming are now dead) and it is in their own business interests and those of their supporters to distinguish their approach from those of their peers, and appear to have all the answers.

It is suggested that any person interested in learning about the approaches and methods of any of these four men goes to the source and consults their original work rather than that of their disciples.

The ways of approaching quality management as suggested by Crosby, Deming, Feigenbaum and Juran are variations on a theme; the essential difference is the focus of their approach. A number of writers (e.g. Bendell 1989; Fine 1985; Gerald 1984; Main 1986) have compared and contrasted the approaches of the four gurus and these commentaries are helpful in assessing the value of each approach. Broadly speaking, the teachings of these four gurus can be characterized by the main focus of their approach, as follows:

- Crosby: company-wide motivation.
- Deming: statistical process control.
- Feigenbaum: systems management.
- Juran: project management.

McBryde (1986) says that the 'golden thread' running through the philosophies of all four (and other, unnamed) gurus is the concept of adopting quality as a fundamental business strategy permeating the culture of the entire organization. Fine (1985) concludes that the teachings of Crosby, Deming and Juran (Feigenbaum is not included in his comparison) have four points in common:

- The importance of top management support and participation.
- The need for workforce training and education.
- Quality management requires careful planning and a philosophy of company-wide involvement.
- Quality improvement programmes must represent permanent, ongoing activities.

The main ideas of all four are orientated to ensuring that organizations survive by making full use of their resources.

Imai

Imai (1986, 1997) is the person accredited with bringing together the various management philosophies, theories, techniques and tools which have assisted Japanese companies over the last four or so decades to improve their efficiency. The published evidence indicates that the impact of Kaizen in Japanese companies has been considerable.

In simple terms Kaizen is the process of incremental, systematic, gradual, orderly and continuous improvement that uses the best of all techniques, tools, systems and concepts (e.g. TPM, JIT, SMED, quality circles and the PDCA cycle). From this it is clear that Kaizen is generic in its application. Improvements take place in steady planned steps in contrast to the usual methods of Western organizations of large-step innovations and efforts. A good idea of what Kaizen encompasses is given by the glossary of Kaizen terminology and concepts at the front of Imai's book.

The aim of Kaizen is to ensure that everyone in an organization is of the frame of mind to pursue naturally continuous improvement in whatever they do. It also encourages people to accept continuing change at the place where action takes place (the *gemba*). Running through the concept are a number of basic principles such as:

- Continuous focus on improvement
- Everyone in the company should be involved
- Delighting the customer
- Everything should be considered from a total system standpoint

The key elements of Kaizen:

- Adaptability of both people and equipment
- Use of existing technology to optimize capacity
- Creative involvement of all employees
- 'Make it a little better each day' attitude

Ishikawa

Ishikawa's contribution is in three main areas: (1) the simplification and widespread use of the seven basic quality control tools; (2) the company-wide quality movement; and (3) quality circles. His thinking covers a number of aspects of modern-day TQM.

An underlying theme throughout Ishikawa's work (Ishikawa 1979, 1985, 1991) was that people at all levels of the organization should use simple methods and work together to solve problems, thereby removing barriers to improvement, co-operation and education and developing a culture which is conducive to continuous improvement.

Ishikawa developed the cause-and-effect diagram and was also responsible for bringing together the selection of tools which are now known as the seven basic quality control tools. His argument was that these seven tools, when used together, could help solve most problems.

He was an original member of the quality control research group of the Japanese Union of Scientists and Engineers (JUSE). In this activity he became involved in the teaching of JUSE total quality control (TQC) courses and was involved in this activity until his death in 1989. In Japan, if a company wants to start TQC it is usual for the senior management to attend a course organized by JUSE. This type of course is run by three teachers known fondly as 'the Big Three'. Ishikawa was one of these three. As part of his work with this research group he was involved in studying American methods and helping Japanese companies adapt and develop them for their own environment and operating conditions. He was renowned for working in harmony with his academic colleagues.

Ishikawa is regarded as the 'father of quality control circles'. This was because he was on the editorial staff of the JUSE publication *Gemba to QC*, which when it was launched in April 1962 called for the formation of quality circles. JUSE organized training programmes for shop-floor supervisors – workshop quality control study groups – and this publication was the textbook. Subsequently JUSE started to register the quality circles which then formed in manufacturing organizations. From this start Ishikawa played a great role in the development of quality circles in Japan and assisted with world-wide spread of the concept. Dale (1993), quoting Dr Noguchi (executive director of JUSE), makes the point that Ishikawa claimed quality circles are effective in solving 30–35 per cent of an organization's quality problems.

Shingo

Shingo has had a number of books translated into English (e.g. Shingo 1985, 1986, 1989). He is best known for his work on single minute exchange of die (SMED), the mistake-proofing (poka-yoke) defect prevention system and, in conjunction with Ohno, the development of the Toyota production system. He liked to be known as 'Dr Improvement' and is renowned for his work on improving manufacturing processes.

Shingo advocates the use of the poka-yoke system to reduce and eliminate defects. He classifies poka-yoke systems into two types: regulatory functions and setting functions. Two main functions are performed by the regulatory devices: (1) control methods which when abnormalities are detected shut down the machine thus preventing the occurrence of further non-conformities, and (2) warning methods which signal, by means of noise and/or light devices, the occurrence of an abnormality. There are three main types of poka-yoke setting functions: (1) contact methods in which sensing devices detect abnormalities; (2) fixed-value methods in which abnormalities are detected by counting devices; and (3) motion-step methods where abnormalities are detected by failure to follow a predetermined motion or routine.

The term SMED refers to the theory and technique for performing set-up operations in under 10 minutes. It is a fundamental approach to continuous improvement, bringing benefits in terms of stock reduction, productivity improvements, flexibility, reduction in set-up errors and defects, and improved tool management. The concept of SMED and quick changeover advanced by Shingo challenges traditional wisdom (e.g. economic batch sizes, that set-up always takes a long time, and that the skills required for set-up changes can only be acquired through long-term practice and experience). Shingo identifies three main stages of improvement through SMED:

1 Differentiate and separate internal set-up (which can only be performed when a machine is shut down) from external set-up (which can be done while the machine is running).
2 Shift internal set-up elements to external set-up.
3 Improve the methods involved in both internal and external set-ups.

The contribution he made to the development of the Toyota production system is legendary and his written work outlines a number of methods (e.g. JIT, scheduling, workplace layout, stock control SMED, mistake-proofing) for improving quality and productivity.

Taguchi

Genichi Taguchi is a statistician and electrical engineer who was involved in rebuilding the Japanese telephone system. He was contracted to provide statistical assistance and design of experiment support. Taguchi rejected the classical approach to the design of experiments as being too impractical for industrial situations and revised these methods to develop his own approach. He has been applying Taguchi design of experiments in the Japanese electronics industry for over 30 years.

His ideas fall into two principal and related areas known as 'the loss function' and 'off-line quality control'.

In his ideas about the loss function Taguchi (1986) defines quality as follows: 'The quality of a product is the loss imparted to society from the time the product is shipped.' Among the losses he includes consumers' dissatisfaction, warranty costs, loss of reputation and, ultimately, loss of market share. Taguchi maintains that a product does not start causing losses only when it is out of specification, but when there is any deviation from the target value. Further, in most cases the loss to society can be represented by a quadratic function (i.e. the loss increases as the square of the deviation from the target value). This leads to the important conclusion that quality (as defined by Taguchi) is most economically achieved by minimizing variance, rather than by strict conformance to specification.

This conclusion provides the basis for Taguchi's ideas for off-line quality control. Off-line quality control means optimizing production process and product parameters in such a way as to minimize item-to-item variations in the product and its performance. Clearly this focuses attention on the design process. Taguchi promotes three distinct stages of designing in quality:

- *System design*: the basic configuration of the system is developed. This involves the selection of parts and materials and the use of feasibility studies and prototyping. In system design technical knowledge and scientific skills are paramount.
- *Parameter design*: the numerical values for the system variables (product and process parameters which are called factors) are chosen so that the system performs well, no matter what disturbances or noises (i.e. uncontrollable variables) are encountered by it (i.e. it is robust). The objective is to identify optimum levels for these control factors so that the product and/or process is least sensitive to the effect of changes of noise factors. The experimentation pinpoints this combination of product/process parameter levels. The emphasis in parameter design is on using low-cost materials and processes in the production of the system. It is the key stage of designing in quality.
- *Tolerance design*: if the system is not satisfactory, tolerance design is then used to improve performance by tightening the tolerances.

When seeking to optimize production process and product or service parameters it is frequently necessary to determine experimentally the effects of varying the parameter values. This can be a very expensive and time-consuming process which may produce a lot of redundant information. By using fractional factorial experiments, which Taguchi calls orthogonal arrays, the number of experiments required can be reduced drastically. An orthogonal array from a design of experiment carried out on the corrugator at Rexam Corrugated South-West Ltd. is shown in figure 3.1.

The attention given to what are commonly termed 'Taguchi methods' has been largely responsible for organizations examining the usefulness of experimental design in making improvements. Quite apart from the successes derived from using his methods, the level of awareness he has promoted in design of experiments is an achievement in itself. However, it should not be overlooked that a number of other people have made significant improvements with other approaches to experimental

	Gap	Straw unwind	Gaylord heater	Fluting shower	Liner wrap	Small P/heat	Roll pressure	Strength	Variation
Set 1	6	Off	On	Off	Off	Off	40	58.73	6.93
Set 2	6	Off	On	On	On	On	60	76.27	7.18
Set 3	6	On	Off	Off	Off	On	60	63.26	6.29
Set 4	6	On	Off	On	On	Off	40	67.07	7.53
Set 5	9	Off	Off	Off	On	Off	60	61.65	4.51
Set 6	9	Off	Off	On	Off	On	40	61.19	4.90
Set 7	9	On	On	Off	On	On	40	65.56	4.57
Set 8	9	On	On	On	Off	Off	60	62.73	5.41

Figure 3.1 Design of experiments: liner bond strength
Source: Rexam Corrugated South West Ltd.

design. It should also be mentioned that he provided little advice on the management of the experiments themselves.

Japanese-Style Total Quality

The Japanese define their goal as continual improvement towards perfection. They allocate responsibility for quality and its improvement among all employees. The workers are primarily responsible for maintaining the system, although they have some responsibility for improving it. Higher up, managers do less maintaining and more improving. At the highest levels, the emphasis is on breakthrough and on teamwork throughout the organization.

There are a number of now familiar concepts associated with Japanese-style TQM, or total quality control (TQC) or company-wide quality control (CWQC) as they term it (see Mizuno 1988; Nemoto 1987). CWQC is defined by JUSE (see Deming Prize Committee 1997) as:

> a set of systematic activities carried out by the entire organization to effectively and efficiently achieve company objectives and provide products and services within a level of quality that satisfies customers, at the appropriate time and price.

Earlier work tried to make a distinction between TQC and CWQC, but in Japanese companies today they appear to be one and the same. These concepts include:

- Total commitment to improvement
- Perfection and defect analysis
- Continuous change
- Taking personal responsibility for the quality assurance of one's own processes
- Insistence on compliance
- Correcting one's own errors

- Adherence to disciplines, and
- Orderliness and cleanliness

Various practices facilitate continuous improvement in Japanese companies, including:

- Policy deployment of targets for improvement
- Use of statistical methods
- Housekeeping
- Daily machine- and equipment-checking
- Successive and self-check systems
- Visual management
- Mistake-proofing
- Detailed quality assurance procedures
- Visual standards
- The concept that the next person or process is the customer
- Improvement followed by standardization
- The just-in-time philosophy
- Total productive maintenance
- Quality circles
- Suggestion schemes, and
- Treating suppliers as part of the family

Dale (1999) outlines the following simple facts which he believes can be learnt from the Japanese experience of TQM:

- TQM depends on a systematic approach which is applied consistently throughout the entire organization.
- There are no quick fixes for the TQM success of Japanese companies. Western executives are always on the lookout for the universal panacea; unfortunately there are none. This search for the quick fix is often an irritation to the Japanese. Their success is the result of the application of a combination of procedures, continuous discussion, systems, tools, improvement actions and considerable hard work and dedication from all employees.
- Senior and middle managers must believe in TQM as a key business strategy and be prepared to stick with it over the long term and ensure that it is integrated with other strategies.
- There must be a permanent managed process which examines all products, service processes and procedures on a continuous basis and develops the mindset in all employees that there is no ideal state. Self-assessment against the criteria of the recognized Quality management excellence models are an invaluable means of assessing progress in order to ensure that an organization continues to win customers.
- Each person should take personal responsibility for the quality assurance activities within their area of control and quality assurance must be integrated into every process and every function of an organization.
- Planning for improvement must be thorough.
- Improvement is a slow, incremental process. Companies should not expect quick and major benefits from the application of any single method, system,

procedure and/or tool or technique. To be effective the quality management tools and techniques must be used together, in particular, the seven original quality control tools.

● There must be a fanatical obsession with pursuing perfection, challenging targets, reacting quickly to problems to find out what went wrong and putting in place corrective action.

● The concept of TQM is simple; however, defining, introducing and fostering the process is a considerable task and requires total commitment from all employees.

● TQM is all about common sense. The Japanese put common sense into practice. They manage and apply common sense in a disciplined manner. In European companies a typical saying is 'you cannot teach common sense'; the Japanese have done just that.

Summary

The published writings and philosophies of the eminent people mentioned in this chapter can provide the necessary inspiration and guidance to organizations in introducing and developing a process of continuous improvement. While the slavish following of a guru's teachings or points is no guarantee of success, despite the propaganda, it would be a brave manager who can afford not to learn from their collective wisdom. They should, however, be prepared to adapt and develop these teachings to suit their operating conditions and available resources.

References

Aguayo, R. (1990), *Dr. Deming: The American who Taught the Japanese about Quality*. New York: Simon & Schuster.

Bendell, T. (1989), *The Quality Gurus: What Can They Do for Your Company?* London: Department of Trade and Industry.

Crosby, P. B. (1979), *Quality is Free*. New York: McGraw Hill.

Dale, B. G. (1993), The key features of Japanese total quality control. *Quality and Reliability Engineering International*, 9(1), 169–78.

Dale, B. G. (ed.) (1999), *Managing Quality*, 3rd edn. Oxford: Blackwell.

Deming, W. E. (1982), *Quality, Productivity and Competitive Position*. Cambridge, Mass.: MIT, Centre of Advanced Engineering Study.

Deming, W. E. (1986), *Out of the Crisis*. Cambridge, Mass.: MIT, Centre of Advanced Engineering Study.

Deming Prize Committee (1997), *The Japan Quality Medal Guide for Overseas Companies*. Tokyo: Union of Japanese Scientists and Engineers.

Feigenbaum, A. V. (1956), Total Quality Control. *Harvard Business Review*, 34(6), 93–101.

Feigenbaum, A. V. (1961), *Total Quality Control*, 1st edn. New York: McGraw Hill.

Feigenbaum, A. V. (1983), *Total Quality Control*, 3rd edn. New York: McGraw Hill.

Fine, C. H. (1985), *Managing Quality: A Comparative Assessment*, Manufacturing Issues. New York: Booz Allen & Hamilton Inc.

Gerald, V. (1984), *Three of a Kind: A Reflection on the Approach to Quality*. Eindhoven: Corporate Quality Bureau, Philips Group N.V.

Howard, S. and Gitlow, S. J. (1987), *The Deming Guide to Quality and Competitive Position*. Milwaukee: ASQC Quality Press.

Imai, M. (1986), *Kaizen: The Key to Japan's Competitive Success*. New York: Random House Business Division.

Imai, M. (1997), *Gemba Kaizen: A Commonsense Low Cost Approach to Management*. Milwaukee: ASQC.

Ishikawa, K. (1979), *Guide to Quality Control*. Tokyo: Asian Productivity Organization.

Ishikawa, K. (1985), *What is Total Quality Control? The Japanese Way*, trans. Lu D. J. Englewood Cliffs, NJ: Prentice Hall.

Ishikawa, K. (1991), *Introduction to Quality Control*. Tokyo: Chapman & Hall.

Juran, J. M. (1988), *Quality Control Handbook*, 4th edn. New York: McGraw Hill.

Juran, J. M. and Godfrey B. (1999), *Juran's Quality Control Handbook*, 5th edn. New York: McGraw Hill.

Kilian, C. S. (1992), *The World of W. Edwards Deming*. New York: SPC Press.

Main, J. (1986), Under the spell of the quality gurus. *Fortune*, 18 August, 24–7.

McBryde, V. E. (1986), In today's market: quality is best focal point for upper management. *Industrial Engineering*, 18(7), 51–5.

Mizuno, S. (1988), *Company-Wide Total Quality Control*. Tokyo: Asian Productivity Organization.

Nemoto, M. (1987), *Total Quality Control for Management*. Englewood Cliffs, NJ: Prentice Hall.

Ozeki, K. and Asaka, T. (1990), *Handbook of Quality Tools*. Buckinghamshire: Productivity Europe.

Scherkenbach, W. W. (1991), *The Deming Route to Quality and Productivity: Road Maps and Roadblocks*. Milwaukee: ASQC Quality Press.

Shingo, S. (1985), *A Revolution in Manufacturing: The SMED System*. Cambridge, Mass.: Productivity Press.

Shingo, S. (1986), *Zero Quality Control: Source Inspection and the Poka-Yoke System*. Cambridge, Mass.: Productivity Press.

Shingo, S. (1989), *A Study of the Toyota Production System from an Industrial Engineering Viewpoint*. Cambridge, Mass.: Productivity Press.

Taguchi, G. (1986), *Introduction to Quality Engineering*. New York: Asian Productivity Organization.

Yoshida, K. (1995), Revisiting Deming's 14 points in light of Japanese business practice. *Quality Management Journal*, 3(1), 14–30.

chapter four

The Introduction of TQM

B. G. Dale

Introduction

There are a number of approaches which can be followed in the introduction of TQM. These include:

1 A listing of TQM principles and practices in the form of a generic plan along with a set of guidelines.
2 Prescriptive step-by-step approaches.
3 Methods outlining the wisdom, philosophies and recommendations of internationally respected experts on the subject (i.e. Crosby, Deming, Feigenbaum and Juran).
4 Self-assessment methods such as the MBNQA model for performance excellence and the EFQM excellence model (see chapter 24).
5 Non-prescriptive methods in the form of a framework or model (see chapter 5).

With all this available advice and prescription it is not surprising that there is sometimes inertia on the part of senior management teams who are faced with the task of introducing TQM in their organizations.

It is up to the management team of each organization to identify the approach which best suits their needs and business operation. Indeed, it is not unusual for an organization to find that its TQM approach is not working out as planned and to switch to another approach. Some of the main ways of starting TQM are examined in this chapter. It begins by examining why organizations decide to embark on TQM.

The contribution of Dr David Lascelles contained in the section 'Change and Continuous Improvement' is acknowledged.

Change and Continuous Improvement

Changing the life-long behaviour, customs, practices and prejudices of an organization is not easy. Organizations committed to quality will strive continually to improve the quality of their goods or services, and are committed to change, but in many cases they were intended to be stable and unchanging. Good reasons must exist either inside or outside the organization to precipitate the process of change and get managers to recognize that they need to improve their business.

Dale (1999) reports that in Japanese companies the major motivations for introducing TQM and associated problem points include:

- Environmental, national and business factors and changing circumstances such as: the second oil crisis, exchange rate of the yen, slow economic growth and severe competition.
- A lack of effective long-range planning.
- An organizational emphasis on defensive mechanisms.
- The new products which were launched did not achieve their sales target values.
- A need to develop new products which are attractive to the marketplace. In the past, the tendency was to carry out formal and technological development rather than listening to the real needs of customers.
- Slow growth in sales and market, leading to stagnation of the business.
- Concerns about how to achieve the long-term plan of the organization and the president's plan on quality, cost and delivery.
- Complacency about current profits and a failure to recognize the seriousness of the situation.
- The written and verbal experiences of companies who were already practising TQM, in particular those companies who had received the Deming Application Prize and were major customers of the company in question.
- Organizational, conceptual and business weaknesses such as:

  - Lack of advance planning for quality
  - Lack of liaison between development, design and manufacturing departments
  - Emphasis on manufacturing for quantity without sufficient regard for quality
  - Management policies were not universally understood throughout the organization
  - A poor approach to the solution of problems
  - The morale of workers was poor
  - Only stop-gap measures were employed to cope with customer claims
  - Chronic defects in the manufacturing process
  - Problems at production start-up due to insufficient pre-production planning.

Dale also points out that 'Whenever a Japanese company has faced a crisis of any kind, they have turned to the introduction of TQM as a principal pillar for their management activities.'

Lascelles and Dale (1989) report that the improvement process is often triggered by one or more of the following:

Figure 4.1   Market-led paradigm of TQI
Source: Lascelles and Dale (1993)

- The chief executive
- Competition
- Demanding customers
- Fresh-start situations

Later, Lascelles and Dale (1993) argued that these can be viewed as links in a chain, with competition acting as a catalyst setting off a chain reaction which enhances quality awareness in the market, resulting in demanding customers and chief executives behaving as external and internal change agents respectively (see figure 4.1). Drawing on this work these forces are now examined.

Forces for Change

The chief executive officer

Many writers on the subject of quality management are agreed that unless the CEO plays an active role and takes the lead to improve quality within an organization, attempts and gains made by individuals and departments will be short-lived. The limited success usually surfaces in a lack of empowerment at lower levels of the organizational hierarchy. The role of the CEO has been explored in detail in chapter 2. However, most chief executives want tangible proof of the need for continuous improvement and for their own involvement, because they usually have a number of urgent matters which need their attention. Thus other factors must also be present, of which market pressure (e.g. intense competition, demanding customers) has by far the greatest impact. A restart situation or greenfield opportunity may also aid the process by eliminating some of the barriers to change or reducing their effects.

Competition

Competition is fierce in today's business environment and quality is recognized as a key consideration in many purchasing decisions. There is little doubt that quality is an essential part of the marketing mix as companies seek ways to differentiate effectively their products and/or services from those of their competitors. Many successful companies (in market share terms) now advertise their products and/or services on the basis of quality and reliability rather than price. For example, consider the number of advertisements in which the word quality is featured. There are numerous well-publicized cases (e.g. DTI 1990) in which intense competition has been the change agent compelling companies to develop their quality systems to meet the requirements of the ISO9000 series of quality management system standards and/or to introduce a TQM approach to improve quality. The options may be to go out of business, to lose market share, or to have to withdraw from a particular market. The motivation for improvement is provided here by the need to stay competitive, and the change agent is the customer whose awareness of quality has been enhanced. As a result of such pressures, suppliers of goods and services have, in turn, themselves become demanding customers and seek improved levels of quality conformance from their own suppliers.

Demanding customers

Demanding customers with high product and service quality expectations and an established reputation for quality can be very effective change agents. In addition to providing tangible evidence of the value of reputation and standing, they have the potential for bringing about radical and permanent changes in attitudes towards continuous improvement among their suppliers through the requirements they place on them. Many major purchasers have policies which outline what is required of suppliers in terms of their approach to quality management (e.g. the QS9000 quality system standard). Documents such as these describe fundamentals that must be incorporated into a supplier's quality planning methods and quality system to control and improve quality. Each supplier is responsible for building on these fundamentals to develop an effective quality system, and products and services which are defect-free. Many quality-conscious purchasers assess and evaluate supplier performance. Some also provide resources to help suppliers implement tools, techniques and systems, improve workplace layout, and give guidance on problem-solving. For example, Nissan Motor Manufacturing (UK) Ltd., among others, have a supplier development team who are working with suppliers on a continuous basis to teach them how to make incremental improvements (see Lloyd et al. 1994 for details). Companies that take an active interest in their suppliers are likely to provoke a far-reaching effect on the way in which they manage continuous improvement.

'Fresh-start' situations

The degree of entrenchment of attitudes, and hence the difficulty of changing them, is related to the length of time an organization has been established, its size, staff turnover rate, managerial mobility, markets, competitors, and many other factors which influence the 'performance' of an organization. A fresh-start situation therefore provides excellent opportunities to make rapid, fundamental, changes to attitudes and relationships.

A 'greenfield' venture may be the setting up of a new company, a new operational direction for an existing company (e.g. creation of a new strategic business unit as part of a diversification programme), an established company relocating to a new factory, or a company establishing a new operation in existing premises after rationalizing plant, product lines, manpower, etc. It may be argued that most greenfield ventures are in areas where growth expectations are high and where demanding customers are at their most influential. Furthermore most greenfield companies tend to be small at the outset so that the purchasing power of individual customers is considerable. A greenfield venture provides an opportunity for the introduction of a process of continuous improvement in a situation where there is no prior history of lame excuses, acceptance of non-conformance, shipping non-conforming products in order to meet production targets, providing and accepting a poor level of service, poor delivery performance, and where 'we have always done it this way', 'it will not work here' and other unhelpful attitudes are absent. In a greenfield venture there is an opportunity to start from scratch without any vested interest or inhibiting procedures to overcome. It is an opportunity for senior management to try to do all the things that should be done to engender a culture of continuous improvement.

A hiatus, no matter how brief, brought about by an interruption of a company's operations may present the same kind of opportunity. Intentional temporary dislocation or cessation of normal activities may be another way of breaking with tradition, deflating the pressures of expediency, and removing the barriers to improvement. Moving to a new site, a takeover, management buy-out, large-scale refurbishing of premises or equipment, bankruptcy, or a major catastrophe might also be the catalyst for change.

How Do Companies Get Started?

Once change has been triggered, organizations need to translate enhanced quality awareness and organizational need for improvement into effective action. At this stage an organization's senior management team ask questions such as:

- What should we do?
- What are the priorities?
- What advice do we need?
- From whom should we be taking advice?
- Can we get unbiased advice?
- Should the approach be top-down or bottom-up?
- Do we need an umbrella term? Do we have to use the term TQM? What are the alternatives: quality improvement, continuous improvement, business improvement, customer care, customer focus, customer first, excellence?
- How quickly should we proceed?
- Which tools and techniques should we apply?
- How do we apply these tools and techniques?
- What courses and conferences should we attend?
- Can we make use of one of the recognized excellence models?
- Which companies should we visit?
- Which network of companies should we attempt to join?
- What training do we need?
- What packages and programmes should we buy?
- Should we call in a management consultant and which one?

- Should we develop the quality system to meet the requirements of the ISO9000 quality management system series?
- How important is quality management system registration?
- How do we embrace our current improvement initiatives under the TQM banner?

Their dilemma is often compounded not just by a lack of knowledge of TQM and the process of continuous improvement but also by a lack of experience in managing organizational change. The overwhelming quantity and variety of available advice, which is often conflicting, sometimes biased and sometimes incorrect and misdirected, simply adds to the confusion and chaos. It is not surprising then that there is sometimes inertia on the part of senior management teams who are faced with the task of introducing a formal process of continuous improvement in their organizations.

Approaches to TQM

Each writer on the subject of TQM develops and outlines an approach which reflects their own background, values and experience. These approaches include:

1　Methods outlining the wisdom, philosophies and recommendations of the internationally respected experts on the subject.
2　Prescriptive step-by-step approaches.
3　A listing of TQM principles which are presented in the form of a TQM implementation plan and a set of guidelines.
4　Non-prescriptive methods in the form of a framework or model.
5　Self-assessment methods based on the excellence models on which the Malcolm Baldrige National Quality Award (MBNQA) and the European Quality Award (EQA) are based.

Thus it can be seen that there are a number of ways to get started and it is up to each organization to identify the approach which best suits its needs and business operation. Indeed, it is not unusual for an organization to find that its TQM approach is not working out as planned and switch to another approach. Some of the main ways of starting TQM are now examined in brief.

Applying the wisdom of the quality management experts

The writings and teachings of Crosby, Deming, Feigenbaum and Juran, discussed in chapter 3, are a sensible starting point for any organization introducing TQM. These four men have had a considerable influence in the development of TQM in organizations throughout the world. The usual approach is for an organization to adopt the teachings of one of these quality management experts and attempt to follow their programme. The argument for this approach is that each expert has a package which works, the package gives some form of security, it provides a coherent framework, gives a discipline to the process and provides a common language, understanding and method of communication. To facilitate this some companies have purposely opted for the simplest package. The approach of Crosby is generally recognized as being the easiest to follow. Dale (1991) found that Crosby, followed by Juran and then Deming, were the most frequently used experts. Observations of organizations setting out on this road show that sooner or later they will start to pull into their improvement process the ideas of other quality management experts. This is understandable because none of these experts has all the answers to the problems facing an organization, despite the claims made about the exclusivity of approach.

Whichever man's programme or approach is being followed it should be used as a quality management tool to focus on the improvement process and not treated as an end in itself.

Applying a consultancy package

Some companies (usually large concerns) decide to adopt the programme of one of the major management consultancies on the grounds that it is a self-contained package which can be suitably customized for application throughout their organization. Some companies are very comfortable with consultants, others not so. Most of the 'gurus' have their own consultancy activities to help organizations implement the ideas and principles of the expert in question. Also a number of the consultancy packages are based on the teachings and wisdom of the quality management gurus.

It is important for a company to understand that the use of a consultant organization does not relieve the senior management team of their own responsibilities for TQM; it is their responsibility to own the improvement process and to exercise leadership. Executives should never allow the consultant to become the 'TQM champion' or the company expert on TQM. A key part of consultancy is the transfer of skills and knowledge, and when the project is complete the training and guidance provided by the consultant must remain within the organization in order that the process of improvement can progress and develop. They also help to change the way managers think and behave. The consultant should be perceived by the organization as an 'implementation' tool and not as an initiator of TQM and the improvement process. It may be that the consultant is also learning on the job and that the organization is acting, unknowingly, in the role of guinea pig, and any ideas, proposals and decisions should always be scrutinized carefully by the TQM steering committee for their applicability to the company's operations.

Management consultancies bring their expertise and skills to the company and provide the resources, experience, disciplines, objectivity and the catalyst for getting the process started. An organization can benefit from the use of this expertise providing it is willing to accept the recommendations of the consultants. The consultants are usually involved in a wide range of activities, from planning through to training and project work, facilitation of improvement team meetings and implementation of specific improvement initiatives. There are a myriad consultancies offering a variety of TQM products and packages, and not all of them will suit every organization. It is likely that organizations, in particular large ones, will use more than one consultancy as they make progress on the TQM journey.

A company intending to use a consultancy must carefully consider its selection so as to ensure that the one chosen is suited to its needs; this also applies to the individual consultant(s) who will actually carry out the work. The selection issue generally involves a presentation of the TQM approach used by the consultancy to senior management and other interested parties. There are a number of factors to be taken into consideration, including:

- Presentation of the TQM approach used by the consultancy to senior management and other interested parties.
- Personality of the consultant(s) and the perceived interaction with the people with whom they will work.
- Proposal details.
- Previously published material.
- Availability and adequacy of educational material and supporting systems, programmes and tools, including delivery style of the material.
- Willingness to carry out ongoing reassessment and fine-tune the training programme.
- Reputation, experience and track record of the consultancy and individual consultant(s), with existing clients.
- Knowledge of TQM and its application in practice in similar or related companies – not just in consulting, research and/or teaching.
- Honesty about what can be achieved and the time period.
- Rapport and ability to communicate with staff at all levels in the organization.
- Ability to develop a bond with the organization.
- Training skills and ability.
- Grasp of the client organization's culture and management style, and understanding of the organization's current status with respect to TQM.
- The extent to which the consultancy is prepared to assist in carrying out a quality management diagnosis and tailor and adopt the package and delivery methods to suit the needs of the client.
- Willingness to challenge the senior management rather than simply playing the role of 'yes men'.
- Guarantees on work undertaken and promise of results.

The decision to use a consultant organization is usually made by the CEO with support from the quality director. It is dangerous for the consultant to assume that other board members will contribute more than vocal support to the process of improvement. It is not unusual to find those directors who have not been directly involved or consulted resisting the initiative.

The company needs to understand clearly what it is buying from a consultancy. It is often difficult to define in precise detail what is required in a TQM assignment, with the consequence that the terms of reference are vague. This sometimes results in a difference between what was ordered and what is delivered; wrangling over the deliverables from a TQM contract is a major detractor from a process of continuous improvement. The company should also take care that a TQM assignment is not used to open the door for other consultancy work in problem areas such as manufacturing management, business process re-engineering (BPR), logistics, human resources, organization development, accountancy and business management. The easiest way of selling consultancy is on the back of a short-term successful assignment; this might have a negative influence on the long-term success of TQM.

A major complaint about consultancies is the use of 'off-the-shelf' packages and prescriptive solutions that fail to maximize client involvement and do not reflect the client's business process and business constraints, and the use of prescriptive words and terms which do not suit the culture of the client organization.

For those considering the utilization of an external consultant, the main issues to be addressed and agreed on can be summarized as follows:

1   Clear terms of reference specifying the expected benefits to the organization of the consultancy project, with tangible objectives, milestones and time-scales and the building of follow-up sessions to maintain the improvement momentum.

2   The precise nature of the relationship between the client management team and the consultant. The management team will need to consider the precise form of consultancy input required, and identify success criteria for the project.

3   The mechanism for implementing the improvement strategy and managing the change process, together with the resources required. The issues involved include the role of the senior management team, the amount of time and energy individual senior managers are able or prepared to commit, and who might assume the day-to-day role of project co-ordinator.

A booklet *Choosing and Using a Consultant* produced by the Employment Department (1991), which is aimed at directors and managers, contains a number of useful pointers to identify, select and work with consultants.

Frameworks and models

A framework or model is usually introduced to present a picture of what is required in introducing TQM. They are the means of presenting ideas, concepts, pointers and plans in a non-prescriptive manner and are usually not considered to be a 'how-to' guide to TQM introduction and subsequent development. They are guides to action and not things to be followed in a slavish manner. Step-by-step approaches have a set starting point and usually follow one route and, in general, are rigid. They are more concerned with the destination than the route to it. A framework allows the user to choose their own starting point and course of action and build gradually on the individual features and parts at a pace which suit their business situation and available resources. Aalbregtse et al. (1991) provide an excellent description of what a framework should consist and its objectives. A number of writers (e.g. Burt 1993; Chu 1988; Dale and Boaden 1993; Flero 1992; Johnson 1992) have proposed a range of TQM improvement frameworks. A typical framework for managing continuous improvement is the UMIST improvement framework as described by Dale and Boaden in chapter 5. It provides an indication of how the various aspects of TQM fit together and is particularly useful for those organizations who:

- Are taking their first steps on the continuous improvement journey;
- Have got ISO9001 quality management system and require some guidance and advice on what to do next;
- Are attempting to develop improvement plans and controls across a number of sites;
- Have less than three years operating experience of TQM.

Developing a tailor-made organizational route map

A variation on these approaches is to absorb the 'received wisdom' and the experiences of other companies and extract the ideas, methods, systems and tactics which are appropriate to the particular circumstances, business situation and environment of the organization. Organizations starting with any of the more popular approaches to TQM will eventually use this method.

In this approach management have to think through the issues and develop for themselves a vision, quality objectives, policy, approach, a route map for quality improvement and the means of disseminating the philosophy to all levels of the organization. A feature of organizations following this approach is that senior management will have visited other companies with a reputation for being 'centres of excellence' to see at first hand the lessons learned from TQM, and will have become involved in meetings relating to TQM with executives of like mind from different companies. They are also frequent attendees at conferences and are generally well read on the subject.

When getting started on the improvement process it is always beneficial for organizations to establish contacts with others that have a reputation for excellence in systems and products. There is much to be said for learning by association and sharing information through networks. Companies working with or competing directly against companies with advanced management processes develop their knowledge of TQM and continuous improvement at a fast rate. A case in point is the influence which the Japanese automotive and electronic companies have had on the UK supply base.

From the outset, organizations must accept that TQM is a long and arduous journey, which has no end. Unfortunately there are no short cuts and no one has a monopoly of the best ideas. Furthermore, once started, the momentum needs to be maintained, otherwise even the gains may be lost. Even the most successful improvement process has periods when little headway is made. The method of getting started on TQM is less important than management commitment to continuous improvement and the leadership they are prepared to demonstrate; this is the key determinant of long-term success.

Self-assessment

If a process of continuous improvement is to be sustained and its pace increased it is essential that organizations monitor on a regular basis which activities are going well, which have stagnated and what needs to be improved. Self-assessment (discussed in detail in chapter 24) against a recognized model provides such a framework and it is defined by the EFQM (2001) as:

> a comprehensive, systematic and regular review of an organization's activities and results referenced against a model of business excellence. The self-assessment process allows the organization to discern clearly its strengths and areas in which improvements can be made and culminates in planned improvement actions which are monitored for progress.

Summary

This chapter has argued that a formal approach to TQM is triggered by one or more of four factors, namely the CEO, competition, demanding customers and fresh-start situations.

The point has been made that there is no 'right' way of introducing and developing TQM. There are a number of approaches, and these have been examined in the chapter. It is senior management's responsibility to select the approach which best suits its business and operating environment and any constraints which may exist. The approach should always be tailored to the organization and 'off-the-shelf' packages avoided. Senior management have much to gain by networking with their counterparts in different businesses and this exchange of ideas and concerns and discussion of common issues can help to fine-tune the approach which is being used and to advance the development of TQM.

References

Aalbregtse, R. J., Heck, J. A. and McNeley, P. K. (1991), TQM: how do you do it? *Automation*, 38(8), 30–2.

Burt, J. F. (1993), A new for a not-so-new concept. *Quality Progress*, 26(3), 87–8.

Chu, C. H. (1988), The pervasive elements of total quality control. *Industrial Management*, 30(5), 30–2.

Crosby, P. B. (1979), *Quality is Free*. New York: McGraw Hill.

Dale, B. G. (1991), Starting on the road to success. *The TQM Magazine*, 3(2), 125–8.

Dale, B. G. (ed.) (1999), *Managing Quality*, 3rd edn. Oxford: Blackwell.

Dale, B. G. and Boaden, R. J. (1993), Improvement framework. *The TQM Magazine*, 5(1), 23–6.

DTI (1990), *The Case for Quality*. London: Department of Trade and Industry.

Employment Department (1991), *Choosing and Using a Consultant*. London: HMSO.

EFQM (2001), *The EFQM Excellence Model*. Brussels: EFQM.

Flero, J. (1992), The Crawford slip method. *Quality Progress*, 25(5), 40–3.

Johnson, J. W. (1992), A point of view. Life in a fishbowl: a senior manager's perspective on TQM. *National Productivity Review*, 11(2), 143–6.

Lascelles, D. M. and Dale, B. G. (1989), Quality improvement: what is the motivation? *Proceedings of the Institution of Mechanical Engineers*, 203(B1), 43–50.

Lascelles, D. M. and Dale, B. G. (1993), *The Road to Quality*. Bedford: IFS Publications.

Lloyd, A., Dale, B. G. and Burnes, B. (1994), Supplier development: a study of Nissan Motor Manufacturing (UK) and her suppliers. *Proceedings of the Institute of Mechanical Engineers*, 208(D1), 63–8.

chapter five

A Framework for the Introduction of TQM

B. G. Dale

Introduction

This chapter presents a framework for the introduction of TQM. It is divided into four main sections, all of which need to be addressed once the motivation for TQM has been identified. The motivation will set the overall strategic direction of TQM and influence the relevant importance of each part of the framework. The foundation of the framework is 'organizing' and the two pillars which form its structure are the use of 'systems and techniques' and 'measurement and feedback'. 'Changing the culture' is something which must be considered at all stages, including the initial organizing activities, but primarily results from the other initiatives described, interacts with them throughout the process, and will evolve with the organization's operating experience of TQM. People, both as individuals and working in teams, are central to TQM and without their skills and endeavours continuous improvement will simply not occur. The framework integrates the various aspects of TQM, from 'soft' approaches such as teamwork, employee development and human relations, to the use of 'hard' techniques such as SPC and FMEA. A diagrammatic representation of the framework is given in figure 5.1 and a summary of its features in table 5.1.

The framework provides an indication of how the various aspects of TQM fit together and is particularly useful for those organizations who:

- Are taking their first steps on the TQM journey.
- Have got ISO9000 series registration and require some guidance and advice on what to do next.

Barrie Dale acknowledges the contribution of Dr Ruth Boaden to the development of the framework described in this chapter. He also wishes to thank the directors and managers who have commented on earlier versions of this chapter, in particular, the past and current associates of the UMIST TQM Multi-Company Teaching Company Programme for their invaluable suggestions in the development of the framework.

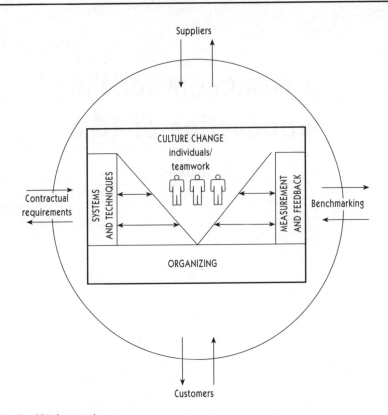

Figure 5.1   The TQM framework
Source: Dale and Boaden (1993)

- Are attempting to develop improvement plans and controls across a number of sites.
- Have less than three years' operating experience of TQM and continuous improvement.

   The framework is not a 'how-to' guide for TQM; there are a considerable number of such guides outlining a step-by-step approach to TQM. These guides usually have a set starting point and follow a single route. The framework is a means of developing and presenting plans in a non-prescriptive manner; it is a guide to action and not to be followed slavishly. In this way it allows an organization to choose an appropriate starting point and course of action and develop TQM and the improvement process at a pace which suits its business situation and available resources. If used in the correct 'manner the framework ensures that there are adequate mechanisms in place to enable continuous improvements to occur. At this stage the organization can turn to the use of self-assessment methods against a recognized model to identify strengths and weaknesses in its approach (for details of self-assessment, see chapter 24).
   The framework was initially developed as a theoretical tool, from the UMIST research experience. The details of the framework as presented here have been based on its use by the senior management teams of a number of major manufacturing

Table 5.1 TQM framework: a summary

Organizing	Systems and techniques	Measurement and feedback	Changing the culture
Long-term strategy for TQM formulated and integrated with other strategies; improvement plans developed	Identification of applicable tools and techniques at each stage of continuous improvement	Key internal and external performance measures identified, defined and developed	Assess the current status of organizational culture before developing plans for change
Definition of quality, TQM and continuous improvement developed and agreed	Training in the use of tools and techniques, for the right people at the right time	Ongoing discussion with customers about expected performance	Recognize the ongoing nature of culture change, and the need to outline specific changes
Choice of approach to TQM	Identification of other systems and standards that may be required by customers or legislation	Means for celebration and communication of success and teamwork developed	Recognize the role of people as an asset
Identification of sources of advice	Use of a formal quality system	Benchmarking, once improvement is under way	Plan change consistently and incrementally
Stages of improvement activity identified, taking the starting point into account	Identification of key business processes and improvement based on these processes	Consideration of the link between results from improvement and rewards	To minimize conflict, consider the inter-relationships of all activities within the organization
Executive leadership and commitment to TQM		Means of assessing the progress towards world-class performance considered, e.g. EFQM or MBNQA models	Identify factors which indicate that culture is changing
Vision and mission statements and values developed and communicated to all members of the organization			Consider the national and local culture
Decide the means by which TQM will be communicated			
Formal programme of education and training for all members of the organization			
Organizational infrastructure established to facilitate local ownership of TQM			
Teamwork established as a way of working and part of the infrastructure			

companies and a number of service organizations, in both private and public environments. In addition, the framework has also been used in syndicate exercises by some 300 people from a wide variety of manufacturing and service organizations, in America, Hong Kong, South Africa and the UK. With its solid research base and practical testing and application, it is a very robust framework.

Organizing

This foundation stage is concerned with the motivation for starting TQM and a process of continuous improvement (which will influence the TQM approach adopted) and the resultant strategies, plans, and means necessary to introduce and develop the process. The appropriate time to introduce TQM must also be considered, as should communication down and across the organization of what TQM is, why it is being adopted and what will be involved, including the cost and required resources.

It is also useful to consider the problems and obstacles likely to be encountered in the introduction of TQM and agree actions to avoid or minimize them: see chapter 7 for details of typical difficulties and obstacles. Similar examples are also provided by Bunney and Dale (1996), Crofton and Dale (1996), Dale (1991) and Dale and Lightburn (1992).

In planning this stage full use should be made of pilot schemes, whether they are in relation to the use of a technique such as SPC or the operation of improvement teams. In this way, problems can be resolved on a small scale and experiences fed back and reacted to before development and advancement of the issue under study.

The key actions in this stage can be described as follows:

1 *A clear long-term strategy for TQM should be formulated and integrated with other key business strategies, departmental policies and objectives. This also includes the development of a quality policy and quality strategy. The aim should be to integrate them with the long-term plans of the business.* Any short-term strategy which the organization needs to pursue (e.g. to cater for rapid turnover of staff, market downturns, exchange fluctuations and supply difficulties) should be consistent and integrated with the long-term strategy. The strategy must then be developed into a series of improvement plans and objectives for each department and function and also for those areas and aspects of the business which have been identified as requiring improvement, and methods of monitoring and assessment developed. Such plans will also result from the other three sections of the framework and also from actions and initiatives which are independent of it. The methodology of policy deployment (e.g. Dale 1990; Akao 1991) is important in this respect; details are given in chapter 8.

2 *A common organizational definition for quality, TQM, and other terms used as part of the continuous improvement process, should be developed, agreed and communicated in simple and non-technical language, after discussion.* Consideration should also be given to the term (e.g. TQM, total quality performance, business excellence, world-class, customer first, business improvement or continuous improvement) used to describe the improvement initiative, or indeed to whether a term is required. The development of a glossary of quality-related terms should be considered; useful guidance is provided in

BS EN ISO9000 (2000). A lack of such definitions can hamper the progress of TQM; it will also help to prevent misunderstanding, competing views and different interpretations being made by the various functions and levels within the business and also with customers and suppliers, improving communication both inside and outside the business. Without clear definition it is difficult to deliver what is espoused as quality. In particular, many people have difficulty in understanding the difference between TQM and quality assurance.

3   *The approach to TQM should be decided.* This will depend on the existing culture of the organization as well as the preferences of senior management but is an important element in its success. Whichever TQM approach is adopted, it should be flexible and capable of fine-tuning to suit the business needs and objectives of the organization. Some of the available options were explored in chapter 1.

4   *The organizations and people (internal and external) who can be sources of advice on the approach to TQM, and its introduction and development, should be identified.* Such advice may also be required to develop the quality management system to meet the requirements of ISO9001 and/or QS9000 and the application of particular tools and techniques. Useful expertise is often available within the organization. Such people know the internal workings of the organization, its processes and the unique problems which exist. This expertise should not be overlooked. It is always beneficial to combine internal expertise with external consultants' knowledge and skills. In service organizations, which have large numbers of relatively small locations, or those manufacturing organizations which have a variety of operating sites spread across a country or throughout a number of countries, it is recommended that a 'directory of resources and experiences' is compiled to encourage co-operation and mutual assistance.

5   *Stages of improvement activity should be identified at the outset, taking into account the starting point of the organization, the motivation for TQM and the tools and techniques which may be applicable.* For example, Newall and Dale (1991) identified six stages of an improvement process – awareness, education and training, consolidation, problem identification and improvement planning, implementation of quality plans and assessment. A formal project-planning methodology, which requires the identification of milestones and their ongoing monitoring, is also a vital tool at this stage.

6   *Executive leadership, tangible commitment and support should be recognized as being crucial at all stages (see chapter 2).* Such commitment should be demonstrated in actions such as allocating time to understanding and involvement in TQM, being visible and accessible ('management by wandering about'), holding discussions with people at the operating level of the business, providing words of encouragement and advice, 'quality' placed at the top of every business meeting agenda, identification of key performance measurements, use of tools and techniques in their everyday work activities, developing personal action plans, seeking feedback on their style of management, acting as a mentor to improvement teams, attending training sessions, writing articles on TQM in the company newsletter, ensuring that any decisions made are consistent with the agreed plans and objectives, and exhibiting a passion for TQM. There is no magic formula for achieving such commitment, although the characteristics of good leaders are currently being researched

with the aim of identifying appropriate management guidelines for the future. Useful guidance is currently provided by Bass (1985), Kotter (1990), Maxwell (1993, 1995), and Townsend and Gebhardt (1997).

7 *Vision and mission statements which are concise and understandable to all employees should be developed, displayed and communicated in company-unique language.* It is also important to outline what needs to be done to make these statements and the associated company values become a reality, including the benefits that will accrue from TQM and how it will affect the way employees go about their jobs. The format and timing of education/awareness-raising events should also be outlined. The influence of the historical culture of the organization, its people, processes, technology, products/services and the views of its current senior executives must not be underestimated in this process.

8 *It is important that everyone in the organization can identify with the vision and mission statements* since this will help to unite and focus employees on where the organization is heading. Employees must feel that the vision statement is achievable. Regular assessments should also be carried out to see whether employees believe that the organization is getting closer to achieving the objectives outlined in these statements.

9 *Communication is a key component of TQM and management cannot communicate too much on issues relating to TQM and the improvements made.* The communication should be based on common sense, be two-way, use jargon-free language and be consistent in the approach adopted. It must be good enough to win the 'hearts and minds' of all employees. The means of communication should include both written and verbal mediums in both group and individual mode (e.g. noticeboards, whiteboards, news-sheets, booklets, team-meeting minutes, team briefings, senior management 'state-of-the-nation' briefings, breakfast and birthday meetings and electronic mail). Communication must be by example, with management doing what they say must be done and they must assess, on a regular basis, to ensure that the messages they wish to convey are getting through. Managers must recognize the difference between the art of communication and its medium. It also means that management must listen and act upon the views of those they manage.

10 *A formal programme of education and training should be established.* This is important in order to build the skills of employees, and should involve basic job skills and process training, including induction, TQM awareness, customer care, and training in the use of tools, techniques and systems. It must provide a common message and encompass the whole organization starting with the senior management team and members of the TQM steering committee. The training should also aim to identify potential improvement projects.

11 *The development of a training matrix* (see figure 5.2) helps to ensure that needs and capabilities are identified, along with the current level of awareness of TQM, quality systems, tools and techniques, etc. Training records also need to be maintained. The training matrix should be reviewed whenever an appraisal is carried out. Consideration should also be given to the concept of a 'learning organization': this would require an internal library of information and the appropriate training aids to be set up.

12 *An organizational infrastructure should be established which will ultimately facilitate local ownership of TQM.* Direction should be provided by the TQM

Person and function	Type of course and duration		
	General awareness	Specific (e.g. FMEA)	Degree of difficulty
Senior management			
Clerical			
Operator			

Figure 5.2 TQM training matrix

steering committee, but the time it sometimes takes for people to accept such ownership for TQM and continuous improvement should not be underestimated. Actions include deciding the membership of the committee, role and meeting frequency, setting up, as appropriate, local steering groups, identification of improvement co-ordinator (full-time or part-time), facilitators and team leaders, along with clear definitions of their roles, ensuring the means by which the actions developed by improvement teams can be carried through and agreeing budgets. In some companies it may be more appropriate for TQM steering committee-type issues to be discussed as an agenda item as part of management/board of directors meetings. Research by Boaden and Dale (1993) has shown that full-time support is essential in order to get the process going and establish a central pool of expertise, particularly in service or multi-site manufacturing organizations. The structure must be appropriate for the business situation. However, it is important that the improvement structure does not duplicate the existing management structure. If it does then questions must be asked about the latter. It is also recommended that the current organizational structure is assessed in terms of its suitability for starting and sustaining TQM.

13 *Teamwork should be established and become part of the organization's method of working.* In the first place it is suggested that a review is undertaken of any teams which are already established, in conjunction with their previous and current projects. Following this, task forces/project teams and cross-functional improvement teams should be established to address the major problems facing the organization, followed by the setting up of departmental improvement teams.

Systems and Techniques

This pillar of the framework involves the development of a quality management system to provide the necessary controls and discipline, and the standardization of improvements. It also involves the use of quality management tools and techniques to, for example, aid quality planning, listen to the 'voices' of customers, capture data, control processes, make improvements, solve problems and involve people. Key actions at this stage include:

1 *The tools and techniques applicable at different stages of the improvement process should be identified.* The areas/projects for the application of these tools and the conditions (organizational and people) necessary for the successful application of each tool and technique have to be identified. In the first place consideration should be given to identifying which tools and techniques employees are familiar with and those which are in regular use. Tools and techniques should be classified as core and optional, depending on their nature and impact and the environment (e.g. manufacturing or service) in which they are being applied.

2 *The right type of training targeted at the right people should be developed; it should emphasize the why and how of the tools and techniques and the benefits of their use.* Many studies (e.g. Payne and Dale 1990; Dale and McQuater 1998) have demonstrated that the right type of training helps to stop the misuse of tools and techniques (e.g. SPC being applied in the wrong areas; only part characteristics being measured, used only for control purposes; lack of reactive disciplines, etc.). When tools and techniques have been used incorrectly, an additional set of problems in the introduction of TQM is created. Suitable training packages on tools and techniques should be developed and customized for the organization – this is perceived to be very important in some situations (e.g. public services). There is no correct 'formula' for training, since each organization will be starting from a different position and will have different needs, audiences, topics and views on the delivery mechanisms, but the superior-performing companies have well-developed, cyclical formal training programmes for TQM and have mechanisms in place for determining the effectiveness of the training.

3 *The use of a formal quality management system should be considered, if one is not in place.* If such a system is already in use, then some evaluation of its contribution to TQM is vital; the objective should be to continually improve and strengthen the quality system and ensure that any improvements are built into the system. The requirements outlined in BS EN ISO9001 (2000) is a good starting point.

4 *Any other systems and standards which may be required as part of future contractual or legislative requirements, or simply in order to compete in certain markets should be identified and implemented.* If relevant systems and standards are integrated with the improvement initiative it is less likely that the organization will have conflicting priorities and policies, and confusion will be reduced. Examples include: ISO14001 (1996), OHSAS 18001 (1999), Investors in People, Charter Mark, the Management Charter Initiative, National Vocational Qualifications, Environmental and Responsible Care programmes, and hygiene requirements. Ethical, social and political issues will also have to be considered.

5 *Process analysis and improvement should be a continual part of the organization's improvement process.* There should be a focus on processes (e.g. business planning and control and order generation) rather than functions within the organization. Process analysis and innovation gives emphasis to the centrality of quality throughout the business process and also focuses attention on customer and supplier relationships. Once key business processes have been identified along with their process owners, rationalization, simplification and identification of key performance measures can occur. This forms the basis for improvement, and despite the difficulties of implementing such improvements

when significant organizational restructuring may be necessary, it can yield significant business results.

Measurement and Feedback

This pillar of the framework enables the 'voice of the customer' to be translated into measures of performance with which the organization can identify, and on which it can improve. It also deals with internal measures of performance, supplier assessment and development and rewards and recognition. Key actions at this stage include:

1   *Key internal and external performance measures should be identified and defined to assess the progress being made with TQM, and to ensure that customers are satisfied.* The measurement process involves a two-way flow of information between the organization and its customers and suppliers, and these parties should be consulted as part of the process of deciding what measurements to make. However, it should be accepted from the outset that measuring customer satisfaction can be difficult and painful. For example, reading and developing responses to negative comments is not easy. Two key questions which need to be addressed in relation to feedback are: To whom is it made? and What level of detail is provided? When traditional financial and accounting-type data measurement criteria are evaluated in terms of their relevance to TQM it is often found that many of the existing indicators are inaccurate, unfocused, unconnected and seen as an end in themselves and therefore obsolete. Care must be taken to ensure that appropriate measures are developed, defined clearly and used. The chosen performance measures should help to facilitate the integration of TQM into the business processes of the organization and encourage all employees to focus on the key business and quality issues. It is suggested that an organization should consider the use of the 'balanced scorecard' method. This employs performance measures that contain different viewpoints and perspectives, typically representing customers, internal processes, continuous improvement and finance.

   The performance indicators must be monitored, displayed and communicated through debriefing sessions on a regular basis, thereby sharing the information with all employees. This also assists with renewing commitment when the improvement process starts to stagnate – 'If we cannot express what we know in numbers, we don't know much about it', and 'You cannot manage what you do not measure.' People are encouraged when they are able to see the results of their activities and efforts on key results areas and measures. This also applies to qualitative evidence such as photographs of shop-floor and office areas before and after a campaign to improve housekeeping. It is also useful to feed back data on typical mistakes and what long-term corrective action has been taken to avoid them being made again; any goals and targets established as part of this should be achievable. It is important to build results and corrective actions into improvement plans and standardize the improvements across the organization. Senior management must recognize that gathering data for external measures is time-consuming, and extra resources may well be needed.

   Assessment of supplier performance and feedback of any measurements along with corrective actions is also a key feature of this pillar of the framework.

2 *Discussion with customers (internal as well as external) about the performance expected and their needs and expectations should be undertaken, using a variety of techniques.* This must be an ongoing exercise to ensure that gaps between actual performance and customer needs and expectations are identified and analysed, and actions put in place for closing the gap. In going about this exercise it is also important to assess the relationship between the sales and marketing functions and the strengths of each. The main objective of all this is to build a partnership with customers and to develop customer loyalty in order to build competitive advantage.

Issues that have to be considered in this marketplace research include:

– How well the organization is meeting customer expectations
– How well the organization responds to customers' comments
– How customers perceive they are treated
– The chief causes of concern to customers
– The main complaints from customers
– Suggestions the customer might have for improvements and what else may be required in terms of products, services and features
– How the organization rates against the competition
– Whether the data which have been collected are actually used to generate improvements which benefit the customer.

In some organizations it may be necessary to initiate suitable systems for identifying customer needs. Customers must also be encouraged and invited to challenge the organization which is delivering the product or service. The trend is for increasing the level of contact with customers (internal and external), and such 'moments of truth' occur far more frequently in commerce, public organizations and service-type situations than in manufacturing organizations (see chapter 11). Systems to identify customer needs include:

– Customer workshops
– Client service and call centres
– Panels and clinics
– Focus groups
– Customer interviews
– Market research
– Surveys: mail (including electronic), telephone, comment cards, point of purchase (survey designs should vary in length, contact and format)
– Trailing the service and/or product
– Field trials of new products
– Using 'test' consumers and mystery shoppers
– Feedback from professional and trade associations
– Product launches
– Field contacts

Often potential sources of information are customers lost and customers gained, the data which the finance and accounts department hold on customers, and field failure and warranty claims.

There must be a methodology and system for analysing and feeding back the data gathered from customers by such means (i.e. customer service measurement); the same applies to data on competitors.

Goodman et al. (1996) report eight common pitfalls identified by Technical Assistance Research Programs Inc. (TARP) that undermine the integrity and value of customer feedback. These pitfalls are useful to keep in mind in tackling the issue of customer feedback data:

- Inefficient and costly data-collection
- Inconsistent classification schemes
- Old data
- Analysis in a vacuum
- Analysis without priorities
- Analysis that is not actionable
- Ineffective presentation of data and findings
- Failure to track the impact of corrective actions resulting from the voice of customer process

A considerable amount of useful guidance on understanding customer needs is provided by Gale (1994), McCarthy (1997), Vavra (1997) and BS EN 12973 (2000).

3 *Benchmarking should be considered once the organization has taken some steps to improve quality.* The benchmarking of a small number of strategic processes helps employees to see the need for change and thereby give impetus to the improvement process. The concept of benchmarking is a proven technique for assisting companies with a process of continuous improvement. It is a process whereby internal performance and practices are compared to those of other companies, including the superior-performing ones, in a bid to develop, improve and achieve the best practice that leads to superior performance (see Camp 1989, 1995, and chapter 21 below for details).

4 *Means of celebrating and communicating success with TQM should be considered, and methods developed for recognizing the efforts of teams and individuals.* The issue of ownership of TQM is linked to providing adequate recognition, rewards and incentives for quality efforts, and in this way the message that quality is a strategic concern is reinforced. Two quotes worthy of mention are 'What gets measured gets done' (Anders Scharp, former CEO, Electrolux) and 'What gets rewarded gets repeated' (Anne Vant Haaff, former corporate quality manager, KLM).

Publishing successes is an effective means of communicating how people have tackled improvements. It helps to build up in people's minds that beneficial changes have started to take place, that things which at one time appeared impossible are now possible, and it helps convert the cynics: with published evidence of success they cannot say that TQM is not working – nothing succeeds like success.

Companies struggle in deciding how to recognize the efforts of teams and individuals for a job well done and often fail to think through the implications of their decisions in an adequate manner. Recognition and communication of success can be facilitated in a number of ways such as quality news-sheets, team briefs, quality action days, team competition/celebration days, quality conferences, presentations by the president and/or CEO, supplier award days, 'how are we doing?' boards, 'thank you' notes, small tokens of appreciation such as mugs, pens, meals, certificates and trophies, publicity in the company newsletter, personal thanks, applause, special functions (i.e. dinner, get-togethers, overseas trips, use of the company resources for personal use), and allocation of shares in the company; there is also recognition of performance by customers. Personal 'thank you' and 'praise' notes from senior management are often seen as a more genuine recognition than buying people through money. Townsend and Gebhardt (1997) present some useful examples of successful recognition programmes which provide a range of thought-provoking ideas.

In some organizations people do not welcome individual recognition as they are made to feel uncomfortable by their peers, but in others tokens of recognition are warmly desired and appreciated. To help in deciding the most appropriate way to celebrate success it is recommended that views from employees are sought and the methods tailored to suit the needs of both the situation and employees.

5 *Linking rewards to improvement activities and results must be considered, although it is controversial.* Financial payment for participation in improvement activities, in particular, those schemes relating to individuals, should be discouraged but perhaps not overlooked. Continuous improvement should be a natural part of every person's job, but people at different levels of an organization have widely differing expectations of what improvement means to them personally and to the company. There is a view, however, that 'links to pay and promotion may still be the most tangible proof that top executives take total quality seriously', (see Troy 1991). An Income Data Services study (IDS 1991) concentrated on those incentive schemes in which quality or customer service are major determinants of bonus payments. It concluded that few companies have sought 'to make a direct link between quality or customer service targets and then payment'. The study did go on to describe how Rank Xerox, Elida Gibbs, Scottish Widows, Companies House, British Steel and 3M have linked bonus payments in this way.

If there is pressure within an organization for financial payment perhaps it could be approached through a Japanese-style suggestion system, or along the lines of the Improvement Opportunity Scheme as described by Piddington et al. (1995). Organizations and individuals have different perceptions of the value of suggestion schemes. Among the common complaints are: 'We did not get any feedback so we are not going to make any more suggestions' and 'The response time to the suggestion was too long'.

6 *Means of assessing the progress of the business towards world-class performance should be used.* For example, the MBNQA criteria for performance and the EFQM excellence model should be considered (see chapter 24).

Changing the Culture

Organizations attempt to change culture for different reasons. Changing the culture is a key element in TQM and has wide-ranging implications for the whole organization; it requires the introduction and acceptance of individual, group, and organizational change. TQM provides the opportunity to make and influence behaviour and attitudes which have real effects on internal and external relationships and the way the organization conducts its business.

Culture change is not just relevant to TQM, although the increased emphasis on customers and their needs makes some form of culture change a must for most organizations. There is, however, a shortage of information and guidance for companies looking for ways to change, plan and facilitate culture change. The change of culture must be planned to avoid ambiguity and facilitate improvement; managers must learn to lead change and useful advice is provided on this issue by Atkinson (1990), Kanter et al. (1991), Schein (1985) and Tichy (1983). The current status from both management and employee perspectives should be established before firm plans for change are developed.

It is not possible to identify key actions for this stage, but there are a number of features which should be considered:

1 *An assessment, from both management and employee perspectives, of the current status of the organizational culture should be undertaken before firm plans for change are developed.* Senior management must be prepared to resolve conflicts, and resistance to change which is identified in the assessment; the personal values of staff and their expectations sometimes presents a problem.

2 *Culture change must be recognized as ongoing, rather than as a prerequisite to the introduction of TQM.* Some degree of culture change in terms of senior management commitment and leadership and provision of adequate resources must, however, take place prior to and as part of the organizing stage. For example, the effective use of tools and techniques, developing the quality management system to meet the requirements of the ISO9000 series, teamwork, the impact of successful improvement projects, presentations, recognition, effective channels of communication, etc. are all activities which can contribute to culture change. There are of course other activities which will contribute to the culture change process (e.g. improving the environment in terms of provision of uniforms and safety shoes, team meeting rooms and lockers) which may not connect directly with TQM and the improvement process. The crucial factor is a recognition of these activities and their contribution to culture change. In planning any changes it is useful to develop thinking along the lines of 'Where are we now?' and 'Where do we want to be?' Middle management must be involved in the planning process, since the burden of change falls on them. Management must create the culture which all employees believe in.

3 *Change should be planned and take place in a consistent and incremental manner.* Experience indicates that if the change is too great and unplanned the organization will revert back to the status quo. Clear and public displays of key indicators and 'how are we doing data' help to ensure that the changes which are made are real and that no slippage occurs. While there may also be some unexpected outcomes, they are no substitute for planned change.

  The planned changes must be outlined in specific terms and, where possible, qualified against a time-scale. Employee attitude surveys, customer surveys and internal customer–supplier workshops are also useful for identifying culture change indicators. Examples of possible changes include:

  – Create a single-status environment: harmonize conditions and eliminate other traditional status symbols, such as reserved car-parking spaces, different types of dining facilities, different terms and conditions of employment (i.e. move blue-collar sick pay towards that of staff) and other forms of demarcation (i.e. seasonal gifts being shared rather than going to individuals).
  – Reduce the number of organizational levels.

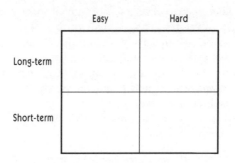

Figure 5.3 Culture change grid

- Delegate decision-making and the responsibility for taking actions down to the lowest possible level and spread the power base.
- Senior managers meet employees of all levels on a regular basis.
- Teach managers to adopt a listening, consulting and learning style of leadership.
- Enable every employee to visit a customer and other parts of the business.
- Operator exchange programmes.
- Operators to 'brief' customers during customer visits to the sites.
- Develop a requirement for senior management to spend a specified amount of time with people at the operating level of the business.
- Require the CEO to attend one meeting of each active quality team on an annual basis.
- Train managers to act as trainers.
- Change the payment system to one which recognizes issues such as the team, acquisition of skills, flexibility, etc.
- Replace supervision by leadership and give staff more freedom to get on with the job.
- Introduce the concept of associates rather than employees.
- Make it possible for operators to move between jobs within the business.
- Introduce cross-functional team activity.
- Provide opportunities for management to listen to the views of staff and customers and develop a listening and learning style of leadership.
- Get staff to tell management where they are going wrong. It is important to put into place a mechanism for ensuring that this happens, and providing guidance to staff in how to go about it, and to management on how to handle such feedback.
- Change to a cellular type of organization.
- Recognize and respect people's contribution to the business.
- Provide financial education for everyone

The grid shown in figure 5.3 can be used to classify the degree of difficulty of each change and its effects.

4 *The role of people within the organization should be recognized.* The way that they are treated is vital, since they are an intellectual asset whose value to the organization can be increased by careful nurturing or decreased by poor management. It should also be recognized that most organizations are made up of people of differing ages, background, skills, abilities, levels of enthusiasm,

levels of flexibility and ability to accept change (in some industries, tradition is very deep-rooted and this presents a specific set of resistance-to-change difficulties). If culture change is to be successful these people-based factors must be taken into account. The means of developing and involving people must be identified; a skills audit is a useful starting point for this. The Investors in People programme provides useful advice on people development.

5 *Teamwork is an important facilitator in culture change, but organizations must ensure that the organizational infrastructure can adapt to the changes which teamwork will bring.* The operating characteristics of the teams to be employed in TQM should be defined and communicated (see chapter 23). It is also essential that participants in teams and other improvement activities are volunteers, not 'conscripts'.

6 *The interrelationship of all activities in the organization, and the way in which they contribute to the overall quality of service and product provided, should be identified, so that conflict is minimized and TQM becomes part of the way in which the business is run.* Such conflict typically arises at middle management level, where the impact of strategic initiatives meets the problems of day-to-day running of the organization. In any large organization there will be a variety of initiatives going on at one time, many of which will affect staff directly (e.g. installation of new computer systems, development of information technology, introduction of Manufacturing Resources Planning (MRP II), cost-cutting exercises, marketing promotions), and these may indirectly contribute to the quality of product and service provided. It is important that management and staff understand the relationship between these and formal improvement initiatives, otherwise they may be perceived as being in conflict, and thus not achieve the desired outcomes. A case in point is a strain on resources resulting in people not attending quality team meetings.

7 *Factors which indicate that TQM has started to change culture should be identified.* Without such factors it is difficult to know whether culture change is taking place, and the concept may be undermined by 'lack of results'. Factors that indicate that culture is changing include:

- People see for themselves the need for tools and techniques.
- Motivators and champions start to emerge from various parts of the organization.
- People talk processes and not functions.
- Changes to procedures and systems are easier to make.
- People are not afraid of expressing their views.
- People show a positive response to recognition.
- Employees are viewed by senior management as an asset and not a cost.
- People volunteer to take on tasks which would previously have involved considerable negotiations between management and unions.
- Shop stewards help management to explain new procedures.
- People asking for their setting-up activities to be videotaped in order to reduce the machine down time.
- Ideas and suggestions start to flow from the shop floor.
- Willingness to serve others.
- Team meetings scheduled outside of shift team, without pay.
- Improvement teams ask management to suggest project themes.
- The distinction between the 'manager' and the 'managed' becomes hazy.

    – Senior management shift their attention from TQM to concentrate on other things and improvement activities continue.
    – Continuous improvement goes on in the face of organizational instability.

8   *In planning for change thought needs to be given to the culture of a country and its people.* A national culture is a set of shared values, beliefs and behaviours which binds people into a relatively cohesive group. However, there may be subcultures (i.e. local cultures) within countries. Details of national culture are provided by Hofstede (1984) in terms of four dimensions – power distance, uncertainty avoidance, individualism and masculinity. For example:

    – Companies in Hong Kong are characterized by paternalistic leadership, power, distance and, to some degree, risk avoidance by employees. In Hong Kong there is also a tendency for Chinese people not to be open in reflecting opinions and ideas, they tend to look first for personal monetary reward and benefits: such attitudes can be in conflict with culture change which is a longer-term process.
    – In South Africa there are a number of issues which have to be considered such as the political/union situation, the use of traditional leaders in an ethnic sense, the inherent suspicion of management by the workforce as a result of historical and political factors, the characteristics of both first and third world cultures and concepts, racial integration of personnel by means of positive assertive actions, and the eleven official languages.

In addition the cultures of different industry types, which are often quite strong, need to be taken into account.

Use of the Framework

The framework should be used as part of a eight-stage process:

1   *Review the organization's adoption of TQM to date.* This should include a presentation by senior management on the progress to date and future plans. The grid shown in figure 5.4 can be used for pinpointing the current position and the features of the four first four levels of the TQM adoption model (see chapter 6) – 'uncommitted', 'drifters', 'tool-pushers' and 'improvers' – are also

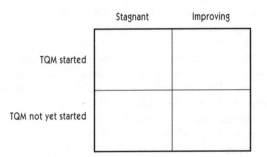

Figure 5.4   TQM grid

Culture Change Section	Yes	In part	No
Commitment			
– Senior management	●		
– Visibility		●	
Current status			
– Questionnaire			●
Employee involvement	●		
Training and people Development			
– Customer appreciation	●		
– Appraisals/objectives	●		
– Skills audit		●	
Conditions of employment			●
People environment		●	

Figure 5.5 TQM framework: feature assessment

of help in positioning an organization. This stage can take the form of a TQM awareness session if the business is relatively immature in its adoption of TQM.

2 *Customize the framework to suit the individual organization.* In the first place, a full presentation of the framework is made to the participants. If the framework is being developed for a single organization, the senior and middle managers are divided into syndicate groups and tasked to consider the features of each section of the framework and customize it to suit the individual organization and its business. If the framework is being used in an open workshop session, and the participants are from manufacturing industry, the syndicate groups can be organized either by size of organization or type of industry. If they are from a mix of sectors they can be organized by sector (e.g. manufacturing, transport, financial, public sector, health care).

3 *Present and debate the customized framework.* A spokesperson from each syndicate group makes a presentation on the framework they have developed, with the features of each group's framework being debated in open forum. In the case of a single company a consolidated framework is developed, based on what has been agreed in the discussion arising from the open forum. If the syndicate group comprises a number of different companies, the participants can take the framework back to their own organization and either debate the framework with their management team and add or delete features as appropriate or repeat the syndicate exercise as a single management team.

4 *Assess which features of the framework are already in place.* Self-audit surveys and internal and external indicators can be employed. A number of methods of measurement can be used, for example, ranking each feature on a 1 to 6 scale or the use of a yes, no, in-part classification (figure 5.5 shows an example of this).

5 *Prioritize the features which are not already in place.* This should be done in accordance with the overall strategy and business plans of the organization. In some cases an organization may wish to accept this generic framework as it stands, thereby skipping steps 2 and 3. The way that this had been handled is to present the organizing section of the framework to the management team

Features Vision			Plans				
What will it look like?	What does it involve?	What is the current situation?	What needs to be done?	Who is going to do it?	What is going to be done?	What are the obstacles/issues?	
1							
2							

Figure 5.6   TQM framework: organizing section

and get them to undertake steps 4 and 5 above. This is repeated for the other three sections.

6   *Develop plans to introduce the prioritized features of the framework identified in the previous stage.* The plans should have a start and finish date, with detailed actions, milestones, resources and responsibilities.

7   *Communicate the details of the framework and the plans derived from it down through the organization.* This helps to gain acceptance. The framework should also be communicated to suppliers and customers.

8   *Identify any potential problems in putting the plans developed at stage 6 into place.* Some typical problems encountered are: lack of structure and how to formalize the existing organization in relation to current management roles and responsibilities, lack of trained personnel, definition of terms (e.g. customer response time), conflict of barriers, traditional attitudes, time conflicts/ constraints and constructing a real and meaningful mission statement which can be owned.

The format shown in figure 5.6 can be used as part of this process.

Summary and Outcomes

The following are the outcomes derived by those organizations who have used the framework:

• Developing the framework provides a mechanism for debating TQM and continuous improvement strategies, plans, actions and initiatives and helps to generate a common level of understanding and reconcile views and opinions. It also assists management in identifying the factors which can slow down the process of improvement (e.g. inconsistent objectives, insufficient involvement and ownership, lack of data, lack of operator involvement, failure to complete projects, break-up of improvement teams, etc.) and helps to pinpoint and eradicate weaknesses in the current TQM approach of the organization.

• The framework, once developed and customized, becomes a reference point for current and future improvement initiatives. It builds on the quality initiatives already in place and guides the organization's development of TQM in a formal manner.

• Use of the framework requires all members of senior and middle management to be involved in the planning process, thereby developing ownership of the resultant plans. The prioritization of the framework features, in conjunction with business and commercial needs, against a time-scale helps to ensure that TQM is part of the business planning process and integrated with other strategies.

- The framework provides a means of communicating, in the organization's own language, what is involved in TQM and provides the essential logic of why the organization is adopting and progressing TQM and what is involved. It ensures that discussions on improvement are both structured and specific.

- In a multi-site operation the framework provides a common approach and language for all businesses, and those likely to be acquired in the future. In this way it avoids confusion with common suppliers and customers and presents a consistent approach and TQM image to both employees and the market-place. It helps understanding of what each site has achieved in relation to TQM, assists in taking policy decisions (e.g. individual or common vision and mission statements, specific sites taking the lead role in piloting training programmes, quality management tools and techniques, etc.) shares common experiences, and highlights the availability of resources, mutual assistance, training, expertise, experiences, etc. It also helps those businesses which are less advanced in terms of TQM to discuss in a coherent manner common issues of interest with those that are more advanced (i.e. the common language and approach helps to facilitate 'technology' transfer).

- It provides the means for the local management committee and/or the TQM steering committee to assess the progress made by businesses against the plans developed, and ensures that issues are followed through. In undertaking this task problems can be identified and appropriate counter-measures developed.

- It can be used not only to assess the maturity of TQM but to audit whether or not certain features of the framework are firmly in place. In this way the next set of priorities can be identified.

- The correct use of the framework ensures that an organization puts in place the key features of TQM and a process of continuous improvement. Many of these fundamentals are encompassed in the 'TQM packages' offered by consultants. Thus an organization which feels it needs some 'outside' assistance, can introduce and start a process of improvement without necessarily going to the expense of employing a management consultant. The use, if any, of a consultant could come later in the process when more specialized and detailed advice is required.

References

Akao, Y. (ed.) (1991), *Hoshin Kanri: Policy Deployment for Successful TQM*. Cambridge, Mass.: Productivity Press.

Atkinson, P. (1990), *Creating Culture Change*. Bedfordshire: IFS.

Bass, B. M. (1985), *Leadership and Performance Beyond Expectations*. New York: Free Press.

Bunney, H. S. and Dale, B. G. (1996), The effect of organizational change on sustaining a process of continuous improvement. *Quality Engineering*, 8(4), 649–57.

BS EN ISO9000 (2000), *Quality Management Systems: Fundamentals and Vocabulary*. London: British Standards Institution.

BS EN ISO9001 (2000), *Quality Management Systems*. London: British Standards Institution.

BS EN 12973 (2000), *Value Management*. London: British Standards Institution.

Camp, R. C. (1989), *Benchmarking: The Search for Best Practices that Lead to Superior Performance*. Milwaukee: ASQC Quality Press.

Camp, R. C. (1995), *Business Process Benchmarking: Finding and Implementing the Best Practices*. Milwaukee: ASQC Quality Press.

Crofton, C. G. and Dale, B. G. (1996), The difficulties encountered in the introduction of total quality management: a case study examination. *Quality Engineering*, 8(3), 433–9.

Dale, B. G. (1990), Policy deployment. *The TQM Magazine*, 2(6), 321–4.

Dale, B. G. (1991), Starting on the road to success. *The TQM Magazine*, 3(2), 125–8.

Dale, B. G. and Boaden, R. J. (1993), Managing quality improvement in financial services: a framework and case study. *The Service Industries Journal*, 13(1), 17–39.

Dale, B. G. and Lightburn, K. (1992), Continuous quality improvement: why some organizations lack commitment. *International Journal of Production Economics*, 27(1), 57–67.

Dale, B. G. and McQuater, R. E. (1998), *Managing Business Improvement and Quality: Implementing Key Tools and Techniques*. Oxford: Blackwell Business.

EFQM (2001), *The EFQM Excellence Model*. Brussels: EFQM.

Gale, B. T. (1994), *Managing Customer Value*. New York: Free Press.

Goodman, J., De Palma, D. and Broetzmann, S. (1996), Maximizing the value of customer feedback. *Quality Progress*, December, 35–9.

Hofstede, G. (1984), *Culture's Consequences*. California: Sage Publications.

IDS (1991), *Bonus Schemes: Part 2*. IDS Study No. 492 (October). London: IDS.

ISO14001 (1996), *Environmental Management Systems: Specification with Guidance for Use*. Geneva: International Organization for Standardization.

Kanter, R. M., Stein, B. A. and Jick, T. D. (1991), *The Challenge of Organizational Change*. New York: Free Press.

Kotter, J. P. (1990), *A Force for Change: How Leadership Differs from Management*. New York: Free Press.

Maxwell, J. C. (1993), *Developing the Leaders Within You*. Nashville: Nelson.

Maxwell, J. C. (1995), *Developing the Leaders Around You*. Nashville: Nelson.

McCarthy, D. C. (1997), *The Loyalty Link: How Loyal Employees Create Loyal Customers*. New York: John Wiley & Son.

Newall, D. and Dale, B. G. (1991), The introduction and development of a quality improvement process: a study. *International Journal of Production Research*, 29(9), 1747–60.

OHSAS 18001 (1999), *Occupational Health and Safety Series Specification*. London: British Standards Institution.

Payne, B. J. and Dale, B. G. (1990), Total quality management training: some observations. *Quality Forum*, 16(1), 5–9.

Piddington, H., Bunney, H. S. and Dale, B. G. (1995), Rewards and recognition in quality improvement in what are the key issues. *Quality World Technical Supplement*, March, 12–18.

Schein, E. H. (1985), *Organizational Culture and Leadership*. Oxford: Jossey-Bass.

Tichy, N. M. (1983), *Managing Strategic Change: Technical, Political and Cultural Dynamics*. New York: John Wiley & Son.

Townsend, P. L. and Gebhardt, J. E. (1997a), *Quality in Action: 93 Lessons in Leadership, Participation and Measurement*. New York: John Wiley & Son.

Townsend, P. L. and Gebhardt, J. E. (1997b), *Recognition, Gratitude and Celebration*. Menlo Park, Calif.: Crisp Publications.

Troy, K. (1991), *Employee Buy-in to Total Quality*, R-97. New York: The Conference Board.

US Department of Commerce (2001), *Baldrige National Quality Program 2001 Criteria for Performance Excellence*. Gaithersburg: US Department of Commerce National Institute of Standards and Technology.

Vavra, T. G. (1997), *Improving your Measurement of Customer Satisfaction*. Milwaukee: ASQC Quality Press.

chapter six

Levels of TQM Adoption

B. G. Dale and D. M. Lascelles

Introduction

From research work carried out world-wide on the subject of TQM by the Manchester School of Management at UMIST during the last 20 years or so, it is clear that the extent to which organizations have adopted and committed themselves to TQM as the ethos of the business is variable. Six different levels of TQM adoption (or lack of it) have been identified, which are termed:

1   Uncommitted
2   Drifters
3   Tool-pushers
4   Improvers
5   Award-winners
6   World-class (see figure 6.1)

These levels of TQM adoptions were first derived by Dale and Lightburn (1992) from empirical observation, and were later refined by Lascelles and Dale (1991). The descriptions underlying each of the levels have since been tested by Dale in a number of workshop sessions for senior management in Europe, Hong Kong and South Africa. The initial descriptions of each level have been refined and added to from this testing and the current descriptions are reported in this chapter.

These levels are not necessarily the stages through which organizations pass on their TQM journey; rather, they are characteristics and behaviours which organizations display at one point in time in relation to TQM. While there are obviously exceptions to these generalized descriptions, with some organizations mid-way between two of the six levels, displaying hybrid characteristics and behaviour, it has been found that these six levels are a useful way of characterizing organizations and helping them to recognize symptoms and develop plans for the future. This positioning has also been found useful in helping to understand how people from a variety of hierarchical levels view the organization's TQM maturity. Some organizations, in

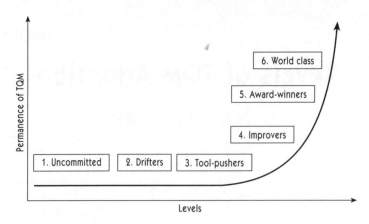

Figure 6.1   Levels of TQM adoption
Source: Lascelles and Dale (1993)

using the levels as a TQM positioning model, have assigned a set of values (i.e. using a likert-type scale) to each of the statements which highlight the characteristics and behaviour for each level, thereby quantifying the perceived level of their TQM adoption.

The six levels are now described.

Level 1 – Uncommitted

Level 1 organizations are those who have not yet started a formal process of quality improvement and, in some cases, can be considered as being ignorant of TQM. Their quality initiatives are usually limited to gaining ISO9001 quality management system registration and perhaps applying a few quality management tools and techniques as a reaction to customer pressure. The extent to which both systems and tools and techniques have been applied is often directly related to the amount of time spent by the client representatives on site, closely monitoring their use. The ISO9001 quality management system will be seen by employees as a quality system and not a management tool. The quality department will be driving the quality management system and the keeping of ISO9001 registration is totally dependent upon their efforts. The success of quality system audits by second- and third-party agencies will be viewed by senior management as an indication of the success of the company's quality initiative. The business will be operating in a detection mode (see chapter 1), but senior management believe a preventative approach is in place.

In this type of organization much talk is likely to be heard on topics such as productivity gains, financial indicators, and ISO9001 and other customer certificates of registration. Quality improvement is seen both as an externally imposed contractual requirement and as an added cost – a twin threat to be avoided whenever possible. Quality is not given priority in terms of either managerial time or resource allocation. The focus will be on the product not on the process, and corrective and preventative action will not be taken intuitively but only in response to client/customer complaints. The priority is given to fire-fighting situations.

Problems are given support for their resolution subject to the level of impact which they may have on sales turnover. In this respect, failures and non-conformances encountered prior to shipment of product will receive the greatest attention, while those which have occurred after the product has been delivered and those problems which have arisen over a period of time will receive progressively less attention. It is also likely that the quality of design in terms of product, service and process will not receive the necessary and appropriate attention at the right time.

Little investment in the education and training of management with respect to quality will have taken place, and managers consider themselves to be above this type of training. Consequently, senior managers in this type of organization are reluctant to take responsibility for or get involved in improvement activities. Evidence of this lack of commitment usually surfaces strongly in an ISO9001 implementation programme. It is usual to find that management makes time available at the beginning of the programme, but as it progresses the attention given will diminish (e.g. non-attendance at meetings, failure to respond to requests for data, and not doing what they had agreed to do).

It is likely that this type of organization will have had some bad experience of TQM or one of its elements, in the form of a programme (i.e. quality circles, ISO9001 registration, empowerment) and consequently the concept will have acquired a less than favourable reputation amongst the senior management team. Some managers will associate TQM with unreasonable demands on them and their time and see it as a costly and bureaucratic system which will limit their autonomy.

Level 1 organizations are termed 'The Uncommitted' because they have no long-term plan for continuous improvement and are not convinced of its benefits. Managers, particularly at senior management level, are usually ignorant of the philosophy and values of TQM, and if they do have some knowledge of the concept they may be sceptical as to its relevance for them and their business. Any knowledge that has been acquired has come through informal sources. They are not necessarily small, immature, unsophisticated or owner-managed organizations. Some 'household name' organizations are at this level and are often characterized by a long and successful trading history with little effective competition and a lack of customer pressure (i.e. market-niche products, protected markets and contracts assured which are subject only to the budgetary constraints of the client).

Particular characteristics of Level 1 organizations include:

- An overwhelming emphasis and gearing of activity on return on sales and net assets employed, at the expense of other measures, both financial and non-financial.
- Meeting output and sales targets is the major objective of the business, whatever the cost.
- There will be a lack of quality assurance and behaviour-regulating systems, and as a consequence alternative methods will be employed to ensure that unrealistic production targets are met. These methods, more often than not, result in quality aspects of the job being discarded, resulting in a high incidence of internal and external failure.
- A pervading attitude of short-termism as evidenced by frequent changes of priority, lack of investment in people, technology, research and development, and infrastructure and cost-cutting.

- The company is inward-looking and its management style tends to be auto-cratic and 'lean and mean', with senior management having sole discretion and decision-making responsibility.
- The potential threat from the competition is not recognized.
- A number of negative elements are embedded in the organizational culture (e.g. 'them and us' attitudes, a limited view of 'on-the-job' expertise, inflex-ible working practices, job demarcation, little recognition of the potential of individuals, individuals are chastised in front of both their peers and subordin-ates and not given a chance to defend themselves, employees are required to wear identification tags to provide visual proof to management that they belong to a specific area, and managers enforce their ideas upon staff to a point where they are not allowed to think or deliver any input to decisions).
- The majority of employees have little concern for quality: it is seen as someone else's job. Employees are not held responsible for the quality of their output. A typical scenario is that inspectors find the defects and workers fix them.
- People hijack ideas and proposals from other employees to ingratiate them-selves with management.
- When quality improvement proposals and suggestions for change are made they are either squashed, not understood or changed to suit management's needs, and there is an unwillingness to instigate any real changes.
- One hundred per cent inspection is carried out on incoming materials, at key points during the production process, and on the finished product. The main focus of the activity is to measure conformance to specification and a con-siderable amount of activity revolves around the acceptable quality level (AQL) concept.
- The data collected from tools such as checksheets and quality control checks tend to be left on file with no effort to identify trends and highlight major non-conformances.
- Ineffective and inaccurate corrective action control procedures.
- A piecework system is in operation for operatives and inspectors, with payment made for non-conforming work.
- Any quality improvement initiatives tend to be 'bottom-up' and are product-related.
- The same problems recur with no formal procedures for pursuing long-term corrective action.
- Processes are not fully understood, documented and/or accessible.
- Employees are encouraged, when things go wrong, to make all efforts to 'cover their backs', and if blame can be passed on to alleviate pressure then it is done without a thought for others. This type of action is condoned, if not encouraged, by management.
- Contact with customers is minimal.
- Suppliers are often blamed for quality problems, although the majority of the problems are of the company's own making.
- A lack of communication up and down the organization.
- Management and people are driven by fear and uncertainty. For example, in a plant of one of the UK's top-performing companies (in profit terms) a defective batch of product was hidden from the plant director by the works manager and a production supervisor so that they could dispose of it when the director was off-site. Another typical example of this characteristic is the

unwillingness of all levels of personnel to express their opinions and ideas in the presence of their manager/director.

It could be argued that such companies, which are often very profitable, do not need TQM when they seem to be doing very well without it. But 'doing very well' is only for the time being and may not be a long-term phenomenon. Certainly, with rising costs due to inefficiency, they will in the future begin to suffer. Such uncommitted companies and their business philosophies are 'dinosaurs' belonging to another age; 'They are unlikely to survive the new economic age' (Deming 1982).

Level 2 – Drifters

Level 2 organizations will have been engaged in a process of continuous improvement for up to three years and have followed the available advice and 'received wisdom' on TQM. The management team will be taking stock of the progress made and it is also likely that initial enthusiasm will have worn off so that ways of reviving the process are under consideration. At this stage, those with a short-term view may be expressing disappointment that TQM has not lived up to their expectations, asking questions such as 'What comes after TQM?' 'What do we need to concentrate on next?' 'What is the next fad?' 'Should we be using business process re-engineering?' 'Should we use the EFQM excellence model?' This type of organization is susceptible to the latest fad and this focus is detrimental to the development of an in-depth understanding of the fundamentals of key concepts. For example, in one utility some management believed that quality was being introduced into their processes by re-engineering them and therefore considered that there was no need for an ISO9001 quality management system.

Senior management perceive that the motivation of employees can be improved but think that this is being suffocated by their supervisors and managers. To facilitate this motivation a form of empowerment programme is put into place, and some senior managers express the belief that this will replace TQM. It will also be assumed by senior management that – in spite of their lack of visible involvement in TQM, recognition for the improvements which have taken place and failure to prioritize improvement activities – continuous improvement will be naturally self-occurring and self-perpetuating.

This type of organization may have followed a programme along the lines of Crosby's 14 steps (1979; see chapter 3 above). Having reached Step 14 – 'Do it all again' – they do not know what to do next and are wary of 'doing it again' because the initiative taken to date has not been perceived as universally successful throughout the organization. In the case of a service, commercial, or public-sector organization they may have started with a customer-care programme, perhaps in a blaze of publicity. It is not unusual to find organizations at this level seeking to employ the philosophy of one of the other quality management experts – a typical comment being 'We started with Crosby and are now viewing the Juran videotapes to see if his philosophy is suitable for our next step forward' – or be considering the use of the EFQM model, taking the line 'This is evidence of our commitment to TQM.'

There is a danger that this type of organization enters a cycle of programme renewal and decline, moving in ever-decreasing circles of false starts, waning enthusiasm, frustration and disappointment.

The characteristics of Level 2 organizations include:

- Continuous improvement is still perceived as a programme, not a strategy or a process, and will have a low profile within the organization. It will not be integrated with business and departmental objectives.
- There is no plan for deployment of the TQM philosophy throughout the organization. Communication is limited and TQM does not penetrate to shop-floor and office levels.
- Management are overly susceptible to outside interventions and easily get distracted by the latest 'fads' which are put to them under various guises (i.e. they are quality fashion victims).
- Management have undue high expectations of ISO9001 and fail to distinguish between meeting this standard and TQM. It is also likely that the procedures of such a system will be cumbersome; control and disciplines engendered by it will have been allowed to slide and documents will have become obsolete, resulting in a superficial application. While there is a belief that staff should work within the system, management cannot accept that they themselves need to accept the same disciplines. Consequently, at first-line supervision and operator levels they tend to be driven by day-to-day actions and quotes rather than compliance with quality management system requirements.
- The quality department has low status within the organization.
- Continuous improvement activities are little more than cosmetic 'off-line' motivation programmes, with little impression on the company's organizational structure, internal relationships, and overall business direction.
- There is inadequate reporting of defects and inaccurate and/or inappropriate feedback, and there is a lack of clarity on what the real non-conformances and defects are.
- The softer aspects of TQM will have been promoted without the underpinning and mastering of the quality assurance basics.
- Any teamworking is superficial and departments only tend to co-operate in order to lay the blame on another department. Considerable in-fighting, rivalry and 'politics' exist between departments.
- A programme of quality circles will have been attempted as a means of developing employees, and middle management told that they are judged by the number of quality circles they have in operation. The initial circles will have flourished, after which they will have floundered and then virtually died.
- No real changes in corporate culture have been made since the start of the TQM initiative. The activities associated with TQM are not given time to come to fruition before they are discarded and replaced by others.
- There is a reasonably high degree of suspicion and scepticism about TQM by management and staff, with a number of senior and middle managers not accepting the concept of TQM. Those at an operating level see TQM as another short-term tool to squeeze more productivity out of them.
- There are gaps in people's understanding of TQM and what it is, and, in addition, some key elements of the improvement process will have been treated superficially. This will not have been helped by an unco-ordinated training programme. A typical scenario is that awareness of TQM exists at the lower levels of the organization, and understanding of the benefits is turned into frustration because they do not get the support of senior management,

because they lack of knowledge of the concept and do not understand the seriousness of the situation facing the organization.

- There is a wide gulf between levels of the organizational hierarchy in perceptions of TQM, benefits achieved and progress to date.
- Self-assessment has been performed against one of the recognized award models, but the areas for improvement identified have not been addressed by developing a time-scaled plan of action. The focus of the self-assessment exercise is likely to have been on scoring mechanisms, 'scoring points' and impressing customers and suppliers, and not on how to facilitate improvement, and is perceived by many in the organization as being of little practical value. There is an overwhelming desire to win a quality award, mainly for PR and marketing reasons.
- A fear of failure and uncertainty pervades the organization and there is the view that TQM will be sidelined in the medium term.

Level 2 organizations are termed 'The Drifters' because they drift, without a clearly defined baseline, from one programme to another in a stop-start fashion, with concepts, ideas and initiatives being reborn and relaunched under different guises. Management teams try a variety of approaches, often in response to the latest trend, consultancy input, what they perceive will impress customers and what has been gained from conference presentations and discussions with other companies. A change of approach may be sparked off when a senior manager who has been a protagonist of the TQM philosophy and a particular line of thinking leaves the organization. Individual initiatives may be very creative because the managers are intelligent and articulate people, and some will be genuinely committed to and enthusiastic about TQM. However, while they are unable or unwilling to place quality improvement within a strategic business framework, it will not yield the desired long-term results.

Level 3 – Tool-Pushers

A Level 3 organization has more operating experience of quality improvement than a drifter, usually between three and five years. They will typically have ISO9001 registration and/or have met the requirements of the quality system standard of one or more of the major purchasers. They employ a selection of quality management tools and techniques such as SPC, the seven basic quality control tools, quality circles, FMEA and mistake-proofing, use a variety of quality improvement groups, and may be in the process of extending their knowledge of some of the more advanced techniques such as design of experiments, QFD and the seven management tools.

It is not uncommon to find that the training on tools and techniques has been aimed at individuals who cannot propagate their further use and application, hence the knowledge is contained. The system certification and use of tools and techniques will usually have been prompted and forced by a customer-driven initiative or based on the initiatives of individual employees. In some cases the tools and techniques will not have been implemented in a strategic and systematic way, but reactively and when necessary. An increasing number of organizations at Level 3 are also looking to the criteria of the TQM and performance and excellence models of MBNQA (2001) or the EFQM (2001) to provide an indication to senior management of what is involved in TQM and give some direction and structure to their improvement process, the quantitative assessment of progress being perceived as of particular benefit.

A detailed examination of the quality assurance procedures, quality planning systems and the use of quality management tools and techniques reveals that, in the main, they are being employed with an almost militaristic mindset (i.e. exacting and stringent quality requirements have been set by the customer and as a result a regulative approach has been built around fulfilling them).

If the organization is owned by an offshore parent company, it is likely it will have made an attempt to address the annual themes in its officially submitted business plans and will have responded to the improvement initiatives put out by regional and corporate headquarters. However, there will be no master plan to integrate and sustain the various initiatives which have been downloaded by headquarters to the various operating businesses.

There are a number of Level 3 organizations which have purchased a particular quality improvement tool (e.g. the Juran training videotapes) and then followed the recommended advice – i.e. training by module, establishment of problem-solving teams, project-by-project improvement, etc. However, even though some of these teams have been highly successful, after a period of up to two years the impetus of this type of training has been lost and the Juran training methodology has fallen into disuse. Such companies buy tools, training packages, programmes, etc. and disregard them once the novelty has worn off, thereby failing to realize the potential afforded by the tool by neglecting to link it into a continuous improvement strategy. It is often the case that the tool itself is then blamed as 'ineffective' when in reality it was its incorrect application which caused it to fail.

The characteristics of this type of organization are:

- They are for ever looking for the latest panacea, for a 'quick fix'. This has happened with quality circles, SPC, FMEA, design of experiments, QFD and benchmarking, The excellence models and BPR are now being used in this way by many organizations.
- Not all members of the senior management team are committed to TQM and those that are will probably not understand its full implications, with considerable variability in their knowledge of the subject. The different interpretations placed on the concept are sometimes wanted and built upon by management to disguise their lack of commitment to TQM. Some of these senior managers do not see it as their responsibility to facilitate improvement, but have a 'What's in it for me?' attitude. This surfaces in the form of autocratic and negative behaviour, particularly in the sales/marketing and finance functions. They have a tendency to delegate TQM responsibilities to the quality department (e.g. customer complaints, issues revolving around administration errors such as pricing, invoicing, duplication of orders, over- and under-supply, and chairing ISO9001 review meetings). Middle managers may say all the right things, but they remain unconvinced in their own minds of the value and strategic importance of TQM, and demonstrate this in their day-to-day actions. In their area of responsibility they give priority to systems and techniques which they consider will have more short-term impact than TQM. These apparently conflicting priorities are communicated through their actions and comments to first-line supervisors and operators, where the understanding of TQM and continuous improvement is usually patchy.

- The continuous improvement effort is concentrated in the manufacturing/ operations departments with other departments remaining less involved in improvement efforts. The tools and techniques will be in a reasonable state of health in those areas most affected by customer audits. The quality department is usually the main driving force of the improvement process and company employees perceive the department owning quality assurance and quality improvement. There will also be a perception within the quality department staff that they themselves own the continuous improvement process.
- A certain amount of inter-departmental/functional friction and lack of communication is likely to be evident.
- Detailed quality procedures are in place and the focus is on control of what exists now. The emphasis is on solving current rather than future problems.
- A quality management information system will exist, but the data provided by the system will not be used to its full potential.
- Meeting output targets is the key priority of the majority of managers, with conflict between the manufacturing/operations and quality assurance departments.
- Short-term results regarding product output and quality are expected, resulting in reactive problem-solving and a neglect of long-term, root-cause, process-improvement actions.
- The management style is reactionary.
- Organizations have acquired a reputation for their products and services but their processes have considerable potential for improvement.
- There are repeated claims from some parts of the organization that TQM is not working, with a tendency to dwell on old practices as being more effective.

This type of organization finds it very difficult to sustain the momentum of its improvement initiatives and is continually on the look-out for new ideas and quick fixes to deploy. The practice followed is often to replace those quality management tools and techniques which have been found to require considerable effort and disciplined application to make them work. The fire-fighting culture tends to suppress those techniques which need more effort to use and apply them successfully. A Level 3 organization gives the right kind of signals and presents the requisite image to its customers and suppliers, but under the surface a 'fire-fighting' culture remains, which is not really committed to TQM.

There are a number of similarities between Level 2 and Level 3 organizations, in that TQM has not affected the pervading organizational culture or achieved significant business results. The difference lies in the way in which organizations react to this, with Level 2 organizations trying a new overall approach, while Level 3 organizations merely turn to another tool or technique within the context of the same overall approach. Level 3 organizations more commonly have well-developed quality management systems, and tend to be concentrated in the manufacturing sector.

Level 4 – Improvers

Level 4 organizations will typically have been engaged in a process of continuous improvement for between three and eight years and during this time will have made important advances. They understand that TQM involves cultural change and have recognized the importance of customer-focused continuous improvement. The chief executive and members of the senior management team have committed themselves to total quality through leadership and their own personal actions. They will have formulated a strategy for TQM, in conjunction with the other business strategies, and have implemented a good deal of it. It is at this level that TQM begins to have a real impact on business performance.

Characteristics of this type of organization include:

- A policy deployment and problem-solving infrastructure is in place, together with a robust and proactive quality system.
- There is a high degree of closed-loop error prevention through the control of basic production/operation and/or service processes.
- A long-term and company-wide education and training programme is in place.
- Process-improvement activities exist throughout the organization with people looking to improve activities within their own sphere of influence, on their own initiative.
- The importance of employee involvement through a variety of departmental and cross-functional teams and other means is recognized, communicated and celebrated.
- Benchmarking studies have been initiated and the data are used to facilitate improvement activities.
- A 'leadership culture' is starting to emerge, with some strong quality improvement champions.
- Trust between all levels of the organizational hierarchy exists.
- The preoccupation with 'numbers' is less marked than with 'drifters' or 'tool-pushers'.
- The 'hype' which is usually associated with TQM is replaced by an acceptance of good management principles and practice.

In Level 4 organizations, TQM is still, however, dependent on a small number of key individuals to sustain the drive and direction of the improvement strategy. There is a danger of lost momentum and failure to 'hold the gains' if key managers or directors leave, if business mergers or organizational restructuring take place, or if the economic environment and trading conditions become difficult. This has been the case for a number of organizations during times of recession, where the long-term nature of TQM and its benefits have been discarded at the expense of short-term 'survival'.

Level 4 organizations are termed 'The Improvers'. They are moving in the right direction and have made real progress, but still have some way to go. TQM is not internalized throughout the organization and the process of improvement is not self-sustaining, with organizations still vulnerable to short-term pressures and unexpected difficulties. The results of improvement projects are not all effectively utilized for improvements and such initiatives are heavily dependent upon the individuals driving them. It is also likely that the change in culture is relatively slow and some contradictory signals are sent out (e.g. people empowerment versus control mechanisms). An overall strategy which pulls all the islands of improvement together is not fully in place, and concerns will also be expressed by management with respect to resources, in particular time. In 'improvers' the more complex quality management techniques must be implemented carefully. They should be handled by employees who are able to understand them, otherwise people will be overwhelmed and the technique rejected.

The next step forward involves the management and co-ordination of quality improvement across entire streams of processes – the point at which quality improvement starts to become total. Process-stream improvement and benchmarking activities of key processes may take between five and 10 years to mature sufficiently, so it is unlikely that the kind of cross-functional culture required to move up to Level 5 will emerge in less than five years; it is more likely to take around 10 years. At this stage of development, TQM will be a focal point but will not necessarily have attained prime strategic importance.

Level 5 – Award-Winners

To date there have been over 220 winners of the Deming Application Prize, the Japan Quality Award, the MBNQA and the EQA.

In their research on the long-term management issues of continuous improvement, Williams and Bersch (1989) conclude that strong, world-class, quality-related competitiveness can only be achieved when an organization has reached the stage of being able to compete for the top quality awards (i.e. Deming Application Prize, Japan Quality Award, MBNQA, and the EQA). Because the challenge is so formidable they estimated that probably only 150 or so companies have reached this level of quality. Williams and Bersch (1996), in discussion with Dale, have suggested that:

> It is now impossible to estimate with any accuracy how many companies are beyond level 5 in your model. This is primarily for two reasons. Firstly due to the tremendous expansion of total quality (TQ) over the past ten years especially in South East Asia where information sources are scarce and often unreliable. And secondly because we are now coming to the view that many companies are practising the basic TQ principles at a high level and yet have never realized that such a thing as TQ exists. To them, such principles are just about effective management. So they never take part in TQ surveys or competitions, apply for Quality Awards or join TQ societies and networks, etc. and are therefore difficult to track down . . .

Level 5 organizations are therefore termed 'Award-Winners'. Not all organizations reaching this level have actually won an internationally recognized or national quality award but they have reached a point in their TQM maturity where the kind of culture, values, trust, capabilities, relationship and employee involvement in their business required to win such an award have been developed; a point at which continuous improvement has become total in nature.

Such organizations have the following characteristics:

- A leadership 'culture' throughout the business that is not dependent on the commitment and drive of a limited number of individuals; all employees are involved in improvement.
- A number of successful organizational changes have been made.
- Business procedures and processes are efficient and responsive to customer needs.
- Effective cross-functional management processes and achieved process-stream improvements that are measurable.

- Strategic benchmarking practised at all levels, in conjunction with an integrated system of internal and external performance measurement.
- A more participative organizational culture than before TQM was initiated.
- Powers of decision-making relinquished by management to people at lower levels of the organizational hierarchy in varying degrees.
- TQM is viewed sincerely by all employees as a way of managing the business to satisfy and delight customers, both internal and external.
- Perceptions of key stakeholders (i.e. people, customers and society) of organizational performance is surveyed and acted upon to drive improvement action.

However, although they may appear to form part of an elite, Level 5-type organizations have not necessarily achieved 'world-class' status. The attainment of Level 5 status marks the end of an organization's TQM apprenticeship and signifies that the organization has the capability and the potential to make an impact at the highest level, world-wide.

Level 6 – World-Class

This level is characterized by the total integration of continuous improvement and business strategy to delight the customer. Williams and Bersch claimed in 1989 that less than 10 companies world-wide, all Japanese, had reached this stage. Smith (1994) in a chapter of his book entitled 'Becoming World Class', says that 'perhaps 50 organizations worldwide earn the world-class label'. However, in discussing numbers the points made by Williams and Bersch under the discussion of award-winners should be noted.

An indication of world-class quality performance is that a company can apply for the Japan Quality Medal five years or more after it has received the Deming Application Prize. This, according to JUSE, is 'When it has been determined that an applicant company's implementation of CWQC has improved substantially beyond when it won the Deming Application Prize' (Deming Prize Committee 2000). They go on to say that 'By setting the goal of applying for the Japan Quality Medal when companies receive the Deming Application Prize, they can expect to prevent their CWQC from becoming stale and sluggish. In this way they can further develop their CWQC practices.' The Japan Quality Medal has currently been awarded on just 16 occasions (2000 data). While it is a clear indicator of TQM maturity, this award is not the sole qualification for Level 6 status.

Closer to home, the Royal Society for the Encouragement of Arts, Manufacturers and Commerce points out in *Inquiry: Tomorrow's Company* (RSA 1995) that there are too few world-class companies in the UK and an insufficient number of such companies are being created. In discussing the approach of 'tomorrow's company' the point is made that:

> The companies which will sustain competitive success in the future are those which focus less exclusively on shareholders and on financial measures of success – and instead include all their stakeholder relationships, and a broader range of measurements in the way they think and talk about their purpose and performance.

The characteristics of such a company, which it is claimed can compete at world-class levels, are examined in the inquiry and summarized as:

- Defining and communicating purpose and value
- Developing and applying a unique success model
- Placing a positive value on relationships
- Working in partnership with stakeholders
- Maintaining a strong licence to operate

The relatively small number of organizations which have truly reached Level 6 epitomize the TQM concept. TQM is concerned with the search for opportunities to improve the ability of the organization to satisfy the customer. By this stage of TQM maturity (which will have probably taken more than 10 years after its initiation), the organization is continuously searching to identify more product and/or service factors or characteristics which will increase customer satisfaction. The focus of its TQM strategy is on enhancing competitive advantage by improving the customer's perception of the company and the attractiveness of the product and/or service. This constant drive to enhance customer appeal through what the Japanese call 'miryokuteki hinshitsu' ('quality that fascinates') is integral to the concept of continuous improvement. Just like the concept of total quality itself 'miryokuteki hinshitsu' is a vision, a paradigm and a value framework which will condition an entire organizational culture.

The never-ending pursuit of complete customer satisfaction to satisfy latent requirements is a personal goal of everyone in the organization and an integral part of their everyday working lives. TQM is no longer dependent on top-down drives to improve motivation and deploy the policy, but it is driven laterally throughout the organization. Kanter's terminology (1989) of 'PAL' – pooling, allying and linking across organizations – is useful here; she describes organizations who *pool* resources with others, *ally* to exploit opportunities and *link* systems in partnerships. Those organizations who PAL while seeking continuous improvement of processes and customer satisfaction are typical of Level 6.

Customer desires and business goals, growth and strategies are inseparable; total quality is the integrative and self-evident organizational truth. The vision of the entire organization is aligned to the voice of the customer in such organizations. Total quality is the single constant in a dynamic business environment – it is a way of life, a way of doing business – for all 'world-class' organizations.

In summary the characteristics of world-class organizations are:

- Company values are fully understood and shared by employees, customers and suppliers.
- Each person in the organization is committed in an almost natural manner to seek opportunities for improvement to the mutual benefit of everyone and the business.
- Dependability is emphasized throughout the organization.
- The right things are got right first time and every time in every part of the company.
- Waste is not tolerated.
- The key processes of the organization are aligned to create common and shared objectives and to facilitate an environment conducive to improvement.
- There is total willingness and inherent capability to predict and respond to changing market conditions and customer needs and requirements.
- They constantly compete and win against the best world-wide.

Attaining Level 6 status is not the end, for none of the levels described here represents a 'steady state'. In particular, 'world-class' status is often attainable for only a few years, and it is dangerous for an organization to become complacent and blinkered to environmental changes. It is possible for such organizations to 'slip' to Level 5, or even lower.

Summary

Total quality management is a strategy for change in an environment where the accepted paradigms are subject to constant challenge. It is a strategy concerned with developing an organizational culture in which people are able to meet these challenges and realize the opportunities of change. The six levels described in this chapter are intended as a positioning model to aid organizations in identifying their weaknesses and addressing them, as part of the continual challenge of continuous improvement throughout the organization. The characteristics underpinning the six levels are also helpful in highlighting different perceptions of progress with continuous improvement at different levels of the organizational hierarchy of a firm. The characteristics of the more advanced adoptions should also provide the requisite inspiration to those less advanced to highlight the type of issues to which attention needs to be given.

References

Crosby, P. B. (1979), *Quality is Free.* New York: McGraw Hill.

Dale, B. G. and Lightburn, K. L. (1992), Continuous quality improvement: why some organisations lack commitment. *International Journal of Production Economics*, 27(1), 57–67.

Deming, W. E. (1982), *Quality, Productivity and Competitive Position.* Massachusetts: MIT Press.

Deming Prize Committee (2000), *The Deming Prize Guide for Overseas Companies.* Tokyo: Union of Japanese Scientists and Engineers.

EFQM (2001), *The EFQM Excellence Model.* Brussels: EFQM.

Kanter, R. M. (1989), *When Giants Learn to Dance.* London: Simon & Schuster.

Lascelles, D. M. and Dale, B. G. (1991), Levelling out the future. *The TQM Magazine*, 3(2), 125–8.

Lascelles, D. M. and Dale, B. G. (1993), *The Road to Quality.* Bedford: IFS Publications.

Smith, S. (1994), *The Quality Revolution: Best Practice from the World's Leading Companies.* Oxfordshire: Management Books.

RSA (1995), *RSA Inquiry: Tomorrow's Company.* London: Royal Society for the Encouragement of Arts, Manufacturers and Commerce.

US Department of Commerce (2001), *Baldrige National Quality Program 2001: Criteria for Performance Excellence.* Gaithersburg: US Department of Commerce, National Institute of Standards and Technology.

Williams, R. T. and Bersch, B. (1989), *Proceedings of the First European Quality Management Forum*, 163–72. European Foundation for Quality Management.

Williams, R. T. and Bersch, B. (1996), Personal discussion, London, 8 May.

chapter seven

Sustaining TQM

B. G. Dale

Introduction

Total quality management is a long-term process. It can take an organization up to 10 years to put the fundamental principles, practices, procedures and systems into place, create an organizational culture that is conducive to continuous improvement and change the values and attitudes of its people. It requires considerable effort and intellectual input by the senior management team, and a clear strategic direction and framework. It is also unfortunate that misconceptions abound with regard to what TQM and quality improvement are and how to achieve them. Therefore it is little wonder that the vast majority of organizations do encounter problems in their continuous improvement efforts. In recent times there have been a number of reports outlining the lack of success of some TQM initiatives and the problems which have been encountered (e.g. Boyett et al. 1991; Develin and Partners 1989; Harari 1997; Kearney 1992; Economist Intelligence Unit 1992; Miller 1992, on a survey by Ernst and Young; Naj 1993; Redman and Grieves 1999; and Tice 1994). However, the vast majority of such reports, based on questionnaire surveys, contain flaws in the interpretation of the findings since they do not usually define what they mean by TQM.

This chapter describes the main issues which impact on sustaining TQM. 'Sustaining' in this context means maintaining a process of continuous improvement. The issues have been grouped into five categories: internal/external environment, management style, policies, organization structure and process of change. The categories and issues are summarized in table 7.1.

The issues described have been identified from work carried out over a period of three years on an Engineering and Physical Sciences Research Council (EPSRC)-funded project (Dale and Boaden 1991). They were initially identified from fieldwork

Barrie Dale acknowledges the contribution of Dr Ruth Boaden, Mr Mark Wilcox and Ms Ruth McQuater to the material contained in this chapter. He also acknowledges the support of the EPSRC for their funding of research contract GR/H.21499.

Table 7.1   TQM sustaining categories and issues

Environment	External:
	  a. Competitors
	  b. Employee resourcing, development and
	    retention
	Internal:
	  a. Customer focus
	  b. Investment
	  c. The 'fear' factor

Management style	a. Industrial relations b. Management/worker relationship
Policies that may conflict with TQM	HRM Financial Maintenance Manufacturing
Organization structure	a. Positioning of the quality function b. Departmental, functional and shift boundaries c. Communication d. Job flexibility and cover e. Supervisory structure
Process of change	a. Improvement infrastructure b. Education and training c. Teams and teamwork d. Procedures e. Quality management system f. Quality management tools and techniques g. Confidence in management

carried out in six organizations (12 sites) and then refined and developed by reference to relevant theories, in the form of a TQM sustaining audit tool (TQMSAT); for more detail, see Dale et al. (1997). The issues reflect a variety of perspectives on business operation, including continuous improvement, organizational behaviour, human resources management, industrial relations and the labour process. The objective of the audit tool is to identify the issues that impact on sustaining TQM. The issues are investigated by discussion of aspects of the organizations under each of the five mentioned categories. The audit tool does not prescribe 'solutions' to the issues raised. The use of the information revealed is organization-dependent, but it has most commonly been used as an input to planning the advancement of the improvement process, sometimes as part of self-assessment against one of the internationally recognized models of excellence (i.e. MBNQA and EFQM). The audit tool is primarily intended for use by a skilled interviewer who is knowledgeable in TQM, but can be used in self-assessment mode depending on the level of openness and trust in the company. The audit tool has been validated and tested at seven manufacturing sites: four first-line automotive component suppliers (UK, USA, Germany and Spain), a manufacturer of bearings and two packaging manufacturers; one example of this testing is provided by Kemp et al. (1997). Examples are used from each of these seven case studies to outline and highlight the issues underlying each of the five sustaining categories. However, before describing each of the categories and the examples, the development and methodology of the audit tool is outlined.

TQM Sustaining Audit Tool: Development and Methodology

The majority of the self-assessment methods and audit tools which are in common use focus on the review of an organization's activities and results against a predetermined model, framework or system standard (see Lascelles and Peacock 1996; Conti 1997). In this way progress made by them to meet a specification of business excellence can be assessed. Such assessments are, in general, focused on looking for positive factors, although organizational weaknesses are also identified. For example, in using the EFQM excellence model strengths and areas of improvement are identified for each of the individual criteria (see chapter 24).

The TQM sustaining audit tool is different in that it is looking for a specific set of predetermined negative factors, that is, those factors identified from the research which have been seen to have a detrimental effect on sustaining TQM. Companies are often reluctant to face up to failures as they usually require actions which have far-reaching effects; the audit tool forces companies to address these types of issues. It can also be argued that focusing on the negative issues is probably the best way to understand the strengths and weaknesses of TQM within an organization. However, during the interview process carried out to determine if the negative issues are in place, some areas of strength are also identified.

In five of the organizations where the audit tool was tested, self-assessment against either the MBNQA or EFQM excellence models was taking place at the same time. The feedback from the collaborating organizations was that the findings from use of TQMSAT made a useful input to the collection of data with respect to some of the criteria, in particular with obtaining views from a cross-section of the organization.

The audit tool should be used by either (1) an outside agency such as a management consultant or (2) an organization in self-assessment mode. If it is being used by an outside agency a plant tour is recommended to gain an insight into the improvement initiatives in operation, the process and technology being used, and the general operating environment of the business. It is also recommended that historical information such as reports and presentations are collected and analysed.

Interviews, which should last for about one hour, are conducted with between 10 and 20 people, depending on the size of the organization, from a cross-section of the organizational hierarchy. The time needed for each interview will depend on the person's position and knowledge of the company; it needs to be kept flexible to enable areas of the audit to be dealt with in depth. In deciding the selection of people to be interviewed some consideration should be given to the inclusion of TQM champions, since the negative influences are likely to have been identified by them. The person being interviewed should be informed of the purpose of the interview at least one week prior to it taking place. The interviewee should be encouraged to seek views from their area on the issues which people believe are affecting the sustaining of TQM. Using the guidelines provided, the interviews should explore the issues which comprise each of the five sustaining categories. In this way the questioning draws out the history and background which may be inhibiting TQM and highlight areas to be improved. Some of the issues can be explored in greater or less detail depending on the person being interviewed and their knowledge of the business and TQM. By discussing these issues with a variety of people, most of the factors which impinge on the sustaining of TQM will be uncovered. A small number of questions are given under each of the five categories as examples for each of the issues. The questions have been prepared in TQM jargon-free language and thus should be universally understood, irrespective of the approach taken to TQM. These questions have proved useful in unlocking the thought processes of the interviewee in order to facilitate a discussion about the degree of difficulty caused by the issues being explored. Questions can, of course, be developed and tailored to suit the organization under examination and also the person being interviewed. The strength of TQMSAT is in the categorization of issues; the individual questions asked are not in themselves significant.

Once the interviews have been completed a summary report outlining the findings for each of the issues should be produced. A half-day seminar should then be held to feed back and discuss the findings, and assist the organization in developing an action plan to overcome the difficulties identified. The people attending the seminar should include all the employees who have been interviewed. In presenting the findings it should be remembered that it is the perceptions of people with respect to difficulties which are being reported. If senior management believe the perceptions to be incorrect then they need to consider how they can change the perceptions.

The interpretation of results is crucial. As the line of questioning is essentially 'negative' to draw out positive action plans for the future, it is important that the outcomes which are reported do not encourage the semantics of blame. The 'problem' statement should be explained as the relatively 'easy' bit; the solutions take longer and need the full continued participation and co-operation of everyone, not just management, who it is easy to blame for all the problems identified.

Category 1 – Internal/External Environment

A common method of distinguishing between the internal and external environment and their influencing factors is to use the strength, weaknesses, opportunities and threats (SWOT) framework. Opportunities and threats are viewed as external variables:

> The **external environment** consists of variables (opportunities and threats) that exist outside the organization and are not typically within the short-term control of top management. (Wheelan and Hunger 1988)

Strengths and weaknesses are part of the internal environment:

> The **internal environment** of a corporation consists of variables (strengths and weaknesses) within the organization itself that are also not usually within the short-term control of top management. (Wheelan and Hunger 1988)

The point of making these distinctions is that there are a number of environmental variables which are often outside the direct control of managers, although they can affect a business through the perceived negative and destabilizing effect which they have on both employees and the improvement process. Therefore managers need a knowledge of these variables so that they can, where possible, plan around them. The factors in this sustaining category are therefore split into external and internal environment.

External environment

Competitors

This relates to the ability of the organization to understand and react to the threat posed by competitors (e.g. building a state-of-the-art plant in greenfield conditions and competing directly with the organization for its current customers) and to compete in global markets which have high technical, quality and performance standards and measures, and involve new technologies.

Typical questions include:

- Can you identify which companies and/or products comprise the competition?
- What is your knowledge of the competition in terms of quality performance and technology employed?
- How are data on the competitors collected and analysed?
- How are data on the competitors communicated to non-management employees?
- What concerns do you have about the competitors?
- Where is the company's advantage in the marketplace vis-à-vis the competitors and from the point of view of its suppliers?

In a bearings manufacturer the main competitors were known to employees, but there was a genuine interest in having more data about them. It was felt that this would stop some employees becoming complacent and alert others to the threat. There was some concern about the competition; this did not appear to be a major worry, but there was an awareness that some orders had been lost. There was a strong view that the company had a good name in the industry and this gave it a competitive advantage. The biggest weakness was recognized to be delivery performance. It was felt that if the competition focused their attention on reducing lead time this would result in a loss of market share.

Employee resourcing, development and retention

The inability to recruit and retain employees of sufficient calibre to maintain an organization's growth can threaten the strategic direction of the business. New employees, in particular, in the case of the recruitment of a relatively large number over a short time-frame, also have to be integrated into the improvement culture of the organization, otherwise they can have a disruptive effect on the improvement process. Another factor in this issue is the retention of employees and the efforts made by management to develop them.

Typical questions include:

- What difficulties do you have in recruiting employees of the right calibre?
- In which type of skill/function do you experience recruitment difficulties?
- What difficulties do you experience in retaining key personnel?
- What external labour-supply problems exist that could affect the business?
- What policies and procedures do you have to develop employees?
- What are the main reasons people give for leaving?

One of the packaging manufacturers experienced no difficulty in recruiting people of sufficient calibre. However, in some functions the training given to people had increased their market potential and they had moved to competing organizations to improve their salary and job prospects.

In some cases the development of people was taking place through training and increasing job flexibility. Much of this stemmed from departmental heads' initiatives, rather than being a company policy. The development through formal training courses was recognized and these were regarded as plentiful, typified by the comment 'people seem to do lots of courses'. In other cases little development of people had taken place (e.g. new operators being recruited on a six-month contract and just used as a pair of hands).

Internal environment

Customer focus

Meeting the needs and requirements of customers is the main thrust of TQM. It is important to have measures in place to assess how well the products and services meet the customer requirements and to identify their future needs. In some organizations TQM is not introduced for these reasons and the motivation for introducing TQM needs to be assessed.

Typical questions include:

- What methods do you use to ensure that you are the supplier of choice of your customers?
- How do you ensure that you meet the needs and requirements of your customers?
- What type of feedback do you receive from the customer?
- What are the weaknesses in how you deal with the customer?
- Is the internal customer concept recognized?
- Is the TQM initiative perceived to be a good thing?
- Is TQM seen as an imposition and resented?
- Is TQM seen as long-term or a fad?
- What do you believe are the major factors motivating quality improvement?

The Spanish automotive component suppliers were extremely well focused on their major customers (SEAT and VW) and were proud of their quick reactions to responding to meet their needs and requirements. The positive feedback from customer second-party audits and surveys was perceived as an indication that their performance, in the eyes of the customer, was along the right lines. The practice of customer visits by operators was well entrenched. For example, the marketing manager, when making visits to SEAT, usually took operators with him, and members of the assembly cell had spent time on the assembly-line at SEAT observing how the connector assembly was fitted to the end-product. These visits had helped to build up confidence amongst the operating staff.

There was good knowledge of the internal customer concept amongst the operators (e.g. when they encountered a non-conformance with a part, they had no hesitation in going to the supplying process and discussing the problem with them). However, this concept was less well understood in the non-manufacturing departments.

Investment

The willingness of a business to finance new machinery and equipment, to invest in education, training and recruitment and to improve the fabric of buildings and the associated environment, can affect TQM in many ways. Adequate resources to meet the business plans and quality improvement actions that have been developed are also needed, as well as positive responses to improvement team suggestions to implement the findings from their projects.
    Typical questions include:

* Are you satisfied with the level of investment in the business?
* Are the investments made by the right people?
* Who is consulted about the investment?
* Have the investments made been worthwhile?
* Is the investment which has been made recognized by employees?
* Are you satisfied with the way in which investment priorities are determined?
* What is the market share–market growth profile of the organization?
* To what extent do non-management employees understand the process of investment decision-making?
* What feedback is given to non-management employees about the progress of ongoing investment decisions?

    In one of two packaging manufacturers the majority of people interviewed had a lot to say about the apparent unwillingness to invest in new machinery. This was claimed to influence confidence in the future of the business and employee morale. The perceived reason for the lack of investment was considered to be the relatively low levels of profitability, which were a common occurrence in the first quarter of each year, and the policies of the plc. Some people were aware of what was required to obtain investment through the capital equipment request process, others less so. There was also a lack of feedback regarding the progress of the investment requests. The general view was that the investments made were prudent and the benefits were clearly evident. However, it was felt that the company could be penny wise and pound foolish in terms of ongoing investment in machinery (e.g. a cheaper equivalent of belting specified by the manufacturer being purchased which, in the long term, increased the cost of maintenance). It was also considered that more could be done to get the views of the users of equipment prior to its proposed acquisition.

The 'fear' factor

The 'fear factor', or loss of control, describes the uncertainty felt by employees about their future. It may be caused by plant closures within the group, redundancies, restructuring, relocation, low volume of work within a business, mergers and takeovers, and a lack of trust between managers and the workforce. The type of corporate control used – strategic planning, financial control and strategic control – can also influence this factor, as can morale. Where the 'fear' factor is present a survival/protectionist attitude may develop with short-term decisions taken on a reactive basis.
    Typical questions include:

* Does the 'fear factor' exist in your organization? If so, describe it, and where and when it occurs.

- What major organizational changes (e.g. takeovers and mergers) have taken place recently?
- How have these changes affected the long-term improvement plans of the business?
- Is the change process seen as threatening?
- Have management been open, direct and honest in communicating issues relating to change?
- What plant closures, redundancies or restructuring have there been recently?
- To what extent have these type of events caused uncertainty/insecurity among employees?
- How is this uncertainty/insecurity being managed and how are people being involved and contributing to the change?

This factor was firmly in place at the German automotive component supplier. Typical was the view that 'If we cannot reduce wages and salaries the plant will close and the equipment will be transferred to Spain and England.' The fear factor was attenuated because of the increase in the unemployment rate in Germany and the lack of experience of the majority of German people of this level of unemployment. There was a good slice of realism, typically expressed by the comment 'Germans cannot live as well as we have done in the past.' Senior management have used the fear factor to get people to increase their efforts. Another example of the 'fear factor' was some employees putting roadblocks in front of those at a lower level in the organization who were taking the initiative to make improvements, expressed in terms of being worried about 'stepping on people's area of responsibility'. When ideas were not followed up and projects not completed there was little explanation given to the people who had originally taken the initiative.

Category 2 – Management Style

This category distinguishes between macro- and micro-levels and implications of management style, using the sub-categories of industrial relations and management–worker relationships respectively. The former defines the way in which a business manages employee relations, as outlined typically by Fox (1974) and Marchington and Parker (1990). The latter concerns the attitudes, values and interpersonal skills of managers and supervisors, and their interaction with their subordinates.

Industrial relations

As already outlined in this book, one of the basic tenets of TQM is that managers and workers share the same objectives. This management style has been described as unitarist by Fox (1974). Writers such as Burrell and Morgan (1979) developed Fox's work to define two alternative styles, termed pluralist and radical. To sustain TQM, the shift from a radical or pluralist management style to a unitarist position is necessary. However, this transition is often problematic and the path is potentially strewn with conflict, in particular where there is existing trade union recognition and collective bargaining procedures are in place. The following three categories of industrial relations are summarized below:

- A 'unitary' management style emphasizes a sense of teamwork and pulling together and having common goals for all employees.
- A 'pluralist' management style recognizes the 'rights' of individuals and groups. Procedures for collective bargaining are in place and mechanisms used via trade union representatives.
- The 'radical' concept of industrial relations is based on the notion of opposing class interests. The organization is seen as overtly political, where managers and workers strive to achieve incompatible goals (Morgan 1986).

The relationship between management and the workforce at the manufacturer of bearings was not adversarial and there was an effort on both sides to work together; the point was made that they had been clear of industrial relations disputes for many years. However, there was still a considerable degree of 'them and us' in play, brought about by previous decisions and actions, false starts, and changes in senior management. There was also a feeling that some people, albeit a minority, would reject anything put forward by management.

Management–worker relationship

This issue centres around the notion of trust and discretion within the relationship. TQM is often said to lead to high-trust/high-discretion roles and relationships through the use of teamwork in all its various forms within a process of continuous and company-wide improvement. Self-managing work groups, empowerment, increased participation and the involvement of employees in decision-making are related factors. The management–worker relationship is also concerned with the potential confusion and contradictions in management style resulting from an approach based on scientific management with low trust/low discretion (Taylor 1964). Even where companies believe that they have moved away from such a style, remnants of the principles are often found to be embedded in the operating practices of the organization.

At the UK-based automotive component supplier, 'them and us' was only raised in terms of the relationship between project managers and the shop floor in terms of the initiation of new products. It was claimed that project managers were not willing to seek or listen to ideas from the operating level of the business, and that when suggestions had been made there was often no feedback to operators. It was also felt that the senior management team should be seen more on the shop floor. Recognition and rewards for commitment to improvement were also raised in probing this issue with personal 'thank you' notes and 'pats on the back' from managers emerging as the key responses.

Category 3 – Policies

It is not unusual to find policies within the organization which conflict, are inconsistent with, or overlap with, TQM. Typical of such policies are:

- *Human resources management (HRM)*, where the policy is to pursue individualistic practices supported by the reward system which undermine the teamwork ethos of TQM. Other aspects of HRM policies, which may conflict with TQM, include the level of salaries in relation to the type of work done, lack of transparency of salaries across the organization, perceived discrimination in relation to reward and effort, a complex salary grading structure, performance-related pay, and levels of salaries relative to those within the geographical area. Other examples of conflicting HRM policies include a lack of consistency in applying appraisal systems, performance assessment and discrimination between shop floor and staff on issues of sickness and leave of absence.

- *Financial policies* that encourage short-term decision-making and business results in order to maintain stock-market credibility and benefits to shareholders. These prevent managers from pursuing the longer-term objectives of TQM.
- *Maintenance policies* which, owing to a need to reduce costs, limit the amount of work carried out on planned maintenance. This in turn impacts on the performance of the machinery and its ability to produce conforming product.
- *Manufacturing policies* that focus on and encourage output rather than quality performance and customer satisfaction. This focus also has a detrimental effect on training which, as a consequence, may be perceived as unnecessary or time-wasting, and on the holding of improvement team meetings.

Below are examples of such policies identified at one of the packaging manufacturers.

Human resources

- The policy of part-time contracts. While management gave considerable emphasis to explaining the reasoning behind this policy, the communication needed to be reinforced and maintained.
- The operation of the staff appraisal system and, in particular, ensuring consistency between employees.

Production

- Maintaining production output and quality, in terms of conforming product. When under pressure to meet production targets there was a temptation to increase the machine running speed on the corrugator even though this was known to have a detrimental impact on board quality.
- The pressure to meet production targets was also having an adverse effect on the meetings of quality teams. While the company was prepared to pay people to meet in teams after their shift, the view expressed by employees was that they wished to hold their quality team meetings in company time. A comment which encapsulated this view was: 'If the company cannot make available the time for us to meet during normal working hours, why should we give up our time to the company?'
- The time which people have available. If a person was involved in a quality team there was a perception that they were short of work in their day-to-day job and consequently they would be given more work to do.

Maintenance

- There was a view that maintenance was not given the attention it deserved and since the machinery was a key determinant of quality, this conflicted with TQM.

Category 4 – Organization Structure

This category is concerned with the issues that arise from the way in which a business is structured and includes functions, roles, responsibilities, hierarchies, boundaries, flexibility and innovation. Structure has been defined by Wilson and Rosenfield (1990) as:

> the established pattern of relationships between the component parts of an organization, outlining both communication, control and authority patterns. Structure distinguishes the parts of an organization and delineates the relationship between them.

Positioning of the quality function

The size and role of the quality function within the organization, and its relation to other departments, influences the deployment of the quality policy and its integration with other aspects of the organization. The principles which underpin TQM (i.e. everyone taking personal responsibility for quality assurance, pursuing continuous improvement in their day-to-day work activities and being reorientated towards the customer; see chapter 1) pose a problem for the positioning of the quality function. The quality department can deflect people from practising these types of principles by retaining responsibility for quality improvement. On the other hand, it is often charged with implementing the quality policy, which involves managing the process of change, providing guidance to departmental heads and 'empowering' employees.

Typical questions include:

- What position does the quality manager/director have in the organization? Who reports to them and how do they relate to other functions, especially production?
- Has a supporting infrastructure been created?
- Is the quality function in a position to develop and influence business policy and changes in the business?
- Do you consider that the role and responsibilities of the quality department are understood?
- Can the quality manager/director help to influence a change in the business to make the environment more conducive to improvement?
- To what extent is the quality manager/director responsible for quality, or have they delegated this responsibility to line managers?
- How much do individuals take responsibility for their own quality assurance and quality improvement?

At the bearings manufacturer there were some different views about the degree to which people had accepted responsibility for ownership of quality assurance and quality improvement and had 'pride' in their job. A lot of discussion centred around production and inspection responsibilities. Overall, only in a minority of cases did people hold the view that final inspection would take the responsibility for product quality. It was also felt that the quality department should work more closely with the engineering and production departments to give advice and guidance on the more preventative aspects of quality management.

Departmental, functional and shift boundaries

The boundaries and barriers which are built up between departments, functions and shifts are obstacles to teamwork and cross-functional/interdepartmental working and co-operation. These barriers are often a legacy of the hierarchical structures and bureaucracies established under scientific management which promoted functional foremen and specialists. They typically lead to empire-building and a lack of understanding of other departments which hinder the sustaining of TQM.

Typical questions include:

- How much of a problem are departmental barriers and empire-building in the organization?
- Which department do you consider presents the most barriers?
- How do these barriers affect cross-functional co-operation and communication?
- What steps are being taken to break the barriers down?
- Are people sympathetic to what is involved in jobs undertaken by others?
- To what extent are there problems between shifts?
- To what extent are cross-functional teams in operation?

At the bearings manufacturer the departmental barriers issue was perceived as a major problem in both a physical and mental sense, described as 'hand grenades thrown over the wall'. There was also a lack of sympathy on the part of some people about what was involved in the jobs undertaken by people outside their immediate departmental function: 'I do a better job than you'; 'My skills are greater than yours'; 'I have pride in my work but it is just a job to them'; 'We're doing our job right, why is this not the case with you?' The view was expressed that the service departments were more inclined to help production when things were going smoothly and not when problems were being experienced. The fact that a number of the procedures in the service departments were set up when the company employed more people was given as a potential cause of a lack of responsiveness.

The main problems in relation to shift boundaries were the failure of one shift to accept the set-ups of another, and that any difficulties resulted from person-to-person conflict rather than shift-to-shift conflict.

Communication

The issue here is the way in which communication is practised, both up and down and across the organization. The methods by which achievements are recognized and communicated is also examined.

Typical questions include:

- What evidence is there of a communication policy (e.g. newsletters, team brief, quality noticeboards)?
- What is the predominant direction of transfer of information – up or down the organization?
- How effective is the flow of information in terms of two-way transfer?
- Are business objectives communicated so that the business plan is understood at all levels of the organizational hierarchy?
- Are individual and team objectives aligned to the business plan?
- What potential communication problems exist?
- What means are used to recognize and communicate the achievements of both individuals and teams?

In the German automotive component supplier the general view was that people were told rather than being given the reasons for a particular course of action and situation and that there was a lack of systematic information. A comment which typified this view was: 'Why did management do it that way, why did they take that course of action?' Senior management did not appear to communicate company objectives down through all levels of the organization by, for example, quarterly 'state-of-the-nation briefings' in order to fully explain to every employee the situation and the key decisions and through team briefings.

Job flexibility and cover

This serves to highlight the reliance of a business on key people in specialized functions. Both numerical and task flexibility are important if a business is to respond to changing demand and circumstances.

Typical questions include:

- Which areas and skills are particularly vulnerable to problems if key people are unavailable or leave the company?
- What steps have been taken to encourage job flexibility?
- Is there a policy of succession planning in place within the organization?
- What barriers are there to making the changes (e.g. trade union resistance, demarcation, working practices, protectionism)?

The small size of the Spanish component supplier made it particularly vulnerable to this issue. It had a succession planning process in place and this was of some help, as was training to increase flexibility.

Supervisory structure

This concerns the limitations of the traditional supervisory role, and the reorganization to a team leader-type structure, which is considered more suitable to improvement initiatives, in particular at the operating level of the business.

Typical questions include:

- What types and levels of supervision exist?
- How do supervisors treat and deal with their staff on a day-to-day basis?
- What type of activities do supervisors undertake on a daily basis?
- To what extent do supervisors control or lead in order to gain employee commitment to continuous improvement?
- What features (e.g. setting direction, steering, aligning people in the common direction, motivating, communicating) of a team leader-type structure are in place?
- To what extent do supervisors, in the event of a crisis, revert back to the traditional supervisory role?

In the UK automotive component supplier the team leader structure was reasonably well developed, but the outcomes arising from the daily meetings held at the start of the shift between the team leaders and their teams and those between the team leaders and the production manager were not fed back to the respective teams. There is also little evidence of the team leaders attempting to align their people in an agreed common direction and motivating and inspiring their staff. In addition, the training given to team leaders and their teams was often not followed through and used.

Category 5 – Process of Change

The issues underpinning this category relate to the improvement process itself and/or are a direct result of some form of improvement activity and action. They refer to the training, coaching and development of employees (i.e. skills, attitudes and behaviours) as well as changes in organization structure and management style, and the adoption of new working practices which are required as part of the TQM initiative. Many of the issues in this category relate to the ability of management to implement change and integrate TQM into the working practices of the organization.

The process of change involved in integrating the philosophy of TQM into an organization is complex and wide-ranging. If the process is to be effective it requires the creation of an environment where employees are motivated to want to improve on a continuous basis. If the managers cannot create this environment then any systems, tools, techniques or training employed will be ineffective.

Improvement infrastructure

This considers the adequacy of the improvement infrastructure in terms of steering committee, co-ordinator and facilitators and assesses 'hype' versus real ownership.

Typical questions include:

- Is there a steering committee? Is its membership and role communicated across the company?
- Is there an improvement co-ordinator?
- What is his or her role?

- Are there designated improvement facilitators?
- If so, in which areas and functions?
- To what extent have the co-ordinator and facilitator got the right type of skills and knowledge to undertake these types of roles?

In one of the packaging manufacturers the full-time facilitator was seen as the key link in the improvement chain, and his promotion was perceived to have weakened the improvement infrastructure and left a void, with a consequential loss of focus. There was a lack of knowledge about the TQM steering committee, its membership and role. While the role of the part-time facilitator was recognized there were not enough people taking on this role. It was found that the team leaders were not forceful: they needed to feel they had the total backing of top management behind them and to exercise this support.

Education and training

This considers the appropriateness of the training programme in relation to the needs of the individual and the organization. It includes the design, delivery and evaluation of the programme.
Typical questions include:

- What type of training – job, management, TQM – have you had?
- Are you satisfied with the level of education and training opportunities which exist within the company?
- To what extent have you put the skills and knowledge acquired to use?
- Are the trainers effective?
- What coaching and counselling have you had from your immediate managers and functional staff to assist in putting skills and knowledge acquired through training into practice?

The standard training programme which was in place at the UK component supplier was recognized to be excellent. However, the mixing together on training courses of people from all levels of the organizational hierarchy was not effective, and some scaling down of the range of levels attending a particular training course was needed. It was evident that refresher training was required from time to time. Attention to individuals' training needs was also required, and a systematic method needed to be put into place to identify these needs.

Teams and teamwork

This considers the health of teams and teamwork within the organization and the mechanisms in place to support and encourage teams.
Typical questions include:

- What types of improvement teams are in operation?
- How effective are these types of teams?
- What are the major reasons for the lack of success of teams?

- To what extent is teamwork practised as part of normal business activities?
- To what extent do you think teamwork is beneficial for you and the organization?
- What are your major frustrations about teams both in general and, in particular, ones you have been involved with?
- To what extent is there a conflict between teams, e.g. competing for rewards and putting forward ideas and suggestions for improvement?
- Do improvement teams prevent individuals from pursuing personal improvement initiatives?

In one of the packaging manufacturers there had been a number of projects completed successfully through improvement team activity and there was good support for the teamwork ethic. The value of the projects completed was recognized, along with their value in increasing quality awareness. However, there had been cases in which teams had been less successful. The main reasons included: project findings accepted but not implemented, project terminated due to a lack of investment, the team stopping meeting due to increased production pressure, and a lack of back-up and support. There were currently no teams in operation. They had fizzled out when the improvement facilitator took up another post and production volumes increased.

Procedures

This considers the procedures, or lack of them, which are in place to counteract problems and abnormalities. The ability of people to understand and follow procedures and the willingness of management to respond effectively to ideas and suggestions for improvement are also factors considered.

Typical questions include:

- To what extent do problems recur? If so, why?
- What sort of problems recur?
- How do you report any potential concerns which you have?
- How are these concerns responded to?
- Is there any evidence of ideas and concerns being reported but nothing being done to correct and prevent them from recurring (i.e. the 'sponge' syndrome)?
- What type of corrective and preventative mechanisms are in operation?

At the bearings manufacturer problems tended to recur, particularly at the operating level of the business. This tended to be brought about by people not being prepared to go to the trouble of requesting changes to be made, the ineffectiveness of the short-term corrective actions taken, and the failure to standardize the changes.

Quality management system

This considers the effectiveness of the quality management system and the need to ensure that quality manual and procedure owners seek continuous improvements to the system. It also investigates the degree to which the system has been developed using a process management approach.

Typical questions include:

- Is the quality management system reactive or proactive?
- Are the procedures underpinning the system followed in everyday work activities?
- To what extent are the systems and procedures presented as processes?
- Are the processes independent of the organization?
- Are process owners identified?
- How can the quality management system be strengthened?

The quality management system of one of the packaging manufacturers tended to be reactive and the procedures cumbersome. For example, it was claimed that, when an audit was undertaken, 'People dust down the procedures, follow what is in the manual and then revert to their normal way of doing things.'

Quality management tools and techniques

This issue considers the need for a planned approach to identify and apply quality management tools and techniques, and to integrate their use into the day-to-day operations of the business.
Typical questions include:

- What type of quality management tools and techniques do you use in your everyday work routines? And in improvement teams?
- How do you decide which tools and techniques to apply?
- Why are tools and techniques used in your department?
- Which tools and techniques have the greatest impact?
- To what extent is there resistance to the introduction and use of tools and techniques?

The overwhelming view at the German component supplier was that tools and techniques were not used in any systematic way, and a number of the ones in use tended to be used in static mode and were not well understood. There was also a failure by managers to use the tools and techniques in their day-to-day decision-making.

Confidence in management

This considers the extent of confidence in senior management by both managers and workers. Lack of confidence can be brought about by, amongst other things: the lack of success of previous TQM initiatives; the inability to see projects through to a conclusion; actions not mirroring promises; changes in management; and conflicting priorities that suggest that TQM is not as important as previously thought.
This factor also considers the negative effects on sustaining TQM of those managers who are resistant to change and tend to suppress continuous improvement activities. Typical questions include:

- How confident are you that management are serious about TQM?
- Is there stability at the top of the organization?
- Describe examples of areas where you have a lack of confidence: are these in play within the organization?
- Is confidence in management growing or decreasing?
- How effective are management in prioritizing the various ongoing improvement initiatives within the organization?
- Do management underestimate the time needed for improvement results to become visible?
- Do people in the organization block improvement initiatives?
- Are you confident that management will reverse the attitudes and behaviour of the people who are resistant to improvement?

The considerable number of changes in senior management at the bearings manufacturer had led to a lack of confidence, attenuated by the style of some previous managers, and the inability to see projects and initiatives through to a satisfactory conclusion. This had led to a tendency to blame any problems on management and a certain degree of apathy. The current management team were suffering from the attitudes created by their predecessors. To build up confidence it was said that 'Management must be seen to be straight-talking and their actions must always mirror their words.'

Summary

Total quality management is a long-term process which requires considerable dedication and hard work to achieve the vision; along the journey there are many pitfalls to avoid and barriers to surmount. The typical pitfalls have been explored in this chapter and include: inadequate leadership, fear and resistance to change, lack of problem-solving skills, failure to complete projects, break-up of improvement teams, lack of resources devoted to continuous improvement, inadequate information and its analysis, poor communication, and underestimating the time before results become visible. These pitfalls impact negatively on the sustaining of TQM and they have been grouped into the five categories of internal/external environment, management style, policies, organization structure, and the process of change, and developed in the form of a TQM sustaining audit tool. These categories have been described along with their underlying issues.

Using the methodology outlined in the chapter, TQMSAT has been piloted at seven manufacturing sites. In each case it succeeded in identifying a range of issues which had the potential to have a negative impact on sustaining TQM, and helped management to identify fundamental causes rather than just see symptoms. The trailing of the tool indicates that its relevance and value depends on the status of TQM in the company at the time of its application.

References

Boyett, J., Kearney, A. T. and Conn, H. (1991), What's wrong with total quality management? Tapping the network quality. *Quality* 3(1), 10–14.

Burrell, G. and Morgan, G. (1979), *Sociological Paradigms and Organisational Analysis.* London: Heinemann Educational.

Conti, T. (1997), *Organisational Self-Assessment.* London: Chapman & Hall.

Dale, B. G. and Boaden, R. J. (1991), *Total Quality Management: Integration and Development.* Swindon: Engineering and Physical Sciences Research Council, GR/H.21449.

Dale, B. G., Boaden, R. J., Wilcox, M. and McQuater, R. E. (1997), Total quality management sustaining audit tool: description and use. *Total Quality Management,* 8(6), 395–408.

Develin and Partners (1989), *The Effectiveness of Quality Improvement Programmes in British Industry.* London: Develin and Partners.

Economist Intelligence Unit (1992), *Making Quality Work: Lessons for Europe's Leading Companies.* London: Economist Intelligence Unit.

Fox, A. (1974), *Beyond Contract: Work, Trust and Power Relations.* London: Faber & Faber.

Harari, O. (1997), Ten reasons TQM doesn't work. *American Management Association – Management Review,* January, 38–44.

Kearney, A. T. and the TQM Magazine (1992), *Total Quality: Time to Take off the Rose-Tinted Spectacles.* Bedfordshire: A. T. Kearney/TQM Magazine.

Kemp, A., Pryor, S. and Dale, B. G. (1997), Sustaining TQM: a case study at Aeroquip Iberica. *The TQM Magazine,* 9(1), 21–8.

Lascelles, D. M. and Peacock, R. (1996), *Self-Assessment for Business Excellence.* Berkshire: McGraw Hill.

Marchington, M. C. and Parker, P. (1990), *Changing Patterns of Employee Relations.* London: Harvester Wheatsheaf.

Miller, C. (1992), TQM's value criticized in new report. 9 November, American Marketing Association.

Morgan, G. (1986), *Images of Organisation.* London: Sage.

Naj, A. (1993), Some manufacturers drop efforts to adopt Japanese manufacturing techniques. *Wall Street Journal,* A1.

Redman, T. and Grieves, J., 1999, Managing strategic change through TQM: learning from failure. *New Technology, Work and Employment,* 14(1), 45–61.

Taylor, F. W. (1964), *The Principles of Scientific Management.* New York: Harper & Row.

Tice, L. (1994), Report card on TQM. *Management Review,* January, 22–5.

Wheelan, G. and Hunger, H. (1988), *Strategic Management and Business Policy,* 3rd edn. California: Addison Wesley.

Wilson, D. C. and Rosenfeld, R. H. (1990), *Managing Organisation.* London: McGraw Hill.

part two

The Business Context of TQM

The purpose of part 2 of the book is to introduce the reader to some activities which have an influence on TQM in a business context. It contains six chapters:

Chapter 8 – Policy Deployment
Chapter 9 – Quality Costing
Chapter 10 – Managing Human Resources for Quality Management
Chapter 11 – Managing Service Quality
Chapter 12 – Supplier Development
Chapter 13 – Business to Business, Old-Economy Businesses and the Quality Function

Policy deployment is the Western translation of 'hoshin kanri', the Japanese strategic planning and management process involving setting direction and deploying the means of achieving that direction, with appropriate involvement at all levels of the organizational hierarchy. Chapter 8 reviews the history and concept of policy deployment and proposes a policy deployment model. It is argued that this model will enable an organization to deploy, in an effective manner, its vision, mission, goals, objectives, targets and means.

Quality-related costs commonly range from 5 to 25 per cent of an organization's annual sales turnover, depending on the 'industry' and the way in which it manages quality. The reduction of costs is an important part of any business plan. Chapter 9 explains why quality costs are important to management, defines quality costs and outlines how to identify, collect, analyse, report and use them to best advantage. The typical pitfalls in quality cost collection are also aired.

Chapter 10 argues that a number of organizations have not achieved the success they expected with TQM because they failed to give sufficient attention to its so-called 'soft' aspects. It is also pointed out that HR considerations are dealt with in a limited way by the TQM literature. The chapter goes on to review the need to consider these issues and, drawing on recent research, outlines the key role that the HR function can play in the development and success of TQM.

Chapter 11 examines the implications for service quality in a changing business environment. It explores definitions and characteristics of services, the service quality GAP model, dimensions and determinants of service quality, measurement of service quality, customer service and service encounters and service delivery processes and the role of personnel.

Organizations cannot consider TQM in isolation; they need to involve their customers and suppliers in the improvement process. Chapter 12 outlines the importance and role of supplier development in TQM and the need to develop long-term collaborative business partnerships between customer and supplier. It identifies the typical barriers in supplier development and draws on best practice to outline how organizations should start and advance the partnership concept.

Chapter 13 explores the major ways in which old economy companies are attempting to integrate the new economy as extensions of their current businesses. It also examines the possible implications of the changes for the quality function and how quality management expertise can help companies adapt and thrive in the dot.com revolution.

chapter eight

Policy Deployment

R. G. Lee and B. G. Dale

Introduction

An increasing number of organizations, as part of a strategic planning approach to continuous improvement, are starting to use policy deployment. It has been found that this concept is an excellent means of engaging all employees in the business planning process, obtaining harmony across functions, focusing an organization on the vital few objectives (VFO) to achieve business results, and turning strategic intent into an annual operating plan. The methodology is aimed at being consistent in target-setting and achievement, not just in magnitude but in overall organizational effectiveness. Figure 8.1 is an illustration of the policy deployment system from a manufacturer of ceramic products. According to Newcombe (1989), policy deployment 'helps create cohesiveness within a business that is understood throughout the company; it provides a structure with which to identify clear organizational goals'.

In the late 1980s the concept of policy deployment was little known outside Japan. Dale (1990) recalls leading study missions of European executives and management consultants to leading exponents of TQM in Japanese manufacturing industry in 1988 and 1989, and it was clear that, when the concept of policy deployment was introduced by the Japanese host organization, this was something new to the study mission participants. This prompted Dale to write an introductory piece on the concept.

Policy deployment is the Western translation of 'hoshin kanri', the Japanese strategic planning and management process involving setting direction and deploying the means of achieving that direction; the PDCA cycle is used extensively in the process. The concept was developed in Japan in the early 1960s to communicate a company's policy, goals and objectives throughout its hierarchy. It was the Bridgestone Tire Company in 1962 which conceived the concept (see Akao 1991; Kondo 1997). The company visited a number of the Deming Application Prize winners and, in 1965, published a report which described best practices and put forward ideas to resolve the perceived problems by the use of policy deployment. By 1975, hoshin kanri was widely accepted in Japan, proving to be effective in motivating employees

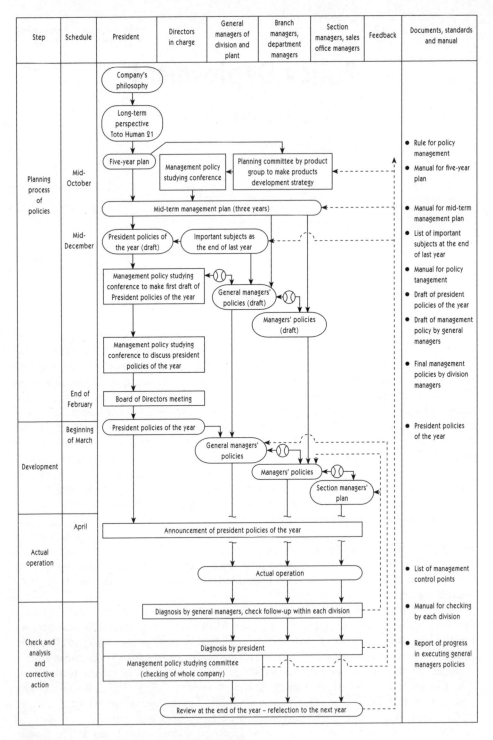

Figure 8.1   An example of the policy management system
Source: Toto Ltd., Chigasaki Works, Chigasaki City, Japan

and uniting them in their respective improvement processes as Japanese companies moved to increase 'their overall strength and character' (Kondo 1997).

By the early 1980s hoshin kanri had begun its journey across the Pacific Ocean on a wave of Deming Application Prize-winning Japanese subsidiaries such as Hewlett-Packard's YHP Division and Fuji-Xerox. MBNQA- and EQA-winning companies started to use policy deployment successfully in the early and mid-1990s respectively in order to link medium- to long-term policy to annual plans to achieve significant improvements in business results. Woll (1996) outlines the benefits of the use of hoshin planning by three American organizations as:

> Analog devices, for example, identified new product sales as one of its hoshins three years ago and was able to go from shipping $125 million in new products in 1995 to shipping $300 million in 1996. One Hewlett-Packard product group realized $8.4 million in manufacturing cost reductions within one year. Teradyne reports that hoshin planning helped them to ensure that its more than 1,000 active quality improvement teams work on meaningful activities that are aligned with its business goals.

There is little academic literature on policy deployment which is based on empirical research, despite its popularity in large multinationals with Japanese subsidiaries (see Lee and Dale 1998). Van der Wiele et al. (1996a) say 'In recent times policy deployment has been a topic in which organizations have shown an increasing interest', but 'it is still not a well known technique in many companies', which is 'typical of those organizations who are not very well advanced in their quality management activities'. However, having made this point, it should be said that it features as a topic in texts such as Imai (1986) and Juran (1964): the latter was probably one of the first contributors to the development of the policy deployment concept.

This chapter reviews the definition, concept, and characteristics of policy deployment and proposes a policy deployment model based on the catch-reflect-improve-pass process (Mulligan et al. 1996). The model, based on research described in Lee and Dale (1999), demonstrates how policy deployment, business results and self-assessment are inextricably linked into the PDCA cycle of business operations, and it is argued that this will enable an organization to deploy its vision, mission, goals, objectives, targets and means more effectively.

Definitions: Policy Deployment

Hoshin kanri was developed in Japan to communicate a company's policy, goals and objectives throughout its hierarchy; its main benefit is to focus attention on key activities for success. Kano (1995) provides some background on the difficulties in the English translation of the term, making the point that 'a considerable semantic gap exists between the English policy and the Japanese word hoshin'. A literal translation of hoshin kanri provides an insight into its concept (Total Quality Engineering 1997):

> Hoshin   = a compass, a course, a policy, a plan, an aim;
> Kanri   = management control, care for;
> Together = 'management control of the company's focus'.

The popular term 'policy deployment' is often used interchangeably with hoshin kanri. While the translation is useful as an insight, and in particular attention should be drawn to the 'management', 'control' and 'focus' as elements, there are a number of widely varying definitions of hoshin, hoshin kanri, management by policy and policy deployment which expand the concept. Watson (1991) simply states that 'Perhaps the most accurate term for hoshin kanri would be target-means deployment.' Total Quality Engineering (1997) say hoshin kanri is:

> A system of forms and rules that encourage employees to analyse situations, create plans for improvement, conduct performance checks, and take appropriate action.

Integrated Quality Dynamics (1997) define hoshin as:

> A one-year plan for achieving objectives developed in conjunction with management's choice of specific targets and means in quality, cost, delivery, and morale.

or, in 'catch-phrase' form,

Hoshin = Target + Means

While these definitions offer variations on the themes of plans, targets and means, the most comprehensive and 'encompassing' definition, and one that emphasizes the importance of the PDCA cycle and feedback, is that of Mizunode quoted in Eureka and Ryan (1990):

> Deploy and share the direction, goals, and approaches of corporate management from top management to employees, and for each unit of the organization to conduct work according to the plan. Then, evaluate, investigate and feed back the results, or go through the cycle of PDCA continuously and attempt to continuously improve the performance of the organization.

The following are the main characteristics which emerge from this discussion of policy deployment definitions:

- Clear organizational goals understood by employees from each level of the organization.
- Involvement of employees in the development of action plans.
- All employees and functions are working in the same direction to achieve the organization's objectives.
- Regular review mechanism using the PDCA cycle thereby promoting an environment of continuous improvement.
- Visible display of information.

Another significant point to draw from the preceding definitions is that they 'interpret' hoshin kanri and often fail to mention feedback. Interpretation of hoshin kanri as policy deployment by Western writers often leads to a watering down of the concept, and although 'catch-phrase' versions may make Western managers' jobs easier, it can lead to inadequate application of the method and unsatisfactory results.

What is Policy Deployment?

Kendrick (1988) provides one of the earliest Western articles on policy deployment, discussing how it was used by the Florida Power and Light Company to reshape the corporate objective-setting process to conform to customers' needs. However, one of the first articles by a Western author to thoroughly summarize the Japanese approach to policy deployment was produced by Dale (1990): 'Policy Deployment within a process of long-term planning is one of the features of "the approach" to Total Quality Control (TQC) by Japanese companies.' He described the deployment of the president's annual management policy plan through the levels of the organizational hierarchy. The process involves developing plans, targets, controls and areas for improvement based on the previous level's policy and an assessment of the previous year's performance. The plans and targets are discussed and debated at each level until a consensus on plans and targets is reached, along with the methods for meeting the goal – Dale called this 'play catch', but it is now more commonly known as 'catchball'. Once agreement has been reached at all levels, in a strictly controlled six- to eight-week policy deployment period, individual, plans, targets, control points, improvement areas and corrective actions are recorded and, perhaps more importantly, prominently displayed around the workplace as part of the visible management system. Control of the deployment process and subsequent implementation of the policies is conducted through quarterly, monthly, weekly and daily reviews depending on the level of the individual involved. Dale (1990) says the PDCA cycle 'is extensively used in these diagnoses' and that 'the discipline of policy deployment and agreement at each level' ensures everyone is working in the same direction.

The concept of policy deployment as providing a bridge between the corporate 'plan' and the 'do' steps in continuous improvement is re-emphasized by Robinson (1994), who says that at Harris Semiconductor (USA), the process:

> Embraces the concept of empowerment as a balance between alignment of activities to the goals and the freedom people have to take action. The ultimate purpose of this process is to empower people to make meaningful improvements.

More recently, Kondo (1997) described hoshin kanri as 'a system of management in which the annual policy set by a company is passed down through the organization and implemented across all departments and functions'. There are a number of elements in Kondo's article which are key to the Japanese approach, support the foregoing summary of Dale's (1990) description of the process, and which are often overlooked or underplayed by those describing Western systems of policy deployment. The key points made by Kondo (1997) are:

- Policy deployment is effective in motivating employees.
- The aim of the process is 'give and take'.
- For a top-down approach to work senior managers have to be highly respected.
- Results are checked by means of individual managers' control items.
- The process is an important strategy for allowing top managers to exercise leadership.
- Policy is not determined only by short-term considerations.
- Top management must 'lead the way in whipping up everyone's energy and enthusiasm'.

- The purpose of the top management audit is to find and solve problems, discover and build on strengths, and standardize and institutionalize improvements.
- If management audits are carried out in the wrong way, there is a danger they will become superficial and ritualistic.
- It is important for top managers to talk directly to ordinary workers.

Thiagarajan and Zairi (1997) concluded that:

> Management of the best organizations are using the process of policy development and deployment to make sure that employees understand the objectives of the company, and how they will contribute to meeting the objectives.

Kondo (1998) notes that 'Hoshin Kanri proved extremely effective in furthering company wide improvement plans by uniting the efforts of all employees.'

The most important policy deployment concepts to be drawn from the writings of Dale (1990) and Kondo (1997) are:

- Leadership
- Communication
- Control
- Review

And that there are four stages:

- Policy-setting
- Policy deployment
- Policy implementation
- Evaluation and feedback

However, despite the defined process and benefits to be gained from effective policy deployment, even in Japanese companies there are some fundamental problems with its application. Kogure (1995) defines them as:

1 Ambiguity of relations between goal and policy.
2 Unfitness of content of management policy between superiors and subordinates in terms of a policy's abstractness and concreteness.

Kogure (1995) describes the first problem as one of distinguishing between policies and goals, the order in which they are issued and how they relate to each other. With respect to the second problem, Kogure (1995) discusses how there is an imbalance between content of policy and level of issuer – the higher the policy-issuer the more abstract the policy should be; it is the role of the subordinate to develop plans and not policy. He describes the following four patterns where:

1 Management policies of superiors and subordinates are both quite abstract and deployment of policy is carried out only perfunctorily.
2 Content of superior manager's policy is too concrete.

3 A gap between the superior manager's policy and the subordinate manager's policy is quite conspicuous because the former is too abstract and the latter is too concrete.

4 The matching of the subordinate manager's policy to the superior manager's policy is very appropriate and policies are deployed properly from top to bottom.

Pattern 4 is where true policy deployment occurs. However, as Kogure (1995) states, patterns 1, 2, and 3, and especially pattern 1,

> Frequently appear at the stage of introducing TQC; however, sometimes these patterns still remain even in companies advanced in applying TQC, because employees in these companies have no full knowledge of how to balance abstractness and concreteness when deploying policy.

What Policy Deployment is Not

At first glance, policy deployment looks very similar to management by objectives (MBO); and, as Akao (1991) and Fortuna and Vaziri (1992) highlight, hoshin kanri was initiated by the emergence of MBO in Japan. However, although there are some similarities, there are more significant differences, Eureka and Ryan (1990) refer to hoshin kanri as MBO done right. From the work of Akao (1991) and Fortuna and Vaziri (1992) a number of similarities and differences between policy deployment and MBO are revealed: these are outlined in table 8.1.

Policy deployment is not a solution to all planning problems but a process which enables managers to plan effectively and translate those plans into actions. Furthermore, although Integrated Quality Dynamics (1997) consider the description of hoshin kanri as policy deployment as 'not the best translation' (they describe hoshin as a one-year plan with targets and means and state that hoshin management is not only 'deployment'), their 'myths' are worth repeating:

Hoshin myths
- Hoshin is part of QFD.
- Hoshin is only for the top management of an organization.
- Hoshin is the corporate policy.
- Hoshin is following the direction of the shining needle.

Hoshin management myths
- Hoshin management is part of QFD.
- Hoshin management works successfully only in Japanese organizations.
- Hoshin management is strategic planning.
- Hoshin management can be implemented without any other TQM methods and systems.
- The key to successful hoshin management is deployment of targets.
- When implementing hoshin management the starting point is to determine the corporate vision.

These 'myths', offered by Integrated Quality Dynamics, give valid insights into misconceptions perpetuated by some writers on the subject. Policy deployment is not just about corporate philosophy and management jargon, it provides a positive

Table 8.1 Main similarities and differences between policy deployment and MBO

Similarities	*Differences*
self-determination of goals	policy deployment focuses on a general improvement plan for the organization and not on an individuals's performance
attainment of goals	
setting continuously higher goals	policy deployment ensures an individual's goals are congruent with company objectives
improvement in performance	
self-evaluation of results	policy deployment encourages employee participation in objective-setting rather than acquiescence to a superior's bidding and direction
co-ordination, discussion, and exchange of ideas	
inducement of creativity and morale improvement	policy deployment focuses on timely and relevant feedback, not an annual or bi-annual review of progress
	policy deployment focuses on the process of getting there, how the objectives will be met and what actions an individual must take
	policy deployment emphasizes process and quality tools and techniques to solve problems
	policy deployment encourages the formulation of management teams
	policy deployment encourages the establishment and implementation of TQM
	policy deployment emphasizes customer focus and quality of products and services

process which engages all employees in the cycle of planning, implementing, and reviewing policy. In terms of this, the authors believe that policy deployment is not:

- An excuse to pay lip-service to employee feedback during the catchball process.
- An opportunity for 'empowered' employees to take decisions without adequate direction, support, checks and balances.
- A permit for managers to abdicate their responsibility for the plan and the results.

The Policy Deployment Process

Policy deployment works on two levels to manage continuous improvement and achieve business results: strategic objectives and daily control of the business. The key features of the process are now examined.

Five- to 10-year vision

A challenging, customer-focused vision, pertinent to people at all levels and appropriate for the next five to 10 years, is required. According to Goal/QPC Research

(1994) a draft of the vision should be given to the organization for a reality check and then communicated to everyone at all levels. Unfortunately, this is easier said than done, as visions are generally created at top management level and any reality check is likely to receive middle management filtering of employee comments to prevent unfavourable views reaching top management (i.e. the 'sponge' effect). The most effective way of overcoming this problem is to gather accurate information on the company, its customers, competitors and market, and then hold workshops between top management strategists and employees without middle management interference (i.e. play catchball without middle management). However, this method needs to be treated with caution because it is not usually a good approach to ignore middle managers.

Mid-term three- to five-year objectives

Translating the vision into mid-term objectives, together with the broad means to achieve them, is the next step. Wood and Munshi (1991) suggest that the objectives should be prioritized, and from this the critical ones are selected with a focus on a small number of breakthrough objectives (a maximum of three). Then, determine the means by which the objectives will be achieved and cascade the objective and means through a catchball discussion. The process of catchball provides the opportunity to ensure commitment to objectives at each hierarchical level and produces an organization which is focused and committed to the same goals. However, these medium-term goals, as extensions of past performances, are of little value without analysis of critical problems, current practices and changes inside and outside the company. Mulligan et al. (1996) say a holistic perspective is required, including:

- Business objectives
- Environmental conditions
- Resources constraints
- Definitions of core business processes

Annual plan and objectives

Annual, short-term objectives are determined from the mid-term goals and the annual plans should be actionable and specific. This one-year plan includes the targets, means and measures that each manager will work on during that year. The managers will develop their annual policies, improvement targets and plans for every section and department which are within their remit of responsibility. Goal/QPC Research (1996) say it is necessary to choose a small number of targets areas on which to focus (six to eight maximum) and half of these should be related to the manager's participation in the strategic plan and the other half to the critical process of the person's regular job. However, Mulligan et al. (1996) suggest that departments should have only three or four goals so line management can have the appropriate level of focus and resources assigned. Regardless of the number of objectives, all must be measurable, with monthly numerical targets, and the reasons for selection must be compelling and obvious (Watson 1991). Furthermore, they should be owned by the organization through the process of catchball, and the plan, objectives,

blackburn challenge 98

Our aim is to defy inflationary pressures in all areas of our business. Our measure of success will be – achieving profitability at an output level of 7000 housings a day.

NSK-RHP blackburn – Hoshin Kanri 1998

We will all take ownership for achieving Profitability Without Volume

blackburn mission

Our aim is to give unrivalled stakeholder satisfaction – by ensuring product conformance, on time delivery, minimal environmental impact and competitive costing. Always developing our people to their full potential and involving them to ensure their safety and well being.

	Objectives	Targets
Quality	Reduce Incident Of Audit None Compliance	–50%
	Reduce Customer Complaints	–50%
	Conformance To Specification	Fdry 97.6% M/c 99.2%
	Reduce Ferrybridge Returns	0.05%
Cost	Reduce Casting Cost	£2.07
	Reduce Expenditure Cost	–10%
	Reduce Labour Cost	–10%
Delivery	Improve Schedule Adherence	TBA
	Foundry & Machine Shop	TBA
People	Validation Of Skills Levels	40%
	Personal Development Reviews	1/year
Health & Safety	Achieve BS8800	Q4
	Reduce Lost Time Accidents	–50%
	Reduce Accident Incidents	–50%
	Introduce Smoking Policy	Q3
Environment	Reduce Waste	–10%
	Reduce Energy Usage	–10%
	Hold An 'E' Day	June 98

Danny McGuire
(Plant Manager)
Issue Level 1:1

Strategies

* Through the application of Teamworking, involving everyone in Kaizen and CANDO activities, we intend to develop Total Productive Maintenance (TPM) in all areas of the site.
* The achievement of Target 160 actions will ensure we achieve profitability in 1998.
* Through achievement and maintenance of standards – ISO9002, ISO14001, BS8800 & IIP we will ensure Customer/Neighbour/Employee satisfaction.

Enablers

* Improve our productivity performance through,
  - key machine productivity status displayed throughout the factory – on line OEE's
  - all key machines taken to TPM stage 3 by Q2 and to stage 5 by Q3
  - key machine breakdown history (6 months) input to MAINPAC by Q4
  - 80% of our people involved in TPM activities by Q4
* Improve our cost performance by,
  - breaking down the factory into natural work groups, identifying all cost elements and setting targets for reduction
  - displaying sample housing costs at each stage of the production process to increase the cost awareness of our people
  - involving the Kaizen TPM Teams in the implementaiton of all *Target 160* activities
* Improve our customer/neighbour/employee satisfaction by,
  - maintenance of ISO9002 and ISO14001 working to improve our audit compliance
  - promoting a positive effect on the environment both inside and outside of our business
  - improving our employee's health standard and well being through achievement of BS8800
  - raising the skills level of our people in line with the business needs through IIP and application of our training plans, working always towards accreditation of the training to NVQ standards

Figure 8.2 NSK-RHP top-level policy deployment annual plan
Source: NSK-RHP Blackburn foundry

and targets should not be constrained at management level, but cascaded down to each individual team or employee.

There is a set time-scale (usually six to eight weeks) for this policy management deployment activity to be cascaded down through all organizational levels. It is usual to commence the policy deployment process at a set time in the calendar year. The long negotiations which are involved in the deployment helps to ensure that there is consensus and a genuine commitment at all levels to meet the agreed targets.

The NSK-RHP Bearings, Blackburn Foundry's top-level policy deployment annual plan, is shown in figure 8.2. This has been developed from the RHP Bearings European Division policy deployment plan. An example of a breakdown of this into an environmental policy is shown in figure 8.3.

Deployment/roll down to departments

Clear, disciplined action plans with direction for improvement, what is to be measured, and the processes to be improved are generated through a continuous catchball between all organizational levels and around chosen targets. Corporate and division/department planning cycles should be synchronized and annual plans should present a prioritized set of actionable tasks, designed to achieve breakthrough in critical areas (Wood and Munshi 1991). A significant aspect of policy deployment is the extent to which the targets and means initiated at the top level are extensively modified through negotiation by the creativity of the lower levels of employees through bottom-up feedback. This involvement of everyone results in full ownership and understanding of the plan at all levels of the organization. The goal of catchball is to prevent sub-optimization, and local optimization may have to be forsaken in the interests of the company as a whole, even if this appears to rebuff the concept of 'empowerment' which pervades modern companies. Ideally, policy deployment should be a shop-floor process, with no off-site management retreats and/or staff-level planning. Once the goals, objectives and plans have been agreed, along with the methods and means to reach the goal, they should be openly displayed in the work area adjacent to the progress charts that are tracking achievement and targets.

Execution

The actionable tasks, following the deployment phase, should be taken up by teams and individuals, departmentally and cross-functionally, depending on the task. When using the cross-functional approach it is essential to determine the lead department to determine responsibility for and supervision of the task. The team/individual should have a clear statement of target and means and follow a PDCA cycle, with periodic checks from senior management (Wood and Munshi 1991). It is usual for a department to keep a register of the improvement action agreed with staff.

In this way the improvement activities of an organization are focused on carrying out projects to meet these policies. This ensures integration and the internalization of objectives. Every employee understands their manager's policy and therefore knows what to do and that everyone is working in a common and unified direction to achieve the goals of the business. In addition, employees understand the issues which are important to the company, helping to facilitate relations between the different sections of the business.

NSK–RHP *blackburn* Environmental Policy 1998

'Breaking the Mould' to ensure our ENVIRONMENTAL future.

Strategies

➤ Through the Continuous improvement cycle, we will develop strategies to reduce our energy usage.

➤ Through our philosophy of **'Cost Down'** we will identify all waste and set out a programme to eliminate, minimise, recycle or make good use of all waste within the site.

➤ Through improved communications, we will involve our people, customers, suppliers, neighbours, regulatory bodies and other interested parties in minimising our impact on the environment.

Enablers

➤ Establish Programmes and systems for pollution prevention – specifically carry out trials to establish viable alternative products for solvent based paints and rust preventatives.

➤ Ensure compliance with all relevant environmental laws and legislation to which our organisation subscribes.

➤ Work with our local authority to ensure compliance with the Environmental Protection Act.

➤ Use the TMC process for setting and reviewing environmental targets and objectives.

➤ Inform, instruct and train our people in environmental issues, thereby ensuring continuous environmental awareness with the use of competency based training plans.

➤ Build on our 'best practice' recognition for incorporating environmental issues into existing management systems.

➤ Through communications and teamwork, involve our people to minimise our impact on both local and global environment.

➤ Contribute to the reduction of global warming through the reduction of, reuse of or recycling of all waste.

Objectives

Quality	Set up review meetings with local Environmental Officer to agree compliance with all legislative regulations, e.g. EPA.
Cost	Install bulk storage of paint, amine and resins by Q4 98 Target 10% energy & waste disposal reduction CAPEX proposal for site sub-metering Q4 98
Delivery	Audit waste disposal suppliers annually Deploy environmental TMC to work groups
People	Introduce formal start-up and shutdown procedures across site, complete Q2 98 Specific environmental issues to be posted on notice boards and briefed as necessary. Site to have an Environmental open day for employee's children during 1998.
Safety	Test and refine all Emergency Procedures. Complete ALL environmental aspects assessments Q1 98 Reduce Pollard noise levels to below 85 dec.
Environment	Investigate re-use of waste coolant, proposal by Q3 98. Carry out trials on alternative Rust Inhibitors, proposal by Q2 98 Install abatement equipment – amine

Danny McGuire
(Plant Manager)
Issue Level 1:1

Figure 8.3 NSK–RHP environmental policy
Source: NSK–RHP Blackburn foundry

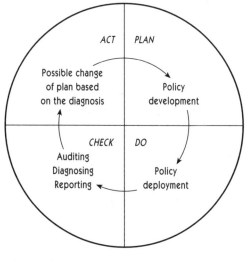

Figure 8.4 The plan-do-check-act cycle
Source: Dale and Cooper (1992)

Progress review (monthly and quarterly)

The control and review of policies are necessary to compare actual to planned performance of each activity that is supporting the organization's goals and objectives; identify gaps, problems and root causes; determine counter-measures; and recognize and reward achievement. The regular reviews are generally made through:

- Senior management diagnosis.
- Plant manager and section manager diagnosis and monthly review of plant activities.
- Discussion of achievements and improvements at plant conferences on quality, cost, and delivery (QCD).
- Each section's daily management and records in terms of clarity of the section's function in the organization and the role of each person, clear points of control, activities for improvement, standardization and taking corrective action.

The progress reviews stress the importance of self-diagnosis of targets and process to ensure that there is an alignment of activities in the cascading of organizational objectives and operating methods. Problems should be identified and corrective action implemented. PDCA is built into the policy deployment process and regular checking will assure continuous improvement and reduce costs (see figure 8.4). The results of these activities are reflected in the following year's policy and assist in improving the process of deployment. In some organizations, the process of policy deployment is also subject to diagnosis by outside experts.

Annual review

Wood and Munshi (1991) suggest the review process should focus upon the following:

- Achievements of the past year
- Lessons learned in the past year
- The gap between goals and achievements in the past year
- Root cause analysis of the problems
- Environmental factors
- Future plans for the organization

This forms the basis of policy deployment for the succeeding year, the check being undertaken at the start of the cycle. However, one important review should not be forgotten, the review of the policy deployment process itself, to learn from mistakes made and improve it for the following year; the process can also constitute a useful theme for a benchmarking project.

Mulligan et al. (1996) say that the most tangible aspect of policy deployment is the four sets of reports that support the organization's planning process:

Hoshin plan summary
- Articulated objectives
- Objective owners
- Long- and short-term goals
- Implementation strategy
- Specific improvement focus

Hoshin action plan
- Detailed links between core objectives and implementation initiatives

Hoshin implementation plan
- Records progress as the plan is implemented
- One plan for each objective
- Incorporates: task ownership; milestones and due dates

Hoshin implementation review
- Charts post-implementation results relative to company goals
- Competitive benchmarks
- Accepted world-class benchmarks

Visible display

It is good practice for a department or section to have a visible display of the outcomes from the policy deployment process, as part of their visible management system; figure 8.5 illustrates the key points of the typical format of such a display.

The left-hand side of the chart shows the tree of policy deployment from the plant manager down to the level of each section. The overall rate of imperfection for each section is related to the different processes, with information being provided on individual problems. A proportion defective (p) control chart is used to monitor the rate of imperfection against the set target. The right-hand side of the chart indicates the annual improvement targets for quality, cost, delivery, safety and morale. A slogan relating to the improvement is displayed at the head of the problem to be solved. The names of the workers who are responsible for the various activities

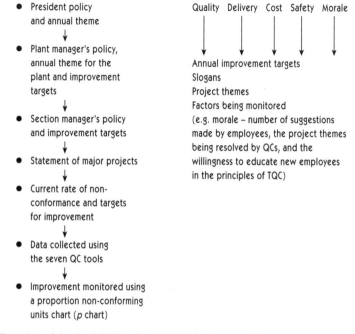

- President policy
  and annual theme
  ↓
- Plant manager's policy,
  annual theme for the
  plant and improvement
  targets
  ↓
- Section manager's policy
  and improvement targets
  ↓
- Statement of major projects
  ↓
- Current rate of non-
  conformance and targets
  for improvement
  ↓
- Data collected using
  the seven QC tools
  ↓
- Improvement monitored using
  a proportion non-conforming
  units chart (*p* chart)

Quality Delivery Cost Safety Morale

Annual improvement targets
Slogans
Project themes
Factors being monitored
(e.g. morale – number of suggestions
made by employees, the project themes
being resolved by QCs, and the
willingness to educate new employees
in the principles of TQC)

Figure 8.5 Key points of the visual display of policy deployment for a section
Source: Dale and Cooper (1992)

relating to the policy deployment are also displayed. It is usual to position at right angles to the board and completing the policy deployment 'corner' examples and pictures of typical imperfections in the section together with an improvement book. This book logs each improvement which has been made helps to promote standard-ization; it also serves as a point of reference as to what type of improvements have been made in the past. Some organizations keep the specific details of the deployment within the relevant offices, posting only the specific key actions, responsibilities and measures on the shop-floor policy deployment display. It is argued that in this way employees' attention is focused on the specifics rather than elaborate details.

A Check-Reflect-Improve-Scrutinize-Pass (CRISP) Approach to Policy Deployment

From an analysis of the research carried out into the policy deployment process of a 'world class' organization and observations of the use of policy deployment by a variety of organizations, including Japanese manufacturing companies based in the UK, it is clear that the key to ensuring the effectiveness of the process is leadership and communication (see Lee and Dale 1999).

In the literature on policy deployment there is consistent reference to cascade and catchball as essential elements. However, based on research and practical experience, deployment is the area where management can have the most impact but often fail to deliver what is necessary. The cascade process often does not work because line

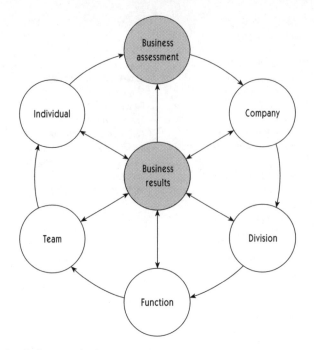

Figure 8.6   The policy deployment wheel

managers fail to communicate with their teams in an effective manner due to lack of time, skills or management style. Catchball fails to work because employees do not see the results of the process and it becomes over-reliant on individual management style. Policy deployment can be viewed in the form of a wheel (see figure 8.6), with business results at the hub, targets and means as the spokes, and catchball as the rim. What is required is an effective application of the PDCA cycle, as described by Akao (1991) and Kondo (1997), throughout this policy deployment wheel.

Mulligan et al. (1996) make a valid and astute observation: 'The image of catchball involves a group of children passing a ball (idea) amongst themselves while standing in a circle.' They go on to say that an alternative mnemonic – 'CRIP' – embodies the catchball concept more clearly. CRIP stands for catch, reflect, improve and then pass the idea. Preferably, no one should pass on the idea immediately on receipt without first improving it. In this way they believe a consensus is achieved with maximum participation and minimal conflict. However, more importantly, it prevents 'passing the buck' and, combined with PDCA, it can be used throughout the policy deployment process to monitor progress and the continued relevance of objectives. Indeed, this whole cycle can become CAPD, when policy deployment begins with annual self-assessment and the monitoring cycle begins with the 'check' step to ensure goals remain viable and appropriate (see Akao 1991).

One solution to the 'management' problem encountered with policy deployment is for organizations to adopt the CRISP approach. This is a development of the mnemonic CRIP, as briefly described by Mulligan et al. (1996) in relation to their discussion of hoshin kanri as a strategic planning method. CRISP stands for catch, reflect, improve, scrutinize and then pass. The addition of 'scrutinize' is an innovation which would solve the problems of unsatisfactory, incomplete policy deployment and lack of management commitment and attention to the process, which, from our research, are believed to be the main issues. Furthermore, as well as being a memorable mnemonic, the word CRISP has the added advantage of suggesting the brisk, decisive manner in which the process is conducted.

Essentially, CRISP entails each individual and team catching the policy, reflecting and improving upon it, but, before passing the policy up and down the hierarchical chain, having their work scrutinized by the previous level to ensure the reflection and improvement are in line with the original policy (see figure 8.7).

This is the all-important 'check' aspect in the PDCA cycle which often does not occur in an organization's deployment process. Although, at first sight, this approach may appear to add unnecessary bureaucracy to policy deployment and extend the process time-frame, the addition of scrutiny does not have to be a viewed as a burden, because the CRISP approach has the following advantages:

- Senior managers are required to demonstrate and use their leadership and communication skills.
- Senior managers can ensure that the right policy is being cascaded down the chain by checking their subordinates' planning activities.
- Senior managers can ensure that there is commonality of policy deployment throughout the organization, that policy deployment is pervasive and that the whole organization is pulling together as one team in the same direction.
- Cross-functionality of plans and purpose will be facilitated.
- Managers can 'check employees' understanding' of the policy through scrutiny of their planning output and terms of reference.
- Middle and first-line managers are required to perform catchball-cascade because their teams' plans and terms of reference will be checked by senior managers and middle managers respectively.
- Managers are required to communicate effectively in a team forum to ensure they meet senior management's scrutiny requirements.
- Managers would not be able to 'pass the policy deployment buck' without tailoring it, in conjunction with their team, because of senior management scrutiny.
- Managers would have an opportunity to demonstrate their leadership skills to senior managers throughout the process.
- Leadership and communication skill gaps can be identified and personal development programmes organized during the process.
- Teams and individuals will see the catchball process in action when they are involved in scrutiny of the next level's improvement of their objectives.
- Teams and individuals will 'buy in' to policy deployment when they see management using their feedback, become involved in its scrutiny, and have plans and objectives linked to company goals.
- It provides a 'closed loop' for policy deployment.

The CRISP approach does not necessarily elongate the policy deployment process if it is done efficiently. Much of the work should be done pre-policy deployment, with individuals and teams working cross-functionally to draft their VFO, plans and roles, responsibilities and objectives, after carrying out a self-assessment against a recognized excellence model, such as EFQM or MBNQA. In this manner the pre-policy deployment work will be the basis of the catchball feedback up the chain and form the framework for the final policy deployment activities. If CRISP is executed

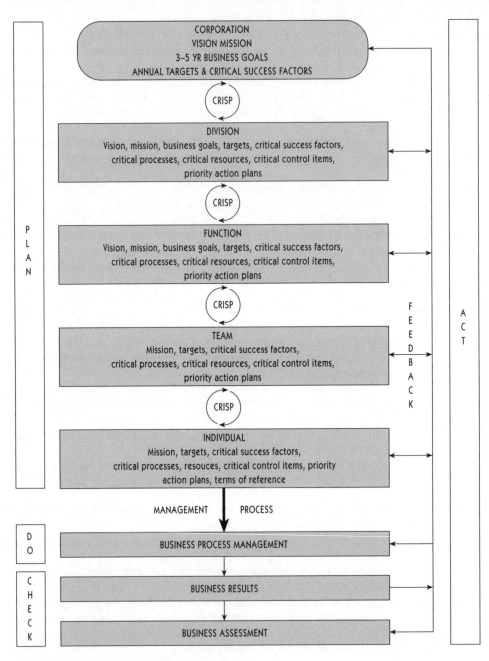

Figure 8.7 A CRISP approach to policy deployment

correctly, after undertaking a self-assessment, the workload during the policy deployment phase should be reduced. If the self-assessment and pre-policy deployment CRISP process has been successful there should be no surprises or major reworks following the actual policy deployment.

An example of the application of a CRISP approach to policy deployment in a typical business unit (BU) would follow the process outlined below:

1   Prior to receiving the policy from the corporate organization, following self-assessment, each team/individual in the BU would go through a cross-functional process of defining their prioritized VFO, drafting plans and their terms of reference (TOR) for the following year. This would be fed up the chain through the BU using CRISP. Each higher level would catch the input from the subordinate teams/individuals, reflect upon it, improve upon it by co-ordinating all cross-functional inputs, give the results of the improvement back to the originating teams/individuals for scrutiny to ensure that the original sense has not been subverted and then pass it on to the next level. Finally, the general manager (GM) of the BU would pass on the BU prioritized VFO to the corporate organization for incorporation into their planning process.

2   On 'catching' the corporate organization's VFO, the senior management team, led by the GM, would reflect upon it in relation to the BU VFO they had already determined, noting complementary and conflicting points. The senior management team would then improve the corporate organization's VFO using the previously determined BU VFO to produce the final version. The senior management team would pass their improved and BU-specific VFO back to the corporate organization for scrutiny to ensure that the original sense of the deployed policy had not been distorted. On confirmation from the corporate organization that the BU VFO are acceptable, the senior management team would pass on the BU prioritized, cross-functionally co-ordinated policy – via the appropriate communication channels – to subordinate teams.

3   At the next function level, the team of line managers, led by a senior manager, would 'catch' the BU policy. The function team would reflect upon this policy, led by a senior manager, who would show where their original input to the BU policy has been used to determine the BU VFO (highlighting catchball) and how the BU VFO are linked to the corporate organizations VFO. The team would then improve upon the BU VFO by linking their original and draft VFO to the BU VFO and determining a revised set of function-specific VFO. Again, before the line managers deployed this policy to their teams, the function-specific VFO would be passed back to the senior management team for scrutiny to ensure the interpretation and improvements were valid, there were no cross-functional conflicts and that the senior management's direction had been followed at the function level. As part of this scrutiny the senior management team would check function, vision, mission, goals, objectives, tar-gets, critical processes, resources, priority action plans, critical control items, and TORs. On passing scrutiny, the function line managers would communicate the deployed policy to their teams.

4   At team level, a similar process to that at the function level would occur and this would be finally deployed down to an individual level as necessary.

Following the successful use of the CRISP approach to policy deployment, each individual and team should see how their original input to the planning process, following self-assessment, has been used to generate the VFO and how their role is linked to the company policy. In this way, each employee will possess TORs that they have developed with their manager and are specifically tailored to support the

VFO. They will also have a vision, mission, goals, objectives, targets and means that they have contributed to and can understand in terms of their work and the company policy. Most of all they will have played their part in policy deployment, been involved in catchball and bought in to the process.

The CRISP approach is a generic management technique and can be applied to any organization involved in a communication and feedback process, a model which shows the CRISP approach applied specifically to policy deployment is provided at figure 8.7. The model highlights how the PDCA cycle overlays the business process; that using a CRISP approach policy is deployed throughout the company; and following the policy deployment process, how business process management results and self-assessment are linked to this cycle.

Summary

Policy deployment is a structured planning process that uses fact-based and participative methods to deliver achievement of objectives through continuous improvement. There are three common phases:

- Definition of the vision, mission, goals and objectives of the company.
- Deployment of the objectives throughout the organization.
- Management of the achievement of objectives.

The following are the key concepts which underpin policy deployment:

- Clear organizational goals understood by all employees.
- Involvement of employees in the development of action plans.
- All employees and functions are working in the same direction to achieve the organization's objectives.
- Regular review mechanism using the PDCA cycle, thereby promoting an environment of continuous improvement.
- Visible display of information to all concerned.

To ensure that the policy deployment process is effective everyone in an organization needs to have proactive involvement in the cascade and catchball process, and this should be led by the senior management team. BUs, departments and sections need to prioritize and co-ordinate their VFOs in an effective manner and then use these to identify and prioritize the processes which need to undergo improvements.

During the PDCA cycle of policy deployment, managers should focus on the 'check' rather than the 'act', which employees should be empowered to do. However, this check should not be used as an excuse for management to neglect their responsibility to inspect their subordinates' work. One method of ensuring that the cascade and catchball of policy deployment is effective and closed loop is to adopt the CRISP approach as described here and encourage managers to demonstrate effective leadership and communication.

Throughout the policy deployment literature (e.g. Dale 1990; Akao 1991; Hill 1994; Kondo 1997) there is a constant emphasis on the PDCA cycle in strategic planning and daily control. CRISP strengthens the catchball process which represents the PDCA cycle between organizational levels, and facilitates Kogure's (1995) 'pattern 4' of policy content and level of issuer, by forcing managers to conduct policy deployment and to have their activities scrutinized before passing the improved targets and means up or down the hierarchy. At each management level they are having their work checked by superiors and checking that of their subordinates (and vice versa) and, in this way, allowing everyone to exercise and demonstrate leadership and commitment.

Hoshin kanri, or policy deployment, is simply PDCA applied to the planning and execution of a few critical strategic organizational objectives. It is an essential element of TQM and is slowly being acknowledged by authors such as Lascelles and Peacock (1996) and van der Wiele et al. (1996a) as an essential link with self-assessment against an excellence model. Although policy deployment is best used by sophisticated organizations that are a long way down the TQM road, the authors believe that fundamental elements such as catchball can be used by less advanced companies to develop leadership and employee involvement and lay the foundation for future use of the full policy deployment approach.

References

Akao, Y. (1991), *Hoshin Kanri: Policy Deployment for Successful TQM*. Cambridge, Mass.: Productivity Press.

Dale, B. G. (1990), Policy deployment. *The TQM Magazine*, December, 321–4.

Dale, B. G. and Cooper, R. (1992), *Total Quality and Human Resources: An Executive Guide*. Oxford: BPI.

Eureka, W. E. and Ryan, N. E. (1990), *The Process-Driven Business: Managerial Perspectives on Policy Management*. Dearborn, USA: ASI Press.

Fortuna, P. M. and Vaziri, K. H. (1992), *Orchestrating Change. Policy Deployment, Total Quality: A Manager's Guide for the 1990s*. London: Ernst and Young Quality Improvement Consulting Company/Kogan Page.

Goal/QPC Research (1996), Hoshin planning. <http://www.goalqpc.com.80/RESEARCH/plan.htm/>.

Hill, D. (1994), Policy deployment (hoshin kanri) in Durham. In *Philips Quality Matters*, ISS56, 11–13. Eindhoven, The Netherlands: Philips Electronics.

Imai, M. (1986), *Kaizen: the Key to Japan's Competitive Success*. New York: Random House Business Division.

Integrated Quality Dynamics (1997), TQM: hoshin. <http://www.iqd.com:80/hoshin.htm>.

Juran, J. M. (1964), *Managerial Breakthrough*. New York: McGraw Hill.

Kano, N. (1995), A perspective on quality activities in American firms. In J. D. Hromi (ed.), *The Best on Quality: Targets, Improvements, Systems*, vol. 6, ch. 16. Milwaukee: ASQC Quality Press.

Kendrick, J. J. (1988), Managing quality: lighting up quality. *Quality*, 27(6), 16–20.

Kogure, M. (1995), Some fundamental problems on hoshin kanri in Japanese TQC. In J. D. Hromi (ed.), *The Best on Quality: Targets, Improvements, Systems*, vol. 6, ch. 23. Milwaukee: ASQC Quality Press.

Kondo, Y. (1997), The hoshin kanri: Japanese way of strategic quality management. *Proceedings of the 41st Congress of the European Organization for Quality*, June, vol. 1, 241–50. Trondheim, Norway.

Kondo, Y. (1998), Hoshin kanri: a participative way of quality management in Japan. *The TQM Magazine*, 10(6), 425–31.

Lascelles, D. and Peacock, R. (1996), *Self-Assessment for Business Excellence*. Maidenhead: McGraw Hill.

Lee, R. G. and Dale, B. G. (1998), Policy deployment: an examination of the theory. *International Journal of Quality and Reliability Management*, 15(5), 521–40.

Lee, R. G. and Dale, B. G. (1999), Policy deployment: modelling the process. *Production Planning and Control*, 10(5), 493–501.

Mulligan, P., Hatten, K. and Miller, J. (1996), From issue-based planning to hoshin: different styles for different situations. *Long-Range Planning*, 29(4), 473–84.

Newcombe, J. E. (1989), Management by policy deployment. *Quality*, 28(1), 29–30.

Robinson, R. (1994), Goal deployment: getting everyone aiming at the same target. *Tapping the Network Journal*, 5(3), 8–11.

Thiagarajan, T. and Zairi, M. (1997), A review of total quality management in practice: understanding the fundamentals through examples in best practice, part 1. *The TQM Magazine*, 9(4), 270–86.

Total Quality Engineering (1997), Hoshin planning. <http://www.tqe.com:80/tqehelp/hoshin.html>.

van der Wiele, A., Williams, A. R. T., Dale, B. G., Carter, G., Kolb, F., Luzon, D. M., Schmidt, A. and Wallace, M. (1996a), Self-assessment: a study of progress in Europe's leading organizations in quality management practices. *International Journal of Quality and Reliability Management*, 13(1), 84–104.

van der Wiele, A., Williams, A. R. T., Dale, B. G., Carter, G., Kolb, F., Luzon, D. M., Schmidt, A. and Wallace, M. (1996b), Quality management self-assessment: an examination in European business. *Journal of General Management*, 22(1), 48–67.

Watson, G. (1991), Understanding hoshin kanri. In Y. Akao (ed.), *Hoshin Kanri: Policy Deployment for Successful TQM*. Cambridge, Mass.: Productivity Press.

Woll, T. (1996), Mutual learning has corporations sharing good ideas. *Boston Business Journal*, 16(41), 22–3.

Wood, G. R. and Munshi, K. F. (1991), Hoshin kanri: a systematic approach to breakthrough improvement. *Total Quality Management*, 2(3), 213–26.

chapter nine

Quality Costing

B. G. Dale

Introduction

This chapter defines quality costs and explains why they are important to management. It also outlines how to determine, report and use quality-related costs.

Ideas of what constitute quality costs have changed rapidly in recent years. Whereas only a few years ago the costs of quality were perceived as the cost of running the quality assurance department and the laboratory, plus scrap and warranty costs, it is now widely accepted that they are the costs incurred in designing, implementing, operating and maintaining a quality management system, the costs involved in introducing and sustaining a process of continuous improvement, plus the costs incurred owing to failures of systems, processes, products and/or services. Quality costs arise from a range of activities: for example, the functions of sales and marketing, design, research and development, purchasing, storage, handling, production planning and control, production/operations, delivery, installation and service make, in some way, a contribution to these costs. Suppliers, subcontractors, stockists, distributors, agents, dealers, and especially customers can all influence the incidence and level of these costs.

Quality-related costs commonly range from 5 to 25 per cent of a company's annual sales turnover or operating costs in public sector-type operations, depending on the 'industry' and the way in which the company manages quality and the improvement process. Ninety-five per cent of this cost is expended on appraisal and failure. Reducing failure costs by eliminating causes of failure can also lead to substantial reductions in appraisal costs. Quality costs may be reduced to one-third of their current level by the use of a cost-effective quality management system (Dale and Plunkett 1990).

Barrie Dale is indebted to the late Dr Jim Plunkett for the use of some of his research findings to be used in this chapter.

Definition and Categorization of Quality Costs

The importance of definitions to the collection, analysis and use of quality costs cannot be over-stressed. Without clear definitions there can be no common understanding or meaningful communication on the topic. The definition of what constitutes quality costs is by no means straightforward, and there are many grey areas where production and operation procedures and practices overlap with quality-related activities. Quality costs may be regarded as a criterion of quality performance – but only if valid comparisons can be made between different sets of cost data. Clearly the comparability of sets of data is dependent on the definitions of the categories and elements used in compiling them. If definitions are not established and accepted, the only alternative would be to qualify every item of data so that at least it might be understood, even though it may not be comparable with other data. The value of much of the published data on quality-related costs is questionable because of the absence of precise definition and lack of qualification.

Many definitions of quality-related costs are in fairly specious terms. Admittedly there are difficulties in preparing unambiguous acceptable definitions and in finding generic terms to describe tasks that have the same broad objectives in different cases. It should also be appreciated that problems of rigorous definition arise only because of the desire to carry out costing exercises. Consideration of quality in other contexts (e.g. training, supplier development, design and engineering changes, and statistical process control) does not require such a sharp distinction to be made between what is quality-related and what is not. But there is ample practical and research evidence in the literature to show that, even when collecting costs, collectors do not feel constrained to stick to rigorously defined elements. By and large collectors devise their own elements to suit their own industry and/or particular situation. The result is a proliferation of uniquely defined cost elements which preclude comparisons between data from different sources.

Accounting systems do not readily yield the information needed, as it is presently defined, and rigorous definitions of quality activity elements are necessary only for costing purposes. Thus there is an apparently absurd situation of defining elements in a way which makes them difficult to cost. Given that accounting systems are unlikely to change radically to accommodate quality costing difficulties there should be greater consideration of the accounting aspects when defining quality cost elements. However, the use of activity-based costing (ABC) systems should make it easier to gather quality-related costs. In simple terms ABC breaks down products and services into elements, called 'cost drivers' (e.g. machine set-up) and for each cost driver an overhead rate is determined. The cost drivers are then added together for a particular product or service. This results in more accurate product costs, since costs are not just related to volume of production but to the environment (e.g. variety, change, complexity) in which they are produced. Details of ABC are provided by Innes and Mitchell (1990) and Cooper and Kaplan (1991). These systems are used to enable more accurate calculations of product costs, and tend to focus on values at an activity level. This enables the quality cost associated with an activity to be more easily obtained. It also aids the inspection of the detailed activity analysis and consideration of the cost drivers affecting these activities. ABC is of particular benefit in identifying costs in non-manufacturing areas. A process management structure in which a manager is responsible for a complete process regardless of functional structures is also an aid to the identification, collection and reporting of quality cost data.

Over-ambition or over-zealousness may prompt people, including management consultancies, to try to maximize the impact of quality costs on the CEO and members of the senior management team. Consequently they tend to stretch their definitions to include those costs which have only the most tenuous relationship with quality. This attempt to amplify quality costs can backfire. Once costs have been accepted as being quality-related there may be some difficulty in exerting an influence over the reduction of costs which are independent of quality management considerations. It is not always easy to disown costs after one has claimed them, especially if ownership is in a 'grey area' and no one wants them. In relation to this point of over-ambition the following questions are posed:

- Is the typically quoted figure of quality costs as 25 per cent or so of annual sales turnover or operating costs realistic?
- What is the basis for figures which are frequently quoted in excess of this 25 per cent?
- What are the likely reactions of senior management when the calculated quality costs are less than this figure? For example, figures of this order of magnitude tend to be remembered by senior management. If the calculated quality costs for their organization turn out to be less than this figure, there is sometimes a tendency for them to believe they have nothing to worry about in terms of continuous improvement; this is clearly a dangerous assumption.
- What can be said to executives whose response to this claim of 25 per cent is along the lines, 'If the organization is incurring costs of this magnitude how are we managing to survive?'

Definitions of the categories and their constituent elements are to be found in most standard quality management texts. Detailed guidance is given in specialized publications on the topic: BS6143 (1990), Campanella (1999), Campanella and Corcoran (1983), Dale and Plunkett (1999) and Grimm (1987).

The widespread use and deep entrenchment of the prevention-appraisal-failure (PAF) categorization of quality costs (Feigenbaum 1956) invites analysis of the reasons for it. After all, arrangement of data into these categories is usually done for reporting purposes, after the collection exercise. It adds nothing to the data's potential for provoking action, except perhaps by facilitating comparison with earlier data from the same source (and even this may not be valid because of their relationship to current warranty costs, where these are included, and to other current costs).

However, there are some general and specific advantages to be gained from the PAF categorization. Among the general advantages are that it may prompt a rational approach to collecting costs, and it can add orderliness and uniformity to the ensuing reports. The specific advantages of this particular categorization include:

- Its universal acceptance.
- Its conferral of relative desirability of different kinds of expenditure.
- Most importantly, its provision of keyword criteria to help to decide whether costs are, in fact, quality-related or basic work (e.g. essential activities in producing and supplying a company's products and/or services); in this way it helps educate staff on the concept of quality costing and assists with the identification of costs.

The last-mentioned point may explain why earlier literature on the subject (e.g. Feigenbaum 1956; ASQC 1974 – this booklet has now been withdrawn) defines the term 'quality costs'. Matters are judged to be quality-related if they satisfy the criteria set by their definitions of prevention, appraisal and failure.

However, as TQM has developed, the need to identify and measure quality costs across a wider spectrum of company activities has arisen, and the traditional prevention-appraisal-failure approach is, in some respects, unsuited to the new requirement. Among its limitations are:

1   The quality activity elements as defined do not match well with the cost information most commonly available from accounting systems.
2   There are many quality-related activities in grey areas where it is unclear which category they belong in (this is not detrimental to the process of cost collection, provided the decision-making is consistent).
3   It is not broad enough to account for many of the activities of non-manufacturing areas.
4   In practice the categorization is often a post-collection exercise done in defer-ence to the received wisdom on the topic.
5   The categorization seems to be of interest only to quality assurance personnel.
6   It is not an appropriate categorization for the most common uses of quality-related cost information.
7   To the unwary, because of the distribution of cost elements, it can lead to more focus on the prevention and appraisal components rather than on failure costs.

In these circumstances a broader categorization which measures only the cost of conformance and the cost of non-conformances, as in Crosby's (1979) philosophy, is gaining recognition. The principal arguments in its favour are that it can be applied company-wide and it focuses attention on the costs of doing things right as well as the costs of getting them wrong. This is considered to be a more positive all-round approach which will yield improvements in efficiency. In theory all costs to the company should be accounted for under such a system. In practice, departments identify key-result areas and processes against which to measure their performance and costs. Details of one such process cost model are incorporated into BS6143 (1992).

Machowski and Dale (1998), reporting the main findings of a questionnaire survey which assessed, in an organization involved in the design and manufacture of telecommunications equipment, the level of understanding of quality costing in a cross-section of employees together with their attitudes and perceptions of the concept, concluded that:

> The respondents had a better understanding of the price of conformance and price of non-conforma-tion categorization than the traditional PAF model. This should be noted by those cost collectors deciding on the best ways of categorizing quality costs and seeking alternatives to the traditional PAF model. The main advantage of the broader POC and PONC categorization is that it can be applied company-wide and focuses attention on the cost of doing things right as well as the costs of getting them wrong.

Other alternatives include:

- Controllable and uncontrollable
- Discretionary and consequential
- Theoretical and actual
- Value adding and non-value-adding

Clearly the prospects for success of a costing system will depend on how well the system matches and integrates with other systems in the company and the way that the company operates. Categorization of costs so that they relate to other business costs, and are easy for people to identify with, must have distinct operating advantages. From observations of quality departments at work, it is suggested that a supplier-in-house-customer categorization would have such advantages. Another such practical alternative, based on investigations carried out into one company's total cost of ownership of supplied parts, is: attaining, possessing and sustaining costs, for details see Nix et al. (1993). However, whatever categorization is preferred there is no escaping the need to decide what is quality-related and what is not. In attempting to do so there are no better passwords than prevention, appraisal, and failure (despite their limitations as cost categories).

When defining and categorizing costs it is important to try to define the quality activity elements to align with the business activities of the company and fit in with existing costing structures. Warranty cost is an example of just such an element. Clearly it is quality-related, it is part of the business agreement between a company and its customers, and the company must make financial provisions to meet its possible liabilities under the agreement.

In the matter of definitions of quality and their ease of costing, accountants have a preference for definitions which are confined to meeting specification. Open-ended definitions such as 'fitness for purpose' admit too many intangibles and make costing more difficult. If, say, 'fitness for purpose' is the quality objective, it must be met through suitable specifications and detailed requirements, and the cost collectors must not be left in the difficult situation of trying to decide what parameters affect the product's or service's suitability for its purpose.

Collecting Quality Costs

Purpose

Among the main purposes of collecting quality-related costs are:

1. To display the importance of quality-related activities to company management in meaningful terms (i.e. costs).
2. To show the impact of quality-related activities on key business criteria (e.g. prime cost, and profit and loss accounts).
3. To assist in identifying projects and opportunities for improvement.
4. To enable comparisons of performance with other divisions or companies to be made.
5. To establish bases for budgets with a view to exercising budgetary control over the whole quality operation.
6. To provide cost information for motivational purposes at all levels in the company.

There is little point in collecting quality-related costs just to see what they may reveal. It must not be seen as just another cost-monitoring exercise. Getting the purposes of the exercise clear at the outset can go a long way towards avoiding pitfalls and unnecessary work.

Pursglove and Dale (1996), in a study of the setting up of a quality costing system in an organization involved in the manufacture of PVC-based oil coatings and moulding compounds, provide an interesting angle on making the case for quality costing. First they give the following reasons why no attempt had previously been made by management to gather quality costs:

- A lack of understanding of the concept and principles of quality costing amongst the management team.
- An acute lack of information and data.
- The profitable nature of the business.

They go on to relate the reasons why the new managing director, whose only experience of a quality costing system was at his previous company, decided to set up a quality costing system. They quote him as saying: 'This system was perceived as making good sense of the data gathered' and he particularly liked the way that the costs were expressed as a percentage of raw material usage costs.

The justification for setting up a quality costing system included:

- Quality problems with the company's main business account, resulting in the return of significant amounts of material and subsequent claims.
- Inadequate methods of measurement and control of materials through the production process.
- Ineffective control over raw material ordering.
- Amount of non-conforming finished product.

They go on to say that:

> It was hoped by senior management that the quality costs system would help to identify the areas of costs and highlight those on which to focus improvement effort. Another objective was to set and monitor departmental targets in order to promote and manage reductions in the main costs.

Strategies

Clearly the strategy to be adopted will be influenced by the purpose of the exercise. If, for example, the main objective is to identify high-cost problem areas then approximate cost data will suffice. If the CEO and members of the senior management team already accept that the organization's cost of quality is within the normally quoted range and are prepared to commit resources to improvement there is no point in refining the data. If, on the other hand, the objective is to set a percentage cost reduction target on a particular aspect of the company's activity, it will be necessary to identify all the contributing cost elements carefully and ensure that corrective action produces real gains and does not simply transfer costs elsewhere. If the intention is only to get a snapshot from time to time as a reminder of

larger companies have accounting systems from which it is relatively easy to extract quality-related costs. Often such companies have large, immutable accounting systems and practices imposed by a head office and have little flexibility to provide quality costs. On the other hand, smaller companies are less likely to have a full-time professionally qualified person responsible for management accounting. Some of the difficulties in obtaining quality costs data are related to organizational structures and accounting systems. For example, it has been found on more than one occasion that in a functional structure there is no real incentive to report and reduce costs of quality, and, in relation to the accounting system, activity-based costing has been found to be useful in identifying costs of quality in non-manufacturing areas.

A noticeable feature of accounting systems is the greater accountability the nearer one gets to the production/operations areas. This has implications for the cost-collection exercise because a number of quality costs are incurred close to the production/operations area. Hence the accountability bias is in the quality cost collector's favour. A factor working in the opposite direction is the involvement of personnel from a wide spectrum of functions. It is important that the quality costing exercise does not concentrate purely on the production/operations: a considerable amount of non-value-added activity and waste is incurred in the non-producing or service functions.

When seeking to measure costs under quality-related headings it is sometimes easy to overlook the factor that the task is primarily a cost-collection exercise and that these exercises have other, different, criteria to be considered which are sensibly independent of the cost topic. It is suggested by Plunkett and Dale (1985) that an appropriate set of criteria for any cost-collection exercise is:

- Purpose
- Relevance
- Size of costs
- Ease of collection
- Accuracy of data
- Potential for change
- Completeness

A set of back-up criteria like these can often provide a useful way out of the dilemma about whether or not particular activities and costs should be included in a costing exercise.

Some Cost Aspects of Manufacturing Industry

There are a number of cost aspects – hidden in-house quality costs, scrap and rework, appraisal costs and warranty costs – which occur in manufacturing industry and which warrant discussion. Commercial organizations and those providing a service will have their equivalents of these types of costs.

Hidden in-house quality costs

Hidden quality costs occur in two forms:

1   Those owing to inbuilt inefficiencies in processes and systems.
2   Activities which are clearly quality-related but do not carry a quality tag.

There are many inbuilt inefficiencies such as excess materials allowances, excess paper and forms, excess production/operation starts, poor material utilization, deliberate overmakes and production overruns. These, though, are sometimes not regarded as costs; they may in fact have their origins in engineering, technical, manufacturing and operating inefficiency. The same may also be true of the provision of standby machines, equipment and personnel, additional supervision, some safety stocks and items and other contingency items. Similarly excess and selective fitting owing to variability of machined parts is often an accepted practice. This can be considerably reduced or even eliminated by the use of SPC and design of experiments.

Phua and Dale (1997), in an examination of overmakes in a small company manufacturing complex high-technology printed circuit boards for the aerospace and defence industries, identified a number of company practices such as two-panel loading, step and repeat factors and an outdated overmake planning grid which contributed to the excessive number of overmakes being manufactured and put into inventory as stock boards. The implementation by the company of a number of improved planning measures reduced the number of overmakes by one-third.

Another type of inbuilt inefficiency which is frequently encountered in the packaging industry is where customers change, at the last moment, their order requirements of the packaging manufacturer. In this situation manufacturers usually do their very best to respond to prevent a line stop situation at the customer's, but this exceptional service response incurs additional costs which will not be recovered from the customer.

Snagging facilities to avoid stopping production in line manufacturing are a form of inbuilt inefficiency. Many people would reason that because systems are imperfect it is necessary to provide contingency facilities, such as snagging areas, and that their operating costs are just another built-in burden. But there is no reason why the principle of accountability should not apply and the function responsible for the failure (purchasing, stores, planning, etc.) made accountable for the cost.

Inattention to maintenance of process performance may result in built-in costs by acceptance of lower levels of capability and more non-conformances than are necessary. Maintenance budgets are frequently decided on an arbitrary or general experience basis without having due regard to the particular process needs. Maintenance should be preventative in the sense of prevention of non-conformances rather than preventing breakdown. Failure to do this is tantamount to building in unnecessarily high levels of non-conformance, with consequential inbuilt costs. The use of techniques such as SPC and TPM will draw attention to changes in capability and cause maintenance work to become more process- than machine-oriented.

Commercial organizations and those providing a service have their equivalents of these types of costs. These include: service queries in relation to a problem which the customer has experienced with the service provided, service recovery in which the service provider takes certain steps to demonstrate to the customer that they are sorry for the problems created, rework with respect to issues such as incomplete first-call services, process changeovers and penalty payments.

Junk mail advertising a myriad services, from insurance policies, financial deals and arrangements to double glazing and offers on foodstuff, while loosely classed as marketing, can be considered to be another example of inbuilt inefficiency and waste. In a similar vein there is also a series of costs associated with customer loyalty programmes.

The principal problem arising from built-in inefficiencies, apart from their direct costs, is that they distort the base values against which important judgements are made; ironically, the more the base values are used the more firmly entrenched and accepted the built-in inefficiencies become.

Major activities in the second category are concessions, modifications and engineering changes. It is suspected that in many companies concessions are an expedient way of maintaining production schedules and that little account is taken of the disadvantages incurred in deciding to overlook non-conformances. Not least among these are proliferation of paperwork and lax attitudes towards quality and its improvement among managers, supervisors and operatives. In fact, frequent concessions on non-conforming goods are a positive disincentive to operators and first-line supervisors to get it right first time.

In many companies goods passed on concession do not feature in quality reporting systems because they have escaped the company's defect reporting system. In some companies goods are supposed only to be passed on concession if they cannot be rectified. It is often easier to find reasons why goods cannot be rectified than it is to rework them. Hence concession systems may become an engineering/technical expediency, or, equally, they may be seen as a production expediency to avoid impediments to output or delays in delivery.

To anyone investigating costs in manufacturing industry, striking features are the large amount of time and money spent on modifications and engineering changes, and an apparent acceptance that they are facts of engineering life that one must learn to live with. Thus they might justifiably be categorized as inbuilt costs. The costs, though hidden, are believed to be substantial and, quite apart from the costs of personnel directly involved, there can be serious implications for inventory, and even impediments to output if modifications and changes are not kept to a minimum or processing the modifications or changes becomes protracted.

There is a need for a new set of specific definitions and elements to help determine the costs associated with these types of activities.

Other examples of hidden costs are provision of 'clean areas' and 'protection' for components and assemblies, segregation, marking, and handling of scrap, movement of goods for inspection purposes, the activities of purchasing and accounting personnel in dealing with rejected supplies, the effects of order-splitting (for quality reasons) on planning and manufacture, and the costs of machine downtime for quality reasons.

Scrap and rework

These costs are collected and reported in most companies. They are frequently regarded as important costs which feature in companies' business decisions. Yet the economics of scrapping or rectification are by no means clear in many companies.

The first difficulty is the valuation to be placed on scrapped goods. Some popular views encountered are that the value should be the factory selling price, the market price, the raw materials price or the materials cost plus the cost of processing to the point of scrapping, or the materials cost plus 50 per cent of the cost of processing, irrespective of the point of scrapping. These different bases will obviously give rise to very different valuations. The second difficulty is that the decision about whether to scrap or rework is often taken by personnel who do not have access to the financial information necessary to make an economic choice. And in any case the economics will vary depending on workload, urgency of delivery, etc. It will often be found that scrap vs. rework decisions are based primarily on ease of rework and output and delivery targets rather than on cost.

The practice, found in some organizations, of deducting from quality costs the income from sales of scrap is to be discouraged because it makes the overall quality cost appear to be better than it really is. Also, the type and quantity of scrap sold at a particular time may bear no relation to current production.

Appraisal costs

Though appraisal costs cover a wider range of activities, the majority of the expenditure is on in-house inspection and test activities. Opinions differ about whether testing is an appraisal cost. Carson (1986) is positive that testing is about detecting defects, that it is an appraisal cost, and that there is an onus on the manufacturing department to 'get it right first time'.

Testing is effectively proving the fitness for purpose of the product in one or more respects. There may well be cases where such testing ought not to be necessary but is, and it hence incurs a quality cost. However, in many cases the state of the technology may be such that testing is unavoidable. A manufacturer may be unable to give guarantees without testing the product, he may be unable to get insurance cover without testing, and it may be a contractual requirement of the customer. In the end, the decision whether to test or not may be taken out of his hands, whatever he thinks he can achieve without testing. Whether testing is a quality-related or a purely production activity is a matter to be decided in individual cases.

The economics of appraisal are not known in most companies. High costs of failure are apparently used to justify inspection and its frequency, without any attempt being made to determine the true economic balance. It is somewhat surprising that the economics of inspection are not well established and widely known considering that inspection-oriented approaches have predominated in manufacturing industry for many decades. There is evidence of the potential for cost reductions through drastic reductions in inspection forces, apparently without loss of quality (e.g. Kohl 1976; Richardson 1983). It is expected that there would be little change in first-off inspection unless the capability of machines and tools to sustain tolerances was improved, but that the patrol and final inspection activity can be reduced through SPC. This is all part of the change of philosophy from detection to prevention, as discussed in chapter 1.

Warranty costs

Warranty costs are usually met from a provision set aside for the purpose. Care needs to be taken when determining costs from changes in provisions because the provision may be used to meet some other charge or may be topped up from time to time with arbitrary amounts of money. Hence it is necessary to know about all the transactions affecting the provision.

Reporting Quality Costs

Quality cost reporting is not yet widely accepted as one of the normal activities in the reporting of quality performance. Duncalf and Dale (1985) report that only 36 companies out of 110 respondents to a questionnaire survey of quality-related decision-making claimed to collect quality costs, and of these there were few that collected them across all the categories of prevention, appraisal and failure.

An important consideration in the presentation of quality-related costs is the needs of the recipients, and it may be worth presenting information in several different formats. For example, weekly reports of the cost of scrap and rework may be of greatest value to shop-floor supervisors, monthly reports of total costs high-lighting current problems and progress with quality improvement projects would be suitable for middle management, while total costs and costs on which to act are needed by senior managers. While selective reporting of this kind has its merits, it should always be done against a background of the total quality-related cost. Ideally quality cost reports should show opportunities for cost savings leading to increased profits or price reductions.

For maximum impact quality costs should be included in a company's cost-reporting system. Unfortunately, the lack of sophistication of quality cost collection and measurement is such that it does not allow quality cost reporting to be carried out in the same detail and to the same standard as, for example, reporting on the production/operations and marketing functions. Reporting of quality costs is, in the main, a subsection of the general reporting of quality department activities, and as such loses its impact. Often quality reports do not separate out costs as an aspect of quality which is worthy of presentation and comment in its own right. This usually results in cost information not being used to its full potential. Separating costs from other aspects of quality and discussing them in the context of other costs would improve the clarity of reports and help to provide better continuity from one report to the next.

Good standards of reporting are essential if the costs are to make an impact and provoke action. Managers are like everyone else in wanting easy decisions to make. Having costs, which are the basis of business decisions, tangled up with technical information makes the data less clear than they could be and may provide a reason to defer action. The manager's problem should not be to disentangle and analyse data in order to decide what to do; it should be to decide whether to act, choose which course of action to pursue and ensure provision of the necessary resources. Problems, possible solutions and their resource requirements should be presented in the context of accountability centres which have the necessary authority to execute the decisions of the senior management team.

Many manufacturing companies make goods for stock, and it may be many months or possibly years after manufacture that a product goes into service. This raises the issue of the comparability (or even relevance) of categories of cost one to another. Much has been written about definition, categorization, and reporting of quality costs, and the implication is always that the reported costs are concurrent and relevant to each other. Clearly prevention costs should have a bearing on appraisal and failure costs, and expenditure on appraisal may influence the magnitude and distribution (between internal and external) of failure costs, but not necessarily concurrently. In some industries the time lags arising between action and effect are such that concurrent expenditures on, say, prevention and warranty bear no relation whatever to each other. Reporting only concurrent costs in isolation can be misleading, and in some cases it is perhaps worth considering contemporary costs as well as concurrent costs.

The long intervals which may occur between manufacture and receipt of warranty claims can have some special implications for cost reporting. Warranty costs in any period may bear no relation to other quality costs incurred in the same period, and should not be reported in the same context. To include them can distort considerably the quality performance of the company or department as depicted by the levels and ratios of quality-related costs. The delays may also mean that the causes underlying the failures leading to the claims may no longer be a problem.

One of the maxims of cost-collecting seems to be that, in general, costs need to be large to attract attention. This creates something of a dilemma for the cost collector because large costs are often insensitive to change. But the collector cannot omit large costs and concentrate only on smaller costs which may readily be seen to change. Hence cost groupings need to be chosen carefully so that cost reductions achieved are displayed in such a way that both the relative achievement and the absolute position are clearly shown. Another dilemma arises from the fact that one-off estimates do not change and that there is no point in collecting costs which do not change.

The format for the collection of costs should make provision right at the outset for all those elements and cost sources which are thought to be worth collecting. The creation of a quality-related cost file, integrated with existing costing systems but perhaps with some additional expense codes, should not present many problems. As stressed earlier, it is important to make provision in the file for collecting data which are not readily quantifiable even though it may take a long time to obtain satisfactory returns on a routine basis.

When reporting costs at regular intervals it is important to ensure that sets of data remain comparable. If additional cost elements are introduced as an organization becomes more experienced in quality costing, these must be reported separately until an appropriate opportunity arises to include them among related costs. It is also worth coding each cost element to indicate its source and status (e.g. accounting records, calculation from standard data, calculation through surrogates, average rates, estimates, etc.).

Presentation of costs under prevention, appraisal, and internal and external failure, as advocated by BS6143 (1990) and Campanella (1999), is the most popular approach, albeit with different cost elements appropriate to different industries, whether manufacturing, commercial or service-related. This format is favoured by quality managers perhaps because, on the face of it, it forms a quality balance sheet for the quality management function with prevention equivalent to investment, appraisal to operating cost, and failure to losses. This categorization of costs is of interest and some value to quality managers, but less so to other functional managers on the grounds that they do not relate directly to the activities of the business.

The influence of senior management is vital in the reporting of quality costs. If there is no pressure to reduce costs against mutually agreed targets then the reporting will become routine and people, quite naturally, will devote their efforts to what they believe are the most important activities. It is important that senior management develop a quality cost reduction strategy.

Uses of Quality Costs

According to Morse (1983): 'The potential uses of the information contained in such a [quality cost] report are limited only by imagination of management.' Many of the uses can, however, be grouped into four broad categories:

- First, quality costs may be used to promote product and service quality as a business parameter.
- Secondly, they give rise to performance measures.
- Thirdly, they provide the means for planning and controlling quality costs.
- Fourthly, they act as motivators.

The *first* use – promoting quality as a business parameter – is usually interpreted as gaining the attention of higher management by using their language – i.e. money. But costs can also be used to show that it is not only the quality department that is involved in quality, that everyone's work can impinge on quality and that it is indeed an important business parameter – especially if the influences of suppliers and customers are made clear. Clearly knowledge of quality-related costs will enable decisions about quality to be made in an objective manner.

The *second* use – giving rise to performance measures – includes a wide variety of activities. Among them are:

1   *Trend analyses* to show changes in costs or cost ratios with time. Diagnosis of the cause of change can often prompt pilot exercises in the use of specific tools and techniques.
2   *Pareto analyses* to identify quality improvement projects. This is the quickest route to the exploitation of quality cost data.
3   *Identification of investment opportunities.* Progressive companies are always looking for profitable ways to invest in quality improvement projects and initiatives, but their task is made very difficult by the lack of data and under-standing of the economics of investment in quality. While it may be axiomatic that prevention is better than cure, it is often difficult to justify investment in prevention activities. To some extent such investments are regarded as acts of faith. Little is known and nothing has been published on the appropriate levels and timing of investments, payoffs or payback periods. However, there are many opportunities for investment in prevention, with consequential real cost savings. Employing qualified, experienced staff, encouraging continuing education and providing training are examples of investment in personnel. Investment in supplier quality development activities is claimed by many com-panies to pay handsome dividends (Galt and Dale 1990). Of more direct interest to engineers and technical personnel are the possibilities of effect-ive savings through investment in tooling, equipment and machinery and mistake-proofing devices (for details of mistake-proofing see Shingo 1986). A poor standard of tools is frequently responsible for non-conforming product, and the extra costs of providing a higher standard of tooling is often a worthwhile investment. Quality considerations also enter into the selection of machinery and equipment inasmuch as a premium is paid for machine tools with the potential to achieve a capable process, thus avoiding failure costs,

and maybe some appraisal costs. Kaplan (1983) takes this line of argument further when he suggests that if manufacturing costs decrease as quality increases (and there is evidence of this), then the financial justification for new capital equipment, including robots, should include the savings in manufacturing costs from achieving a lower incidence of defects.

4   *Performance indicators and quality efficiency indexes.* Business efficiencies are commonly analysed and expressed using a variety of criteria (mostly financial). Maintenance and improvement of quality are not among the criteria used. Quality managers' efforts to persuade fellow managers and directors of the value of continuous improvement to a company are often frustrated by a lack of well-known and accepted indices or standards. Some companies have developed measures for the purpose of internally monitoring improvement, but no general guidelines or methods of calculation exist which would readily allow a company to assess its standards against a norm or other companies' performances. The most popular comparative measure against which quality costs are measured is gross sales, followed by manufacturing or operating costs and value added. Other useful bases are hours of direct production labour, units of product, and processing costs. It is widely held that single ratios do not tell the whole story and may always need to be considered alongside other ratios. BS6143 (1992) recommends that at least three comparison bases should be used, and urges care and caution in the selection of bases. Other useful guidance is contained in Campanella (1999) and Feigenbaum (1991).

Quality cost data may also be used to assist with vendor-rating. Winchell (1987) lists 'visible' and 'hidden' quality costs. Included in the visible quality costs category are the following:

- Receiving or incoming inspection
- Measuring equipment calibration
- Qualification of supplier product
- Source inspection and control programme
- Purchased material reject disposition (material review)
- Purchased material replacement
- Rework of supplier-caused rejects
- Scrap of supplier-caused rejects

The visible costs, if tracked, are perhaps most significant because they can be good indicators of problem areas.

Hidden quality costs include:

- Those that are incurred by the supplier at his plant.
- Those incurred by the buyer in solving problems at the supplier's plant.
- Those costs which usually are not allocated to suppliers, but are incurred by the buyer as a result of potential or actual supplier problems – including loss of business from customers who don't come back.

In much of the foregoing it is implicit that placing costs on activities and quality management data somehow enhances the underlying data and shows something which might otherwise not be revealed. While enhancement of data in this way may be useful, it may not always be necessary. Sometimes only translating numbers into costs is sufficient to provoke action (e.g. Richardson 1983). Similarly, the mere collection of data may provoke investigative action. In one case study (Dale and Plunkett 1999), it was only when the company began to collect quality costs and analyse its warranty payments that it became aware that its policy of automatic payment of warranty invoices for less than £1,000 was being seriously abused by customers. By the simple expedient of a knowledgeable person checking all invoices over £400 many tens of thousands of pounds were saved. Perhaps more importantly, word soon got around that invoices were being checked and the incidence of attempted abuse reduced rapidly.

The *third* use of quality costs – as a means of planning and controlling quality costs – is widely mooted in the literature. Costs are the bases for budgeting and eventual cost control. Contributions from the quality fraternity tend to see establishment of quality cost budgets for the purpose of controlling costs as the ultimate goal which may be achieved after accumulating data over a long time in pursuit of quality improvements of specific cost reductions. Campanella and Corcoran (1983), drawing on ASQC's (1974) *Quality Costs: What and How?* (now withdrawn), summarize the uses of quality costs for budgeting thus:

> Once quality cost elements have been established and costs are being collected against them, you can generate a history with which to determine the average cost per element. These averages can serve as the basis for future quotes and 'estimates to complete'. Budgets can be established for each element. Then, going full circle, the actuals collected against these elements can be used to determine budget variances and, as with any good system of budget control, action can be taken to bring variances into line.

However, Morse (1983), giving an accountant's view, is not so positive:

> After quality cost information has been accumulated for several periods, it may be possible to budget certain quality costs.

These views appear to reflect the general situation that the quality management fraternity is much more optimistic about the potential for achieving fairly sophisticated uses of quality costs than are accountants. And, despite the popularity of the topic with contributors to the quality literature, there are relatively few examples of its application to quality costing.

In the research experience of UMIST the state of development of quality costing in most companies is not advanced enough to establish budgetary control over quality costs other than within the quality department.

Fourthly, quality costs can be used for motivational purposes at all levels in a company. Costs have traditionally been used to motivate senior managers to become interested and take part in the promotion of quality. As companies move towards TQM the use of costs as a motivator becomes more widespread. Thus, for example, costs of scrapped goods are displayed to line supervision, operatives and clerical staff because they can see the relevance of them to their work. It is found that this group of people responds positively in terms of increased quality awareness, improved handling of the product, housekeeping disciplines, etc. Although the costs may be relatively small in company terms, they are usually large in relation to operatives' salaries. Thus a strong impact is made, in particular when poor trading conditions result in restrictions being placed on salary increases and even in freezes or reductions being imposed, without disclosing sensitive cost information.

Finally, while it is clearly important to make good use of quality-related costs it is equally important to avoid misuse of them.

- It must be remembered that in some industries quality costs are not susceptible to conventional cost-reduction techniques and quality may not be compromised to save money, e.g. where there is a possibility of severe loss of life or ecological disaster. Only in those situations where the consequence of failure is merely loss of profit is a manufacturer in a position to trade off quality expenditure against potential loss of profit resulting from product failures (Cox 1982).
- Costs alone must not be used to determine an optimum level of quality as suggested by 'economic cost of quality' models which appear everywhere in the literature. Such models have been heavily and widely criticized in recent years. For example, Plunkett and Dale (1988) have observed that, though well-intentioned in warning against extravagance in pursuing quality, the models are only notional and do not reflect actual experience. Many of the published models are ambiguous, inaccurate and misleading. While there is no objection to trying to optimize quality costs, quality should not be compromised. Quality should be determined by customer requirements, not optimum quality costs. The real dangers are that the taking cognizance of the model will inhibit the development of TQM and quality improvement in the company and that the company will perhaps settle for a standard of quality which is less than what the customer requires. The form of the model, shown in figure 9.1 from BS6143 (1990), resembles real situations much more closely than the classical optimum-quality cost models which are usually portrayed in quality management and production and operations management textbooks.
- Comparisons with other cost data should be avoided. Comparisons should only be made after it has been shown that the data are genuinely comparable (i.e. sources, computation, accounting treatment, and reporting methods are identical).

Summary

The value of cost data should not be underestimated. Costs are a most effective way of drawing attention to and illuminating situations in ways that other data cannot. It has been found that even the most rudimentary attempts at quality costing have been beneficial in identifying areas of waste and trends in quality improvement performance. It should also not be forgotten that quality costs are already being incurred by an organization; the whole purpose of the quality costing exercise is to identify these 'hidden costs' from various budgets and overheads, the objective being to allocate these indirect costs to a specific cost activity.

Unfortunately, the whole process of definition, collection, reporting, and use of quality-related costs is not yet well enough developed to be used in the same way as many other costs. A major influence in this is undoubtedly the solid entrenchment

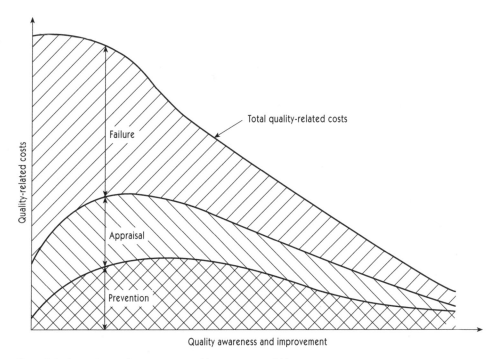

Total quality-related costs

Failure

Appraisal

Prevention

Quality-related costs

Quality awareness and improvement

Figure 9.1   Increasing quality awareness and improvement activities
Source: BS6143-2 (1990)

of the prevention-appraisal-failure categorization of quality-related costs. The potential uses of cost data derived from elements defined via this categorization are restricted and do not fit well with companies' day-to-day operating modes and experience. Nor do they lend themselves to sophisticated business uses. However, even with restricted potential, there is still much to be gained, as shown in this chapter. Sizes and proportions of costs can be used successfully as criteria for deciding whether to act, what resources should be committed, priorities to be allocated, etc.

As things stand now, the most widely accepted and used categorizations and definitions of quality cost elements cause the definition-collection-reporting-use process sequence to be definition-driven, with companies making the best use they can of the outcome. But companies should be looking for more effective ways of using quality cost data. Perhaps taking a different approach to the categorization and definition of costs will assist with this.

However, what is more important is to make the process sequence dynamic. Use is the most important part of the sequence, but at present there is little or no feedback from uses to definitions. There is a need for use-driven definitions which will in turn affect the collection and reporting stages. The system can then become dynamic, changing as business requirements change. It is a task which needs to be tackled jointly by accountants and the manager responsible for quality in the company. The question to be answered is: 'How can cost information be used to improve the company's quality status, keeping in mind that quality status is determined by customers, supplier performance and in-house quality management?'

References

ASQC (1974), *Quality Costs: What and How?* Wisconsin: American Society for Quality Control. This booklet has now been withdrawn, and the material is included in Campanella (1999).

BS6143 (1990), *Guide to the Economics of Quality,* part 2: *Prevention Appraisal and Failure Model.* London: British Standards Institution.

BS6143 (1992), *Guide to the Economics of Quality,* part 1: *Process Cost Model.* London: British Standards Institution.

Campanella, J. (ed.) (1999), *Principles of Quality Costs: Principles, Implementation and Use.* Milwaukee: ASQC Quality Press.

Campanella, J. and Corcoran, F. J. (1983), Principles of quality costs. *Quality Progress,* 16(4), 17–22.

Carson, J. K. (1986), Quality costing: a practical approach. *International Journal of Quality and Reliability Management,* 3(1), 54–63.

Cooper, R. and Kaplan, R. (1991), Profit priorities from activity-based costing. *Harvard Business Review,* 69(3), 130–5.

Cox, B. (1982), Interface of quality costing and terotechnology. *The Accountant,* 21 June, 800–1.

Crosby, P. B. (1979), *Quality is Free.* New York: McGraw Hill.

Dale, B. G. and Plunkett, J. J. (1990), *The Case for Costing Quality.* London: Department of Trade and Industry.

Dale, B. G. and Plunkett, J. J. (1999), *Quality Costing,* 3rd edn. Aldershot, Hants.: Gower Press.

Duncalf, A. J. and Dale, B. G. (1985), How British industry is making decisions on product quality. *Long-Range Planning,* 18(5), 81–8.

Feigenbaum, A. V. (1956), Total quality control. *Harvard Business Review,* 34(6), 93–101.

Feigenbaum, A. V. (1991), *Total Quality Control.* New York: McGraw Hill.

Galt, J. D. and Dale, B. G. (1990), Customer–supplier relationships in the motor industry: a vehicle manufacturer's perspective. *Proceedings of the Institution of Mechanical Engineers,* 204 (D4), 179–86.

Grimm, A. F. (1987), *Quality Costs, Ideas and Applications,* vol. 1. Milwaukee: ASQC Quality Press.

Innes, J. and Mitchell, F. (1990), *Activity-Based Costing: A Review with Case Studies.* London: The Chartered Institute of Management Accountants.

Kaplan, R. S. (1983), Measuring manufacturing performance: a new challenge for managerial accounting research. *The Accounting Review,* 58(4), 686–705.

Kohl, W. F. (1976), Hitting quality costs where they live. *Quality Assurance,* 2(2), 59–64.

Machowski, F. and Dale, B. G. (1995), The application of quality costing to engineering change. *International Journal of Materials and Product Technology,* 10(3–6), 378–88.

Machowski, F. and Dale, B. G. (1998), Quality costing: an examination of knowledge, attitudes and perceptions. *The Quality Management Journal,* 5(3), 84–95.

Morse, W. J. (1983), Measuring quality costs. *Cost and Management,* July–August, 16–20.

Nix, A., McCarthy, P. and Dale, B. G. (1993), The key issues in the development and use of total cost of ownership model. *Proceedings of the 2nd International Conference of the Purchasing and Supply Education Group.* University of Bath, April, 247–54.

Phua, L. and Dale, B. G. (1997), The effects of overmakes on company performance. *IEE Proceedings,* 144(2), 57–62.

Plunkett, J. J. and Dale, B. G. (1985), Some practicalities and pitfalls of quality-related cost collection. *Proceedings of the Institute of Mechanical Engineers,* 199(B1), 29–33.

Plunkett, J. J. and Dale, B. G. (1988), Quality costs: a critique of some 'economic cost of quality models'. *International Journal of Production Research,* 26(11), 1713–26.

Pursglove, A. B. and Dale, B. G. (1995), Developing a quality costing system: key features and outcomes. *OMEGA,* 23(5), 567–75.

Pursglove, A. B. and Dale, B. G. (1996), The influence of management information and quality management systems on the development of quality costing. *Total Quality Management*, 7(4), 421–32.

Richardson, D. W. (1983), Cost benefits of quality control: a practical example from industry. *BSI News*, October.

Shingo, S. (1986), *Zero Quality Control: Source Inspection and the Poka-Yoke System*. Cambridge, Mass.: Productivity Press.

Winchell, W. O. (ed.) (1987), *Guide for Managing Supplier Quality Costs*. Wisconsin: American Society for Quality Control.

chapter ten

Managing Human Resources for Quality Management

A. Wilkinson and A. Brown

Introduction

This chapter is concerned with the human resource (HR) issues relating to quality management (QM). Proponents of QM define quality in terms of customer requirements. Those employees who do not have direct contact with external customers are encouraged to view their colleagues as customers, linked ultimately via a chain of internal customer relationships to the final (external) customer. In this way, employees in the organization are to be customer-driven, with the aim of continuously improving customer satisfaction. There are implications for human resources, as employers are urged to move away from supervisory approaches to quality control towards a situation where employees themselves take responsibility (Oakland 1993). Thus, the effective implementation of QM requires that all employees, from top management to the shop or office floor, develop a commitment to continuous improvement as an integral part of their daily work. There is a need to develop a 'quality culture' (Dale et al. 1997). We argue that, while QM does have far-reaching implications for HR, this is dealt with in a limited way by the conventional QM literature. But it is also argued that HR practice has significant implications for reinforcing QM. In this chapter we discuss how HR practices have been adopted by quality-focused organizations to support their quality efforts.

QM: The HR Concerns

The 1990s produced strong evidence that QM did not achieve its objectives (Hill and Wilkinson 1995; Wilkinson 2002), with a failure to achieve changed attitudes and culture being part of this (Wilkinson et al. 1998). Systems- and procedures-driven QM, where the focus is on the production process, conformance to requirements and achieving zero defects, has been criticized for being inward looking and bureaucratic, less concerned with producing 'quality' goods and services than with conforming to internal procedures. HR issues are often not deemed very significant, with employees taking a role of following clearly laid down instructions.

Central to this chapter is the 'human factor': however brilliant a strategy QM is, it needs to be implemented, and this depends on people. A failure to change attitudes and culture can be partially attributed to the neglect of HR policies in the organization and a failure to align the HR policies with QM to ensure integration. However, the prescriptive literature on QM says more about what employers are trying to achieve in terms of employee commitment than about how this is to be achieved or the problems that may be faced in attempting to do this (Wilkinson et al. 1998; Snape et al. 1995; CIPD 1996). The usual argument in the QM literature is that employees, including supervisors and managers, are to be won over, not by compulsion, but by leadership, training and recognition (Oakland 1993). The assumption is that employees in general will derive satisfaction from involvement in continuous improvement and from doing a job well. There is a notion of reciprocal commitment here, with the QM organization meeting the individual's needs for job satisfaction and receiving commitment to organizational goals in return.

Proponents of QM have understated the difficulties in getting staff at all levels in the organization to 'buy in' to the ideals of QM, and focus on an overly limited range of change levers (Hill 1995). Traditional working practices and management styles may be inconsistent with QM, and resistance to the ideals of QM may be encountered not only at shop-floor level, where it may cut across traditional working and industrial relations practices, but also amongst professional, supervisory and managerial staff. This is due partly to a lack of understanding of the issues involved, but also to the emphasis quality professionals place on systems rather than the individual (Waldman 1994). However, despite this general lack of attention given to the people element of quality, there are organizations which have used HR policies to support QM (e.g. Blackburn and Rosen 1993; Wilkinson et al. 1993; Brown 1995).

The arguments behind QM fit with broader developments in terms of the notion of a high-commitment HR strategy (Walton 1985). As markets become more competitive, due partly to the globalization of competition and liberalization by governments, while customers are becoming more demanding – not only on price but more particularly in terms of choice, quality, service and design – companies are now targeting their products at niche markets and attempting to respond quickly to ever-changing customer demands, rather than selling standard mass-produced goods (Piore and Sabel 1984). In consequence, there is a greater emphasis on flexible, responsive organizations with multi-skilled workers and flexible technology, rather than on simple economies of scale. There is in consequence a need to win employee commitment to the goals of quality and flexibility (see table 10.1). QM implies the adoption of flexible organization structures, with an open management style, the devolution of responsibility, and the establishment of problem-solving teams (Wilkinson et al. 1998).

The Two Sides of QM

QM has both 'hard' and 'soft' sides. The former may involve a range of tools and techniques, including SPC, and the basic quality management tools. The soft side of QM is concerned with HR and cultural change. The soft side thus puts the emphasis on the management of HR: a well-trained and motivated 'quality' workforce is more

Table 10.1   Management styles for the future

Traditional management	*Future management*
Policeman	Guide
Disciplinarian	Cheerleader/coach
Paper-shuffler	Enthusiast
Office-bound	Verbal communicator
Allocates jobs	Delegates tasks
Focus on control	Focus on quality
Focus on markets	Focus on customers
Maintains bureaucracy	Sheds bureaucracy
	Creates a vision

Source: Rosenfeld and Wilson (1999)

likely to contribute to organizational success. However, QM writers tend to have a rather unitary view of the organization and, hence, some barriers to change are underplayed (Wilkinson and Witcher 1991; Yong and Wilkinson 1999). There is little acknowledgement that there may well be tensions between the production-oriented 'hard' aspects of QM (which tend to emphasize working within prescribed procedures) and the 'soft' aspects (which emphasize employee involvement and commitment). Furthermore, Powell (1995) goes so far as to suggest that competitive advantage comes more through tacit behaviour and imitable factors (e.g. open culture, employee involvement and executive commitment), than the factors more commonly associated with QM (e.g. benchmarking and process improvement).

In this chapter, some of the soft issues which remain undeveloped within the QM literature are examined. We first look at the QM gurus' approach to HRM (see also chapter 3). Second, we examine a range of issues relating QM to HR practice. These issues have arisen from a number of research projects examining links between QM and HR issues over the last 10 years; see Wilkinson et al. (1992, 1998), Marchington et al. (1993), Brown (1995), CIPD (1996), Godfrey and Wilkinson (1998), and Godfrey et al. (1998), and including some ongoing Australian research examining HR practices in quality award-winning organizations (Brown 1995).

QM and the Management of People

Oakland (1989) states that:

> QM is concerned with moving the focus of control from outside the individual to within; the objective being to make everyone accountable for their own performance, and to get them committed to attaining quality in a highly motivated fashion. The assumptions a director or manager must make in order to move in this direction are simply that people do not need to be coerced to perform well, and that people want to achieve, accomplish, influence activity and challenge their abilities.

Each of the quality gurus places a rather different emphasis on the people-management aspects of the system (Dale and Plunkett 1990; Oakland 1993; Coyle-Shapiro 1993). For Crosby, Juran, and Taguchi, the role of employees in continuous improvement is minimal. While Crosby (1979) recognizes a need for quality awareness to be raised among employees and for more personal concern to be generated, his approach suggests that employees should be encouraged to communicate to management the obstacles they face in achieving their improvement goals. Moreover, he rejects outright the redesign of work, regarding work itself as a secondary motivator to how employees are treated.

Juran, in fact, argued in the 1940s that the technical aspects of quality control were well covered and 'an understanding of the human situation associated with the job will go far to solve the technical problems; in fact such an understanding may be a prerequisite to a solution'. However, he saw little role for ordinary shop-floor employees, with the primary responsibility lying with quality professionals and, to a lesser extent, middle management, although he warned against exhortation. His emphasis is on training and top management leadership (Juran 1989) and he has also discussed the notion of self-supervising teams, arguing that the 'winning' quality companies have begun to develop these concepts (Juran 1991).

Taguchi (1986) argues that quality is achieved by minimizing variance; his methods have been concerned with enabling quality to be designed into a product or process. Thus quality and reliability are pushed back to the design stage where they belong. He has little to say about HR issues.

Deming (1986), Feigenbaum (1983), and Ishikawa (1985) offer a rather more positive approach to people management. Deming is critical of exhortations, slogans and targets. In particular, he has criticized (Deming 1986) the notion of zero defects as a motivational programme:

> Eliminate slogans, exhortations and targets for the workforce asking for zero defects and new levels of productivity. Such exhortations only create adversarial relationships as the bulk of the causes of low quality and low productivity belong to the system and thus lie beyond the power of the workforce.

While Deming has been known for his advocacy of statistical techniques, he also believes that employees should be trained to spot defects, and to improve quality; they should be offered rewarding and challenging jobs, and he argues (Deming 1982) for the creation of high-trust relations: 'Posters like these [zero defects] never helped anyone do a better job. What is needed is not exhortations, but a road map to improvement.'

However, Deming's advocacy of rewarding and challenging jobs does not encompass a radical redesign of work. Central to his philosophy is 'pride in workmanship', subsequently refined as 'joy in work'. The implicit rationale is that, if individuals enjoy work, their motivation will be intrinsic rather than extrinsic, with the former being a prerequisite for continuous improvement. 'Joy in work' seems mainly to encompass the removal of obstacles preventing individuals from accomplishing the best possible job.

Feigenbaum (1983) also argues that workers need a good understanding of what management is trying to do: 'improvement can only be achieved by everyone's participation' and the workforce must have a good understanding of management aims. 'Quality control begins with education and ends with education.' This is seen to be achieved through teamwork. Ishikawa (1985) places a strong emphasis on the internal customer and hence stresses the importance of employees being involved; he points out that Western companies need to overcome their professional 'expert' culture, suggesting that employees may be unwilling to co-operate given a lack of organizational consensus. Ishikawa (1985) writes of respect for humanity as a management philosophy. In his view,

Top Managers and Middle Managers must be bold enough to delegate as much authority as possible. That is the way to establish respect for humanity as your management philosophy. It is a management system in which all employees participate from the top down and from the bottom up, and humanity is fully respected.

Thus QM has important implications for people management. If quality is to be 'built in' rather than inspected, quality must be the responsibility of all employees rather than specified departments. QM proponents have highlighted the need to increase the involvement of all employees in monitoring their own work with the aim of constantly maintaining and improving quality, 'getting it right first time', and removing the need for retrospective quality checks (Crosby 1979). The aim is for zero defects rather than an 'acceptable' quality level. QM is also said to minimize the costs of poor and uncertain quality because it is a way of making everyone improve the quality of their work. Every person has a common focus, based on the customer, so that people with different jobs, abilities and priorities are able to communicate in pursuit of a common organizational purpose (Wilkinson and Witcher 1991).

In short, QM is supposed to place a greater emphasis on self-control, autonomy and creativity, expecting active co-operation from employees rather than mere compliance with the employment contract (Wilkinson et al. 1991). The principles underlying certain versions of both QM and HRM theory have some common themes. Both emphasize commitment, self-control and trust, and take McGregor's Theory Y view that workers, if given responsibility, will be motivated and committed and hence identify with company goals. (Theory X was the traditional view of workers as essentially lazy and hence needing close monitoring and control.) The HRM literature emphasizes that people are a key asset. In summarizing the HRM philosophy, Guest (1987) states the case thus:

Because they are the most variable, and the least easy to understand and control of all management resources, effective utilization of human resources is likely to give organizations a significant competitive advantage. The human resource dimension must therefore be fully integrated into the strategic planning process.

Much of the HRM literature puts the emphasis on individuals and their performance, with systems of performance management, including Performance Related Pay (PRP), prominent. However, there is also an alternative version of the relationship between TQM and HRM; what we might call the 'Deming-TQM' view. The key issue here is whether the main source of variation in organizational performance is the system or individual performance. The view implicit in the performance management approach is that organizational performance can be effectively managed by focusing on the performance of individual workers. In contrast, Deming (1986) argues that differences in the performance of individuals belong to the category of 'special causes' of variation in work performance, and as such are minor relative to the 'common causes' of performance variation. He argues that the latter are endemic to the system of work and are primarily attributable to system design rather than to the day-to-day work effort of particular individuals. The implication is that attempts to manage organizational performance through the performance of individual workers are mistaken.

Thus, we have contrasting approaches: one focusing on the management of individual performance, the other on improving the system. Indeed Deming goes further and argues that individual appraisal and incentives divert attention from the true causes of performance variation and actually undermine those employee behaviours which contribute towards continuous improvement. He thus appears to argue that the two approaches are mutually exclusive.

Deming is surely correct to counsel against blaming individual workers for deficiencies in the work system, and it is widely recognized that evaluating workers against targets that are beyond their control is likely to demotivate. However, we have already seen that the proponents of TQM have given too little attention to the question of individual motivation and commitment, and that there is a need to examine more clearly how HRM affects the implementation of TQM. One possibility is a synthesis of the two views. Waldman (1994), for example, proposes a theory of work performance in terms of both 'person factors' (knowledge, skills and attitudes, and individual motivation) and 'system factors' (including the work system constraints and demands). Aside from determining work performance, these two sets of factors are said to interact, for example with the work system impacting on skills development and motivation and with people also influencing the design of the system. Thus HR policies can be adapted to underpin the development of the necessary motivation, attitudes and competencies required for TQM (Wilkinson et al. 1998).

HR Policies and Practices

If the soft side of QM is accorded importance, then it is clear that a re-examination of existing HR policies is required. The 'quality of people' is vital, with quality within the HRM model seen broadly, incorporating quality of work, quality of workforce (including investment in training and development) and quality of treatment of the workforce by management (Guest 1987).

There are a number of critical HR issues:

- Employee involvement
- Organizational culture
- Training and education
- Selection
- Appraisal
- Pay
- Employee well-being
- Industrial relations
- Employment security

Employee Involvement

A number of the QM gurus advocate employee involvement in decision-making – see, in particular, Deming (1982), Feigenbaum (1983) and Ishikawa (1985) – and this is reflected in the standard texts. Oakland (1989) writes of 'total involvement':

> Everyone in the organization from top to bottom, from offices to technical service, from headquarters to local sites must be involved. People are the source of ideas and innovation and their expertise, experience, knowledge and co-operation have to be harnessed to get these ideas implemented.

Employee involvement is thus fundamental to QM ideas, in terms of both an educational process and more direct involvement in quality issues and how they relate to the job (Wilkinson 2001). Three separate but integrated elements make up the participative structure of QM.

First is the educative process at corporate level. This may be through a number of vehicles: papers, videos, briefing, 'walking the talk', etc. For example, at a fibres plant, workers attended workshops which provided them with some insight into what the manufacturers made out of the product they were given. Some manufacturing organizations have posters and signs on the shop floor stressing that 'Customers make paydays possible' and 'The next person you pass your work to is your customer', etc. However, some of these initiatives can backfire: Ben Hamper's account (1992) of his time at General Motors (GM) includes a story of how, as part of the quality initiative, a man dressed up as a cat – 'Howie Makem' – to patrol the shop floor and urge workers to produce better quality. At GM, workers found it all too easy to see the gap between the rhetoric and the reality, and, indeed, there were suggestions that if there was a quality cat there should also be a quantity cat since this was the other god that GM worshipped.

Second, there may be changes in the organization of work. This may involve organizing work units into cells, the creation of semi-autonomous work groups, or some less fundamental restructuring, which involves the removal of inspectors, with workers taking responsibility for QA.

Third, committees, QCs, quality improvement or action teams which may be established on an ad hoc basis to solve particular problems or may be more permanent fixtures. These may be either based on the work group or cross-functional in structure. Like QCs, however, QM tends to offer involvement in a rather limited way since it is largely confined to the operational process. It does not then extend involvement over wider issues of corporate strategy (Wilkinson et al. 1997).

An emphasis on teamwork pervades the quality literature. According to Hill (1991a, 1991b), teamwork offers real opportunities to bring about more collegial relationships within the managerial group, a decline in resistance to change due to sectional interests and less organizational rigidity. Oakland (1989) argues that:

> much of what has been taught previously in management has led to a culture in the west of independence, with little sharing of ideas and information. Knowledge is very much like organic manure, if it is spread around, it will fertilize and encourage growth, if it is kept covered, it will eventually fester and rot.

He further argues that teamwork devoted to quality improvement changes independence to interdependence through improved communications, trust, and the free exchange of ideas, knowledge, and information.

Juran's (1988) notion of self-control suggests that responsibility for quality be assigned to those who control the quality of what they do. This is said to improve motivation by encouraging employees to find satisfaction in their own work. Furthermore, the supervisory climate is meant to support this with fear of failure discouraged in favour of a search for failure. As Deming has argued, a drive through fear is counter-productive. Individuals blamed for mistakes are unlikely to search for them to put them right, and thus key systems failures will not be addressed. QM theory suggests that individuals and teams should have the power to improve their quality and this must represent real authority and the ability to regulate what they do. They must not take on responsibility for something that is beyond their control. Semi-autonomous work groups can help create the conditions for self-control, as advocated by Juran. The concept of self-regulation of task activities has not only been demonstrated to sustain effort but, more importantly, has contributed to self-development. This may itself reduce employees' dependence on tasks assigned by superiors (Robertson et al. 1992). Thus, not only might the utilization of HR in this way assist in the implementation of QM, but it should also develop the self-confidence and competence of those involved. Research evidence from writers outside the quality field (e.g. Hackman and Oldman 1976) suggests that these attributes are key causal variables in determining levels of performance, motivation and job satisfaction.

Robertson et al. (1992) argue that, given the right setting, employees will generally welcome the opportunity to contribute to quality improvement. However, in creating the right 'setting' for these activities, a number of principles are important (French and Caplan 1973).

- The change process must not be used as a manipulative tool, e.g. employees' advice is sought but subsequently ignored.
- The decisions to be made should not be seen as trivial because this may undermine the motivation of those involved.
- The activities undertaken must be relevant to both the needs of workers and the quality improvement process.
- Workers involved must have the authority to implement any decisions made (Robertson et al. 1992).

Participative decision-'making' is more likely to be accepted by those affected by it, and it is associated with higher satisfaction and may also lead to higher-quality decisions (Bass 1990).

Teamworking, at its best, involves employees being willing to undertake a range of tasks, irrespective of job title, so as to meet customer requirements. There may be an absence of formal job descriptions and *all* employees (especially managerial staff) are prepared to be flexible when needed. This is sometimes referred to as 'working beyond contract' or a 'can do' state of mind. It is exemplified by the idea that workers have two jobs; one is to do their designated task, the other is to search for continuous improvements and changes (Morton 1994). In research undertaken by one of the authors, an organization was visited where cell-based teamworking had been developed to the extent that it was viewed as the standard way of working, with the teams having a great deal of autonomy, largely controlling task allocation, monitoring of attendance, health and safety issues and, to a lesser extent, the flow of production. The teams were responsible for choosing the areas to measure (within certain guidelines) and setting their own year-on-year improvement targets. Some of the more advanced teams also had responsibility for the recruitment and training of temporary staff as well as controlling overtime levels (Godfrey et al. 1998). But there may be potential contradictions between increased employee influence over management decision-making and the limited impact of employee involvement on underlying organizational structures (Marchington and Wilkinson 2000).

Finally, middle management need to be given more attention: QM has implications which can affect the organization's traditional power culture because it is about empowering people to improve systems (thus bottom-up), but this may be unsettling. In many of the UK organizations we have researched, it is clear that managers are unwilling to relinquish power. Clearly, QM is likely to require new propensities, attitudes and abilities. Bradley and Hill (1987) have argued that the burdens involved in operating participative management are usually ignored by its advocates so that, while the language of teamwork may be widespread, the reality is that, in practice, it can be little more than exhortation. As Schuler and Harris (1992) point out, 'If middle managers were not included in designing the quality improvement programme in the first place, and if they are neither trained adequately nor offered sufficient incentive to change, they can be expected to resist the change process.' Placing responsibility for implementing QM in the hands of those whose future is threatened by QM is likely to shape the manner and enthusiasm with which they perform, and is clearly a major issue. The concerns of supervisors have been well documented. Fears of job security, job definition and additional workloads may mean the withholding of support and consequent damage to quality initiative (Klein 1984; Marchington and Wilkinson 2000).

Organizational Culture

Williams et al. (1993) state the case thus:

> Culture influences what the executive group attends to, how it interprets the information and the responses it makes to changes in the external environment. Culture is a significant contributor to strategy analysis and the development of strategy. Since culture influences what other members of the organization attend to, how they interpret this information and react, it is a significant determinant of the success of strategic implementation. Culture influences the ability of the organization both to conceive and to implement a new strategy.

In the long term, there is a necessity for the introduction of both quality systems and a quality culture to facilitate the quality process. A quality culture has been defined as 'a culture that nurtures high-trust social relationships and respect for individuals, a shared sense of membership of the organization, and a belief that continuous improvement is for the common good' (Hill 1991a). Quality management implies an open management style, with a devolution of responsibility. The aim is to develop a 'quality culture', whereby everyone in the organization shares a commitment to continuous improvement aimed at customer satisfaction.

Much of the academic literature emphasizes the difficulties in changing organizational culture, and recent years have seen a debate on the issue of 'Can culture be managed?' (Salaman 2001; Hope and Muhlemann 2001; Grugulis and Wilkinson 2002). Schein (1985), for example, sees culture as very deep-seated, consisting of three levels. First, 'artifacts and creations' are the visible manifestation of an organization's culture. This refers to the visible environment and behaviour of people in the organization, including such things as the layout of offices (open-plan or closed doors?), dress norms, and the way in which people in the organization tend to express and deal with disagreements. On the second level, we can identify the 'values' of an organization: views on what 'ought' to be, and how things 'should be done here'. Such values often emerge early in the life of an organization, or when it faces a novel challenge, and will gain acceptance and be incorporated into the culture of the organization to the extent that they provide workable solutions to the problems which the organization faces. Gradually, certain core values increasingly come to be taken for granted by members of the organization, and are transformed into 'basic underlying assumptions'; this is the third level of culture, which operates at the pre-conscious level. Schein's (1985) account thus underlines the complex nature of organizational culture, and counsels against the view that it is something which can easily be manipulated by management.

Williams et al. (1993) note that attempts to manage culture are likely to be more successful where change is preceded by some sort of 'precipitating crisis', such as a market slump, new competition, privatization, or financial problems. This helps to convince people of the need for change. Such developments are also often associated with a change in the leadership of the organization, introducing fresh ideas and often acting as the catalyst and champion of change. Schein (1985) appears to be in agreement with this, seeing structure, systems and procedures as significant but secondary mechanisms of change, with leadership and education, along with 'the deployment of organizational rewards and punishments', as the key levers of change.

Thus cultural change, in practice, is problematic. The corporate culture of the organization and existing ways of doing things might be too strong for QM. Indeed, existing ways of doing things constitute the main barriers to QM's successful adoption in the first place. Thus, it may be that rather than viewing QM as a process for changing organizations, conversely organizations must change to accommodate QM (Wilkinson and Witcher 1993)!

Training and Education

Training plays a particularly important role in a QM environment for several reasons, including communicating the vision of QM, training in QM tools and training in job skills (Brown 1993). Introducing QM requires awareness training to help develop appropriate attitudes and values relating to quality and the skills and techniques of quality improvement, including teamwork. Most large organizations have found that training tends to become more focused in a quality context. Modularized programmes which identify the various types of training which each employee will be given are generally developed. Training programmes used by award-winning companies usually incorporate:

- *Quality concepts*: continuous improvement, awareness of quality (for new employees), understanding quality management.
- *Quality techniques*: quality measurement, quality tools, problem-solving, statistical process control (SPC), process control.
- *Teamwork*: raising the level of interpersonal skills, communication, getting more out of teamwork (how do teams work?), team member/leader training.

Within companies there are also programmes available to develop other skills, such as computer training, negotiating skills, English language, etc. Many organizations are putting effort into effective leadership development programmes in quality-focused organizations.

Education in numeracy and literacy are also often overlooked in efforts to redesign jobs and run improvement teams. Companies with multi-lingual workforces tend to put considerable effort into English or other relevant language courses;

otherwise participating in a team can prove to be rather meaningless for non-English-speakers. Some organizations provide company-sponsored English language courses for their employees.

Training is another activity that most Western managements view as a cost rather than an investment (Dale et al. 1994). However, as QM proponents have pointed out, training of managers and employees is paramount if QM is to succeed, as without a quality-versed workforce, most improvement efforts, even if embarked on, will be short-lived: especially for the managerial level, training can help overcome fears of employee empowerment, as well as offer managers the opportunity to develop their ability to be involved in management decisions. Besides the basic QM understanding or awareness courses, there should also be a balance of the hard technical skills (such as problem-solving tools) and the soft skills related to dealing with human resources and leadership. However, much to the detriment of QM, training is usually conducted in a vacuum, with little thought being given to how the training ought to be followed up and reinforced in daily activities (Dale et al. 1997). To counter such criticisms, it is argued that companies therefore also have to be more conscious of marrying the formal training programmes and the cultural change introduced by QM initiatives.

Introducing QM can also highlight inadequacies in existing training programmes, or simply the lack of them, illustrating the significance of Deming's point 6 (Deming 1982) – institute training on the job. One manufacturer discovered that introducing QM required its employees to have a greater understanding of their job and of the equipment which they were using in order to consider improvement opportunities through QM. They developed an induction programme which included job roles, people, machinery and safety. Induction programmes take on an increased import-ance in both quality awareness-raising and job-specific skills. Apart from including QM/quality in their induction programmes, employers usually give more attention to other information concerning job roles, health and safety, and so on.

Commitment to learning seeks to ensure continuing training and development for all employees. It demonstrates employer willingness to encourage and facilitate employee development rather than just provide specific training to cover short-term crises. Different types of measure can be employed, ranging from fully fledged 'learning companies' through to employment development assistance programmes, and task-based and interpersonal skills training. One large Australian public utility established a joint development agreement with the unions which provided scope for continuous learning. This learning encompassed skill enhancement, competency training and both on- and off-the-job learning opportunities.

Selection

Recruiting high-quality, committed and appropriate staff to the organization is central to the achievement of quality. Competencies often sought at the selection stage include trainability, flexibility, commitment, drive and initiative. Recruitment methods need to attract a pool of high-quality candidates, with a comprehensive induction programme representing the final stage of successful selection. The development and maintenance of the desired culture requires that the new recruits are open to working in that culture. Japanese implants have been noted for the time and effort they take to screen potential employees, often for attitudes as much as for the appropriate skills; this recognizes that attitudes are deep-rooted and difficult to change in the short term (Marchington and Wilkinson 2002).

One Australian vehicle manufacturer uses an extensive selection process for screening new employees and identifying those who are considered the most suitable for the quality culture in the company. A list of factors which are considered to be important was developed by the HR division and includes: teamwork, problem identification, problem solution, work standards, adaptability, initiative, job fit, motivation, communication, production proficiency, and practical learning. Various techniques are used during the recruitment process to assess a potential candidate's strength on each of these, including aptitude tests and assessment centres which incorporate group exercises. New applicants are subjected to about seven hours' testing and interviews before a job offer is made, with only one in four applicants being successful. Beneficial outcomes reported include hiring manufacturing employees who can read and write in English and can articulate views which are seen as fundamental to participating in teams and process improvement activities. Initial analysis has found participation in improvement activities to be substantially higher, along with greater participation in training, with better results for the new recruits.

Modified recruitment and selection criteria are particularly important for managers and supervisors in order to reinforce a participative style of leadership where communication and general people management skills are more or just as important as pure technical skills. In some Australian quality-focused companies, recruitment and selection focuses just as much on a person's values, customer focus and people interaction attributes as on their competencies and technical skills. For managerial positions the emphasis is on management through people skills and on teamwork. They have started to use some tests to measure such attributes, and to look at work methods which are used rather than simply the results which they have achieved. In one case, a recently appointed head of accounting in a large public sector organization was not a qualified accountant but someone who had team and process improvement skills which were regarded as more important than technical skills for this senior management post.

Another method of reinforcing organizational cultures in terms of demonstrating what's important is to build teamwork and process improvement activities into job descriptions and criteria for promotion. Some organizations have, for example, altered their job descriptions for supervisory staff to emphasize team and people skills as equal to technical competence. Job descriptions have been developed by a number of organizations which include a proportion of time allocated to improvement activities and teamwork. Organizations which have been certified to ISO9000 generally find that they need to include quality activities in job descriptions.

Appraisal

The traditional performance appraisal process is heavily criticized by some of the quality gurus, especially Deming, who describes it as one of the 'deadly diseases' of Western management. According to Deming (1982), performance appraisal produces short-term performance, builds fear, demolishes teamwork and nourishes rivalry and politics, none of which enhances quality improvement.

Others argue that performance appraisal has a key role to play as a primary tool to communicate to managers whether quality standards are being met. Furthermore, under

QM, the customer (internal or external) is regarded as supreme; it thus seems a logical step to include customer evaluation of managerial performance in their overall appraisal. However, it seems few organizations which have adopted QM do this formally for either internal or external customers, although there is a growing use of 'mystery shoppers', whereby an individual, either a company employee or someone contracted in, poses as a customer, monitors, and reports on their experience to senior managers. There are some examples of organizations using internal customers, often a manager's subordinates, to evaluate their manager's commitment to QM. There are difficulties here, though, with evidence from the USA that managers are using their own survey data of customer satisfaction with their unit's performance to verify and, if necessary, challenge the surveys and ratings of senior managers (Redman 2001).

With the recent trend towards a focus on performance management, many organizations have strong and explicit linkages between employee and managerial performance and the company business plan and vision and values. This requires managers and employees to outline their annual performance plans, which must be linked directly to the organization's strategic plan. This shift from reliance on output to an input–output link means that performance and development reviews now focus on what you set out to do, what you achieved, how was it done and what you learnt as a result, and is more in tune with the notion of a learning orientation.

In a service organization, managerial performance is assessed by examining three areas, namely business performance, HRM effectiveness, and leadership in deploying and practising leadership through quality. These became generic areas for all management reviews and succession planning. Possible ratings given to managers are: role model, adequate, and needs work, with the last of these being a bar to promotion. In another company values relating to quality have been made more behavioural and are built in to the performance management system for managerial employees. Building and instilling pride in the team, motivating others to achieve common objectives, and communication are important attributes for managers.

In one case, team performance is appraised. The team performance recognition system is designed to provide an incentive for improving team operation and not simply focusing on the results which teams produce. It illustrates how performance can be measured on a team basis. Some of the criteria for assessment include: goals and objectives, leadership, communication, meeting format, and use of the continuous improvement steps.

Appraising performance for promotion purposes is another area where organizations with quality management can make modifications. Factors such as facilitating teamwork, communication skills, etc. rather than the ability to meet set targets can be used as criteria for promotion. Some organizations use 360° feedback processes for managerial and supervisory performance management (Redman 2001).

Pay

A key element in the HRM cycle is to retain and motivate employees through the rewards system. The retention of high-quality employees will require an innovative approach to rewards, particularly in competitive labour markets. Single-status terms and conditions can help to break down 'us and them' attitudes and promote a sense of shared responsibility for continuous improvement, while incentives may also have a role to play. However, incentive pay has been a controversial issue in the quality management literature. There is general agreement that output-related payment-by-results systems can undermine employee commitment to quality, but some of the quality gurus have gone further. Deming (1986) is strongly opposed to attempts to underpin quality improvement with pay incentives, and argues that performance appraisal and management by objectives (MBO) are inconsistent with the kinds of behaviours necessary for continuous improvement. Although they are popular among employees, some of the QM gurus have argued that the key to the development of the quality culture is the provision of recognition rather than reward, and have suggested the use of award schemes as a way of recognizing outstanding performance or achievements. Such schemes may involve either tokens or prizes of significant financial value, but in either case the aim is to provide recognition.

Work improvements that lead to less stressful jobs are seen as rewarding in themselves. Such writers (e.g. Deming 1986) also believe that rewards, especially those of a monetary nature, can undermine teamwork. For example, when companies come up with schemes for paying for employees' suggestions, employees may seek their own self-interest and capitalize on this new scheme, instead of volunteering to collaborate with peers in team-oriented activities. Besides dampening the enthusiasm for teamwork, these rewards can also place a ceiling on continuous improvement as employees are less motivated to try harder once their quotas have been reached. Conversely, organizations that reward managers on the number of teams or quality circles operating in their departments may find that the role of the individual employee in problem-solving may become overshadowed, as there is a constant push by managers to increase the participation rate of employees in teams; in such circumstances, the 'quality' from individuals' contributions becomes eclipsed by the 'quantity' of teams formed.

Others have questioned this view, suggesting that pay and appraisal may be used as part of the implementation of QM, provided that management realize that incentives alone are unlikely to be sufficient to build the quality culture. Furthermore, employers could be well advised to link pay and quality. There may be an expectation amongst employees that they should receive increased pay in return for taking on greater responsibility for quality, and that they should share directly in the financial benefits of quality improvement (Drummond and Chell 1992; Yong and Wilkinson 2001). Where this is not forthcoming, there may be a risk of employees becoming disillusioned with QM. One US commentator has suggested that quality management programmes often 'run out of steam' three to five years on, as employees begin to lose interest in token rewards and praise amid a growing expectation that they are due a share of the financial benefits of their quality improvement efforts (Walker 1992; Snape et al. 1996).

Clearly, this is a controversial area, and the implementation of QM is likely to involve a search for new forms of reward. Developments such as group-based incentives, aimed at encouraging teamwork, and skills-based pay, aimed at encouraging individuals to broaden their skills, are likely to be consistent with QM, and may provide a complement or even a substitute for more traditional types of incentive (Bowen and Lawler 1992: 37–8). Some companies have linked a bonus to customer service or quality. Many large Australian companies have also used enterprise industrial relations agreements to link pay with quality performance. The link is reinforced through the performance management process where individual employees and managers align their own plans with departmental and organizational strategies.

According to Snape et al. (1996), pay incentives cannot be used as a 'stand-alone issue'; instead financial incentives should be used sensitively as part of a broader QM implementation strategy involving leadership, training, communications, and a review of human resource practices, such that employees' awareness of key improvement areas and quality issues is enhanced. To address the problem of compensation systems being counter-productive in terms of teamwork and continuous improvement, one trend amongst Australian quality-driven companies is the movement away from hourly pay rates towards annual salaries for operations and process employees. Some manufacturing and process-type companies have found that continuous improvement activities usually result in fewer problems and breakdowns so that employees on hourly rates often experience pay reductions as less overtime is available. Ultimately, employees begin to question the benefits of quality improvement if they are personally financially disadvantaged. The movement to enterprise agreements in Australia over the past decade has also promoted gainsharing and profit-sharing schemes which addresses the issue of how any monetary benefits resulting from quality improvements might be shared.

The use of bonus schemes is quite common in the Australian Quality Award (AQA)-winning companies. A service company uses bonus schemes in both the sales/service area and the production area. In the sales/service area bonuses are based on (among other things) customer retention. Other bonuses are based on team performance. In the production area the bonus is based on workplace teamwork attendance. A manufacturing company developed a bonus system because employees felt that they were not rewarded fairly for the extra effort put into quality improvements. There is now a bonus system that covers all the employees and is based on bottom-line profit, and there are plans to add warranty savings to the bonus (a total failure cost incentive) and maybe health-related targets. This is partly done because performance improvements are exponential (that is, big gains in the beginning, smaller gains later on). For middle and senior management there is also a bonus tied to non-financial objectives.

Employee Well-Being

The notion of employees being internal customers is a core principle of quality management. Their welfare and satisfaction has considerable impact on the quality culture, so keeping track of this through measurement is seen as equally important as measuring external customer satisfaction. This is included as a criterion in national quality award models such as the AQA, and EFQM.

Many of the AQA-winning companies use as a direct measure of employee satisfaction an attitude/satisfaction survey conducted on either an annual or six-monthly basis. Indirect measures of employee satisfaction being used include staff turnover, absenteeism and freedom from industrial disputes. Usually the results of the surveys are communicated to the employees, and often departmental managers may be required to discuss the findings with their employees in order to develop strategies to deal with problems, should there be any. Results may also be linked to performance reviews for managers. In other cases, these survey findings provide improvement opportunities for teams.

Other activities, quite common in AQA-winning companies, for improving well-being and morale of employees are sponsoring sporting groups, recognizing long-term membership of the company, supporting social gatherings, on-site medical facilities, rehabilitation consultants, banking facilities, company-subsidized canteens, and free pick-up of employees at train stations by bus. Many Australian companies have a multicultural workforce. This can lead to communication problems as these employees do not always speak English, so almost all the award-winning companies have an English as a second language course in place. Besides having an English-language course, Bilcon engineering and Ford (Australia) translate key documents into foreign languages.

Labour turnover

A fluid workforce makes change management initiatives like QM difficult to develop successfully. Turnover of employees disturbs the organizational routine of firms. These routines within an organization are the basis of what Cole (1993) refers to as 'organizational memory', which when disrupted has an adverse effect on quality improvement:

> The memories of individual organizational members are a primary repository of an organization's operational knowledge and trust. When an individual leaves a job or an organization, some of this knowledge may be replaced through documentation and through supervisors and co-workers who have similar knowledge . . . [but] it is [also] often the case that the memory of a single organizational member may be the sole storage point of knowledge that is idiosyncratic and critical for the organization. It is not easy to document or share the sales representative's knowledge of a major customer's specific preference with regard to quality, cost, and delivery trade-offs. (Cole 1993)

While a documented manual can serve a company well in the light of labour turnover, it needs to be said that documentation is of limited use when the jobs are demanding or fast-paced; in such circumstances, the written rules and records would not supply all the correct information or be accessed quickly enough (Nelson and Winter 1982). Special non-routine situations are difficult to meet except by long-term employees, as they require 'skills based on accumulated experience of unusual patterns and trust relationships and a knowledge of the surrounding factors (equipment, fellow employees, suppliers, and customers)' (Cole 1993). Employees build up trust with their customers over time, and this bond between employees and customers cannot be replicated in some documented manual or be easily passed on to the new recruits once employees leave the company. A large turnover problem subsequently also affects the morale of the remaining employees as they end up shouldering the interim responsibilities of the employees that have left the company. Managerial job-hopping and high turnover rates can affect teamwork and generally undermine organizational stability.

Although turnover is seen as a greater threat to quality in small organizations (as they have fewer resources to carry out massive documentation) and those that are at the leading edge of technology (here people don't document as much as the technology is changing so fast) (Cole 1993), this apprehension is also very acute in environments where there is a scarcity of labour. For example, in research on QM in Singapore, employees leave their jobs in search of better pay, working conditions, and greater job satisfaction creating a discontinuation in an organization's QM efforts and its daily working routine (Yong and Wilkinson 2001). While training can be used to alleviate the problems of turnover in the case of Singapore, there is an inverse relationship to this turnover–training linkage. As a result of the high turnover problem, Singapore employers are less willing to spend money and effort to train their employees, for fear that, once skilled, these employees will be tempted away by other employers who offer better pay, working conditions, welfare benefits, or career prospects. This training deficit is inevitably detrimental to the quality improvement efforts of organizations.

Industrial Relations

QM seems to require widespread organizational changes and a re-examination of production/operations methods and working practices, and this has implications for industrial relations. However, the whole question of the problems faced in implementing QM at a working level is neglected by the literature, and there is little systematic discussion of the conditions necessary for such an approach to be successful. Indeed, the quote from Oakland (1989: 5) seems to imply implementation is unproblematic for management, and unitarism – a perspective based on assumptions that the organization comprises a group of people with a single set of values and loyalty and with management's 'right to manage' seen as rational and legitimate – is an underlying theme. Implementation is seen as a matter of motivation, with the correct attitudes being instilled by simple training programmes and education. Possible conflicts of interest are not addressed.

These issues are ignored in most texts on QM – Oakland's (1989, 1993) standard work does not mention trade unions at all – and are not understood by many organizations. However, unions are likely to be a countervailing source of power and loyalty. Moreover, while the literature suggests that persuading workers to take responsibility for quality and improvement and adjusting traditional job roles requires simply a dose of motivation and training, these are areas which may involve issues of job control and working practices and possibly monetary issues as well. These are more fundamental issues than the usual 'teething problems' of the management of change because of fear of the unknown.

To what extent have trade unions resisted the implementation of TQM? In some cases, union representatives have taken the view that the introduction of TQM is a management issue which does not directly concern the unions (Dawson 1994; McCabe 1999; Wilkinson et al. 1992), but as TQM is implemented and the organizational and industrial relations implications become clearer, union representatives can be expected to become increasingly concerned. Unions may fear that such developments threaten to marginalize their role in the workplace by establishing rival channels of communication, and emphasizing the individual and small group over collective concerns (Marchington et al. 2001).

However, unions are not necessarily opposed to TQM. In recent years there have been suggestions that management and unions can engage in a co-operative partnership in designing and implementing organizational change, and a report from the Involvement and Participation Association, endorsed by senior managers and union leaders, also urges a partnership at workplace level (Sparrow and Marchington 1998). Such views presumably envisage a form of enterprise unionism committed to the enhancement of productivity and quality, based on a firm acceptance of the common interests of management and employees. How widespread such a model can become depends as much on the precise nature of organizational changes and their handling by management, as on national union policy.

Workers' reactions to TQM are complex. While QM may be seen as facilitating a greater say in the way they work and the ability to influence their work environments, it may also be seen as increased responsibility and therefore pressure. Furthermore, it is one thing for workers to be encouraged to come up with ideas, but it is entirely another that they should be expected to do so (Dawson and Webb 1988). The failure of QM is usually attributed in the literature to either technical difficulties – e.g. a lack of training or inadequate resource support – or the fact that it is not fully integrated into management strategy and practice. However, there may be more fundamental problems relating to the different conceptions of management and the workforce, with management seeing QM as a set of 'neutral' techniques and tools like any other while, as Deming (1986) points out, the system is often seen as repressive by workers. While workers may find it difficult to challenge the logic of management action in principle, they almost invariably interpret, evaluate and react towards managerial initiatives and, in their own way, 'audit' their introduction and operation. As Glover (2000) noted, workers were not compliant, docile consumers of TQM. They observed management actions with a sceptical eye and were not surprised when management failed to deliver. Where management were successful in meeting the expectations of TQM, workers responded positively.

Despite these challenges there are examples of Australian companies who have developed enterprise-based industrial relations agreements through union–management negotiations, and such agreements are used in tangible ways to reinforce QM. During the late 1990s a number of quality-focused companies developed agreements which explicitly provided for periodic salary increases based on movements in specific indicators which included productivity but also customer satisfaction and quality measures. One example incorporates three performance indicators, namely conversion costs per tonne, complaint costs per tonne and frequency of complaints. The agreement also provides a bonus pay system for linking improvements in these performance indicators with pay. Employee involvement through process improvement teams provides the vehicle for continuous improvement. In subsequent agreements, these have been refined to link with managerial and employee performance management processes.

A number of enterprise agreements which incorporate QM have been negotiated in the Australian public sector. These typically include measures aimed at reducing demarcation problems and improving labour flexibility to permit productivity improvements. This requires specification of measures to assess productivity gains and how these will be distributed. Other examples show negotiated enterprise deals which actively promote quality improvement. Some agreements include productivity and payment measures; some incorporate QM as part of a total package which includes workplace and job redesign, flexibility and productivity improvements. QM offers a mechanism for achieving productivity and efficiency gains to deliver pay increases.

Union officials can act as drivers both as parties to enterprise agreements and in actively promoting involvement to their members. In some instances unions can become so supportive of QM that they drive the process with the same vigour as management. A mining company, faced with five unions at one of its mineral-processing plants, gave the opportunity for all unions to be involved in planning and implementing changes which included QM. Only one union, representing about half of the 1,200 employees (mainly process workers) chose to be actively involved from the outset. The second largest, representing tradespeople, oscillated between being and not being involved. Over time, the proactive union was able to secure improved benefits for its members under a workplace agreement. While the non-participation of three unions hindered some process improvement teams since the members weren't allowed to participate, it didn't create too many problems in most areas of the operation of the plant.

Employment Security

This is one way in which employers can demonstrate to employees that they really are their 'most important resource' and one which has come under intense pressure during the last decade of major organizational changes. Unlike some of the other 'best practices', this one has to be qualified slightly. It does not mean that employees can stay in the same job for life, nor does it prevent the dismissal of staff who fail to perform at the required level. Similarly, a major collapse in the market which necessitates reductions in the labour force should not be seen as undermining this principle. The principal point about this practice is that it asserts that job reductions will be avoided, wherever possible, and that employees should expect to maintain their employment with the organization. A key factor which facilitates the achievement of employment security is a well-devised and forward-looking system of HR planning and an understanding of how organizations may be structured to achieve flexibility. It is perhaps summed up best by the view that workers should not be treated as a variable cost, but rather viewed as a critical asset in the long-term viability and success of the organization (Marchington and Wilkinson 2002).

Integration

Most of the studies on best-practice HRM conclude that there needs to be horizontal integration (Marchington and Wilkinson 2002), i.e. the policies must be mutually reinforcing and not adapted on a 'pick and mix' basis. Indeed, Pfeffer (1994) argues that there needs to be an 'overarching philosophy' that 'provides a way of connecting the various individual practices into a coherent whole'. Without an overriding philosophy, policies are undermined and diluted (Godfrey and Wilkinson 1998). In research undertaken at UMIST, this was a typical view of employers:

- Employees are to be developed, informed and given greater responsibility.
- Management style should be open, friendly and participative.
- Teamworking, both cell-based and cross-functional, should be the normal way of working.
- The vision is of a committed and capable workforce, working in teams and requiring little in the way of direct external control. This common vision needs to be evident across all levels of management and, in particular, it must be shared by all senior managers.

The acceptance of such a common vision will predetermine many company activities and attitudes in the areas of QM and the management of HR. It results in an acceptance of the importance of the HR dimension of QM. The presence of an overall management vision influences both the HR practices implemented and the way in which they are implemented. Where this common vision is missing, managers often had difficulty describing the type of company culture they would like to see, and employees complained about inconsistencies in management approach and a lack of commitment to QM from senior management. Without this overall vision or strategy, there is a lack of direction in QM and HR policies, and they may both fail to link in to business strategy. Moreover, there is a lack of urgency in changing HR policies which conflict with QM, and business strategy decisions may be taken which conflict with the QM initiative.

However, simply referring to a common vision is insufficient, as there must also be understanding. In one organization, a manager complained that there had, in the past, been 'commitment without understanding'. There was a tendency for managers to say what they thought they should say without actually understanding the implications. This led to inconsistent management behaviour and actions that conflicted with espoused company values, e.g. putting extreme pressure on employees to increase production because they were falling behind target. This common vision can be reinforced by management training and the appraisal system. If the performance of managers is appraised solely on output and cost factors, then these will be deemed to be the most important aspects of management behaviour. At one site, a production manager was achieving high output figures through an autocratic management style with minimum employee involvement. His 'success' was rewarded with no direct challenge to the fact that his style failed to match the espoused management approach. The end result was that other managers were inclined to copy his style and the attempt to increase employee involvement and introduce teamworking at the site failed.

As well as having an overall vision, there also needs to be an infrastructure which links HRM, QM and business strategy. This is provided through the development of a strong policy deployment process which is designed to ensure the senior management policy plan is deployed to all levels of the organization, thus facilitating the management vision (Godfrey and Wilkinson 1998).

Issues of implementation require the involvement and ownership of middle managers. However, feelings of role ambiguity and insecurity have been reinforced by the events of the past two decades, during which many supervisors and middle managers have lost their jobs or found that their existing skills are irrelevant to organizational needs. Supervisors often doubt the sincerity of support from senior management, an anxiety that is fuelled as their own job security is lessened and they find little attempt to 'involve' them in management decisions. An important step in any change programme may well be to involve line managers in the process and give them increased responsibility and authority (Fenton O'Creevy 2001: 37).

Line managers and supervisors may also be suffering from work overload, conflicting requirements from senior management, and a lack of explicit rewards for undertaking the human resource aspects of their jobs. Like most staff, supervisors are being asked to take on extra duties, and are finding it difficult to squeeze more out of their working hours. Fenton O'Creevy (2001: 36) found that delayering and job loss put even greater pressures on line managers by reducing the time and energy available for implementing new initiatives. However, rather than seeing negative attitudes as the problem, and therefore regarding supervisors as scapegoats, Fenton O'Creevy (2001: 37) argues that it is management systems that are to blame. He questions whether or not reward and appraisal mechanisms are appropriate to encourage positive behaviours or if there is sufficient time left in the working day to devote to staff development. It is hardly surprising if line managers concentrate on the achievement of targets they know will be used to assess their performance at appraisal (Bach 2000). If meeting production deadlines or having zero defects has higher priority when they are appraised than the regularity of team briefings or opportunities for their staff to engage in self-development, then they are bound to focus on the former.

Converting strategy into practice is also difficult if there is a lack of training provided for line managers and supervisors. More worrying is the view that line managers and supervisors may not be sufficiently competent in interpersonal skills to cope with the responsibilities required to lead change programmes at workplace level (Cunningham and Hyman 1995; Marchington et al. 2001). Too often, it would appear, insufficient time is allocated to the training of first-line managers because senior managers are keen to implement new initiatives with a minimum of delay. This has been particularly apparent from our own studies of employee involvement over the years. Training in how to run a quality circle, for example, could consist of little more than a half-hour session on 'how not to communicate' followed by an amusing video illustrating how things went wrong elsewhere. Occasionally, a speaker may be invited from another organization to explain their approach and answer questions, but there is little attempt to give supervisors the chance to practise their skills (Marchington and Wilkinson 2002).

Based on research at UMIST funded by the EPSRC, an audit tool was developed to facilitate self-assessment of HR policies and practices. It follows the people management structure of the EFQM excellence model (see table 10.2). It is not intended to score criteria but to provide a basis for an informed discussion of organizational policy. These are the key concerns (Dale et al. 1998):

- Reducing 'them and us' barriers between managers and employees
- Increasing the commitment of employees
- Improving the performance of employees
- Dealing with incentives and rewards
- Increasing employee involvement

The emphasis on HR issues implies that the HR department should have an input. Recognition of the significance of HR issues in principle is, by itself, inadequate. In her classic work, Legge (1978) points out that:

> the personnel management considerations involved in production, marketing and finance decisions were not so much overruled as went by default. In other words, non specialists, while formally recognising the importance of effectively utilising human resources, lacking as they did the expertise to develop a systematic view of what this entailed in terms of personnel strategies and actions, in practice tended to underestimate the importance of the human resource variable in decision making on issues that were not explicitly personnel management.

Thus, Giles and Williams (1991) point out that personnel people have much to offer quality management. They are guardians of key processes such as selection, appraisal, training and reward systems, which go right to the heart of achieving strategic change. In research carried out for the Institute of Personnel Management it was suggested that there were five phases or areas of intervention (Marchington et al. 1993).

Table 10.2 An audit tool to facilitate self-assessment of HR policies and practices

	Reducing 'us and them' barriers	Increasing commitment	Improving performance	Rewards and incentives	Employee involvement
Section 1: Planning and improving HR					
1a Aligning HR and business strategy					
1b Employee surveys					
1c Single status and harmonization					
1d Rewards and employment security					
1e Innovative work organizations					
Section 2: Sustaining and developing capabilities					
2a Identifying and matching competencies					
2b Managing recruitment and career development					
2c Training plans					
2d Evaluating training					
2e Developing employees through work experience					
2f Developing team skills					
Section 3: Performance management					
3a Aligning targets					
3b Reviewing and updating targets					
3c Appraisals					
Section 4: Involving and empowering employees					
4a Encouraging participation					
4b In-house ceremonies					
4c Empowering people					
4d Recognition system supports involvement					
Section 5: Communications					
5a Identifying communication needs					
5b Sharing information					
5c Evaluating communication					
5d Effective communication structures					
Section 6: Caring for employees					
6a Health and safety and environmental issues					
6b Other benefits					
6c Social and cultural activities					
6d Employee facilities and services					

The first stage at which the personnel function may make a contribution is in the shaping of QM initiatives at the formulation or developmental phase, and the second area is at the implementation phase of the QM process. Having shaped and implemented a new QM initiative, the personnel function can play an effective part in attempting to maintain and reinforce its position within the organization. Interventions in the third area are designed to ensure that QM continues to attract a high profile and does not lose impetus. The fourth area in which the personnel function may be able to make a contribution to QM is at the review stage, either on a regular (perhaps annual or biennial) basis or as part of an ongoing procedure for evaluating progress. Fifth, and to some extent in conjunction with each of the above contributions, personnel functions can apply QM processes to a review of their own activities, along the lines of the review undertaken by the internal contractors analysed above.

It is not assumed that the more of these that are undertaken the better. Indeed, employing such a strategy might result in poorer performance because resources are spread too thinly or the function comes to be seen as the purveyor of the latest fads and fashions which are irrelevant for organizational needs. The key question must be: How can the function continually improve its contribution to quality management initiatives and organizational success?

Summary

QM comprises both hard production/operations-oriented and soft employee relations-oriented elements and, while QM proponents have tended to emphasize the 'hard' aspects of the theory, there is some attention paid to 'softer' issues.

Involvement and cultural issues present the greatest challenges or are dealt with in a somewhat cursory way, while increasing attention has been given to industrial relations and HR practices to reinforce the quality drive. Organizational restructuring, downsizing, outsourcing and other changes have placed more pressure on the HR department to maintain employee support for quality initiatives, yet this is often where workforce reductions take place. There needs to be both a general improvement of the HR variable, with employees seen as a resource to be developed rather than a cost to be controlled, and integration with QM within the organization. Until a closer alignment between the ideas and practices of QM and HRM takes place, it is unlikely that QM will achieve its aims.

These points should be considered:

- QM and HRM practices should and can be integrated to mutually reinforce quality efforts.
- Middle management and supervisory concerns should be addressed; they are key actors in the QM process.
- Culture is a complex concept and not easily manipulated. In attempting to change culture, senior management should utilize a wide array of 'tools'.
- The context of change should be considered. QM introduced in a climate of recession, and associated with job losses and intensification, is likely to be perceived in a negative way by employees.
- Issues of power and conflict need to be addressed rather than ignored or dealt with only when they openly obstruct the programme.
- The HR department has an important role to play in all these areas, and can make a contribution to QM at a number of phases.

References

Australian Quality Council Ltd (2001), *Australian Business Excellence Awards 2001: Application Guidelines*.

Bach, S. (2000), From performance appraisal to performance management. In S. Bach and K. Sisson (eds), *Personnel Management: A Comprehensive Guide to Theory and Practice*. Oxford: Blackwell.

Bass, B. (1990), *Bass & Stodghill's Handbook of Leadership: Theory, Research and Managerial Applications*. New York: Free Press.

Blackburn, R. and Rosen, B. (1993), Total quality and human resources management: lessons learned from Baldrige award-winning companies. *Academy of Management Executive*, 7, 49–65.

Bowen, D. E. and Lawler, E. E. (1992), Total quality-orientated human resource management. *Organizational Dynamics*, 20(4), 29–41.

Bradley, K. and Hill, S. (1987), Quality circles and managerial interests. *Industrial Relations*, 26 (Winter), 68–82.

Brown, A. (1993), TQM: implications for training. *Industrial and Commercial Training*, 25, 20–6.

Brown, A. (1995), Quality management: issues for human resource management. *Asia Pacific Journal of Human Resources*, 33(3), 117–29.

CIPD (1996), *The People Management Implications of Lean Ways of Working*. London: Chartered Institute of Personnel and Development.

Cole, R. (1993), Introduction to special issue on total quality management. *Californian Management Review*, 35(3), 7–11.

Collinson, M., Rees, C. and Edwards, P. (1997), *Involvement but No Empowerment: A Case Study Analysis of Quality Management*. London: DTI.

Coyle-Shapiro, J. C. (1993), The quality guru's working paper. Unpublished.

Crosby, P. B. (1979), *Quality is Free*. New York: McGraw Hill.

Cunningham, I. and Hyman, J. (1995), Transforming the HRM vision into reality: the role of line managers and supervisors in implementing change. *Employee Relations*, 17(8), 5–20.

Dale, B. G., Cooper, C. and Wilkinson, A. (1994), *Managing Quality and Human Resources*, 2nd edn. Oxford: Blackwell.

Dale, B. G., Cooper, C. and Wilkinson, A. (1997), *Managing Quality and Human Resources*, 3rd edn. Oxford: Blackwell.

Dale, B. G., Godfrey, G., Wilkinson, A. and Marchington, M. (1998), Aligning people with processes. *Measuring Business Excellence*, 2(2), 42–6.

Dale, B. G. and Plunkett, J. J. (eds) (1990), *Managing Quality*, 1st edn. Hemel Hempstead, Herts.: Phillip Allan.

Dawson, P. (1994), *Organizational Change: A Processual Approach*. London: Chapman.

Dawson, P. and Webb, J. (1988), New production arrangements: the totally flexible cage? *Work, Employment and Society*, 3, 221–38.

Deming, W. E. (1982), *Quality, Productivity and Competitive Position*. Cambridge, Mass.: MIT Press.

Deming, W. E. (1986), *Out of the Crisis*. Cambridge, Mass.: MIT Centre for Advanced Engineering Study.

Drummond, H. and Chell, E. (1992), Should organizations pay for quality? *Personnel Review*, 21(4), 3–11.

Feigenbaum, A. V. (1983), *Total Quality Control*, 3rd edn. New York: McGraw Hill.

Fenton O'Creevy, M. (2001), Employee involvement and the middle manager: saboteur or scapegoat? *Human Resource Management Journal*, 11(1), 24–40.

French, J. and Caplan, R. (1973), Organisational stress and individual strain. In A. J. Marrow (ed.), *The Failure of Success*. New York: AMACOM.

Giles, E. and Williams, R. (1991), Can the personnel department survive quality management? *Personnel Management*, April, 28–33.

Glover, L. (2000), Neither poison nor panacea: shopfloor responses to TQM. *Employee Relations,* 22(2), 142–5.

Godfrey, G. and Wilkinson, A. (1998), *Adopting Best Practice HRM in a TQM Context.* Working Paper, Manchester School of Management, UMIST.

Godfrey, G., Wilkinson, A., Marchington, M. and Dale, B. (1998), *Vision, Deployment and Practice: TQM and HRM in Manufacturing.* Quality Management Centre Occasional Paper, Manchester School of Management, UMIST.

Grugulis, I. and Wilkinson, A. (2002), British Airways: hype, hope and reality. *Long-Range Planning,* 35(2), 179–94.

Guest, D. (1987), HRM and industrial relations. *Journal of Management Studies,* 24(5), 503–22.

Hackman, R. and Oldman, G. (1976), Motivation through the design of work: test of a theory. *Organisational Behavioural and Human Performance,* 16(2), 250–79.

Hamper, B. (1992), *Rivethead.* London: Fourth Estate.

Hill, S. (1991a), How do you manage a flexible firm? The total quality model. *Work, Employment & Society,* December, 397–415.

Hill, S. (1991b), Why quality circles failed but total quality might succeed. *British Journal of Industrial Relations,* 29 December, 541–68.

Hill, S. (1992), People and quality. In K. Bradley (ed.), *People and Profits.* Aldershot, Hants.: Gower.

Hill, S. (1995), From quality circles to total quality management. In A. Wilkinson and H. Willmott (eds), *Making Quality Critical: Studies in Organizational Change.* London: Routledge.

Hill, S. and Wilkinson, A. (1995), In search of TQM. *Employee Relations,* 17(3), 8–25.

Hope, C. and Muhlemann, A. (2001), The impact of culture on best-practice production/operation management. *International Journal of Management Reviews,* 3(3), 199–217.

Ishikawa, K. (1985), *What is Total Quality Control? The Japanese Way,* trans. D. J. Lu. Englewood Cliffs, NJ: Prentice-Hall.

Juran, J. M. (ed.) (1988), *Quality Control Handbook.* New York: McGraw Hill.

Juran, J. M. (1989), *Juran on Leadership for Quality.* New York: Free Press.

Juran, J. M. (1991), Strategies for world class quality. *Quality Progress,* 24(3), 81–5.

Klein, R. (1984), Why supervisors resist employee involvement. *Harvard Business Review,* September–October, 87–95.

Legge, K. (1978), *Power Innovation and Problem Solving in Personnel Management.* New York: McGraw Hill.

Legge, K. (1994), *Human Resource Management: Rhetorics and Realities.* London: Macmillan.

Marchington, M. (1995), Fairy tales and magic wands: new employment practices in perspective. *Employee Relations,* 17(1), 51–66.

Marchington, M. and Wilkinson, A. (2000), Direct participation. In S. Bach and K. Sisson (eds), *Personnel Management.* Oxford: Blackwell.

Marchington, M. and Wilkinson, A. (2002), *People Management and Development: HRM in Action,* London: CIPD.

Marchington, M., Wilkinson, A., Ackers, P. and Dundon, T. (2001), *Management Choice and Employee Voice.* London: Chartered Institute of Personnel and Development.

Marchington, M., Wilkinson, A. and Dale, B. (1993), *The Case Study Report in Quality and the Human Resource Dimension.* London: Institute of Personnel Management.

Mayerson, D. and Martin, J. (1987), Cultural change: an integration of three different views. *Journal of Management Studies,* 24(6), 623–47.

McCabe, D. (1999), Total quality management: anti-union Trojan horse or management albatross? *Work, Employment and Society,* 13(4), 665–91.

Morton, C. (1994), *Becoming World Class.* London: Macmillan.

Nelson, R. and Winter, S. (1982), *An Evolutionary Theory of Economic Change,* Cambridge, Mass.: Belknap Press of Harvard University.

Oakland, J. S. (1989), *Total Quality Management*. London: Heinemann.

Oakland, J. S. (1993), *Total Quality Management: The Route to Improving Performance*, 2nd edn. London: Butterworth Heinemann.

Pfeffer, J. (1994), *Competitive Advantage through People*. New York: Free Press.

Piore, M. J. and Sabel, C. (1984), *The Second Industrial Divide*. New York: Basic Books.

Powell, T. C. (1995), Total quality management as competitive advantage: a review and empirical study. *Strategic Management Journal*, 16(1), 15–37.

Redman, T. (2001), Appraisal. In T. Redman and A. Wilkinson (eds), *Contemporary Human Resource Management*. Hemel Hempstead: Financial Times/Prentice Hall.

Robertson, I., Smith, M. and Cooper, M. (1992), *Motivation: Strategies, Theory and Practice*. London: Institute of Personnel Management.

Rosenfeld, R. and Wilson, D. (1999), *Managing Organizations*, 2nd edn. New York: McGraw Hill.

Salaman, G. (2001), Corporate culture. In J. Storey (ed.), *HRM: A Critical Text*, 2nd edn. London: Thomson Learning.

Schein, E. H. (1985), *Organisational Culture and Leadership*. Oxford: Jossey-Bass.

Schuler, R. and Harris, D. (1992), *Managing Quality: The Primer for Middle Managers*. New York, Mass.: Addison-Wesley.

Snape, E., Wilkinson, A., Marchington, M. and Redman, T. (1995), Managing human resources for TQM: possibilities and pitfalls. *Employee Relations*, 17(3), 42–51.

Snape, E., Wilkinson, A. and Redman, T. (1996), Cashing in on quality? Pay incentives and the quality culture. *Human Resource Management Journal*, 6(4), 5–17.

Sparrow, P. and Marchington, M. (1998), *HRM: The New Agenda*. London: Financial Times/Pitman.

Taguchi, G. (1986), *Introduction to Quality Engineering*. New York: Asian Productivity Organization.

Waldman, D. (1994), The contributions of total quality management to a theory of work performance. *Academy of Management Review*, 19(3), 511–36.

Walker, T. (1992), Creating quality improvement that lasts. *National Productivity Review*, Autumn, 473–8.

Walton, R. E. (1985), From control to commitment in the workplace. *Harvard Business Review*, 63 (March–April), 77–84.

Wilkinson, A. (1992), The other side of quality: soft issues and the human resource dimension. *Total Quality Management*, 3(3), 323–9.

Wilkinson, A. (2001), Empowerment. In T. Redman and A. Wilkinson (eds), *Contemporary Human Resource Management*. London: Financial Times/Prentice Hall.

Wilkinson, A. (2002), Total quality management. In T. Redman and A. Wilkinson, *The Informed Student Guide to HRM*. London: Thomson Learning.

Wilkinson, A., Allen, P. and Snape, E. (1991), TQM and the management of labour. *Employee Relations*, 13(1), 24–31.

Wilkinson, A., Godfrey, G. and Marchington, M. (1997), Bouquets, brickbats and blinkers: total quality management and employee involvement in practice. *Organization Studies*, 18(5), 799–819.

Wilkinson, A., Marchington, M., Ackers, P. and Goodman, J. (1992), Total quality management and employee involvement. *Human Resource Management Journal*, 2(4), 1–20.

Wilkinson, A., Marchington, M. and Dale, B. (1993), Enhancing the contribution of the human resource management function to quality improvement. *Quality Management Journal*, 2, 35–46.

Wilkinson, A., Redman, T., Snape, E. and Marchington, M. (1998), *Managing through TQM: Theory and Practice*. London: Macmillan.

Wilkinson, A. and Witcher, B. (1991), Fitness for use? Barriers to full TQM in the UK. *Management Decision*, 29(8), 46–51.

Wilkinson, A. and Witcher, B. (1993), Holistic total quality management must take account of political processes. *Total Quality Management*, 4(1), 47–56.

Williams, A., Dobson, P. and Walters, M. (1993), *Changing Culture*. London: Institute of Personnel Management.

Yong, J. and Wilkinson, A. (1999), The state of quality management: a review. *International Journal of Human Resource Management*, 10(1), 137–61.

Yong, J. and Wilkinson, A. (2001), In search of quality: the quality management experience in Singapore. *International Journal of Quality and Reliability Management*, 18(8), 81–3.

Yong, J. and Wilkinson, A. (2002), The long and winding road: the evolution of quality management. *Total Quality Management*, 13(1), 101–21.

chapter eleven

Managing Service Quality

B. R. Lewis

Introduction

Managing service quality is concerned with understanding what is meant by service quality, what its determinants are and how they may be measured, and identifying the potential shortfalls in service quality and how they can be recovered. Responsibility for quality service lies with operations, marketing, human resources and other management – working together within an organization.

Service quality issues have been of academic and practitioner interest, and to marketers in particular, for more than two decades. This results from the increasing importance of the services sector in both developed and developing economies – to embrace both public and private, profit and not-for-profit organizations. This includes industries such as financial services, health care, tourism, professional services, government, transport and communications – where the focus of business activity is on 'services' rather than 'products'.

Services are characterized as being different from products along a number of dimensions that have implications for the quality of service provided to customers.

- They are typically intangible: there is usually little or no tangible evidence to show once a service (e.g. investment advice, consultation with a doctor) has been performed.
- Secondly, the production and consumption of many services are simultaneous; the service may not be separable from the person of the seller, and the customer may be involved in the service performance (e.g. legal advice, hairdressing). Thus, the service process, including staff at the customer interface, becomes integral to service quality.
- Related to this is heterogeneity: variability often exists in services as a function of labour inputs and non-standardization of delivery, and so the use of quality standards in the conventional sense is more difficult.
- Many services cannot be stored to meet fluctuations in demand (e.g. a doctor's time, hotel rooms, purchase of shares in a privatization issue), so companies need to develop systems to manage supply and demand.

Further to this, as product and process quality and total quality management have become prime concerns in the manufacturing sector, is the acknowledgement that service is critical for all organizations. In the manufacturing sector, quality is related not only to the product itself but also to all aspects of its supply and delivery through the non-manufacturing functions and, often, after-sales use/service. Customer service and service quality are now a focus for any corporate or marketing strategy, and high levels of service are typically seen as a means for an organization to achieve competitive advantage. Consequently, it is clear that service quality concepts and frameworks developed for the services sector are applicable to all organizations, and that attention needs to be focused on products/services and their production and delivery, together with all those personnel who are instrumental to quality service.

In this chapter some comments will be made on the changing business environment, which has implications for service quality. The focus will then turn to defining service quality, measurement of service quality and the role of personnel in service delivery. The final sections are concerned with the service delivery process, the need to monitor service quality, and the development of service recovery strategies.

The Service Environment

Environmental trends that impact on service and quality issues relate to consumers' awareness and expectations, technological developments, and competitive elements.

Consumers, be they individuals, households or businesses, are more aware of the alternatives on offer (in relation to both services/products and provider organizations) and rising standards of service. Their expectations of service and quality are therefore elevated, and they are increasingly critical of the quality of service they experience. Expectations are what people feel a service/product should offer and what they relate to the company and its marketing mix, both the traditional elements (product, price, place and promotion), and the extended elements of physical evidence, process and people (see Booms and Bitner 1981). The physical environment includes tangible clues which might be essential (computers in a travel agency) or peripheral (decor, uniforms) to a service being bought. The service process is also critical: if systems are poor (e.g. breakdown of computer access to customer accounts in a bank) employees get blamed and consumers perceive poor-quality service. Personnel are also integral to the production of a service and, although their degree of contact with the customer varies, all have a contribution to make.

Advances in technology include: management information systems; marketing information systems to include customer databases; banks' automated clearing systems; tourism reservation/booking systems; and the development of the internet for accessing information and for shopping. These advances provide a major contribution to facilitate customer–company exchanges and increase levels of service. Increased mechanization and computerization, including the use of the internet, can depersonalize services, but also results in increases in speed, efficiency, accuracy and improved services. The other side of the coin is that depersonalized service could lead to reduced customer loyalty. But, generally, high-tech and high 'touch' go hand in hand, better personal service with enhanced technological efficiency. Technology can free employees' time and allow them to concentrate on the customer and enhance customer–staff interaction. Technology will not replace people in the provision of services.

In addition, the business environment is increasingly complex and competitive as a result of economic conditions, legislative activity (e.g. deregulation in financial services and air travel; the Citizens' Charter in the public sector in the UK) and increased customer choice and sophistication. Corporate reaction has been to emphasize operations and financial efficiency, and/or more focused product and market strategies. In addition, companies may also have an appreciation of the importance of customer service and quality, and the possible opportunities for attaining differentiation and achieving a competitive edge by providing superior service. Consequently, service quality is seen as a mechanism to achieve pre-eminence in the marketplace and the battle for market share, and so becomes a factor in strategic planning.

The benefits of good service

Without a focus on service quality, organizations will face problems and complaints from both employees and customers, and associated financial and other costs. Further, a proportion of dissatisfied customers will complain and tell others, generating adverse word-of-mouth publicity and possibly accusations of blame between personnel in the organization, and some will switch to competitors. With a service quality programme, an organization can expect a number of benefits relating to customers, employees and corporate image.

- The most often mentioned benefit is enhancing customer loyalty through satisfaction. Looking after present customers can generate repeat *and* increased business and may lead to the attraction of new customers from positive word-of-mouth communication. This is significantly more cost-effective than trying to attract new customers (see e.g. Rosenberg and Czepiel 1984).
- A number of organizations highlight the additional benefits of increased opportunities for cross-selling (see Lewis 1990). Comprehensive and up-to-date product knowledge and sales techniques among employees, combined with developing relationships and rapport with customers, enables staff to identify customer needs and suggest relevant products.
- In relation to employees, benefits may be seen in terms of increased job satisfaction and morale and commitment to the company, good employer–employee relationships, and increased staff loyalty, all of which contribute to reducing the rate of staff turnover and the associated costs of recruitment, selection and training activities. Further to this, Heskett et al. (1994) in their service–profit chain, model the impact of employee satisfaction and performance and employee loyalty and retention on customer satisfaction and retention and organizational success.
- In addition, good service quality enhances corporate image and may provide insulation from price competition; some customers will pay a premium for reliable service quality. Overall, successful service quality leads to reduced costs (of mistakes, operating, advertising and promotion) and increased productivity and sales, market share, profitability and business performance.

Defining Service Quality

At this point it is useful to introduce the concept of 'service encounters', which may also be referred to as 'moments of truth' or 'critical incidents' (see Albrecht and Zemke 1985; Czepiel et al. 1985). A service encounter is any direct interaction between a service provider and customers and may take varying forms. For example, a bank customer wishing to make an account enquiry may choose between an interaction with an automated teller machine, or over the internet, or with a bank employee by phone, letter, or face to face in a branch. Every time a customer comes into contact with any aspect of the bank and its employees he or she has an opportunity to form an impression of the bank and its service. Service encounters have a high 'impact' on consumers and the quality of the encounter is an essential element in the overall impression and evaluation of the quality of service experienced by the customer.

Service encounters also have an impact on employees in relation to their motivation, performance and job satisfaction, and their rewards. Consequently, all organizations need to manage their service encounters effectively for the benefit of customers and employees and for the achievement of corporate goals. This concept is developed further by Lewis and Entwistle (1990), who illustrate the variety of encounters which may prevail and which together impact on customer service and quality.

Further, one can witness the extent to which technology is impacting on and improving service encounters. Bitner et al. (2000) have examined the ability of technology to effectively customize service offerings, recover from service failure and spontaneously delight customers. They examine the infusion of technology as an enabler of both employees and customers in efforts to achieve these three goals. Service quality is variously defined, but essentially is to do with meeting customer needs and requirements and with how well the service level delivered matches customers' expectations. Expectations are desires/wants, i.e. what we feel a service provider should offer, and are formed on the basis of previous experience of a company and its marketing mix, awareness of competitors and word-of-mouth communication.

Consequently, service quality becomes a consumer judgement and results from comparisons by consumers of expectations of service with their perceptions of actual service delivered (see Gronroos 1984; Berry et al. 1985, 1988). If there is a shortfall, then a service quality gap exists which providers would wish to close. However, one needs to bear in mind that:

- Higher levels of performance lead to higher expectations.
- To find expectations greater than performance implies that perceived quality is less than satisfactory. This is not to say that service is of low quality: quality is relative to initial expectations – one of the issues to take into account when measuring service quality.

The concept of service quality gaps was developed from the extensive research of Berry and his colleagues (Parasuraman et al. 1985; Zeithaml et al. 1988). They defined service quality to be a function of the gap between consumers' expectations of a service and their perceptions of actual service delivery by an organization, and suggested that this gap is influenced by several other gaps which may occur in an organization.

Gap 1. Consumer expectations – management perceptions of consumer expectations
Managers' perceptions of customers' expectations may be different from actual customer needs and desires, i.e. managers do not necessarily know what customers (both internal and external) want and expect from a company. This may be remedied by market research activities (e.g. interviews, surveys, focus groups, complaint monitoring), and better communication between management and personnel throughout the organization.

Gap 2. Management perceptions of consumer expectations – service quality specifications actually set
Even if customer needs are known, they may not be translated into appropriate service specifications, due to a lack of resources, organizational constraints or absence of management commitment to a service culture and service quality. The need for management commitment and resources for service quality cannot be overstated.

Gap 3. Service quality specifications – actual service delivery
This is referred to as the service performance gap and occurs when the service that is delivered is different from management's specifications, owing to variations in the performance of personnel – employees not being able or willing to perform at a desired level. Solutions are central to human resources management and will be returned to.

Gap 4. Actual service delivery – external communications about the service
What is said about (the) service in external communications is different from the service that is delivered, i.e. advertising and promotion can influence consumers' expectations and perceptions of service. Therefore it is important not to promise more than can be delivered (or expectations increase and perceptions decrease), and not to fail to present relevant information. Success in this area requires appropriate and timely information/communication both internally and to external customers. Gaps 1 to 4 together contribute to consumers' expectations and perceptions of actual service (Gap 5). Organizations need to identify the gaps prevalent in their organization, determine the factors responsible for them, and develop appropriate solutions.

Dimensions of service

Dimensions of service quality are diverse and relate to both a basic service package and an augmented service offering (Gronroos 1987). A basic or core service product might be hotel accommodation, with associated services which are required to facilitate consumption of the core service (e.g. hotel reception and check-in), and supporting services which are not required but may enhance the service and differentiate it from competition (e.g. a restaurant in the hotel) (see also Lovelock et al. 1999: 290–311). The augmented service offering includes how the service is delivered (process), and the interaction between a company and its customers. The latter include: the accessibility of the service (e.g. number of hotel receptionists and their skills, hotel design); customer participation in the process (e.g. the need to fill in forms); and the interaction between employees and customers, systems and customers, and the physical environment and customers.

Dimensions of service (quality) have been research and discussed for 20 years. Gronroos (1984) referred to the technical (outcome) quality of service encounters, i.e. what is received by the customer, and the functional quality of the process, i.e. the way in which (the) service is delivered – typically, this includes the attitudes and behaviour, appearance and personality, service-mindedness, accessibility and approach-ability of customer-contact personnel. In addition, there exists the corporate image dimension of quality, which is the result of how customers perceive a company, and is built up by the technical and functional quality of its services. This model was later synthesized with one from manufacturing which incorporated design, production, delivery and relational dimensions of quality (see Gummesson and Gronroos 1987).

Other key contributors have been Lehtinen and Lehtinen (1982), who referred to process quality (as judged by consumers during a service) and output quality (judged after a service is performed). Edvardsson et al. (1989) presented four aspects of quality which affect customers' perceptions:

- *Technical quality*: to include skills of service personnel and the design of the service system.
- *Integrative quality*: the ease with which different portions of the service delivery system work together.
- *Functional quality*: to embrace all aspects of the manner in which the service is delivered to the customer, including style, environment and availability.
- *Outcome quality*: whether or not the actual service product meets both service standards or specifications and customer needs/expectations

An investigation in the manufacturing sector (Lewis and Craven 1995), that focused on the relationship between a major supplier and its business customers (also manufacturers), found three dimensions of service quality. These related to: products (e.g. quality of products, record of technological innovation, range of products, technical specifications, product availability); the organization and its personnel (e.g. reputation, previous experience, helpful personnel, technical support, after-sales services, location of supplier, communication/response times); and operations/systems (e.g. delivery reliability and speed, ease of contact, administrative efficiency, and electronic aspects of ordering).

However, the most widely reported set of service quality determinants is that proposed by Parasuraman et al. (1985, 1988). They suggested that the criteria used by consumers that are important in moulding their expectations and perceptions of service fit 10 dimensions:

- *Tangibles*: physical evidence
- *Reliability*: getting it right first time, honouring promises
- *Responsiveness*: willingness, readiness to provide service
- *Communication*: keeping customers informed in a language they can understand
- *Credibility*: honesty, trustworthiness
- *Security*: physical and financial; confidentiality
- *Competence*: possession of required skills and knowledge of *all* employees
- *Courtesy*: politeness, respect, friendliness
- *Understanding*: knowing the customer, his needs and requirements
- *Access*: ease of approach and contact

These 10 dimensions vary with respect to how easy or difficult it is to evaluate them. Some, such as tangibles or credibility, are known in advance, but most are experience criteria and can only be evaluated during or after consumption. Some, such as competence and security, may be difficult or impossible to evaluate, even after purchase. In general, customers rely on experience properties when evaluating services. Subsequent factor analysis and testing by Parasuraman et al. (1988) condensed these determinants into five categories (tangibles, reliability, responsiveness, assurance and empathy) to which Gronroos (1988) added a sixth dimension, recovery.

Service providers should also consider the contribution of Johnston et al. (1990) and Silvestro and Johnston (1990), who investigated service quality in UK organizations and identified fifteen determinants which they categorized as hygiene, enhancing, or dual threshold factors.

- *Hygiene* factors are those that are expected by the customer; failure to deliver will cause dissatisfaction (e.g. cleanliness in a restaurant, train arrival time, confidentiality of financial affairs, lack of queues, return of phone calls).
- *Enhancing* factors lead to customer satisfaction; failure to deliver will not necessarily cause dissatisfaction (e.g. bank clerk addressing you by name, welcome of a waiter in a restaurant).
- *Dual threshold* factors are those for which failure to deliver will cause dissatisfaction, and delivery above a certain level will enhance customers' perceptions of service and lead to satisfaction (e.g. explanation of a mortgage service repayment level, interest charges, payback period and other relevant conditions).

More recently, Zeithaml et al. (2000) researched the delivery of service quality over the web. They studied out focus groups of consumers with varying experience of internet buying, assessing their expectations and perceptions of buying on the web, and found eleven dimensions of e-service quality: access, ease of navigation, efficiency, flexibility, reliability, personalization, security/privacy, responsiveness, assurance/trust, site aesthetics, and price/knowledge. Personal service was not considered critical in e-service quality except when problems occurred or when consumers had to make complex decisions. They also discussed service quality gaps or shortfalls which may occur when companies interact with their customers through the internet. These are:

- *An information gap*, owing to insufficient or incorrect information about website features desired by customers
- *A design gap* to include aspects of site design and functioning of the website
- *A communications gap*, to include inaccurate or inflated promises

The combined effect of these gaps leads to a fourth, fulfilment, gap which relates to stock availability, the reordering process and delivery: this may occur as a result of deficiencies in the design and operation of the website.

Zones of tolerance

Consumers' expectations with respect to dimensions of service are generally reasonable: for example, they expect luggage to arrive with them on an aircraft, and planes to arrive on time most of the time. They also expect basics, for example, from a hotel in terms of security, cleanliness, and being treated with respect. However, expectations vary depending on a host of circumstances and experiences and they also rise over time. Further, experience with one service provider (a hotel or a doctor) can influence expectations of others (a bank or a lawyer).

In addition, consumers have what Parasuraman et al. (1991a) refer to as 'zones of tolerance', the difference between what is desired and what is considered adequate. The desired level of service is what the consumer hopes to receive, a blend of what 'can' and 'should' be, which is a function of past experience. The adequate level is what they find acceptable; it is based in part on their assessment of what the service will be, the 'predicted' service, and it depends on the alternatives that are available. Tolerance zones vary between individuals, service aspects and with experience, and tend to be smaller for outcome features than for process dimensions. In addition, if options are limited or non-existent (for example, the choice of general practitioner services, or of rail and plane routes or hotels) desires may not decrease but tolerance levels may be higher. Conversely, if many alternatives are available (for example, the choice of restaurants in a city), it is easy to switch and tolerance zones are more limited. Further, expectations are higher in emergency situations (for example the theft of a chequebook or loss of a credit card) and when something was not right the first time.

Measurement of service quality

The measurement of service quality has also been the focus of research interest and debate over the last 20 years. Parasuraman's dimensions of service provided the basis of the SERVQUAL questionnaire (Parasuraman et al. 1988), which was designed to measure service quality, i.e. the comparison between consumers' expectations of service (E) and their perceptions of actual service delivered (P). This is a 22-item scale with reported good reliability and validity which can be used to better understand service expectations and perceptions of consumers. The original scale items were of the form:

	strongly agree				strongly disagree	
	1	2	3	4	5	6	7

service expectations: e.g. 'customers should be able to trust bank employees'
   (E)   'banks should have up-to-date equipment'

and perceptions: e.g. 'I can trust the employees of my bank'
   (P)   'my bank has up-to-date equipment'

Following some discussion in the research literature, Parasuraman et al. (1991b) offered a revised SERVQUAL, in which negatively worded statements were changed to a positive wording; respondents were required to indicate 'what an excellent service would provide' rather than 'what firms in an industry should provide'; some of the items were changed; and the relative importance of SERVQUAL's five dimensions was assessed by asking respondents to allocate 100 points between the five dimensions.

In response to criticism, Parasuraman et al. (1991b, 1993, 1994) continued to defend SERVQUAL over other methods of evaluation of service quality, for its practical and diagnostic value. They claim that SERVQUAL is a measure relevant to a broad spectrum of services and is based on their five generic service quality dimensions: reliability, responsiveness, assurance, empathy and tangibles. Further, they suggest that SERVQUAL may be used to track service quality trends and improve service; categorize customers, compare branches/outlets of an organization and compare an organization with its competitors. However, it is limited to current and past customers, as respondents need knowledge and experience of the company.

During the last 15 years, a host of research studies have used SERVQUAL or similar instruments to assess the dimensions of service quality. Of particular interest are those researchers who have debated SERVQUAL and related methodologies (see e.g. Smith 1995; Buttle 1996a for a review of some of the evidence). Areas of concern have focused on conceptual/theoretical, operational and interpretative issues, to include for example:

- The disconfirmation paradigm. Should service quality measurement be based on an assessment of performance minus expectations, or is attitude a better description of service quality?
- The relative focus on the process and outcome of service delivery.
- The measurement of expectations: what is being measured? Ideal, desired or adequate expectations etc.
- The dimensionality of service quality and its applicability to all service industries and situations.
- The scaling techniques incorporated and associated importance weightings of service quality dimensions.
- Changes in attributes and importance, expectations, and perceptions over time.
- The timing of measurement: before, during or after a particular service encounter.

For example, Cronin and Taylor (1992) investigated the conceptualization and measurement of service quality and the relationships between service quality, customer satisfaction and purchase intention. They found that a performance-only-based measure of service quality (SERVPERF) may be an improved means of measuring the construct as opposed to the gap-based SERVQUAL scale. Their views have subsequently been supported by others and recently Brady, Cronin and Brand (2002) re-examined and found strong support for the superiority of the performance-only approach to the measurement of service quality.

Babakus and Boller (1992), in their review of the suggested methodological shortcomings of the SERVQUAL construct, found that the dimensionality of SERVQUAL may depend on the type of services under study. Again, there is support for this opinion in continuing research. Some of the most recent research also incorporates the potential impact of cultural setting on the dimensionality of service quality, for example in financial services where Lewis et al. (2002) found eight dimensions of service quality in retail banking in Cyprus: tangibles, reliability, responsiveness, customer contact personnel, commitment to customers, services portfolio, access and image. This followed from earlier evidence (Lewis 1991), in an international comparison of retail bank customers in the US and UK, of cultural differences in attitudes and behaviour which impact on expectations and perceptions of service quality.

Finally, researchers such as Cottam and Lewis (2001) have considered the extent to which consumer expectations, perceptions and satisfaction may change during the course of extended service delivery and consumption. In particular, they found, from repeated measures of expectations throughout a year-long service experience, that levels of expectation, both ideal and predicted, changed during the process of service consumption, and that expectations were not a key variable in predicting satisfaction with the service.

There thus remains a considerable challenge for both academics and practitioners to refine the methods used to identify and measure appropriate dimensions of service quality and the gaps that exist for organizations.

The Role of Personnel in Service Delivery

Having assessed customer needs, organizations must set standards/specifications and systems for service delivery to include the relevant dimensions of customer service, i.e. to avoid Gap 2. This implies a requirement for management commitment to a service culture and service quality, and the allocation of appropriate resources – in relation to products, systems, environment and people.

The subsequent challenge is to ensure that the service delivered meets the specifications set. This depends on the performance of *all* employees, who must be able and willing to deliver the desired levels of service. Employees' contributions in meeting customer needs and, thus, influencing customer perceptions of service cannot be overstated. Success depends on the development of enlightened personnel policies for recruitment and selection, training, motivation and rewards for all employees – both customer-contact and back-room staff.

Internal marketing

An understanding of the concept of internal marketing is central to personnel policies. Internal marketing views employees as internal customers and jobs as internal products (see Berry 1980), and a company needs to sell its jobs to employees before selling its service to customers: satisfying the wants of internal customers upgrades the capability to satisfy the needs of external customers. Gronroos (1981) refers to three objectives of internal marketing:

- *Overall*: to achieve motivated, customer-conscious and care-orientated personnel.
- *Strategic*: to create an internal environment which supports customer-consciousness and sales-mindedness among personnel.
- *Tactical*: to sell service campaigns and marketing efforts to employees – the first marketplace of the company – via staff training programmes and seminars.

Berry (1981) developed the concept in terms of the possibilities for market research and segmentation. He suggests that organizations should carry out research among employees to identify their needs, wants and attitudes with respect to working conditions, benefits and company policies. Further, he indicates that people are as different as employees as they are as consumers and might be segmented in a number of ways. For example, with respect to flexible working hours, which lead to increased job satisfaction, increased productivity and decreased absenteeism. In addition, 'cafeteria benefits' could be appropriate with respect to health insurance, pensions, holidays, etc. – the notion being that employees use 'credits' (a function of salary, service, age,. etc) to choose their benefits.

The concept of internal marketing has been researched by Varey (1996), who studied the origins, nature, scope and application of the concept and considered how it might be developed to take greater account of the social and non-economic needs and interests of people working in an organized enterprise. From extensive review of the literature in various disciplines, organizational case studies, expert academic opinion and in-depth interviews with managers, some limitations of the popular concept of internal marketing were addressed and consideration given to the structural impact of internal marketing which leads into a presentation of a broader conception of internal marketing. A number of themes that offer a contribution to this broader conception were identified. They include: marketing-oriented service employee management; organization as an internal market; internal marketing as a social process; the individual person in an internal market; a relational perspective on communication; and empowerment.

Further, Ahmed and Rafiq (2002: 4–24) discuss the development and evolution of the internal marketing concept, models of internal marketing, and links with service quality, customer satisfaction, customer loyalty and profitability.

Personnel policies

Personnel issues are addressed by Lewis and Entwistle (1990), who develop the concept of service encounters to include encounters or *relationships* within the organization, at *all* levels and *between* levels – which contribute to the quality of service delivered to the final customer. This includes relationships between: customer contact and backroom employees; operations and non-operations staff; and staff and management at all levels and locations.

Successful personnel policies include recruitment and selection of the 'right' people. Key characteristics for employees to perform effectively may relate to: process and technical skills; interpersonal and communication skills; flexibility and adaptability; and empathy with the customer. It is also vital to identify the training needs of new *and* present employees with respect to technical and interpersonal dimensions, and to consider employment conditions, i.e. employees' wants and attitudes with regard to working conditions, benefits and welfare. This is undertaken, typically, via a training audit. Subsequently, training programmes may be developed to provide product, company and systems knowledge and also interpersonal and communication skills. Zeithaml et al. (1988), in relation to Gap 3, indicate that success will depend on:

- *Teamwork*: evidenced by a caring management and involved and committed employees.
- *Employee–job fit*: the ability of employees to perform a job.
- *Technology–job fit*: are the 'tools' appropriate for the employee and the job?
- *Perceived control*: e.g. do employees have flexibility in dealing with customers? If not stress levels may rise and performance decrease.
- *Supervisory control systems*: based on behaviours rather than 'output quality'.

- *Avoidance of role conflict*: for employees in satisfying their expectations of the company *and* the expectations of customers.
- *Avoidance of role ambiguity*: i.e. employees should know what is expected of them and how performance will be evaluated and rewarded.

A project by Lewis and Gabrielsen (1998) included a survey of front-line employees in a number of banks. The research objectives included the identification of organizational variables which affect the service quality process, and the survey of employees focused on attitude and opinion statements pertaining to: organizational culture and internal working environment; the role of management; role perception; training; organizational structures; evaluation and rewards; and service recovery. The findings stressed the need for and importance of management concern for the organizational culture, the acknowledgement that human resources are an intrinsic part of the service and quality delivered, and that the potential of employees (to be customer-aware, innovative, and to use initiative) needs to be enhanced/maximized with appropriate leadership.

Customer service training programmes are typically designed to move a company to a service-oriented culture by breaking down barriers and improving internal communications. Advantages are seen to be: creating an atmosphere of all working towards a common goal; understanding the work of others; and encouraging all staff to have responsibility and authority for achieving corporate objectives – which includes empowering employees to exercise judgement and creativity in responding to customers' needs.

Employees also need to be supervised and systems set to monitor and evaluate their performance (e.g. product knowledge tests, mystery shoppers) *and* satisfaction. In addition, organizations have a variety of recognition and reward schemes for excellent employees: customer-service awards may be financial or not, and may involve career development.

Service Delivery

In relation to service delivery, organizations need to avoid Gap 4, i.e. a failure to deliver the service as promised. Once a company has successfully assessed customer needs, translated them into service systems and standards, and recruited and trained employees, it must then manage its 'promises'. Quality systems are of benefit in helping to ensure this. Further, a company needs appropriate advertising and promotion so that the service that is offered in external communications matches the service that the organization is able to deliver. Advertising and promotion affect customers' expectations and perceptions of the delivered service, so it is important not to promise more than can be delivered. Realistic communications are needed so as not to increase expectations unnecessarily and decrease perceptions of quality: the hotel that advertised 'there are no surprises' was deemed to be over-promising.

Monitoring service quality

A critical element in any service strategy is for a company to have in place systems to measure and monitor success. These include research and evaluation among employees and customers, using focus groups, discussions, surveys and interviews, and sometimes mystery shoppers and 'control' branches. Collection and analysis of customer complaints and complimentary letters is also valuable, and for some organizations key indicators are provided by service guarantees and recovery activities.

Many, if not most, service providers now make promises and/or offer guarantees with respect to products/services, delivery and aspects of performance. In the private sector, these may be an element in a company's competitive armoury, for example: hotels which offer cash compensation or free accommodation if difficulties are not resolved in 30 minutes; a pizza delivery which becomes free after a certain time delay; UK organizations providing financial services publicizing their codes of practice including, for example, their 'promises to students' and 'commitments to you'; and a shopping centre which publishes promises to customers, including information on consumer rights with respect to faulty goods and the return of goods (<www.meadowhall.co.uk>).

Utility companies in the UK have been actively developing and promoting, for competitive and consumer-oriented reasons, their service guarantees. For example, 'TXU Energi aims to deliver faultless customer service . . . if our service doesn't match our promise we want you to *tell* us. If we have slipped up, you'll see a credit on your bill' (<www.txuenergi.co.uk>). United Utilities publish standards for all their services and make various promises, for example, with respect to planned mains repairs, they make promises relating to provision of information, timing and restoration of water supply, and cash compensation is available and levels clearly specified if these promises are not met (<www.unitedutilities.co.uk>).

In addition, in the UK the Citizen's Charter has spurred the development of various service charters: the National Health Service has a Patients' Charter with guaranteed Patients' Charter Rights (promises) relating to the provision of health care, access to information and information on quality standards, together with national and local charter standards; local authorities have charters of rights; and the Department for Education has a Parents' Charter, outlining parents' rights on what they can expect. The Royal Mail and Parcel Force both have codes of practice, and publish their service standards, for example with regard to delivery times, and compensation levels for delays and for lost and damaged items.

Finally, Virgin Trains have a detailed Passengers' Charter which sets out their commitment to passengers with respect to customer care, service improvement, quantified standards (i.e. reliability and punctuality of trains), keeping passengers informed, and what happens when things go wrong (<www.virgintrains.co.uk>). They also include quantified compensation and refund levels.

Hart (1988) summarizes key considerations relating to service guarantees. Some aspects of service and customer satisfaction cannot be guaranteed, for example unconditional on-time arrival of planes, and so guarantees must be realistic. A good service guarantee is unconditional, easy to understand and communicate, easy to invoke and easy to collect on. It should also be meaningful, in particular with respect to pay-out which should be a function of the cost of the service, seriousness of failure and perception of what is fair, for example, 15-minute lunch service in a restaurant or a free meal. Ideally, a service guarantee should get everyone in the company to focus on good service, and to examine service delivery systems for possible failure points.

Service failure

To turn to service failures and customer complaints, service providers now appreciate that only a small proportion of dissatisfied customers complain, so that complaint data are not a true reflection of the extent of customer dissatisfaction. The reasons why dissatisfied people keep quiet are discussed by Goodman et al. (1986) and Horovitz (1990) and include:

- Fear of hassle or too much trouble to complain.
- No one is available to complain to or there is no easy channel by which to communicate disquiet.
- No one cares and it won't do any good.
- Do not know where to complain.
- Customers seeing themselves as a source of service problems by their failure to perform in the creation of the service.

Hart et al. (1990) discuss the additional costs of replacing customers over those of trying to retain customers who may be dissatisfied. There is also evidence of customers who complain and who then receive a satisfactory response subsequently being more likely to buy other services or products, engage in positive word-of-mouth communication, and be loyal (e.g. Hart et al. 1990; Blodgett et al. 1997). Further, Mattila (2001) has shown that effective service recovery can have a strong positive influence on recovery satisfaction and loyalty.

Organizations should strive for zero defects in their service delivery – to get things right the first time (see Reichheld and Sasser 1990). Consequently, many companies develop service quality systems that tend to be rigid, with sophisticated techniques and structured personnel policies – to try to provide consistent high-quality service. However, all service organizations will find themselves in situations where failures occur in their encounters with customers with respect to one or more dimensions of service quality, and where they need to deal with customer dissatisfaction and complaints. For example, problems do occur (e.g. bad weather may delay an airline flight, or employees may be sick and absent) and mistakes will happen (e.g. a hotel room not ready on time, a dirty rental car, a lost chequebook or suitcase).

One should note, however, that a service failure may not only relate to a flawed outcome. A service failure can still occur if the service fails to live up to the customer's own expectations (Michel 2001). In fact, Lewis and Spyrakopoulos (2001) define a service failure as 'any dissatisfaction or problem that a customer perceives in relation to a service or a service provider'.

A number of researchers have investigated service failures and several have attempted to classify them (e.g. Bitner et al. 1990, 1994; Kelley et al. 1993; Hoffman et al. 1995; Johnston 1994; Armistead et al. 1995) in relation to: problems in the service organization (e.g. with regard to employees, equipment and systems); those which may be customer induced; and those that are a result of the actions of other organizations.

Others have highlighted the consequences of service failure (e.g. Kelley et al. 1993) to include dissatisfaction, decline in consumer confidence, negative word of mouth, and the inability to retain customers. Armistead et al. (1995) also include the increased costs of putting services right, providing compensation and recruiting new customers to replace lost ones. In addition, there is evidence that service failure can lead to decline in employee morale and service performance (Bitner et al. 1994).

Service recovery

The actions that a service provider takes to respond to service failures are referred to as service recovery. Service recovery is defined by Armistead et al. (1995) as 'specific actions taken to ensure that the customer receives a reasonable level of service after problems have occurred to disrupt normal service', and by Zemke and Bell (1990) as 'a thought-out, planned, process for returning aggrieved customers to a state of satisfaction with the organization after a service or product has failed to live up to expectations'. The response from an organization to service failures needs to be the result of a conscious, co-ordinated, effort of the firm to anticipate that service flaws will occur, and to develop procedures, policies and human competencies to deal with them.

When something does go wrong, what do customers expect from the service firm? Zemke and Bell (1990) and Zemke (1994) concluded that customer expectations for service recovery are: to receive an apology for the fact that the customer is inconvenienced; to be offered a 'fair fix' for the problem; to be treated in a way that suggests the company cares about the problem, about fixing the problem, and about the customer's inconvenience; and to be offered value-added atonement (i.e. compensation) for the inconvenience. Service recovery is 'emotional and physical repair': organizations need to fix the customer first and then fix the customer's problem.

Critical to the service recovery process is the empowerment of front-line employees. It is essential to give personnel the authority, responsibility and incentives to identify, care about and solve customer problems and complaints; to allow them to use their initiative and judgement to respond flexibly, and to act with respect to the best solutions to satisfy customers. The personnel implications are highlighted by Schlesinger and Heskett (1991): empowerment is seen to lead to better job performance and improved morale – it is a form of job enrichment, evidenced by increased commitment to jobs and reflected in attitudes towards customers. Knowing that management has confidence in employees helps to create positive attitudes in the work place and good relationships between employees and between employees and customers.

A number of research studies have focused on service recovery. For example, Johnston (1994) produced, from customer anecdotes, a list of factors that led to satisfactory recovery to include attention, helpfulness, care, responsiveness, communication and flexibility. These would appear to be intrinsic to the actions found by Armistead et al. (1995), in a survey of managers across the services sector, to be most effective in satisfying customer complaints: namely, immediate and speedy response, listening, courtesy, caring and honest responses, getting it right and solving the problem, and financial compensation.

A recent study by Lewis and Spyrakopoulos (2001) investigated service failures and service recovery strategies used by banks to respond to them. A survey questionnaire was developed to measure customers' perceptions of the magnitude of service failures and the effectiveness of service recovery strategies. Service failures related to banking procedures, mistakes, employee behaviour and training, technical failures and omissions of the banks: they were found to vary in importance and some were more difficult to deal with satisfactorily than others. Different service recovery strategies (e.g. corrections, compensation, apologies and explanations) were more effective for particular failures. Further, customers with long relationships and higher deposits with their banks were more demanding with respect to service recovery.

A recent interesting stream of research has emerged in response to the question 'How do customers evaluate companies' service recovery strategies?', and focuses on consumers' evaluation of satisfaction with complaint handling in terms of perceived justice (see Blodgett et al. 1997; Mattila 2001; Michel 2001; Smith and Bolton 1999; Smith et al. 1999; Tax and Brown 2000; Tax et al. 1998). In addition, Smith and Bolton (2002) consider the manager's perspective on recovery efforts in relation to customer perceptions of justice. Perceived justice comprises three elements:

- *Distributive justice*: the perceived fairness of the outcome. What did the offending firm offer the customer to recover from the service failure (e.g. refund or replacement)?
- *Interactive justice*: this refers to the perceived fairness of the manner in which the customer is treated during the complaint-handling process and includes courtesy and politeness of personnel, empathy, effort in resolving the situation and the firm's willingness to apologize and provide an explanation for the service failure.
- *Procedural justice*: the perceived fairness of the process used to rectify a service failure, e.g. the speed (or delay) in processing and correcting complaints, the accessibility and flexibility of the procedures.

Research by the above authors has shown differences in the relative importance of these justice elements by service type together with evidence of interaction between the dimensions. The main conclusion to be drawn from the available evidence is that, in order to recover effectively from service failure, an organization must provide a fair outcome, with a sincere apology, while taking the blame and acting swiftly to recover from the failure. Further, interactions between the justice dimensions mean that failure to deliver on one of them can impact negatively on the total success of the recovery. The effectiveness of service recovery strategies has also been shown to depend on factors such as the service type, the magnitude of the failure, the type of failure (i.e. process or outcome), prior experience, service recovery expectations, purpose of purchase and attitudes towards complaining.

Overall, from a review of the available research evidence, it is possible to suggest a number of requirements for companies to create an effective service recovery programme:

- Seek out possible failure points. Focus on critical service encounters and try to anticipate problems, in particular as few people complain.
- Educate customers and encourage complaints. Make it easy to complain (e.g. 24-hour customer service hotlines) and offer service guarantees.
- Monitor service process, detect and track service failures, and analyse complaint data. Measure performance against company standards. Use the findings to improve service quality and prevent failures and dissatisfaction from happening again.
- Engage in customer research, focused on both the process and outcome of service delivery, to: identify when things go wrong; track how service recovery

is implemented; and measure again to see if the recovery has satisfied the customer (i.e. follow-up feedback).

- Develop proactive service recovery, to include, in addition to reinstatement, elements such as: initiation of the recovery process, which can enhance customers' evaluation of the service provider; apologies, to show that the customer's problem is being taken seriously and is important to the organization; speedy response; and recompense as appropriate.
- Train, empower and facilitate employees to recover. Service recovery typically involves interpersonal interaction and communication skills, and knowledge skills, with implications for human resources management.
- Show management commitment. Employees need to be supported by senior management who have a commitment to absolute customer satisfaction.

Summary

Today the business environment is characterized by changing customer expectations, technological and product advances, legislative and political developments, and economic and competitive conditions which contribute to an increasing emphasis on service quality for all organizations – in both the services and manufacturing sectors. Managing service quality necessitates an integrated approach from operations, marketing, human resources and other key managers/areas of a business.

Organizations need clearly defined service strategies with top management commitment and leadership. They need to understand their service encounters (both internal and external to the company) and potential failure points, and to avoid service quality shortfalls or gaps. This can be achieved by researching both service personnel and customers, identifying key dimensions of service quality, and developing appropriate service quality initiatives. Successful service strategies will include emphasis on products/services, delivery systems and procedures, technology, and personnel – their skills and commitment to the organization and its customers.

The outcome of a successful service strategy will be satisfied and retained employees and customers, with consequent benefits to the organization. The links between customer retention and profitability have been evident for a number of years (see e.g. Heskett et al. 1994; Buttle 1996b). There is a growing awareness of the 'lifetime value' of retained customers in terms of the revenues and contributions earned from a long-term relationship, i.e. the longer the association between company and customer, the more profitable the relationship for the company.

In conclusion, one can refer to the work of Zeithaml (2000) who has recently reviewed the evidence on the profit consequences of service quality. She offers a substantive and valuable review of research projects and findings on the effect of service quality on profits; the link between perceived service quality and purchase intentions; customer and segment profitability; and the key drivers of service quality, customer retention and profitability. She also develops an inventory of questions for ongoing research.

References

Ahmed, P. K. and Rafiq, M. (2002), *Internal Marketing: Tools and Concepts for Customer Focused Management*. Oxford: Butterworth Heinemann.

Albrecht, K. and Zemke, R. (1985), *Service America: Doing Business in the New Economy*. Homewood, Ill.: Dow Jones–Irwin.

Armistead, C. G., Clark, G. and Stanley, P. (1995), Managing service recovery. In P. Kunst and J. Lemmink (eds), *Managing Service Quality*, 93–105. London: Paul Chapman Publishing.

Babakus, E. and Boller, G. W. (1992), An empirical assessment of the SERVQUAL scale. *Journal of Business Research*, 24(May), 253–68.

Berry, L. L. (1980), Services marketing is different. *Business*, 30(3), 24–9.

Berry, L. L. (1981), The employee as customer, *Journal of Retail Banking*, 3(1), 33–40.

Berry, L. L., Zeithaml, V. A. and Parasuraman, A. (1985), Quality counts in services too. *Business Horizons*, 28(3), 44–52.

Berry, L. L., Parasuraman, A. and Zeithaml, V. A. (1988), The service-quality puzzle. *Business Horizons*, July–August, 35–43.

Bitner, M. J., Booms, B. H. and Tetreault, M. S. (1990), The service encounter: diagnosing favorable and unfavorable incidents. *Journal of Marketing*, 54(1), 71–84.

Bitner, M. J., Booms, B. M. and Mohr, L. A. (1994), Critical service encounters: the employees' viewpoint. *Journal of Marketing*, 58(4), 95–106.

Bitner, M. J., Brown, S. W. and Meuter, M. C. (2000), Technology infusion in service encounters. *Journal of the Academy of Marketing Science*, 28(1), 138–49.

Blodgett, J. G., Hill, D. J. and Tax, S. S. (1997), The effects of distributive justice, procedural justice, and interactional justice on postcomplaint behaviour. *Journal of Retailing*, 73(2), 185–210.

Booms, B. H. and Bitner, M. J. (1981), Marketing strategies and organisation structures for service firms. In J. H. Donnelly and W. R. George (eds), *Marketing of Services*, 47–51. Chicago: American Marketing Association.

Boshoff, C. and Leong, J. (1998), Empowerment, attribution and apologising as dimensions of service recovery: an experimental study. *International Journal of Service Industry Management*, 9(1), 24–47.

Brady, M. K., Cronin, J. J. and Brand, R. R. (2002), Performance-only measurement of service quality: a replication and extension. *Journal of Business Research*, 55, 17–31.

Buttle, F. (1996a), SERVQUAL: review, critique and research agenda. *European Journal of Marketing*, 30(1), 8–32.

Buttle, F. (ed.) (1996b), *Relationship Marketing: Theory and Practice*. London: Paul Chapman Publishing Ltd.

Cottam, A. M. and Lewis, B. R. (2001), *The Measurement of Expectations: Timing and Relevance Issues in Services Consumption*. Manchester: Manchester School of Management, UMIST.

Cronin, J. J. and Taylor, S. A. (1992), Measuring service quality: a re-examination and extension. *Journal of Marketing*, 56(1), 55–68.

Czepiel, J. A., Solomon, M. R. and Surprenant, C. F. (eds) (1985), *The Service Encounter: Managing Employee–Customer Interaction in Service Businesses*. Lexington, Mass.: Lexington Books.

Edvardsson, B., Gustavsson, B. O. and Riddle, D. I. (1989), *An Expanded Model of the Service Encounter with Emphasis on Cultural Context*. Research Report 89: 4, CTF Services Research Centre, University of Karlstad, Sweden.

Goodman, J. A., Marra, T. and Brigham, L. (1986), Customer service: costly nuisance or low-cost profit strategy? *Journal of Retail Banking*, 8(3), 7–16.

Gronroos, C. (1981), Internal marketing: an integral part of marketing theory. In J. H. Donnelly and W. R. George (eds), *Marketing of Services*, 236–8. Chicago: American Marketing Association.

Gronroos, C. (1984), *Strategic Management and Marketing in the Service Sector*. UK: Chartwell-Bratt.

Gronroos, C. (1987), *Developing the Service Offering: A Source of Competitive Advantage*. Helsingfors: Swedish School of Economics and Business Administration.

Gronroos, C. (1988), Service quality: the six criteria of good perceived service quality. *Review of Business*, 9(3), 10–13.

Gummesson, E. and Gronroos, C. (1987), *Quality of Products and Services: A Tentative Synthesis between Two Models*. Research Report 87: 3, Services Research Centre, University of Karlstad, Sweden.

Hart, C. W. L. (1988), The power of unconditional service guarantees. *Harvard Business Review*, 66(4), 54–62.

Hart, C. W. L., Heskett, J. L. and Sasser, W. E. (1990), The profitable art of service recovery. *Harvard Business Review*, 68(4), 148–56.

Heskett, J. L., Jones, T. O., Loveman, G. W., Sasser, W. E. and Schlesinger, L. A. (1994), Putting the service profit chain to work. *Harvard Business Review*, 72(2), 164–74.

Hoffman, K. D. and Kelley, S. W. (2000), Perceived justice and recovery evaluation: a contingency approach. *European Journal of Marketing*, 24(3/4), 418–32.

Hoffman, K. D., Kelley, S. W. and Rotalksi, H. M. (1995), Tracking service failures and employee recovery efforts. *Journal of Services Marketing*, 9(2), 49–61.

Horovitz, J. (1990), *Winning Ways: Achieving Zero Defect Service*. Cambridge, Mass.: Productivity Press.

Johnston, R. (1994), *Service Recovery: An Empirical Study*. Warwick: Warwick University Business School.

Johnston, R., Silvestro, R., Fitzgerald, L. and Voss, C. (1990), Developing the determinants of service quality. In E. Langeard and P. Eiglier (eds), *Marketing, Operations and Human Resources Insights into Services*, 373–400. Aix-en-Provence: First International Research Seminar on Services Management, IAE.

Kelley, S. W., Hoffman, K. D. and Davis, M. A. (1993), A typology of retail failures and recoveries. *Journal of Retailing*, 69(4), 429–52.

Lehtinen, U. and Lehtinen, J. R. (1982), *Service Quality: A Study of Quality Dimensions*. Helsinki: Working Paper, Service Management Institute.

Lewis, B. R. (1990), Service quality: an investigation of major UK organisations. *International Journal of Service Industry Management*, 1(2), 33–44.

Lewis, B. R. (1991), Service quality: an international comparison of bank customers' expectations and perceptions. *Journal of Marketing Management*, 7(1), 47–62.

Lewis, B. R. and Craven, P. (1995), The role of customer service in buyer–seller relationships: evidence from the industrial gases market. In *Interaction, Relationships and Networks*, Proceedings of the 11th IMP International Conference, Manchester, 7–9 September, 762–86.

Lewis, B. R. and Entwistle, T. W. (1990), Managing the service encounter: a focus on the employee. *International Journal of Service Industry Management*, 1(3), 41–52.

Lewis, B. R. and Gabrielsen, G. O. S. (1998), Intra-organisational aspects of service quality management. *The Service Industries Journal*, 18(2), 64–89.

Lewis, B. R., Ioannou, M. and Cui, C. C. (2002), *Service Quality in the Cypriot Banking Sector: Determinants and Gaps*. Manchester: Manchester School of Management, UMIST.

Lewis, B. R. and Spyrakopoulos, S. (2001), Service failures and recovery in retail banking: the customers' perspective. *International Journal of Bank Marketing*, 19(1), 37–47.

Lovelock, C., Vandermerwe, S. and Lewis, B. (1999), *Services Marketing: A European Perspective*. Hemel Hempstead: Prentice Hall Europe.

Mattila, A. S. (2001), The effectiveness of service recovery in a multi-industry setting. *The Journal of Services Marketing*, 15(7), 583–96.

Michel, S. (2001), Analysing service failures and recoveries: a process approach. *International Journal of Service Industry Management*, 12(1), 20–33.

Parasuraman, A., Berry, L. L. and Zeithaml, V. A. (1991a), Understanding customer expectations of service. *Sloan Management Review*, 32(3), 39–48.

Parasuraman, A., Berry, L. L. and Zeithaml, V. A. (1991b), Refinement and reassessment of the SERVQUAL scale. *Journal of Retailing*, 67(4), 420–50.

Parasuraman, A., Zeithaml, V. A. and Berry, L. L. (1985), A conceptual model of service quality and its implications for future research. *Journal of Marketing*, 49(Fall), 41–50.

Parasuraman, A., Zeithaml, V. A. and Berry, L. L. (1988), SERVQUAL: a multiple item scale for measuring consumer perceptions of service quality. *Journal of Retailing*, 64(1), 14–40.

Parasuraman, A., Zeithaml, V. A. and Berry, L. L. (1993), More on improving service quality. *Journal of Retailing*, 69(1), 140–7.

Parasuraman, A., Zeithaml, V. A. and Berry, L. L. (1994), Reassessment of expectations as a comparison standard in measuring service quality: implications for further research. *Journal of Marketing*, 58(January), 111–24.

Reichheld, F. E. and Sasser, W. E. (1990), Zero defections: quality comes to services. *Harvard Business Review*, 68(5), 105–11.

Rosenberg, L. J. and Czepiel, J. A. (1984), A marketing approach to customer retention. *Journal of Consumer Marketing*, 1, 45–51.

Schlesinger, L. A. and Heskett, J. L. (1991), Breaking the cycle of failures in service. *Sloan Management Review*, 32(3), 17–28.

Silvestro, R. and Johnston, R. (1990), *The Determinants of Service Quality: Hygiene and Enhancing Factors*. Warwick: Warwick Business School.

Smith, A. K. and Bolton, R. N. (1999), A model of customer satisfaction with service encounters involving failure and recovery. *Journal of Marketing Research*, 36(3), 356–89.

Smith, A. K. and Bolton, R. N. (2002), The effects of customers' emotional responses to service failures on their recovery effort evaluations and satisfaction judgements. *Journal of the Academy of Marketing Science*, 30(1), 5–23.

Smith, A. K., Bolton, R. N. and Wagner, J. (1999), A model of customer satisfaction with service encounters involving failure and recovery. *Journal of Marketing Research*, 36(August), 356–72.

Smith, A. M. (1995), Measuring service quality: is SERVQUAL now redundant? *Journal of Marketing Management*, 11(1–3), 257–76.

Tax, S. and Brown, S. W. (2000), Service recovery: research insights and practices. In T. A. Swartz and D. Iacobucci (eds), *Handbook of Services Marketing and Management*, 271–86. Thousand Oaks, Calif.: Sage Publications.

Tax, S. S., Brown, S. W. and Chandrashekeran, M. (1998), Customer evaluations of service complaint experiences: implications for relationship marketing. *Journal of Marketing*, 62(April), 60–76.

Varey, R. J. (1996), A broadened conception of internal marketing. Unpublished Ph.D. thesis, Manchester School of Management, UMIST.

Zeithaml, V. A. (2000), Service quality, profitability and the economic worth of customers: what we know and what we need to learn. *Journal of the Academy of Marketing Science*, 28(1), 67–85.

Zeithaml, V. A., Berry, L. L. and Parasuraman, A. (1988), Communication and control processes in the delivery of service quality. *Journal of Marketing*, 52(April), 35–48.

Zeithaml, V. A., Parasuraman, A. and Malhotra, A. (2000), *A Conceptual Framework for Understanding e-service Quality: Implications for Future Research and Managerial Practice*. Cambridge, Mass.: Report 00–115, Marketing Science Institute.

Zemke, R. (1994), Service recovery. *Executive Excellence*, 11(9), 17–18.

Zemke, R. and Bell, C. R. (1990), Service recovery: doing it right the second time. *Training*, 27(6), 42–8.

WEBSITES (ACCESSED IN AUGUST 2002)

<www.meadowhall.co.uk/retailer_promise>
<www.txuenergi.co.uk/domestic/promise>
<www.unitedutilities.co.uk>
<www.virgintrains.co.uk/about/charter>

chapter twelve

Supplier Development

B. Burnes and B. G. Dale

Introduction

The quality of purchased supplies is crucial to an organization's products and services and consequently to its success in the marketplace. In many cases, as outsourcing has become the norm, bought-in components and services can account for some 70 to 80 per cent of the final cost of a product. It is therefore clear that suppliers are critical to the competitiveness and performance of the purchaser's products and services. Many major European companies, following the example of Japan, have during the last 15 years or so started to encourage their suppliers to develop their quality management systems, adopt a continuous improvement philosophy, eliminate non-value-added activity, improve their manufacturing systems, use lean manufacturing techniques, become more flexible and responsive, pursue cost-down activities, and concentrate on their core competencies and product lines. If the major companies wish to become and stay competitive they have to take their suppliers with them; electronic commerce and the internet are also facilitating and encouraging closer links with suppliers.

This process of customers working together with their suppliers to effect these changes is given a variety of names: supplier development, supply-chain management, supplier relationships management, co-makership, partnership sourcing, customer–supplier alliances, and proactive purchasing. This variety of names, and the way different organizations interpret them and the process, has led to much confusion about both the meaning and practicality of the partnership approach to purchasing. As well as the many, many individual initiatives by customers and suppliers there are also currently a number of industry-wide initiatives to facilitate closer relationships between suppliers and customers and reduce costs in the whole value chain, for example, that of the Machine Tool Technologies Association and the Society of British Aerospace Companies (SABAC) to develop collaborative relationships between machine tools suppliers and aerospace companies. This chapter, based on Burnes and Dale (1998), examines the key issues in sustainable partnerships under the main headings of long-term issues of partnership, barriers to developing partnerships, conditions of partnerships, the issues to be considered in partnership, the process of partnership and the potential difficulties. The chapter concludes with a list of dos and don'ts when developing partnerships.

Long-Term Issues of Partnership

The traditional, open-market bargaining approach to customer–supplier dealings has been based on the assumption that the parties involved are adversaries who have conflicting objectives and are engaged in a win-lose and 'dog eat dog' contest, based upon tough negotiations, price-orientation and cost undercutting with no love lost between businesses. This approach, which in reality no one can benefit from, focuses on negative issues, involves power abuse, and is characterized by uncertainty, all of which can seriously undermine, rather than reinforce, the competitiveness of both customers and suppliers.

Partnership demands a new form of relationship. It means working together towards common aims and aspirations. It is based on the principle that both parties can gain more through co-operation than conflict. Partnerships are characterized by mutual trust and commitment, integrity, integration, co-operation, honesty, a willingness to openly declare problems and work together to find answers, the sharing of data and ideas, improvements and best practices, clearly understood responsibilities, collaborative R&D, and a desire to continuously improve products and services. As an example, many first-tier suppliers are no longer being handed a prescriptive design by the original equipment manufacturer (OEM). Instead they are provided with a specification which the component, when assembled, must conform to. Other examples include suppliers setting up a manufacturing facility alongside their customers and a supplier's staff working on the customer's assembly line. In many respects, this form of relationship has similarities with a vertically integrated firm but without the difficulties of managing a complex business across different types of technologies and processes. One of the drivers for closer relationships with suppliers has been the move by OEMs to concentrate on their core competencies and to shift other activities and responsibilities to their suppliers. It must not be forgotten that a partnership does not come about by accident, and it cannot be sustained by inattentiveness. It is a management process which needs to be managed.

To develop a viable long-term business relationship, considerable changes in behaviour and attitude are required and need to be promoted in both customer and supplier organizations. Customers need to be prepared to develop plans and procedures for working with suppliers and commit resources to this. For their part, suppliers have to accept full responsibility for the quality of their shipped product and not rely on the customer's receiving inspection to assess if it meets their requirements. As a prerequisite of partnership, both parties have to reach an agreement on how they will work together, what they want from the relationship and how to resolve any problems which may arise. To ensure that the relationship is sustainable it is important that the objectives of the agreement should be examined and discussed on a regular basis.

The typical benefits of developing a long-term business partnership include:

- Reduction and elimination of the inspection of supplied parts and materials.
- Improved product and service quality, and delivery performance and responsiveness.

- Improved productivity, increased stock turns and lower inventory carrying cost and reduced costs per piece.
- Value-for-money purchases.
- Security and stability of supplies.
- Transfer of ideas, expertise and technology between customer and supplier and dissemination and implementation of best practice.
- Joint problem-solving activities, with the customer providing assistance to the supplier to help improve processes, leading to easier and faster resolution of problems.
- Integration of business practices and procedures between customer and supplier.
- A comprehensive customer–supplier communications network to ensure the supplier is provided with early access to the customer's future designs and manufacturing plans and is kept informed of changing customer requirements. This assists with the planning of workloads and typically opens up wider channels than those in the traditional relationship where the buyer and sales representatives would be the main point of contact.
- Customer and supplier being more willing and open to examine their processes to look for improvements.
- The supplier contributing to the customer's design process, undertaking development work and monitoring technological trends; this can lead to innovative products and services, and other business opportunities.
- Helping to develop sustainable growth of the supplier in terms of investment in equipment and manufacturing resources. Related to this is the reputation and credibility in the marketplace of both partners which arises from the relationship.
- Exposure of the supplier to new tools, techniques, systems and business practices.
- Provision by the customer of an advisory service to suppliers in terms of training, equipment and operating methods.

Barriers to Developing Partnerships

Developing partnerships is not without difficulties. Lascelles and Dale (1990) have carried out research which reveals that certain aspects of the customer–supplier relationship can act as a barrier to supplier development. These include:

- Poor communication and feedback.
- Supplier complacency.
- Misguided supplier improvement objectives.
- Lack of customer credibility as viewed by their suppliers.
- Misconceptions regarding purchasing power.

Poor communication and feedback

In general, communication and feedback between customer and supplier is not good. Sometimes it is even so bad that the parties do not even realize how poor they are at communicating with each other. The main dissatisfactions expressed by suppliers relate to technical specifications and requirements, the lack of consultation on design and product engineering issues and changes to the delivery schedule. There are some strong indications that not all dissatisfied suppliers actually communicate their dissatisfaction to the customer.

Supplier complacency

This covers issues such as: being insular, not being prepared to take a global view of supply and being unconcerned about customer satisfaction. There are two types of measurement relating to a customer's satisfaction with the quality of supplies, reactive and proactive.

Examples of reactive measures include:

- Failure data (e.g. non-conformity analysis, customer rejections, warranty claims).
- Customer assessment rating and audit reports.
- Verbal feedback from meetings with customers.
- Contractual requirements outlined in the customers' vendor improvement plans.

Examples of proactive measures are:

- Customer workshops and forum meetings
- Market research
- Benchmarking key processes
- Competitor evaluation
- Reliability analysis
- Advanced quality planning

Misguided supplier improvement objectives

Customers are often not sure what they want from supplier improvement initiatives and can underestimate the time and resources required to introduce and develop partnerships. There also appears to be a dilution and distortion of the quality message as requirements are passed down the supply chain. For example, when faced with demands to improve quality from customers, first-tier suppliers usually react by implementing specific tools and techniques required by the customer. In turn, the supplier then insists that their own suppliers use the same tools and techniques but fail to understand that these are only fully effective within the context of an organization-wide approach to continuous improvement.

Lack of customer credibility

Suppliers need to be convinced that a customer is serious about continuous improvement. This requires the customer's behaviour and attitudes to be consistent with what they are saying to suppliers. The following are examples of how a credibility gap may emerge:

- Purchasing and supplies management practices such as a competitive pricing policy to force down prices, frequent switches from one supplier to another, unpredictable and inflated production schedules, last-minute changes to schedules, poor engineering design/production/supplier liaison, over-stringent specifications, inconsistent decisions made by supplier quality assurance (SQA) personnel, abuse of power by SQA personnel and the use of 'loss of business' as a bargaining ploy in negotiating a reduction in price. It is not uncommon for a customer to talk quality to its suppliers and then act quite differently by relegating quality to secondary importance behind, for example, price and meeting the production schedule.
- The TQM and business excellence image which major purchasing organizations attempt to create in discussions with suppliers are not reflected in practice when supplier personnel visit their own manufacturing sites.
- A customer accepts non-conforming items over a long period of time, possibly unwittingly, and then suddenly criticizes the supplier for supplying non-conforming materials.
- A lack of a strategy for dealing with the tooling used for supplied parts. For example, a supplier may report to the customer that the customer-supplied tooling is reaching the end of its useful life. The customer then asks the supplier to carry out some minor refurbishment as a short-term measure; the supplier advises against this but is pressurized to do the repairs. When non-conforming parts are found in batches from the 'patched-up' tooling, the supplier acquires quality performance demerits.
- The customer fails to react positively to supplier concerns about design issues and is prepared to let the supplier carry the consequences.
- Failure to respond to a supplier's request for information and provide advice on queries.
- The use of supplied components that have not passed the initial sample approval procedure.
- The customer's SQA personnel are fooled by the camouflage measures, fakes and ruses employed by a supplier in an assessment of a vendor's quality system.
- The supplier is forced to hold stocks to cover a customer's inadequate scheduling and poor systems control.

Misconceptions regarding purchasing power

Purchasing power is a major issue in the buyer–supplier relationship. Lack of purchasing power is a commonly cited reason for the lack of success in improving supplier performance. The general view is that a purchaser's influence on its suppliers varies with its purchasing power, and the greater this is the more effective will be its SQA activities. These power imbalances can cause uneven levels of commitment in the relationship.

However, purchasing power alone is no guarantee of improving supplier performance. Companies with considerable purchasing power may well improve the quality of purchased items but will not necessarily achieve lasting benefits or motivate their suppliers to internalize the benefits of a process of continuous improvement to satisfy all their customers.

Conditions of Partnership

One of the key points which stands out is the wide diversity of partnership arrangements and definitions of partnership which have developed within the UK over the last decade. Although, as might be expected, there are differences between the public and private sector purchasing practices, there are now probably greater differences within the private sector. This is neither surprising nor any cause for alarm. However, to get the best out of partnership it is vital to understand the relationship, its current state and how it can be developed. The main driving force behind the move to customer–supplier partnerships has been the establishment of Japanese transplants in Europe, especially in the UK. However, it has to be recognized that the conditions under which European customers and suppliers operate are markedly different to those in Japan, where many large organizations have dedicated suppliers – companies who supply only them. This has led to the phenomenon, in the motor industry for example, where it is not just Toyota vying with Nissan and Honda for supremacy but the entire Toyota supply chain battling against the Nissan and Honda supply chains. These are clearly not the conditions which operate in the UK and the rest of Europe.

In the UK, dedicated suppliers are few and far between. The leading suppliers will be dealing with most if not all of the main companies in their industry. These suppliers will work closely with a particular customer to develop a product, process or service. The way that this is done varies but includes obtaining a supplier's input on product development and sharing product planning and development data with suppliers. However, the benefit to that customer is likely to be short-lived because, in a commercial environment, the supplier has to work with all its customers in a similar way in order to retain their business. There are, of course, issues of confidentiality which a first-tier supplier needs to respect when dealing with competitors involved in similar activities. It is clear that many UK customers and suppliers are abandoning adversarial relationships in favour of more co-operative partnerships. However, they are correctly attempting to fit these to their circumstances and needs rather than merely copying what worked for Japanese companies in Japan.

Nevertheless, it does mean that customers and suppliers are having, in a relatively short space of time, to learn, adopt and adapt an approach to purchasing which has taken Japanese companies over 40 years to develop. Quite rightly, different companies, industries and sectors are developing partnerships in their own way to meet their own needs and circumstances. However, it must be recognized that no one enters into a partnership with their suppliers or customers out of any altruistic motive or wish to be 'nice' to them. Partnerships are driven by hard-headed business objectives, mainly the need to achieve/maintain competitiveness in an increasingly global and hostile business environment. For example, even partnership suppliers are being told that for an increasing amount of business they are expected to cut costs. Therefore it has to be recognized that customer–supplier partnerships are not an easy option or some sort of panacea. This is particularly the case where a supplier is expected to meet the global requirements of its major customers. Underlying the rhetoric of partnership are difficult choices not only about whether to enter into partnerships and the type to be adopted but also, and perhaps more importantly, the internal upheavals this requires for most organizations.

The Issues to be Considered in Partnership

Burnes and Whittle (1998) show the steps that organizations need to take to decide whether to undertake a partnership initiative. However, even when organizations have examined all the issues involved and decided that the partnership approach is for them, they should not attempt to rush into building new external relationships and mechanisms until they are sure that the internal equivalents are appropriate and effective. In particular, senior management should:

- Outline clear objectives for the partnership initiative and ensure that those involved understand what they are and are committed to the ideals.
- Develop a strategy and plan to accomplish these objectives.
- Establish a procedure for deciding which suppliers to involve.
- Ensure that the philosophy of the organization is in line with, or can be realigned with, the partnership approach to purchasing, especially the need for teamwork.

Though the above will not necessarily be easily achieved, in the first instance, perhaps the most critical task will be for the organization to refocus and restructure those aspects of its own operations which are crucial to effective supplier performance. In effect, what is required is for it to put its own house in order before it asks its suppliers to do the same. In particular, the increasing complexity of the task of obtaining conforming supplies at the right time, at the right price and every time suggests that the conventional form and organization of the purchasing management function may no longer be adequate. Traditional staff structures based on tight functional groups have resulted in compartmentalized attitudes to suppliers which hinder supplier development. Companies will need to restructure their purchasing, quality and engineering departments to ensure that they have the right skills in dealing with suppliers, and that functional accountability and logistics are adequate to the task of supplier development. Enterprise resource planning (ERP) systems that link into personnel files, business functions of payroll, accounting, order-processing and sales, production-planning schedules and engineers' software are most useful in this regard. It is also important to establish a multi-functional team-work approach to purchasing.

To be effective, partnership requires well-trained personnel capable of working with suppliers to achieve the objectives which have been agreed; in effect, these personnel act as change agents. Purchasing and other staff who liaise with suppliers will need to understand the capabilities of suppliers' processes, systems and value streams and have a good working knowledge of the philosophy, principles, techniques of improvement and shop-floor procedures. It is also important that a customer's staff can speak the same language as their supplier's counterparts, whether these be in production, quality, design, finance, or sales activities. Embarking on an action plan for partnership with insufficient regard to the needs of the purchasing organization's skills is likely to result in frustration and possibly eventual failure of the initiative.

It is also important that the most effective mechanisms and linkages for communication and feedback are used. Typically, purchasing, quality, design, engineering/

technical and production personnel all talk to suppliers but with no single functional area accepting total responsibility for the quality, cost and delivery of the bought-out items. The need for clear accountability and co-ordination is a crucial factor in ensuring that channels of communication between customers and suppliers are effective and that suppliers receive a consistent message. Importantly, it must be clear who will be responsible for all negotiations and communications for current and future business with each supplier. An increasing number of organizations are conducting business with their suppliers via electronic transactions and real-time data. Typical of the documents involved in the transmission are planning schedules, goods receipt details and invoices. A number of major purchasers in particular market sectors (e.g. automotive, and defence and aerospace) have combined forces to establish e-marketplace systems that connect manufacturers, suppliers and customers by automating a range of processes and communication mechanisms. The use of the internet is examined in more detail in chapter 13.

For a company with many suppliers and bought-out items, it may take several years to introduce and develop an effective process of partnership. It has to be recognized, however, that not all suppliers will welcome or be capable of accepting this form of approach. Some, for whatever reason, will prefer to maintain a more adversarial approach. Though in the longer term a process of supply-base reduction will eliminate many of these, others may well remain. It will also be the case that while a few suppliers may be world-class, the majority will need to improve if they are to meet the company's expectations. Therefore, most companies will find that they will need to adopt different practices with different suppliers. Probably, in the majority of cases, a partnership approach based on a commitment to supplier improvement will be the order of the day. On the other hand, with those suppliers whose performance is already world-class, it may be the customer who finds itself being improved. However, with some suppliers, relationships may well remain antagonistic.

Therefore, before starting a process of partnership, a company will need to review its supplier base and identify those suppliers with whom it needs to work with in the long term and the type of relationship it will be able to establish. The strategy should reflect core manufacturing expertise. As it will not be possible to launch a partnership approach with all its suppliers at once, the company will need to establish a mechanism for selecting the initial group of suppliers. One approach is to concentrate on new products, product and process modifications and new vendors. Another approach involves the use of Pareto analysis to focus priorities by ranking bought-out components and materials according to some appropriate parameter (e.g. gross annual spend).

To assist their suppliers, some major organizations have documented the fundamental requirements for the control of quality and achievement of improvement, some have even produced explanatory booklets (QS9000, as discussed in chapter 14, is a good example of this). These organizations make it a condition of the purchase order agreement that suppliers' products comply with these requirements. The motor industry, through the Society of Motor Manufacturers and Traders (SMMT), and the aerospace sector, through SABAC, are using specially trained 'master engineers' who carry out weekly shop-floor improvement workshops to spread best practice amongst the respective supplier bases, in particular SMEs.

Assisting suppliers to improve their performance is important; however, it must be recognized that the delivery of non-conforming product from a supplier can often be attributed to an ambiguous purchasing specification and poorly detailed customer requirements. Purchasing specifications are working documents used by both customer and supplier and must be treated as such. The content of material and product specifications has become highly standardized, and usually includes such features as functional physical characteristics, dimensional details, reliability characteristics, methods of test and criteria for acceptance, conditions of manufacture, installation, storage and use, and so on. The purchasing department should review the accuracy and completeness of purchasing documents before they are released to suppliers. It is good practice to send these documents to the quality department for comment prior to transmission to the supplier.

It is also important to recognize that, just as suppliers can learn from customers, the reverse also applies. Suppliers are knowledgeable in their own field of operation and should be given every opportunity to provide a design input to the preparation of the specification. With the reduction in specialist technical staff in many customer organizations, this is now a common occurrence. Suppliers will be more likely to accept responsibility for defects and their associated costs if they are involved in the design of the product or formally agree with the customer the specification and drawing for the part to be produced. This supplier input to the design process is a key factor in cost avoidance and reduction and helps to reduce the product development lead time.

One outcome of partnerships is that an increasing number of major purchasing organizations are awarding more long-term contracts and contracts for the life of a part. Strategic sourcing (i.e. single or dual sourcing) is considered by many writers and practitioners to be a complementary policy. This will inevitably contribute to the reduction in the size of organizations' supplier bases. In the future the number of suppliers a customer uses will decrease as more and more customers buy upper-level assemblies. However, some organizations have sought to avoid single sourcing and being completely dependent on the supplier because of worries about being put into a difficult supply situation should the supplier experience problems or become insolvent. It is a balance of power situation on which careful judgement is needed. A reduction in the supplier base can result in benefits such as:

- Less variation in the characteristics of the supplied product.
- Improved opportunity for improving processes, developing innovations and prototyping and proving.
- Increases in the amount of time the customer's quality assurance and purchasing personnel can devote to vendors, and more frequent interactions.
- Improved and simplified communications with vendors.
- Less paperwork.
- Less transportation.
- Less handling and inspection activity.
- Fewer accounts to be maintained and thus reduced costs for both parties.

It is easier to develop a partnership relationship if the suppliers are in close proximity to the customer. Consequently, a number of customers are now reversing their international sourcing strategies to develop shorter supply lines and are recommending that suppliers set up operations close to their main manufacturing facilities. Closeness is also a vital element in the use of a JIT purchasing strategy.

The Process of Partnership

Having put its own house in order and selected suitable suppliers for inclusion in its partnership programme, the next step for the purchasing organization is to get the selected suppliers involved and obtain their commitment. This entails communicating to suppliers what is required and reaching an understanding with them on a set of common objectives.

The most practical way of setting about this task is to hold presentations to suppliers covering issues such as:

- The approach being taken to partnership.
- What is expected of suppliers and what assistance they can expect from the customer.
- The quality system standard to be used.
- How suppliers' performance will be assessed; how the results will be communicated.
- What assistance will be provided to help suppliers improve.

Presentations to suppliers can be held either on the customer's premises or at individual suppliers' sites. A supplier conference and/or presentation must give those involved an opportunity to air grievances and discuss problems in an open and honest manner and must be aimed at establishing a climate of co-operation and commitment.

Once a supplier's senior management team have agreed to participate in the partnership process, it is usual for the purchasing organization to visit the supplier's factory and carry out a formal vendor-approval survey. The objective of the survey is to assess the supplier's suitability as a business partner, including the identification of strengths and weaknesses, awareness of continuous improvement mechanisms and the cost-effectiveness of collaboration. The survey is a multi-disciplinary task which usually involves the customer's purchasing, quality, engineering and technical personnel. The survey should cover areas such as controls, processes and capabilities, workshop environment, plant, technology, research and development, quality systems, staff attitudes, responses, tooling, and planning and administrative systems.

As part of its audit, a customer must assess the supplier's commitment to advanced product quality planning (APQP). A useful summary of APQP, which consists of five phases – plan and define the programme, product design and development, process design and development, product and process validation and feedback, assessment and corrective action – is provided by Thisse (1998). APQP commences with a joint review of the specification and classification of product characteristics and the production of an FMEA. The supplier should prepare a control plan to summarize the quality planning for significant product characteristics. This would typically include a description of the manufacturing operation and process flows, equipment used, control characteristics, control plans, specification limits, the use of SPC and mistake-proofing, inspection details, and corrective and preventative action methods. The next step is for the supplier to provide initial samples for evaluation; this would be supported by data on process capability on the key characteristics identified by both parties, plus test results. Following successful evaluation of initial samples, the supplier is in a position to start a trial production run prior to routine volume production.

Once the customer has assessed the adequacy of the supplier's policies, systems, procedures and manufacturing methods, and the supplier has been able to demonstrate the quality of its shipped product, the goods inward inspection of suppliers can be reduced considerably; in some cases down to the ideal situation of direct line supply. At this point, 'preferred' or 'certified' supplier status can be conferred on the supplier. Many companies now also operate a supplier award scheme to recognize excellent supplier performance.

This assessment should not be a one-off exercise. An increasing number of major purchasing organizations will audit all their suppliers at regular intervals. This is to ensure that suppliers' systems, processes and procedures are being maintained and improved. The frequency with which each supplier is reassessed is dependent on such factors as:

- The supplier's performance.
- The status awarded to the supplier.
- The type of item being supplied.
- The volume of parts being supplied.
- The occurrence of a major change at the supplier (e.g. change of management, change of facilities and process change).
- The supplier's request for assistance.

The partnership process is ongoing, aimed at building up an effective business relationship based on openness – a relationship which demands a greater and quicker exchange of information between both parties. During the early days, the parameters of the new relationship are never completely clear to either party and it takes time to work out ground rules which are suitable for both of them. A number of major purchasing organizations have introduced electronic ordering and purchasing with their key suppliers and even the electronic sharing of product data. The more that this can be done to transfer data in digital format the better in terms of error reduction and improved communication. This linking of information systems and processes can often test the strength of the relationship, in particular, when incompatibilities in customer and supplier systems are discovered. The electronic data exchange relates to quality data, technical requirements and specifications, schedules, manufacturing programmes, lead times, inventory management, and invoicing. Suppliers are obliged to communicate any changes to materials, processes or methods that may affect the dimensional, functional, compositional or appearance characteristics of the product. Customers are obliged to provide sufficient information and assistance to aid the development of their suppliers' approach to continuous improvement. In some cases this extends to joint problem-solving and cost-reduction activities. When the relationship has developed from problem-solving to problem avoidance, it indicates it has passed a major hurdle.

It is argued by writers such as Fruin (1992) and Morris and Imrie (1992) that the benefits of partnership are best achieved by spreading the concept to all members of the value chain from raw material to end product. This is perhaps best handled by a supplier association. Such an association is usually taken to be a group of first-level suppliers and a particular customer. This is a loose grouping who share knowledge and experience for the purpose of continuous improvement down the supply chain. This is characteristic of the Japanese supply chain, where it is also usual for first-tier supplier to develop its own supplier associations. Fruin (1992) points out that 'the

Toyota Motor Corporation has three regional supplier associations and Nissan Motor has two'. These forms of co-operative supplier network are now starting to develop in Europe. For example, Morris and Imrie (1992) describe a network in place at Lucas Girling, and Hines (1992) describes how the Welsh Development Agency, through its 'Source Wales' initiative, has assisted Llanelli Radiators to form a supplier association.

Potential Difficulties of Operating Partnerships

In a partnership which is regarded as a success by both parties, everyone wins. If only one party is considered the winner, as is the case with typical adversarial purchasing arrangements, there can be little basis for a partnership. A partnership is about a long-term relationship between a customer and a set of suppliers in order to reduce total costs all round, develop and maintain a competitive position and satisfy the end-customer. It is important that the partnership is lived in the way it is articulated. This is far from easy and there are many potential obstacles.

The following, based on our practical and research work, are the main difficulties usually experienced in developing a partnership approach:

- An over-emphasis on cost reduction and piece price down, rather than the total cost of acquisition.
- Variations in the approaches of individuals and a general lack of cohesion.
- A perceived lack of understanding by the customer of the business implications of its actions, e.g. sudden and large-scale changes in production level and work mix, changes in priorities, and a failure to stick with delivery schedules.
- Poor and inconsistent communication.
- An unwillingness by customers to reciprocate openness with the suppliers.
- Poor reliability of information and systems.
- Inadequate project management.
- A tendency for the customer to blame all the problems that are encountered on the supplier.
- Inability to respond to things which have gone wrong and to resolve the problem.
- Failure to respond to suggestions and ideas for improvement.
- A lack of understanding from the customer of a supplier's constraints and problems.
- A customer asking the supplier to do things which they themselves have not achieved.
- A lack of understanding of the minor problems which undermine the credit-ability of the customer.
- A mismatch between what is requested and the existing infrastructure.

Summary

Suppliers are now recognized as an essential part of any organization's competitiveness. There are two major reasons for this: greater global specialization and changes in the nature of competition. Effective partnership requires purchasing organizations to treat suppliers as long-term business partners, and this necessitates a fundamental shift from the traditional adversarial buyer–supplier relationship. Properly implemented partnership will help to reduce costs and increase market share to the benefit of both parties, together with technology transfer issues surrounding product, process, practices, and systems. However, the nature and mechanisms of partnership must be related to the particular circumstances and needs of those involved. In conclusion, the following dos and don'ts developed from the work of Dale and Galt (1990) will help both customers and suppliers establish the type of partnership that is most appropriate for them:

Do

- Look at ways of reducing the size of the supplier base. By reducing incoming material, component and sub-assembly variability, outgoing product and service quality will improve.
- Ensure that, in support of the supplier development process and its various stages, your staff and those in the customer organization use the appropriate engineering quality tools. These tools include statistical process control, the seven quality control tools, the seven management tools, FMEA, FTA, QFD, design of experiments; the tools also facilitate design for manufacturability and cost avoidance.
- Involve suppliers in new product development and investigate the full range of ways of achieving this.
- Encourage suppliers to dispatch only conforming product, thereby eliminating the need to carry out duplicate testing and inspection on incoming goods.
- Award long-term contracts to key suppliers who have shown commitment and improvements in order to demonstrate the tangible benefits that can arise from a partnership.
- Consider implementing an assessment and rating scheme to select and measure the performance of suppliers. Poor selection will lead to increased costs as other suppliers are sought to compensate for the deficiencies of the one chosen without due care.
- Develop procedures, objectives and strategies for communicating with the supply base.
- Treat suppliers as partners, thereby establishing trust, co-operation and dependence.
- Ensure that the staff dealing with suppliers act in a consistent and courteous manner and match actions to words.
- Respond positively to suppliers' requests for information.
- Develop and decide upon mutually agreed purposes and values that define the relationship and measure its success. The approach by the customer must be seen by the supplier as helpful, constructive and of mutual benefit.
- Decide and agree on the best means of promoting and monitoring good communication in order to create a constructive dialogue and ensure the provision of reliable information. This requires defined points of communication to be established.
- Listen and be receptive to feedback and be willing to share information and ideas and discuss problems. Discover and respond to functional perceptions, in both customer and supplier, of the state of the partnership.

- Provide education to raise awareness of the partnership approach and specific training for the new skills required.
- Be honest about the state of the partnership and avoid complacency.
- Ensure that customer and supplier organizations are sufficiently knowledge-able about each other's business, products, procedures, and systems and how the respective organization's worked.
- Remember a flexible and open approach, which encourages positive constructive criticism, is crucial.

Don't
- Begin partnership unless senior management understand what is involved and support the concept.
- Overlook the fact that senior management commitment, in both customers and suppliers, to the ideals of partnership is necessary, along with their active participation in the process, including understanding its importance. Manage-ment must recognize that it is not a 'quick fix' solution to achieve cost reduction.
- Treat suppliers as adversaries.
- Keep suppliers short of information.
- Buy goods on price alone. Ensure other criteria such as quality and delivery performance, R&D potential, competitive manufacturing and engineering excellence are also taken into account.
- Constantly switch suppliers.
- Accept non-conforming goods.
- Talk quality but act production schedule and price per piece.
- Forget that the initial samples procedure is a key factor in receiving conform-ing supplies.
- Forget that the customer and supplier must be prepared to add value to each other's operations, through reducing costs and identifying opportunities for improvement.
- Forget that the move to partnering usually takes longer than expected.
- Overlook the fact that the principles and values of partnership must be cas-caded to all relevant levels in the customer and the supplier and must be fully accepted, in particular by those staff at the day-to-day contact point.
- Forget that the effectiveness of the partnership must be measured and monitored.
- Forget that developments affecting both parties should be carried out with mutual consultation.
- Assume that there will be no problems; ensure that suitable counter-measures are ready to address the obstacles encountered.
- Forget that the partnership process and lean manufacture go together.

References

Burnes, B. and Dale, B. G. (eds) (1998), *Working in Partnership: Best Practice in Customer–Supplier Relations*. Aldershot, Hants.: Gower Press.

Burnes, B. and Whittle, P. (1998), Supplier partnerships: assessing the potential and getting started. In B. Burnes and B. G. Dale (eds), *Working in Partnership: Best Practice in Customer–Supplier Relations*, ch. 6. Aldershot, Hants.: Gower Press.

Dale, B. G. and Galt, J. (1990), Customer–supplier relationships in the motor industry: a vehicle manufacturer's perspective. *Proceedings of the Institution of Mechanical Engineers*, 204(D4), 179–86.

Fruin, W. M. (1992), *The Japanese Enterprise System: Competitive Strategies and Co-operative Structures*. New York: Oxford University Press.

Hines, P. (1992), Materials management for the 21st century: Llanelli Radiators Supplier Association. *Logistics Today*, March–April, 19–21.

Lascelles, D. M. and Dale, B. G. (1990), Examining the barriers to supplier development. *International Journal of Quality and Reliability Management*, 7(2), 46–56.

Morris, J. and Imrie, R. (1992), *Transforming Buyer–Supplier Relationships*. London: Macmillan.

Thisse, L. C. (1998), Advanced quality planning: a guide for any organisation. *Quality Progress*, February, 73–7.

chapter thirteen

Business to Business, Old-Economy Businesses and the Quality Function

R. Williams and R. Visser

Introduction

The so-called new economy has taken a beating over the past few years. The dot.coms have come – and many have also gone. Perhaps the last great white hope of the new revolutionary age, Enron, has filed for bankruptcy. But the phenomenon that is the internet is not going away: it just keeps growing (Kirkpatrick 2001). Slowly but surely an increasing number of individuals and companies are coming to rely on it for doing business. The changes will, perhaps, be more incremental than the instant revolution originally predicted. But they will surely, in the end, be just as radical; it will just take longer before we all realize what is happening. The purpose of this chapter is to look at some of the possible consequences of the current developments for the quality function.

The internet can be used for three main purposes. First, through the use of e-mail and similar derivatives, it is a messaging medium par excellence. Secondly, it is a medium for transactions: for buying and selling. Finally, it can be used as an entertainment or information medium. All three have implications for the effective utilization of the organization's assets, but in this chapter we will concentrate on the area which is likely to impinge most closely on most organizations: the medium of transactions.

What is the Effect of the Internet on Business Transactions?

The internet will have a major impact on business transactions because of the differences it brings. Timmers (1999) has pointed out three major characteristics which distinguish transactions using electronic industrial markets from what has gone before. The first distinguishing characteristic is globalization: the internet increases an organization's possibilities for global sourcing and for global selling. As the noted central banker Greenspan (2000) has concluded, by lowering the costs of transactions and information, technology has reduced market frictions and provided significant impetus to the process of broadening world markets. This means that considerations about location can become secondary and price competition is likely to increase. The second characteristic Timmers notes is a major increase in the possibilities for customization. Internet technologies facilitate specification design and pricing online, which again is likely to increase price competition. A third characteristic of doing business on the internet is that it facilitates the solving of customer demands through using a group of business partners. The traditional linear model from producer to customer no longer holds; value can instead be delivered more quickly and cheaply through a network of partners.

Other experts have argued that transactions using electronic commerce come far closer than do transactions using traditional media to the economist's ideal of perfect competition, in that barriers to entry are lowered, transaction costs are reduced, and buyers have improved access to information (e.g. Shapiro and Varian 1999; Wyckoff 1997).

Such fundamental changes as carrying out transactions using the internet can bring have encouraged major investment from those seeking to exploit them. The pattern up to 2000 was clear. For example, in America revenues from transactions using the internet tripled in 1999; in Europe and Japan they rose faster still. But the biggest growth was expected in the area of transactions between businesses; the so called business-to-business (B2B) sector. *The Economist* (26 February 2000) reported that 'In 1999 global e commerce was worth some $150 billion with around 80 per cent of these transactions being between one business and another.'

It is interesting that, in this business-to-business sector, although the growth rate might have slowed, it is still continuing strongly. Forrester (2001), a respected research organization in the field, expects this sector to reach nearly $2.7 trillion in the US by 2004 and to reach $7 trillion or 27 per cent of total US trade by 2006. Another respected market researcher, Gartner (2001), forecast in March 2001 that by 2004 the global business-to-business e-commerce market would have continued growing and would be worth £4.8 trillion. As James (2000) has remarked, it is hard to know how seriously to take these dramatic predictions, but major growth in this area, despite the downturn both in the world economy in general and in internet-related stocks in particular, seems inevitable.

The growth will be important for quality management because it is expected to be concentrated in medium and large old-economy companies. Forrester, for example, reports that 79 per cent of large companies expected to be trading online by 2002. And it is in medium and large old-economy companies that most quality professionals are still concentrated. Therefore it is on these types of companies that we will concentrate in this chapter.

Medium and Large Old-Economy Companies and the New Economy

Medium and large old-economy companies can be involved in transactions within the new economy in three major ways:

- First, by making investments in and even taking over new-economy companies. For example, Nortel Networks Corporation, a telecommunications equipment giant, had, by 2000, a minority interest in 86 high-technology companies which allowed it to incorporate the smaller companies' products into its own broader product offering. It also made seven major acquisitions in the first half of 2000 for a total of more than $11 billion and had a process in place which, at the height of the boom, was monitoring hundreds of technology start-ups and resulted in between 20 and 30 potential acquisitions coming up for serious consideration every week.
- The second way in which large old-economy companies can be involved in transactions is by starting up their own subsidiaries to operate within the new economy. A typical example would be the banking sector. It was not in the best interest of banks to encourage their offline customers, from whom they largely derive their current profits, to migrate over to the internet. So it was in their own interests to set up small separate companies to cover the fledgling world of online financial services (see Wenninger 2000).
- The third way is by attempting to incorporate the new economy into their old-economy organization. It is this third area which is probably the most interesting from the point of view of the effective utilization of organizational assets. This is because old-economy companies who invested in new-economy companies, or who started up their own, normally ran them as separate entities. Clearly financial reasons played an important part in this decision, but so also did organizational considerations. The organization and culture of new-economy companies were often very different from those of the mother company, and running the new-economy companies as separate entities was felt to minimize any possible cross-pollution from new to old or vice versa. In contrast, when large and complex old-economy companies attempted to integrate business-to-business e-commerce into their own existing organization, interesting problems, and thus possibilities for the quality function to increase effective utilization, arose. This chapter examines these interesting problems and possibilities.

Although the field is complex and still changing fast, there seem to be three major ways in which large old-economy companies are attempting to integrate the new economy as extensions of their current businesses:

- The first way is by treating the internet as an extension of their normal market. They therefore use it primarily to improve current customer relations and as a medium to sell more product or service and to buy cheaper. For every business the net – at minimum – offers opportunities for reducing operating cost levels and/or enhancing services (Venkatraman 2000).
- The second way in which old-economy companies are attempting to integrate the new economy is by using the net to expand and improve their current partnership relationships amongst their key suppliers. As Timmers (1999) has suggested, the net can encourage very close integration between the partners throughout a value chain.
- Finally, we would suggest there is also a third approach which is much more fundamental and which requires that old-economy organizations re-evaluate their business models before deciding on their e-commerce strategy and

practice. This third approach requires that management should re-examine why customers buy from them, look at all stages in the processes involved and consider how the net could impact each stage, and then, if necessary, develop new business models, with their required reorganization.

We will outline each of these areas in turn, and consider their possible implications for quality management.

There is a dearth of reliable information about this whole area. Most publications at the time of writing this chapter are based more on experience than research and tend to quote as examples the same few companies, who are often not only reorganizing to accommodate the new internet economy but are also intimately involved in selling related equipment or services. This chapter is therefore based on personal experience of working in the field, plus interviews with others more experienced than us, in addition to the available literature sources. The comments made must therefore be taken as possibilities rather than probabilities.

Companies Buying and Selling on the Internet

The first major developments in this area started in the mid-1990s and saw major firms such as Walmart and General Electric (GE) moving buying and selling online to cut costs and speed supplies. The aims of cutting paperwork and time may have been simple, but the results were impressive. GE, for example, has built up a trading process network which is a web-based link to suppliers so that they can bid for GE components contracts. This global supplier network links 1,500 corporate buyers and around 16,000 suppliers. According to information issued in 2000 by GE, the system cut procurement cycles in half, processing costs by one-third and the cost of goods purchased by between 5 and 50 per cent. In the 18 months up to December 2001 around 2,000 e-auctions worth $416 billion have been completed through this route. Every GE company now has targets for e-auctioning of around 60–70 per cent of total spend, and this e-procurement model is applied not just to indirect spend but to many services as well (*Financial Times*, 5 December 2001). Indeed the GE CEO Jeff Imelt has been reported (Useem 2001) as going even further in suggesting that his managers should either digitalize or outsource all parts of their business which do not touch the customer directly.

IBM provides another good example of the savings to be made. By 1999 it had plugged 6,700 suppliers into its online procurement system and bought more than $12 billion-worth of goods over the net, eliminating around five million invoices. This, together with sharper purchasing as a result of increased transparency etc., resulted in IBM saving $240 million on the $11 billion it spends. Customer support is another area where major savings can be made in some companies through putting customer technical advice online. IBM, for example, estimates that, for every service call handled through ibm.com, it saves 70 to 90 per cent of the cost of having a person take that call. In 1999 it expect to handle 35 million online service requests, thus saving $750 million.

Since much of these benefits in savings can be achieved without connectivity, these applications do not imply major organizational change for the old-economy organization involved, but they can of course put price and on-time delivery pressure on suppliers. They also put major strain on the systems involved, since many business-to-business transactions tend to be critical to the functioning of a business, and often carry high financial penalties in the event of a failed delivery. Business-to-consumer transactions can go wrong without threatening the supplier's future. But failure of an important business-to-business transaction can mean not just heavy legal costs but also the loss of a key customer and credibility in the marketplace.

However, despite this potential danger, attempts by individual companies to buy and sell through the net were quickly followed by neutral independent firms bringing together a multitude of buyers and sellers to create genuine markets to help spread this process. Attention was originally called to this new class of businesses by Hagel and Singer (1999), who referred to them as 'infomediaries'. Although the field is complicated and changing fast, three major groupings within this general business model have been distinguished:

- *Aggregators.* This grouping initially grew rapidly but is now declining. Aggregators helped buyers in fragmented markets select products by providing up-to-the-minute price and product information and a single contact point for service.
- *Online auctioneers* are the second major grouping within this general business model. The service they provide is to dispose of surplus goods and services at the best price. An example would be 58K.com, which is an online print procurement auction site that is free to printers and their customers. Print buyers submit jobs, specifying the length of the auction, their preferred bidders and the number of bids they wish to receive. Printers, who must be authorized by 58K.com, then submit bids anonymously in an open auction process. 58K.com takes a fee of 2 per cent of the total print order. The company suggests that print buyers can save at least 10 per cent on their procurement costs and often 25 per cent of their time. Printers gain access to a far wider spread of business and, given more information about demand in their specific market, have the ability to find work to fill excess and expensive capacity on their presses. And the 2 per cent charge is clearly much less than they would normally have spent on sales staff.
- *Exchanges* are the third major grouping. Their service is to create liquidity in fragmented markets, by matching bids and offers and by acting as neutral enforcers of the rules. A typical example would be NTE, which sells surplus load space in lorries. These exchanges can aid a company's profitability, for example by enabling it to buy more effectively as well as to eliminate surplus capacity. But since they are global and open to all, then they also put major pressure on prices in the markets in which they operate even though they may be managed by neutral third parties.

The rapid initial spread of business exchanges was followed by a realization by many large customers that if they combined their individual buying power with that of large-scale competitors into a separate buying and selling exchange it would have a major effect on their procurement costs. For example, General Motors, Ford and Daimler Chrysler merged their individual exchanges in early 2000 to create Covisint, a virtual marketplace for the automotive industry which it is estimated will eventually buy $240 billion-worth of parts from tens of thousands of suppliers. The result, it has been reported, according to a study by Goldman Sachs, would be cost savings averaging just over $1,000 per vehicle (*Financial Times*, 14 June 2000). It is therefore hardly surprising that other major manufacturers moved to join this consortium, with Renault/Nissan already committed. Perhaps even more surprisingly, some major tier one suppliers (see Dyer 1996) such as Delphi Automotive Systems, Johnson Controls, Dana, Federal Mogul and Siemens, who build major sub-assemblies, are also reported to be interested. In 2001 Covisint reported it had already handled procurement transactions worth more than $45 billion.

Major companies can use the internet like this to put themselves at the centre of new e-business ecosystems that will transform their way of doing business. Car-makers have long used electronic data interchange (EDI) to link with big suppliers. But EDI is inherently rigid; it provides basic information about transactions but it cannot adapt to rapidly changing markets. It is also too expensive for small firms. In contrast the internet is more flexible, cheap to access and open to all.

So in the business-to-business arena it is hardly surprising that there has been a shift in emphasis from industry-wide marketplaces to private single-company ex-changes. Many companies have found it difficult to co-operate with competitors to build an exchange. Such co-operation can be complicated. For example, the automobile manufacturers found that working together in Covisint involved the integration of back-end systems, the harmonization of processes, agreement on strategic priorities and the creation of a management structure acceptable to all parties. In contrast many organizations have quickly realized that building a private exchange on which they can easily conduct reverse auctions with suppliers is relat-ively straightforward.

Suppliers quickly learn that it is not only price which is important in the new exchanges. Since many companies now have a just-in-time manufacturing and invent-ory process, they are totally dependent upon a completely reliable supply chain. So the new on-demand no stock procurement policies of the market site owners will also place major demands on supplier reliability, production speed and flexibility of response. This means that a high level of systems integration will be needed. The companies involved will have to integrate their internal manufacturing warehousing, inventory and shipping systems. Many such systems will have to be upgraded so that they can send and receive the new extensible markup language (XML) data and thus become part of an end-to-end solution. This is likely to give many organizations major problems since many of these internal systems are still implemented on older mainframe and mini computers which could be difficult to upgrade because they are based on architectures that were defined before XML was invented. If they have not reorganized in order to get their major internal processes under full control, and if they themselves have not become web-based, in the opinion of at least one very influential management figure, Jack Welch, late of GE, they will experience major problems (*Fortune*, 1 May 2000).

The interconnectivity demanded internally will have a major influence upon the organization. For example, order-taking systems have to be customer-friendly and closely linked with planning and production systems to ensure just-in-time delivery and zero stocks as far as possible. Marketing is likely to increase in status and power at the expense of the sales function as customer relationships become more import-ant and more and more conventional sales are taken over by the net. Also, procure-ment will have to be online to ensure adequate supplies of whatever may be needed. Closer links will also be required with the total administrative system to ensure that as far as possible the whole paper chain from order to invoice and payment should proceed without any man hours being involved. Finally, logistics and distribution must also be linked into the system since delivery windows agreed with customers have to be precisely met. These functions are also likely to gain heavily in status and importance.

The recent growth of outsourcing will merely add to the complexity of the necessary systems integration. Over the past few years, as co-ordination costs have been cut with the help of information and communications technology, firms have been moving to outsource more of what were perceived as their non-core competencies such as design, procurement, marketing, distribution and after sales support as well as finance and human resources (Sarkar et al. 1995). Since the internet considerably reduces transaction costs between buyer and seller, the possibility of outsourcing is even greater. But, even if only non-core supplies are involved, the organization still needs to ensure close and smooth-running interconnectivity. It is probable that, once an organization is seeing 15 to 20 per cent of sales go through the web, it will be forced to move rapidly to the kinds of internal process integration outlined. And the overview described above shows that most of the major business processes will be affected.

But many companies still have a long way to go. For example, airlines have long been regarded as leading in their use of the internet for doing business and yet Delta, a major American carrier, has recently been reported by Kirkpatrick (2001) as having no fewer than 25 different databases containing customer information. It is estimated that eventually it will only need one or two. It is only by combining these individual function-based databases that companies will be able to move to a situation where a customer's order automatically triggers reactions in relevant areas throughout the company, let alone all the way down a supply chain.

The effects of moving to selling sizeable amounts through the net are so profound that they raise the question as to which industries these business exchanges are most likely to develop and thus leave little freedom for suppliers to opt out. They will expand fastest when suppliers are either forced into joining them by their customers or when they see joining as having clear advantages accruing to themselves as well as to their customers. They will be forced to join when an industry has a large fragmented group of suppliers serving a few major customers, such as in the auto industry. Under these circumstances suppliers are likely to be forced to join, whether they fear for lower prices or for competitors sharing information on pricing and supply deals.

Again business-to-business exchanges will grow fast in a situation where everyone saves money through lower processing costs when they use an intermediary, for example, when markets are complex and fragmented and where no one has dominant power, such as in the life sciences, or in complex industries with sophisticated supply chains like electronic components or forest products (Kaplan and Sawhney 2000).

Within these special market situations, the business-to-business exchanges which will grow fastest will probably be those concentrating on maintenance, repair and operating (MRO) goods. These items are not related to the core business of the customer but this can be a vast business in its own right. The Ford Motor Company, for example, estimates its own non-core purchasing business at $16 billion annually, covering everything from simple janitorial and office supplies to huge welding machines. It is this area which lends itself most easily to being obtained through the transparency and global reach of business-to-business exchanges (Kaplan and Sawhney 2000).

Virtual Communities or Total Value Chain Integration

The second way in which old-economy larger companies will react to the new challenges and opportunities posed by the growth of business transactions using the internet is to attempt either to set up or to join supply-chain communities. Most often these will be a vertical chain of all the key suppliers involved in servicing one major customer.

Bovet and Martha (2000) have estimated that the supply chain accounts for 60 to 80 per cent of many companies' total costs and so it is highly likely that they will focus on extracting greater value from these operations. The ultimate aim of any manufacturer of complex equipment must be to build to order and not to stock, since the financial savings are so large. Probably this level has only been reached by a very few companies such as Dell Computer and Cisco Systems (Hartman and Sifonis 2000). However, it has been reported that, although it takes on average between 60 and 100 days to make a car and deliver it to the customer, manufacturers such as General Motors and Toyota are planning systems to bring this down to five days (*Economist*, 8 January 2000). Car manufacturers expect cutting cycle time to this extent will result in taking around 50 per cent out of overall inventory. With at least $20 billion in parts on hand at any one time to support assembly systems, the savings on carrying costs alone could add up to several hundred million dollars per year.

The revolution which this will demand not just from their own systems but also from those of their whole supply chain is obvious. It will require forming web-based links not just between internal departments but also between suppliers and customers right down the chain. It means integration of the whole value chain into what different experts have given different names, although they appear to be describing the same phenomenon. For example, Timmers (1999) calls them a 'virtual business community', Rayport and Sviolka (1995) a 'Virtual Value Chain' and Bovet and Martha (2000) 'Value Nets'.

Manufacturers use such digital networks to tie together suppliers who work in concert to deliver tailored solutions, often making the product simultaneously at a variety of plants to co-ordinate production to keep inventories light and costs low (Bovet and Martha 2000). Cisco Systems is a classic example of a manufacturer using such a network. Cisco develops and manufactures high-performance networking products that link geographically dispersed local and wide-area networks. The company has created an elaborate web of partners on the net, including manufacturers, assemblers, distributors, OEMs strategic partners, and sales channels. Products are conceived, designed, developed, manufactured, sold, serviced and enhanced from multiple locations, all on the web. Cisco transfers its strategic knowledge (i.e. customer requirements and company strategy) and product knowledge assets to its strategic partners. In turn, Cisco receives system design input and planning knowledge from these partners. With Cisco's active encouragement, participants lubricate the system by freely exchanging knowledge and opinions. On an hourly basis the net is the channel for these exchanges. This community enables dramatically low cycle times, reduced costs and fast innovation. Cisco's value network is drenched in intangible value exchanges which create its strategic advantage in the market (Tapscott 1999). At Cisco, the whole process of ordering, outsourced contract manufacturing and shipping, payment, help desk and support centre has been automated: 64 per cent of all Cisco orders passed through the system without being touched by anyone in 1999 (Venkatraman 2000). According to the finance director, the company can now close its books in one day instead of 10, and it saves $4,500 million a year by using the web (Hartman and Sifonis 2000).

Dell, a major producer of computers and user of the direct selling method, is pursuing a similar policy. Many of Dell's business customers use the internet to order computers, a process that automatically spawns the design, manufacturing and shipping of customized products. Although Dell still carries out some of its own manufacturing, if manufacturing assets are looked at in dollar terms they are small, roughly six to seven weeks of cashflow. But Dell is connected with capital-intensive suppliers like Intel and Solectron, who supply Dell's factories in real time. This system led to the company, in 2000, making returns on invested capital of 292 per cent and each Dell employee has been reported as generating more than $750,000 in revenue, compared to an industry average of around $525,000 (James 2000).

In the computer business, with model changes occurring very rapidly, Dell considers that inventory devalues at 1 per cent per week. So the company operates with a maximum of six to seven days of inventory whereas it estimates its competitors to have ten times that level.

Cisco and Dell sit at the centre of net-based webs of partners. In such situations information about all elements in the value chain has become widely available and no one partner in the network has to own the elements to know what is going on (Rayport and Sviolka 1995). Close, trusting partnership-type collaboration between the partners is essential. No business involved can afford to have even one weak link in the chain because, increasingly, the competitiveness of firms will not depend on their resources and capabilities alone but will be decided by their ability to mobilize their whole value chain. And it is value chains or constellations rather than businesses which will compete against each other (Cool 1997).

In a virtual supply-chain community, the relationship between partners will be one of partnership based on long term relationships and involvement in joint new product development. As van Alstyne (1997) has suggested, value chain constellations are critically dependent on affiliation, loyalty and trust. Ideally, to build these there should be shared values and social norms of loyalty as well as frequent trading and collaboration. But not only will values be shared but also costing and profit margins. Therefore suppliers, in order to justify their place in the community, will have to place a major premium on continually improving their performance and developing leading-edge new products and services. They should also possess service skills which clearly in the eyes of the customer exceed those of the competition (Bovet and Martha 2000).

Disaggregation and Organizational Revolution

The third possible reaction of old-economy companies to the growth of the net economy is to step back and reassess how it might affect their business. Schwartz (1997) indeed argues that the major opportunities posed by the net economy lie in first deconstructing the value chain in order subsequently to reassemble it, if necessary, with new roles and new business actors. Companies are thus being counselled to rethink the strategic fundamentals of their business (Evans and Wurster 1999). These authors argue that information defines supplier relationships. Having a relationship means that two companies have established certain channels of communication and information. When information is carried by things (e.g. by a salesman or piece of direct mail), it goes where the things go and no further. But once everyone is connected electronically, information can travel by itself. The traditional link between the flow of product-related information and the flow of the product itself can be broken. The net enables information to be unbundled from its physical carrier. This means that information can cheaply reach many more people in a form which can be easily made personally appealing to them. This changing economics of information, as Evans and Wurster (1999) call it, threatens to undermine established value chains, requiring many companies to rethink their strategies fundamentally, which will often result in unbundling vertically integrated value chains.

The rethinking always starts with the customer. It will involve going back to the basic value proposition and understanding why end-customers actually buy from the organization concerned as opposed to the competition. Having established this, everything that makes this possible has to be separated out. For example, the goods or services involved, the key business processes, the financial and human resources required, the organizational structures and the major systems and procedures. These are the molecular elements that can be redesigned, added to and reconfigured to transform the value proposition. And what needs to be examined is how transacting business using the net can help add new forms of value at each step on the way.

Such disaggregation can be a highly threatening exercise for many senior managers. They may need strong encouragement before they are willing to undertake such an exercise. For example, in 1999 General Electric recruited an estimated 100 external top e-commerce experts to be used as 'black belts' or team leaders of 'Destroy your business teams'. These teams were set up in every GE unit with the objective of disaggregation; of examining how the net could be used to annihilate the unit's mainstream business. The task was hard. Many units were run by senior managers with years of success in running businesses under pre-net conditions. Such individuals often did not have much understanding of e-commerce, and had difficulty envisaging that the net could have any impact on their thriving businesses.

The need for this radical rethinking of strategy and unbundling of vertically integrated value chains is greatest, according to other experts (e.g. Tapscott et al. 2000) in what they refer to as distributive networks. These are the key organizations supporting business transactions on the web. They allocate and deliver goods, whether information, objects, money, or other resources, from providers to users. They facilitate the exchange and delivery of information goods and services.

A distributive network uses mediating technologies to facilitate exchanges across time and space (Stabell and Fjelstad 1998). Transportation companies used to use trucks and roads, then Federal Express (Fedex) moved ahead with an intelligent software which enabled an air/truck network. In late 1998 Fedex decided that its physical distribution system of trucks and airplanes was less valuable than its internetworked information resources; its digital capital was gaining value over its physical capital. Fedex decided to focus on value-added context services like online package tracking and logistics outsourcing and leave the actual driving jobs to outsourcers. Essentially the company started to move away from physical capital in favour of relationship and structural capital. It began selling its transport network, marshalling a web of truck and air transporters to handle the physical delivery.

In Europe, distributive networks such as power companies, postal and telecommunications services, and railroads tended to be government-regulated monopolies. They reflected a physical capital asset-based mindset, a view that to deliver value to a customer the company should own its entire value chain, for example in the case of electricity supply, generating facilities, transmission lines, local distribution networks, and access to end customers.

Rethinking strategy concentrating on the opportunities and threats posed by transactions using the net would raise the possibility of disaggregating the businesses of generation, transmission and marketing. So disaggregation can be a radical revolution. It is thus, despite the enthusiasm with which some consultants sell it, a high-risk strategy, as Enron found out to its cost. But for some businesses the greater long-term risk may in fact be to do nothing. However, being a high-risk strategy, a key to success will be the way in which the whole process of disaggregation and subsequent repositioning of the business is managed. The key is, through disaggregation, to increase effective use of the organization's assets. This is an area in which quality management should be able to play a crucial role since the essence of a quality approach is that all corporate assets, both hard and soft, should be used to optimum effect and all inefficient waste eliminated (see the discussion on quality in Stern and Shiely (2001) and in the other chapters of the present volume).

What will the Speed of Change Be?

It is difficult to predict the speed with which business-to-business transactions will move onto the internet. Possible technical, organizational and societal problems which might slow the process can easily be identified. The technical problems are likely to be solved relatively quickly. The organizational and societal ones might well stay much longer.

The technical problems fall into three categories:

- Businesses cannot easily integrate their existing systems with the net. The net was originally set up as an information superhighway. The web was designed to help people get information out of computers, so it is ideal for business to consumer. Now it is being used by business for carrying out transactions and not just searching for information.
- The net is insecure.
- There is the problem of speed.

All three of these weaknesses are being addressed and should be of far less importance in the near future. For example, the problem of integration of current systems with net-based operations. The current major net language, HTML, describes how to lay out a page, but not what the page is describing. So a page on the subject Apollo can be a page on a Greek god or a page on moon landings. This problem should be eased with the launch of the long-awaited XML. This will tell the searcher what the page is describing. XML adds invisible metatags describing the objects contained in the web page and this will help internet searches to become faster and more accurate.

XML also helps make data meaningful so it can be used in a business process. Data items such as customer account numbers can carry definitions of themselves so that other applications can identify and process them. XML is in schemas. So if a company wants to invoice another company it could download an XML schema and send an invoice in the appropriate form. But XML is very complicated. It will not be complete until each industry has the electronic schemas that describe common processes for each industry. Each industry will have to develop as it were its own accepted dictionary for the industry-specific business terms it uses. Thus some experts consider that there will be rapid agreement on the simple things like invoices and payments. But some of the advanced EDI areas will be much harder to standardize. At the time of writing this chapter (early 2002) there were several proposed standards for harnessing XML, so that computers could talk to computers across companies and industries – but none had won widespread agreement.

The second problem is that of security. Public key infrastructure (PKI) is expected to be the answer to this problem. This comprises digital certificates – the online equivalent of a handwritten signature – and will enable secure payments to be made.

The third problem, that of speed and effectiveness of communication, should be solved with the impending rapid spread of broadband connections in the business-to-business area and the ease with which systems like bluetooth, once their initial problems are ironed out, should enable different appliances to communicate with one another.

Organizational problems might be more difficult to solve. There is, for example, the problem of trust. It has many facets in carrying out business transactions using the internet. For example, although initial information search costs can be greatly reduced, uncertainty often remains as to whether the right information has been found. Usually many responses are returned and the reliability of the information found is unclear. Using search agents or shopping booths can decrease the search time and number of responses but they are far from perfect (see Brown and Duguid 2000). There can also be uncertainty about a product. For example, with some perishable products the appearance and smell can be very important and has a clear subjective element.

A final possible problem concerns uncertainty about the trustworthiness of a supplier or customer. This can be decreased by creditworthiness checks, establishing a contract or obtaining insurance or using certification bodies, all of which, however, increase external co-ordination costs.

The problems discussed above have resulted to date in many businesses compensating for the degree of risk involved in doing business on the net either by concentrating only on lower-value items or by increasing their mark-up as a kind of insurance (Timmers 1999).

Many of these new hubs may well experience other kinds of organizational problems. For example, some of the proposed exchanges demand co-operation between companies who have spent years fighting each other in the marketplace, and this co-operation is hardly likely to be easy (Henig 2000). And there will always be companies who will be very loath to allow any third party, including any business exchange, to come between them and their key customers (Wigand and Benjamin 1995). As businesses get more used to working on the net, it might be that these problems could be expected to diminish, but it is likely to take some time.

However, there is another group of problems which are only just beginning to surface. These we refer to as the societal problems. Again there are three main types:

- First, the influence of those individuals and communal bodies who are increasingly worried about the effect on individual and organizational privacy and basic liberties of the spread of the transparency of net-based transactions (Lessig 2000).

- Secondly, there is the issue of patents. The United States Patent Office has recently been granting a number of patents involving business methods. Such patents cover a business process rather than a physical invention or a software programme. They increased dramatically in number after a 1998 US federal appeals court ruling upheld their validity – and the fastest-growing category of these patents involves the internet. Amazon.com, for example, has patented one-click shopping and has successfully sued to keep its competitor Barnes & Noble.com Inc. from using it. Critics maintain that many of these patents should never have been granted because they either cover obvious processes or are simply electronic forms of traditional activities. However, their existence could alter the financial attractiveness to many companies of doing business over the net, and thus, until the legal issues are resolved, it is suggested that they will delay expansion of transactions using this medium.

- Thirdly, there are now clear signs that many governments are concerned about the effects of the rapid expansion of business on the net (Symonds 2000). Such expansion can have major monopolistic, taxation and service delivery implications. It can also have major implications in other areas (e.g. employment legislation). For example, Greenspan (2000) has suggested that most of the return from the newer technologies results from cost reduction, which on a consolidated basis largely means the reduction of labour costs. And as he points out, European and Japanese governments have a lower level of high-tech capital investment than the United States because these countries have chosen in the past to make discharging employees a difficult and costly process in comparison with the USA. It is questionable, given the availability of new technology and the increased globalization of trade which is resulting, how long such differences can continue to exist without the issue of protectionism again coming to the forefront. Such governmental problems are likely to remain for a long time.

Possible Effects on the Quality Function

Buying and selling on the net

The implications for the quality function of the three situations we have outlined are very different. The first situation, the simple move to more buying and selling on the net, means more of the same for the quality function. In contrast, it is probable that the development of virtual supply chains and of disaggregation attempts will bring the major changes.

The first stage of simply moving basic transactions like buying and selling onto the net is likely to force Western-based companies to lower their costs since they will be competing with companies from across the globe, many of whom will have lower operating costs. However, cost-cutting by itself will seldom be enough to ensure a place in the new market situation. In order to avoid being classified as just another commodity supplier companies will also have to endeavour to add some unique value in their customers' eyes by being able to offer exceptional levels of customer service.

Companies aiming to reduce costs while at the same time increasing flexibility and speed of response to customers are virtually forced to adopt a lean production approach. By lean production we mean a focus on minimization of buffers and a concentration on a just-in-time supply approach (see Womack and Jones 1996; Taylor and Brunt 2001). The research findings are not crystal clear, and some criticism of the original Japanese approach has been strongly voiced (e.g. Cusumano 1994), but what evidence there is suggests that to achieve top-level results a lean production approach has to be accompanied by high-performance management together with the kinds of team-based organizational change programmes in which the quality function plays a pivotal role, such as 6 Sigma. Such programmes emphasize process management, customer focus, organizational learning and self-managed teams (Wood 1999).

Since this is such a well-known area to quality professionals and well described in this book we will not elaborate further, save to say that what is becoming important is the degree to which the environment allows such systems to develop (e.g. Cooke 2001).

Virtual supply-chain networks

If an organization is to successfully become a member of a virtual supply-chain network then it will have to maintain the discipline of its high-performance systems but also develop in other areas as well. What is needed is a combination of rational and orderly organization resulting from the high-performance systems with a willingness to constantly consider change and, where necessary, implement innovation. This balance between, on the one hand, strong routines and, on the other hand, the freedom to experiment and innovate is difficult for any organization to achieve. And yet it is not impossible. For example, the most definitive study of why Toyota was able to achieve such a dominant position in the world automotive market has concluded that this balance was the major reason for its success (Fujimoto 1999).

However, despite Toyota's apparent success, many other organizations are likely to find the demands such virtual chains place on systems integration and flexibility very challenging. Business process re-engineering (BPR) is not a promising answer. That can only work really well where there are defined clearly measurable inputs and outputs and where a linear process is involved (Brown and Duguid 2000). And enterprise resource planning (ERP) applications are also not likely to help much since they are mostly concentrated on the internal business processes of the organization and have limited ability to collaborate with other enterprises. And successful hard-wiring, such as has been implemented in ERP systems, is exactly what does not, according to Hagel and Brown (2001), work well when flexibility or collaboration are necessary.

What is now needed, Hagel and Brown (2001) maintain, are loosely coupled business processes where the focus is on the specification of end-products at various stages in the process and not on defining in detail the activities within any one business process. Rather than seeking to control every step, the designers of such processes aim to qualify appropriate service providers and to create appropriate economic incentives and penalties to ensure performance.

The new systems focus on defining key milestones throughout the process, then systematically query service providers throughout the supply chain to confirm that the milestones are met. In this way an organization can quickly and cost-effectively implement an approach that does not require integration with diverse databases. It simply provides the necessary visibility to determine whether the expected end-products will be delivered on time.

Because of their flexibility, loosely coupled business processes create the potential for much more frequent and significant performance improvements. By focusing on milestones and creating visibility on performance against milestones, designers of loosely coupled business processes can provide continuous benchmarking.

Hagel and Brown (2001) point out that Toyota has pioneered innovative collaborative business processes with key suppliers in the automotive industry. In its major assembly plants it has set aside a room where it brings suppliers together each week and posts each supplier's performance against specific milestones. The visibility of performance among all suppliers creates rapid feedback on performance gaps and enormous social pressure for suppliers to act to close these gaps. They also refer to Li and Fung, which is a $3.2 billion Hong Kong trading company. It co-ordinates the activities of 7,500 suppliers in 37 countries who it knows can deliver apparel and other products for designers and retailers looking for low-cost but reliable sources. It begins by lining up sources of raw material and then mobilizes as many as five supply levels to make the product, and couples these with appropriate logistics and packaging companies to deliver the product to its customers. It continually reallocates work among its many service providers based on recent performance trends and results. If one provider develops a performance advantage for a specific task, it sees a quick return on its performance investment, while others see an equally quick decline in their workloads as performance gaps appear.

As long as companies rely on conventional enterprise-centric hard-wired business processes, they will be blocked from exploiting the advantages offered by web services technology. Loosely coupled business processes are much more suitable for co-ordinating across companies, letting each one more effectively leverage the resources of others. But the culture as well as the systems change required for those used to operating classic ERP systems is considerable.

As already described in this book, the quality function has always played an important role in supporting the effective management of internal processes. This task will continue to be of crucial importance. But the function will now face a new challenge. It has to move outside its own employing organization to co-operate with others in the network. It has to learn how to support the loosely coupled cross-organizational processes essential for virtual network development.

Disaggregation and Maximizing Assets

Although there is little previous experience to draw on in this area, some logical conclusions can be drawn. Classic total quality (TQ) practice was based on managing variation through a PDCA learning cycle. This required a degree of routine. It required that the organization should at least have the same situation and process tomorrow as today, and it also required the causes of variation to be predictable. Indeed it could be said that quality was primarily backward-looking and was mainly concerned with getting rid of what was wrong.

But there is little routine in the new situation. Rather it involves high volatility with little predictability. So there can be little reliance on classic TQ contract-based tools such as a traditional ISO 9000 approach. The use of a contract-based approach depends on the contract's ability to predict every situation that will happen. That is impossible in fast-change situations. In such situations, rather than use contracts, because of the many unpredictable variables involved, organizations need a variety of options/alternatives which can cope with the unpredictability – and which can then be used as needed.

The choice of alternative is most likely to be dictated by whichever will create the most shareholder wealth. And the measure which seems most likely to dominate this field will be economic value added (EVA). EVA is, simply put, the profit that remains after deducting the cost of the capital invested to generate that profit. It has been reported (Stern and Shiely 2001) that, by 2001, over 300 companies world-wide had already adopted this discipline, including such market leaders as Coca Cola, Siemens, Herman Miller and the US Postal Service.

So it is important for the quality function to be aware of how they can play a key role, in creating this shareholder value. In the haste to adopt the new measurement system, it is all to easy to forget lessons learnt over the years. For example, a possible alternative could be the customer valuation approach which might help stabilize customer unpredictability. It involves organizations analysing the customers they currently serve and then structuring their service level offerings and charges according to the profitability of each customer. The quality function can play a key role in such analysis.

Again most firms assign substantial capital spending rights to senior executives and almost none to shop-floor employees. But, as the quality function knows all too well, some elements of the production process are well within the control of shop-floor workers, and, if well managed, can contribute significantly to creating share-holder wealth. Such value drivers include such old favourites as productivity improvement, scrap reduction, work in process inventory reduction and reduction in key cycle times. All are, of course, measurable and at least to some extent within the control of shop-floor employees.

Finally, an Open Systems approach may help cope conceptually with unpredictability. This may aid in organizing complexity into the coherent story that is so essential before the situation can be managed. As Deming (1994) concluded, management of a system requires a model of the interrelationships between all components within the system and of the people that work in it. And again, the quality function could have a key part in such an approach.

Summary

As this chapter has pointed out, the uncertainties, problems and complexities for many organizations of moving business-to-business transactions onto the internet will mean that the pace for many will be slow but sure. At the outset organizations will have both internet-based and non-internet-based systems running in parallel. So the quality function will have to move in the directions we have suggested while at the same time continuing to fulfil its more traditional roles.

To summarize, we have suggested, in this chapter, that there are three major ways in which old-economy companies are attempting to integrate the new economy as extensions of their current businesses.

The first way is by treating the net as an extension of their normal market. They are using it primarily to sell more product or service and to buy cheaper. This will involve many organizations in operating primarily through business-to-business exchanges. The transparency and global reach of these exchanges will put major pressure on suppliers' costs and the speed and flexibility of response. As suggested, the major accepted way for Western companies to achieve these needed cost savings and performance increases is to adopt a lean management approach combined with a high-performance organization – a clear role for the quality function.

The second way in which old-economy companies are attempting to integrate the new economy is by using the net to expand and improve co-makership and partnership relationships amongst their key suppliers. We envisage many business-to-business suppliers becoming members of fully integrated virtual supply chains. In such a situation, what is needed is a combination of the high-performance systems rationale and orderly organization with a willingness to constantly consider change and, where necessary, implement innovation in an agile manner. This balance between, on the one hand, strong routines and, on the other, the freedom to experiment and innovate is difficult for any organization to achieve. The most likely solution is the development of loosely coupled business processes across the whole virtual value chain. So again the role of the quality function is clear. Having built up their expertise in supporting the effective management of key business processes within the organization, they must now adapt this expertise to the new, more loosely coupled environment.

Finally, we have suggested there is also a third approach which may be merely temporary, but is much more fundamental. This approach requires that old-economy organizations should totally rethink their business models before deciding on their e-commerce strategy. It requires old-economy organizations to re-examine why customers buy from them, look at all stages in the processes involved and consider how the net could impact each stage in the processes, and then, if necessary, develop new business models with their required reorganization. This is again a possible quality role. The key driver in this process is likely to be the need for creating maximum shareholder value and the key measures will be EVA. The quality function will have to ensure that, in the rush to disaggregate, the hard-earned lessons of the past are not forgotten.

This chapter has outlined three major ways in which organizations may adapt to carrying out transactions on the internet. Few companies can be easily slotted into one category or another. Subunits of many companies may well be spread across different categories, and some may be moving from one category to another. The speed of change will vary across business sectors. Also there are many and varied problems involved in the moving of business-to-business transactions onto the net. But the move of business transactions to the net is coming and there is therefore a need for business to act fast in order to be ready.

There is one more important role which the quality function can play. The coming of transactions using the net will affect asset performance. As has already been signalled, the relative value of fixed assets such as property and machinery will decline whereas the relative value of intangible assets such as relationships with customers and suppliers, intellectual capital, and abilities such as the organization's innovative capacity or its ability to adapt to major change, will increase.

This move has resulted in a large gap between companies' value on the stock market and that given by normal accounting information. It has been reported that the market value of S&P 500 companies is more than six times what is on their books. The balance sheet number reflects only 15 per cent or so of the value of these companies. And these are hardly new-economy stocks but include about

80 per cent of corporate America, most of which consists of low-tech or service companies (Lev 2001). Even the renowned Federal Accounting Standards Board in the USA has produced a report on this problem and is conducting four studies in the field of non-financial metrics and intangible assets.

These newly valuable intangible assets nearly all involve people. But people are free agents. People may be central to many of the new assets, but people can and do change employers frequently. What can be regarded as much more fixed are the systems that lie behind people's successful behaviour. That is the systems which stimulate and support the new desired behaviours. These systems and procedures are what the quality function needs to play a role in discovering and then to guide management in adapting the systems to fit their own organization and then further improve them.

These systems and procedures are increasing in importance now that there are signs that the finance community is beginning to value an organization's internal systems, an area in which the quality function plays an important part, and is not just basing valuations on the organization's external policies. In the past valuation has mainly depended on external aspects such as market strategy and mergers and acquisitions, matters on which the influence of quality has seldom been strong. But now this may be changing. The internal improvements necessary for successful transference of business to the internet may at last enable the quality function to justify its existence in financial terms.

Typical of this new approach by financial experts is Braunschvig (1998), writing from a position as a managing director at Lazard Freres in New York. He suggests that productivity increases can have an impact on how companies are valued. He suggests that recent unfortunate experiences with the internet sector have resulted in the investment community's becoming increasingly sensitive to a firm's capacity to generate earnings. So the adoption of initiatives promoting a company's productivity growth should appeal to them.

Methods that measure a company's ability to leverage its resources, human, financial, or technical, in order to expand its output while controlling its use of inputs could be used alongside growth-driven valuation approaches. Investors foresee organizations spending much more time than they do now assessing the internal systems, both technical and managerial, of the enterprise (Braunschvig 1998). They will be seen as drivers of productivity growth, thus of earnings potential and therefore of valuation. This focus on productivity appeals particularly to companies in economies now approaching the margin of their present efficiencies and facing increasing competition from foreign players in domestic markets and abroad.

American companies have been protected from the world-wide commercial environment by advantages arising from the commercial environment in which they operate, the size and scope of the internal US market, its openness, relatively benign government interference and the willingness to invest and thus the subsequent strength of its innovation processes. Though these advantages remain, it is clear that technological innovations in production processes are being adopted abroad in areas such as South-East Asia with increasingly short time-lags.

The best means of drawing this chapter to a close is perhaps provided by Braunschvig's (1998) conclusion that both American and, especially, European economies have to leverage their human and technological resources with higher productivity growth. This could well be, he writes, the opportunity of last resort for mature economies challenged by companies from younger, hungrier cultures and countries.

References

Bovet, D. and Martha, J. (2000), *Value Nets*. New York: Wiley.

Braunschvig, D. (1998), Work remade. In D. Leebaert (ed.), *The Future of the Electronic Marketplace*, ch. 6. Boston, Mass.: MIT.

Brown, J. S. and Duguid, P. (2000), *The Social Life of Information*. Boston, Mass.: Harvard Business School.

Bunnell, C. (2000), *Making the Cisco Connection*. New York: Wiley.

Cooke, F. L. (2001), Human resource strategy to improve organisational performance: a route for firms in Britain? *International Journal of Management Reviews*, 3(4), 321–39.

Cool, K. (1997), The competitiveness of European industry. Inauguration address for the BP Chair in European Competitiveness, INSEAD, 3 June.

Cusumano, M. A. (1994), The limits of lean. *Sloan Management Review*, Summer, 27–32.

Deming, W. E. (1994), *The New Economics*, Cambridge, Mass.: MIT.

Dyer, J. H. (1996), How Chrysler created an American Keiretsu. *Harvard Business Review*, July–August, 42–56.

Evans, P. B. and Wurster, T. S. (1999), Getting real about virtual commerce. *Harvard Business Review*, November–December, 84–94.

Federal Accounting Standards Board (FASB) (2001), *Business and Financial Reporting: Challenges for the New Economy*. Washington.

Forrester (2001), <www.Forrester.com>, 8 December.

Fujimoto, T. (1999), *The Evolution of a Manufacturing System at Toyota*. New York: Oxford University Press.

Gartner Corporation (2001), *E-Business Services Worldwide Market Size and Forecast, 2000–2005* (March). New York.

Greenspan, A. (2000), Global economic integration: opportunities and challenges. <www.federalreserve.gov.aug 25>.

Hagel, J. and Brown, J. S. (2001), Cut loose from old business processes. <www.optimizemag.com.Dec>.

Hagel, J. and Singer, M. (1999), *Net Worth: Shaping Markets when Customers Make the Rules*. Boston, Mass.: Harvard University Press.

Hartman, A. and Sifonis, J. (2000), *Net Ready*. New York: McGraw Hill.

Henig, P. D. (2000), Revenge of the bricks. *Red Herring*, August, 121–34.

James, G. (2000), B2B: hot or hype? Supplement to *Business*, 20 August.

Kaplan, S. and Sawhney, M. (2000), E. hubs: the new B2B marketplaces. *Harvard Business Review*, May–June, 97–103.

Kirkpatrick, D. (2001), Great leap forward. <www.Fortune.com. Dec 10>.

Lessig, L. (2000), *Code and Other Laws of Cyberspace*. New York: Basic Books.

Lev., B. (2001), *Intangibles: Management Measurement and Reporting*. Washington, DC: Brookings Institution.

Rayport, J. F. and Sviolka, J. J. (1995), Exploiting the virtual value chain. *Harvard Business Review*, November–December, 75–85.

Sarkar, M., Butler, B. and Steinfeld, C. (1995), Intermediaries and cybermediaries: a continuing role for mediating players in the electronic marketplace. *Journal of Computer Mediated Communication*, 1(3), 249–72.

Schwartz, E. (1997), *Webonomics*. New York: Broadway Books.

Shapiro, C. and Varian, H. R. (1999), *Information Rules*. Boston, Mass.: Harvard Business School.

Stabell, C. B. and Fjelstad, O. J. (1998), Configuring value for competitive advantage. *Strategic Management Journal*, 19, 420–31.

Stern, J. M. and Shiely, J. S. (2001), *The EVA Challenge*. New York: Wiley.

Symonds, M. (2000), Government and the internet. Supplement to *The Economist*, 24 June.

Tapscott, D. (1999), *Creating Value in the Network Economy.* Boston, Mass.: Harvard Business School.

Tapscott, D., Ticoll, D. and Lowy, A. (2000), *Digital Capital.* London: Nicholas Brealey.

Taylor, D. and Brunt, D. (2001), *Operations and Supply Chain Management: The Lean Approach.* London: Thomson Learning.

Timmers, P. (1999), *Electronic Commerce.* New York: Wiley.

Useem, J. (2001), It's all yours Jeff. *Fortune,* 17 September, 28–32.

van Alstyne, M. (1997), The state of network organisations: a survey in three frameworks. *Journal of Organisational Computing,* 7(3), 221–46.

Venkatraman, N. (2000), Five steps to a dot.com strategy. *Sloan Management Review,* Spring, 15–18.

Wenninger, J. (2000), The emerging role of banks in e commerce. *Current Issues in Economics and Finance,* 6(3), 1–5 (New York: Federal Reserve Bank).

Wigand, R. J. and Benjamin, R. I. (1995), Electronic commerce: effects on electronic markets. *Journal of Computer Mediated Communication,* 1(3), 353–62.

Womack, J. R. and Jones, D. T. (1996), *Lean Thinking.* New York: Simon & Schuster.

Wood, S. (1999), Human resource management and performance. *International Journal of Management Reviews,* 1(4), 367–414.

Wyckoff, A. (1997), Imagine the impact of electronic commerce. *The OECD Observer,* 208 (October/November).

part three

Quality Management Systems, Tools and Techniques

Quality management systems, tools and techniques are a fundamental part of an organization's approach to TQM. This part of the book deals with their use and application. In the individual chapters dealing with tools and techniques, each tool and technique is described, together with an indication of its range of application and how it is constructed and deployed. Part 4 contains the following chapters:

Chapter 14 presents an overview of quality management systems and argues that such a system is a key building-block in an organization's approach to TQM. The review includes the fundamental purpose of a quality management system and the development of quality system standards. The ISO 9000 series of quality management system standards is reviewed, including implementation issues and guidelines, the assessment and registration process, and their benefits and limitations.

Chapter 15 explores the subject of integrated management systems (IMS) in terms of quality, environment, and occupational health and safety management. The chapter opens by examining definitions of IMS. It then goes on to discuss the linkages between ISO 9001 and ISO 14001, the integrated and aligned approaches, arguments for and against integration and some of the common problems. A comparative analysis of the current integration models is presented and a model described which addresses the issues of scope and culture which none of the existing models of IMS addresses.

Chapter 16 opens by examining the role of quality management tools and techniques in the introduction and development of TQM. It then goes on to explore the issues which should be considered in selecting tools and techniques, and the typical problems found in their use and application. It describes a number of the basic quality control tools – checklists, flowcharts, checksheets, tally charts and histograms, graphs, Pareto analysis, cause-and-effect diagrams, brain-storming and scatter diagrams. It then describes and outlines the use of the seven management tools (relations diagram method, affinity diagram method, systematic diagram method, matrix diagram, matrix data-analysis method, process decision program chart and the arrow diagram method). Departmental purpose analysis and mistake-proofing, which are not covered elsewhere in the book, are outlined. In all cases the focus is on describing the tools and their uses, avoiding excessive detail of their construction. Examples of the tools and techniques are taken from a variety of organizations and situations.

Chapter 17 outlines the concept of quality function deployment (QFD). The methodology is fully explained, in particular the construction of the House of Quality, and the planning, organiza-tion and management of QFD projects is reviewed. The benefits of QFD are examined, potential pitfalls identified, and guidelines provided for its effective use.

Chapter 18 provides a review of design of experiments. It opens by describing the historical background of design of experiments before going on to explain details of the methods. The key steps in setting about undertaking an experimental design are explained in simple language.

Chapter 19 gives an overview of the concept of failure mode and effects analysis (FMEA), together with its value as a planning tool to assist with building quality into an organization's products, services and processes. FMEA is described, along with the procedure. Drawing on expe-rience from Allied Signal, the development of both design and process FMEA are outlined, and guidance to effective use is examined.

Chapter 20 provides an overview of statistical process control (SPC) and its concepts. The main factors in the plan and design of a control chart are examined and details of how to construct the more popular type of control charts are given. The issues involved with the implementation of SPC are described and typical problems encountered in the introduction and application of SPC highlighted.

Chapter 21 outlines the history of benchmarking, summarizes the main types of benchmarking and gives an overview of the main steps in a formal benchmarking process. The main learning experiences from a number of diverse benchmarking projects carried out within North-West Water are also explored in the chapter, mentioning success factors, difficulties and pitfalls.

Chapter 22 outlines the concept of business process re-engineering (BPR), traces its history and development, and examines how it complements TQM. The benefits and potential problems of BPR are reviewed and guidance given on how to set about a BPR project.

Chapter 23 deals with the use of teams and teamwork in TQM. The operating characteristics of project teams, quality circles and quality improvement teams are outlined. A set of guidelines to help ensure that teams are both active and effective is provided, along with a simple assessment methodology.

Chapter 24 deals with quality awards and self-assessment and its role in the advancement of TQM. Drawing on a number of recent studies, it examines the influence of TQM and business performance. The key points of the Deming Application Prize, Malcolm Baldrige National Quality Award and European Quality Award are reviewed. The various ways of undertaking self-assessment against a Business Excellence Model are outlined. Drawing on a major European research study on self-assessment, the key lessons from the use of self-assessment by European business are highlighted.

chapter fourteen

Quality Management Systems

B. G. Dale

Introduction

This chapter opens by examining the concept of quality assurance and the responsibilities of people within an organization for carrying out the activity. A quality system is defined and the background of quality system standards traced, the key features of the ISO9000 series (1994) are examined, implementation guidelines and issues outlined, the quality system assessment and registration reviewed and the benefits and limitations highlighted. A model is also presented which outlines what is required for a small company to successfully achieve ISO9000 series registration. Much has already been written about quality systems and standards (Dale and Oakland 1994; Davies 1997; Hall 1992; Jackson and Ashton 1993; Lamprecht 1992, 1993; Rothery 1993), and there are the standards themselves. This chapter is therefore restricted to an overview of the key features and issues.

What is Quality Assurance?

Quality assurance is defined in BS EN ISO9000 (2000) as:

> Part of quality management, focussed on providing confidence that quality requirements will be fulfilled.

Quality assurance is often regarded to be discreet policing by the quality assurance department. This is not so. The ideal role of the department is to oversee the whole process of quality assurance within an organization, provide guidance, advise on the assignment of roles and responsibilities to be undertaken by each function and person, and address weaknesses in the system. Quality assurance needs to be an integral part of all of an organization's processes and functions, from the conception of an idea and throughout the life-cycle of the product or service: determining customer needs and requirements, planning and designing, production, delivery and after-sales service.

The objective should be to get every person in the organization to take personal responsibility for the quality of the processes for which they are accountable. This includes treating following processes as 'customers' and endeavouring to transfer conforming products, services, materials and documents to them, monitoring quality performance, analysing non-conformance data, taking both short- and long-term action to prevent the repetition of mistakes, and promoting the feed forward and feedback of data. The emphasis should be on the pursuance of corrective and preventative actions and procedures and non-conformance investigation in a thorough manner with closed-loop effectiveness. It is also necessary for everyone to perform their tasks in accordance with their training, their procedures and as defined by the quality management system.

The main objective of quality assurance activity is to build quality into the product and/or service during the upstream design and planning processes and in this way give confidence to a customer that a product and/or service performs as they expect. Quality function deployment, FMEA, design of experiments, design reviews, design for manufacturability/assembly and quality audits are all part of an advanced product quality planning process, and of considerable assistance in the pursuance of this goal.

Quality assurance activity which is planned and managed along these lines will strengthen an organization's TQM efforts.

What is a Quality Management System?

A quality management system is defined in BS EN ISO9000 (2000) as:

a management system to direct and control an organization with regard to quality.

The purpose of a quality management system is to establish a framework of reference points to ensure that every time a process is performed the same information, methods, skills and controls are used and applied in a consistent manner. In this way it helps to define clear requirements, communicate policies and procedures, monitor how work is performed and improve teamwork.

Documentary evidence about the quality management system is fundamental to quality assurance and takes several forms.

- A company quality manual (sometimes called a level 1 document) provides a concise statement of the quality policy and quality management objectives as part of the company objectives. ISO10013 (1995) provides useful guidelines on the development and preparation of quality manuals. A quality manual is defined in BS EN ISO9000 (2000) as:

    a document specifying the quality management system of an organization.

    A procedures manual (sometimes referred to as a level 2 document) describes how the system functions, gives the structure and responsibilities for each department/unit and details the practices to be followed in the organization.
- Work instructions, specifications, methods of performance and detailed methods for performing work activities for a third level of documents.
- In addition there is often a database containing all other reference documents (e.g. forms, standards, drawings, reference information, supplier list, etc.).

The quality management system documentation helps to ensure that employees know what they should be doing, along with appropriate means. It also provides evidence to those who wish to assess the system.

The quality management system should define and cover all facets of an organization's operation, from identifying and meeting the needs and requirements of customers to design, planning, purchasing, manufacturing, packaging, storage, delivery, installation and service, together with all relevant activities carried out within these functions. It deals with organization, responsibilities, procedures and processes. Put simply, a quality system is good management practice.

A quality management system, if it is to be comprehensive and effective, must cover all these activities and facets and must be developed in relation to the corporate strategy of the company. The system developed can be tested against a reference base and improvements made. This reference base is a 'quality management system standard' which describes demonstrable features or conditions that are assessable. An organization's quality management system is usually assessed by the customer (known as second-party certification) or by a party which is independent of the customer and organization (known as third-party certification). It is usual to certify that the system conforms to a specific quality management system standard (e.g. ISO9001) and whether the system is fully implemented and effective. This process is known as certification.

A quality management system which embraces quality management objectives, policies, organization and procedures, and which can demonstrate, by assessment, compliance with ISO9001 or that of a major purchaser, provides an effective managerial framework on which to build a company-wide approach to a process of continuous improvement.

The Development of Quality Management System Standards

Irrespective of the approach taken to TQM and the quality management maturity of the organization, a business may need to demonstrate to customers that its processes are both effective and under control and that there is effective control over procedures and systems. The pressure for proof that systems and procedures are in place, and working in an effective manner, led to the demand for quality assurance based on the development of quality management system standards. The origins of this can be traced back to the 1950s when the US Department of Defense and the UK Ministry of Defence saw a need for greater reliability in purchased products and a reduced reliance on customer or purchaser inspection as the main assurances of quality.

The early standards were contractual requirements by major purchasers of their suppliers. Such standards were customer- and sector-specific and designed to be used in contractual situations in the industries for which they were designed and in which they operated; the standards had a strong bias towards internal quality control, which was primarily inspection. Many purchasers developed their own requirements and methods of assessment, which involved visiting the supplier to examine the degree to which their operating procedures and systems followed their requirements. This method of assessment is called second-party certification.

The current quality management system standards evolved from military standards, for example, the American Military Standard MIL-Q-9858(a), the North Atlantic Treaty Organization (NATO) Allied Quality Assurance Publications (AQAPs), and nuclear and power industry requirements such as the Canadian Standards Association (CSA) CSA-Z299. There had also been a considerable contribution to formalized quality assurance procedures by NASA, the controlling body for the American space programme, the Polaris submarine programme and the nuclear power-generating industry. There has been considerable co-operation between America, Canada and Britain in relation to quality system development.

The UK defence standard for quality systems was first published in 1973 by the Procurement Executive of the British Ministry of Defence (MOD) – the DEF-STAN O5-21 series. This was a result of its change in policy on the acceptance of contractor-manufactured product. The previous acceptance policy of the MOD involved inspecting the manufactured product by its own team of inspectors. This policy required considerable resources involved with the inspection and the paperwork associated with contract release forms. These standards were virtual copies of the American-derived NATO AQAPs used by NATO in defence procurement, which were based on MIL-Q-9858(a). The AQAP standards (AQAP 1–14) addressed the problem of achieving consistency and total product interchangeability in the supply of standardized weapons and ammunition coming from many different suppliers and intended for the different national military units which make up NATO. The MOD used the DEF-STAN O5-21 series to approve potential suppliers and audit current suppliers in contractual situations. It was a requirement that a supplier developed their quality management system to meet the clauses set out in these standards for them to be included on the MOD defence contractors list. These standards made the contractor responsible for the quality and reliability of his product; they became the basis for contracts with the MOD from April 1973. One principle is that the prime contractors must conduct assessments of their own suppliers in line with the requirements of these standards. The O5-21 series was withdrawn in 1985 and MOD assessments were carried out using the similar AQAP standards. From September 1991, the MOD have, in the main, relied on third-party assessment against the ISO9000 series of standards. This type of situation relates to specific military applications such as aircraft construction, ammunition and explosives, packaging and software. A new set of defence standards (the 05-90 series, 05-91 to 05-95), which includes the ISO9000 series plus special military purchase requirements, is used to assess suppliers in contractual situations.

In 1972 the British Standards Institution (BSI) published BS4891 (1972), *A Guide to Quality Assurance*, which set out guidance to organizations on quality and its management, and was intended as a guide to companies developing their quality management systems; this standard was withdrawn in 1994. This was followed in 1974 by the issue of BS5179, which was a three-part standard *A Guide to the Operation and Evaluation of Quality Assurance Systems*; this standard was withdrawn in 1981 after being superseded in 1979 by the first issue of BS5750.

During the mid-1970s there was a proliferation of quality system standards produced by a variety of second- and third-party organizations. The Warner report (1977), *Standards and Specifications in the Engineering Industries*, stressed the need for a national standard for quality management systems, to reduce the number of assessments to which suppliers were being subjected by their customers. It pointed to the shortcomings and fragmented nature of the British system of standards. It was recommended that British Standards be produced to provide the single base document for quality systems. Subsequently, in 1979, the British Standards Institution issued the BS5750 series of quality management system standards.

It was the British Standards Institution which formally proposed the formation of a new technical committee (ISO/TC 176) to develop international standards for quality assurance, techniques and practices (this committee is responsible for developing and maintaining the ISO9000 family of standards). Some 20 countries originally participated in the development of what was to become the ISO9000 series. In 1987 the series of international standards on quality management systems was first published by the International Organization for Standardization (ISO) (the ISO is a federation of some 140 countries' national standards institutes) This initial version of the standards, while reflecting various national approaches and international requirements, was based largely on the 1979 version of the BS5750 series and the eight or so years of UK user experience, mainly in manufacturing industry, and the Canadian CSA Z299 series. The text of these international standards was approved as suitable for issue as a British Standard with dual numbers – BS5750: Parts 0 to 3 (1987) and extended in 1991 to services and software as Parts 8 and 13 (1991), but these were as guidance-only documents.

The ISO9000 series was adopted by CEN (the European Committee for Standardization) and CENELEC (the European Committee for Electrotechnical Standardization) as the EN 29000 series, thus harmonizing the approach to quality systems in the European Community, the standard at this stage having three numbers: national, European and international. It has perhaps had the most significant and far-reaching impact on international standardization of any set of standards. An excellent account of the historical background of the ISO9000 series is provided by Spickernell (1991).

The ISO9000 series has been revised on the basis of international implementation experience and was reissued in summer 1994. This revision was meant to be interim, involving minor changes pending a full revision (ISO standards are meant to be reviewed and, if necessary, revised every five years). All ISO standards go through at least three phases – working draft (WD), committee draft (CD) and draft international standard (DIS) – during their development. This process aims to get as much feedback as possible from users. Drafts at any stage can be circulated many times until the required consensus is reached. The phase 1 minor revisions (1994) were undertaken with the aim that no new requirements should be introduced, and that the standards should be clarified to aid implementation and assessment and to remove internal inconsistencies. The second and more thorough set of revisions in the 2000 version has seen a major rewrite which has enhanced the existing standards by including requirements for concepts typically associated with TQM and continuous improvement. The standards, which are now more in-depth, represent a business-oriented approach and will be more demanding for many organizations.

Government initiatives

In July 1982 a UK government White Paper was published on standards, quality and international competitiveness which triggered a National Quality Campaign and suggested that, to maintain standards, more independent certification should be encouraged and that accreditation by a central agency would uphold the standards of certification bodies. The National Accreditation Council for Certification Bodies (NACCB) was set up in June 1985 by the Department of Trade and Industry as the national statutory body with the task of assessing the independence, integrity and technical competence of any certification bodies applying for government accreditation in four areas: approval of quality systems, product conformity, product approval, and approval of personnel engaged in quality verification. At the same time the National Measurement Accreditation Service (NAMAS) was set up to register laboratories and test houses. NAMAS was formed by the amalgamation of the British Calibration Service (BCS) and the National Testing Laboratory Accreditation Service (NATLAS), also in 1985, and both parts of the Civil Service. In August 1995 and in response to market demand, NACCB and NAMAS merged to create a single accreditation authority – the United Kingdom Accreditation Service (UKAS), which is recognized and promoted by the DTI. The objective is to bring economies of scale and improved efficiency to UK accreditation. Accreditation allows a certification body to demonstrate its competence and independence. The accreditation of certification bodies by UKAS is to enhance mutual recognition of test results and certification among those certification bodies operating to an agreed set of principles and methodologies. UKAS is also subjected to assessment by similar bodies elsewhere in the world for multilateral recognition with other accreditation bodies. To be eligible for accreditation, third-party certification bodies are required to meet criteria outlined in three European (CEN) standards, available in the UK as British Standards, based on the European EN 45000 series for certification bodies issuing certificates of product conformity; for certification bodies certificating that suppliers' quality systems comply with appropriate standards, normally BS EN ISO9001, 9002 and 9003; and for certification bodies certificating the competence of personnel. These standards will be incorporated into International Standards, as ISO already have guides such as ISO62 and ISO25.

This set of standards helps to promote confidence in the way in which product and quality system certification activities are performed and in the accreditation systems and bodies themselves. From the accreditation granted it will be clear whether the certification body is accredited for quality system assessment only, and in which fields, or whether it has the additional qualification of being accredited to certificate conformity of product.

Those companies which have been assessed by an accredited certification body can use the symbol of the Royal Crown if the scope of the certification applied for falls within the scope of accreditation of the accredited certification body. The use of this Royal Crown lends authority and assurance. This is known as the National Accreditation mark. However, there is a degree of independent accreditation and, in the UK, a number of certification bodies are registered with the Accreditation Service for Certifying Bodies, providing an alternative to UKAS. International accreditation is now well established through the International Accreditation Forum (IAF) and a range of mutual recognition agreements (MRAs). The aim is for audit, certification and accreditation to be accepted across the world.

The Department of Trade and Industry, through the National Quality Campaign initiated as a result of the 1982 White Paper, and its 'Managing into the 1990s' programme, actively encouraged British industry to consider its approach to quality management more seriously; one of the methods advocated is registration with the BS EN ISO9000 quality management system series. They issue a central register of quality-assured companies. This register lists the firms whose quality management system has been approved by major users or independent third-party assessment bodies, which means the investigation is done by an independent organization, unrelated to buyer or seller. It also identifies the assessment standard used – the BS EN ISO9000 series or its equivalent – and details of the certification body.

Acceptance of the ISO9001 series of standards

The set of requirements outlined in ISO9001 can be supplemented for specific industries or products by 'quality assurance specifications', 'ISO guidance notes and codes of practice' which provide more detail.

The Chrysler Corporation, Ford Motor Company and General Motors Corporation (the so-called 'Big Three') have produced a common quality system assessment standard (QS9000) which is an industry-specific scheme. This standard, on which development work started in 1988, was first released in August 1994, with a world-wide version in February 1995. It harmonizes the separate quality system standard requirements of these three companies and will reduce the current level of duplication in terms of information requested from suppliers leading to economic advantage. These three organizations have had comprehensive quality assurance systems in place at their sites for some considerable time, and have required suppliers to meet the standards of these systems. They view this as a platform to enhance the quality and performance of their suppliers. The first section of QS9000 aligns itself with the elements of ISO9001. This industry standard has recently been incorporated into the ISO network and issued as ISO TS16949. The following are some examples of the prescriptive requirements:

- Advanced product quality planning shall be in place, supported by a multi-disciplinary approach for decision-making.
- Trends in quality, operational performance, current quality levels and customer satisfaction shall be determined and documented. These should be compared by competitive analysis and/or benchmarking and be reviewed by management.
- Failure mode and effects analysis shall be used.
- Capability studies are mandatory and minimum capability indices are stipulated.

The second (sector-specific) section contains additional but common and harmonized requirements of Chrysler, Ford and General Motors covering the production part approval process, continuous improvement, identification of key product and process parameters, process capability performance and measurement system studies on product and process parameters, and development of control plans. Sixteen typical examples are cited of areas of such activities, together with 14 techniques/ methodologies to support them. The third section addresses customer-specific additional and non-general requirements.

QS9000 was initially confined to the first-tier suppliers of manufacturing plants in the US, but its implementation has spread world-wide and down the supplier chain. Registration to QS9000 has now become the norm in the automotive industry.

Other similar sector-specific derivatives of ISO9001 include TL9000, which is the world's first quality system metrics for the global telecommunications industry developed and managed by the Quality Excellence for suppliers of Telecommunications Forum and AS9000 in the aviation and aerospace industry. The ISO has a policy and commitment to sector versions of ISO9001 where a need is demonstrated.

Registration to ISO9001 is a useful foundation leading to the development of a quality system to meet the independent system requirements of customers. A number of major purchasers use this registration as the 'first pass' over a supplier's quality system. They will take ISO9001 as the base, and only assess those elements of the system which they believe are particularly sensitive to them as purchasers (e.g. those clauses which are not covered in the ISO9000 series – customers often require the supplier to have additional features to the series supplanted within the system or those clauses without sufficient detail amended to the satisfaction of the customer).

In 1993 Dr John Symonds (internal consultant for environment, health and safety, and quality of Mobil Services Company) launched the first world-wide survey of ISO9000 certificates issued in different countries by independent quality system certification bodies. The International Organization for Standardization has taken over responsibility for this annual survey, which has been extended to cover the ISO14000 environmental management systems standards. The survey report details world, regional and country breakdowns of registrations and also industry-sector breakdown by country. The tenth cycle of the survey (ISO2000) shows that up to the end of 2000 at least 408,631 ISO9000 certificates had been awarded in 158 countries. The survey also shows that in the same time-frame at least 22,897 ISO14000 certificates had been awarded in 98 countries. The trend in registrations is upwards.

The ISO9000 Series of Standards: An Overview

Introduction

In simple terms, the objective of the ISO9000 series is to give purchasers an assurance that the quality of the products and/or services provided by a supplier meets their requirements. The series of standards defines and sets out a definitive list of features and characteristics which it is considered should be present in an organization's management control system through documented policies, manual and procedures, which help to ensure that quality is built into a process and is achieved. Amongst other things it ensures that an organization has a quality policy, that procedures are standardized, that defects are monitored, that corrective and preventative action systems are in place, and that management reviews the system. The aim is systematic quality assurance and control. It is the broad principles of control, in general terms, which are defined in the standards, and not the specific methods by which control can be achieved. This allows the standard to be interpreted and applied in a wide range of situations and environments, and allows each organization to develop its own system and then test it against the standard. However, this leads to criticisms of vagueness.

The series of standards can be used in three ways:

- Provision of guidance to organizations to assist them in developing their quality systems.
- As a purchasing standard (when specified in contracts).
- As an assessment standard to be used by both second-party and third-party organizations.

Functions of the standards and their various parts

The ISO9000 family of standards consists of four primary standards: ISO9000, ISO9001, ISO9004 and ISO19011 (see below):

- ISO9000: Quality Management Systems: Fundamentals and Vocabulary
- ISO9001: Quality Management Systems: Requirements
- ISO9004: Quality Management Systems: Guidelines for Performance Improvement
- ISO19011: Guidelines on Quality and Environmental Auditing

The standards have two main functions. The first function identifies the aspects to be covered by an organization's quality system and gives guidance in quality management and application of the standards. The second function defines in detail the features and characteristics of a quality management system which are considered essential for the purpose of quality assurance in contractual situations.

ISO9000 outlines the fundamentals of quality management systems and provides the definitions of the key terms used in ISO9001 and ISO9004.

ISO9001 presents quality management system requirements applicable to all organizations' products and services. It is used for demonstrating system compliance to customers, for certification of quality management systems, and as the basis for contractual requirements. It requires the following:

- A detailed documentation of quality requirements, processing steps and results.
- Implementation of a set of controls to maintain the system.
- Compliance with the requirements of the 22 sub-elements.

ISO9004 is a quality management system guidance specification that embraces a holistic approach to performance improvement and customer satisfaction.

ISO9001 and ISO9004 are based on a process model that uses the following eight quality management principles that reflect best practice:

- Customer focus
- Leadership
- Involvement of people
- Process approach
- System approach to management
- Continual improvement
- Factual approach to decision-making
- Mutually beneficial supplier relationship

These two standards employ common vocabulary and structure to facilitate their use and are intended to be used together by organizations wishing to develop their systems beyond the minimum requirements of ISO9001.

ISO19011 will provide guidance on managing and conducting environmental and quality activities. This standard combines the quality system auditing standard (ISO10011: Parts 1 to 3) with the environmental system audit standards (ISO14010, ISO14011 and ISO14012).

With respect to auditing the ISO10011 series contains three standards:

- ISO10011-1: Provides guidelines for auditing a quality system and for verifying the ability of the system to achieve defined objectives.
- ISO10011-2: Gives guidance on the education, training, experience, personal attributes and management capabilities to carry out an audit.
- ISO10011-3: Provides guidelines for managing quality system audit programmes.

Principal elements of ISO9001

The format of the new standard has now just five requirement clauses rather than the 20 of the 1994 version. However, while there are some additional and important requirements in the new standard, all the 20 clauses in the 1994 version can be recognized.

The five main elements are:

1 *Quality management system*

- General requirements ('The organization shall establish, document, implement and maintain a quality management system and continually improve its effectiveness in accordance with the requirements of this international standard' – BS EN ISO9001 (2000))
- Documentation requirements

2 *Management responsibility*

- Management commitment
- Customer focus
- Quality policy
- Planning
- Responsibility, authority and communication

3 *Resource management*

- Provision of resources
- Human resources
- Infrastructure
- Work environment

4 *Product realization*

- Planning of product realization
- Customer-related processes
- Design and development
- Purchasing
- Production and service provision
- Control of monitoring and measuring devices

5 *Measurement, analysis and improvement*

- General ('The organization shall plan and implement the monitoring, measurement, analysis and improvement processes needed:(a) to demonstrate conformity of the product; (b) to ensure conformity of the quality management system and (c) to continually improve the effectiveness of the quality management system': BS EN ISO9001 (2000))
- Monitoring and measurement
- Control of non conforming product
- Analysis of data
- Improvement.

The set of requirements outlined in ISO9001 can be supplemented for specific industries or products by 'quality assurance specifications', 'quality assurance guidance notes' and 'codes of practice' which provide more detail in their form as sector guides.

It is worth mentioning that ISO14001 (1996) *Environmental Management Systems: Specification with Guidance for Use*, shares many management principles with the ISO9000 series. The 2000 revision of ISO9001 has ensured closer compatibility and synergy with the ISO14001. A number of organizations are considering how they may develop their quality management system as a basis for environmental management: see Wilkinson and Dale (1999) and chapter 15.

Implementation Guidelines for ISO9001

At this point in the chapter it is useful to quote the guidelines, with some development by the author, advanced by Long et al. (1991), based on their research into the application and use of the ISO9000 quality system series in small and medium-sized enterprises; the guidelines are also applicable to larger organizations.

- An organization should be clear on the reasons for seeking ISO9001. Implementation for the wrong reasons will prevent the organization from receiving the full benefits. In addition, it may be found that implementing and maintaining the requirements of the chosen standard is a burden in terms of costs and extra paperwork with no compensating benefits. ISO9001 registration must therefore not be sought just to satisfy the contractual requirements of major customers or for marketing purposes. Indeed when most competitors have ISO9001 registration there is little marketing advantage, and in many markets it is now a qualifying criterion.

- The development of a quality management system to meet the requirements of ISO9001 should be managed as a project, with the identification of key steps, milestones and time-scales. This will prevent progress being sporadic and variable.

- Prior to a programme of ISO9001 implementation it is important that an internal quality audit is conducted of the existing quality management system by a qualified auditor. This will determine the initial status of the company's quality management system, enable management to assess the amount of work required to meet its requirements and also to plan for systematic implementation of the standard (i.e. a gap analysis). Without this knowledge the project-planning process mentioned above would be impossible. It is important that a realistic timetable is established, because if it is too tight there will be a tendency to do things artificially and this will result in considerable time spent later in debugging the system. On the other hand, if it is too relaxed there may be a tendency to do little in the initial period. Involvement of the appointed management representative during the quality audit is essential.

- For those organizations developing a quality management system for the first time a steering committee should be established comprising all the heads of departments and chaired by the CEO. This type of representation is essential to gain cross-functional support for the project and to help ensure the smooth development and implementation of the system. Participation and commitment from all the heads of department is essential in order to gain employee

Enhancement of the quality system

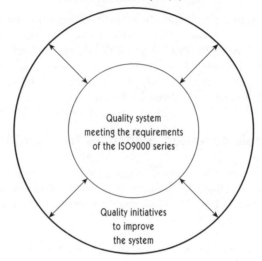

Figure 14.1   Quality system development

support for the project, and this will help to ensure the smooth implementation and subsequent maintenance of the standard. In extremely small companies where there is little or no second-tier management the whole-hearted
commitment and involvement of the CEO is critical and essential.

- ISO9001 should be considered as the minimum requirement. Without a
  documented quality management system there is neither basis nor connected
  reliable data to monitor the process of quality improvement. Organizations
  should, however, aim to have a quality system which surpasses the standard's
  requirements, with new quality initiatives built into the system, as illustrated
  in figure 14.1 (this is the objective of ISO9004). A quality management
  system which meets the requirements of ISO9001 should in no sense be
  regarded by senior management as the pinnacle of their quality management
  achievements. All it says to the outside world is that the organization has
  controls, procedures and disciplines in place. The organization should treat
  ISO9001 registration as a precursor to developing its approach to TQM.
- There is a need to create a conducive environment for the development of a
  quality management system which meets the requirements of ISO9001. This
  can be achieved by the formulation of organizational quality policy and quality objectives. The responsibility of executives in the establishment, maintenance, and development of an ISO9001 system cannot be over-emphasized.
  The leadership of senior management and their total commitment to the
  process of quality system registration to ISO9001 are vital: it is only they
  who can deliver the resources and co-operation of appropriate personnel and
  provide the necessary direction. The CEO, while accepting ultimate responsibility, has, as one would expect, to delegate a variety of tasks. Senior management must not only understand the principles of the ISO9000 series but
  should ensure that the quality policy is implemented and understood by all
  employees, and that everyone in the organization has quality improvement

objectives for their jobs. They also need to react positively to the actions resulting from quality audits.

- Training at all levels within the company is required on the importance of product and service quality in general, and the reasons for the quality system and its benefits in particular. This will help to facilitate the right type of behaviour, attitude and values of employees towards the ISO9000 series and will encourage total participation. It not only provides the opportunity to answer any questions which employees may have about the standard and the process and the reasons for registration; a systematic approach to quality, education and training will also reduce resistance to change and other obstacles. An element of this awareness can occur if the initial audit is well explained and sympathetically carried out, explaining the reasons for recommendations.

- Once all the above steps have been taken the organization is in a position to commence developing its system to meet the requirements of ISO9001. Accurate procedures, including operating and working instructions, are required. These procedures must be practical, workable and easily implemented. Wherever possible, they should document what employees are currently doing; they are then most likely to continue in the same way, enabling assessment requirements to be met naturally. Only where the standard would suggest that some modification is required should it be introduced. In writing procedures it is worthwhile to keep in mind how to demonstrate to the auditor that the ISO9001 requirements have been fulfilled. In simple terms this can be condensed into three principles:

  - Write down what you do
  - Do what you have written down
  - Be in a position to prove it.

- 'Ownership' of the procedure is important as personnel who are given responsibilities for writing the procedures must be familiar with the requirements of the ISO9000 series and be fully conversant with the procedures they are drafting. The use of consultants and management specialists to write procedures is undesirable as they are unlikely to understand fully the 'style' of the company. It is often found that when procedures are written in isolation and then pushed into the working environment as required mandates, it leads to two main problems. Initially there is the problem of changing the way that people work without any perceived gain and benefit. Secondly a formal assessment of the system may reveal differences between what is written and what is actually done. Also with respect to this, it is helpful to document a procedure before trying to improve it, unless the change is easy to make. The use of others to write procedures does not allow for the positive factor of employee involvement and the related communication issues, and the 'ownership' of the processes by those operating them is lessened. This also happens when there is an over-use of technological aids in producing the procedures. The procedures as they are being developed and/or documented need to be checked to see that they meet the requirements of ISO9001 and how they impact on other procedures, systems and activities.

- The quality management system must become an integral part of the management process. When it is treated in this way it will ensure that business improvements are incorporated into the system.

Quality Management System Assessment and Registration

When the organization has endorsed its process controls, written the necessary procedures and instructions, and developed its system to meet the requirements of ISO9001 for which registration is sought, the following key activities need to be accomplished.

- Train and educate staff in the workings and operation of the system and test out the procedures which have been developed. Education and training is a key element for people following procedures, completing the appropriate documentation, taking corrective action seriously, providing timely and accurate information and being aware of what their responsibilities are. The internal audit process must identify any non-conformity with the procedures. In some companies, plans for training are supplemented by people's involvement, for which departmental achievements are rewarded. For example, snapshots of audit requirements undertaken by an implementation team and recognition of performance given by rewards such as mugs, writing blocks, pens, etc.
- It may be beneficial to arrange for a pre-assessment of the system to be carried out by the selected certification body.
- Decide the most appropriate time to go for assessment.
- ISO9001 registration is conferred by certification bodies who have, in turn, been accredited in the UK by UKAS. The list of accredited certification bodies should be consulted and a 'supplier audit' of them carried out. It is important to establish the scope of the certification body's approval, its fee structure, relevant experience and knowledge in the organization's field of work, reputation, current workload, etc. Goodman (1997) and the British Quality Foundation (BQF) (1997) have published guidance on choosing a certification body, which serve as useful checklists. In addition to specifying how to conduct the search for a certification body the BQF provides considerable details on five factors in making this selection, namely cost, scope, sector or general, credibility of the certification body and comfort factors.
- Upon completion of the necessary forms, the chosen certification body will provide a quotation and details of fees. After agreeing a contract, the appropriate documentation is then sent to the certification body to check initial compliance against the standard. In general, a certification body will usually want to see proof that the quality system has been in effective operation for a period of six months. However, this depends on the size of the company and the maturity of its quality management system.
- If the documentation is acceptable as it stands, some certification bodies proceed to the on-site assessment for a preliminary review (pre-audit assessment). At this stage, the company is able to make appropriate modifications and establish corrective actions to take account of the assessors' initial findings and comments.
- The formal assessment involves an in-depth appraisal of the organization's quality management system for compliance with the appropriate part of the standard (see ISO19011). This is carried out by a small team of independent assessors appointed by the certification body and generally under the supervision of a registered lead assessor, although increasingly for the smaller enterprise only one assessor is used. If the assessors discover a deviation from

the requirements or identify a non-conformity with the procedures, a non-conformity report is raised. At the end of the assessment, the non-conformities are reviewed and the assessors make a verbal report to management with their recommendation. The recommendation can be unqualified registration, qualified registration and non-registration. Any non-conformity with the appropriate part of the standard or within the company's system must be rectified, within a prescribed time, before approval is given.

- Once registered the certification bodies have a system of routine surveillance. The frequency of these surveillance visits varies with the certification body but is generally twice a year. The certification body has the right to make these visits unannounced but rarely does so. The registration usually covers a fixed period of three years, subject to the successful surveillance visits. After three years a quality system reassessment is made. However, the main approach these days is continuous assessment during the surveillance visits. Continuing assessment is planned so that the cumulative effect over a three-year cycle is a complete audit of the quality system. This not only reduces the cost of registration but also minimizes the inconvenience caused to the organization. The continued registration is confirmed in writing following the site visit.

Long et al. (1991), from their research into the implementation of the ISO9001 by organizations, have identified four factors that determine the time taken:

1 The status of the quality management system prior to seeking registration. This status is determined by the presence or otherwise of activities which are in accordance with one of these three standards and their existence in a documented form. When few activities are in place and/or activities are not documented then more time is required first to document and then to develop the system to meet the appropriate requirements.

2 The complexity of the company in terms of work locations, products manufactured, services offered, type of production and the type and number of production processes and operating instructions. With increasing complexity more procedures and work instructions are required to be documented.

3 The priority given by management to implementing the requirements of the standard and the time they are prepared to set aside for the activity from their normal day-to-day work responsibility affects the progress of implementation. This is especially the case when there are no full-time personnel responsible for quality assurance.

4 A conducive environment is required for the implementation and development of the standard. Resistance to change, lack of understanding about product and service quality and poor attitudes among employees towards quality improvement are major obstacles in implementing the requirements of the chosen standard.

ISO9000 Series Registration: A Model for Small Companies

McTeer and Dale (1996) have developed a model which outlines what is needed for a small company to successfully achieve ISO9001 registration. The model, which is shown in figure 14.2, consists of the domains of motivation, information, resources

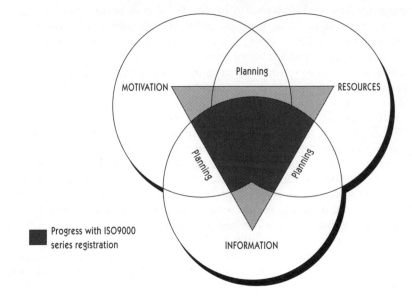

Figure 14.2   An active quality management system regime
Source: McTeer and Dale (1996)

and planning; by examining the interaction between them it highlights how progress towards ISO9001 registration can be enhanced or diminished. The dynamics of the model require that the four domains are raised from their latent state through internal and external motivations. As the factors inflating or deflating the domains strengthen or weaken, so the rate of progress towards installing a quality management system to meet the requirements of ISO9001 increases or decreases. It is argued that progress by a company towards ISO9001 registration is only made when the demands of motivation, information and resources occlude. The union of only two domains is insufficient to generate sufficient momentum to promote progress towards registration, and if all the domains are sufficiently deflated the progress to ISO9001 is halted. Drawing on the paper by McTeer and Dale (1996) the model is now described.

Motivation

In a small company's journey from a primitive quality management system to attaining registration to ISO9001, the degree of motivation can be regarded as the most important driving force. The degree of motivation can be influenced, both positively and negatively, by internal and external factors. The most powerful motivating force is demand from customers, in particular large ones, for registration and the fear of losing orders; this ensures that the momentum to introduce an ISO9001 quality management system is maintained. Head office pressure and the impact of senior management are also factors influencing the degree of motivation, for example in making appropriate resources available. The motivation is also affected by employee attitudes and behaviour. Antagonism or apathy from employees towards the company's endeavours to obtain ISO9001 registration makes it difficult to progress quality management system development.

In addition to the primary forces there are a number of secondary forces, including the enhancement of company status in the marketplace, the urge to gain a commercial advantage, and advertising opportunities.

Information

As well as educating the company's quality management system champion to the requirements of ISO9001, education and training on quality management system principles and practices must also be given to apprise the workforce of what is required from it. This can help to alleviate or avoid many of the problems associated with the acceptance of new working procedures, practices and disciplines. The solution for many companies is to employ management consultants to ensure that the detailed requirements of developing an ISO9001 system are achieved, and this can help to overcome many of the problems of comprehending the requirements of the standards. By strengthening the reservoir of quality management knowledge the quality management system champion is better able to communicate effectively with their consultant and better placed to understand the problems and pitfalls of introducing a quality management system. In this way delays in the process of documenting the system, nugatory work and over-documented and bureaucratic quality manuals can be avoided.

If a company is already able to build upon established quality assurance and quality control procedures (no matter how basic) this also helps to speed things up. Failure to raise the level of quality awareness and understand the demands of ISO9001 leads to confused, frustrated and neglected employees and poorly briefed managers who will tend to restrict the progress towards registration.

Resources

Three resources are significant: time, finance and availability of personnel.

In failing to make or allocate time to the process of introducing a quality management system, programmes will slip, leading to suspension or abandonment as other more urgent tasks appear and take precedence. Time and the availability of personnel are closely coupled. If the quality management system champion is able to delegate work to staff or a management consultant, time pressures can be eased. Extra resources devoted to the development of a quality management system are also instrumental in increasing the pace of progress.

In small companies there is usually little slack time available in the owner's or managing director's day-to-day work activities to dedicate to the development of a quality management system. Further, there is a shortage of staff time to assist in this process and the problem becomes more acute as the number of employees in the company diminishes. Unless compensated by a greater stimulus to produce a quality management system, a lack of time or conflicting priorities will delay or lead to termination of progress. Also for many small companies the budgeting for the process of introducing and then maintaining an ISO9001 system requires some minor restructuring of finances.

Planning

Planning is crucial to the successful introduction of an ISO9001 system. Only by formulating a sensible plan which details a timetable of achievable events, milestones and target dates will a company succeed in this objective. This includes recognizing the need for education and training, additional skills, the use of external resources and, in some cases, the need to apprise company employees of the need for ISO9001 registration. This domain is seen as both the magnet which draws the motivation, information and resources domains together and the glue that binds them.

Only by drawing together motivation, information and resources can progress be made towards the installation of a quality management system to meet the requirements of the ISO9001. Figure 14.2 illustrates the situation where the progress of a small company towards ISO9001 registration is advancing and maturing: the three elements are overlapping and locked together by the planning element. The size of the area of occlusion between these four elements provides a portrayal of the intensity of a small company's progress towards acquiring ISO9001 registration.

Benefits and Limitations of the ISO9000 Series of Standards

Since its introduction, the ISO9000 quality system series has been widely accepted throughout the world. A number of benefits are claimed for the system, including:

- Improved controls, discipline (e.g. prevents the use of short cuts and duplication of activities), procedures, documentation, communication, dissemination and customer satisfaction, quicker identification and resolution of problems, greater consistency (i.e. the job is done the same way, time after time and best practices are shared), increased quality awareness, in particular from those departments and people who traditionally perceived 'quality' not to be their major concern.
- A reduction in errors, customer complaints and non-conforming products, services and costs and the retention of customers.
- Assistance with the liberalization of trade through common rules and language.
- Responsibility for quality issues is placed firmly where it belongs, with the supplier and not the customer.
- Reduction in the number of customer audits and assessments and also a reduction in the time taken, leading to a saving in resources need for such activities.
- Identification of ineffective and surplus procedures and documents and other forms of waste.
- A better working environment.

For details see various BS, ISO and certification body literature, and also Atkin (1987), Bulled (1987), Collyer (1988), Dale and Oakland (1994), DeAngelis (1991), Ford (1988), Hele (1988), Long et al. (1991), Marquardt et al. (1991), Perry (1991) and Rayner and Porter (1991).

A survey carried out by PERA International and Salford University Business Services Limited (1992) of 2,317 firms who had completed a quality consultancy project under the DTI Enterprise Initiative prior to 31 December 1990 found the following benefits:

> Overall, 89 per cent of all clients surveyed believed that the introduction of quality management systems had a positive effect on their internal operating efficiency.
> Some 48 per cent of firms claimed increased profitability, 76 per cent improved marketing and 26 per cent improved export sales – all attributed the effect to the introduction of quality management systems.

A survey carried out in 1993 by Research International Ltd. for Lloyds Register Quality Assurance assessed the impact of the ISO9000 series on British business. Some 400 managers from companies of varying size and industrial type were interviewed. Amongst the main findings were the following:

- 89 per cent of companies which had gained ISO9000 series registration said it met or exceeded their expectations.
- 86 per cent of companies said registration had improved management control, 69 per cent said it had increased their efficiency and productivity and 40 per cent claimed it had reduced their costs.
- Disappointment expressed about the ISO9000 series was relatively low. Only 3 per cent reported that it had increased their paperwork and 6 per cent said gaining approval was too costly.

A survey carried out by Vanguard Consulting Ltd. (1994) obtained responses from 647 organizations. The conclusion reached was that organizations which achieved success with the ISO9000 series took a broader view with respect to its implementation than those which sought it because of some form of obligation. Since then there have been numerous surveys (e.g. Brown and van der Wiele 1995; Vloeburghs and Bellens 1996) in various parts of the world. A survey by Buttle (1996), which claims to be 'the most comprehensive national omni-sectoral survey into the impact of ISO9000 on UK business', obtaining data from 1,220 organizations, found, using factor analysis, that the three most important benefits sought from certification were profit improvement, process improvement and marketing benefits. The survey also pointed out widespread willingness to recommend the ISO9000 series of standards to other firms. On the other hand, a number of difficulties, problems and shortcomings have been reported and discussed. These include:

- Deciding whether registration should be sought for the whole company or just one unit/division/site/premises or even a specific operation carried out on one site or certain defined activities, as in the case of local authorities.
- Applicability of the standards to certain situations, particular sectors of business, and management styles.
- Interpretations of various sections of the standard and understanding the requirements of the standards.
- Terminology used.
- Lack of flexibility and perceived restrictions on creativity.
- Lack of relevance to the real needs of the business, resulting in a view that it was bureaucracy gone mad (e.g. paper-shuffling) and a why bother attitude from people at the operating end of the organization.

- The time and resources needed in writing procedures and training and re-training staff in the requirements of the ISO9000 series and the internal auditing of the system.
- The bureaucracy involved in documentation and accreditation and the lack of mutual recognition of certificated bodies between countries.
- The cost involved in achieving ISO9001 registration and then maintaining it. This applies, in particular, to small companies. The cost comprises the additional workload incurred by company personnel in writing the procedures, managerial time, increased paperwork, etc., the fee of the management consultancy (if a consultant is used to assist with the process of registration) and the certification body's fees.
- Perceived by small companies to be only applicable to large companies.
- Considered by those companies who have mature TQM approaches to be of no value.
- In some cases, in particular sales/service situations, the rigour and applicability of the standards are perceived as restrictive and barriers to providing a flexible and responsive service to customers.
- Lack of internal and external audit rigour.

Details are given in the following sources: Association of British Certification Bodies and the NACCB (1994), BSI Policy Committee for Small Businesses (1994), Batchelor (1992), Brennan (1994), Burgess (1998), Campbell (1994), Commerce (1994), Dale and Oakland (1994), Hersan (1990), Jennings (1992), Long et al. (1991), Oliver (1991), Owen (1988), Rayner and Porter (1991), Sayle (1987) Terziovski et al. (1997), and Whittington (1989). Some of these reported difficulties have been eased by the 1994 and 2000 revisions of the ISO9000 series in terms of clearing up the ambiguity regarding implied requirements, consistency of clause numbering between ISO9001, ISO9002 and ISO9003, process control requirements and the emphasis given to preventative action and the provision of advice for small businesses (e.g. the BSI handbook *ISO9000 for Small Businesses* (1997)). In addition, a number of the certification bodies have introduced a special service of assessment and surveillance to reduce the cost of ISO9001 registration to small businesses. The fee structure of such services has been developed to help smaller businesses.

Seddon (1997) has launched what is almost a one-man crusade against the ISO9000 series, and his recent book provides some interesting reading of views of what he considers to be the damage inflicted on companies that adopt and implement the requirements of this series of standards.

The revised standards, with their provision for performance improvement; greater emphasis on the involvement of senior management; suitability for all sizes of organizations; increased compatibility with ISO14001; and user/customer-friendliness, should lead to a reduction in these types of difficulty and criticism; however, only time will tell.

What now follows is an overview of the benefits and limitations of the ISO9000 series as seen by the author.

- A quality management system is a fundamental pillar in an organization's approach to TQM and it helps to ensure that any improvements made are held in place (see figure 14.3). However, ISO9001 registration is not a

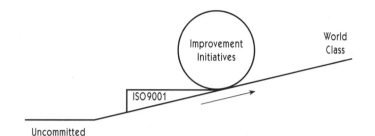

Figure 14.3   Quality improvement and the ISO9000 series

prerequisite of TQM. Some organizations, in particular, those from the non-manufacturing sector, have analysed and improved their systems and working practices and have then gone straight to TQM.

- The guidance provided in the requirements of ISO9001 and ISO9004, and the independent assessment surveillance, is an indisputable aid in developing and maintaining the procedures, controls and discipline required in a quality management system. This is of particular value for those companies which are just commencing their quality journey. The system should help to ensure that more people within the organization are touched by quality, and in this way quality awareness is raised. However, there is a tendency to encourage the separation of a business into areas that complete the recording of requirements and those areas which do not. For example, functions such as finance, management information systems and human resources are little affected, except for training requirements. It is TQM which stimulates the business by creating the understanding that all its component parts have customers, that waste must be systematically eliminated, and that improvement is a continuous process. To help eradicate these weaknesses relating to the separation of functions BSI Quality Assurance introduced in 1991 company-wide registration to extend quality system accreditation to the whole of the company (core businesses as well as supporting functions) (see Perry 1991 for details).

    Experience indicates that, in most companies, it is not easy to get every function and person involved to take responsibility for their own quality assurance and to make quality improvements in the processes for which they are responsible. The ISO9000 series of standards, albeit limited in respect of the point made above, can assist in making this happen.

- It is a contractual requirement of many customers that their suppliers are registered to ISO9001; registration is also required to get on bid lists. Once a company has become registered, it is more than likely that it will ask its suppliers, distributors and providers of service to do the same, setting into motion a chain reaction or what might be classed as a form of pyramid selling. Therefore, in many sectors of industry and government procurement agencies, it is necessary from a marketing viewpoint, and without it a company will simply not get orders. In much of the world it is now a prerequisite condition of doing business and in some sectors of industry (e.g. the automotive industry) the rate of certification is very high. An increasing number of long-standing suppliers to companies have been told by them that they must get ISO9001 registration to continue to be a supplier. This is in spite of the supplier having been the supplier of choice for a considerable period of time. Once ISO9001 registration has been achieved an organization may not be able to afford to lose it. Within the European Union, directives (controlling the production and use of most safety-related products, from toys to pressure vessels) call up ISO9001 as mandatory QA or QC.

- Suppliers have a habit of doing what their customers want and many organizations have achieved ISO9001 registration to provide documented proof that they have an adequate quality system in place just to satisfy the demands of their major customers. This may not produce the required improvement ethos naturally, and any gains made will be short-lived if registration is perceived as a contractual condition rather than a foundation for ongoing improvement. Some suppliers also use it to demonstrate to customers (actual and potential) that they are committed to quality and have achieved what they often call 'the right level of quality'.

- A system based on the ISO9000 series provides only the foundation blocks, and registration to ISO9001 should be viewed as the minimum requirement; the objective should be to develop and improve the system in relation to the needs of the organization. An organization does not achieve superior-performing company status merely by ISO9001 registration. It is clearly a pre-competitive issue, and separate from the ability to compete, which depends on many other factors. The winners will be those who have a dedicated commitment to company-wide improvement through continuous self-assessment of what they do.

- The preparation of systems, procedures, working instructions, etc., to meet the requirements of ISO9001 will have a beneficial effect on a company's performance in terms of improved process yields, reduced levels of non-conformance, improved management control, etc. However, the underlying mechanisms of the ISO9000 series are such that they will tend towards a steady-state performance. The ISO9000 series of standards is designed to produce consistency in actions, products and services. An organization can have a consistent performance with a high level of non-conformance. In the words of one executive, 'ISO9000 is an excellent system for telling us where we have produced rubbish.' The achievement of consistency, while meritorious, leads to a goal which, once achieved, can result in complacency. A consequence of this is that management may pay lip-service to the quality system.

- The question 'Does the quality system reflect the needs of the customer?' should for ever circulate in the minds of senior management.

  Only if there is strong leadership and a written commitment to improvement in the management review of the system will an improvement cycle be triggered. Some organizations have done this by building on and widening their quality systems management review meetings – which deal with issues such as quality audit; corrective and preventative action; production rejections, concessions and corrective actions; waste levels; supplier performance/concessions; customer complaints; and market trends and requirements – into monthly steering meetings for quality improvement. In this way the quality system is integrated into the quality improvement process; it is not uncommon to find they are operated in parallel.

- Having an ISO9001 certificate of registration does not as a matter of course imply that non-conformities at all stages of the process will not occur, and there is no consensus to suggest that companies working to the same management system generate the same standard of quality. The standard is not prescriptive as to the means of prevention. Detection methods which rely very heavily on inspection techniques, human or mechanical, would appear to satisfy the standard in many aspects. This may be an acknowledgement of the fact that there are many processes where, given the state-of-the-art technology, it is not possible to achieve 'zero defects'. The standard does clearly indicate that corrective and preventative actions and procedures should be established, documented and maintained to prevent recurrence of non-conforming product, and that the system should be maintained and developed through the internal audit and management review, but there is a lack of evidence to suggest that improvement is an explicit criterion by which ongoing registration is monitored. In general, ISO9001 tends to measure the effectiveness of documentation, paperwork and procedures (the requisite assessments are often termed a paperchase); this leads to the claim that it encourages bureaucracy and a complex process of documentation.

- Experience indicates that the ISO9000 series has a limited impact on the total improvement operation of an organization simply because it does not get to the root cause of problems. Most problems are resolved at branch level, and this is a failure in a number of businesses.
- In some quarters there is confusion about the relationship between the ISO9000 series and TQM. They are not alternatives; a quality system is an essential feature of TQM. However, some organizations see ISO9001 registration as the pinnacle of their TQM achievements and no plans are laid for building on this registration; a small number of people even believe that improvements driven through internal audits of the ISO9001 will lead their organization to TQM. As previously mentioned, registration often results in a sense of complacency, in particular after successful third-party assessment of the system.
- It should be obvious from the above discussion that ISO9001 registration, or for that matter any other quality system registration or certification or approvals, will not prevent a supplier from producing and delivering non-conforming products and/or services to its customers. The standards are a specification for the management of quality; there is clear distinction between registration and capability, and this fundamental fact needs to be recognized. Product and/or service quality is determined by the individual organization and its people and processes and not by a quality management system standard.
- Many organizations and executives have inflated views of the ISO9000 series; these are often picked up from the hype generated by those selling advisory services. These views can lead to high expectations of what the standard can achieve which, in the long term, may do it a disservice. The following are typical of the comments (not referenced or attributed to individuals):

  - 'Quality recognition of the ISO9000 series from a national accredited certification body is prized nationwide because it is known to be difficult to achieve the high standards required by their impartial testing procedures.'
  - 'It will give the car-buying public a guarantee of complete satisfaction or their money back. What it aims to achieve is the world's coveted benchmark

of quality: BS5750. . . . it is a standard that is recognized as being truly superb and is a move that no other rival car maker can afford to ignore.'
- 'How can it be coveted and difficult to achieve when many thousands of companies in the UK have already met this requirement?'
- 'Such and such a company is the first in its industrial sector to obtain the prestigious ISO9001, ISO9002 or ISO9003 registration – tremendous achievement, very proud to have achieved to the registration, the most significant event in the company's history, breaking new ground for quality, etc., etc. (write-up and picture in the local paper).'

To the informed what these motherhead statements and platitudes are saying is that the organization has taken the first step down the TQM journey.

Summary

A quality management system is one of the key building-blocks for an organization's TQM activities. ISO9001 and ISO9004 define and set out a definitive list of features and characteristics which should be present in an organization's quality management system through documented policies, manual and procedures, whatever the product manufactured or offered, or the service provided, or the technology used. In this way sound advice is provided on how an organization may develop a quality system.

In addition to incorporating the clauses of ISO9001 a quality system design must: maximize ownership, allow flexibility without loss of control, be able to be developed to cope with changes in the business and capture improvements; above all it must be 'user-friendly'.

Seeking registration for the wrong reasons and a system which is too inflexible and bureaucratic are some of the major pitfalls. Assessment to ISO9001 may improve an organization's systems, procedures and processes but on its own will not deliver continuous and company-wide improvement. To make best use of the ISO9000 series it is important that the implementation is carried out in the right spirit and for the right reasons. This is an area in which management commitment is vital. The solution to many of the reported difficulties, shortcomings and criticisms of the standard lies in the hands of an organization's senior management team. The saying 'you only get out what you put in' is so relevant to the ISO9000 series and it is so important that the system is seen as being alive. All too often the ISO9001 system is left solely in the hands of the quality department, often just one individual.

Registration to ISO9001 is not the only way to achieve quality assurance, neither is it a prerequisite for TQM. It is, however, sometimes necessary to have the appropriate registration in order to do business at both a national and international level, and in this respect it is a key marketing tool. It is the fear of loss of business and substitution in the marketplace that have caused many organizations to obtain ISO9001 registration. The ISO9000 series provides a common benchmark for good-quality management system practice which is recognized throughout the world. An organization which is registered to ISO9001:2000 should be working in an organized, structured and procedural way with defined methods of operating. It is important that organizations do not view ISO9001 registration as their pinnacle of success in relation to quality assurance and quality management. It only provides the basic foundation blocks, and they must have strategies and business plans in place to move on and cater for areas which are not addressed by the standard and develop to TQM. This is particularly important in smaller businesses which, in a number of cases, attain ISO9001 registration and have no interest in or vision of developing further their quality management activities.

References

Association of British Certification Bodies and the NACCB (1994), *Quality Systems in the Small Firm: A Guide to the Use of the ISO9000 Series*. National Accreditation Council for Certification Bodies. London: Institute of Quality Assurance.

Atkin, G. (1987), BS5750: practical benefits in the factory. *Works Management*, November, 38–42.

BS EN ISO9000 (2000), *Quality Management Systems: Fundamentals and Vocabulary*. London: British Standards Institution.

BS EN ISO9001 (2000), *Quality Management Systems: Requirements*. London: British Standards Institution.

BS EN ISO9004 (2000), *Quality Management Systems: Guidelines for Performance Improvement*. London: British Standards Institution.

Batchelor, C. (1992), Badge of quality. *Financial Times*, 1 September, 16–17.

Brennan, S. (1994), Death or Honour. *Commerce Magazine*, April, 8–9.

British Quality Foundation (1997), *Choosing a Certification Body*. London: BQF.

Brown, A. and van der Wiele, A. (1995), Industry experience with ISO9000. *Asia Pacific Journal of Quality Management*, 4(2), 8–17.

BSI (1997), *ISO9000 for Small Businesses*. London: British Standards Institution.

BSI Policy Committee for Small Businesses (1994), *The Application of BS5750 to Small Business: Initial Report*. London: British Standards Institution.

Bulled, J. W. (1987), BS5750: quality management, systems and assessment. *General Engineer*, November, 271–80.

Burgess, N. (1998), Lessons learned in quality management: rational role for certification. Institution of Electrical Engineers Symposium, London, 31 March.

Buttle, F. (1996), An investigation of the willingness of UK-certificated firms to recommend ISO9000. *The International Journal of Quality Science*, 1(2), 40–50.

Campbell, L. (1994), BS5750: what's in it for small firms? *Quality World*, March, 377–9.

Collyer, R. (1988), BS5750 and its application. *Polymer Paint Colour Journal*, 177(4191), 318–20.

Commerce, C. (1994), BS5750. *Commerce Magazine*, May, 16–18.

Dale, B. G. and Oakland, J. S. (1994), *Quality Improvement Through Standards*, 2nd edn. Cheltenham: Stanley Thornes.

Davies, J. S. (1997), *ISO9000 Management Systems Manual*. New York: McGraw Hill.

DeAngelis, C. A. (1991), ICI Advanced Materials implements ISO9000 programs. *Quality Progress*, 24(11), 49–51.

Ford, E. (1988), Quality-assured fabrication. *The Production Engineer*, October, 36–8.

Goodman, S. (1997), Tips on how to choose your certification body. *Quality World*, February, 114–15.

Hall, T. J. (1992), *The Quality Manual: The Application of BS5750, ISO9001, EN 29001*. Chichester: John Wiley.

Hele, J. (1988), BS5750/ISO9000 and the metals processor. *Metallurgia*, March, 128–34.

Her Majesty's Stationery Office (1982), *Standards, Quality and International Competitiveness*. Government White Paper, Cmnd 8621. London: HMSO.

Hersan, C. H. A. (1990), A critical analysis of ISO9001. *Quality Forum*, 16(2), 61–5.

ISO10011-1 (1990), *Guidelines for Auditing Quality Systems*, Part 1: *Auditing*. Geneva: International Organization for Standardization.

ISO10011-2 (1991), *Guidelines for Auditing Quality Systems*, Part 2: *Qualification Criteria for Quality Systems Auditors*. Geneva: International Organization for Standardization.

ISO10011-3 (1991), *Guidelines for Auditing Quality Systems*, Part 3: *Management of Audit Programmes*. Geneva: International Organization for Standardization.

ISO10013 (1995), *Guidelines for Developing Quality Manuals*. Geneva: International Organization for Standardization.

ISO14001 (1996), *Environmental Management Systems: Specification with Guidance for Use*. Geneva: International Organization for Standardization.

ISO19011 (2000), *Guidelines on Quality and Environmental Auditing*. Geneva: International Organization for Standardization.

ISO (2001), *The ISO9000 Survey of ISO9000 and ISO14000 Certificates (Tenth Cycle)*. Geneva: International Organization for Standardization.

Jackson, P. and Ashton, D. (1993), *Implementing Quality through ISO9000*. London: Kogan Page.

Jennings, G. M. (1992), ISO9001/ISO9002: use, misuse and abuse. *Quality Forum*, 16(2), 61–5.

Lamprecht, J. L. (1992), *ISO9000: Preparing for Registration*. New York: Marcel Dekker.

Lamprecht, J. L. (1993), *Implementing the ISO9000 Series*. New York: Marcel Dekker.

Lascelles, D. M. and Dale, B. G. (1993), *Total Quality Improvement*. Bedford: IFS Publications.

Long, A. A., Dale, B. G. and Younger, A. (1991), A study of BS5750 aspirations in small companies. *Quality and Reliability Engineering International*, 7(1), 27–33.

Marquardt, D., Chove, J., Jensen, K. E., Petrick, K., Pyle, J. and Strahle, D. (1991), Vision 2000: the strategy for the ISO9000 series standards in the 90s. *Quality Progress*, 24(5), 25–31.

McTeer, M. M. and Dale, B. G. (1996), How to achieve ISO9000 series registration: a model for small companies. *Quality Management Journal*, 3(1), 43–55.

Oliver, B. (1991), Further thoughts on ISO9000. *Quality News*, 17(3), 122–3.

Owen, F. (1988), Why quality assurance, and its implementation in a chemical manufacturing company. *Chemistry and Industry*, August, 491–4.

PERA International and Salford University Business Services Ltd. (1992), *A Survey of Quality Consultancy Scheme Clients, 1988–1990*. London: The Enterprise Initiative/DTI.

Perry, M. (1991), *Company-Wide Registration: A Foundation for Total Quality*. Milton Keynes: BSI Quality Assurance, British Standards Institution.

Rayner, P. and Porter, L. J. (1991), BS5750/ISO9000: the experiences of small and medium-sized firms. *International Journal of Quality and Reliability Management*, 8(6), 16–28.

Research International Ltd. and Lloyds Register Quality Assurance (1993), *BS.5750/ISO9000: Setting Standards for Better Business*. London: Lloyds Register Quality Assurance.

Rothery, B. (1993), *ISO9000*. Hampshire: Gower Press.

Sayle, A. J. (1987), ISO9000: progression or regression? *Quality News*, 14(2), 50–3.

Seddon, J. (1997), *In Pursuit of Quality: The Case Against ISO9000*. Middlesex: Oak Tree Press.

Spickernell, D. G. (1991), The path to ISO9000. Third Business Success Seminar, London, November.

Terziovski, M., Samson, D. and Dow, D. (1997), The business value of quality management systems certification: evidence from Australia and New Zealand, *Journal of Operations Management*, 15(1), 1–18.

Vanguard Consulting Ltd. (1994), BS5750/ISO9000/EN 29000: a positive contribution to better business. *The TQM Magazine*, 11(2), 60–3.

Vloeburghs, D. and Bellens, J. (1996), Implementing the ISO9000 standards in Belgium. *Quality Progress*, June, 43–8.

Warner, F. (1977), *Standards and Specifications in the Engineering Industries*. London: National Economic Development Office.

Whittington, D. (1989), Some attitudes to BS5750: a study. *International Journal of Quality and Reliability Management*, 6(3), 54–8.

Wilkinson, G. and Dale, B. G. (1999), Manufacturing companies' attitudes to system integration: a case-study examination. *Quality Engineering*, 11(2), 249–56.

chapter fifteen

Integrated Management Systems

G. Wilkinson and B. G. Dale

Introduction

The need to assure customers that products and services satisfy requirements for quality has led to the introduction of quality management systems (QMS), and registration to QMS standards, such as ISO9001 (1994 and 2000), has become the norm for many organizations. However, responsible organizations have also to be concerned about the well-being of their employees, their working environment, the impact of operations on the local community, and the long-term effects of their products while in use and after they have been discarded. They cannot ignore legislation such as the Environmental Protection Act 1990, the Health and Safety at Work Act 1974 and the Control of Substances Hazardous to Health Regulations 1988, where failure to have effective management systems in place can lead to heavy fines, a prison sentence, loss of operating licence or even plant closure. Customers, employees, shareholders and the community are also concerned about these matters. In addition to benefits, such as less waste, lower energy costs and reduced absence and employee turnover levels, creating an 'image' that meets customer expectations can help an organization improve market share. This has led to the introduction of EMAS, the European Commission's Eco-Management and Audit Scheme (European Commission 1993); ISO14001 (1996) – the specification for environmental management systems (EMS); and BS8800 (1996) and BSI-OHSAS18001 (1999) – guides/specifications for occupational health and safety management systems (OH&SMS). Dealing with separate management systems covering quality, environmental, and health and safety issues, and ensuring that they align with the organization's strategy has not proved easy, however, and from the mid-1990s, an integrated management system (IMS) addressing these three areas of management has become of interest to business. Research studies by Riemann and Sharratt (1995), Hillary (1997) and Wilkinson and Dale (1998, 1999), and survey results examined by Daniel (2001), show increasing interest by companies in integration and an IMS is now seen as part of the organization's management portfolio. Although the design of ISO14001, BS8800, BSI-OHSAS18001 and ISO9001 (2000) has been undertaken to facilitate their integration, the introduction of an IMS has presented problems, and writers such as Shillito (1995), Tranmer (1996), Beechner and Koch (1997), Karapetrovic and Willborn (1998) and Dalling (2002) have suggested how they might be overcome.

The chapter opens by examining the word 'integration' and an IMS in four areas of literature, the case for integration, and some of the problems that an IMS raises. Five current models of integration – the ISO9001 and ISO14001 matrix; the integrated and aligned approaches; an interlinked or system of systems model, and the European model for total quality management (TQM) are then analysed and compared, and the key issues affecting integration are identified. Finally, a model of an IMS which overcomes the limitations of these models and offers an alternative to an approach which is based on the standards is described.

The Case for Integration and Some of the Problems

In the field of organizational behaviour, the terms integration and co-ordination are used in a similar sense. The principle of co-ordination – 'The need for people to act together with unity of action' (Mullins 1996: 40) – forms a part of the classical approach to organization theory, and techniques for achieving co-ordination include the standardization of work processes, outputs and targets, skills and knowledge, and establishing a culture that guides what employees do. Much of the thinking about integration is also built on the work of Lawrence and Lorsch (1967), who found that each department in an organization operated in its own environment, which led to differences in their structure, goals and attitudes. Integration, which was needed to overcome this differentiation, was described as the degree of co-ordination and co-operation between departments.

The systems concept treats organizations as open systems – see for example Mullins (1996), where the elements/parameters of the system are input, process, output and feedback control. The concept indicates that the elements should be compatible with each other and both the elements and the boundary of the system should be defined:

> All the subsystems necessary to a system describe the systems boundary. The boundary of the system defines its scope. The boundary determines the totality of inputs, processes and outputs required to operate a system. (Optner 1975: 38)

> In an integrated system, the subsystem outputs all contribute to the final system output, and the subsystems and their elements lose their independent character. (Optner 1965: 40)

The systems concept treats compatibility, harmony and alignment of subsystems as important, and Cummings and Worley (1997) offer co-ordination and integration as solutions to the problem of unalignment. They describe alignment as how well the elements of a system or subsystems fit together, and believe that good alignment leads to increased organizational effectiveness. However, unlike the literature on organizational behaviour, the systems concept makes little mention of organizational culture. Nevertheless, culture can be seen as a restriction on the output or objective of the system, which Optner (1975) says can be imposed either internally or externally. It is therefore possible to view culture as a constraint in the same way that financial restrictions and legal requirements can influence the output.

In the field of quality management, integration is closely related to deployment, and Garvin (1991) believes that the terms are sometimes used interchangeably. For Garvin, integration refers to the degree of alignment or harmony in an organization: 'whether different departments and levels speak the same language and are tuned to the same wavelength' (1991: 87). He sees horizontal deployment as a measure of the extent of quality effort across an organization; similarly, Dale and Oakland (1994) say that 'company-wide registration relies on the introduction of a fully integrated quality system . . . company-wide registration can be thought of as a Total Systems Audit and provides a firm foundation for TQM' (1994: 163). Integration and deployment are both used when assessing the criteria of the European Foundation for Quality Management (EFQM) excellence model (EFQM 1999), and the use of the model is normally associated with organizations operating at the higher levels of Dale and Lascelles' (1999) six levels of TQM adoption, and Sandholm's (1999) stages of quality culture. Both include stages/levels where there is little interest in quality; where there is a culture which relies on trendy methods and the use of the latest management fad; where there is a realization that these methods have not produced the results expected; and finally, where quality and the focus on customers' requirements becomes a natural part of the organization's culture, and is integrated into everything that it does.

In the management system standards literature, MacGregor Associates (1996) make a clear distinction between the concepts of integration and alignment. Integration is seen as 'a single top level management "core" standard with optional modular supporting standards covering specific requirements'; alignment is: 'Parallel management system standards specific to an individual discipline, but with a high degree of commonality of structure and content' (1996: 9). This has resulted in two separate approaches to integration:

1   The integrated approach, where the core elements cover the QMS, EMS and OH&SMS, plus possible future management systems.
2   The aligned approach, which has similar common elements and allows adoption of 'that part of the common elements appropriate to the standards under immediate consideration' (1996: 9).

MacGregor Associates say the aligned approach is deemed the more flexible of the two approaches; it satisfies the demand from users for harmonization of the standards, makes documentation simpler and allows one-stop assessments, with the expectation that system audit and administration costs will be reduced. They also see differences in the scope of the standards as important and, because of this, suggest that it is unrealistic to consider their integration, but alignment is possible.

When recommending that the ISO9000 and 14000 series of standards should not be merged, but made more compatible, the ISO technical advisory group, ISO/TAG 12 (1998), said that compatibility

> means that common elements of the standards can be implemented in a shared manner, in whole or in part, by organizations without unnecessary duplication or the imposition of conflicting requirements. Compatibility does not mean that the text of the common elements of the standards needs to be identical, although they should be whenever practical.

The 'common elements' referred to are those shown in the tables provided in the annexes to the ISO14001, BS8800 and BSI-OHSAS18001 standards, but while writers such as Beechner and Koch (1997) and Puri (1996) see the links between the standards as strong, others, such as Shillito (1995), Hoyle (1996) and Stapleton (1997), only see similarities, and differences that cannot be ignored. For these writers, organizational culture and differences in culture in the disciplines within an organization present a problem when attempting to integrate systems.

Although implementation of the individual standards can contribute to culture change in the organization (Dale 1999), culture is not addressed by ISO9001 and ISO14001. Boiral (1998) believes that not only do the ISO standards fail to recognize differences in organizational culture, they also give little specific guidance on the promotion of employee commitment, empowerment and consultation. Wilkinson and Dale (2002) also found that differences in the standards and the failure to address culture had not been overcome with the introduction of ISO9001 (2000). They found significant differences in the scope of the standards, particularly in those areas dealing with the communication of policy, involvement in continual improvement activity, consultation about the setting of objectives and awareness of procedures. Although issues such as motivation, morale and co-operation are included in ISO9004 (2000), the guidelines provided are not intended for certification purposes, and are only recommended for use by organizations wishing to move beyond the requirements of ISO9001. These differences indicate that integration which is based on the requirements of the standards is proving difficult to achieve, and further work and changes will be needed. On the other hand, merging the documentation is less difficult and may be encouraged by ISO9001 (2000).

The results of the above examination are summarized and compared in table 15.1 which shows that, in addition to the need for a definition of an IMS:

- All the areas of literature agree that systems should fit well together.
- The literature on organizational behaviour associates integration with co-ordination and co-operation, and the words alignment and compatibility are not used.
- In the management system standards literature, integration and alignment are two separate approaches rather than associated terms. The association between integration and performance improvement is also less clear in this area of the literature.
- Culture in the organizational behaviour literature is portrayed as 'a common outlook' and 'differences in attitudes', but while quality management recognizes the importance of culture, the standards and system concept do not address it.
- The literature on management system standards suggests that differences in the scope of the standards is important.

Returning to the advantages of an IMS and the problem of integration. Karapetrovic and Willborn (1998) believe that integrating systems, in whatever form, should always lead to a more effective system. The benefits include:

- Improved operational performance, internal management methods and cross-functional teamwork
- Higher staff motivation

Table 15.1 Integration in four areas of literature: a comparison and summary of the findings

Integration: In organizational behaviour	Integration In systems concept	Integration In quality management	Integration In management system standards
Is associated with co-ordination	*Is associated with* co-ordination, compatibility and alignment	*Is associated with* deployment	*Is associated with* alignment, harmonization and compatibility
Co-ordination – unity of action and effort – is achieved by: standardization and a guiding culture	*Co-ordination and integration* increase alignment (how well systems fit together)	*Integration* refers to the degree of alignment and harmonization	*Integration* implies a single top-level system
Integration – is the degree of co-ordination and co-operation needed to overcome differentiation (differences in structures, goals and attitudes) and establish a common outlook	*Integration and alignment* increase efficiency and effectiveness. In an integrated system, subsystems lose their independence *The systems concept does not mention culture.*	*Integration/deployment* are associated with the European Model for TQM; levels of TQM activity and stages of quality culture *Quality management recognizes the importance of culture.*	*Alignment* implies parallel systems *Compatibility* refers to the common elements in the standards *Culture* is thought to be important by some; others say it is not *Differences in the scope of systems may be important. The standards do not mention culture and culture change.*

- Fewer multiple audits
- Enhanced customer confidence
- Reduced costs

Seghezzi (2000) argues that, although keeping systems separate reduces internal complexity, it increases the danger of conflict and reduces effectiveness. Integration avoids these disadvantages, improves effectiveness and efficiency, and creates synergy through improved communication between departments, better co-operation, and working in processes. Integration also allows single audits, which saves time and money, and allows problems at interfaces to be identified.

Seghezzi (2000) suggests three ways to integration:

1 *Addition* requires the individual systems to be kept separate, but the individual system manuals are made more comparable by cross-reference lists.
2 *Merger* involves the use of one standard (normally ISO9001) as the basis for the design of a merged system, where the works instructions are fully integrated; the procedures are partially integrated and the processes are integrated only to a small degree. This results in the creation of a total system, but the partial systems are still visible.
3 *Integration* requires the development of a generic management system 'with high integrative power' (Seghezzi 2000: 164) and models of TQM are said to meet this requirement.

Aschner (1999) also sees TQM as offering a solution to the problem of integration, but Jonker and Klaver (1998) suggest that five different integration levels have to be considered:

1 Having decided that an IMS is needed, managers must start to integrate policy.
2 A conceptual model is then needed, such as the EFQM excellence model.
3 This model should be used as the basis for developing a system, which addresses the principle of feedback and improvement.
4 A system based on the standards is required but, for integration, both the similarities and differences in the standards have to be recognized.
5 Finally, instructions and manuals have to be considered, where integration is achieved by merging instructions and procedures.

The idea of using the EFQM excellence model for developing a system which is also based on the standards presents problems. The British Quality Foundation (1996) has tried to compare and assess the ISO9000 series, the Charter Mark Award for Excellence, and Investors in People against the EFQM business excellence model (EFQM 1996),[1] but differences in concept have made this difficult. The conclusion is that, even if ISO14001 and BS8800 are included in the comparison, the standards still fall short of what the model offers. The standards provide a useful framework on which to build further improvements and to secure what has already been achieved (Dale 1999), but the EFQM model involves an assessment which looks at:

• How the organization approaches each of the criteria and the extent to which that approach has been integrated into normal operations.
• The degree to which the approach has been deployed to its full potential.
• The degree of excellence and the scope of the results achieved.

There are clearly similarities between the 'approaches' of MacGregor Associates (1996), Jonker and Klaver's (1998) 'integration levels' and Seghezzi's (2000) 'ways', but while MacGregor Associates make no mention of TQM, Aschner (1999), like Jonker and Klaver and Seghezzi, recognizes its importance when trying to achieve integration. However, none of them have developed and tested models of an IMS which are based on TQM.

---

[1] The EFQM business excellence model (EFQM 1996) is also known as the European model for total quality management. The EFQM continues to promote TQM, but the current version of the model, the EFQM excellence model (EFQM 2002), makes no reference to it.

The ISO9001/ISO14001 Matrix

This matrix is based on the links between ISO9001 (1994) and ISO14001 (1996) and is shown in table 15.2. It has been used by Puri (1996), Beechner and Koch (1997) and Karapetrovic and Willborn (1998), but they use the sub-clause numbering of an earlier ISO14001 draft rather than the 1996 version. In comparing the linkages suggested by ISO with those used by these writers, it is therefore necessary to amend the numbering to match that of ISO14001:1996. The ISO view is that shown in ISO14001:1996, table B2, and they indicate that the links between the two standards are strong for policy; organization, and structure and responsibility; management review; document control; process control and operational control; inspection and testing/control of inspection equipment, and monitoring and measurement; records; internal audits; and training.

However, table 15.2 also shows that there are different views on the strength of some linkages:

- ISO14001 does not link quality planning with environmental planning and associates all the environmental planning elements (4.3.1 to 4.3.4) with management responsibility and quality policy. In doing so, however, it is made clear that the link between ISO14001 and ISO9001 for objectives and targets and legal requirements is weak. Puri and Beechner and Koch link some environmental planning elements with quality policy and others with quality planning, design control and contract review. Karapetrovic and Willborn, however, associate no environmental planning elements with quality policy and link them to contract review, design control or quality planning.
- Beechner and Koch see the ISO9001 sub-clauses dealing with design control, control of customer-supplied product, product identification and traceability, handling/storing, and servicing as not being applicable to ISO14001, but ISO14001 associates all these elements, except product identification and traceability, with operation control. Karapetrovic and Willborn see the position similarly to ISO14001 but they also see a connection between design control and environmental programmes, while Puri links design control with legal and other requirements; product identification with monitoring and measurement and servicing with communication.
- ISO14001 indicates that statistical techniques in ISO9001 has no counterpart in ISO14001, but both Beechner and Koch, and Karapetrovic and Willborn, associate it with monitoring and measurement.
- ISO14001 sees communication as having no counterpart in ISO9001, but Puri links it with servicing; Beechner and Koch link it with contract review, and Karapetrovic and Willborn with process control.
- ISO14001 sees emergency preparedness and response as having no counterpart in ISO9001, but Puri links it with corrective and preventative action; Beechner and Koch link it with control of non-conforming product, and Karapetrovic and Willborn with process control.

The requirements of each standard and the meaning of the relevant sub-clauses are therefore being interpreted differently, and some writers see the links as stronger than indicated in table B2 of ISO14001:1996. While stronger links help to support

Table 15.2   Sub-clause linkages between ISO9001:1994 and ISO14001:1996

ISO9001:1994		ISO14001:1996 *ISO view (ISO14001:1996 Annex B Table B2)*	*Puri (1996)*	*Beechner & Koch (1997)*	*Karapetrovic & Willborn (1998)*
Management responsibility					
Quality policy	4.11	4.2 Environmental policy	4.2	4.2	4.2
	–	4.3.1 Environmental aspects	4.3.1	–	–
	4.4.4 part	4.3.2 Legal & other requirements	–	–	–
	4.1.1 part	4.3.3 Objectives & targets	4.3.3	4.3.3	–
	–	4.3.4 Environmental programmes	–	–	–
Organization	4.1.2	4.4.1 Structure & responsibility	4.4.1	4.4.1, 4.3.4	4.4.1
Management review	4.1	4.6 Management review	4.6	4.6	4.6
Quality system					
General	4.2.1 part	4.1 General requirements	–	4.1	4.1
	4.2.1 part	4.4.4 Environmental management system documentation	4.4.4	–	–
Quality system procedures	4.2.2	4.4.6 Operational control	–	4.4.4, 4.4.6, 4.3.1	4.4.4
Quality planning	4.2.3	–	4.3.4	4.3.1, 4.3.4	4.3.4
Contract review	4.3 part	4.4.6 Operational control	4.3.2, 4.4.6	4.3.2, 4.4.3	4.3.1, 4.3.2, 4.3.3
Design control	4.4	4.4.6 Operational control	4.3.2, 4.4.6	N/A	4.3.4, 4.4.6
Document & data control	4.5	4.4.5 Document control	4.4.5	4.4.5	4.4.5
Purchasing	4.6	4.4.6 Operational control	4.4.6	4.4.6 part	4.4.6
Control of customer-supplied product	4.7	4.4.6 Operational control	4.4.6	N/A	4.4.6
Product identification & traceability	4.8	–	4.5.1	N/A	–
Process control	4.9	4.4.6 Operational control	4.4.6	4.4.6	4.4.3, 4.4.6, 4.4.7
Inspection and testing	4.10	4.5.1 part Monitoring & measurement	4.5.1	4.5.1	4.5.1
Control of inspection, measuring equipment	4.11	4.5.1 part Monitoring & measurement	4.5.1	4.5.1	4.5.1
Inspection and test status	4.12	–	–	4.5.1	–
Control of non-conforming product	4.13	4.5.2 part Non-conformance, corrective & preventative action	4.5.2	4.4.7, 4.5.2	4.5.2
Corrective and preventive action	4.14	4.5.2 part Non-conformance, corrective and preventative action	4.4.7, 4.5.2	4.5.2	4.5.2
	–	4.4.7 Emergency preparedness			
Handling, storing etc.	4.15	4.4.6 Operational control	4.4.6	N/A	4.4.6
Control of quality records	4.16	4.5.3 Records	4.5.3	4.5.3	4.5.3
Internal quality audits	4.17	4.5.4 Environmental system audit	4.5.4	4.5.4	4.5.4
Training	4.18	4.4.2 Training, awareness & competence	4.4.2	4.4.2	4.4.2
Servicing	4.19	4.4.6 Operational control	4.4.3, 4.4.5	N/A	4.4.6
Statistical techniques	4.20	–	–	4.5.1	4.5.1
	–	4.4.3 Communication			

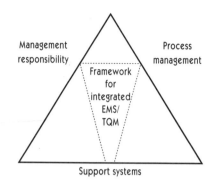

Figure 15.1   The components of an integrated EMS/TQM system
Source: Puri (1996)

their views, the differences underline the views of others, such as Hoyle (1996) and Stapleton (1997), who point to the danger of trying to find links that do not exist. The differences also indicate a fundamental weakness in the matrix model as a means of integrating the two standards. Where the linkages are strong and widely accepted as such, they offer the possibility of some form of integration, but where they are weak and open to a range of interpretations, they can be seen as no more than a stapling together of the standards.

As discussed earlier in the chapter, the ISO/TAG 12 (1998) recommendations indicate an awareness of the difficulties presented when trying to achieve integration in this way and conclude that ISO9001 and ISO14001 should not be merged, but should be made more compatible. However, as discussed above, an examination of ISO9001 (2000) by Wilkinson and Dale (2002) has shown that there are still differences which make integration difficult.

The matrix model is clearly the cross-reference list needed for 'Addition', which is the first of Seghezzi's (2000) three ways to integration, and Puri (1996) uses it in the framework shown in figure 15.1, to which three broad components have been added.

Puri says that each of these additional components (management responsibility, process management and support systems) has its place in an EMS and TQM, and identifies a checklist of the elements of ISO9001 and ISO14001, which he says will show how an integrated EMS/TQM system can be developed. It is primarily a matrix model which offers the possibility of integrated procedures and processes, and the emphasis in his suggested checklist is still on the standards.

In the integrated approach the core elements are intended to cover quality, environmental and any other management systems, which, for MacGregor Associates, means that organizations must implement all systems even though this might not be their immediate plan. (It should be noted that the model shown in figure 15.2 still shows the core as separated into three parts, even though the MacGregor Associates definition calls for a single 'core' standard.) They say that

One danger of an integrated approach is that it could be interpreted as imposing upon an organization the form of management system which it should have. It could also prove a burden in meeting requirements that were not necessary for the discipline being immediately contemplated, e.g. 'continual improvement' when certification to ISO9001 is being sought. (MacGregor Associates 1996: 7)

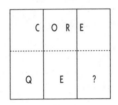

Figure 15.2 Model of an integrated standard
Source: MacGregor Associates (1996)

Figure 15.3 Model of aligned standards
Source: MacGregor Associates (1996)

They therefore do not see continual improvement as a requirement of ISO9001:1994, but presumably accept that it is for ISO14001. In which case, continual improvement could clearly not be a core integrated element.

In the aligned approach (figure 15.3), the common elements of each standard are similar, and it allows organizations to only adopt that part of the common elements which are appropriate to the standard under immediate consideration.

Although the term 'core elements' is used in the integrated approach and 'common elements' is used in the aligned approach, they are treated as meaning the same thing, and are those elements in ISO9001 (1994) and ISO14001 'which are similar at least superficially' (p. 8). Following the integrated approach is said to mean that 'the requirements of the common elements would become progressively more complex', but in the aligned approach, 'the subsequent incorporation of other disciplines e.g. OH&S, would not invalidate the structure previously established in respect of quality and environment' (p. 8).

The common elements identified by using the linkages shown in Annex B of ISO14001 are:

- Policy
- Organization and management responsibility
- Management review
- Implementation and operation
- Human resources and training
- Measuring and monitoring (including internal audits)
- Corrective action
- Preventative action

They are therefore subject to the same views and interpretations discussed earlier, but the real problem, which MacGregor Associates recognize, is the differences, and they still see consistent terminology and principles, which they describe as harmonization, as essential requirements in both approaches.

In proposing the two approaches, MacGregor Associates also believe that the differences in scope in ISO9001 and ISO14001 are much deeper than the differences in discipline, and the similarities in the elements have tended to obscure this. They believe that the aligned approach can cope with these differences but the integrated approach cannot.

Although the concept of a single standard covering quality, environment, and health and safety may be seen as attractive, there are difficulties in trying to make it a reality and these become clearer by applying the systems concept (Optner 1965, 1975) to the problem.

As single management systems, quality, the environment, and health and safety each has its own set of elements and the elements of each individual system must be compatible with each other. It does not matter if the elements of the quality system differ in some way from those of the other systems, and each system can have different restrictions placed on its output, i.e. it does not matter if, in setting the objectives of each system, different restrictions are imposed, and the definitions of the elements and the boundary (scope) of each system can differ. Therefore, while harmonization might be desirable, it is not essential.

For the aligned approach, the system elements and boundaries can differ because the systems are parallel and not integrated, but the requirements for each individual system must still be met. Harmonization is now required, however, because the documentation is based on similarities and the identified linkages. One of the objectives of the aligned approach is simplification, and without harmonization the documentation becomes more, rather than less, complex.

For the integrated approach, the boundary of each subsystem in the core must be the same. As a single integrated system, the core system would be audited and certificated as one rather than three separate systems, and the three parts of the core and their elements would no longer be independent. The non-core parts of the system would require harmonization as indicated above for the aligned approach, and there is no reason why the non-core parts could not be given different boundaries.

The systems concept therefore suggests that the integrated approach, with its integrated core and aligned supporting subsystems, will be more complex than either the aligned approach or a fully integrated standard. However, a single system/standard which addresses the requirements of three existing systems/standards looks difficult to achieve, and an approach proposed by Karapetrovic and Willborn (1998), which is said to avoid these difficulties, is now considered.

Interlinked Systems

Karapetrovic and Willborn (1998) have suggested a simple model of a system (see figure 15.4) which they believe overcomes problems caused by the lack of clarity in the quality vocabulary. It uses a seven-point decision cycle which is similar to Deming's (1982) plan-do-check-act (PDCA) cycle and helps to show the interrelationships between systems.

They suggest that interlinked or integrated systems can be seen as forming a 'system of systems' where the individual systems do not lose their identity and can still be audited and certificated. While this approach avoids some of the

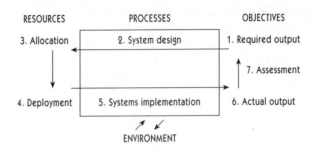

Figure 15.4   Simple graphical model of a system
Source: Karapetrovic and Willborn (1998)

problems presented by a single integrated standard, there are features that require consideration.

Although Karapetrovic and Willborn (1998) agree that integrating two systems leads to a loss of independence, they then associate interlinking with integration, and state that 'interlinked or integrated systems form a so-called "system of systems"' (1998: 207). This concept allows the QMS and EMS to be related to another system in the same organization, but 'individual systems are interlinked without relinquishing their individual identities' (1998: 207). Their 'system of systems' is therefore not a true integrated system as defined by the systems concept.

Their model (figure 15.5) shows how the elements of ISO9001 and ISO14001, which have been derived from the linkages shown earlier in table 15.2, can be integrated.

It should be noted that the linkages given by Karapetrovic and Willborn in table 15.2 are not all the same as the associations shown in figure 15.5. 'Statistical techniques' (4.20) is linked to 'monitoring and measurement' (4.5.1) in the table, but in the systems model it is seen as a 'system-wide supporting element' and part of 'resources for performance improvement'. Similarly, 'organization' (4.1.2) is linked to 'structure and responsibility' (4.4.1) in the table, which is shown as part of 'Allocation' in the systems model and placed alongside 'purchasing, control of customer-supplied product', and 'control of inspection equipment'. In table 15.2, however, 'purchasing' (4.6) and 'control of customer-supplied product' (4.7) are linked to 'operational control' (4.4.6), and 'control of inspection equipment' (4.11) is linked to 'monitoring and measurement' (4.5.1). These changes arise because part of 'structure and responsibility' (4.4.1) in ISO14001 deals with management's responsibility to provide resources, while the other part deals with defining roles and responsibilities, and the reporting of performance. Therefore, while the model aids understanding of the relationships between elements of each standard that are not obvious from either the standards themselves or the ISO9001/ISO14001 matrix, the positioning of the sub-clauses in the model and the linkages are not always clear and are open to interpretation.

The EFQM Model

The European model for total quality management (see p. 292 n. 1; figure 15.6) is intended to show that customer satisfaction, people satisfaction (employee satisfaction)

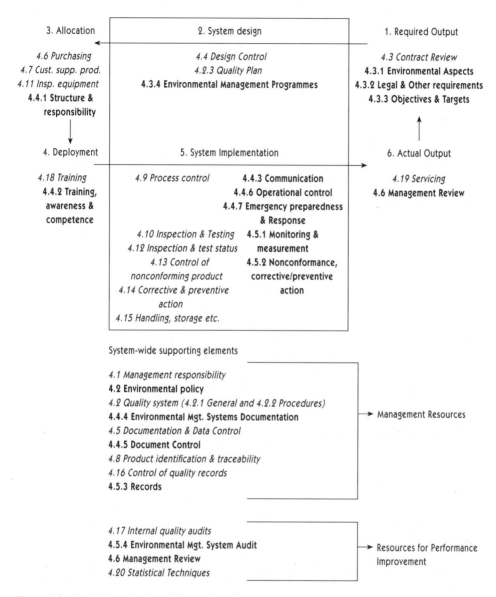

Figure 15.5   Graphical model of an IMS based on ISO9001 and ISO14001
Note: ISO9001 elements in italics; ISO14001 elements in bold
Source: Karapetrovic and Willborn (1998); amended for ISO14001:1996 elements

and impact on society (stakeholder satisfaction) are achieved through leadership driving policy and strategy, the management of people (employees), and the management of resources, which will ultimately lead to improved/excellent business results. Leadership, people, policy and strategy, processes and resources are seen as the enablers which can secure improved people, customer and stakeholder satisfaction and lead to improved business results. The model is based on the TQM philosophy, which requires a total quality approach to be implemented throughout

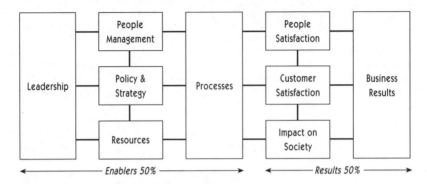

Figure 15.6   The European model for Total Quality Management (1996)

the whole organization, and the self-assessment and scoring processes emphasize the importance of deployment of the enabler criteria at all levels, and across all activities in the organization. The approach used should be integrated into normal operations and planning, and the scope of the results criteria should cover all relevant areas of the organization. The value of both deployment and integration is therefore made clear in the assessment process.

An examination of the assessment criteria also shows that the model is very much concerned with the assessment and shaping of the organization's culture and climate, the part that leadership plays in doing this, and the influence that culture and climate have in securing improved business results.

Although the model is not intended to represent a total quality system, and the 1999 version has removed references to TQM, it has been seen as a standard, and a model on which an integrated system could be built, by Jonker and Klaver (1998). As a TQM model it could also form a basis for an IMS, as suggested by Aschner (1999) and Seghezzi (2000). However, as discussed earlier, differences in concept have made a comparison between the model and the standards difficult. While the standards provide a useful framework on which to build further improvements and to secure what has already been achieved, the model does not demand their implementation, but it would, for example, look at how quality, the environment, and health and safety were managed. The standards are more concerned with satisficing, but the model drives improvement and is concerned with optimizing, and integration can be either based on the requirements of the standards or on TQM. In the latter case, the standards are still necessary for quality assurance and quality control, but improved business performance is the main aim. Integration through the standards, however, is generally associated with the reducing of audit fees, and administration costs.

A Comparative Analysis of the Current Integration Models

The results of an analysis of the current integration models are summarized in table 15.3, which shows that none of the models meets the requirements of a fully integrated system which addresses both the ISO certification needs and promotes business improvement. Although the European model for total quality management addresses culture and offers the opportunity to facilitate business improvement, it

Table 15.3 A comparison of the IMS models

Model	Scope	Requirements	Objectives	Limitations for integration
ISO9001/ 14001 Matrix	As required by each standard	Harmonization of elements & standards	Meeting certification requirements of each standard. Reducing audit & admin. costs	Addition of other standards adds to complexity Linkages open to different interpretations Ignores culture
Aligned standards	As required by each standard	Harmonization of elements & standards	Meeting certification requirements of each standard. Reducing audit & admin. costs	Offers potential for the addition of other standards but adds to complexity Ignores culture
Integrated core standard with aligned subsystems	Must be same for each 'part' of the core As required by each standard for subsystems	Harmonization of elements in the core Harmonization of elements & standards in subsystems	Meeting certification requirements of the core standard & sub-systems. Reducing audit & admin. costs	Core elements must be defined at the outset Complex Ignores culture
Interlinked standards through a systems approach	As required by each standard	Harmonization of elements & standards	Meeting certification requirements of each standard. Offers potential for addition of certificated systems	Addition of other systems adds to complexity Ignores culture
EFQM Model (1996)	'Total' company-wide	Implementation of TQM 'Harmonization' of approach Development of IMS models	Business excellence; improving performance in all areas	Does not address ISO certification requirements

cannot replace the standards or be seen as an alternative to them. The differences in concept between the standards and the model also mean that the standards, either individually or collectively, cannot readily be compared with the model.

The analysis has also shown that true integration through the ISO9001/ISO14001 matrix is seen as increasingly unlikely, and alternative approaches, such as the 'aligned', 'integrated core with aligned subsystems' and 'interlinked' standards, are being suggested. All these approaches require harmonization of the standards and their elements; they fail to address culture and differences in the scope of the standards, and the addition of other systems is likely to increase their complexity. Furthermore, while harmonization of the standards should satisfy demands for integrated documentation and help to reduce administration and audit costs, the other deficiencies will still remain because they are inherent in the standards themselves. Overcoming them will require standard writers to address matters such as the motivation of employees, and there is no indication of a desire by ISO or BSI to do this, at least in the short term. It is therefore possible that no single approach is likely to meet all of the requirements, but the EFQM model and an approach based on TQM could offer a solution to the problem.

The Key Integration Issues

From analysis of the literature and the above models of integration, Wilkinson and Dale (2000) have identified five key issues which have been tested in the field in order to assess their relevance and determine their importance. They are:

1   There are differences in understanding of the term integration and the two approaches being adopted suggest that integration is taking place in two ways and at different levels. The two approaches are: a merging of the documentation through the aligned approach, and implementation of the integrated system through a TQM approach. Merging of the documentation through the aligned approach is adequate for certification purposes, but the scope of the IMS and the level of integration will also be reflected by the organization's needs and its culture.

2   Integration into a single merged standard is not favoured by standard writers, and the current focus of attention by BSI and ISO is on achieving compatibility between the standards in order to bring about their alignment. The objective is to increase understanding of and to simplify the terminology used, and, as a result of this, many organizations believe that a reduction in administration and audit costs will be possible. However, the lack of compatibility in the standards has not prevented organizations from combining their documentation, and some are looking for more than reduced audit and administration costs from their IMS.

3   Differences in the scope of the systems do not hinder a merging of the documentation through the aligned approach, but implementation of an IMS is likely to be adversely affected by these differences. This suggests that differences in scope are more important than differences in terminology and definitions.

4   Focusing on alignment and the possibility of reducing administration and audit costs has distracted attention from the view that integration through a TQM approach could offer more substantial benefits.

5   Culture is seen as important and an enabler for the improvement of business performance, but neither the standards nor the systems concept addresses issues such as motivation and co-operation. Increasing the compatibility of the standards will therefore not overcome their failure to address culture.

The findings support the views of Aschner (1999) and Seghezzi (2000) that there is a need to develop and test models of an IMS based on a TQM approach, which recognizes the issues identified, offers potential for overcoming the limitations in the current models of integration, and gives guidance on how organizations should implement an IMS.

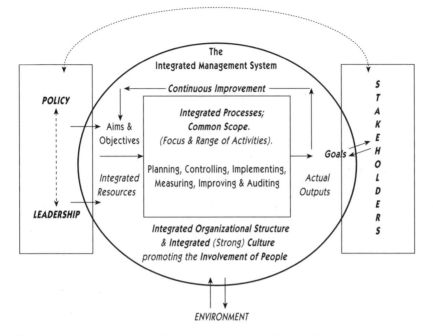

Figure 15.7   A model of an integrated quality, environment and health and safety management system

An Integrated Management Systems Model

The model shown in figure 15.7 provides a definition of an IMS which is based on existing and accepted definitions of a QMS, EMS and OH&SMS given in the relevant standards. It shows the elements of an IMS and what organizations need to consider when implementing such a system. The model, which has been tested for value and validity by Wilkinson and Dale (2001) in a survey of British Standards Society (BSS) members, also indicates that integration of the documentation and audits forms only a part of a fully integrated management system, and that other factors are likely to influence successful integration. It can be used by any organization wishing to implement an integrated quality, environmental, and health and safety management system, but particularly by those who have recognized and accepted the difference between an IMS manual, which is based on the requirements of the standards, and the need to exceed those requirements for full integration. Since the model is based on a TQM approach, experience in introducing TQ initiatives is likely to make implementation of an IMS easier.

The model shows a combined system containing a QMS, EMS and OH&SMS, where each of these three systems/subsystems has lost its independence; their outputs contribute to the final output, and the boundary of each is the same. The resources, and processes and procedures interact through the organization's structure and culture to carry out the activities of planning, controlling, implementing, measuring, improving and auditing, and transform inputs into outputs. The outputs are then compared with the organization's goals, which have been determined by its policy and the needs of all its interested parties (stakeholders). The results of this comparison are then fed back to the input, so that the aims and objectives can be revised and the resources adjusted, if necessary, in a sequence of activities which forms a cycle of continuous improvement. The driving force in the system is leadership and the resources used are the combined resources of the QMS, EMS and OH&SMS, which include people, finance, equipment, the tools and techniques used, information and documentation, and training. Integrating these resources helps to ensure that everyone and everything used is involved with and contributes an input to the combined quality, environment, and health and safety processes.

The processes used have a common scope, i.e. they have a common focus and aim, which is satisfying stakeholders' requirements, and a common range of activities, and each of these activities addresses quality, environment, and health and safety needs and policy.

The resources and activities of the IMS operate through an integrated organizational structure and culture, where the structure is a common set of relationships, responsibilities, authorities and communication channels, which promote the key elements of TQM, such as teamworking, involvement and co-operation. The culture is a strong one; the organization's core values are based on the TQM philosophy and approach, and they are widely shared by everyone involved in the quality, environmental, and health and safety activities.

From this description the following definition of an IMS is proposed:

> The part of the overall management system that includes the combined resources, processes and structures for planning, implementing, controlling, measuring, improving and auditing the combined quality, environment, and health and safety requirements of the organization.

Summary

There is a growing interest in the integration of management systems which is supported by organizational theory, but differences in understanding about integration indicate a need for a definition of an IMS. In the quality management literature, integration is associated with deployment and the scope of the QMS, and in the management system standards, integration and alignment are two separate approaches rather than related terms. It is therefore not surprising to find that integration is viewed in a number of different ways; from the implementation of a single system throughout the whole organization; to combining two or more systems through similarities in their structure, and to organization-wide integration of all management systems with the policy and objectives of each system aligned to the overall policy.

The integration of standards, such as ISO9001 and ISO14001, requires harmonization of their clauses and sub-clauses, and the current view of ISO is that the standards should be made more compatible and aligned, with the objective of reducing audit and administration costs. Alignment results in independent parallel systems which have similarities in content, and a single merged standard is not favoured by standard writers, because it is seen as imposing a requirement, which some organizations may feel they do not need. A single integrated standard would also require the scope/boundary of each system to be the same and would lead to the merged standards losing their independence. To overcome these difficulties, the integrated approach, which uses an integrated core and aligned subsystems, has been proposed, but the systems concept shows that the scope of the systems within the core would still have to be the same, and the outcome would be more complex than a single integrated standard. Interlinking the two standards to form a system of systems has been suggested as an alternative which overcomes the lack of clarity in the terms used, but analysis suggests that the linkages will still be open to interpretation and such a system would not be a true integrated one.

By focusing on alignment and the possibility of reducing audit and administration costs, attention has been distracted from the view that integration through a TQM approach could offer more substantial benefits. Because they are based on the requirements of the standards, the aligned, integrated and interlinked approaches to integration are concerned with satisficing rather than optimizing. On the other hand, although the EFQM model does not address the integration of management systems and cannot replace ISO9001 or ISO14001 for certification purposes, it embraces the TQM philosophy, is concerned with the assessment of culture and climate, and encourages business improvement. This indicates that achieving a common philosophy, approach and aims is more important than achieving compatibility of terms and definitions, and it is helpful to view scope in a wider sense than the physical boundary of a system. Scope can then be seen as including the philosophy and aims of the IMS, where compatibility means more than making the terminology and definitions consistent, and a TQM approach offers a way of doing this.

Culture is seen as an important tool and an enabler for the improvement of business performance, but neither the standards nor the systems approach to integration addresses issues such as motivation and co-operation. Since increasing the compatibility of the standards will not overcome their failure to address culture, it is an issue for organizations to address. In doing so, it is important to consider the degree of culture change achieved prior to introduction of the IMS, and support, ownership, training and the successful implementation of existing systems will also need to be considered. Similarly, since integration through the standards is unlikely to bring about a culture change beyond that already achieved by implementing the individual standards, an organization looking to bring about a further culture change by this approach is likely to be disappointed. On the other hand, the implementation of an IMS which is based on total quality offers potential for a lasting and significant change in the organization.

In order to address these issues and the limitations of current models of integration, a definition of an IMS has been suggested, and a model of integration which is based on a TQM approach has been described. The model, which has been tested in the field, can be used by any organization wishing to implement an integrated quality, environmental, and health and safety management system, but particularly by those who have recognized the difference between an IMS manual that is based on the requirements of the standards, and the need to exceed those requirements for full integration.

References

Aschner, G. B. (1999), Meeting customers' requirements and what can be expected. *The TQM Magazine*, 11(6), 450–5.
BS8800 (1996), *Guide to Occupational Health and Safety Management Systems*. London: British Standards Institution.

BSI-OHSAS18001 (1999), *Occupational Health and Safety Series Specification*. London: British Standards Institution.

Beechner, A. B. and Koch, J. E. (1997), Integrating ISO9001 and ISO14001. *Quality Progress*, 30(2), 33–6.

Boiral, O. (1998), Against the tide of modern management. *Journal of General Management*, 24(1), 35–52.

British Quality Foundation (1996), *Quality Links*. London: BQF.

Cummings, T. G. and Worley, C. G. (1997), *Organizational Development and Change*, 6th edn. Cincinnati, Ohio: South-Western College Publishing.

Dale, B. G. (1999), Quality management systems. In B. G. Dale (ed.), *Managing Quality*, 3rd edn, ch. 13. Oxford: Blackwell.

Dale, B. G. and Lascelles, D. M. (1999), Levels of TQM adoption. In B. G. Dale (ed.), *Managing Quality*, 3rd edn, ch. 1. Oxford: Blackwell.

Dale, B. G. and Oakland, J. S. (1994), *Quality Improvement through Standards*, 2nd edn. Cheltenham: Stanley Thornes.

Dalling, I. (2002), The future is unified, integrated and minimalist. *Quality World*, 28(1), 10–13.

Daniel, F. J. (2001), ISO9001: 2000 – direct hit? *Quality World*, 27(10), 28–30.

Deming, W. E. (1982), *Quality, Productivity, and Competitive Position*. Massachusetts: MIT Centre for Advanced Engineering Study.

European Commission (1993), *Eco-Management and Audit Regulation: Council Regulation (EEC) No. 1863/93*. Brussels: European Commission.

EFQM (1996), *Self-Assessment, 1996 Guidelines for Companies*. Brussels: EFQM.

EFQM (1999), *The EFQM Excellence Model*. Brussels: EFQM.

Garvin, D. (1991), How the Baldrige award really works. *Harvard Business Review*, November/December, 80–93.

Hillary, R. (1997), Environmental management standards: what do SMEs think? In C. Sheldon (ed.), *ISO14001 and Beyond*. Sheffield: Greenleaf Publishing.

Hoyle, D. (1996), Quality systems: a new perspective. *Quality World*, 22(10), 710–13.

ISO9001 (1994), *Quality Systems: Model for Quality Assurance in Design, Development, Production, Installation and Servicing*. Geneva: International Organization for Standardization.

ISO9001 (2000), *Quality Management Systems: Requirements*. Geneva: International Organization for Standardization.

ISO9004 (2000), *Quality Management Systems: Guidelines for Performance Improvements*. Geneva: International Organization for Standardization.

ISO14001 (1996), *Environmental Management Systems: Specification with Guidance for Use*. Geneva: International Organization for Standardization.

ISO/TAG 12 (1998), ISO/TAG 12, ISO9000/ISO14000 Compatibility. <http://www.iso.ch/presse/presse19.htm, July>.

Jonker, J. and Klaver, J. (1998), Integration: a methodological perspective. *Quality World*, 24(8), 21–3.

Karapetrovic, S. and Willborn, W. (1998), Integration of quality and environmental management systems. *The TQM Magazine*, 10(3), 204–13.

Lawrence, P. and Lorsch, J. (1967), *Organization and Environment*. Cambridge, Mass.: Harvard University Press.

MacGregor Associates (1996), *Study on Management System Standards*. London: British Standards Institute.

Mullins, L. J. (1996), *Management and Organizational Behaviour*, 4th edn. London: Pitman Publishing.

Optner, S. L. (1965), *Systems Analysis for Business and Industrial Problem Solving*. Englewood Cliffs, NJ: Prentice Hall International.

Optner, S. L. (1975), *Systems Analysis for Business Management*, 3rd edn. Englewood Cliffs, NJ: Prentice Hall.

Puri, Subhash, C. (1996), *Integrating Environmental Quality with ISO9000 and TQM*. Portland, Oreg.: Productivity Press.

Riemann, C. and Sharratt, P. (1995), Survey of industrial experience with environmental management. In P. Sharratt (ed.), *Environmental Management Systems*. Rugby: Institution of Chemical Engineers.

Sandholm, L. (1999), Trendy versus effective quality strategies. *The TQM Magazine*, 11(6), 437–44.

Seghezzi, H. D. (2000), Total management systems: why and how? In *Proceedings of the 4th European Quality Congress*, Budapest, 1, 158–68.

Shillito, D. (1995), Grand unification theory: should safety, health, environment and quality be managed together or separately? *Environmental Protection Bulletin* (Institution of Chemical Engineers), 039, November, 28–37.

Stapleton, P. (1997), Many possibilities exist for ISO9001 and ISO14001 integration. *Quality Progress*, 30(7), 8–10.

Tranmer, J. (1996), Overcoming the problems of integrated management systems. *Quality World*, 22(10), 714–18.

Wilkinson, G. and Dale, B. G. (1998), Manufacturing companies' attitudes to system integration: a case study examination. *Quality Engineering*, 11(2), 249–56.

Wilkinson, G. and Dale, B. G. (1999), Integration of quality, environmental, and health and safety management systems: an examination of the key issues. *Proceedings of the Institution of Mechanical Engineers*, 213(pt. B), 275–83.

Wilkinson, G. and Dale, B. G. (2000), Management system standards: the key integration issues. *Proceedings of the Institution of Mechanical Engineers*, 214 (pt. B), 771–80.

Wilkinson, G. and Dale, B. G. (2001), Integrated management systems: a model based on a total quality approach. *Managing Service Quality*, 11(5), 318–30.

Wilkinson, G. and Dale, B. G. (2002), An examination of the ISO9001:2000 standard and its influence on the integration of management systems. *Production Planning and Control*, 13(3), 284–97.

chapter sixteen

Tools and Techniques: An Overview

B. G. Dale

Introduction

To support, develop and advance a process of continuous improvement it is necessary for an organization to use a selection of tools and techniques. Some of these tools and techniques are simple (sometimes deceptively so), while others are more complex. There is a considerable number of tools and techniques; the following are perhaps the most popular and best known:

- Checklists
- Flowcharts
- The seven quality control tools (QC7: cause-and-effect diagram, checksheet, control chart, graphs, histogram, Pareto diagram and scatter diagram)
- Quality costing
- Statistical process control
- Failure mode and effects analysis
- Fault tree analysis
- Design of experiments
- Quality function deployment
- The seven management tools (M7: affinity diagrams, relations diagrams, systematic diagrams, matrix diagrams, matrix data analysis, process decision programme chart, and arrow diagrams)
- Departmental purpose analysis
- Mistake-proofing
- Benchmarking
- Total productive maintenance
- Housekeeping

Tools and techniques have different roles to play in continuous improvement and if applied correctly give repeatable and reliable results. Their roles include:

- Summarizing data and organizing its presentation
- Data-collection and structuring ideas
- Identifying relationships
- Discovering and understanding a problem
- Implementing actions
- Finding and removing the causes of the problem
- Selecting problems for improvement and assisting with the setting of priorities
- Monitoring and maintaining control
- Planning
- Performance measurement and capability assessment

A number of the tools and techniques in the above list have a separate chapter in the book devoted to them. This chapter provides an overview of the tools and techniques which are not given such coverage but are likely to be used in an organization's improvement process. The focus is on describing the tools and their uses and avoids detail on construction. Where appropriate, guidance for further reading is provided for those who may wish to extend their knowledge of a particular tool or technique. A deliberate attempt has been made to choose examples from a variety of situations to give the reader a flavour of their applicability in a wide number of situations.

Selecting Tools and Techniques

The potential user must always be aware of the main uses of the particular tool and technique they are considering applying. There is often a danger of using a tool and technique in a blinkered manner, almost expecting it to solve the problem automatically.

When selecting tools and techniques there are two factors which organizations should keep in mind:

1 The application of any tool and technique in isolation without a strategy and plan will only provide short-term benefits. If tools and techniques are to be effective over the longer term, appropriate employee behaviour and attitudes are needed to make effective improvements.
2 No one tool or technique is more important than another – they all have a role to play at some point in the improvement process. It is a mistake to single out one tool or technique for special attention and to become over-reliant on it; the Japanese make the point that a warrior should never have a favourite weapon. A common saying used to emphasize this is 'If you only have a hammer, it is surprising how many problems look like nails.'

A number of companies use tools and techniques without thinking through the implications for TQM or how the concept will be developed and advanced within the organization. This can give rise to misconceptions and misunderstandings which eventually become barriers to progress. Many companies who use tools and techniques as the springboard to launch an improvement process usually single out a specific tool or technique, sometimes at random, and apply it with undue haste without giving sufficient thought to the following issues:

- What is the fundamental purpose of the technique?
- What will it achieve?
- Will it produce benefits if applied on its own?
- Is the technique right for the company's product, processes, people and culture?
- How will the technique facilitate improvement?
- How will it fit in with, complement or support other techniques, methods and quality management systems already in place, and any that might be introduced in the future?
- What organizational changes, if any, are necessary to make the most effective use of the technique?
- What is the best method of introducing and then using the technique?
- What are the resources, skills, information training, etc. required to introduce the technique successfully?
- Has the company the management skills and resources and the commitment to make the technique work successfully?
- What are the potential difficulties in using the technique?
- What are the limitations, if any, of the technique?

It is important for managers to address these questions when considering the introduction of any tool or technique. Unfortunately, some managers are always looking for tools and techniques as a quick-fix solution to the problems facing their organization at a particular point in time. In general, management teams that are 'technique reactive' tend to be unclear on the concept of TQM. They often confuse the implementation of a particular technique with TQM and tend to use the technique as an end in itself rather than as a means to an end.

If the management team is preoccupied with specific techniques and lacks an adequate understanding of TQM and the improvement process, the risk is that tools and techniques are picked up and discarded as fashion changes; an analogy can be made to a magician producing balls out of the air or pulling rabbits out of a hat (see figure 16.1). When this happens and a tool or technique fail to meet expectations, disillusionment sets in and the company experiences considerable difficulty convincing its employees that it is serious about improvement. This, of course, has an adverse effect on the use of techniques in the organization in the future.

One of the main reasons that companies fall into this trap is that they have unduly high expectations of the benefits arising from the use of a single tool or technique which stem from the lack of clarity and in-depth understanding of it. Much of this is a result of the publicity and selling which often accompany a specific tool or technique. In general, on its own a single tool or technique may simply indicate or signify the presence of a problem which must be identified and resolved to produce only a small incremental improvement. It is only as a result of the cumulative effect of a series of tools and techniques within a TQM approach that the organization starts to see long-term benefits from its improvement endeavours (see figure 16.2). Therefore, organizations should resist the temptation to isolate the benefits arising from any one tool or technique.

Motivation for the use of any particular tool or technique is a key factor in the success of its implementation. They could be those specified as a contractual requirement by a major customer, they may be what management believe the marketplace will be expecting in the future, or the view may be taken that their use will give the organization an edge over its competitors. We have found (Dale and Shaw 1990)

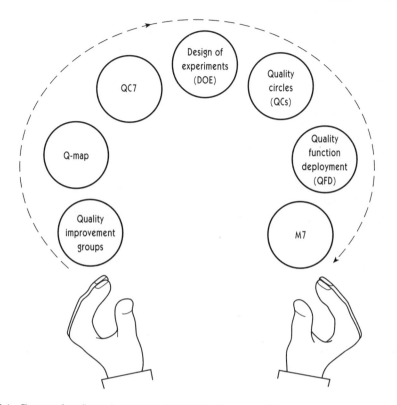

Figure 16.1 The use of quality management tools and techniques

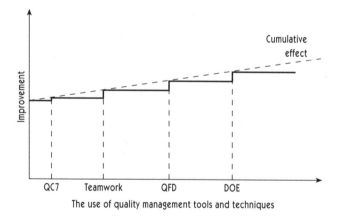

The use of quality management tools and techniques

Figure 16.2 Incremental improvement through the use of quality management tools and techniques

that when a major customer insists on the use of a specific technique as a contractual requirement of its suppliers, two phases can be identified in its use.

1 The technique is applied by the supplier simply to satisfy the demands of the customer in order to maintain the business. To emphasize this they point out

a case in which SPC has been used on a process for a particular customer's product, though when other customers' products were made with the same process SPC was not used. During this phase the supplier often resorts to a number of camouflage measures, fakes and ruses to convince the customer that the technique is being applied effectively and beneficially. The emphasis in this phase is on satisfying the customer's paperwork requirements. This phase is wasteful of time and resources, but suggests that suppliers appear to need this phase to develop their own awareness and understanding of the technique which is being applied.

2   The second phase begins when the supplier's management team starts to question how they might best use the technique to enhance the company's competitive position. This is when real improvements begin to occur. They also point out that motor industry suppliers appear to have reached this phase in a shorter period of time with FMEA than they did with SPC, and suggest that this is due to the learning experience and also the depth of intellectual demands of each technique. Those organizations using techniques such as SPC for the sole reason of satisfying the quality system audits of major customers are missing the direct benefits of the correct use of the technique and also the opportunity that it affords to launch a process of quality improvement. The danger in adopting this approach is that the improvement process goes only as far as the customer requires.

Because of the variety of starting points and motivations for improvement it is not possible to identify a universal implementation plan detailing the order in which specific techniques should be used by an organization. However, one piece of advice is that organizations should start with the simpler techniques, such as checklists, flowcharts and the seven original quality control tools. Simple tools and techniques can be just as effective as the more complex ones. In the West there is a tendency to ignore the simple tools and to use tools and techniques in isolation, whereas the Japanese companies tend to use the seven original quality control tools together and give high visibility to the results. In this way they are not only listening to the process through control charts, but taking action to improve it. This combined use of the seven tools facilitates problem resolution and improvement action.

Difficulties and Issues Relating to the Use of Tools and Techniques

Research carried out by Dale et al. (1998) into the difficulties relating to the use of tools and techniques discovered that the critical success factors relating to the successful use and application of tools and techniques could be grouped into four main categories:

- Data-collection
- Use and application
- Role in improvement
- Organization and infrastructure

They also identified a number of issues which relate to the difficulties experienced with all tools and techniques, including management support, user understanding,

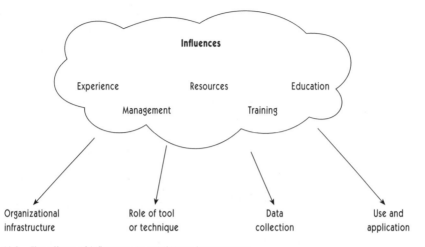

Figure 16.3 The effects of influences on continuous improvement

integral approach, discipline and application. A number of issues which relate to specific tools and techniques were also highlighted, including, level of complexity, visual display, initial investment and overall status of TQM.

Building on this initial work, Dale and McQuater (1998) have identified five main influences on each of the four success factors (see figure 16.3). The influences are experience, management, resources, education, and training. Based on these influences an assessment methodology has been developed for identifying potential difficulties that impinge on the effective use of tools and techniques in an organization and for providing a diagnostic analysis. The methodology, described by Dale and McQuater (1998), consists mainly of an assessment grid, questionnaire and semi-structured interviews. These approaches can be used separately as well as in combinations, depending on the organization's objectives for carrying out the assessment. The assessment grid, which can be used on its own to undertake a 'health check' of potential areas for concern, is reproduced in table 16.1.

Problem-Solving Methodology

The use of tools and techniques should be employed within a problem-solving approach for maximum effectiveness and efficiency. Probably the best-known problem-solving cycle is PDCA.

The *plan* aspect of the cycle is usually considered in four stages:

1 Define the problem or improvement opportunity and specify objectives.
2 Identify the likely causes of the problem.
3 Pinpoint the root causes of the problem.
4 Prepare solutions and develop and agree an action plan.

The *do* is concerned with implementing the action plan; *check* monitors the effectiveness of the actions which have been implemented and *act* relates to standardization of the results and transferring the practices to other processes.

Table 16.1 An assessment grid for a health check:
(a) recognition and use grid; (b) application grid

Please indicate on the grid ONLY the techniques and tools you recognize. For those that you have recognized, if you use them for *any* purpose, not only for quality-related matters, please tick the box marked use.

Example	Recognize	Use
QC7		
Cause and effect	✓	
Check sheets		
Control charts		
Graphs/charts	✓	✓
Histograms	✓	✓
Pareto analysis	✓	✓
Scatter diagrams	✓	

	Recognize	Use
QC7		
Cause and effect		
Check sheets		
Control charts		
Graphs/charts		
Histograms		
Pareto analysis		
Scatter diagrams		
M7		
Affinity diagrams		
Arrow diagrams/critical path analysis		
Matrix data analysis methods		
Matrix diagrams		
Process decision programme chart		
Relation diagrams		
Systematic diagrams/tree diagrams		
Techniques		
Benchmarking		
Brainstorming/brainwriting		
Departmental purpose analysis		
Design of experiments (Taguchi)		
Failure mode and effects analysis		
Flow charts		
Force field analysis		
Problem solving methodology		
Quality costs		
Quality function deployment		
Questionnaire		
Sampling		
Statistical process control		
*		
*		
*		
*		
*		

* Add any company-specific techniques and tools not indicated on the list

Table 16.1 (cont'd)

Please complete the grid ONLY for the techniques or tools you indicated on the recognition and use grid. Do not attempt to fill it in its entirety. They may be occasions when some of the categories cannot be allocated a score; in that case insert 9 (not applicable)

Score out of 5 in each of the categories where:

1 = No value
2 = Low value (e.g. little used, not understood, little or poor training, etc.)
3 = Some value (e.g. basic understanding, small benefits, basic training, etc.)
4 = High value (e.g. good understanding, some benefits, reasonable training, etc.)
5 = Very high value (e.g. complete understanding, excellent benefits, effective traing, etc.)
9 = Not applicable or no training

	Importance	Relevance	Use	Understand	Application	Resources	Management	Training	Benefit
For example: *Pareto analysis*	5	4	2	3	3	2	1	1	4
	Importance	Relevance	Use	Understand	Application	Resources	Management	Training	Benefit
QC7									
Cause and effect									
Check sheets									
Control charts									
Graphs/charts									
Histograms									
Pareto analysis									
Scatter diagrams									
QC7									
Affinity diagrams									
Arrow diagrams/critical path analysis									
Matrix data analysis methods									
Matrix diagrams									
Process decision programme chart									
Relation diagrams									
Systematic diagrams/tree diagrams									
Techniques									
Benchmarking									
Brainstorming/brainwriting									
Departmental purpose analysis									
Design of experiments (Taguchi)									
Failure mode and effects analysis									
Flow charts									
Force field analysis									
Problem solving methodology									
Quality costs									
Quality function deployment									
Questionnaire									
Sampling									
Statistical process control									
Other techniques, tools, systems									
For example:									
ISO9000 series									
Quality operating system QS9000									
Other awards (e.g. EQA)									

At each stage of the cycle a range of tools and techniques is employed. The Ford Motor Company has been at the forefront in developing a step-by-step process of ensuring that any improvement action is permanent. This is known as the TOPS (team-orientated problem-solving) 8D (eight-discipline) approach. The following is a summary of the eight disciplines.

- D1   Use a team approach (see chapter 23)
- D2   Describe the problem:

   - Review and analyse existing data
   - Establish problem definition and statement
   - Develop the problem profile
   - Confirm problem with the customer.

- D3   Implement and verify interim containment actions (ICA):

   - Choose best ICA
   - Test for feasibility
   - Develop action plan and implement ICA to isolate the problem from the customer until permanent corrective action is available
   - Monitor and report effectiveness of ICA.

- D4   Define and verify root cause(s):

   - Review, improve and update problem definition and description
   - Identify possible causes by comparison to the problem description
   - Select likely causes
   - Verify root causes
   - Report.

- D5   Choose and verify permanent corrective actions (PCA):

   - Choose best PCA
   - Re-evaluate ICA
   - Verify PCA
   - Make choice
   - Report.

- D6   Implement permanent corrective action:

   - Develop implementation plan
   - Remove ICA
   - Implement PCA
   - Monitor process and assess the effectiveness of problem elimination
   - Formalize changes, and update documents and system
   - Notify affected personnel
   - Report.

- D7   Prevent recurrence:

   - Review current process
   - Identify critical areas or supporting PCA
   - Make recommendations for improvement current processes
   - Report.

- D8   Congratulate the team (see chapter 23).

Checklists

Checklists (sometimes called inspection or validation checklists) are used as prompts and aids to personnel. They highlight the key features of a process, equipment, system and/or product/service to which attention needs to be given, and ensure that the procedures for an operation, housekeeping, inspection, maintenance, etc. have been followed. Checklists are also used in audits of both product and systems. They are an invaluable aid for quality assurance and, as might be imagined, the variety and style and content of such lists is immense. Table 16.2 is used in the internal audit of the quality management system.

The basic steps in constructing a checklist are:

- Study the activity for which the checklist is to be drawn up.
- Drawing on observations of the process, discussions with operatives, and appropriate working instructions and procedures, construct the checklist.
- Walk the checklist through the process by following what happens at each stage.
- Ask the person who is carrying out the process to check its accuracy.
- Display it next to the process.
- Assess its use in practice.

Flowcharts

Process mapping (sometimes called 'blue printing' or process modelling) in either a structured or unstructured format, is a prerequisite to obtaining an in-depth understanding of a process, before the application of quality management tools and techniques such as FMEA, SPC and quality costing. A flowchart is employed to provide a diagrammatic picture, often by means of a set of established symbols, showing all the steps or stages in a process, project or sequence of events and is of considerable assistance in documenting and describing a process as an aid to understanding examination and improvement.

A chart, when used in a manufacturing context, may show the complete process from goods receipt through storage, manufacture, and assembly to dispatch of final product, or simply some part of this process in detail. What is important is that each 'activity' is included, to focus attention on aspects of the process or subset of the process where problems have occurred or may occur, to enable some corrective action to be taken or counter-measure put into place.

Traditionally charts (called process charts) have employed conventional symbolsto define activities such as operation, inspection, delay or temporary storage, permanent storage and transportation, and are much used by operations and methods and industrial engineering personnel (see Currie 1989 for details). In more recent times they have witnessed considerable use in business process re-engineering (see chapter 22).

There are a number of variants of the classical process flowchart, including those tailored to an individual company's use, with different symbols being used to reflect the situation under study. What is important is not the format of the chart and/or flow diagram, but that the process has been mapped out with key inputs, value-adding steps and outputs defined, and that it is understood by those directly involved and responsible for initiating improvements. Analysing the data collected on a flowchart can help to uncover irregularities and potential problem points. It is also a useful method of dealing with customer complaints, providing traceability by

Table 16.2 Checklist: quality management systems

Document/record		QM-13 Ref.
Quality Manual (QM-13) Boiling Water Treatment Feed Manual Cooling Water Treatment Feed Manual Pre-treatment Feed Manual Plant and Equipment Schedule	Maintained with all revisions	Para. 1.2.3
Customer service reports All filed at regional office and consultant's home office in client's files, separated and in chronological order	Countersigned by client Checked and initialled by unit sales manager Dates of visit/last visit Highlight non-conformities Stock levels Control limits	Para. 3.5 Para. 7.1.2
Quality plans Inside front cover of client's files at regional offices and consultant's home office	Must be reviewed on a minimum 12-month basis Checked and initialled by unit sales manager Plant, programme frequency of visits, etc.	
Non-conforming letters retained in client's files and also in a separate file or at least summary log	Issues as and when non-conforming situations are noted and as per guidelines reference interpretation of results	Para. 3.3
Client's files	Quotations/proposals containing quality plans Customer service reports Sales orders Laboratory reports, technical service reports boiler reports, etc. Non-nonforming letters Complaints Audits	Para. 2.5 Para. 3.1 Para. 4.0 Para. 3.6 Para. 3.7 Para. 5.0 Para. 3.4
Calibration records	Held by consultant and regional offices Retain for five years Audit by unit sales manager every six months	Para. 3.2
Complaints	Follow procedures in Quality Manual (QM-12) Retain copies in client's files and also separate file for complaints Retain for five years	Para. 5.0
Home office audits	Once per year by unit sales manager	Para. 1.2.3
Random audits	Unit sales manager to make every six month for each consultant	Para. 3.7 (v)
Training records	Retain for five years	Para. 4.0 Para. 7.0

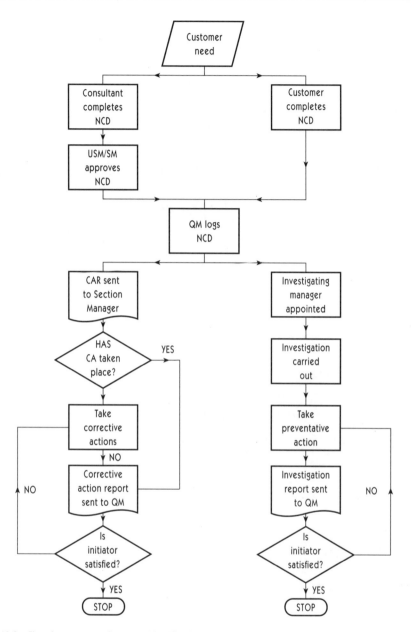

Figure 16.4   Flowchart: non-conformance identification and preventative action process
Key: CA = corrective action; CAR = corrective action request; NCD = non-conformance document;
QM = quality manager; SM = service manager; USM = unit sales manager

establishing the point in the customer–supplier chain where a break or problem has occurred, its potential cause and corrective action. In a number of cases, processes are poorly defined and documented. Also in some organizations people are only aware of their own particular aspect of a process and process-mapping helps to facilitate a greater understanding of the whole process: it is essential to the development of the internal customer–supplier relationship. Figure 16.4 is an example of

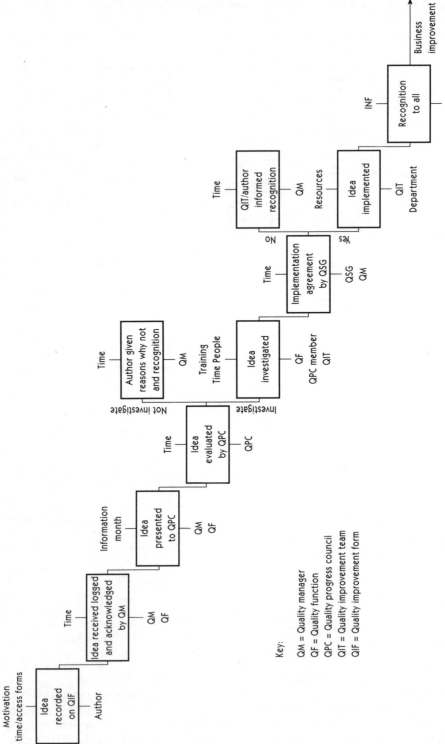

Figure 16.5 Quality management activity planning: quality improvement idea – customer needs awareness

Key: QF = quality function; QIF = quality improvement form; QIT = quality improvement team; QM = quality manager; QPC = quality progress council

flowcharting for the process of non-conformance identification and preventative action.

A specific kind of process mapping – quality management activity planning (Q-MAP) – was developed by Crossfield at the Allied Signal Garrett Automotive plant in Skelmersdale. It is used to map out and analyse organizational procedures to examine what needs to be done, by whom and when (i.e. 'as is' to 'as desired'). The methodology is described in detail by Crossfield and Dale (1990), who outline how Q-MAP has been applied successfully in modelling major aspects of Allied Signal Garrett Automotive's quality assurance systems and procedures, including incoming inspection of material, initial sampling of goods, gauge control/planning, advanced quality planning, new product introduction, implementation of SPC, supplier certification, final view inspection, skip lot sampling, customer initial sample inspection reporting, warranty analysis, and FMEA. It cuts through the complexities of procedural mapping by simple graphical analysis. Each area of interest starts with one 'activity box' which identifies the inputs, outputs, resources required and constraints that apply to that interest. Figure 16.5 is a typical example of Q-MAP.

The following are the main steps in constructing a flowchart:

- Define the process and its boundaries, including start- and end-points.
- Decide the type and method of charting and the symbols to be used, and do not deviate from the convention chosen.
- Decide the detail with which the process is to be mapped.
- Describe the stages, in sequence, in the process using the agreed methodology.
- Assess if these stages are in the correct sequence.
- Ask people involved with the process to check its veracity.

Checksheets

These are a sheet or form used to record data. The checksheet is a simple and convenient recording method for collecting and determining the occurrence of events. The events relate to non-conformities, including the position in which they appear on the non-conforming item (when used in this way they are sometimes referred to as a 'measles' chart or defect position or concentration diagram, or areas for concern chart), non-conforming items, breakdowns of machinery and/or associated equipment, non-value-adding activity or, indeed, anything untoward which may occur within a process. Checksheets are helpful in following the maxim of 'no checking or measurement without recording the data', and are effective in making the first attack on a problem.

They are prepared, in advance of the recording of data, by the operatives and staff being affected by a problem. Checksheets, in table, process, diagram or picture format, are extremely useful as a data-collection device and a record to supplement quality control charts. The data from a checksheet provide the factual basis for subsequent analysis and corrective action. There are many different kinds of checksheets: figure 16.6 is one example.

The following are the main steps in constructing a checksheet:

- Decide the type of data to be illustrated. The data can relate to: number of defectives, percentage of total defectives, cost of defectives, type of defective, process, equipment, shift, business unit, operator, etc.
- Decide which features/characteristics and items are to be checked.

Check item	Week no. Day						
	1	2	3	4	5	6	7
Warp board							
Board delamination							
Surface defect							
Incorrect board spec.							
Incorrect print density							
Shouldering							
Incorrect ink weight							
Off square feeding							
Print mis-registration							
Split bends							
Deep slots							
Narrow slots							
Ink smudging							

Figure 16.6 Checksheet: gluing/stitching department

- Determine the type of checksheet to use (i.e. tabular form or defect position chart).
- Design the sheet; ideally it should be flexible enough to allow the data to be arranged in a variety of ways. Data should always be arranged in the most meaningful way to make best use of them.
- Specify the format, instructions and sampling method for recording the data, including the use of appropriate symbols.
- Decide the time period over which data are to be collected.

Tally Charts and Histograms

Tally charts are a descriptive presentation of data and help to identify patterns in the data. They may be used as checksheets with attribute data (pass/fail, present/absent) but are more commonly used with measured or variable data (e.g. temperature, weight, length) to establish the pattern of variation displayed, prior to the assessment of capability and computation of process capability indices (see chapter 18 on SPC for details). Tally charts are regarded as simple or crude frequency distribution curves and provide a quick way of recording and displaying data.

Statisticians would tend to construct histograms rather than tally charts, but for general analysis purposes they are more or less the same. A histogram is a graphical representation of individual measured values in a data set according to the frequency or relative frequency of occurrence. It takes measured data from the tally sheet and displays its distribution using the class intervals or value as a base – it resembles a bar chart with the bars representing the frequency of data over a range of values. The histogram helps to visualize the distribution of data and in this way reveals the amount of variation within a process, and/or other factors such as edited data and poor sampling techniques. It can be used to assess performance to a given standard,

pH	Frequency	Total
4.75–5.25		0
5.25–5.75		0
5.75–6.25	I	1
6.25–6.75	IIII	4
6.75–7.25	HH III	8
7.25–7.75	HH HH III	13
7.75–8.25	HH HH III	14
8.25–8.75	HH HH II	12
8.75–9.25	IIII	4
9.25–9.75	III	3
9.75–10.25	I	3
10.25–10.75		1

Figure 16.7 Tally chart: effluent analysis – pH

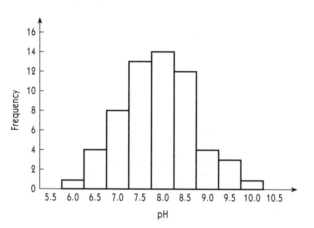

Figure 16.8 Histogram: effluent analysis – pH

specification or tolerance. There are several forms which should be recognized – normal, skewed, bimodal, isolated island, etc. There are a number of theoretical models which provide patterns and working tools for various shapes of distribution. The shape of distribution most often encountered is called Normal or Gaussian.

Figure 16.7 shows a tally chart; figure 16.8 is a histogram which has been constructed from the data collected on the tally chart.

There are several ways of constructing histograms depending upon whether the data are discrete or continuous, whether they are single or grouped values, and whether there is a vast amount of data or not. The following guidelines are given for the treatment of continuous data of sufficient quantity that grouping is required.

- Subtract the smallest individual value from the largest.
- Divide this range by 8 or 9 to give that many classes or groups.
- The resultant value indicates the width or interval of the group. This should be rounded for convenience, e.g. 4.3 could be regarded as either 4 or 5 depending upon the data collected.

- These minor calculations are undertaken to give approximately eight or nine group class intervals of a rational width.
- Each individual measurement now goes into its respective group or class.
- Construct the histogram with measurements on the horizontal scale and frequency (or number of measurements) on the vertical scale.
- The 'blocks' of the histogram should adjoin each other, i.e. there should be no gaps unless there is a recorded zero frequency.
- Clearly label the histogram and state the source of the data.

Graphs

Graphs, be they presentational (i.e. to convey data in a pictorial way), or mathematical (i.e. into which data may be interpolated or from which it may be extrapolated), are used to facilitate understanding and analysis of the collected data, investigate relationships between factors, attract attention, indicate trends and make the data memorable (a picture is worth a thousand words). There is a wide choice of graphical methods available (line graphs, bar charts, pie charts, Gantt charts, radar charts, band charts) for different types of application. Figure 16.9 is a line graph which illustrates right-first-time production; figure 16.10 is a bar chart showing right-first-time production; figure 16.11 is another version of a bar chart which gives the reasons for quality control failure.

The following are the type of issues which need to be considered in the construction of graphs:

- Use clear titles and indicate when and how the data were collected (i.e. the theme of the graphs and the source of data).
- Ensure that the scales are clear, understandable and represent the data accurately.
- When possible, use symbols for extra data to provide clarity of explanation.
- Always keep in mind the reason why a graph is being used (i.e. to highlight some information or data in striking and unambiguous way); anything which facilitates this objective is desirable.

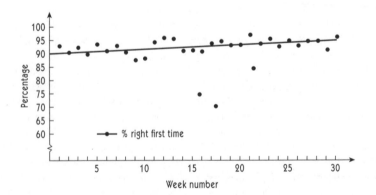

Figure 16.9 Line graph: right-first-time production

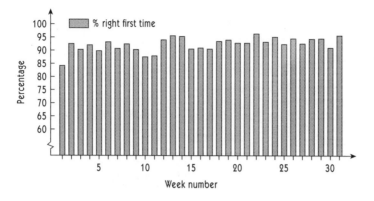

Figure 16.10   Bar chart: right-first-time production

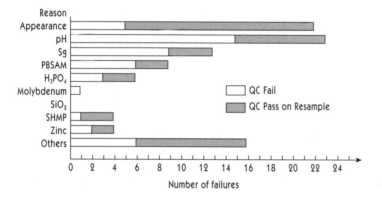

Figure 16.11   Reason for QC failures

Pareto Analysis

This is a technique employed for prioritizing problems of any type, for example quality, production, complaints, stock control, sickness, absenteeism, accident occurrences and resource allocation. The analysis highlights the fact that most problems come from a few causes, and it indicates what problems to solve and in what order (e.g. Juran's (1988) 'vital few and trivial many'). In this way improvement efforts and resources are directed where they will have the greatest impact. Pareto analysis is an extremely useful tool: it can be used to compare before and after situations and data over different time periods. In these ways it can provide insights or problem-solving and process improvement. A Pareto diagram can be considered as a special form of bar chart, comprising a simple bar chart with a cumulative percentage curve overlaid on it.

The diagram is named after a nineteenth-century Italian economist, Wilfredo Pareto, who observed that a large proportion of a country's wealth is held by a small proportion of the population (hence the expression 'the 80/20 rule'). Early in the twentieth century Lorenz produced a cumulative graph, based on these observations, for demonstrating the dominance of the 20 per cent. In the 1950s Juran, using a similar analogy, observed that a large proportion of quality problems were attributable

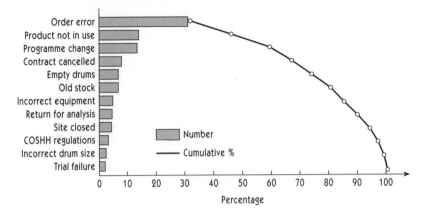

Figure 16.12   Pareto analysis: reasons for returned goods

to a small number of causes (i.e. 80 per cent of rejections are caused by 20 per cent of defect types).

The technique involves ranking the collected data, usually via a checksheet, with the most commonly occurring problem at the top and the least common at the bottom. The contribution of each problem to the grand total is expressed as a percentage, and cumulative percentages are used in compounding the effect of these problems. The ranking of the problems is usually in terms of occurrence and/or cost – just because one defect type happens more frequently than another it does not necessarily mean that it is the costliest or the one that should be tackled first. The results are often presented in two ways: (1) ranked data as a bar chart and (2) cumulative percentages as a graph. Figure 16.12 is an analysis of the reasons for returned goods.

Pareto analysis, while simple in terms of its construction, is extremely powerful in presenting data by focusing attention on the major contributor(s) to a quality problem in order to generate attention, efforts, ideas and suggestions to hopefully gain a significant overall reduction in these problems. It is not a 'once and for all' analysis. If used regularly and consistently, the presentational part of the technique is extremely useful in demonstrating continuous improvement made over a period of time.

The following are the basic steps in constructing a Pareto diagram:

- Agree the problem which is to be analysed.
- Decide the time period over which data are to be collected.
- Identify the main causes or categories of the problem.
- Decide how the data will be measured.
- Collect the data using, for example, a checksheet.
- Tabulate the frequency of each category and list in descending order of frequency (if there are too many categories it is permissible to group some into a miscellaneous category, for the purpose of analysis and presentation).
- Arrange the data as a bar chart.
- Construct the Pareto diagram with the columns arranged in order of descending frequency.
- Determine cumulative totals and percentages and construct the cumulative percentage curve, superimposing it on the bar chart.
- Interpret the data portrayed on the diagram.

Cause-and-Effect Diagrams

This type of diagram was developed by Ishikawa (1976) to determine and break down the main causes of a given problem. Cause-and-effect diagrams are often called Ishikawa diagrams, and sometimes 'fishbone' diagrams, because of their skeletal appearance. They are usually employed where there is only one problem and the possible causes are hierarchical in nature.

The effect (a specific problem or a quality characteristic/condition) is considered to be the head, and potential causes and sub-causes of the problem or quality characteristic/condition to be the bone structure of the fish. The diagrams illustrate in a clear manner the possible relationships between some identified effect and the causes influencing it. They also assist in helping to uncover the root causes of a problem and in generating improvement ideas.

They are typically used by a quality control circle, quality improvement team, kaizen team, problem-solving team, etc. as part of a brainstorming exercise to solicit ideas and opinions as to the possible major cause(s) of a problem, and subsequently to offer recommendations to resolve or counteract it.

It is important to define the problem or abnormality clearly, giving as much detail as possible to enable the identification of potential causes. This can be quite a difficult task, and the team leader must assume responsibility for defining a manageable problem (if it is too large it may need subdividing into a number of sub-problems) to ensure that the team's efforts and contributions are maximized in a constructive manner. There are three types of diagram:

1 *5M cause-and-effect diagram.* The main 'bone' structure or branches typically comprise machinery, manpower, method, material and maintenance. Often teams omit maintenance, and hence use a 4M diagram, while others may add a sixth M (Mother Nature) and so use a 6M diagram. The 4M, 5M, or 6M diagram is useful for those with little experience of constructing cause-and-effect diagrams and is a good starting point in the event of any uncertainty. In non-manufacturing areas the four Ps (policies, procedures, people and plant) are sometimes found to be more appropriate. As with any type of cause-and-effect diagram, the exact format is not so important as the process of bringing about appropriate counter-measures for the identified and agreed major cause(s) of the problem.

2 *Process cause-and-effect diagram.* This is usually used when the problem encountered cannot be isolated to a single section or department. The team members should be familiar with the process under consideration; therefore it is usual to map it out using a flowchart and seek to identify potential causes for the problem at each stage of the process. If the process flow is so great as to be unmanageable, the sub-processes or process steps should be separately identified. Each stage of the process is then brainstormed and ideas developed, using, for example a 4M, 5M, or 6M format. The key causes are identified for further analysis.

3 *Dispersion analysis cause-and-effect diagram.* This diagram is usually used after a 4M/5M/6M diagram has been completed. The major causes identified by the group are then treated as separate branches and expanded upon by the team.

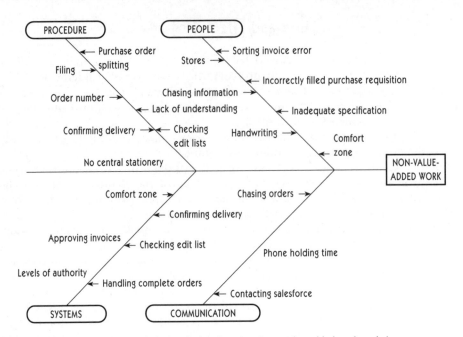

Figure 16.13   Cause-and-effect analysis: purchasing department non-value-added work analysis

Figure 16.13 shows an example of a cause-and-effect diagram for a non-value-added work analysis carried out by a purchasing department.

Cause-and-effect diagrams are usually produced via a team approach and involve the following basic steps:

- Define with clarity and write in a box to the right the key symptom or effect of the problem and draw a horizontal line from the left of the box.
- Ensure that every team member understands the problem and develop a clear problem statement.
- Decide the major groupings or categories for the causes of the effect; these form the main branches of the diagram.
- In a brainstorming session, the group members speculate on causes of the effect and these are added to the branches or sub-branches of the diagram.
- In a following session the causes are discussed and analysed to determine those which are most likely to have caused the effect.
- The most likely, or major causes of the problems are ranked, by the group, in order of importance. This can be done by Pareto voting: 80 per cent of the votes should be cast for 20 per cent of the causes. (If, for example, there are 35 causes, using the figure of 20 per cent gives each member seven votes to allocate to what they believe are the causes of the effect.)
- Additional data are sometimes gathered to confirm the key causes.
- Improvement plans, actions, tests and experiments are decided upon to both verify and address the key causes.

The conventional cause-and-effect diagrams have been developed and refined by Ryuji Fukuda (1990) at Sumitomo Electric, and they are termed cause-and-effect diagrams with addition of cards (CEDAC) – the cards being used to reflect the team's continually updated facts and ideas.

Brainstorming

Brainstorming is a method of free expression and is employed when the solutions to problems cannot be deduced logically and/or when creative new ideas are required. It is used, as highlighted in the above discussion on cause-and-effect diagrams, with a variety of quality management tools and techniques.

Brainstorming works best in groups. It unlocks the creative power of the group through the synergistic effect (e.g. one person's ideas may trigger the thoughts of another member of the group) and in this way stimulates the production of ideas. It can be employed in a structured manner, in which the group follows a set of rules, or in an unstructured format which allows anyone in the group to present ideas randomly as they occur.

The following are some factors to be considered in organizing a brainstorming session:

- Prepare a clear and focused statement of the problem – on some occasions it may be worth sending this to members of the brainstorming group prior to the session taking place.
- Form a group and appoint a leader/facilitator. A team will always produce a greater number of ideas than the same number of individuals working in isolation.
- Elect someone to record the ideas as precisely and explicitly as possible, ideally on a flipchart to maintain a visible and permanent record or on a white board.
- Review the rules of brainstorming (i.e. code of conduct) for example:
  - Each member in rotation is asked for ideas
  - A member can only offer one idea in turn
  - The ideas are stated in as few words as possible
  - Where a member has no ideas they say 'pass'
  - Strive for an explosion of ideas and build on the ideas of other group members
  - Accept all ideas as given and record them; questions are only asked to clarify issues
  - No criticism, discussion, interruptions, comments or judgement
  - Ideas are not evaluated during the brainstorming session
  - Good-natured laughter and informality enhance the environment for innovation
  - Exaggeration adds humour and often provides a creative stimulus.
- Review the problems encountered in brainstorming, in order to prevent or minimize their occurrence. The typical problems include:
  - Attempting to evaluate ideas during brainstorming
  - Criticism of individuals and a lack of cohesion amongst group members
  - A person trying to play the role of an 'expert'
  - A tendency to state 'solutions' rather than possible 'causes'
  - Arguments

- Side discussion and members trying to talk all together
- Members shouting out ideas when it is not their turn
- Poor management of the process (e.g. leader dominates the group)
- Sessions being too long
- Failure to use flipcharts, whiteboards, etc. to visually display the data
- Omission of ideas. The person noting the ideas suppressing those with which they disagree.

- As ideas are suggested these are written down so that they can be seen by all members of the group.
- Allow the ideas to incubate for a period of time before they are evaluated.
- Determine the best ideas by consensus. This can be done in a number of ways – majority voting or polling, Pareto voting, paired comparisons, ranking on a scale of say 1 to 10, or each team member ranking the items in order of priority with 5 points given to the first idea and 3 and 1 points respectively to the second and third ideas, and so on.

There are a number of variations on the classical brainstorming method, for example:

- *Brainwriting*: each person writes down ideas on cards and these cards are placed to the right of the person. After a defined period of time and when stimulation is needed a person takes cards from their left and uses the data on these to both develop the idea and encourage new ideas.
- *Braindrawing*: when stimulation is needed each person does a drawing of an idea and passes it to another person in the group who continues the drawing.

Scatter Diagrams and Regression Analysis

Scatter diagrams or scatter plots are used when examining the possible relationship or association between two variables, characteristics or factors; they indicate the relationship as a pattern – cause and effect. For example, one variable may be a process parameter (e.g. temperature, pressure, screw speed), and the other may be some measurable characteristic or feature of the product (e.g. length, weight, thickness). As the process parameter is changed (independent variable) it is noted, together with any measured change in the product variable (dependent variable), and this is repeated until sufficient data have been collected. The results, when plotted on a graph, will give what is called a scatter graph, scatter plot or scatter diagram. In very simple terms, variables that are associated may show a linear pattern and those that are unrelated may portray an obvious or non-linear random pattern. An example of a linear scatter plot of an effluent analysis for solids/chemical oxygen demand is given in figure 16.14.

Analysis should concern itself with the dispersion of the plots, and if some linear, or known non-linear, relationship exists between the two variables. In this way the scatter diagram is a valuable tool for diagnosis and problem-solving. Regression analysis would subsequently be used not only to establish lines of 'best fit', but to provide the basis for making estimates or predictions of, say, the product variable for a given value of the process parameter. In this way, it is possible to reduce the amount of data which is measured, collected, plotted and analysed.

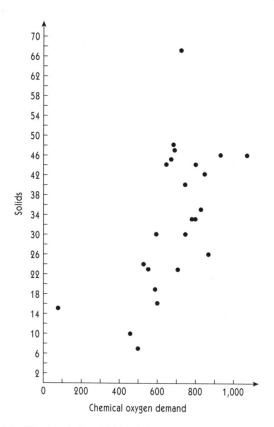

Figure 16.14   Scatter plot: effluent analysis: solids/chemical oxygen demand

How valid or reliable such estimates are is largely a function of the degree of correlation which exists between the two variables (if indeed only two variables are under consideration), and whether the estimates are interpolated (i.e. from within the range of collected data) or extrapolated (i.e. outside that range).

Where there are more than two variables, multivariate regression analysis should be used, but a good background of statistical knowledge is required to undertake this analysis.

The Seven Management Tools

The so-called 'seven new management tools' of quality control were developed by the Japanese to collect and analyse non-qualitative and verbal data, in particular from sales and marketing and design and development activities. Most of the tools have seen previous use in other than TQM applications (for example, value engineering and value analysis, critical path analysis, programme evaluation and review technique (PERT), organizational analysis); the choice of the term 'new' is unfortunate). In Japanese companies these tools are typically used by quality control circles in sales and design areas, and in quality function deployment. It is usual to find some of the tools used together (e.g. a systematic diagram being produced from the data contained in an affinity diagram). A full description of these tools is outside the scope of this chapter; however, they are covered in detail by Mizuno (1988), Ozeki and Asaka (1990) and Barker (1989). The tools are listed briefly below.

Relations diagram method (relationship digraph or linkage diagram)

This is used to identify, understand and clarify complex cause-and-effect relationships to find the causes of and solutions to a problem and to determine the key factors in the situation under study. They are also employed to identify the key issues for some desired result. Relations diagrams are used when the causes are non-hierarchical and when there are multiple interrelated problems; they tend to be used when there is a strong feeling that the problem under discussion is only a symptom. They allow the problem to be analysed from a wide perspective, as a specific framework is not employed, and allow for the use of multi-directional rather than linear thinking. Relations diagrams can be considered to be a more free and broad version of a cause-and-effect diagram. Figure 16.15 is an example in relation to the handling ability of a 'shrinkbag' project.

The major steps in constructing a relations diagram are:

- The central idea problem or issue to be discussed is described clearly and accepted by those concerned.

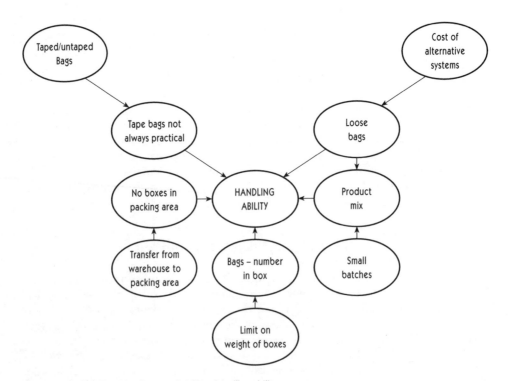

Figure 16.15   Relationship diagram: shrinkbag handling ability

- Issues, causes and related problems which are believed to be affecting the central problem(s) are identified. These are written, in summary form, on cards – one issue, cause, or problem per card.
- The cards are then placed around the central problem/issue in a cause-and-effect relationship. This is done by placing the card believed to have the strongest relationship closest to the central problem/issue, with other cards ranked accordingly.
- The cause-and-effect cards are enclosed within rectangles or ovals, and arrows are used to highlight which causes and effects are related. The relationships are indicated by arrows pointing from cause to effect. The key causes and effects are emphasized by double lines, shading, etc.
- Appropriate revisions are made to the diagram.
- The resulting diagram is analysed for principle causes.

Affinity diagram method (kj – kawakita jiro – method)

This is used to categorize verbal and language data about previously unexplored issues, problems and themes which are hazy, uncertain, large, complex and difficult to understand, thereby helping to create order out of chaos. It is used in conjunction with or as an alternative to brainstorming and is useful when new thoughts and ideas are needed. This diagram uses the natural affinity between opinions and partial data from a variety of situations to help understand and structure the problem. It tends to be a creative rather than a logical process. The diagram helps to organize data, issues, concerns and ideas for decision-making, and to find solutions to previously unresolved problems. Figure 16.16 shows an example for the typical difficulties encountered in new product formulation.

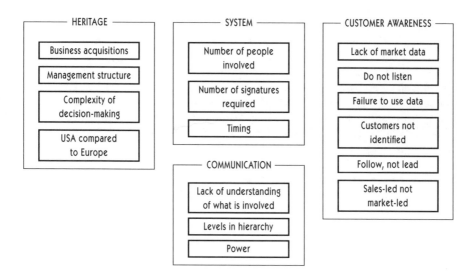

Figure 16.16   Affinity diagram: typical difficulties encountered with new product formulation

The basic steps for developing an affinity diagram are:

- Decide and clarify the theme, issue or opportunity.
- Collect whatever data are currently available on the theme. This could involve interviews with relevant personnel, customers, suppliers, etc. an examination of previously made notes and reports, brainstorming, getting people to express opinions, etc.
- Each idea, note, need, etc. is written on a card or 'Post-It' note.
- The card is placed in a random fashion on the table, board, wall or whatever means is being used to display the data.
- Those cards with related ideas are placed together and separated from the remaining cards. This development of related issues and natural clusters is often done by the team members moving the cards around the board in silence. The idea of this is to allow the more creative right-hand part of the brain to be used. Team discussion can help to develop the individual statements, ideas, etc. on the cards within the cluster. Each group of cards is given a title which reflects the characteristics of its group. The group of stacked cards is then treated as one card. This group card is usually termed the affinity card.
- This process is repeated until all ideas are clustered within different groups.
- The group affinity cards, usually around 5 to 10, are arranged in a logical order and a broad lines drawn around them.

Systematic diagram method (tree diagram)

This is used to examine, in a systematic manner, the most appropriate and effective means of planning to accomplish a task ('how to') or solve a problem; events are represented in the form of a root-and-branch relationship. It displays in increasing detail the means and paths necessary to achieve a specific goal or to clarify the component parts which lead to the root cause of a problem. They are used when the causes that influence the problem are known, but a plan and a method for resolving the problem have not been developed. They can also be useful when a task has been considered to be simple but has run into implementation difficulties. A systematic diagram is usually used to evaluate several different methods and plans for solving a problem and thereby assist with complex implementation. It is used to identify dependencies in a given situation and to search for the most suitable improvement opportunities, and also when there are major consequences for missing key tasks. Figure 16.17 is an example in relation to a project to eliminate waste.

The major steps in constructing a systematic diagram are:

- The problem to be solved or task to be accomplished is written on a card. The card is placed on the left-hand side of the board, table, wall or whatever means is being used to display the data.
- The primary methods and tasks to accomplish the objective or primary causes of the problem are identified. A typical question used in this identification is: 'To achieve the objective, what are the key means?' Each of these methods, tasks, etc. is written on a card and placed directly to the right of the problem statement. In this way the first level of a root-and-branch relationship is created.

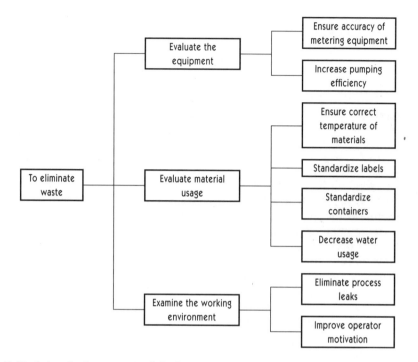

Figure 16.17 Systematic diagram: waste elimination

- Each primary method, task, idea, cause, etc. is treated as the objective and the previous step repeated, with these secondary methods placed to the right of the ones to which they relate, in this way forming the tertiary level. This process is then repeated until all the ideas are exhausted. It is unusual to go beyond four levels in development of the means.
- Working back from the right-hand side of the completed diagram through the levels, the relationship between objectives and means, or problem and causes, is checked to ensure that the means and causes are each related to the objectives and problem respectively – 'Will such and such objective be accomplished if a particular method or task is implemented?'

Matrix diagram method

This is used to clarify the relationship and connecting points between results and causes or between objectives and methods and, by the use of codes, to indicate their relative importance and the direction of the influence. The diagram is also useful to draw conclusions between consequences and their causes. They are used when there are two sets of factors and methods which may have no relationship with each other and when there is a need to get a cumulative numerical score to compare one item to another. The factors are arranged in rows and columns on a chart with the intersections identifying the problem and its concentration; the intersecting points are the base for future action and problem-solving. By seeing, in a graphical manner, the complete problem or picture and its essential characteristics and the actions

Key function	Incorrect completion of forms	Sorting invoicing errors	Levels of authority	Chasing suppliers	Inadequate specification	Chasing information
Procedure						
Systems						
People						
Communication						

Figure 16.18   L-type matrix: eliminating non-value-added work – purchasing department

which may impact on the problem is of considerable help in developing a strategy for its resolution and in prioritizing present activities. Symbols are used to depict the presence and strength of a relationship between sets of data. There are a number of types of matrix diagram (e.g. L-type, T-type, Y-type), each having a specific range of applications. Figure 16.18 shows the structure of an L-type matrix for use by the purchasing department in eliminating non-value-added work.

The major steps in constructing a matrix diagram are:

- Decide the format of the matrix – L-type, T-type, C-type, etc. – and the characteristics, tasks, problems, causes, methods, measures to be mapped and displayed.
- Decide how to arrange the problems and their causes. For example, in an L-shaped matrix for relating customer needs and design features, the customer needs are listed in the rows and the design features relating to each need are listed in the columns.
- Define and specify the symbols which are to be used to summarize a relationship.
- The relationships between, say, the needs and features or problems and causes are identified and discussed and symbols used to indicate the strength of the relationship where a column and row intersect.
- Review the completed diagram for accuracy.

Matrix data-analysis method

This is used to quantify and arrange the data presented in a matrix diagram in a clear manner. It is a numerical analysis method and employs techniques such as multivariate analysis.

Process decision program chart (PDPC) method

This is used to select the best processes to obtain the desired outcome from a problem statement by evaluating all possible events, contingencies and outcomes that can occur in any implementation plan. Considering the system as a whole, it is used to anticipate unexpected events and develop plans, counter-measures and actions for such outcomes. It is used to plan each possible chain of events that might occur when the problem or goal is unfamiliar, new, or unique, particularly when the stakes of potential failure are high. In this it is similar to failure mode and effects analysis and fault tree analysis. However, it is claimed to be more dynamic than these two methods since the relationship between the initiating condition/event and terminating condition/event has been thought out and mapped. It is based on a systematic diagram and uses a questioning technique – for example, 'What could go wrong?', 'What are the alternatives?' – and lists actions or counter-measures accordingly. The PDPC has no prescribed set of rules. Figure 16.19 is an example in relation to a bottleneck engineering problem.

The key steps in constructing a process decision program chart are:

- Describe the problem.
- Identify the issues, anticipated results, likely undesirable outcomes, alternative solutions and approaches.
- Determine the relationships between the issues, solutions and desired goal. These relationships and events are arranged in chronological order and indicated with arrows.
- In the event of a new problem, additional data, etc. that occur, without prior warning, during the course of events the process are reviewed and changes made to reflect the new set of conditions.

Arrow diagram method

This method applies systematic thinking to the planning and execution of a complex set of tasks. It is used to establish the most suitable plan and schedule for a series of activities in a project, and to monitor its progress in an efficient manner to ensure adherence to the schedule. Arrow diagrams are necessary to describe the interrelationship and dependencies of tasks within a job or project which is complex. They are deployed at the implementation planning stage of a project. The sequence of the steps involved and their relation to each other are indicated by an arrow, and in this way a network of activities is developed. This method, its form of construction, calculations and identification of critical path are well known and used in project management in relation to critical path analysis (CPA) and programme evaluation and review technique (PERT). Figure 16.20 is an example of an arrow diagram constructed by quality improvement facilitators for a quality notice board project.

The key steps in constructing an arrow diagram are:

- Identify all the activities needed to complete the plan.
- Decide the feasible sequence of the activities:

  - Which activities must precede certain activities (consecutive activities)
  - Which activities must follow an activity (consecutive activities)
  - Which activities can be done at the same time (concurrent activities).

- Arrange the diagram from left to right according to the above logic with each activity represented by an arrow.
- The beginning or end of an activity or group of activities is called an event or node and these are represented as circles at the tail and head of an arrow. The events should be numbered in the order in which activities occur.

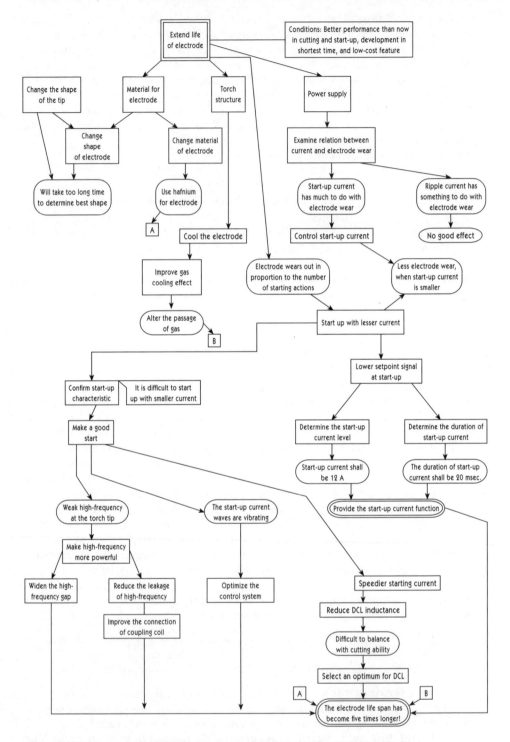

Figure 16.19   An example of a bottleneck engineering problem solved by the PDPC method

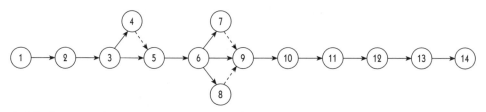

Activities Key

1–2 Choose locations

2–3 Assign responsibilities (deleted: facilitators will action)

3–4 Determine size and configuration of displays needed

3–5 Consider health and safety implications of potential locations

5–6 Establish public relations department's stock of displays and their availability

6–7 Determine method of display (free-standing/wall-mounted)

6–8 Determine preferred 'editorial content' of displays

6–9 Action update of display contents

7–12 Obtain costings for additional/alternative displays

9–10 Source initial display items (e.g. graphs, photos, successes)

10–11 Agree format and action the 'design a logo' competition

11–12 Arrange for displays to be sited/mounted

12–13 Review cost implications

13–14 Seek verbal feedback from site employees

Figure 16.20 Arrow diagram: project quality noticeboards – project management

- The time required for each activity is indicated under the appropriate arrow.
- Analyse the network to find the critical path and to establish in which activities there is free time (float). This is achieved by determining the earliest and latest event times.

Housekeeping

The discipline of cleanliness and housekeeping is a prerequisite for effective quality assurance. It creates a working environment which is comfortable and in harmony with all employees. Organizations need to spend sufficient effort to define and quantify their housekeeping requirements. It is also necessary to ensure that employees local to an area accept that the condition of housekeeping is their responsibility. A variety of aids can be used to promote housekeeping under what is termed the 5s; the strength of this methodology is its simplicity. The 5s are Japanese words (seiri, seiton, seiso, seiketsu and shitsuke), which translate approximately as shown below.

- *Seiri*. Organization: separating what is required from that which is not, eliminating those which are not required and/or tidy them away.
- *Seiton*. Neatness: arranging the required items in a tidy manner and in a clearly defined place, so that be accessed quickly.
- *Seiso*. Cleaning: keeping the surrounding area and environment clean and tidy.

- *Seiketsu*. Standardization: clean the machinery and equipment according to laid down standards and routine in order to identify deterioration.
- *Shitsuke*. Discipline: follow the procedures and previous four steps which have been laid down and continuously improve them.

The 5s evaluation form used by NSK-RHP (Aerospace) is given in table 16.3.

Nissan Motor Manufacturing (UK) refer to this form of housekeeping as the 5 Cs:

- Clean out – determine what is necessary and unnecessary and dispose of the latter.
- Configure – provide a convenient, safe and orderly place for everything and keep it there.
- Clean and check – monitor the condition of the area during cleaning.
- Conformity – develop the habit of routinely maintaining cleanliness.
- Custom and practice – train people in the disciplines of the 5 Cs.

NSK-RHP (Blackburn) use the acronym CANDO – cleanliness, arrangement, neatness, discipline, orderliness.

Departmental Purpose Analysis

Departmental Purpose Analysis (DPA) is a structured quality management tool. Perhaps its main value is in facilitating the internal customer–supplier relationship, determining the effectiveness of departments, and extending quality improvement initiatives to non-manufacturing areas. The concept of DPA originated at IBM in 1984. The key features of DPA are:

- A departmental task analysis is undertaken to determine what needs to be achieved by a department in order to meet company objectives. In this way, a department's objectives are aligned to those of the company and this helps to ensure uniformity of opinion on both departmental and company objectives.
- Identifies in a clear manner the purpose, roles, responsibilities and total contribution of a department to adding value to an organization's activities; non-value-adding work is highlighted.
- Identifies the workload of departmental staff and the current utilization of skills.
- Describes the relationship between a department and its internal customers/suppliers.
- Provides the basis for applying and establishing performance measures by which a department can ensure that it is focusing on satisfying the needs and expectations of its internal customers. From the measurements, improvement objectives and targets can be agreed with all those concerned.
- Identifies interdepartmental problems which can be the subject of a cross-functional team.

Part of a DPA of a sales office is shown in tables 16.4 and 16.5.

Table 16.3 The 5s evaluation form

Item # and description	5S Evaluation Form	Item Score (0–5)	What is the team doing to improve to next level?
1. Removing unnecessary items	All items not required for performing operations are removed from the work area, only tools and products are present at work stations.		
2. Storage of cleaning equipment	All cleaning equipment is stored in a neat manner; handy and readily available when needed.		
3. Floor cleaning	All floors are clean and free of debris, oil and dirt. Cleaning of floors is done routinely – daily at a minimum – posted schedule.		
4. Bulletin boards	All bulletins are arranged in a neat and orderly manner. No outdated, torn or soiled announcements are displayed.		
5. Emergency access	Fire hoses and emergency equipment are unobstructed and stored in a prominent easy-to-locate area. Stop switches and breakers are marked or colour-coded for visibility.		
6. Items on floor	Work-in-process, tools and any other material are not left to sit directly on the floor. Large items such as tote boxes are positioned on the floor in clearly marked areas, identified by painted lines.		
7. Aisleways – markings	Aisles and walkways are clearly marked and can be identified at a glance; lines are straight and at right angles with no chipped or worn paint.		
8. Aisleways – maintenance	Aisles are always free of material and obstructions; nothing is placed on the lines, and objects are always placed at right angles to the aisles.		
9. Storage and arrangement	Storage of boxes, containers and material is always neat and at right angles. When items are stacked, they are never crooked or in danger of toppling over.		
10. Equipment – painting	All machines and equipment are neatly painted; there are no places in the plant less than two metres high that are unpainted.		
	Subtotal pg 1		

Table 16.3 *(cont'd)*

Item # and description	5S Evaluation Form	Item Score (0–5)	What is the team doing to improve to next level?
11. Equipment – cleanliness	All machines and equipment are kept clean by routine daily care.		
12. Equipment – maintenance	Controls of machines are properly labelled and critical points for daily maintenance checks are clearly marked. Equipment checksheets are neatly displayed and clean.		
13. Equipment – storage	Nothing is placed on top of machines, cabinets and equipment; nothing leans against walls or columns. Guards and deflectors are used to keep chips and coolant from falling to the floor.		
14. Documents – storage	Only documents necessary to the operation are stored at the work stations and these are stored in a neat and orderly manner.		
15. Documents – control	All documents are labelled clearly as to content and responsibility for control and revision. Obsolete or unused documents are routinely removed.		
16. Tools and gages arrangement	Tools, gages and fixtures are arranged neatly and stored, kept clean and free of any risk of damage.		
17. Tools and gages convenience	Tools, gages and fixtures are arranged so they can be easily accessed when changeovers or setups are made.		
18. Shelves and benches – arrangement	Arranged, divided and clearly labelled. It is obvious where things are stored; status and condition is recorded.		
19. Workbench and desk – control	Kept free of objects including records and documents. Tools and fixtures are clean and placed in their proper location.		
20. 5S control and maintenance	A disciplined system of control is maintained at the highest possible level. It is the responsibility of everyone to maintain this system and environment.		
	Subtotal pg 2 + Subtotal pg 1 Total	÷ 20 = 5S Score	

Table 16.4 Departmental purpose analysis: sales office main tasks – suppliers

Task	What is the input?	Who provides it?	Is it right?	How can it be modified?
Taking of orders	Phone calls, telexes, fax messages, ansafone, postal orders	Clients, salespersons, unit offices	In the main yes, but some aspects such as packaging sizes, address detail, order numbers, are sometimes given with the assumption we know what is missing.	Personnel placing orders could be more explicit with details. Some detail could be checked at unit offices prior to passing to sales office. Ansafone could be replaced by the Wang electronic mail system.
Processing orders	Computer via VDUs and internal sales office order input form	Sales office	Yes, within our abilities and constant interruptions by phone calls and visitors, which, by causing distractions, can lead to errors.	A CSP is in the system to assist with efficiency. Sales department could specify if the checking of product programme is required as some require it and others do not.
Answering enquiries and liaison with shipping & transport, warehousing & customer stores	Phone calls to engineering technical, purchasing, production, credit control, customer stores, shipping & transport and warehousing	Clients, unit offices & salespersons	Generally yes, but clients sometimes require miracles, are annoyed and sometimes abusive if they do not get them.	Sales office is manned 9 a.m.–5 p.m. Technical back-up and stores are often not available during the working day. Warehouse is unmanned after 4 p.m., which makes transport ineffective as they can only answer in the main based on information from the warehouse.
Daily booked order figures	Edit list	Computer department	Yes	Computer could produce the same data but would have to run in parallel for one year while it built up a year's record.
Outstanding order list – Chemicals	Computer listing 106	Computer department	No	Glassware & reagents should be on engineering list. Due date is required.
Outstanding order list – Engineering	Computer listing 109	Computer department	No	Glassware & reagents should be on this list, not on chemical list.
New account raising	Orders	Clients, salespersons, unit offices	No	Sales office often get passed around in obtaining territory numbers; responsible sales units/offices should know their own prospects.
Process confirmatory orders	Postal orders	Clients, unit offices, salespersons	No	These are confirmatory to verbal instructions. They are not required from unit offices and sales persons.

Table 16.5 Departmental purpose analysis: sales office main tasks – customers

Task	What is the output?	Who receives it?
Processing orders	A Works order set	Warehouse, stores, production control, purchasing & manufacturing plants
Answering enquiries and liaison with shipping & transport, warehousing & customer stores	Fast, accurate response	Clients, unit offices, salespersons, credit control, transport & stores
Daily booked order figures	Accurate booked sales figures	Sales management and Operations Management
Outstanding order list chemicals	That all booked orders are progressed to invoices	Sales office
Outstanding order list engineering	That all booked orders are progressed to invoices	Sales office
New account raising	The facility to process client orders	Sales office
Process confirmatory orders	Processed client orders	Sales office
Ordering and progress of engineering bought out items	Purchase requisitions and progress sheet	Engineering and purchasing departments
Price list maintenance	Special price lists	Sales office and sales management
Forward order diary	Orders raised to client's requirements	Sales office
Water treatment service and supervisory contracts	Memos annotated with account numbers and account special instruction facility displaying contract	Sales office and accounts department

Mistake-Proofing

Mistake-proofing is a technique which is used to prevent errors being converted into defects. The concept was developed by Shingo (1986). The technique is based on the assumption that, no matter how observant or skilled people are, mistakes will occur unless preventative measures are put in place. Shingo argues that using statistical methods is tantamount to accepting defects as inevitable, and that instead of looking for and correcting the causes of defective work, the source of the mistake should be inspected, analysed and rectified. He places great emphasis on what he calls source inspection, which checks for factors which cause mistakes, and then on using poka-yoke or mistake-proofing devices to prevent their reoccurrence.

Mistake-proofing has two main steps: preventing the occurrence of a defect and detecting the defect. In short the purpose is to stop processes from operating when conditions exist that will lead to defects. The system is applied at three points in the process:

1   In the event of an error, prevent the start of a process and shut it down.
2   Prevent a non-conforming product from leaving a process.
3   Prevent a non-conforming part being passed to the next process.

The mistake-proofing technique employs the ingenuity and skills not only of the engineers and/or technical specialists who may develop and fit the devices, but also of the operators who have first identified the cause of the mistake and participated in the corrective action measures. In Japanese companies, quality control circles are very active in developing and using mistake-proofing devices. The devices may be simple mechanical counters which ensure that the correct number of parts are fed into a machine, or they may be cut-off switches, limit switches or float switches which provide some regulatory control of the process or operation, thereby stopping a machine or process automatically. They may be devices which prevent a part being incorrectly fed into the machine, assembled incorrectly, fabricated incorrectly, or placed incorrectly into fixturing. In other words, the assumption is made that, if the part can possibly be fed in wrongly it will be unless some preventative measure is taken. This is the essence of mistake-proofing. Patel et al. (2001), in work based on a study of four precision component manufacturing companies, found that the main types of control method used were jigs, pegs or guidepins, beam sensors, reset and interlock devices and gauges. It is usual to supply the mistake-proofing device and signal with some audible or visual display or mimic diagrams and/or warning light to indicate that something has gone wrong, and not to plan and bring the abnormality to the attention of the operator. They are a relatively cheap and effective way of preventing defects.

Dale and Lightburn (1992), based on their research into mistake-proofing in a European motor industry supplier, offer the following guidelines to organizations approaching the development of mistake-proofing:

- Mistake-proof at the earliest possible opportunity, certainly at the development stage and before any pre-production activities are undertaken.
- Involve manufacturing and quality department personnel in the research and development activity and ensure that there is a forum for the discussion of manufacturing and design problems and their interfaces; cross-functional teams, and concurrent and simultaneous engineering should facilitate this.
- The design and process FMEA, analysis of customer reject returns, warranty claims, field failure reports, in-house scrap and rework, and inspection data should help to pinpoint potential problems that could be resolved by mistake-proofing.
- It is much easier to mistake-proof new products than develop devices for existing products.
- A team approach should be taken to study potential problems and likely causes of mistakes, and the development of mistake-proofing ideas and devices. The team should be multi-disciplinary and involve operators. Customers should also be involved as this helps to build up relationships and provides concrete proof that long-lasting improvement action is being taken. However, some suppliers are sensitive to their problems being exposed to customers.

- There should be some basic training in the principles, techniques, applications, and use of mistake-proofing as well as other activities such as problem-solving and team-building.
- To broaden the experience of mistake-proofing techniques and applications, information should be shared with other companies using the concept.

Total Productive Maintenance

The Japanese have evolved the concept of total productive maintenance (TPM), based on the planned approach to preventative maintenance (PM). Nakajima (1986) outlines how in 1953 20 Japanese companies formed a PM research group and, after a mission to the US in 1962 to study equipment maintenance, the Japan Institute of Plant Engineers (JIPE) was formed in 1969, which was the predecessor of the Japan Institute of Plant Maintenance (JIPM). In 1969 JIPE started working closely with the automotive component manufacturer Nippondenso on the issue of PM, and when the company decided to change the role of operators to allow them to carry out routine maintenance it was the beginning of TPM. Tajiri and Gotan (1992) point out that, while TPM was communicated throughout Japan, only a small number of factories took up the challenge. It was the severe economic situation in the early 1970s that accelerated the adaptation of TPM, propagated by the seven-step programme developed by the Tokai Rubber Industries (see Nakajima 1988).

TPM combines PM with TQM and employee involvement and is considered as a total method of management. Dale (1999), after missions to study Japanese manufacturing organizations, reports that in Japan 'TPM is considered as an additional driver which is complementary to TQM.' The condition of the equipment has a considerable influence on the quality of production output and is a key element in manufacturing a quality product. The machine needs the input of people to keep it lean and to improve its efficiency and operation, thereby promoting a sense of 'plant ownership' by the operators and a feeling of shop-floor goodwill. This is the purpose of TPM.

TPM is a scientific, company-wide approach in which every employee is concerned about the maintenance, quality and efficiency of their equipment. The objective is to reduce the whole-life cost of machinery and equipment through more efficient maintenance management, and as far as possible to integrate the maintenance and manufacturing departments. Teamwork is a key element of TPM. By analysis of each piece of equipment it focuses on reducing manufacturing losses and costs (i.e. the six major losses: breakdown, set up/adjustment, speed, idling and minor stoppages, quality defects and start-up; see Nakajima 1988), and establishes a system of preventative maintenance over a machine's working life. The emphasis of TPM is to improve the skills of operators in relation to machine technology and to train and educate them to clean, maintain and make adjustments to their machine. The training and education of operators is carried out by maintenance and engineering staff. In this way machinery is kept at optimal operating efficiency. The 5Ss are essential activities in TPM, and they also promote visible management.

The main organizational characteristics of TPM are:

- Integration of maintenance and production departments.
- Small teams of operators/maintainers.

- Training is undertaken to make operators feel like owners.
- Good habits are developed:
    - Cleaning becomes checking
    - Cleaning highlights abnormalities
    - Abnormalities are rectified
    - Continuous improvement of environment and equipment.

The seven key steps of a TPM programme are usually considered to be:

Step 1   Initial cleaning, to identify problems with equipment that are not noticed during normal operations.

Step 2   Counter-measures at the source of problems, to minimize accumulation of dirt and other contaminants and put in place improvements to make it easy to access parts of the equipment which need cleaning.

Step 3   Set maintenance, cleaning and lubrication standards for groups of equipment and carry out appropriate training.

Step 4   General inspection procedures and schedules.

Step 5   Autonomous inspection procedures and schedules.

Step 6   Orderliness and tidiness.

Step 7   Full autonomous maintenance.

Summary

Irrespective of the TQM approach chosen and followed, an organization will need to use a selection of tools and techniques to assist with the process of continuous improvement. It is recommended that the more simple tools and techniques, such as the seven quality control tools, are used in the beginning, and that it should be ensured that the tools and techniques which are currently employed are used effectively before attempts are made to introduce other tools.

A planned approach for the application of tools and techniques is necessary. The temptation to single out one tool or technique for special attention should be resisted, and to get maximum benefit from the use of tools and techniques they should be used in combination. It should be recognized that tools and techniques play different roles, and management and staff should be fully aware of the main purpose and use of the tools and techniques they are considering applying in the organization; if this is not the case they could well be disappointed if a tool or technique fails to live up to expectations. It is also important to understand the limitations of how and when tools and techniques can best be used.

The tools and techniques should be used to facilitate improvement and be integrated into the way the business works rather than being used and viewed as 'bolt-on' techniques. The ways in which the tool or technique is applied and how its results are interpreted are critical to its successful use; a tool or technique is only as good as the person who is using it.

Tools and techniques on their own are not enough; they need an environment and technology conducive to improvement and to their use. An organization's CEO and senior managers have a key role to play in the effective use of tools and techniques. They should, for example:

- Develop their knowledge of the tools and, when appropriate, use them in their day-to-day activities and decision-making.
- Be fully aware of the main purpose and use of the particular tools and techniques which are being applied.
- Delegate responsibility for their promotion to suitable individuals.
- Maintain an active interest in the use of tools and the results.
- Endorse expenditure arising from the education and training required and the improvement activities resulting from the employment of tools.
- Recognize and reward those employees who utilize tools and techniques in their day-to-day work activities.

References

Barker, R. L. (1989), The seven new QC tools. In *Proceedings of the First Conference on Tools and Techniques for TQM*, 95–120. Bedford: IFS Conferences.

Crossfield, R. T. and Dale, B. G. (1990), Mapping quality assurance systems: a methodology. *Quality and Reliability Engineering International*, 6(3), 167–78.

Currie, R. M. (1989), *Work Study*. London: Pitman.

Dale, B. G. (1999), *Managing Quality*, 3rd edn. Oxford: Blackwell.

Dale, B. G., Boaden, R. J., Wilcox, M. and McQuater, R. E. (1998), The use of quality management techniques and tools: an examination of some key issues. *International Journal of Technology Management*, 16(4–6), 305–25.

Dale, B. G. and Lightburn, K. (1992), Continuous quality improvement: why some organisations lack commitment. *International Journal of Production Economics*, 27(1), 57–67.

Dale, B. G. and McQuater, R. E. (1998), *Managing Business Improvement and Quality: Implementing Key Tools and Techniques*. Oxford: Blackwell.

Dale, B. G. and Shaw, P. (1990), Failure mode and effects analysis in the motor industry: a state-of-the-art study. *Quality and Reliability Engineering International*, 6(3), 179–88.

Fukuda, R. (1990), *CEDAC: A Tool for Continuous Systematic Improvement*. Cambridge, Mass.: Productivity Press.

Ishikawa, K. (1976), *Guide to Quality Control*. Tokyo: Asian Productivity Organisation.

Juran, J. M. (1988), *Quality Control Handbook*. New York: McGraw Hill.

Lewis, L. (1984), *Quality Improvement Handbook*. Hampshire: IBM.

Mizuno, S. (1988), *Management for Quality Improvement: The Seven New QC Tools*. Cambridge, Mass.: Productivity Press.

Nakajima, S. (1986), A challenge to the improvement of productivity by small group activities. *Maintenance Management International*, 6(1), 73–83.

Nakajima, S. (1988), *Introduction to Total Productive Maintenance*. Cambridge, Mass.: Productivity Press.

Ozeki, K. and Asaka, T. (1990), *Handbook of Quality Tools*. Cambridge, Mass.: Productivity Press.

Patel, S., Dale, B. G. and Shaw, P. (2001), Set-up time reduction and mistake-proofing methods: an examination in precision component manufacturing. *The TQM Magazine*, 13(3), 175–9.

Shingo, S. (1986), *Zero Quality Control: Source Inspection and the Poka Yoke System*. Cambridge, Mass.: Productivity Press.

Tajiri, M. and Gotan, F. (1992), *IPM Implementation: A Japanese Approach*. New York: McGraw Hill.

chapter | **seventeen**

Quality Function Deployment

I. Ferguson and B. G. Dale

Introduction

The Quality Function Deployment (QFD) methodology was developed in Japan at Kobe Shipyard, Mitsubishi Heavy Industries, as a way to incorporate knowledge about the needs and desires of customers into all stages of the design, manufacture, delivery and support of products and services. It is an integrated methodology where all relationships and priorities can be understood and reconciled to the benefit of the customer and producer company. It arose out of a need to achieve simultaneously a competitive advantage in quality, cost and delivery (QCD). These, along with people and environmental factors, are the key performance measures of superior-performing Japanese companies and such organizations use QFD as a matter of course in design and new product development. To take the conception of the product or service into reality requires choices of many aspects of product or service design, which means 'trading off' the high performance of one aspect of the design against another so that the product will be successful for the business and also in the market. This requires good, reliable, benchmarked information available from areas such as:

- Customer needs
- Functionality
- Costs and capital
- Reliability
- Reproducibility
- Manufacturing needs to satisfy postulated quantities per time period

These are critical demands of any design, and how well each separate demand is integrated within the whole determines the success of the product in meeting its horizons.

QFD is a technique which is used in the first place for translating the needs of customers and consumers into design requirements, being based on the philosophy that the 'voice of the customer' drives all company operations. In turn these are translated into component parts and processes which are necessary for producing the end-product. Consequently the final product is one that has been driven by the voice of the customer. In carrying out activities it uses a number of information collection, dissemination and decision-making techniques.

QFD is well suited to manage the integration of the techniques in the design process with its related matrices and focus on business and customer needs. Within the business plan, the function of QFD is to translate the needs of the customer and consumer into product and process design, and through the related matrices of capital, cost and reliability ensure that the 'best choice' of parameters such as functionality, reliability, reproducibility, etc. are met. It employs a step-by-step approach from customer needs and expectations through the four planning phases of:

- Product planning
- Product development
- Process planning
- Production planning through to manufactured products and delivered services

The technique of QFD seeks to identify those features of a product or service which satisfy the real needs and requirements of customers (market- or customer-required quality). A critical part of the analysis is that it takes into account discussions with the people who actually use the product in order to obtain data on issues such as:

- What do they feel about existing products?
- What bothers them?
- What features should new products have?
- What is required to satisfy their needs, expectations, thinking and ideas?
- How and where is the product used?

QFD is a systematic procedure which is used to help build quality into the upstream processes and also into new product development. When used in this way it helps to avoid problems in the downstream production and delivery processes and will consequently shorten the new product/service development time. The concept helps to promote proactive rather than reactive development.

Figure 17.1 shows the close relationship that QFD, functional analysis, FMEA, FTA and design of experiments (DOE) have with each other. Each technique provides information to the design process to make the required outputs a reality.

Some of the major decisions which have to be made before QFD can be used include:

- Deciding which functions and personnel should be represented on the team and who is to be the team leader. This applies, in particular, at the product planning stage.
- Overcoming the usual issues of team members saying they are too busy to attend team meetings, so that the team fails to meet on a regular basis. The need for good teamwork practices should also be recognized as a critical element in the success of the QFD exercise.
- Ensuring that the supporting tools and techniques of quality management are in place before QFD is used.

This chapter now goes on to outline some of the fundamentals of QFD.

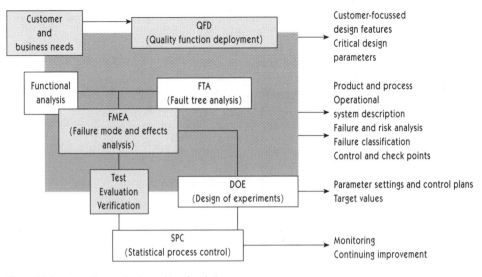

Figure 17.1 Integration and relationship of techniques
Source: Ian Ferguson Associates

Understanding Customer Needs

The voice of the customer is the cornerstone of QFD. Therefore an important issue in carrying out a QFD exercise is to determine who actually is the customer and what is the market sector. The external customer can include companies in the supply chain, distributor, wholesaler, retailer and the consumer. However, as outlined in chapter 1, it should not be forgotten that there are also customers inside the organization (e.g. the related sub-assembly and manufacturing processes, and those affected in the supply chain). It is important to identify the customer chain or hierarchy, as each level will have its own particular needs and bias. This hierarchy needs to be understood and where necessary allowed for in interpretation with respect to design. A list of needs from each level of the hierarchy will usually show some area of conflict and a decision on a trade-off, if any, will need to be made. The customer and consumer groups who are to be involved in the QFD exercise should be targeted, with factors such as type of users, age-groups, areas and social factors being considered. A plan should be formulated for gathering the data in terms of the categories of customers to be contacted, resources needed for gathering the data and the methods to be used. There is a variety of methods for understanding customer needs, and preference should be given to the use of diverse, meaningful data (i.e. 'investigative listening'). To talk and listen to the customer is paramount to understanding their real needs and requirements; of the three methods of achieving this outlined below the preferred method is therefore direct contact with the customer.

1   Direct contact with the customer:

- Customer questionnaires
- Face-to-face discussions with customers
- Consumer contact

2   Failure-related information shows where customer needs are not being met and includes:

- Field-failure data
- Warranty returns
- Customer complaints
- Consumer association reports.

3   Survey:

- Market surveys
- Dealer information
- Trade shows
- Test marketing
- Product reports, as typically reported in trade magazines
- Product to market share trend information
- Competitive data.

In using these methods for understanding customer requirements typical issues that need to be considered include:

- What is wrong with the product and/or service.
- Performance features that delight the customer.
- The 'if only . . .' factor and, in particular, when, how, and by whom it is used.

It is usual to express customers' needs in their original words and then to translate them into the technical language of the organization. Working with the original statements of consumers and customers can be difficult, but offers more insight into their needs and requirements. The reason for this is that they have not been forced to make the choice between predetermined options inherent in a structured, questionnaire-type approach. These original statements will typically relate to a mixture of desires, problems, potential solutions to problems, dissatisfactions, and negative statements, as well as important items that are not stated. However, some interpretation of the customer's words will at times be necessary. The sorting of these often confusing statements so that the wishes of the customer are understood is crucial to the realization of a design which meets their needs and requirements. Affinity and tree diagrams, as outlined in chapter 16, are extremely useful in facilitating this task.

As outlined above, by assembling customer needs in a systematic manner, three levels of customer expectation may be identified:

- The basic functional expectation
- The expectation of performance
- The unexpected items

However, it must be said that, in endeavouring to meet the objective of delighting the customer, conflicting issues often arise and some trade-offs need to be made in a logical manner.

Organizations which use QFD in an effective manner do so to identify product and service features (including additional features) which customers will find attractive and to help 'charm and delight them'. They use the customer voice to distinguish important from not so important features and to separate generic from special features. In this way a differentiation of quality characteristics, features and/or technical advantages can be established between the organization and its competition. The requirements, features and specifications which are identified can then be translated into design requirements as part of the product planning phase and subsequently deployed through the other three phases to ensure that what is delivered to the customer truly reflects their wants or needs. In this way QFD provides the mechanism to target selected areas where improvement would enhance competitive advantage.

The QFD Road: The Main Steps

Stage 1: Product planning

The main objectives of the product planning phase are to:

- Identify customer requirements.
- Determine competitive opportunities.
- Determine substitute quality characteristics.
- Pinpoint requirements for further study.

This enables a complete picture, with a customer focus, to be made of product and/or service.

An example of the 'house of quality' derived from the product planning phase of QFD is shown in figure 17.2.

In simple terms, the key elements of the product planning stage comprise.

The project

The project to be studied in product development should be identified and defined by senior management and the decision made to use QFD. The scope of the project should be clearly outlined, including targets, operating constraints and time-scale. Following on from this a clearly defined mission statement should be produced and a team formed. At this stage of the project it is useful to create a business model which includes market definition and size, product life history, competitive products and prices, projected sales, prices and costs, and the estimated capital requirements and likely payback.

Customer needs

Gathering the voices of customers can be done in the ways described above, by formal questionnaires, focus clinics, direct questioning, listening in a prepared environment, and so on. The information gathered in this way can be entered into a chart similar to that shown in figure 17.3, complete with full information on why the product is needed, for what purposes, who uses it and when, and where and how it is used. This information provides the basis for more easily translating the customer's voice into customer needs which can be satisfied by design features. For example, 'In the UK, mainly men will use the mobile phone while on the move' will translate the needs of that group of customers into a requirement for one-handed operation of the phone, including the ability to dial and hold from the same hand. The phone will then conveniently have design features of the width and depth of the mobile phone, button areas and depression forces, etc. (see figure 17.2).

Relationships Needs v Features

- Strong ● 9
- Medium ○ 3
- Weak △ 1

Relationships Features v Features

- Positive ●
- Negative ✕

Needs v Features	1. ON/OFF RESPONSE TIME	2. ON/OFF DEPRESSION FORCE	3. ON/OFF BUTTON AREA	4. BATTERY CONTACT AREA/FORCE	5. WIDTH × HEIGHT × LENGTH	6. CALL BUTTON COLUMN DISTANCE	7. CALL BUTTON AREA	8. CALL B. DEPRESSION/RELEASE FORCE	9. START/OFF BUTTON FORCE	10. AERIAL LOCK FORCE	11. No. POINT SIZE/CONTRAST COLOR	12. SCREEN POINT SIZE/CONTRAST	13. CHARGER CONNECT FORCE	14. VOLTS/SEC	15. BATTERY LIFE – HOURS	16. BATTERY CHANGING FORCE	Customer rating	Customer rating – Us	Cust. rating – Company 1	Cust. rating – Company 2	Planned level	Improvement ratio	Ranking factor	Importance weight	Relative weight
1. OPERATION																									
2. QUICK TO TURN ON	●	○	●	○													3.0	2	3	3	3	1.5	1.0	4.5	7.6
3. ALWAYS TURNS ON		○	○	●													4.0	3	4	4	4	1.3	1.0	5.2	9.1
4. HOLD IN ONE HAND		○	○		●												5.0	5	4	3	5	1.0	1.1	5.5	9.3
5. OPERATE BY THUMB		●	●		●	●	●	●									3.0	4	2	2	3	1.0	1.1	3.3	5.6
6. OPERATE BY FINGER		○	○		△		○	●									5.0	5	5	4	5	1.0	1.0	5.0	8.5
7. AERIAL LOCKS EASILY					△					●							3.0	2	3	3	3	1.5	1.0	4.5	7.6
8. OPERATE CALL DIRECT																									
9. EASY TO READ No's											●	●					5.0	5	5	5	5	1.0	1.0	5.0	8.5
10. CUT OFF AT CALL FINISH								●									5.0	4	5	4	5	1.3	1.0	6.5	10.6
11. CHECK DIAL START						○	○	●		○							4.0	4	4	4	4	1.0	1.0	4.0	6.8
12. BATTERY																									
13. EASY CHARGER CONNECT													●	●			5.0	5	5	5	5	1.0	1.0	5.0	8.5
14. QUICK TO RECHARGE														●	△	△	5.0	5	4	4	5	1.0	1.1	5.5	9.3
15. EASY BATTERY CHANGE																●	4.0	4	4	5	5	1.0	1.0	5.0	8.5

	1	2	3	4	5	6	7	8	9	10	11	12	13	14	15	16
Importance Weight	69	154	200	104	151	50	96	147	157	69	97	76	76	160	9	86
Relative Weight	4	9	12	6	9	3	6	9	9	4	6	4	4	9	1	5
TARGET VALUES	'x' mils/sec	0,04 N	5 mm Dia		50mm × 5mm × 40mm	10,25 : 32mm	5 × 14mm rnded	0,03 N		0,1 N	12pt Bold	14 pt 1,5:1	0,3 N	'x' milvolts/sec	'y' hours	0,5 N
Ideal value (T,–,+)	T	–	T	T	T	T	T	T	T	T	+	+	T	T	+	T
Technical comparison																
Our Company	W	S	S	S	S	S	S	S	S	W	S	S	S	S	S	S
Company 1	S	S	S	S	W	S	W	S	S	S	S	S	S	S	S	S
Company 2	S	S	S	S	W	S	W	S	S	S	S	S	S	S	S	S
Service info																
Special requirements																
Safety																
Govt/Ind standards																
Environmental																

Project No : 1234
Desc : MOBILE PHONE
Status : Draft

Issue : 1
Date : MAY 1995

Dist : ....
Orig : I A Ferguson

Figure 17.2 The house of quality
Source: Ian Ferguson Associates

Customer classification EXTERNAL/INTERNAL	Voice of customer Actual information	Why needed	What	Who	When	Where	How
SOCIO ECONOMIC GROUP	SPOKEN or WRITTEN WORDS	The answer to: WHY do you want, need this product?	The answer to: WHAT is or will it be used for?	The answer to: WHO uses or will use it?	The answer to: WHEN do or will customers use it?	The answer to: WHERE do or will customers use it?	The answer to: HOW is or will the product be used?
AGE SEX							
1							
2							
3							
4							
5							

Figure 17.3 Gathering the voice of the customer and interpreting it into customer needs
Source: Ian Ferguson Associates

Customer reference	Statement			Basic	Performance	Esteem	Safety	Reliability
	Level 1	Level 2	Level 3					
1								
2								
3								
4								
5								

Figure 17.4 Developing customer needs from analysis of customer statements
Source: Ian Ferguson Associates

Table 17.1 Customer need, design feature and target value matrix

	Customer needs	Design features	Target value
1	Quick to turn on	On/Off response time On/Off button area	'*x*' mil.secs 5 mm dia
2	Always turns on	On/Off depress force Battery contact force	'*y*' N '*z*' N
3	Hold in one hand	Width × length × height	50 × 5 × 40 mm
4	Operate by thumb	Call button area	14 mm dia

Source: Ian Ferguson Associates

Once the customer statements have been produced and further rationale provided in terms of the why, what, who, etc. using the format shown in figure 17.3 we have additional insights into customer needs and market niche requirements. In relation to the case of the mobile phone these statements and their back-up information now need to be reduced to a single and individual customer need from which a design feature can be developed with a target value assigned to it in order to satisfy the need. Thus, for example, 'using the mobile phone while on the move' has a special connotation with mobile phone size and depression forces, as shown in figure 17.2.

Tree diagrams and fishbone diagrams (see chapter 16) are useful tools for developing these customer needs to their most detailed level. For further analysis and cross-referencing purposes it is convenient to summarize the various needs into the most basic categories as shown in figure 17.4. Not only does this give assurance that the basic functional needs of the customer are understood, but also that the key performance, safety, reliability, and cosmetic-related needs are taken into consideration.

In some cases it is necessary to understand the relationship between the various groups of customers and where, when, and how frequently each group is involved with the particular need attributed to the product. Such analysis can easily be made on the basis of the information contained in figures 17.3 and 17.4.

The customer needs ('whats'), taken from the customer logic tree, and the means of satisfying them, or design features ('hows') are then entered in the house of quality (figure 17.2) from a table (see table 17.1) designed to ensure that each need has a design feature that can have a target value assigned to it.

The customer needs are those that are considered to be a priority of the customer; on a scale of 1 to 5, those that are rated from 3 to 5 would be considered important. The appropriateness to the particular house of quality will be taken into account, as will those unexpected or unusual needs, whatever their priority. In determining customer needs it is also important to establish a product and customer hierarchy, as each level will have its own particular needs and bias. A list of needs from each level will usually show some areas of conflict and a decision on a trade-off, if any, will need to be made.

Customer priorities and competitive comparisons and planned improvements

This is the key to prioritization and decision-making on critical design features, which will be a common thread throughout all the stages of the QFD process. The columns in figure 17.2 are used in the following way:

1	*Degree of importance.* Information gathered during customer surveys together with team knowledge is the key for grading each 'need' on a scale of 1 to 5 with 5 being the most important.
2	*Our company rating.* Listed here is an objective view of the company's standing against each customer need from the perception of the customer on a scale of 5 to 1 with 5 being very good and 1 being poor. As much information as can be obtained from impartial sources should be used in this analysis.
3 and 4	*Competitors' rating.* Similar sources as used in 2 will obtain this information for the major competitors. Benchmarking should be used to supplement the information acquired in this way.
5	*Planned level.* This is the company's strategy for the new or modified product, influenced by competitive issues and strategic policy objectives.
6	*Improvement ratio.* This is obtained by dividing the planned level by the company rating.
7	*Sales point.* A maximum of 1.5 is given for a strong marketing feature down to 1.0 for the expected features. Only two or three such points should feature in this analysis. It is in this analysis that 'excitement' qualities are taken into consideration.
8	*Importance weight.* The result of multiplying the degree of importance by the improvement ratio and by the sales point.
9	*Relative weight.* This figure is obtained by taking each importance weight as a percentage of all the weights.

Design features or requirements

This is a very challenging step for engineers. The key is to look for characteristics, features and technical requirements that express the customers' needs and are recognisable as quality features of the product, rather than finite design specifications. This assists in examining the best option for a number of criteria.

The central relationship matrix: the whats v. the hows

The centre block of the house of quality shown in figure 17.2 represents the relationship strength of each customer need with every design feature. The solid circle symbol represents a strong relationship, the open circle a medium relationship, and the triangle a weak relationship. These relationships are usually equated to numbers 9, 3, and 1 respectively. The difference between them represents a means of emphasizing a design feature that is very important over one that is less so.

If there is no relationship between a customer need and a design feature, this will be highlighted by an empty row, indicating that the need will not be satisfied. On the other hand, if there is no relationship between a design feature and a customer need, it will result in an empty column, indicating that the design feature is not necessarily required from a customer perspective.

Relative weights of importance

This calculation indicates the strength of each design feature required in relation to other design features, and the priority from the customer's perspective of the need that created the design feature. To achieve these two parts the weight of importance of each design feature is the multiplication of the relative weight of the customer need and the particular relationship that has been designated in the central matrix. For example, from figure 17.2, 'aerial locks easily' is 7.6 in customer relative weight, satisfied by the one design feature of aerial lock force. The relationship between them (9) is strong. Thus $7.6 \times 9 = 69$.

Design feature interactions: the hows v. the hows

Each design feature needs reconciling with other design features. This is recorded in the roof of the house of quality. Its purpose is to relate the interactions to the proposed target values of design features. A positive relationship is an opportunity to reduce a value that may help to reconcile an interacting negative relationship. Negative relationships require determined design alternatives to weaken the relationship as they are potential sources of conflict and quality assurance problems.

Target values

Each design feature should have a target value assigned to it in order to act as a benchmark in the choice of design concepts at a later stage in the process. The target value will normally be best in class and one that will satisfy the customer to the point of delight. The values are not design specifications and could well be enhanced as the QFD process proceeds. They will certainly be equal to or better than any competitively benchmarked design. These target values may be modified in the light of the information contained in the roof of the house. The reconciliation between relationships is helped by declaring the feature that is a constraint and adjusting the other value according to its ideal value.

Technical comparisons

Technical comparisons are made with the design features, both from the company's existing product range and also those competitive ranges which are under investigation.

The comparisons may be made on some form of quantitative scale or on a 'same', 'better', and 'not so good' basis. Reference will be made to competitive designs where the feature has a higher assessment, and if this cannot be bettered it should be adopted. The customer's evaluation of the company's product and that of its competitors should also be considered. In theory, the engineer's technical evaluation and the customer's evaluation should agree. If this is not the case then the target value chosen is not perceived as the best one.

Service information and special requirements

Service information affecting design features from warranty, complaints, field failures, defect records, internal quality costs, product performance, etc. is recorded. The purpose of this is to ensure that concepts and design work later in the process will eliminate these faults. Safety items, special regulatory items, and environmental issues affecting any design feature are also recorded. The purpose of this is that any concept or product definition must be seen to satisfy these requirements.

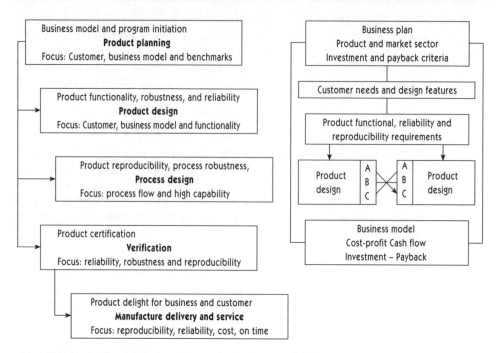

Figure 17.5   Customer needs deployed into product and process definition
Source: Ian Ferguson Associates

Deploying Customer Needs into Product and Process Definition

Figure 17.5 highlights some of the aspects which need to be taken into account, in particular, the main linkages.

Stage 2: Product design, concurrent to a degree with Stages 3 and 4

The product planning carried out in Stage 1 enables a variety of critical design features to be derived which reflect the needs of the customer. This second stage involves translating the Stage 1 design features into component part design features or characteristics.

One aspect of the power of QFD is to enable the customer-derived design features to be reconciled with the product functional requirements. In addition to this, QFD demands that all the relationships between functional requirements and part features are understood, for a part feature that is required to carry out many functions will be more of a risk in the accomplishment of its task than a part feature with only one function to perform.

The output of this stage is a set of target values for part features. These values, together with other sets from the customer-derived design features, reliability engineering, and process design characteristics from Stages 3 and 4, form a standard by which any concept of product design, existing or new, may be judged to determine whether or not it meets all the required criteria.

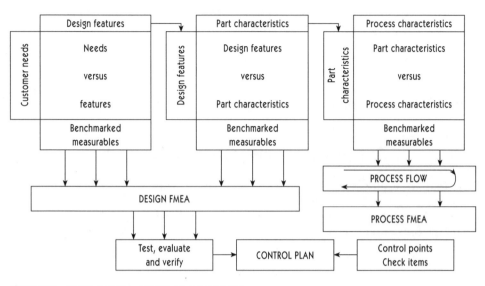

Figure 17.6 Quality function deployment and reliability
Source: Ian Ferguson Associates

The final task of Stage 2 is to prioritize the part characteristics of the chosen concept from a customer's point of view. This should ensure that process designers are in no doubt as to those features which must be reproduced to a high capability in the manufacturing process. A product design is not a design if it cannot be manufactured. Accordingly product concepts leading to designs are, at this stage, subjected to processability, risk and cost analysis. Product design decisions are best taken concurrently with process design decisions; see BS7000 (1989) for further details.

By deriving critical design characteristics of both product and process design the QFD process is ideally suited to provide critical functions that should be treated as part of the FMEA process of risk analysis (see figure 17.6).

Stage 3: Process design, concurrent to a degree with Stages 2 and 4

This third stage ensures that the part characteristics identified as a priority are related to process characteristics, whose target values will ensure their reliability and reproducibility. The process design, which may be an existing process, an existing process with additions and modifications, or a completely new process, will be the subject of intense cost and risk analysis.

The output of this stage will be a prioritized list of process characteristics which the production operating system of Stage 4 will be capable of reproducing with a high degree of capability.

Stage 4: Manufacturing operating systems

The purpose of this stage is to ensure that operational production planning uses those systems which are complete, reliable and will give the high capability requirements that have been identified in Stage 3. This involves areas such as operational specifications and control plans, training, preventative maintenance, gauging methods, audit inspections, SPC, etc.

This section has provided only an overview of the mechanics of QFD. The following are suggested reading for those wishing to develop their knowledge of QFD: Akao (1990), Bossert (1991), Eureka and Ryan (1988) and the transactions of the QFD Symposium from 1990 to 2002.

The Benefits of the Four-Stage Approach

The four-stage integrated approach outlined above, with the customer needs and priority ratings reflected at each stage by the use of integrated importance weights, ensures that what is being moulded, machined, coated, filled, assembled, etched, etc. at the manufacturing stage will more than meet the customer's needs and requirements when they receive the product. This is a sound basis for advanced quality planning.

The analysis is progressive and can be stopped at any of the four stages. However, the experience of the Japanese companies is that the greatest benefit is derived when all stages are completed and the process is carried out in an integrated manner. Each stage obviously has a use and a value of its own, but one stage by itself is limited in its impact with the customer. Thus the Stage 1 house of quality is extremely useful in understanding customer needs and properly identifying their key priorities. The needs are then developed into design features, providing an excellent opportunity to assess target values chosen in comparison with customer's perceptions and competitive products. However, if the product and process design work thereafter is not integrated, all the knowledge and understanding which has been generated can still lead to the development of a product with reliability or cost problems.

A multi-disciplinary team is used to prepare the QFD. The membership of the team is likely to change depending on the stage of QFD being addressed. A number of the seven new quality control tools (relationship diagram, affinity diagram, matrix diagram and systematic diagram; see chapter 16) are also used to assist with the QFD process.

QFD and the Service Sector

QFD is increasingly being used in the service sector because of its ability to integrate needs, features that satisfy needs, relationships, priorities and most significantly the integrated deployment of needs and features throughout the organization. A typical format of this deployment is shown in figure 17.7.

Difficulties Associated with QFD

The following is a summary of the main difficulties which are typically experienced with QFD:

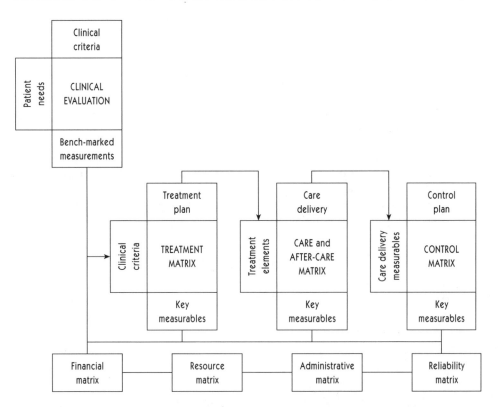

Figure 17.7 Example of a service QFD deploying clinical evaluations into the hospital organization
Source: Ian Ferguson Associates

- Determining who is the customer and identifying their needs; in particular, when the market is new, the customer is not certain of what they want, and knowledge of the market is sketchy. Also related to this is reconciling the various customer needs at various levels in the supply chain.
- A belief that QFD cannot begin until customer needs have been totally defined, leading to a loss of momentum.
- Customer information gathered by marketing department alone, causing engineers difficulty in interpreting customer needs.
- Deciding which chart format best suits the project under consideration.
- Matrices are developed which are too large.
- Failure to extend QFD past the product planning stage thereby missing the integration of best performance with reliability and cost.
- Mixing of 'whats' with 'hows' and 'hows' with 'whats'.
- Skipping some of the steps and failing to pay attention to detail.
- Not addressing fully the issues arising from analysis of the various matrices.
- No internal feedback of the findings.
- Too wide a scope of project causing difficulty of focus.
- A desire by engineers to arrive at a design specification too soon, thereby closing out other potential worthwhile options.
- Non-attendance at meetings and shifting priorities.

The following are the types of issues which can help to overcome the difficulties:

- Team-based training on the project being followed up with regular facilitation by an outside expert.
- A logical system of collecting customer information.
- Adequate analysis undertaken over the complete range of customer needs.
- Use of the expertise of team members to overcome any inertia in identifying customer needs and requirements.
- Make full use of relevant data on warranty claims, field failures, previous products and competitive data in order to develop target specifications.
- Ensure that the QFD charts and matrices are incorporated into the organization's systems and used on an ongoing basis.
- Refine the analysis by sharing the data, and any subsequent discussions which may take place, with customers.

Implementation of QFD

The following are key steps in the effective implementation of QFD:

- *Management issues*
  - The process must be driven by senior management.
  - Appropriate resources and the provision of training need to be allocated and actioned by management.
  - Appoint a steering committee and a QFD champion.
  - Use of a project management system to act as a communication vehicle.

- *Project issues*
  - Select the first project with a limited time-frame and a good chance of an early success.
  - Establish a time-frame for the project at the outset and keep to it.
  - Have a clear project definition and objectives and always have them in view; it is also important to identify any project limitations and operating constraints. This helps to create a focus on what is being done.
  - Develop a clear market definition and business model.
  - Provide a glossary of terms used in the QFD process.

- *The QFD team*
  - Train as a team using as many as company-specific examples as possible.
  - Establish a core team, which is multi-disciplinary, of between five and seven people.
  - Hold short, regular team meetings.
  - Do detailed work outside the meeting and use the meeting for analysis, and decision-making. It is important that each member of the team is prepared to make a significant time commitment to the project.
  - One of the cornerstones of QFD is the customer's voice – it is best for all the team to be part of the data-collection process which is involved in listening to that voice.

- It takes longer, but consensus decisions generally work best.
- Team energy can be created by paying attention to: direction, structure, project management, human issues.

● *Methods of working*

- Do as much concurrent work as possible (e.g. competitive benchmarking with existing product and process designs).
- Create a planning matrix of customer needs to decide what should go into a house of quality; some items will be better achieved by traditional means.
- Keep a realistic perspective on the detail entered about customer needs. Focus on the important, the difficult, and the new.
- Try and ensure that the house of quality is kept to within an approximately 30 × 30 matrix.
- Use the customer's voice and benchmarks as major decision-makers to achieve best in class.

Summary

The QFD process provides a powerful structure for product and process development. When it is used in an effective manner it can bring a correct customer focus to designs that will perform to a high degree of satisfaction with reliability and cost-worthiness. It shortens the development cycle for the design and results in fewer engineering changes. In this way the product/service which the customer receives not only meets their needs but, if the customer interface has been done correctly, there can be unexpected product features which will cause delight and product loyalty. There will also be a common thread through all operations which is traceable back to what the customer really wants.

The discipline of the various matrices used in QFD is to ensure that, apart from satisfying the customer, designs give optimum performance and reliability and maximize the value-to-customer ratio. The application of clear objectives, logical thinking and analysis by the team using the QFD methodology as a framework will help to achieve these goals. A by-product of this type of activity is that it promotes teamwork across functions and levels of the organizational hierarchy.

Understanding customer needs and the acceptable value-to-cost ratio is an effective means of developing a product which will gain market share. The logical integrated planning disciplines involved with the QFD framework replace the 'quick-fix' approach to design and new product development. With perseverance and attention to detail QFD will help to bring products to market on time, and which are best in class, and ensure product acceptability for both market and producer.

The use of QFD is not a magic wand. It is a methodology and by itself it won't solve bad designs, eliminate waste, solve resource problems, or prevent engineering changes being made. It requires a realistic programme and an understanding that it needs considerable attention to detail. Moreover, management commitment, an adequate understanding of the technique, cross-functional teamwork, good training, and an effective champion are vital ingredients for success.

References

Akao, Y. (ed.) (1990), *Quality Function Deployment: Integrating Customer Requirements into Product Design*. Cambridge, Mass.: Productivity Press.

Bossert, J. L. (1991), *Quality Function Deployment: A Practitioner's Guide*. New York: Marcel Dekker.

BS7000 (1989), *Design Management Systems: Part 1: Guide to Managing Product Design*. London: British Standards Institution.

Eureka, W. E. and Ryan, N. E. (1988), *The Customer-Driven Company: Managerial Perspectives on QFD*. Michigan: ASI Press.

Ferguson, I. (1992), Delighting the customer. *Manufacturing Breakthrough*, September–October, 277–84.

Ferguson, I. (1995), *Quality Function Deployment: Developing a Color TV*. Michigan: QFD Institute Transactions.

chapter eighteen

Design of Experiments

I. Ferguson and B. G. Dale

Introduction

The design of experiments is a series of techniques which involve the identification and control of parameters which have a potential impact on the performance and reliability of a product design and/or the output of a process, with the objective of optimizing product design, process design and process operation, and limiting the influence of noise factors. The methodology is used when we need to analyse the significance of effects on system outputs of different values of design parameters. The objective is to optimize the values of these design parameters to make the performance of the system immune to variation. The concept can be applied to the design of new products and processes or to the redesign of existing ones, in order to:

- Optimize product design, process design and process operation.
- Achieve minimum variation of best system performance.
- Achieve reproducibility of best system performance in manufacture and use.
- Improve the productivity of design engineering activity.
- Evaluate the statistical significance of the effect of any controlling factor on the outputs.
- Reduce costs.

Design of experiment techniques, in particular for process improvement, involve the identification and control of those parameters or variables (termed factors) which have a potential influence on the output of a process, choosing two or more values (termed levels) of these variables and running the process at these levels. Each combination of factors and levels, or experimental run, is known as a trial. The basic idea is to conduct a small number of experiments with different parameter values and analyse their effect on a defined output such as plating thickness. On the basis of the analysis a prediction of system performance can be made.

This chapter explores some of the fundamentals and mechanics of design of experiments. Those seeking more knowledge of the topic should consult the following specialist texts: Barker (1990), Bendall et al. (1990), Lochnar and Matar (1990) and Taguchi (1986) and the design of experiment course notes of Ferguson (1995).

Methods of Experimentation

Most people in business, to a greater or lesser extent, experiment in some way. For example, adjusting a variable to produce a desirable result, taking an action to discover a reaction, and testing a hypothesis. There are a number of methods of experimentation – the trial-and-error method, the step-by-step method of changing one factor at a time, the full factorial (i.e. the classical method) and the fractional factorial. One of the objectives of industrial experimental design is to be confident that a difference in output attributable to a change in the level of a factor is significant in relation to any experimental error and other factors that were part of the experimental design.

The trial-and-error method

The trial-and-error method usually means unsystematic changes of factor levels using the experience of the experimenter(s) as the guiding principle. In the one factor at a time method, the first experiment is run with all the factors at the first chosen level and the results of the run are recorded. The second experiment is run by changing the first factor to its second option and again recording the results of the run. Then, keeping this factor at that optimum level, variations are made to another factor to find its optimum, with the other factors being kept constant, and so on. Assumptions are then made about the preference for the lower or higher levels for each of the factors. This approach is familiar and easy to use and understand. However, it is widely criticized, not least for the fact that no information is provided about any interactions which may occur between any two of the factors tested, and so reproducibility is poor. It is also inefficient, resource-intensive and costly. In addition, it is not easy to hold the factors constant from experiment to experiment, and this in itself creates variation.

The full factorial method

The full factorial approach is to consider all combinations of the factors which are being tested. In this way all possible interactions between the factors are investigated to find the best combination. For example, three factors with two levels each (i.e. level 1 and level 2) would need $2^3 = 8$ trials, as shown in table 18.1.

This may be feasible for a small number of factors and when experimentation is easy, but even with say seven factors at two levels, the minimum number of trials would be 2^7 (i.e. 128). Despite the fact that both the main effects and interactions can be measured in a thorough and pure scientific manner, the time and costs associated with running such a large number of experiments are usually considered to be prohibitive and unrealistic in industrial situations. Also much of the information obtained from the trials would be from combinations of factors which are of little practical value. This problem may be overcome by the use of fractional factorial designs.

Table 18.1 The full factorial method

Trial number	Control factors		
	A	B	C
1	1	1	1
2	1	1	2
3	1	2	1
4	1	2	2
5	2	1	1
6	2	1	2
7	2	2	1
8	2	2	2

Source: Ian Ferguson Associates

The fractional factorial method

To overcome the disadvantage of the number of trials necessary in a full factorial design, fractional factorial designs are used where the chosen fraction of the full design gives an even and balanced spread throughout all the factors being studied. Typically a quarter of the 128 experiments required for seven factors at two levels would involve just 32 experiments.

It was three Englishmen who took the lead on this problem of experimental size. Fisher (1925), in the 1920s primarily in agriculture and Plackett and Burman (1946) in process-orientated manufacturing in the 1940s. Their method of experimentation was to change several factors at the same time in a systematic way so as to ensure the reliable and independent study of the main factors and interaction effects. They constructed orthogonal arrays with a limited number of runs as a subset of the full factorial layout. The subsets are 'balanced' in such a way that an even number of each level of each factor is tested during the running of the experiment (i.e. the array is balanced between columns rather than between trials). The technique of orthogonal arrays enables the size of the experiment to be reduced to a practicable level by carrying out only a fraction of the total number of combination of factors. However, in doing this some interaction information will be sacrificed. It is therefore important to use the technical knowledge of those involved in the experiment to ensure that this loss of information is relatively insignificant. A typical Fisher array is shown in table 18.2.

It can be seen that in the array the columns represent the independent variables or factors to be studied and tested at one of two levels and the rows represent the tests or experiments to be performed. In an experiment which has eight experimental runs (i.e. L_8), the first option or level of factor A is tested four times, and the second option or level of factor A is also tested four times. In addition to this, during the experimental run, the array tests all the combinations of options or levels of any two factors. Thus A1 is tested against both B1 and B2, as well as A2 similarly testing B1 and B2. The other property that orthogonal arrays have, due to their full factorial heritage and balance, is the ability to study the effects of interactions

Table 18.2 A typical Fisher array

Runs	Factors						
	A	B	C	D	E	F	G
1	1	1	1	1	1	1	1
2	1	1	1	2	2	2	2
3	1	2	2	1	1	2	2
4	1	2	2	2	2	1	1
5	2	1	2	1	2	1	2
6	2	1	2	2	1	2	1
7	2	2	1	1	2	2	1
8	2	2	1	2	1	1	2

Source: Ian Ferguson Associates

between factors. The number of interactions that can be studied is dependent on the size of the array.

The simple analysis of an orthogonal array is done by averaging the responses that are applicable to the level of each factor. Therefore in the Fisher array shown above, factor A at level 1 is given by averaging the results obtained from running experiments numbers 1 to 4 and factor A at level 2 by averaging the results obtained from running experiments numbers 5 to 8. The difference between level 1 and level 2 of each factor is an indication of the significance of that factor in influencing the response measured. Generally the larger the difference the greater the significance.

Analysis of the orthogonal array enables the strength of each level of each factor to be measured, and their relative significance in influencing the designated output (e.g. bond strength) to be assessed. Analysis of variance is used to estimate the significance that any factor has in influencing the measured response in relation to 'error' (e.g. measurement and inconsistency in the setting of factor levels) in the experimental system.

The efficiency of these orthogonal arrays in addition to the L_8 already described, is further illustrated by the example of L_4–3 independent factors at two levels and involving four experimental runs, L_{12}–11 factors at two levels and 12 experimental runs and L_9–4 factors at three levels and nine experimental runs. The experiments are not necessarily performed in the order 1, 2, 3, 4. Instead the preference is to perform them in random order, unless it is advisable that they be carried out in subgroups. Undertaking the runs in random order is the best way to protect the experiment from the occurrence of unforeseen changes.

The arrays suggested by Taguchi (1986) give economies of scale and time in the cost of experimentation. They are also practical to use in a team environment where maximum use is made of technical knowledge which exists within the team for detail such as the choice of factors, the setting of the levels, whether to study an interaction between factors, and not least the choice of responses of the experimental runs. There are a small number of orthogonal arrays or experimental designs that constitute a fundamental set of arrays: they are sometimes referred to as the 'cookbook'.

Table 18.3 Experimental layout: powder granulation

	Control factors	*Level 1*	*Level 2*
A	Mixing speed	High	Low
B	Drying temperature	High	Low
C	Chopping speed	Long	Short
D	Drying mechanism	Type A	Type B
E	Drying time	Long	Short
F	Mixing time	Long	Short
G	Solution addition rate	Fast	Slow

Source: Ian Ferguson Associates

Table 18.4 Results of experimental runs

	A	*B*	*C*	*D*	*E*	*F*	*G*	*Particle size*
1	High	High	Long	Type A	Long	Long	Fast	3.8
2	High	High	Long	Type B	Short	Short	Slow	4.5
3	High	Low	Short	Type A	Long	Short	Slow	5.3
4	High	Low	Short	Type B	Short	Long	Fast	4.9
5	Low	High	Short	Type A	Short	Long	Slow	4.4
6	Low	High	Short	Type B	Long	Short	Fast	2.9
7	Low	Low	Long	Type A	Short	Short	Fast	2.3
8	Low	Low	Long	Type B	Long	Long	Slow	3.6

Source: Ian Ferguson Associates

The following experiment outlines the concept of orthogonal arrays. It concerns part of the process used in the pharmaceutical industry in the manufacture of medicines in tablet form. To produce uniform tablets in terms of size and content, the initial process of mixing the drug solution and the carrying medium is paramount. It is vital that the particle size, the even distribution of the drug (content uniformity) and the moisture content are controlled with small variation around the target value prior to feeding into the tablet-making part of the operation. The three measured responses are therefore particle size, content uniformity, and moisture content. Table 18.3 shows the layout of the experiment; the orthogonal array is an L_8. The results of each experimental run from the particular combination of the factors in the run are also given in table 18.4. The results of each experiment are an average from a satisfactory sample size.

The experiment will indicate the combination which gives the best result, but there may be a better combination. This is done by analysing the effect of each factor. The output or response of the relevant experiment where the information occurs is simply added up and averaged so that comparisons may be made between level 1 and level 2 of each factor. Comparisons of the relative difference between level 1 and level 2 and between each factor can then be made as to the significance of each factor in affecting the response or output of the experiment. An example of the calculations made is shown in tables 18.5 and 18.6. The average of the experimental run is 3.96.

Table 18.5   Response table: means

$$A1 = \tfrac{1}{4}(3.8 + 4.5 + 5.3 + 4.9) = \tfrac{18.5}{4} = 4.625$$

$$A2 = \tfrac{1}{4}(4.4 + 2.9 + 2.3 + 3.6) = \tfrac{13.2}{4} = 3.300$$

$$B1 = \tfrac{1}{4}(3.8 + 4.5 + 4.4 + 2.9) = \tfrac{15.6}{4} = 3.900$$

$$B2 = \tfrac{1}{4}(5.3 + 4.9 + 2.3 + 3.6) = \tfrac{16.1}{4} = 4.025$$

Source: Ian Ferguson Associates

Table 18.6   Analysis of the experiment

	A	B	C	D	E	F	G
Level 1	4.625	3.9	3.550	3.950	3.900	4.175	3.475
Level 2	3.300	4.025	4.375	3.975	4.025	3.750	4.450
Difference	1.325	0.125	0.825	0.025	0.125	0.425	0.975

Source: Ian Ferguson Associates

Table 18.7   Analysis of the experiment

A2	Mixing speed	$= 3.96 - 3.300 = 0.660$
G1	Solution add. rate	$= 3.96 - 3.475 = 0.485$
C1	Chopping speed	$= 3.96 - 3.550 = 0.410$
F2	Mixing time	$= 3.96 - 3.750 = 0.210$
Total below average		$= 3.96 - 1.765 = 2.195$

Source: Ian Ferguson Associates

Because of the balanced construction of the orthogonal array it is permissible to view the significance of each of the factors in relative value to each other in terms of their effect on influencing the value of the output or response, in this case 'particle size'. Thus mixing speed, solution addition rate, chopping speed and mixing time have the greatest effect in that order, and drying time and drying temperature are, in this example, of no relative significance at all. It is helpful to look at these effects graphically and in comparison with the factorial effect on the variation of the responses within the sample of each experimental run. The other useful property that the balance of the array gives is the additive effect of each of the main control factors in the value of the response, beyond the experimental average. In this example particle size is required to be as small as possible. The effect below average is shown in table 18.7.

If the experiment has been conceived properly and shows variation in the results of the different combination of factors in each experimental run, we would expect to see approximately half of the control factors having some additive effect on the output for a two-level array. The total below average, in this case, can now be used as a prediction of the result if the process is set up using a combination of factor level settings that reflect their best effect on the output, in this case A2, C1, F1, G1. The other factors B, D and E can be set at the level where least cost is incurred. This may be B2 (lowest temperature), E2 (shortest drying time) and perhaps either D1 or D2 according to the lower capital cost, or the lower operating cost.

As the orthogonal array is only a subset of the full factorial array (in this case 8 or 128) it is obligatory to conduct a confirmation run and compare the results which are obtained with the prediction. The closer the confirmation run is to the prediction the better has been the team thinking in the construction of the experiment in terms of: the response chosen, the factors affecting the responses, the levels chosen for the factors and their accurate setting, the measurement system and accuracy, considerations of interaction and uncontrollable factors that may affect the response.

From the analysis of the experiment it is clear which level of each factor would be preferred for a desired output. By looking at what happened to the output when each factor was moved from level 1 to level 2 it can also be seen which factors have the greatest effect on the output. Where there is only a small difference the factor has little effect. On the other hand, where the difference in levels of a factor is greatest, this is the factor which is most significant. It is always helpful to present the results in graph form to facilitate understanding and communication of the data.

Taguchi: An Overview of his Approach

As mentioned earlier, design of experiments dates back to the agricultural research of Sir R. A. Fisher in the 1920s, and historically required a great deal of statistical knowledge and understanding, which most industrial users of experiments found somewhat intimidating. Over the years much effort has been devoted to simplifying the task of experimentation. In the late 1970s, the work of Genichi Taguchi on experimental design made what is regarded by many as a major breakthrough in its application. Taguchi is a statistician and electrical engineer who was involved in rebuilding the Japanese telephone system, and has been involved in applying design of experiments in the Japanese electronic industry for over 30 years. He promotes three distinct stages of designing in quality:

- *System design*: the basic configuration of the system is developed. This involves the selection of parts and materials and the use of feasibility studies and prototyping. In system design technical knowledge and scientific skills are paramount.
- *Parameter design*: the numerical values for the system variables (product and process parameters – termed factors) are chosen so that the system performs well, no matter what disturbances or noises (i.e. uncontrollable variables) are encountered by the system (i.e. robustness). The objective is to identify optimum levels for these control factors so that the product and/or process is least sensitive to the effect of changes in noise factors. The experimentation pinpoints this best combination of product/process parameter levels. The emphasis in parameter design is on using low-cost materials and processes in the production of the system; it is the key stage of designing in quality.
- *Tolerance design*: the third stage in the design process, not to be confused with 'tolerancing'. The tolerance design process uses experimental design to investigate the effect on the variance of the output characteristic of:

- Product design: choosing the upper specification limit (USL) and lower specification limit (LSL) around the nominals of key design parameters that have been prescribed by the parameter design study. Having done this, reconciling the choice of limits of the factors in the design that are predicted to cause most variation, with, typically, the cost of reducing the tolerance gap, or the choice of more expensive materials.
- Process design: choosing the USL and LSL around the nominals of key process factors that have been prescribed by the parameter design study. Having done this, reconciling the choice of limits of the factors in the process that are predicted to cause most variation, with, typically, the cost of reducing the tolerance gap, or the choice of more expensive methods.

Taguchi's approach addresses the following:

- Determining the quality level, as expressed in his loss function concept.
- Improving the quality level in a cost-effective manner by parameter and tolerance design.
- Monitoring the quality level using SPC. A feedback/feed-forward closed-loop system is also recommended.

His 'off-line' approach to quality control is well thought of in the West, in particular by the engineering fraternity, but inevitably there are many criticisms of some of his statistical methods and rather surprisingly of the philosophy he advocates, with claims that it is flawed: for details see Gunter (1987), Kackar (1985) and Howell (2000). What the critics seem to forget is that Taguchi's methods (i.e. engineering, experimental design and data analysis) have proven successful both in Japan and the West, and those organizations which have adopted his methods have succeeded in making continuous improvement; it is this which is important and not the methods used. There is little doubt that his work has led to increased interest by engineers in a variety of approaches and methodologies relating to design of experiments. He has provided a tool to analyse the effects of control factors on variability with respect to noise. However, it should not be overlooked that a number of other people have made significant improvements with the other approaches to experimental design. The maxim to be applied should be 'If it works for you, use it.'

Achieving Robust Design: An Example from Tile Manufacturing

An interesting example of the principles of parameter design and robustness is provided by the case study of the Ina Seito company which manufactures tiles, washbasins and related products, first published in the 1950s. In 1953 they purchased a new oven for a reputed $500,000. The operation and oven layout are illustrated in figures 18.1 to 18.3. The tiles are loaded into compartments in a carrier, which is then transported through the oven on a conveyor belt. The heat to fire the tiles is provided by elements which are placed around the periphery of the tunnel kiln. Air circulates the heat around the oven. There are four different temperature zones in the oven through which the carrier of the tiles passes for different lengths of time. For convenience the oven carrier sections have been numbered 01–09 and I1–I6.

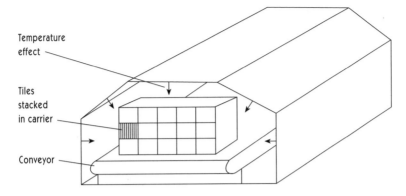

Figure 18.1 Tile manufacture: a reconstruction based on a 1953 problem of Ina Seito
Source: Ian Ferguson Associates

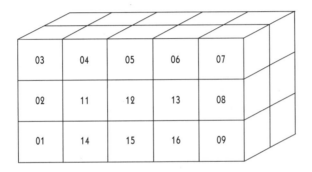

Figure 18.2 Tile manufacture: location in oven carrier
Source: Ian Ferguson Associates

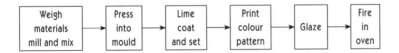

Figure 18.3 Tile manufacture: production sequence
Source: Ian Ferguson Associates

The commissioning trials for the new oven consisted of batches of normal production tiles sent through the oven at the usual known temperature conditions. Samples of tiles from each compartment were then measured for length, width, strength and warp. The results of measurements of length and width are displayed in histogram form in relation to specifications in figure 18.4. Those tiles in locations 11 to 16 are within specification and centred on the target value of 150 mm, while the tiles in location 01 to 09 have a wide distribution of size, with the average being below target value and outside the lower specification limit. They had been exposed to more heat through their position in the carrier and had experienced greater contraction in size.

The Japanese engineers decided that rather than attempting to cure the cause (i.e. the effect of temperature and position) it would be more efficient and economical

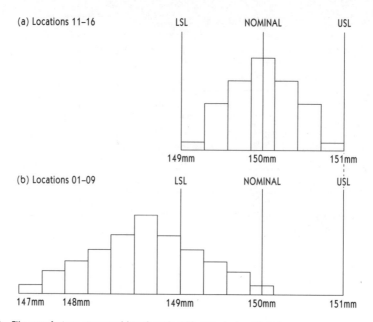

Figure 18.4 Tile manufacture: measured length and width prior to experiment
Source: Ian Ferguson Associates

Table 18.8 Case study: experimental design for tile manufacture

		Control factors	Level 1	Level 2
1	A	Quantity of lime	5%	1%
2	B	Additive particle size	Coarse	Fine
3	C	Quantity of clay	53%	43%
4	D	Clay supplier	S1	S2
5	E	Glazecoat thickness	Thick	Thin
6	F	Quantity of recycled material	4%	0%
7	G	Quantity of feldspar	5%	0%

Source: Ian Ferguson Associates

to accept the present conditions. Their strategy was to find a solution that would render the tiles robust to the effect of temperature and position. They decided to experiment with the formulation of the tile ingredients. As a means of comparison some of the existing formulation is included as one of the options. The experimental matrix was an L_8 orthogonal array with each trial having a different combination of the ingredients (see table 18.8). After each experimental run measurements of length, width, bow and strength were taken, the results are shown in tables 18.9 and 18.10.

The choice of level of the various ingredients that made up the tile recipe was proven by the confirmation run to ensure that the length and width of the tile were acceptably close to the target value of 150 mm, whatever the position of the tile in the oven carrier. There was a robustness in the final mixture of ingredients in relation to the effect of position and oven temperature.

Table 18.9 Experimental layout and runs

	Control factors							Noise factor				Average	σ_{n-1}
	A	B	C	D	E	F	G	11....	16	01....	09		
1	1	1	1	1	1	1	1	147	148	147	145	147.5	1.517
2	1	1	1	2	2	2	2	145	146	145	148	146.2	1.169
3	1	2	2	1	1	2	2	153	152	149	153	151.8	1.941
4	1	2	2	2	2	1	1	151	151	154	154	151.8	1.722
5	2	1	2	1	2	1	2	148	147	148	145	147.3	1.211
6	2	1	2	2	1	2	1	149	147	146	150	147.7	1.633
7	2	2	1	1	2	2	1	147	147	145	146	146.5	1.049
8	2	2	1	2	1	1	2	148	147	146	147	147.5	1.049

Noise factor: N1 = Oven carrier locations 11–16
N2 = Oven carrier locations 01–09
Source: Ian Ferguson Associates

Table 18.10 Response table: mean

	Quantity lime A	Add part size B	Quantity clay C	Clay supplier D	Glazecoat thick E	Quantity RCM F	Quantity Fspar G
Level 1	149.333	147.167	146.917	148.292	148.625	148.542	148.375
Level 2	147.25	149.417	149.667	148.292	147.958	148.042	148.208
Difference	2.083	2.25	2.75	0	0.667	0.5	0.167
Rank	3	2	1	7	4	5	6
Significant level	5%	Fine	43%	S2	Thick	4%	5%
Response	149.333	149.417	149.667	148.292	148.625	148.542	148.375

Source: Ian Ferguson Associates

Steps in Experimental Design

Based on Ferguson (1995) the key steps in designing and running a fractional factorial experiment are now outlined in brief.

Step 1: Define the project objectives

This should include the following:

- A background statement
- The goal to be achieved
- Why the experiment is being considered
- Clear objectives which will result in the goal being achieved
- The area of performance to be achieved
- Available and relevant background statistical information

Step 2: Select critical characteristics

Critical characteristics affect performance. When the mathematical relationship is known between the setting of the characteristic and the performance level, usually by some method of experimental design, it is then possible to improve performance to a benchmark level. Typical critical characteristics are, for example: thickness of plating affecting the protection performance of the article, spring depression forces affecting the release forces available, and component flexibility affecting assembly weights and strengths. This step should be undertaken by people who are knowledgeable about the process under investigation, using engineering and technical know-how, and supported by intuitive, empirical evidence. It is also useful to construct a critical characteristic hierarchy chart. From this the interactive and dependent characteristics should be noted and the critical characteristics decided upon by asking questions such as:

- Is there an accurate measurement system available, with a known acceptable capability of measurement?
- Are the critical characteristics 'pure' and energy-related and not confounded? For example, in a central locking sub-system of a car, the electric motor which provides rotational torque to the plastic gear train, which in turn provides linear motion to the rack and which provides the locking motion, is confounded if the linear motion is measured as a function of the revolutions per minute of the motor spindle. This is an indirect relationship. The 'pure' and functional characteristic in this case is the torque applied to the gear train.
- Can the critical characteristics be improved in value by their controlling factors?

The output of the system should also be decided upon in terms of 'nominal the best', 'larger the better' or 'smaller the better'.

Step 3: Determine the issues that affect the critical characteristics

Brainstorming should be used to identify the issues that affect the critical characteristics. It is useful to think in terms of what would not create the characteristic and what would happen if the characteristic were to be changed. From this exercise an affinity diagram should be considered to group the items and help make sense of the data. It is also useful to arrange the items on a cause-and-effect diagram, adding appropriate items as relevant, with each item being rated on a scale of 1 to 10 for 'appropriateness' to the project objectives (e.g. technical, manufacturability, etc.).

Step 4: Identify control factors and noise factors

From the factors affecting the performance defined in Step 3, make two separate lists of the control factors and the noise factors. The definition of a noise factor is something that either cannot be controlled or for economic reasons is not to be controlled (e.g. different batches of materials, parts and materials that are at the top and bottom specification limits, atmospheric conditions, etc.). It is usual to categorize noises into three groups: external noise (variations in the manufacturing

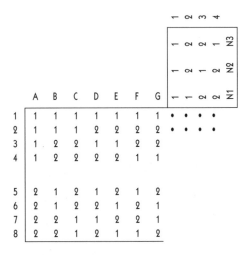

Figure 18.5 Using an orthogonal array for noises being studied
Source: Ian Ferguson Associates

environment, for example ambient temperature and relative humidity); internal noise (variations due to deterioration, wear, fatigue, corrosion or ageing); and piece-to-piece noise (variations in parts manufactured to the same specification). A fundamental aspect of parameter design is to experiment with the control factors which are to be tested against the noise conditions likely to be experienced in practice. If it is economically possible, control factors are tested against individual major noise factors, which for the purposes of the experimental runs only have to be controlled to their upper and lower limits, and are separated from the control factors in a simple outer array. If it is not economically possible to do this, then the sample size of the experiment should be increased and time/order randomization used, to take into account the extreme conditions of noise. For this reason noise factors are controlled for the experimental runs only, and are separated from control factors in a convenient outer array. To minimize the size of the experiment it is usual to select a small outer array for the noise factors (see figure 18.5). Interactions between noise factors are of little interest, but arranging for the noise to be outside the control factor array enables the interaction of each control factor with the noise to be evaluated for significance.

Control factors are factors which may be controlled during production (e.g. temperature, speed, tension, pressure and material type). The basic idea of parameter design is to be able to define control factor level settings that will ensure minimum variation of output under known noise conditions and have the output distribution centred on a value that will be mutually acceptable to other critical characteristics affecting overall performance. Achieving these twin objectives gives what is sometimes called 'a robust design'.

To mix a noise factor with control factors during an experiment would defeat the purpose of achieving a robust design. If they are mixed, then decisions on the best level of control factors would be taken when their optimum level has been influenced by a factor which in reality cannot be guaranteed in normal production to be at the level which was used in the experimental runs, making accurate analyses impossible ('confounded' is the usual term used to describe this situation).

Step 5: Select the control factors to be optimized during the experiment

From the list of control factors set out in Step 4, select the control factors to be used in the experiment to influence the output or critical characteristic. The relative rating of the factors carried out in Step 3 is a useful guide to this.

Step 6: Choose the orthogonal array and assign factors to columns in the array

The choice of the orthogonal array depends on a number of conflicting demands:

- The likely costs of the experiment.
- The number of control factors to be studied.
- The number of levels of the various control factors.
- Whether or not an interaction is to be studied.
- Whether a screening experiment is to be used for differentiating between the vital factors and the less significant ones in terms of their influence over the specified response(s). This kind of experiment, which may, if engineering knowledge demands it, study an interaction between two factors, is usually run at two levels of control factor in order to screen a set of variables. It is an experiment in which those factors deemed not to be significant are discarded and those deemed to be significant are retained for future probing in a second experiment. This second experiment, which may be run at three levels of control factors, may consider interactions between control factors. When a large number of factors are being considered, the concept of performing a sequence of experiments in a step-by-step manner is a useful strategy to adopt.
- Whether the experiment is used for setting ideal levels for the significant factors.
- Whether it is required to break the experimental design into smaller sets of runs, called blocks. A typical reason for this is it is not possible to accomplish all the runs of the design at one time.

Sometimes what to allocate columns to is not a straightforward decision, especially when interactions are to be studied. The orthogonal array is constructed in such a way that, say, column 3 will indicate whether or not the factor in column 1 and the factor in column 2 have an interaction or are independent. If interactions are to be studied a larger design is required, using different columns to study the main effects. If a factor is allocated to every column, it is termed a 'saturated' design; this is often the case in a screening experiment.

The facility for minimum change in a column is most useful when one of the factors being studied is inconvenient and difficult to change from one level to another (e.g. temperature in a process oven). On the other hand, other factors which are easily controlled, such as by adjustment of a lever or knob, have maximum convenience for change. It can be useful to rank factors for their difficulty of change on a scale of 1 (easy) to 5 (difficult). This problem of convenience of change can also be helped by running the experiment in a random sequence.

In all the orthogonal arrays column 1 has only one change between the levels of a factor as the experiment proceeds down the array. Thus in an L_8 array, column 1 has four trials at level 1 for the first consecutive four trials, and then four at level 2 for trials from 5 to 8. Columns 2 and 3 in the L_8 array also exhibit a pattern of changing from one level to another. Column 2 has three changes during the eight trials, while column 3 has only two changes. Columns 4 to 7 do not exhibit such a convenient pattern of level change, with column 4 having seven changes if the experiment is run in the order of trial 1 to 8.

Step 7: Choose the levels of the control factors

Apart from any economic considerations, there are four main objectives in the choice of control factor levels:

- To produce adequate differences between each level so that, as the experiment proceeds, the various combinations of the factors, which are controlled by the orthogonal array, cause sufficient variation to enable the analysis to isolate the significant factors. The reverse condition of too little difference between factor levels nullifies the strength of an experimental design.
- The failure to have an uneven balance between factor levels, such that any one factor becomes so significant that it 'swamps' the effect of other factors.
- A level chosen for a factor should be such that it does not result in information which cannot be measured.
- The levels chosen for factors should be capable of being set to the chosen level during the course of the experiment.

Step 8: Choose sample size

The main purpose of industrial experimental design is to make a product or process 'robust' to the variability caused by a variety of items that are not controlled or are uneconomic to control during the experiment (i.e. noises). Examples include:

- Parts used that are at the top and bottom of their specification limits
- Variability in the performance of machines used in a process
- Environmental aspects of cleanliness, temperature and humidity

To achieve a 'robust' design it is necessary to be assured that these noises have an opportunity to influence the various control factor combinations governed by the orthogonal array. One way of doing this is to have a sufficiently large sample size to ensure that all the noises have impacted on the design, the point at which this constant pattern occurs indicating a preferred sample size – typically 10–30. It is sometimes helpful to take the combination of control factors most likely to cause variation and then generate sufficient responses from that combination so that the cumulative standard deviation results in a reasonably constant pattern around the average of the cumulative standard deviation.

This pattern (i.e. the signature of the combination of control factors) should vary for each experimental run. The differences in the signatures help to provide the answer to those control factors most susceptible to the effect of noise. The size of samples needed in this method depends upon the stability of the design and process, and the degree of accuracy required.

One way of reducing the sample size is to identify the highest and lowest level of the noise and control this at these levels during the course of the experiment. The control factor combinations will then be tested once at the high level of noise and once at the low level of noise, with a sample size being typically reduced to as little as 5 at each noise level. This gives the full signature spectrum of the design and process caused by the noise factors in the various experimental runs. Design layouts for this system require the identified noises to be arranged in an array which will combine the highest and lowest levels of each of the noises.

If the high and low levels of noise are not used, care should be taken to see that the sample size is large enough to enable the noise in the system to have sufficient opportunity to act upon the control factors and influence the experimental output, using a statistically based method, for example the cumulative standard deviation previously described.

Step 9: Organize the experiment and carry it out

This is a multi-disciplined task, and involves considerable organization in scheduling the logistics required by the experiment and tracking the products involved. Typical decisions that need to be taken include:

- Are the facilities available when required and will the environmental surroundings of the experiment be free from external disturbances?
- Who is overseeing the experiment?
- Have all those involved in running the experiment agreed to the experimental plan?
- Have the objectives of the experiments been fully explained to all those likely to be involved?
- Has an initial trial of one of the runs been done for affirmation?
- What will be the procedure employed if a trial run fails?
- Who is measuring and collecting the data?

Once the experiment has been conducted it is necessary to analyse the data using appropriate signal-to-noise ratios and averages and interpret the results, examining relevant interactions. However, interactions tend to be unstable and are not preferred for reproducibility. A better strategy is to have some assurance that the critical characteristic (i.e. the output) is not confounded and then to find factors that can be directly controlled to improve the critical characteristics. Optimum conditions should be chosen and a prediction made for the results of the confirmation trial and run. A confirmation run should be carried out at the optimum settings to validate the conclusion. If a confirmation trial fails to produce the predicted result it may be as a result of 'confounding'.

Step 10: Analysing the data

To be able to fully understand the best settings for control factors from the experiment data, it is necessary that the significance of each factor be known in relation to all the factors. This includes the significance of each factor in influencing the output from both a variation and a location perspective. Coupled with this, it is necessary to understand what effect each factor has on the output distribution when set at the best setting in terms of robustness. There are four possibilities:

- To minimize variation (reducing the spread of the distribution).
- To change the location or average of the distribution.
- To both minimize the variation and change the location of the distribution.
- To have little effect at all.

The effective relative significance of each factor can be conveniently determined by the use of analysis of variance, which Taguchi (1986) extends into quantifying each factor and residual as a percentage contribution to variation.

To categorize each control factor into one of these four categories the data of each experimental run is first summarized into both an average and standard deviation for that run. The average response for each factor for both location and variation is then calculated from these single experimental run figures, using the pattern of the orthogonal array to determine level 1, level 2, etc. as set out above.

Apart from standard deviation there is a choice of metric for determining the variation. The other choices are:

- Logarithmic transformation of standard deviation.
- Taguchi's signal-to-noise ratios that combine location and variation into one relative metric. It should be noted that some information is lost by combining both location and variation into one metric; this approach may not be so useful in very sensitive designs. These ratios can also reflect the different requirements between output characteristics, which ideally should be:
  - Smaller is better (e.g. shrinkage, porosity and vibration)
  - Larger is better (e.g. weld strength, yield and product life)
  - Target is better (e.g. a dimensional characteristic such as diameter, length and width).

For more advanced experiments Taguchi (1986) has recommended a variety of dynamic signal-to-noise ratios for situations where different inputs require a different output, for example, the turning radius for a car via the input of a steering wheel.

Whichever system is used for computing the significance and ability of a factor to influence variation, the resultant tables should show the two situations simultaneously, so that the final choice of setting will result in primarily reducing variation to a minimum, while defining means of adjusting the location to the ideal target value. Response graphs are very useful for achieving this. It is also recommended that a Windows™-based software package such as *Design of Experiments* by Total Quality Software (Nix and Ferguson 1995) be used for this calculation work. Where a conflict of control factor setting occurs, a reconciliation of setting is necessary. Reconciliation methods include loss function comparison of critical characteristics, pair-wise comparison for set criteria and an engineering judgement.

The case study given in tables 18.11–18.13 shows the use of analysing for variation as well as means when using design of experiments in a Taguchi-style parameter design.

Table 18.11   Case study: release times for an anti-depressant compound

	Control factor	Level 1	Level 2
A	Mixing speed	Slow	Fast
B	Mixing temperature	High	Low
C	Interaction temp × speed		
D	Mixing time	Short	Long
E	Feed temperature	High	Low
F	Material type	Type A	Type B
G	Screen size	094	125

Notes: Responses: Particle size, % release per time period
        Noise factor: 5 different runs at different times
Source: Ian Ferguson Associates

Table 18.12   Experimental layout and runs

	Control factors							Noise factor – Batch No.					Result	
	A	B	A × B	D	E	F	G	B1	B2	B3	B4	B5	Avg.	Var.
1	1	1	1	1	1	1	1	1.50	1.51	1.49	1.49	1.48	1.49	0.011
2	1	1	1	2	2	2	2	1.53	1.52	1.53	1.52	1.51	1.52	0.008
3	1	2	2	1	1	2	2	1.47	1.46	1.46	1.44	1.45	1.46	0.011
4	1	2	2	2	2	1	1	1.42	1.42	1.43	1.44	1.42	1.43	0.009
5	2	1	2	1	2	1	2	1.61	1.59	1.54	1.63	1.55	1.58	0.038
6	2	1	2	2	1	2	1	1.71	1.69	1.70	1.69	1.68	1.69	0.011
7	2	2	1	1	2	2	1	1.55	1.53	1.58	1.53	1.52	1.54	0.024
8	2	2	1	2	1	1	2	1.45	1.46	1.45	1.45	1.44	1.45	0.007
										Experimental Average			1.52	0.015

Source: Ian Ferguson Associates

Table 18.13   Analysis leading to prediction of 1.49:9.004

	Mixing speed A	Mixing temp. B	Inter. A × B	Mixing time D	Feed temp. E	Material type F	Screen size G
Variation							
Level 1	0.010	0.017	0.013	0.021	0.010	0.016	0.014
Level 2	0.020	0.013	0.018	0.009	0.020	0.014	0.016
Difference	0.010	0.004	0.005	0.012	0.010	0.002	0.002
Average							
Level 1	1.47	1.57	1.50	1.52	1.52	1.49	1.54
Level 2	1.57	1.47	1.54	1.52	1.52	1.55	1.50
Difference	0.10	0.10	0.04	0.00	0.00	0.06	0.04

Source: Ian Ferguson Associates

Step 11: Predicting the result of the confirmation run

An orthogonal array is only a subset of the full factorial array so it is necessary to confirm that the choice of factor level settings is the best choice and is repeatable. To do this a prediction is made of the improvement over the average of the experimental output, whereby each significant factor adds to the whole improvement. A confidence limit may also be calculated for the given size of the confirmation run.

With this knowledge a confirmation run is made, with the product or process design set with the control factors at the preferred level. The size of the confirmation run needs to be sufficient to give confidence that it represents what will happen in reality.

Step 12: Interpreting the confirmation run and deciding if the project is finished

The confirmation run should reflect the prediction and confidence limits. If it is outside the limits, it is advisable to ask such questions as:

- Were the control factors set as required for the whole of the run?
- Were the required procedures followed?
- What was the influence of the measurement capability?
- Were the noise factors allowed for in the experimental design?
- Has another factor had more influence than expected? If this is suspected then the cause-and-effect diagram should be re-examined.
- Is an unstudied interaction between two or more factors influencing the output?

Finally reference should be made to Step 1 to decide if all the goals and objectives have been met and that the performance level is satisfactory.

Summary

This chapter has given an appreciation of the concept and practice of robustness in both product and process design as the cost-effective way of reducing variation. Experimental design using a variety of matrices which suit different conditions is a key technique for understanding the effect of each controllable factor, be it a product or a process design, in minimizing variation while centring the output on a target value. It is a major technique in investigating quality problems. Statistical design of experiments is a complex subject, but it is possible to develop 'easy-to-use' methods, and we hope this chapter has encouraged this.

The role of experimental design is to build quality into the upstream process by optimizing critical characteristics. A key aspect of experimental design is parameter design. This identifies what parameters are important in a design, be it a product or process, and where each one should be set to achieve minimum variation in a consistent and repeatable manner. Thus robust design experimentation is concerned with identifying as many factors as possible which will enable the system to perform as designed, whatever the various uncontrollable events or noise with which it has to contend.

Taguchi has raised the awareness of engineers and technical staff regarding the fact that many of the problems associated with design, production costs and process control can be resolved using experimental design and analysis methods. This contribution to both awareness and the knowledge base of the subject should not be overlooked.

References

Barker, T. B. (1990), *Engineering Quality by Design*. New York: Marcell Dekker.

Bendall, A., Wilson, G. and Millar, R. M. G. (1990), *Taguchi: Methodology within Total Quality*. Bedford: IFS Publications.

Ferguson, I. (1995), *A Practical Course in Parameter Design*. Birmingham: Ian Ferguson Associates.

Fisher, R. A. (1925), *Statistical Methods for Research Workers*. Edinburgh: Oliver & Boyd.

Gunter, B. (1987), A perspective on the Taguchi method. *Quality Progress*, June, 44–52.

Howell, D. (2000), The variable merits of Taguchi. *Professional Engineering*, 13(2), 30–1.

Kackar, R. N. (1985), Off-line quality control, parameter design and the Taguchi method. *Journal of Quality Technology*, October, 176–209.

Lochnar, R. H. and Matar, J. E. C. (1990), *Designing for Quality: An Introduction to the Best of Taguchi and Western Methods of Statistical Experimental Design*. London: Chapman & Hall.

Nix, A. and Ferguson, I. (1995), *Design of Experiments Software Program*. Lincolnshire: Total Quality Software.

Plackett, R. L. and Burman, J. P. (1946), The design of optimum multifactorial experiments. *Biometrika*, 33(3), 305–25.

Taguchi, G. (1986), *Introduction to Quality Engineering: Designing Quality into Products and Processes*. Tokyo: Asian Productivity Organization.

chapter nineteen

Failure Mode and Effects Analysis

J. R. Aldridge and B. G. Dale

Introduction

This chapter provides an overview of the concept of failure mode and effects analysis (FMEA), and its value as a planning tool to assist with building quality into an organization's product, service and processes. The purpose of FMEA is described and the procedure for the development of both design FMEA and process FMEA is outlined. In examining the use of FMEA reference is made to the work carried out in developing the use of FMEAs at Allied Signal Automotive's Skelmersdale operation. This plant is a manufacturing and assembly facility producing turbochargers for the automotive industry. The company is the world's largest producer of automotive turbochargers, with a current market share of 50 per cent. The lessons learnt in the use of FMEA are fully examined in the chapter.

What is Failure Mode and Effects Analysis?

The technique of FMEA was developed around 1962 in the aerospace and defence industries as a method of reliability analysis, risk analysis and risk management. It is a systematic and analytical quality planning tool for identifying, at the product, service and process design and development stages, what might potentially go wrong, either with a product (during manufacture, or during end-use by the customer), or with the provision of a service, thereby aiding fault diagnosis. The use of FMEA is a powerful aid to advanced quality planning of new products and services, and can be applied to a wide range of problems which may occur in any system or process. Its effective use should lead to a reduction in:

- Defects during the production of initial samples and in volume production.
- Customer complaints.
- Failures in the field.

- Performance-related deficiencies (these are less likely if a detailed development plan is generated from the design FMEA).
- Warranty claims.
- Safety concerns.

In addition, there will be improved customer satisfaction and confidence as products and services are produced from robust and reliable production and delivery methods. It has also relevance in the case of product liability.

There are two categories of FMEA: design and process. A design FMEA assesses what could, if not corrected, go wrong with the product in service and during manufacture as a consequence of a weakness in the design. Design FMEA also assists in the identification or confirmation of critical characteristics. On the other hand, process FMEAs are mainly concerned with the reasons for potential failure during manufacture and in service as a result of non-compliance with the original design intent, or failure to achieve the design specification. Cotnareanu (1999) presents details on how a process FMEA can be modified for use in preventative maintenance.

The procedure involved in the development of FMEA examines ways in which a product service or process can fail and is known as progressive iteration. In brief, it involves the following steps:

- The function of the product, service and/or process is agreed, along with suitable identifications.
- Potential failure modes are identified.
- The effects of each potential failure are assessed and summarized.
- The causes of potential failure are examined.
- Current controls for the detection of the failure mode are identified and reviewed.
- A Risk Priority Number (RPN) is determined, the details are provided below.
- The corrective action which is to be taken to help eliminate potential concerns is decided.
- The potential failure modes in descending order of RPN are the focus for improvement action to reduce/eliminate the risk of failure occurring.
- The recommendations, corrective actions and counter-measures which have been put into place are monitored and reviewed for effectiveness.

The RPN comprises an assessment of occurrence, detection and severity of ranking and is the multiplication of the three rankings:

- The *occurrence* is the likelihood of a specific cause which will result in the identified failure mode, and is based on perceived or (in the case of process capability) estimated probability. It is ranked on a scale of 1–10.
- The *detection* criterion relates, in the case of a design FMEA, to the likelihood of the design verification programme pinpointing a potential failure mode before it reaches the customer; a ranking of 1–10 is again used. In the process FMEA, the detection criterion relates to the existing control plan.
- The *severity of effect*, on a scale of 1–10, indicates the likelihood of the customer noticing any difference in the functionality of the product or service.

The resulting RPN should always be checked against past experience of similar products, services and situations.

The requisite information and actions are recorded on a standard format in the appropriate columns. An example of a process FMEA from Allied Signal Automotive is shown in figure 19.1. The procedure used at the plant for design and process FMEA has been mapped using the Q-MAP technique (for details of Q-MAP, see Crossfield and Dale 1990), as shown in figures 19.2 and 19.3. The FMEA is a live document and should always be modified in the light of new information or changes.

From the design FMEA, the potential causes of failure should be studied and actions taken before designs and drawings are finalized. Likewise, with the process FMEA, actions must be put into place before the process is set up. When used in the proper manner, FMEA prevents potential failures occurring in the manufacturing, producing and/or delivery processes or end-product in use, and will ensure that processes, products and services are more robust and reliable. It is a powerful technique and a number of well-publicized product recall campaigns could conceivably be avoided by the effective use of FMEA. However, it is important that FMEA is seen not just as a catalogue of potential failures, but as a means for pursuing continuous improvement. Nor should it be viewed as a paperwork exercise carried out to retain business, as this will limit its usefulness.

The concept, procedures and logic involved with FMEA are not new: every forward-thinking design, planning and production engineer and technical specialist carries out, in an informal manner, various aspects of FMEA. In fact, most of us in our daily routines will subconsciously use a simple informal FMEA However, this mental analysis is rarely committed to paper in a format which can be evaluated by others and discussed as the basis for a corrective action plan. What FMEA does is to provide a planned systematic method of capturing and documenting this knowledge. It also forces people to use a disciplined approach, and is a vehicle for obtaining collective knowledge and experience through a team activity.

In service-type operations it is often the case that the first time an organization is aware that something has gone wrong with delivery of the service is when the customers complain. It is clear that a simplified version of FMEA would also be of benefit in non-manufacturing situations. A pilot study carried out at Girobank within the data capture services of the headquarters operations directorate has confirmed that FMEA is of benefit in paper-processing-type activities. The technique has since been incorporated into an interdepartmental improvement project to address sub-process improvement relating to a particular stream of work. One of the main benefits of process FMEA is that it has helped to address the complex internal customer–supplier relationship while improving sub-process procedures. The application of process FMEA is considered by the bank as a valuable improvement tool and will be developed alongside other such tools with Girobank's ongoing training initiatives (see Gosling et al. 1992).

The FMEA technique is described in BS5760 (1991). Major purchasing organizations have published their guidelines on FMEA (see e.g. Ford Motor Company 1988; Jaguar Cars 1996; Garrett Automotive Group 1990), as has the Society of Motor Manufacturers and Traders (1989). It features as a subject in textbooks on quality and reliability management (e.g. Groocock 1986; O'Connor 1991), and a number of FMEA software programs, designed on a hierarchy structure, are available.

Process Function / Requirements	Potential Failure Mode	Potential Effect(s) of Failure	Sev	Class	Potential Cause(s)/ Mechanism(s) of Failure	Occur	Current Process Controls	Detec	R.P.N.	Recommended Action(s)	Responsibility & Target Completion Date	Action Results				
												Actions Taken	Sev	Occ	Det	R.P.N.
Kit parts to the Assembly line	Incorrect parts used on build	Turbo failure	7		Wrong parts presented to the line at change over	2	Visual check by setter to the shop Packet. Introduced from the bulk issue area set up on the line Marking of the part number on the 'A' surface on Compressors to ID. Marking of the part number on the Turbine flange.	3	42							
Kit parts to the Assembly line	Contaminated parts	Turbo failure	7		Contaminated parts due to lack of cleanliness of holding containers, Organic material in spacer (GT)	2	Visual check, work instructions by Station describing method of Assembly.	7	98	Introduce cleaning process for all the boxes, which the parts are presented to the line. Euroboxes 300mm × 200mm, 400mm × 300mm & 600mm × 250mm	LM, DN, PE, BW, mid December 1997	Quotes collected, Capital approval sanctioned Delivery 12 December 1997	7	2	3	42
Check cross over holes	Cross over hole not drilled	no oil flow Turbo failure	8		Broken drill, missed operation	5	Air Gauge on assembly 100% prior to build; work instructions by Station describing method of Assembly.	3	120	New poka yoked fixture provided for an 'in process' end of line check. Will pressure test the Centre Housing and check that the cross over hole is present. If OK a letter 'T' will be stamped.	PC, DC, MB Oct 1997	New end of line test fixture, pressure tests CH and checks for Cross over hole, being debugged at supplier to be on stream 1st Dec 1997	8	2	3	48
Affix label to Center Housing	Wrongly orientated to Customer requirements or on Wrong side of Center Housing	Unable to read the customer no on the engine, reject unit which customer will have to adjust label to correct orientation and record ppm	5		Process controlled by the operator and is capable of producing defects	4	100% Visual check by operators; work instructions by Station describing method of Assembly.	5	100	Design new fixture to mistake proof, by Interlocking the fixture to prevent Assembly. Will prevent the Stick Screws from being supplied with air on the detection of incorrect label orientation.	LM, AM, FW, 15 November 1997	Design and detail drawings being modified to suit CH with Backplate assembled	5	2	3	30
Affix label to Center Housing or Compressor Hsg	Incorrect data on label	Customer Dissatisfaction Could use the wrong turbo	7		Wrong input	2	Software provides for a checksum so that the data has to be inputted twice to verify; work instructions by Station describing method of Assembly.	5	70							
Affix label to Center Housing or Compressor Hsg	Label not properly affixed	label will fall off	5		Hole oversize from machining, stripped thread	4	100% Visual check by operators when recording the Serial Number on audit sheet; work instructions by Station describing method of Assembly.	3	60							
Affix label to Center Housing or Compressor Hsg	Label Missing	Unable to ID unit	5		Operation carried out incorrectly	4	100% Visual check by operators Serial Number recorded on audit sheet; work instructions by Station describing method of Assembly.	2	40							

Figure 19.1 Potential failure mode and effects analysis (process FMEA)
Source: Allied Signal Automotive

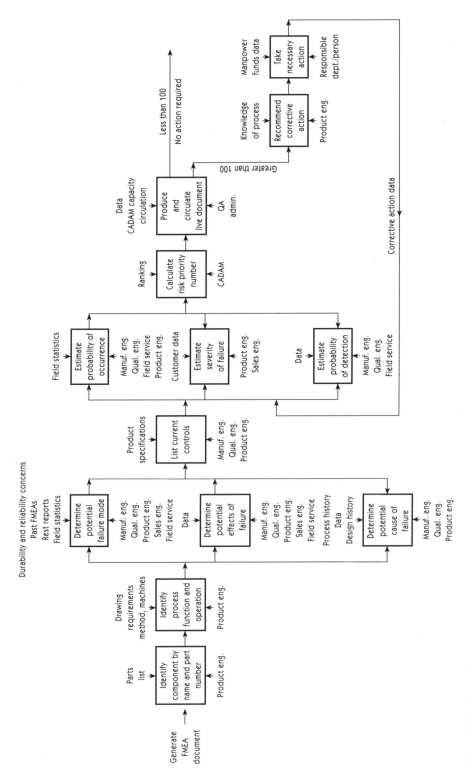

Figure 19.2 Q-map: design FMEA

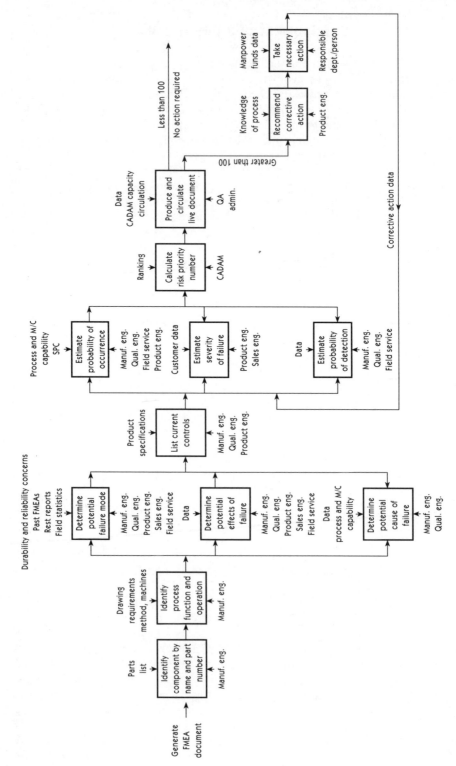

Figure 19.3 Q-map: process FMEA

Development of a Design FMEA

For a design FMEA the potential failure mode may be caused, for example, by an incorrect material choice, part geometry, or inappropriate dimensional specification.

The procedure then identifies the effects of each potential failure mode, examines the causes of potential failure and reviews current controls for the design FMEA, which usually include some form of design verification programme. In the case of a turbocharger this includes items such as material pull tests, heat-cycling tests of components subject to high temperatures, life-cycle fatigue tests to failure, static engine testing, and dynamic engine testing on development vehicles. With regard to the latter, these tests are often carried out by the customers as part of their overall engine/vehicle evaluation programme. Past experience on similar products is often used to verify the validity of certain component parts for a design.

The occurrence for a design FMEA is an estimate, on a scale of 1–10, of the potential failure occurring at the hands of the customer, a ranking of 1 indicating that the failure is unlikely (typifying a possible failure rate of < 1 in a million), and a ranking of 10 indicating an almost inevitable failure (typically 1 in 2).

The detection criterion rests on the likelihood of a current design verification programme highlighting a potential failure mode before it reaches the customer. A ranking of 1 indicates almost certain detection, and a ranking of 10 indicates that the current controls are very unlikely to detect the failure mode before dispatch to the customer.

The severity of effect ranking is again on a 1–10 basis. A ranking of 1 indicates that the customer is unlikely to notice any real effect, in the case of a vehicle, on performance or the performance of the sub-system. A ranking of 10 implies that a potential failure mode could affect safe vehicle operation and or non-compliance with government regulations. A severity ranking cannot be altered by any means other than by redesign of a component or assembly; it is a fixed feature. Clearly serious implications exist under product liability legislation (Consumer Protection Act 1987) for high-severity rankings and these high rankings must be addressed as a matter of urgency.

The activity following the evaluation of current controls is the determination of the RPN.

Development of a Process FMEA

In the case of a process FMEA the potential failure mode may be caused by, for example, the operator assembling the part incorrectly, or by variation in the performance of the equipment or data entered incorrectly into a system by an operator.

The procedure then, as in the case of a design FMEA, identifies the effects of each potential failure mode, examines the causes of the potential failure mode, and reviews the current controls. For a process FMEA the current controls might be operator-performed inspection or SPC information on the capability of the process.

The occurrence for a process FMEA is again based on a 1–10 scale, with a ranking of 1 indicating that a failure in the manufacturing process is almost certain not to occur. This is based on past experience of a similar process, both within the factory and in the field with the customer, typically identified by a high process capability value. Conversely, a ranking of 10 indicates that the failure is almost certain to occur and will almost definitely reach the subsequent operation or customer if counter-measures and controls are not put into place. An occurrence ranking of 10 suggests, and indeed demands, that corrective action be undertaken because it highlights a potentially incapable process.

Detection rankings for a process FMEA indicate for a ranking of 1 that the potential failure mode is unlikely to go undetected through the manufacturing process. A ranking of 10 suggests that current manufacturing inspection controls and procedures are unlikely to detect the potential failure mode in the component or the assembly before it leaves the factory, and that urgent corrective action is required. It is interesting to note that a successive inspection check (e.g. bolt torque conformance) does not result in the detection ranking being markedly reduced; it would still be assigned a ranking of between 7 and 10 since experience indicates that 100 per cent subsequent inspection is only capable of detecting 80 per cent or so of defects. The situation would be assessed differently in the case of automated inspection.

A much better method of detection is to introduce a successive check at a sub-sequent operation whereby the operator is unable to perform his or her operation unless the previous operation has been correctly executed. This can be achieved by designing fixturing in such a way that it will only accept conforming parts from a previous operation. Another method is to install error-proofing devices (for details see Shingo 1986 and chapter 14 above) at source to perform the inspection auto-matically. Examples are the modification of fixturing with fouling plates to prevent mis-assembly, or counting devices to dispense into a dish the correct number of bolts, so that the operator can clearly see if any have been missed.

The criterion for the severity of effect ranking is determined in a similar manner to that for a design FMEA.

The activity following the evaluation of current controls for a process FMEA is again the determination of the RPN.

Analysis of Failure Data

To apply FMEA effectively it is necessary to obtain some real figures for the calcu-lation of the RPN, in particular for internal and external failure rates. These can then be used for compilation of the occurrence ranking. This was achieved at the plant by analysing and summarizing external failure and internal reject data. External failure data are collated using computer aids by field service engineers. The data are obtained from visits to customers to review units which have failed, the disposition of which is determined (i.e. whether the failure liability is due to the plant or the customer or if, in some cases, there is in fact no fault found). Internal process failure rates are collated weekly by the quality assurance department. The data are obtained from rejection notes attached to non-conforming parts by production and inspection personnel.

It is important to realize that if a process FMEA is being compiled for a new product, for which no internal or external failure rate history is known, then it is acceptable to use judgement on failure rates for a similar product. At the plant an analysis was performed of the external failure rates over a five-year period using a spreadsheet programme on a personal computer. These failure rates were then ranked highest to lowest to identify the highest occurring items. The external data were then compared with the internal failure rate data and comparisons made to identify trends in which external and internal failure rates were correlated. When looking at external failure rates, a degree of caution needs to be exercised. In terms of the company's products, a guarantee is given, from the time a product is sold, to the end-user. It is impractical to consider the previous year of warranty data only, since for many applications, particularly for the commercial diesel business, the completed vehicle may not be put into use for up to 18 months following the date of manufacture. Additionally some customers are relatively slow in requesting visits for claims evaluation. This obviously leads to a distorted overall picture – which makes the five-year evaluation more realistic. Consideration must also be taken of any high occurrence failures attributable to one cause. Investigation should be undertaken to see if the cause has been eliminated and, if so, then these should be ignored. The emphasis should be placed on identifying consistent patterns of regularly occurring effects of failure. These types of failure are the ones to which corrective action should be applied.

Recommended Actions for Design and Process FMEA

Following the determination of the RPN it is usual to perform a Pareto analysis and address the potential failure modes in order of decreasing RPN. Determining the figure for an acceptable RPN is really a matter of the application of common sense. If 100 is assumed to be the acceptable maximum then this should be checked against past experience. The rule to be applied is to adopt a consistent approach for each of the rankings, and generally it will be found that the high RPNs are as expected. This takes the form of identifying recommended action(s) and assigning personnel to take appropriate improvement measures by a particular date, which should be before scheduled product release to the customer.

Following satisfactory completion of the actions the RPN can be recalculated, and if it is below the agreed acceptable limits then the corrective action can be assumed to be adequate. If this is not the case, then the design or process must be readdressed by appropriate corrective actions.

For a design FMEA the potential failure causes must be studied before drawings are released to production status. In the case of the process FMEA, all the controls and measures to ensure design intent which are carried forward into the final product must be implemented. If this is not done properly then problems relating to identified failure modes will occur during manufacture. In the case of a new process, potential failure modes may be overlooked because of lack of experience. However, if this is discovered at a later date, these must be included in both process and design FMEAs for future consideration.

Background to the Use of FMEA at Allied Signal Automotive

While large original equipment manufacturers in the automotive industry demand that FMEAs are prepared for their products, there is an almost irresistible temptation for suppliers just to use the FMEA as a paperwork exercise to retain the business. This unfortunately seems to be a commonplace activity within the European motor supplier industry (see Dale and Shaw 1990 for details). This state of affairs dulls the perceived value of the technique, since the lack of thought, plus the usual lack of practical and realistic corrective actions, can easily be spotted by an experienced supplier quality assurance engineer.

This was indeed the early experience at the plant in the late 1980s. FMEA had been used as an activity that was initiated by the quality assurance department to satisfy a number of customer-supplier quality assurance requirements. The use was not widespread amongst other departments within the organization, although some pressure from the quality manager and the Allied Signal Group had been put on the manufacturing engineering department to utilize the technique, and a number of manufacturing engineers had been trained in the use of FMEA via external courses. This had resulted in some marginal attempts to use the technique. However, little or no emphasis was placed on positive corrective actions to reduce potential failure modes. The design FMEAs were being compiled by product engineering in a similar manner to those generated by the quality assurance department – that is to say, to satisfy customer demand.

This historical method of FMEA generation resulted in it being thought of, by those who had come into contact with it, as merely a window-dressing exercise. Consequently the full benefits of using the technique in a structured manner had been missed. From discussions with customers and engineering personnel, and also the findings of Dale and Shaw (1990), it is clear that this situation typifies the European motor industry and is still the case in the vast majority of suppliers.

The main deficiencies observed in the preparation and use of FMEA were:

- The design FMEA was undertaken retrospectively and not early in the product development.
- The design FMEA was being completed by the product engineer alone, with little or no input from experienced personnel of other functions.
- Design verification programmes were poorly documented; they were, however, generally executed in a reasonably satisfactory manner.
- The design FMEA was not made available to the manufacturing engineer as an aid to compiling the process FMEA, and this was often used as an excuse as to why a process FMEA had not been completed.
- Problem areas identified by the FMEA were often not addressed adequately, or they were given unrealistic RPNs to avoid them worrying the customer and perhaps jeopardizing business. In fact the customer often would identify these omissions during a quality system survey and in relation to a delivered non-conforming product.
- Recommended actions tended to be poorly identified or omitted, even when a high RPN identified that they were required.

Developing the Use of FMEA at Allied Signal Automotive

The responsibility for the preparation of the FMEA must be assigned to an individual who has a good working knowledge of the process or design. To obtain a meaningful working document there must also be inputs from a variety of functions, e.g. quality engineering, supplier quality assurance, purchasing, field service/warranty engineering, or sales/application engineering, using a team approach The selection of a team is a key feature in ensuring that the document is complete and agreement has been reached on proposed corrective actions for improvements. The people chosen to be members of the team should have the relevant experience, be well motivated and have the time to carry out the full range of tasks involved with FMEA.

Design FMEA

The initial preparation of the design FMEA is by the product engineer responsible for a particular project. The product engineer completes the first six columns of the FMEA form, namely part function and number, potential failure mode, potential cause of failure, potential effect of failure and current controls (design verification); a design FMEA form is shown in figure 19.4. This should be done when the first draft of a drawing or conceptual design is available, and not when the design has been converted into a development part, when it would be much more difficult to effect any major changes. A failure to observe this fundamental rule of 'think first, not do first' allows potential unnecessary mistakes to be made and costs to be incurred.

Once the product engineer has satisfactorily completed the form, the design FMEA team then meets to discuss the prepared FMEA by analysing, in turn, each part of the form. This procedure allows for any omissions to be included and for rankings to be assigned in order to calculate the RPN. Additionally, and most importantly, the adequacy of the design verification can be reviewed to prevent the potential failure mode from reaching the customer.

The key members for the design FMEA team are shown in figure 19.4. The sales engineer is the interface between the customer and the plant and provides most of the information on customers' needs and wants to the design FMEA. The quality engineer, in normal circumstances, would take the role of facilitator as the link for the administration of the FMEA into the computerized FMEA database. He also provides an input on the assessment of a particular design feature during the production process. The manufacturing engineer is an important member of the team and exerts a strong influence on development of the design in relation to design for manufacturability.

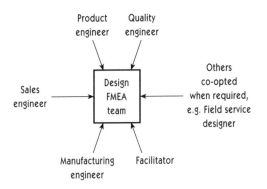

Figure 19.4 Structure of a design FMEA team

Field service engineers and designers are co-opted when required to provide a specialist or more detailed input to a design change or detailed product history based on field experience. This outline of the main activities played by the team members is also similar to that used for a process FMEA and is by no means conclusive. However, experience indicates that large teams are not as effective as small ones; a key factor in the preparation of the design FMEA revolves around total involvement and interaction of all team members.

The meetings to review a design FMEA are best kept to a fixed time of about one hour, and any material not covered during this time should be reviewed at a subsequent meeting. The essential ingredient for success is to hold regular meetings throughout the initial stages of product testing and verification. A meeting should be called to review the FMEA when any significant change is taking place, or if the outcome of a test, for example, proves a part to be incapable of meeting the design criteria.

Process FMEA

The process FMEA should ideally commence with the design FMEA available and to hand. In this way the design intent can be transferred through to the manufacturing stage, before the purchase of any specific tooling and equipment, with an already determined process route and early enough to allow time to implement any specific controls to ensure product quality conformance. However, some organizations have not got the design authority and customers are not always prepared to make the design FMEA available.

The process FMEA team structure at the plant is shown in figure 19.5. The manufacturing engineer performs a similar task to that of the product engineer in the preparation of a design FMEA: the completion of the part name and number, the potential failure mode which, for the process FMEA, relates to a process failure caused by an incorrect machining or assembly operation, the potential effect of the failure, which may relate to either a subsequent process or its effect on the customer in service. The potential cause of failure can either relate to an error made at source or a preceding operation and the current controls indicating both proposed manufacture and quality conformance measures.

The process FMEA team proceeds in a similar manner to that for a design FMEA, by reviewing the FMEA form as prepared by the manufacturing engineer, adding

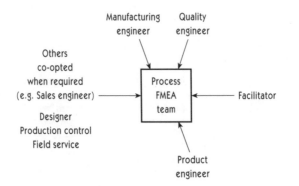

Figure 19.5   Structure of a process FMEA team

any additional information, and determining the RPN on the basis of past experience, and then recommending corrective actions. These are reviewed at a later stage when they have been tested on an initial sample batch. Examples of recommended actions for a process FMEA are typically the execution of a process potential capability study and the subsequent institution of SPC control for non-capable processes, improvement of tooling, additional operator instruction sheets, the use of mistake-proofing devices, application of successive check systems, and the commencement of a planned preventative maintenance programme.

The major difficulties of process FMEA development have been caused by a reluctance, until recently, by the manufacturing engineering function to take a leading role in the preparation and use of FMEA. The reasons for this include a perceived lack of time to allocate to the use of the technique, ignorance of what the technique can do to improve the quality of the product and robustness of the manufacturing processes, and a certain scepticism about quality management techniques, since SPC, although in widespread use, has not been an instant cure for all quality ills as was naively expected by some management and staff.

These difficulties are similar to the four main difficulties identified by Dale and Shaw (1990) in their study of the use of FMEA by automotive component suppliers: time constraints in preparing FMEA, lack of understanding of the purpose of FMEA, lack of training, and lack of management commitment. They go on to comment that 'these tend to be management and concept orientated difficulties rather than technical difficulties in the preparation of FMEA'.

The major factor affecting the adoption of FMEA and its development as an effective advanced quality planning technique has been consistent pressure by the FMEA facilitator, pressure from the quality manager, and the onset of increased customer pressure for evidence of FMEA use. Today some very worthwhile use is being made of the FMEA technique to readdress long-standing problem areas and, much to the surprise of some sceptics, it has yielded a satisfactory solution.

Summary

The major driving force to improve the design and process FMEA procedures at Allied Signal has been a combination of two factors: the use of a FMEA facilitator as a change agent identifying weaknesses in the procedure and suggesting methods for improvement, and the increasing number of customers in the automotive industry requiring the use of the technique.

Finally, a few dos and don'ts are given which may help organizations to avoid some of the difficulties and traps typically encountered in the preparation and use of FMEA.

Do
- Develop a strategy for the use of FMEA.
- Drive the implementation with the full support of senior managers; it is the responsibility of the senior management to see that there is a positive attitude in the organization to FMEA.
- Ensure that all personnel who are to be involved with the FMEA are made aware of the potential benefits arising from the procedure and the necessity for corrective action to be implemented if improvements are to be made.

- Try to ensure that engineers feel that FMEAs are an important part of their job.
- Make FMEA meetings short but regular throughout the early stages of the product life-cycle.
- Consider producing FMEA for product families, material categories, main assemblies and process routes (i.e. generic FMEA) rather than for each component.
- Put into place a procedure for review/update of the FMEA; it should always be treated as a living document.

Don't
- Overlook the benefits of involving customers and suppliers in the preparation of FMEA.
- Start the FMEA process when the design has reached an almost fixed state, when changes will be that much harder to effect.
- Allow the preparation of FMEA to be carried out in isolation by one individual.
- Allow important failure modes to be dismissed lightly with comments such as, 'we've always done it like this', or 'that will involve a considerable investment to change', without considering the feasibility and cost of the change.
- Use the technique as just window-dressing for the customer. There is little difference in the effort made when using FMEA in this way from that required when using it in the correct manner.

Acknowledgements

The authors wish to thank Catie Gosling for the use of her material in describing the use of Process FMEA of Girobank.

References

BS5760 (1991), *Reliability of Systems, Equipment and Components*, Part 5: *Guide to Failure Modes, Effects and Criticality Analysis (FMEA) and FMECA*. London: British Standards Institution.

Consumer Protection Act (1987), London: HMSO.

Cotnareanu, T. (1999), Old tools – new users: equipment FMEA – a tool for preventive maintenance. *Quality Progress*, December, 48–52.

Crossfield, R. T. and Dale, B. G. (1990), Mapping quality assurance systems: a methodology. *Quality and Reliability Engineering International*, 6(3), 167–78.

Dale, B. G. and Shaw, P. (1990), Failure mode and effects analysis in the motor industry: a state-of-the-art study. *Quality and Reliability Engineering International*, 6(3), 179–88.

Ford Motor Company (1988), *Potential Failure Mode and Effects Analysis: An Instruction Manual*. Brentwood: Ford Motor Company.

Garrett Automotive Group (1990), *Guide to the Use of FMEA*. Torrance, Calif.: Allied Signal Inc.

Gosling, C., Rowe, S. and Dale, B. G. (1992), The use of quality management tools and techniques in financial services: an examination. *Proceedings of the 7th OMA (UK) Conference, UMIST, June*, 285–90.

Groocock, J. M. (1986), *The Chain of Quality*. New York: John Wiley & Sons.

Jaguar Cars Ltd. (1996), *Instruction Guide to the Use of FMEA*. Coventry: Jaguar Cars.

O'Connor, P. D. T. (1991), *Practical Reliability Engineering*. Sussex: John Wiley & Sons.

Shingo, S. (1986), *Zero Quality Control: Source Inspection and the Poka-Yoke System*. Cambridge, Mass.: Productivity Press.

Society of Motor Manufacturers and Traders Ltd. (1989), *Guidelines to Failure Mode and Effects Analysis*. London: SMMT.

chapter twenty

Statistical Process Control

B. G. Dale and P. Shaw

Introduction

In recent years statistical process control (SPC) has become a fashionable buzz-word in 'industry', but the concept is not new; its roots can be traced back to the work of Shewhart (1931) at Bell Laboratories in 1923. The control charts in use today for monitoring processes are little different from those developed by Shewhart for distinguishing between controlled and uncontrolled variation, albeit statisticians continue to argue their theoretical foundations. Also in the late 1920s Dudding, a British statistician, was carrying out work along similar lines to those of Shewhart. The British Standards Institution published two early standards on SPC – BS600 (1935), which was their first standard on quality control, and BS600R (1942). Statistical process control was used by American industry during the Second World War to assist with the quality control of war materials, and the now defunct British Productivity Council produced, over 30 years ago, a film entitled *Right First Time* which provides a vivid illustration of the use of SPC by a UK automotive manufacturer.

The 1980s witnessed a resurgence in statistical quality control in general, and SPC in particular. Many words have been written about it and a considerable number of training courses have been offered on the technique by a wide variety of organizations. The trend is such that it might appear to a casual observer that an entire industry has emerged to provide a myriad consultation services on SPC.

What then has caused SPC to become such a popular technique amongst American and European manufacturing companies?

To answer this question it is necessary to go back to the economic recovery of Japan after the Second World War. The Japanese, stimulated by the teachings of Deming (1982, 1986), quickly became skilled exponents of SPC. Western industrial managers visiting Japan during the late 1970s and seeking to learn the lessons

In preparing this chapter, the authors have drawn on their experience of working on behalf of the Ford Motor Company, since 1984. They have also drawn on the data contained in the Ford SPC instruction guide and the SPC course notes used on the three-day course.

behind the international success of the Japanese manufacturing companies identified several key reasons for it. One of the most important was the significant use of statistical methods by employees at all levels of the organization, resulting in low piece-to-piece variability of their manufactured parts. Today, in the West, there is considerable interest in quality and how it might be improved effectively and economically. It is the pursuit of quality improvement that has promoted the revitalized interest in SPC.

The aim of this chapter is to give an overview of SPC and its concepts, both statistical and philosophical, to examine the issues involved with implementation, and to illustrate some typical problems encountered in the introduction and application of SPC.

What is Statistical Process Control?

Statistical process control is generally accepted to mean (management) control of the process through the use of statistics or statistical methods. Perhaps because of this generalized definition of SPC, or people's poor understanding of the subject, some misconceptions have arisen about its applicability and usefulness.

There are four main uses of SPC:

- To achieve process stability.
- To provide guidance and understanding on how the process may be improved by the reduction of variation and to keep it reduced.
- To assess the performance of a process.
- To provide information to assist with management decision-making.

SPC is about control, capability and improvement, but only if used correctly and in a working environment which is conducive to the pursuit of continuous improvement, with the full involvement of every company employee. It is the responsibility of the senior management team to create these conditions, and they must be prime motivators in the promotion of this goal and provide the necessary support to all those engaged in this activity.

It should be recognized at the outset that on its own SPC will not solve problems; the control charts only record the 'voice of the process' and SPC may, at a basic level, simply confirm the presence of a problem. There are many tools and techniques (see chapter 16) which guide and support improvement and, in many instances, they may have to be used prior to the application of SPC, and concurrently with it to facilitate analysis and improvement.

The application of SPC can potentially be extensive. It is not simply for use in high-volume 'metal-cutting'; it can be used in most manufacturing areas, industrial or processing, and in non-manufacturing situations, including service and commerce.

The Development of Statistical Process Control

A brief history of SPC was presented in the introduction. What now follow are some perceptions of the development of control charts into the broader issues of SPC.

When first evolved, the control chart, using data which provided a good overall picture of the process under review, had control limits set out from the process average, which reflected the inherent variation of the process. A process with more variation than another will have wider limits (i.e. the greater the variation the wider the limits). This variation was established from an accurate review or study, and consequently the limits were deemed to reflect the actual 'capability' of the process. The charts so constructed were actually called 'charts for controlling the process within its known capability'. As the word 'capability' has in the last decade been taken to mean something slightly different, the charts tend now to be called 'performance-based' charts (i.e. to control the process within its known performance).

When this idea was discussed with potential users, the question was asked, 'But what if the control limits are outside the specification limits?' This resulted in the development of a chart where the control limits were set in from the specification limits. The distance these limits are set in is a function of the inherent variation in the process. Those processes with greater variation will have limits which are set in further from the specification limits than those with less variation. To reflect this these charts were called 'modified' control charts or 'charts to control the process to specification limits'. These charts tend now to be called 'tolerance'-based charts. A further derivation of this type of chart is one where 'alternative modified limits' are used.

If an organization's quality objective is to produce parts or services to specification, the so-called tolerance-based chart may prove useful, and signals are given to alert operational personnel of the likelihood of producing out-of-specification products. This type of chart does not encourage the pursuit of improvement in process performance.

Using the performance-based charts with limits which reflect the inherent variation of the process and having some statistical estimate of this variation, the objective is to establish its source(s), perhaps using experimental design tools and appropriate tools and techniques, and strive to reduce it on a continuous improvement basis. The consequence of this is that control limits should, over time, reduce, reflecting the reduction in process variation and thereby demonstrating an organization's commitment to continuous improvement. This reduction in variation is confirmed by increased values or measures of process capability.

This situation is where Western companies should be now, that is, striving to reduce variation by using control charts to monitor their processes, and the data generated from the charts to aggressively pursue continuous improvement. If an organization is not using SPC in this manner, management need to critically evaluate their use of SPC and see what is going wrong.

Some Basic Statistics: Averages and Measures of Dispersion

Measures of central tendency

These are numerical values that tend to locate the middle of a set of data. There are many such measures of central tendency or 'average', some of which can be omitted from this discussion of SPC, leaving the mean (arithmetic), median and mode.

- The *arithmetic mean* (x) is determined by adding all the values together and dividing by the number of values. It can be distorted by extreme values and when calculated it may not correspond to any one particular value in the set of data.

$$\bar{x} = \frac{\Sigma x}{n}$$

where Σ means 'the sum of', and n is the number of values or sample size.
- The *median* is the middle value in a group of measurements when they are arranged into an array, e.g. from lowest to highest. Fifty per cent of the values are equal to or less than the median and 50 per cent are equal to or greater than the median – the mid-point.
- The *mode* is often interpreted as that part of the measurement scale where values occur most frequently, or the most commonly occurring value.

These averages or measures of central tendency give an indication of where most of the values tend to cluster. In the context of SPC, it is the 'arithmetic mean' which attracts most attention, be it the mean of a sample, the mean of a series of samples or the mean of a series of sample means. This average may provide information about the accuracy or setting of a machine or a process and may give an indication of how well a target or some nominal value is being achieved.

Measures of dispersion

These are numerical values that describe the amount of variability or spread that is found amongst data. This dispersion may be quite small or it may be large, so some measure of this is required. There are several measures of dispersion which can be used; the most common are the range and the standard deviation. The former is easy to calculate while the latter is a little more difficult. The range and/or the standard deviation give an indication of the variability of the data; they are measures of precision.

- The *range* (denoted by R) is the difference between the smallest and the largest values within the data being analysed (there may be circumstances where this simple approach can be troublesome, but provided some common sense is used, it can be regarded as an acceptable definition).
- The *standard deviation* (denoted by S, σ or $\acute{\sigma}$ depending upon the data under analysis) is a measure which conveys by how much, on average, each value differs from the mean.

Variation and Process Improvement

Products manufactured under the same conditions and to the same specification are seldom identical; they will most certainly vary in some respect. The variation, which may be large or almost immeasurably small, comes from the main constituents of a process – machine, manpower, method, material, and mother nature. The measuring system itself may also give rise to variation in the recorded measurement; this is why repeatability and reproducibility studies are so important.

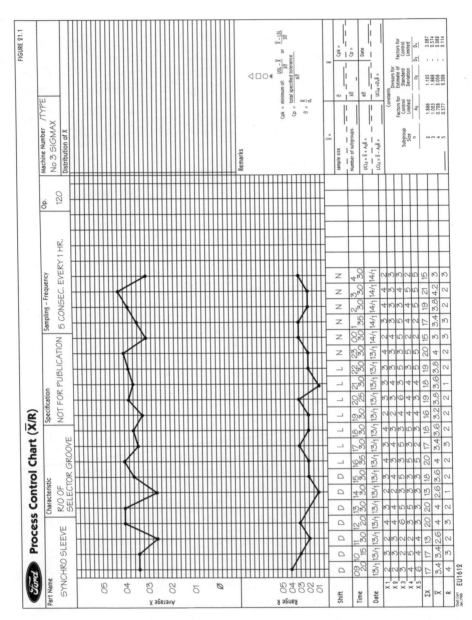

FIGURE 21.1

Figure 20.1 Ford process control chart

Source: Based on a format used by Ford Motor Company

- *Repeatability* is the closeness between results of successive measurements of the same characteristics carried out under the same conditions.
- *Reproducibility* is the closeness between the results of measurement of the same characteristic carried out under changed conditions of measurement.

An important means of improvement is the reduction of variation. SPC is a very useful tool because, given the capability of the measuring system, it ascertains the extent of the variation and whether it is due to special or common causes of variation, process improvement being achieved by removal of either or both causes. It should be stressed that while SPC, if properly used, will give an indication of the magnitude of the variation, it will not give the source. The efforts of management, technical, engineering, and management services and site service activities should be directed at establishing the likely source or sources of variation and, more importantly, reducing them continuously. A number of management decisions are based on interpreting variations in data, whether they be sales, output or financial, and if a variation is misinterpreted it could lead to incorrect decisions being made. It is therefore important that managers improve their knowledge of variation and its causes.

The first step in the use of SPC is to collect data to a plan and plot the gathered data on a graph called a control chart (see figure 20.1). The control chart is a picture of what is happening in the process at a particular time: it is a line graph. These data are then used to calculate control limits which are the main means of determining whether or not the process is in a state of statistical control. Once the process is rendered stable by the identification and rectification of special causes of variation, its process capability can be assessed. The next task is to reduce, as much as possible, the common causes of variation so that the output from the process is centred around a nominal or target value. This is a continuing process in the pursuit of continuous improvement. It is not the natural state of a process to be in statistical control, and a great deal of effort is required to achieve this status and a great deal more to keep it so. The amount of this effort and its focus is a function of senior management within their overall remit. Consequently, engineering, economic and financial considerations, among others, must and do play their part in eliminating variation.

What are special and common causes of variation?

Special (or assignable) causes of variation influence some or all the measurements in different ways. They occur intermittently in the form of shocks and disturbances to the system and reveal themselves as unusual patterns of variation on a control chart. Special causes should be identified and rectified and hopefully, with improved process or even product design, their occurrence will in the long term be minimised. In the short term, their presence should be highlighted and a response programme established to deal with them. It is imperative in the management and control of processes to record not only the occurrence of such causes, but any remedial action that has been taken, together with any changes that may occur or have been made in the process. This provides a valuable source of information in the form of a 'process log', to prevent the repetition of mistakes and enable the development of improved processes. Typical special causes may be:

- Change in raw material
- Change in machine setting
- Broken tool or die or pattern
- Failure to clean equipment
- Equipment malfunction
- Keying in incorrect data

Common (or unassignable) causes influence all measurements in the same way. They produce the natural or random pattern of variation observed in data when they are free of special causes. Common causes arise from many sources and do not reveal themselves as unique patterns of variation; consequently they are often difficult to identify. If only common cause variation is present, the process is considered to be stable, hence predictable. Typical common causes may be:

- Badly maintained machines
- Poor lighting
- Poor workstation layout
- Poor instructions
- Poor supervision
- Materials and equipment not suited to the requirements

In the pursuit of process improvement it is important that a distinction is made between special and common cause sources of variation because their removal may call for different types and levels of resources and improvement action. Special causes can usually be corrected by operational personnel – the operator and/or first-line supervisor. Common causes require the attention of management, engineering, technical, management services, or site services personnel. Teams made up of relevant personnel are often set up to eliminate special and common causes of variation. Operational personnel often have a considerable knowledge of process parameters and they should be included in such teams.

Variable and Attribute Data

Variable (or measured) data

These data are the result of using some form of measuring system (e.g. vernier or pressure gauges, thermometer, odometer). The accuracy and precision of the measurements recorded is a function not only of the measuring system, but also of the personnel engaged in the activity. Therefore it is essential to ensure the capability of the measuring system to minimize the potential sources of error which may arise in the data.

The measurements may relate to product characteristics (e.g. length, diameter, weight, torque, arrival times) or to process parameters (e.g. temperature, screw speed, pressure, shot weight, chemical analysis, ph). Control of process variables gives earlier feedback and leads to better diagnosis of the causes for variation than measurement of product characteristics.

Typically, the measurements may be labelled:

$$x_1, x_2, x_3 \ldots x_{n-1}, x_n$$

where n is the sample size or number of measurements collected.

The (arithmetic) mean is given by

$$\bar{x} = \frac{\Sigma x}{n}$$

The range is given by

$$R = x_{largest} - x_{smallest}$$

The standard deviation is given by

$$S = \sqrt{\frac{\Sigma(x - \bar{x})^2}{n - 1}}$$

Attribute (or countable) data

Such data would be the result of an assessment using go/no-go gauges (as a proxy for measured data) or pass/fail criteria (e.g. conforming/non-conforming). It is important to minimize subjectivity when using the pass/fail type of assessment. To assist those employed in this activity the boundaries of acceptance and rejection must be clearly defined; reference standards, photographs, or illustrations may help in this regard, and where possible the accept/reject characteristics should be agreed with the customer. It is also necessary to differentiate between non-conforming items or units and non-conformities. A non-conformity may be a blemish or presence of some non-preferred feature (e.g. a scratch on surface finish or some similar aesthetic characteristic); the product could still be usable but the occurrence would/may be a source of annoyance to the customer. The objective is to minimize or eliminate the source of these problems. A non-conforming item or unit is one which fails to meet the assessment criteria for one or a number of reasons; in other words a non-conforming item may have one or several non-conformities.

With attribute data, again it is the 'average' which is the main source of interest i.e. the number or proportion of non-conforming items or the number of proportion of non-conformities.

Data-Collection

The objective of data-collection is to get a good overall 'picture' of how a process performs. It is important that before any study of the process is carried out, calibrated gauges which are adequate for the purpose are available, and also reference standards or examples, and that all operational personnel fully understand what is going on and what is required of them.

A data-gathering plan (often referred to as a control plan) needs to be developed for collection, recording and the plotting of data on the control chart. The data collected should accurately reflect the performance of the process. The factors to be considered in the plan and design of a control chart are:

- Whether the data are to be collected as variables or attributes.
- The sample or sub-group size.
- The frequency of collection.
- The number of sub-groups to be taken.
- Sampling risks – the risk of a sample indicating that a process is out of control when it is not and, on the other hand, the risk that the sample fails to detect that a process is out of control.
- Costs: of taking the sample, of investigation and correction of special causes, and of non-conforming output.

Different data-gathering plans may give different 'pictures' of a process and there are many formal economic models of control charts. However, consideration of statistical criteria, and practical experience, have led to organizations formulating general guidelines for sample size and intervals between samples. In the automotive-related industries it has led to the widespread acceptance (for variables) of a sample size of 5, a one-hourly sampling frequency, the taking of at least 20 sub-groups as a test for stability of a process, and the use of three standard error-control limits. To obtain a meaningful picture of process performance from attributes data, and to ensure that the statistical theory supporting the design of the control chart is valid, larger samples ($n > 25$) and more sub-groups are often required.

There is nothing sacrosanct about these guidelines, and in selecting the sample size and frequency some experimentation will, in general, be required. If other sample sizes are more appropriate then they should be used. Whatever plan is developed, it must be able to show any changes in the process, so the general maxim of sampling is 'little and often'.

Different sampling methods will yield different kinds of information. If, for example, samples (or sub-groups) of size 5 are taken every hour from a process, and each sample of 5 represents the most recent pieces, it will give the 'latest news' of the process. In this case, any within-sample variation which is present is a measure of process variation.

A sampling frequency of an hour may result in data which suggest a process is both in control and capable, yet some non-conforming parts may be produced. This situation would suggest that the variation is greater than is perceived, and hence the sampling should be done more frequently. However, if output from the process does not have any non-conformance problems it might be prudent to sample less frequently. What is important is that the data collected have helped to increase knowledge about the process and that confidence has been built up in how it is likely to perform.

Control chart design must not only reflect a clear understanding or engineering, technical, or operating knowledge of the process, but be such that those administering the chart (i.e. collecting the data and calculating and plotting data points) can do so with ease and confidence not only in what they are doing but in what the 'voice of the process' (the chart) is saying to them. It is important that senior management realize that the control chart is a formal communication from the 'operator' to them about the state of the process; it can be regarded as their 'window' on the organization's operating processes.

Construction of Control Charts Using Variables Data

Control charts using mean and range are the most popular variables charts in use and they are now used to discuss the methods of control chart construction. Other types of variables charts include: mean and standard deviation; median and range; moving average and moving range; and individual value and moving range.

There are five steps to control charting:

1. Calculate each sub-group average ($\bar{x}$) and range value (R); these data are plotted on the chart.
2. Calculate the process average ($\bar{\bar{X}}$) and process mean range ($\bar{R}$).
3. These statistics are plotted on the chart as heavy broken lines.
4. Calculate and plot on the chart the control limits.
5. Analyse and interpret the control charts.

The process average $\bar{\bar{X}}$ is the mean of all the sample means, and the mean range $\bar{R}$ is the average of all the sample ranges. These are used to calculate control limits and are drawn on the chart as a guide for analysis. They reflect the natural variability of the process and are calculated using constants, appropriate to the sample size, and taken from statistical tables. The formulae used are:

- Mean control chart

$$\text{Upper control limit (UCL}_{\bar{x}}) = \bar{\bar{X}} + A_2\bar{R}$$

$$\text{Lower control limit (LCL}_{\bar{x}}) = \bar{\bar{X}} - A_2\bar{R}$$

  where A_2 is a constant derived from statistical tables and is dependent upon the sample size.

- Range control chart

$$\text{Upper control limit (UCL}_R) = D_4\bar{R}$$

$$\text{Lower control limit (LCL}_R) = D_3\bar{R}$$

  where D_4 and D_3 are constants derived from statistical tables and is dependent upon the sample size.

With small sample sizes there is no lower limit on the range chart.

It should be noted that the distance of the control limits from $\bar{\bar{X}}$ is a measure of the inherent variability of the process. High variability, as measured by $\bar{R}$, will give wide control limits, and low variability will result in narrow limits. The limits simply reflect the performance of the process when the study data were collected.

If, however, the process mean $\bar{\bar{X}}$ is vastly different from the target or nominal value of the specification, it can be advantageous to set the limits out from this target value, after an adjustment to the process setting has been made. Provided care is taken in the interpretation of ongoing data, no fundamental objection can be made to this approach. These control limits (drawn on the chart as solid lines) are often called action limits, and are set at three standard errors or $A_2\bar{R}$ from the reference value. The method is based on American practice and in more recent times has been embodied in BS7782 (1994) and BS7785 (1994). In a way, these control limits indicate the acceptable differences, which may occur at random, from the reference value $\overline{\overline{X}}$. If random variation only is present in the process, most (99.73%) of the plotted values should lie within the boundaries when using action limits calculated on this basis. Assuming that there are no unusual patterns within the action limits, there is a low probability of points occurring outside the limits. Such points cannot be attributed to random variation – a special cause is deemed to be present.

In order to apply SPC to maximum advantage it is essential to have a full statistical understanding of measures of location, measures of dispersion, the normal distribution, and distributions other than normal. These are well covered in the texts of Duncan (1986), Grant and Leavenworth (1976), Montgomery (1996), Oakland (1996), Ott (1975), Owen (1993) and Price (1984).

Interpreting a Variables Control Chart

The range and mean chart are analysed separately, but the patterns of variation occurring in two charts are compared with each other to assist in identifying special causes which may be affecting the process. The range chart monitors uniformity and the mean chart monitors where the process is centred. The range chart is the more sensitive to piece-to-piece variability so it is usually analysed first.

The process shown in figure 20.2 is not in statistical control, as is indicated by data falling outside the control limits. The responses to this condition should be noted. The fact of the data being outside the control limits shows there are special causes present in the process.

Other indications of special causes, based on generalized statistical probability theory, are:

- A run of points in a particular direction, consistently increasing or decreasing. In general, seven consecutive points is used as the guide.
- A run of points all on one side of the reference value $\overline{\overline{X}}$ or $\overline{R}$. In general, seven consecutive points is used as the guide.
- Substantially more or less than two-thirds of the points plotted lie within the mid-third section of the chart. This might indicate that the control limits or plot points have been miscalculated or misplotted, or that data have been edited, or that process or the sampling method are stratified.
- Any other obvious non-random patterns (e.g. 'saw tooth' and cyclic).

All such special causes should be identified and eliminated. To assist in this activity, it is essential that operational personnel record, preferably on the control chart, all changes that may affect the process. For example, a change in raw material, tool or die, fixture change; a change of operator; an addition of chemicals to a process; and shift changeover data.

A process that is not in control or is unstable is not predictable and to consider the capability of such a process is futile and incorrect.

Unlike the process shown in figure 20.2, that illustrated in figure 20.3 is clearly in statistical control as no special causes are manifested. When this is the case, the control chart can now be used for ongoing control because the process is expected

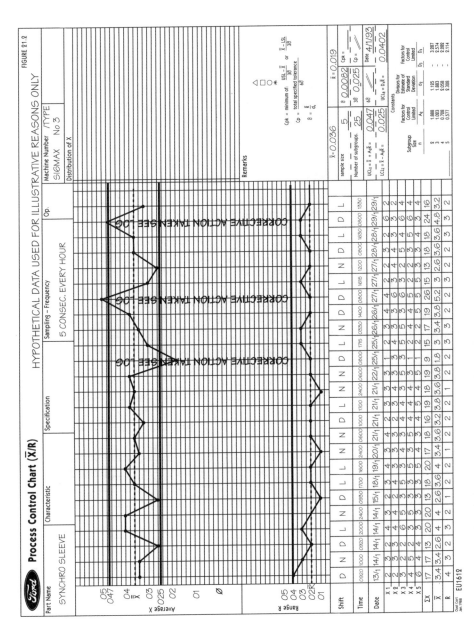

Figure 20.2 Control chart demonstrating 'out of control' condition

Source: Based on a format used by Ford Motor Company

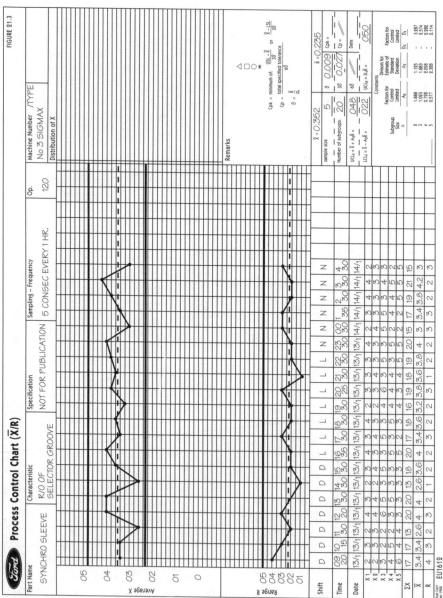

Figure 20.3 Control chart demonstrating 'in control' condition

Source: Based on a format used by Ford Motor Company

to behave as it did when the study was carried out. If properly maintained the chart will indicate to operational personnel when they need to do something to the process and, alternatively, when to do nothing. It discourages operators from interfering needlessly with the process. Over-control occurs when all deviations from the target are attributed to special causes. Under-control occurs when all deviations from the target are attributed to common causes. Either mistake, in general, introduces an extra element of variation into the process. Every time an adjustment is made when it should not have been, production may be lost. On the other hand, when an adjustment is not made when it should have been, the quality of the process output is jeopardized. Statistical control charts should be used to determine when it is appropriate to interfere with the process and when it should be left alone. The control chart should be displayed as close as possible to the process or activity in question. In this way it has greatest value, providing an invaluable means of communication between operating personnel and management.

Construction of Control Charts Using Attributes Data

In order to be able to detect changes in process performance, control charts using attributes data generally require data from quite large sample sizes to obtain the same precision and accuracy as with variables data. For example, a sample or sub-group size of 25 or more is quite common. The sub-group size should be large enough to include several non-conforming items per sample. The sub-groups need to be larger than for measured data and it is often suggested that a minimum of 25 sub-groups should be taken.

An argument in favour of inspection by attributes is that it is not such a time-consuming task as that for variables, so the sample size can be much larger; it is also less costly to undertake. For example, limit gauges or plug gauges are easier for operators to use than more sophisticated measuring devices. In those processes where it is a natural or required part of the process or quality procedure to carry out a 100 per cent inspection or test, the sample size (i.e. the batch size) may well be very large. The same is true in the appraisal of paperwork procedures.

Experience shows that attributes data often exist in a variety of forms in an organization, although it may not necessarily be analysed statistically. The data may be in the form of existing inspection reports, write-ups on rework or rejected items, credit notes, or mistakes made, but they are not analysed in control chart format.

There are a variety of charts which can be used to organize attributes data in order to assist with process control. The choice of chart is dependent on whether the sample size is kept constant and whether the inspection criterion is a non-conforming item or a non-conformity within an item. The main types of attributes chart for non-conforming items are proportion/percentage (p) and number defective (np) charts, while for non-conformities they are proportion (u) and number (c) charts.

The collection and organization of data is almost identical to that described for variables, except that for each sample the number (or proportion or percentage) of non-conforming items or non-conformities are recorded and plotted. The reference value on attributes charts is the process average, with the control limits set at three standard errors from the process average. For example, for a p chart the formulae are the process average ± 3 standard errors:

$$\text{Upper control limit (UCL}_p) = \bar{p} + 3\sqrt{\frac{\bar{p}(1-p)}{\bar{n}}}$$

$$\text{Lower control limit (LCL}_p) = \bar{p} - 3\sqrt{\frac{\bar{p}(1-p)}{\bar{n}}}$$

where $\bar{p}$ is the process average and $\bar{n}$ is the average sample size.

Sometimes the calculation of the lower limit will reveal a negative limit, so no lower limit will be used.

In order to use a p chart effectively for process control, the sample size can vary but should not vary too much. An effective rule of thumb is that the sample size should be within ± 25 per cent of the average sample size ($\bar{n}$) established during the initial data-collection phase.

It can be seen from the formulae that, apart from the statistical criteria in assuming three standard errors, the determinants in the control limits are a function of the process average (i.e. $n\bar{p}$, or $\bar{p}$, or $\bar{u}$, or $\bar{c}$) and the sample size, n.

The formulae for defining the control limits for these other types of attributes control charts can be found in most standard texts on SPC.

The interpretation of attributes data on control charts is similar to that mentioned earlier for variables data, but is worth noting:

- In terms of runs, many people use a run of eight consecutive points rather than seven as with variables data. The distinction should be of no consequence to most users.
- Runs of data points above the process average indicate a deterioration in the process, while a run below the process average indicates an improvement in process performance.
- Unless the sample size is very large, it is unlikely that there will be a lower control limit.

In terms of process improvement, activities should be generated to reduce the process average; this is sometimes referred to as 'the chronic state of the process'. To facilitate this, it is important that in addition to recording and plotting the data points on the chart, additional data-collection and its recording should be made as to the reason or reasons why the item or items were classified as non-conforming – this may be done for one reason or fault or for many faults. To bring about improvement, the cause or causes of rejected work have to be known, and they can then be prioritized for remedial action or counter-measure implementation.

The control charts for non-conforming items and non-conformities are modelled using the Binomial and Poisson probability distributions, so some statistical knowledge of these distributions would enhance the user's understanding of attributes control charts.

Construction and Interpretation of Control Charts: Dos and Don'ts

The following dos and don'ts, developed from Dale and Shaw (1990), may help organizations avoid some of the difficulties and traps encountered in the construction and interpretation of control charts.

Do

- Ensure that the data used to construct the initial control limits are a true reflection of process performance.
- Use the data which are already available to assess the feasibility of using SPC in a particular situation, determine the type of control chart to be used and set up initial control limits. However, don't lose sight of the dangers of using historical data; examine the data, and the means by which they were collected, closely.
- If there is some uncertainty about what can or cannot be measured, use attributes data as a short-term expedient then move on to the use of variables data.
- Ensure that control charts are kept simple.
- Move the data-collection upstream from product characteristic to process parameters.
- Stand back from the data portrayed on the control chart and question what message they are giving. This will help to ensure that some of the fundamentals of control charting have not been ignored.
- Use teams of appropriate personnel in each department to assist in the construction of control charts.
- Try to understand what variation is in general terms and endeavour to understand its likely source or sources in specific terms about the process.
- Use design of experiments to identify the key control factors in the process.

Don't

- Lose sight of the statistical theory on which control charts are based or the underlying logic of SPC.
- Be afraid to experiment with the control chart format, sample size, sampling frequency, and product characteristics and process parameters measured.
- Ignore potential relationships or correlation between product characteristics and process parameters.
- Be tempted to measure and control too many characteristics and parameters.
- Forget that the process can exhibit within-sample and between-sample variation.
- Worry about abandoning control charts which have been based on ill-conceived sampling procedures and making the decision to start afresh.

Process Capability

Because it is easier to understand, the capability of processes using attributes data is mentioned first.

With the np chart (number of non-conforming items), it is usual to express the average number of acceptable items per sample as a percentage to quantify capability, i.e.:

$$\left(1 - \frac{n\bar{p}}{n}\right) \times 100\%$$

With the p chart (proportion or percentage of non-conforming items), it is simply the average proportion of acceptable items expressed as a percentage, i.e.:

$$(1 - \bar{p}) \times 100\%$$

With charts for non-conformities, c and u, it is somewhat meaningless to talk about capability; it is preferable to quantify the average non-conformities per sample or average proportion of non-conformities per item into a measure of 'defects per 100 units' (DHU).

- $\bar{c}$ is the average number of non-conformities per constant sample size. This should be translated into non-conformities per 100 items.
- $\bar{u}$ is the average proportion of non-conformities per item. This figure should be multiplied by 100 to get DHU.

Some organizations translate defects per unit (DPU) into parts per million (PPM), and from this an equivalent in terms of C_p and C_{pk} is obtained; in general, these capability indices are reserved for measured data.

With measured data, the use of indices such as C_{pk}, in particular, and C_p has been increasing during the past decade, and it is for this reason that they are described.

The capability of a process is defined as three standard deviations on either side of the process average when the process is normally distributed. The C_p index is found as the result of comparing the perceived spread of the process with the appropriate specification width or tolerance band.

$$C_p = \frac{\text{total specified tolerance}}{\text{process spread}}$$

Today, customers are specifying to their suppliers minimum requirements for C_p; for example:

$$C_p \geq 1.33$$
$$C_p \geq 1.67$$
$$\text{or} \quad C_p \geq 2.00$$

In simple terms this means that all parts should lie comfortably inside the specification limits.

Given that the process 'spread' is equal to six standard deviations the following should be noted:

$C_p = 1.33$ implies the tolerance band = 8 standard deviations, i.e. $\frac{8}{6} = 1.33$

$C_p = 1.67$ implies the tolerance band = 10 standard deviations, i.e. $\frac{10}{6} = 1.67$

$C_p = 2.00$ implies the tolerance band = 12 standard deviations, i.e. $\frac{12}{6} = 2.00$

It follows that:

1   The specification limits have to be wide – commensurate with excellent physical and functional requirements of the product. *Or*
2   The process variation as determined by the standard deviation has to be small. *Or*
3   Both conditions (1) and (2) apply.

As the C_p index compares the 'spread of the process' with the tolerance band, it is primarily concerned with precision – it takes no account of the accuracy or setting of the process. It is for this reason that C_p is often defined as 'process potential' capability, i.e. what the process is potentially capable of achieving.

The C_{pk} index, however, takes into account both accuracy and precision by incorporating in the calculations, $\overline{\overline{X}}$, i.e. the process (or grand) average. There are two formulae:

$$C_{pk} = \frac{\text{USL} - \overline{\overline{X}}}{3 \text{ standard deviations}}$$

where USL is the upper specification limit, or:

$$C_{pk} = \frac{\overline{\overline{X}} - \text{LSL}}{3 \text{ standard deviations}}$$

and LSL is the lower specification limit.

It is customary to quote the smaller of the two values, giving the more critical part of the measurements distribution. Similar minimum requirements are often prescribed for C_{pk} as for C_p mentioned above.

Because C_{pk} indices assess both accuracy and precision, they are often defined as 'process performance capability' measures. That is, the C_{pk} gives an estimate of how the process actually performs (i.e. its capability) whereas the C_p gives an estimate of its potential (i.e. what it could do if the setting was on the nominal or target value of the specification).

In the calculation of both C_p and C_{pk} it is necessary to know or obtain an estimate of the process standard deviation ($\hat{\sigma}$). The standard deviation can be estimated by using the formula:

$$\hat{\sigma} = \frac{\overline{R}}{d_2}$$

where d_2 is a constant derived from statistical tables and is dependent upon the sample size

This exploits the relationship between the range and the standard deviation which was mentioned earlier in the chapter.

With reference to this the following points should be noted:

- $\overline{R}$ is the average within sample variation. There may be present in the process some considerable between sample variation which should be included in $\hat{\sigma}$. If this is not investigated, $\hat{\sigma}$ could be underestimated, hence any C_p or C_{pk} index will be overestimated.
- The indices implicitly assume that the data (measurements) when drawn out as a histogram or frequency distribution curve, give a reasonable approximation to the Normal (or Gaussian) Distribution Curve. While many processes will offer data which comply with this, there are exceptions, and some modifications in the calculations may be necessary.

The comments made on capability relate to data collected over a long term (many days or shifts) from a stable, in-control and predictable process. Often short-term capability needs to be investigated, particularly for new products or processes (it may be required as part of supplier verification programme, i.e. initial sampling requirements or first article inspection). The time-scale is then dramatically reduced to cover only a few hours' run of the process.

It is recommended that data are collected in the same manner as for initial control chart study, but the frequency of sampling is increased to get as many samples (of size n) as possible to give a good picture of the process (i.e. about 20 samples of size n). Data are plotted on the control chart with appropriate limits, but the following indices are calculated:

$$P_p = \text{preliminary process potential}$$
$$P_{pk} = \text{preliminary process capability}$$

The formula is exactly as for C_p and C_{pk} but the minimum requirements may be higher (e.g. $P_p \geq 1.67$), i.e. 1.67 implies the tolerance band is 10 standard deviations wide and the process 'spread' equals six standard deviations, i.e.

$$\tfrac{10}{6} = 1.67$$

It should not be forgotten that all capability indices are estimates derived from estimates of the process variation (σ). The reliability or confidence in the estimate of the process standard deviation is a function of:

- The amount of data which have been collected.
- The manner in which the data were collected.
- The capability of the measuring system (i.e. its accuracy and precision).
- The skill of the people using the measuring system.
- People's knowledge and understanding of statistics.

Implementation of SPC

Amongst the major manufacturers in the United Kingdom, the Ford Motor Company are considered to be the leaders in the promotion and use of SPC by using it in their own manufacturing plants, and in requiring their suppliers to demonstrate that their processes are in a state of statistical control and capable. To assist their supplier base in meeting the statistical requirements outlined in their Quality System Standard, Ford have established a number of regional training centres in Britain, France, Germany, Spain and the Republic of Ireland. Each centre, using Ford-produced material, offers a three-day SPC course. The School of Management at UMIST is one of four such centres in Britain and the authors have been involved in this training activity since 1984. It is appropriate therefore, when discussing how to get started on SPC, to draw upon the guidelines established by Ford and the experiences acquired by the authors during the last 11 or so years of assisting motor industry suppliers with the implementation of SPC. Some of the most important points are worth enlarging upon.

Awareness

Everybody in the organization should have some basic understanding of SPC and its use. People should not be frightened and intimidated by SPC: the tendency to over-complicate the training should be avoided at all costs. The approach which is recommended is for employees to be exposed to a small amount of training followed by practice, and this sequence should be repeated until adequate knowledge, skills and confidence have been built up.

The training and education programme should start with the senior management team and be cascaded down through the organizational hierarchy using appropriate modes of training at each level. If SPC is to be successful in the longer term, awareness needs to start with senior management and they must take their obligations seriously, providing the necessary commitment, visible leadership and resources. Training for SPC must not be seen as being only for people at the lower levels of the organization.

The time interval between SPC training and the introduction of the technique should be kept to a minimum. The training must always be linked to projects.

Selection of a statistical facilitator

The role of the facilitator is that of a co-ordinator and a source of expertise on the subject of SPC and improvement methods. He or she plays a vital role in the establishment and continued success of SPC and continuous improvement in the organization. The point is made succinctly in the Ford SPC course notes (Anon. 1985): 'The importance of selecting this individual is paramount to the success of the programme and must not be allowed to carry the negative stigma that many "special" assignments do.' The facilitator requires good personal and technical skills and their typical responsibilities include the following:

- Ensure that everyone in the organization is kept informed of progress and developments.
- Assist with developing strategies to advance TQM and the process of quality improvement.
- Monitor progress in individual areas and assist people as and when required.
- Arrange and monitor training on SPC and related techniques.
- Initiate applications of SPC in areas/departments not currently using it.
- Provide advice on all aspects of statistical matters relating to process improvement.
- Assist with all aspects relating to the charting and analysis of data.
- Participate in quality awareness and improvement meetings, workshops and user groups, and liaise with the relevant steering committees.
- Analyse available indicators (e.g. product and process history files) to provide, at regular intervals, a state-of-the-art picture of the benefits and savings achieved as a result of process improvement.

In their guidelines (Anon. 1985), Ford recommend that the appointment of the facilitator should take place early in an organization's SPC programme. Dale and

Shaw (1989) claim that companies who appoint a facilitator are less likely to experience difficulties with the introduction and application of SPC.

From the work of Dale and Shaw it is possible to get an outline profile of an SPC facilitator. The appointment is likely to be made from within the organization, the job will be in addition to the individual's normal workload, the individual will be of middle or senior management status, and their discipline will be either quality or technical.

Setting up a steering committee/arm for SPC

It is useful to establish a steering committee to oversee the programme and develop a strategic plan for implementation. The main function of the committee should be to guide, plan, publicize and manage the progress of SPC and develop diagnostic and improvement actions. This body will give continuity and structure to the programme and ensure that SPC is not dependent on a few people for its direction and future development and will help to establish an improvement infrastructure. It also gives visibility to SPC and shows that management are serious in pursuing its application. To be effective the steering committee needs to be active and plan well ahead.

Selection of an area for a pilot programme

A number of organizations fall into the trap of trying to apply SPC to all areas/ departments at the same time (the 'Big Bang' approach). It is not uncommon to find organizations setting weekly targets for the number of characteristics for which control charts are required to be constructed. If SPC is implemented too quickly and without proper planning, it is probable that many of the key elements necessary for success will be overlooked.

A better approach is to apply SPC in one area where the probability of success is high. This will allow an organization to thoroughly check out its implementation planning and enable it to gather feedback on all the likely pitfalls. Once SPC has been used successfully in one area it is easier to extend its use to other areas and departments. The old adage 'success breeds success' should not be forgotten.

Difficulties Experienced in Introducing and Applying SPC

The purpose behind the application of SPC is straightforward – to reduce variation in process output, first by establishing whether or not a process is in a state of statistical control, and secondly, if it is not, getting it under control by eliminating 'special' causes of variation. Finally, SPC may be used to help reduce 'common' causes of variation.

However, a number of organizations do encounter problems in the introduction and application of SPC. In a recent study of the use of SPC by suppliers in the automotive-related industry, Dale et al. (1990) have reported on the main stumbling-blocks which are typically encountered. These are shown in tables 20.1 and 20.2.

Table 20.1   Main difficulties experienced in the implementation of SPC*

Difficulty	Score (N = 120)
Lack of knowledge/expertise on SPC	149
Poor understanding and awareness within the company of the purpose of SPC	136
Lack of action from senior management	118
Lack of SPC training for operators	106
Lack of knowledge of which parameters to measure and/or control	97
Difficulty in convincing people that SPC is beneficial	94
Negative reaction of operators	87
Negative reaction of senior management	85
Negative reaction of middle management	82
Negative reaction of line management	82
A general lack of encouragement	80
Lack of action from line management	78
Deciding which of the various charting techniques to use	74
Lack of SPC training for senior management	65
Lack of action from middle management	64
Lack of SPC training for line management	58
Poor communication between management and the shop floor	57
Lack of SPC training for middle management	47
Deciding whether to express data in an attribute or variables format	43
Literacy/numeracy of operators	42
Negative reaction of trades union	30
Literacy/numeracy of line supervision	11
Feedback of data	9
Lack of resources devoted to SPC	9
Difficulty in measuring key product characteristics	7
Small batch production	6
An inadequate computer system	5
Organization changes	5
Operators' workload	5
Deciding on manual or computer-aided charting	5
Lack of appropriate gauges	3
Replacement of machinery	2
The nature of product non-conformities	1

* Respondents were asked to select and rank the five main inhibitors to the introduction of SPC. The score was awarded by allocating points of 5, 4, 3, 2 and 1 respectively to the first, second, third, fourth and fifth inhibitor given.

Out of 158 respondents, 122 (77%) indicated that they had experienced difficulties in introducing SPC, and 130 (82%) said they had encountered difficulties with its application and development. The top three difficulties in introducing SPC were:

- Lack of knowledge/expertise of SPC.
- Poor understanding and awareness within the company of the purpose of SPC.
- Lack of action from senior management.

Table 20.2 The difficulties encountered in applying SPC*

Difficulty	*Score (N = 130)*
Applying SPC to a particular process	139
Resistance to change	108
Deciding which characteristic and/or parameter to chart	93
Deciding which charting technique to use	85
Lack of management commitment	85
Lack of problem-solving skills	52
Time restraints	48
Poor understanding of SPC techniques	41
Lack of a company-wide training programme on SPC	35
Attitudes of the workforce	33
Poor understanding of the SPC philosophy	31
An inadequate computer system	3
Unrealistic specifications	3
Difficulty in demonstrating the benefits of SPC	3
Small batch production situation	3
Attitudes of first-line supervision	3
Incapable processes	2
Difficulty experienced in measuring product characteristics	2
Lack of feedback to the workforce	1
Lack of equipment to measure specific characteristics	1
Lack of appreciation of the disciplines necessary to support SPC	1

* Respondents were asked to select and rank the three main difficulties encountered in applying SPC. The score was calculated by allocating points of 3, 2 and 1 respectively to the first, second and third difficulty indicated.

The three main difficulties in its application were:

- Applying SPC to a particular process.
- Resistance to change.
- Deciding which characteristic and/or parameter to chart.

Looking at the variety of difficulties outlined in tables 20.1 and 20.2 it is clear that organizations encounter a wide range of stumbling-blocks in their endeavour to use SPC, indicating that there is no easy recipe for success. When the range of difficulties is studied it is apparent that they can be categorized under two main headings: management commitment, and having the knowledge and confidence to use SPC successfully (including the willingness to experiment and adapt SPC to less well publicized applications, e.g. small-batch production runs and multi-product situations).

It is clear that the majority of difficulties are caused by the lack of commitment, awareness, understanding, involvement and leadership of middle and senior managers. While SPC may be seen to be a bottom-up activity, used by people responsible for controlling a process, it needs management to take their obligations for improvement seriously if it is to be effective over the longer term. They need to devote more intellectual thought and day-to-day attention to SPC. It should not be treated merely as a source of control charts which management use to present to their customers a picture suggesting they are doing something positive about quality improvement.

Dale and Shaw (1991), writing on the common issues and queries which organizations raise in relation to SPC, make the point that a number of people who are considering the use of SPC in their organization and those concerned with its implementation do not understand the fundamentals underlying the concept. They go on to say that there is still a degree of resistance in some industries to its introduction and use. The following profile of an organization which has questioned the use of SPC is presented:

- The Board of Directors and senior management team are not devoting sufficient time and resources to TQM, in general, and SPC, in particular.
- There is a lack of corporate vision, mission, policies and values.
- Meeting the production schedule is the number one priority.
- The emphasis is on firefighting and not on quality planning and prevention-type activities.
- A lack of attention is devoted to the production preparation stage.
- Education and training is accorded a low priority and is not properly assessed and monitored.
- The organization does not have an SPC facilitator.
- Emphasis is on the individual and not on teamwork.
- Engineers are divorced from the realities of the factory shop floor.
- The manufacturing function is not considered a top priority.

Summary

SPC, supported by the positive commitment of all employees in an organization within a framework of TQM, has proved to be a major contribution in the pursuit of excellence. It supports the philosophy that products and services can always be improved. However, it is a technique which, by itself, will do little to improve quality. It is basically a measurement tool and it is only when a mechanism is in place to remove 'special' causes of variation and to squeeze out of the process 'common' causes of variation that an organization will have progressed from simply charting data to using SPC to its fullest potential. Management commitment and leadership and a structured and ongoing training programme correctly used are crucial to the success of SPC.

References

Anon. (1985), *Statistical Process Control Course Notes.* Brentwood, Essex: Ford Motor Company.

BS600 (1935), *The Application of Statistical Methods to Industrial Standardisation and Quality Control.* London: British Standards Institution.

BS600R (1942), *Quality Control Charts.* London: British Standards Institution.

BS7782 (1994), *Control Charts: General Guide and Introduction (ISO7870: 1993).* London: British Standards Institution.

BS7785 (1994), *Shewhart Control Charts (ISO8258: 1991).* London: British Standards Institution.

Dale, B. G. and Shaw, P. (1989), The application of statistical process control in UK automotive manufacture: some research findings. *Quality and Reliability Engineering International*, 5(1), 5–15.

Dale, B. G. and Shaw, P. (1990), Some problems encountered in the construction and interpretation of statistical process control. *Quality and Reliability Engineering International*, 6(1), 7–12.

Dale, B. G. and Shaw, P. (1991), Statistical process control: an examination of some common queries. *International Journal of Production Economics*, 22(1), 33–41.

Dale, B. G., Shaw, P. and Owen, M. (1990), SPC in the motor industry: an examination of implementation and use. *International Journal of Vehicle Design*, 11(2), 115–31.

Deming, W. E. (1982), *Quality, Productivity and Competitive Position*. Cambridge, Mass.: MIT, Centre for Advanced Engineering.

Deming, W. E. (1986), *Out of the Crisis*. Cambridge, Mass.: MIT, Centre for Advanced Engineering.

Duncan, A. J. (1986), *Quality Control and Industrial Statistics*. Illinois: Richard D. Irwin.

Grant, E. L. and Leavenworth, R. S. (1996), *Statistical Quality Control*. New York: McGraw Hill.

Montgomery, D. C. (1996), *Introduction to Statistical Quality Control*. New York: John Wiley & Sons.

Oakland, J. S. (1996), *Statistical Process Control: A Practical Guide*. London: Heinemann.

Ott, E. R. (1975), *Process Quality Control: Troubleshooting and Interpretation of Data*. New York: McGraw Hill.

Owen, M. (1993), *SPC and Business Improvement*. Bedford: IFS Publications.

Price, F. (1984), *Right First Time*. Aldershot, Hants: Gower Press.

Shewhart, W. A. (1931), *Economic Control of Quality of Manufactured Product*. New York: D. Van Nostrand Co. Inc.

chapter twenty-one

Benchmarking

R. Love and B. G. Dale

Introduction

From the late 1980s onwards there has been a growth of interest in the subject of benchmarking as part of the culture of continuous improvement. This has been triggered by the success of the improvement methods used by the Xerox Corporation and by the development of the self-assessment methods promoted by the MBNQA and EFQM models for business excellence. Benchmarking as it is known today originated in Rank Xerox. It is now well documented (e.g. Camp 1989) that when Rank Xerox started to evaluate its copying machines against the Japanese competition it was found that the Japanese companies were selling their machines for what it cost Rank Xerox to make them. It was assumed that the Japanese-produced machines were of poor quality, but this proved not to be the case. This exposure of the corporation's vulnerability highlighted the need for change. In simple terms, the aim of benchmarking is to identify practices that can be implemented and adopted to improve company performance.

The concept of benchmarking was popularized by the seminal work of Camp (1989), based on the experiences of Rank Xerox. In simple terms benchmarking is an opportunity to learn from the experience of others. It helps to develop an improvement mindset amongst staff, facilitates an understanding of best practices and processes, helps to develop a better understanding of processes, challenges existing practices within the business, assists in setting goals based on fact and provides an educated viewpoint of what needs to be done rather than relying on whim and gut instinct.

Since the publication of Camp's work in 1989 many other books of a similar nature have been published (e.g. Codling 1995; Cook 1993; Zairi and Leonard

The authors wish to thank Heather Bunney and Mark Smith for their contribution to the benchmarking projects and material on which this chapter is based. They also wish to thank MCB University Press for allowing material to be extracted from: R. Love, H. S. Bunney, M. Smith and B. G. Dale (1998), Benchmarking in water supply services: the lessons learnt. *Benchmarking for Quality Management and Technology*, 5(1), 59–70.

1994). As pointed out by Zairi (1995), there has been a lack of research on bench-marking and any that has been conducted tends to concentrate on surveys of the concept. Apart from a small handful of papers (e.g. Hanson and Voss 1995; Leonard 1996; Prasad et al. 1996), there is little to prepare the people involved in carrying out a benchmarking exercise for the many issues which need to be faced and the means of resolving some of the main problems which are typically encountered.

Most organizations carry out what can be termed informal benchmarking. This traditional form of benchmarking has been carried out for years, beginning with military leaders. It takes two main forms:

- Visits to other companies to obtain ideas on how to facilitate improvement in one's own organization.
- The collection, in a variety of ways, of data about competitors.

This is often not done in any planned way; it is interesting but limited in its value owing to a lack of structure and clear objectives. This approach is often branded 'industrial tourism'. To make the most effective use of benchmarking and use it as a learning experience as part of a continuous process rather than a one-off exercise, a more formal approach is required.

There are three main types of formal benchmarking:

1 *Internal benchmarking.* This is the easiest and simplest form of benchmarking to conduct and involves benchmarking between businesses or functions within the same group of companies. Many companies commence benchmarking with this form of internal comparison. In this way best internal practice and initiatives are shared across the corporate business.
2 *Competitive benchmarking.* This is a comparison with direct competitors, whether of products, services or processes within a company's market. It is often difficult, if not impossible in some industries, to obtain the data for this form of benchmarking as by the very nature of being a competitor the company is seen as a threat.
3 *Functional/generic benchmarking.* This is comparison of specific processes with 'best in class' in different industries, often considered to be world-class in their own right. 'Functional' relates to the functional similarities of organiza-tions, while 'generic' looks at the broader similarities of businesses, usually in disparate operations. With functional benchmarking the partners will usually share common characteristics in the industry, whereas generic benchmarking is not restricted to an industry. It is usually not difficult to obtain access to other organizations to perform this type of benchmarking. Organizations are often keen to swap and share information in a network or partnership arrangement, particularly when no direct threat is presented to a company's business or market share.

There are a number of steps in a formal benchmarking process. They are now briefly described; more detail can be found in Anderson and Patterson (1996), Camp (1989, 1995).

- Identify what is the subject to be benchmarked (e.g. the invoicing process), decide who will be in the team, the support they require (e.g. training, project champion) and their roles and responsibilities, reach agreement on the benchmark measures to be used (e.g. number of invoices per day, per person), create a draft project plan and communicate with the required internal parties. The process chosen for benchmarking should have a significant impact on customer satisfaction and/or internal efficiency and management must be committed to improving the process.

- Identify which companies will be benchmarked from a set of selection criteria defined from the critical success factors of the project. Research potential partners and select the best partner(s).
- Develop a data-collection plan. Agree the most appropriate means of collecting the data, the type of data to be collected, who will be involved and a plan of action to obtain the data (e.g. explore benchmarking databases, identify contacts in partnering organizations, the questionnaire(s) to be used and the composition, telephone surveys, site visits, etc.).
- Tabulate and analyse data. Determine the reasons for the current gap (positive or negative) in performance between the company and the best amongst the companies involved in the benchmarking exercise. The gap is usually expressed in the form of a percentage.
- Estimate, over an agreed time-frame, the change in performance of the company and the benchmark company in order to assess if the gap is going to grow or decrease, based on the plans and goals of the parties concerned.
- Define and establish the goals to close or increase the gap in performance. This step requires effective communication of the benchmarking exercise findings and gaining acceptance of the data. It is recommended that the audience for the communication should be chosen carefully, as should the means by which it is to be carried out (e.g. presentation, formal report, newsletter, noticeboard).
- Develop action plans to achieve the goals. This step involves gaining acceptance of the plans by all employees likely to be affected by the changes.
- Implement the actions, plans and strategies. This involves effective project planning and management.
- Assess and report the results of the action plans.
- Reassess or recalibrate the benchmark to assess if the actual performance/ improvement is meeting that which has been projected. This should be conducted on a regular basis and involves maintaining good links with the benchmarking partners.

This chapter summarizes the main learning experiences from a number of diverse benchmarking projects carried out within the North-West Water part of the Utility Division of United Utilities (North-West Water is now known as United Utilities).

Company Background

United Utilities is an international company primarily involved in the supply of drinking water, treatment of waste water, and electricity distribution and supply. The company was formed in January 1996 following the merger of North-West Water (NWW) and Norweb. It was England's first multi-utility company and is made up of five divisions. At the time the benchmarking projects were undertaken

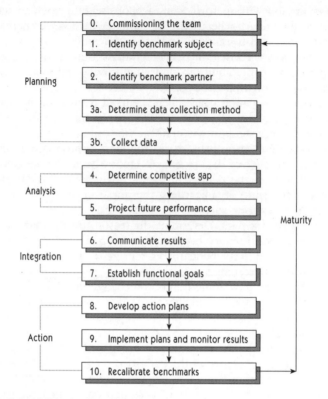

Figure 21.1   The United Utilities benchmarking process
Source: North-West Water

the utility division managed the two regulatory companies, NWW Ltd. and Norweb Distribution.

The main responsibility of NWW is to provide waste water and water services to a population of nearly seven million people in north-west England, servicing an area which covers 14,000 sq. km. They collect, treat and transport water to customers' taps and take away and treat waste water before returning it safely to the environment. NWW run over 200 reservoirs, 150 water treatment works, 600 waste water treatment works, 960 km of aqueducts, 40,000 km of water mains and 30,000 km of sewers.

As part of the company's approach to the management of excellence three benchmarking projects were initiated by the Business Quality Group in early 1995. The purpose of these projects was to promote and trial the use of benchmarking as a business improvement methodology, thereby encouraging further benchmarking projects within the business. This was intended to be done by demonstrating to employees the process of benchmarking and from this provide tangible benefits and cost savings in three high-visibility areas (customer services, operations and laboratory services) through identifying and then adapting and/or adopting external best practices. Benchmarking was also used to demonstrate how a TQM approach to solving a key business issue can deliver bottom-line improvements.

The benchmarking methodology adopted was a modified 10-step process outlined by Camp (1989) (see figure 21.1). The benchmarking teams were encouraged by the Business Quality Group to follow each of the 10 steps and to complete a benchmarking study record when each of the key phases of planning, analysis, integration and action had been completed.

While the '10-step' benchmarking process provides a good outline for benchmarking teams to follow, the ability to understand each of the steps and associated tasks requires some in-depth training. The decision to bring the benchmarking training in house and train all team members using a case-study approach was critical to the success of the projects. Indeed, as the benchmarking process has developed within the utility division, team members have not only received an initial two-day training programme but have also participated in a one-day 'kick-off' workshop involving the team, project leader and project sponsor to ensure that everyone has a clear understanding of the scope and processes involved in the project. The combination of these two events is believed to provide 'best practice' in benchmarking project start-up procedures.

Why Benchmarking?

When NWW started to develop its formal approach to business quality and managing towards excellence it was decided to undertake a minimum of three benchmarking projects each year. The logic underlying this decision included:

- Through the mechanisms of a benchmarking project process owners would focus on what needed to be improved and would be motivated to do so by exposure to the practices seen outside the organization.
- By focusing on high-visibility key processes with the potential of a high return on investment the methodology and practice of benchmarking would be encouraged in diverse areas of the business.
- People would be required to look beyond their current process and, through comparison with other organizations, see and recognize opportunities for improvement.
- It would demonstrate to business unit management that current performance was not as good as initially thought, removing complacency and providing a platform for improvement.
- By focusing on processes rather than individuals the traditional 'blame culture' would be removed.
- It would increase the velocity of change from a public-sector-type approach to management and day-to-day work activities to that of industry leaders in the private sector. As part of this process it was expected to break down insular attitudes and behaviour which, at the time, were typically found in some areas of the business.

In 1995/6 three benchmarking projects were each sponsored by a director of NWW and facilitated by the Business Quality Group. The three projects were in the areas of customer service, laboratory services and operations. The customer services project involved looking at the process of customer call handling with respect to such areas as the time taken to answer calls and query/complaint resolution performance. In laboratory services the area addressed was the process of waste water sampling with consideration of the flow of information through the process, examining such factors as turnaround time of sampling, analysis, validation of results and archiving as well as percentage completion rates. In relation to operations the area of customer satisfaction within planned rehabilitation work was studied (the process of digging up roads to replace and/or repair water pipes, causing a disruption to supply), examining aspects such as communication with customers before, during and after work was carried out together with liaison with contractors.

From these three projects and other more recent projects carried out in the areas of plant services, procurement, employee communications, customer strategy and legal services, it is possible to identify some of the key issues for success, pitfalls and lessons which have been learnt. This information is presented in the form of guidelines to other organizations which may help to ensure that benchmarking projects are successful.

Success Factors

Each of the projects chosen related to key business processes which not only impacted on customers but also had the potential for considerable improvement resulting in a return on investment for the time and resources devoted to benchmarking activities. Each benchmarking team, to a greater or lesser extent, talked to its business partners (i.e. customers and suppliers), when determining the key performance indicators (KPI) for the project. The team reflected as far as possible a wide range of experience of the process being studied and also took into account individual skills and experience. Each team was assisted by a fully trained facilitator in benchmarking.

In each project the process was mapped to help improve understanding of what it was and how it was done. It was often found that, although it was generally thought that everyone involved knew the process being mapped, it was not until it had been mapped 'warts and all' that people actually realized what happened in it. This mapping also helped to communicate the subject area being benchmarked, helping to reflect what happens, and it was found that this was much more effective than simply referring to a set of procedures. This process mapping helped to pinpoint the weak areas of the process, which it is important to do before selecting benchmark partners. For example, the customer services project was able to extrapolate meaningful data from its process allowing the team to determine its current position in relation to the partners benchmarked and where it was being outperformed; this also facilitated a concentration of effort on specific process areas.

At the outset of the data-collection phase it is helpful to consider how the raw data collected are going to be managed and analysed. This involves thinking about what data are required to quantify the process in meaningful terms, how the data are going to be collected, whether they are already available from another source, and what information is needed about the process that is currently not known. It was also found beneficial to summarize the benefits of each benchmarking project into business, process and cost benefits for the area under consideration.

The choice of benchmarking partners is critical in the success and failure of the project, so it is important that due care and attention are paid to the selection. When contacting potential benchmarking partners it is helpful to identify the specific areas of activity and the measurement of success which are to be discussed during the visit. It was found to be important to send out a pack of information to those organizations who, in principle, had agreed to participate in a benchmarking project. The following is typical of the information it needed to include:

- Covering letter including the reason for undertaking the benchmarking project.
- Overview of the organization.
- Details of the process being benchmarked, including KPIs and their definitions and descriptions. For example, the customer services call-handling project included abandoned call rate, profile of calls in relation to peaks and troughs, staffing levels, number of customer services representatives available to take calls, number of calls dealt with by each customer services representative per day, average time to answer calls, call profile, service levels, percentage of enquiries dealt with in first call and percentage of repeat calls per customer on the same issue.
- Benchmarking code of conduct to be signed by both parties; reaching agreement on this encourages openness and trust between the partners.
- Data-collection plan.
- Questionnaire seeking data from the benchmarking partner and a completed questionnaire by the benchmarking team reflecting the state of the art of the process being benchmarked.

The benchmarking teams rated and selected their partners on the basis of their critical success factors in terms of what needed to be achieved by the project as well as such aspects as comparable size, structure, geography (where deemed appropriate), reputation with respect to product and service quality and market position and segmentation using a criteria rating form to focus on the critical few. Consideration was also given to their understanding and experience with benchmaking.

The key findings from each benchmarking visit were related to an action plan with respect to what is/had been implemented. This helped to ensure that the best practices identified were captured and acted upon. In addition, it was found to be important that the analysis identified common threads from the benchmarking visits. Simple graphical displays were used to communicate to all concerned the comparison of the KPI of the process being benchmarked with that of the partners. This assisted with the acceptance of changes that needed to be made, as well as with regular communication of progress, which was built into the project plan after the completion of each phase so that everyone concerned was up to speed before being presented with the project findings.

In the case of the laboratory services project the process being investigated was large and incorporated many different variables and sub-processes, depending on the type of sample. This made it difficult to map and evaluate the process in an effective manner (for example, to track performance measures such as the time taken between each process step). In retrospect the process was not sufficiently well defined to effectively benchmark, owing to its broad nature, scope and size. Also, there were constraints placed on the project which had not initially been understood, such as the technology used in the process. Furthermore, while the team did look outside its own industry, initially only companies with laboratories were considered. As the flow of information through the process was being considered this was perhaps too narrow an approach to selecting partners, and companies who dealt primarily with the analysis and processing of data should have been considered more closely.

The major constraint encountered by the operations refurbishment project was only looking inside the water industry for benchmarking partners. As benchmarking is about breakthrough improvement and the implementation of best practices, looking within the industry is insufficient as often the 'best' at particular practices are from diverse areas. This is a common problem for very specific benchmarking projects such as this, and needs to be watched and the insular attitudes it reflects avoided; teams need to think generically about what is being done rather than literally.

It is important to contact the benchmarking partners early. It can be more difficult than expected with respect to the time involved and the issue of identifying the right partner(s). Desk research into the companies being considered as benchmarking partners should be undertaken before making a decision, although this does depend on time constraints and the type of project being tackled. It has been found useful to visit four to five organizations, and to make all the visits within a period of one month. However, as the company is looking for high gains in the long term from benchmarking it is worthwhile taking the time to ensure that the company being benchmarked is suitable for analysis.

After each visit to a benchmarking partner it is important to detail and collate what has been learnt as quickly as possible while the experience is fresh in the team members' minds. It was also found helpful to summarize what the organization was doing better than the benchmark partner in a report format, identifying key points and providing quantitative as well as qualitative data.

Difficulties and Pitfalls

In order for a benchmarking project to be a success there are certain difficulties and pitfalls which must be avoided. Based on the projects undertaken the most common ones are:

- *Unrealistic assumptions.* When planning the actual project realistic assumptions need to be made about the time required to complete the individual steps of the benchmarking project, the resources needed and the commitment of employees, other than the team members. The planning of the project needs to be as pragmatic as possible. It is also important to 'manage' the expectations at senior management level in respect of quick results and instant benefits as well as their role in the benchmarking process.
- *The team members must be free to participate in the project.* The activities associated with the project should not become something else team members do as part of their normal working week as this will hamper progress and may seriously affect time-scales, commitment, and eventually the findings of the project.
- *Lack of a contingency plan.* If the project plan is based on a single set of circumstances or conditions, it is extremely vulnerable to changes. It is essential that a contingency plan is prepared to support the implementation and prepare for any unexpected major changes to the project. This contingency plan must be developed to cope with both favourable and adverse changes. If implementation is broken down into a number of sequential steps, then it must be possible to bring phase 2 forward if phase 1 takes less time than was initially expected, just as phase 2 would be delayed if phase 1 took longer than expected.
- *Failure to update the plan.* Too often the creation of a plan is seen as a means to an end. Instead the plan should be considered as a living document which

is based on certain assumptions, such as time, cost, resources and levels of commitment, as well as external factors such as the benchmarking partner's response and the time of year. These assumptions will almost certainly change over the period of a benchmarking project, requiring the plan to be updated in terms of what is required and when. In any reconfiguration of the original project the assumptions should be taken into account and any necessary changes made. For example, if the project is to finish on time more money may have to be spent on resources than was originally estimated to achieve any results of significance.

- *Failure to communicate the plan.* Communication of what has been done, what is currently being done and what is planned is vital to the success of a project. If people are not fully aware of what is expected of them, the type of information which has been gathered about best practice, how the benchmark information is to be used to initiate improvements and the changes that will result from the implementation of best practices found from the benchmarking project, then it is highly likely that the plan will fail. It is also important to consider what needs to be communicated and the detail, as well as how it should be done.
- *Inadequate project definition.* If the benchmarking team is not aware of why it is doing a particular project and its capability to change a process then the project will lack direction and focus, leaving the team unsure of what to measure and what best practices it is looking for.
- *Inadequate process understanding.* When documenting a process which is being benchmarked it is important that not only the processes should be described but also each process step plus the main practices. When carrying this out, the question 'How do we know this?' should be asked a number of times (i.e. the 5 'whys' approach) in order to validate what the team considers to be the process with those who are involved at each step. If this is not done then any conclusions drawn from the benchmarking study may be invalid and a potential danger to the present process.
- *Team members try to do everything themselves.* It is important that the team members do not become insular and try to do everything in relation to the project by themselves. At times they will need to seek the advice and help of individuals who are not directly involved in the benchmarking project. This assistance may be in areas such as data-collection, where the data required are already being collected by someone either within a department or externally.
- *The subject area is too large.* Unless the process is within the control of the team and within its comprehension then it is very difficult to both measure, in meaningful terms, what is done and ask the right questions of the benchmarking and business partners (e.g. customers and suppliers).
- *It seems like a good idea to use benchmarking* (i.e. it is the latest fad and fashion). Benchmarking, just like any other quality management technique, when used inappropriately, will not bring the expected benefits to the business. Therefore a balance should be reached between the scope of the problem, the return on investment which is expected and the level of improvement. There is little point in spending considerable time, money and resources on benchmarking a process which will not affect customers in any significant way by bringing breakthrough improvement to business operation.

Key Lessons

Based on the experience of carrying out the three benchmarking projects, the following is a summary of what is considered to be the key role and functions of (1) project sponsors (2) team leaders and (3) team members. Each group of people should be familiar with the role and function performed by the others. These guidelines will provide a form of health check of key considerations to be taken into account by organizations with respect to these type of roles.

Project sponsors

Sponsors should be clear that when carrying out a benchmarking study it is better to focus on a particular business process rather than the product or service. Businesses produce products and services, but it is processes that provide the end-product or service. By focusing on what is done and how it is done rather than just the end-product, more tangible results of a breakthrough nature can be obtained from the study. It should not be forgotten that some managers and directors perceive benchmarking to be simply a competitive analysis of products, services, equipment, factory facilities and operating costs.

The teams should be assembled from a range of skills and areas of expertise from within the process to be benchmarked, with roles and responsibilities assigned at the start in accordance with these skills and responsibilities (e.g. data-gatherers, communicators, etc.).

The narrower the focus of the investigation the greater the chance of success. By focusing on a specific process which has a clearly defined start- and end-point, that is well documented and within the team's ability to change, you will increase the chance not only of learning more about what is presently done but also of improving understanding and appreciation of how other organizations do it better, for example faster, cheaper, or with a better-quality service or product.

Management should be personally involved in the benchmarking process and the project sponsor should encourage their involvement. It is important to be seen to do more than just evaluate the success or failure of a project at its various review stages. They should, particularly in the case of a project sponsor, become involved in the activities of the project, particularly when benchmarking visits and the lessons learned from them are evaluated, so that they can understand more about the reasons for benchmarking and why the organization needs to constantly adapt and adopt best practices. The sponsor is critical to ensure that the project is carried through to the implementation stage, as projects often run in peaks and troughs and on occasions require someone to kick start them again.

It is useful for process 'experts' from outside the team to be involved in the preparation and validation of the questionnaire which will be used when determining who are to be the benchmarking partners and in gleaning information from the eventual partners. These personnel would be made up of both those involved in the day-to-day running of the process and those who are either its suppliers or customers.

When presenting the results of a benchmarking project it is useful not only to define improvements in areas such as customer satisfaction and reduced cycle time, but also to offset measures such as financial and operational savings against the cost of the project.

It is important to remember that it may not be feasible to emulate a world-class organization's processes straight away and, initially, it may be worthwhile benchmarking organizations which are best in class so that an understanding is achieved of the partners process, rather than being dazzled by it, and wondering 'How do we get there?'

Team leaders

The team leader is primarily responsible for the planning of the project and its management. It is useful at the start of each meeting to review the team's progress against the plan, particularly at the stages of collecting and analysing data, organizing visits to benchmarking partners, and recommending and implementing improvements to the process.

Communicate with people and the parties who are outside the team by using newsletters, bulletins on noticeboards, face-to-face discussions, and general updates to those who are required to buy in to the project, and undertake presentations, where appropriate, to individuals and departments who are crucial to successful implementation of the project findings.

Team members

Determine who are the customers and suppliers and hold discussions with them before deciding what are the success criteria and performance measures for the success of the project. Base the measures around what customers/suppliers require, as this is where improvements will be most tangible.

Provide a 'picture' of the process (e.g. a flowchart) to focus ideas and data-collection methodologies. By providing a picture of the process it is easier to identify what you need to know and where to concentrate understanding on what is currently being done.

Describe the process, the process steps and the practice at each step to help understanding of what is currently done and provide a reference point for change in the process at a later date: 'this is what used to be done and this is what is currently done and this is why it was changed and this is the result of the change'.

Balance what can be measured against what you would like to measure. It may be found that once the study has begun there are certain areas of the process which should be measured for the purposes of understanding both what is done and what others do, but that this is beyond current capability. It is beneficial to understand why this is so, and to do something about it before continuing with the benchmarking project. It should always be kept in mind, in particular, when carrying out a benchmarking visit, that the reason for benchmarking is to understand how other organizations and their people do things better.

Use specific measurables in the process to analyse the performance gap. Use simple tools such as a Z-chart (see figure 21.2) so that the position amongst partners can be demonstrated within the areas that have common measures as well as demonstrating what is required to achieve these levels of performance.

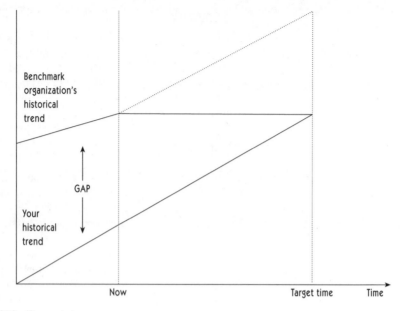

Figure 21.2   Gap analysis

Think generically when looking at other organizations' processes. It is important when considering partners to think beyond the industry in which you are personally involved. In other words, who does what best, or who is perceived to be the best, within the process being studied. This was a particular problem in the operations refurbishment project because of the specific nature of the activities under consideration.

Decide when benchmarking visits are not appropriate. It is important when determining partners that only the relevant few organizations are visited which offer the possibility that something of significance will be learnt. If this is not given adequate consideration, visits can become very much hit and miss, and learning from others becomes a matter of luck rather than the result of a systematic, structured approach.

Throughout the project, the team should be kept informed about what individual members are doing both at an informal and formal level. Team meetings should always have an agenda which is circulated well before the meeting (this should be decided by the team in advance and not dictated to it), with minutes being circulated within a few days of the meeting. As with any agenda the items for discussion/action should be prioritized, with appropriate times allocated to each item, just as would be expected in a project plan.

A record of what has been done, how it was done, and why it was done, should be kept for reference at a later date when a report is being prepared or other benchmarking projects are being started. A benchmarking log book is useful to keep for reference at a later date when producing the report.

Remember to ask the question 'How do we know?' when assessing what is done and what other people do. Hard evidence is needed to back up any assumptions made about internal processes and those of other organizations; this is preferable to saying 'It sounds like a good idea so let's do it!'

Summary

Benchmarking is a technique for the continuous improvement of business processes. It is therefore important to ensure that the process of benchmarking is thought of in a similar vein; the objective is the continual improvement of benchmarking process used for each project by sharing each project's successes, pitfalls, and failures and thereby promoting continuous learning. There is also a need to ensure that benchmarking is incorporated into an organization's culture of continuous improvement.

A benchmarking project is likely to generate other additional benchmarking projects within the process studied or with interfacing processes. A project, in addition to the savings generated, is also helpful in promoting understanding of key performance indicators and measures of quality; in other words, what do we need to have in place to understand what we do, how we do it, why we do it, and how well we do it.

The reasons for NWW undertaking a series of benchmarking projects were communicated across the organization and included:

- It solves problems which are important to the business rather than leaving people to pursue 'pet' projects.
- It is based on a systematic approach and reality, not history or gut instinct.
- Benchmarking projects are proactive rather than reactive.
- The results allow for controlled change rather than frantic catching up.
- They are focused on objective evaluation rather than subjective perceptions.

The main benefits achieved were:

- Average annual savings of £1 million.
- The identification of where North West Water was in relation to the outside world.
- It demonstrated the potential to improve key processes, thereby increasing motivation and facilitating the commitment to change. This is very important in facilitating improvement in a monopoly supplier environment.
- It proved the usefulness of benchmarking as a concept and quality management technique.
- It removed complacency and the 'not invented here' syndrome ('They do that but we can't because we're different').

It became clear as the benchmarking studies progressed that, while lots of organizations and people use the benchmarking jargon, much of the discussion relates to competitive analysis of product and equipment and not the benchmarking of processes. While the benchmarking concept is relatively simple, the difficulties involved in progressing a benchmarking project are not often realized. A case in point is step 3 in the benchmarking process, 'Identify best in class': experience from this study indicates that it takes some degree of investigation and analysis to identify best-in-class organizations, particularly if the project has been poorly defined, with no clearly identifiable process; the more unusual the process being benchmarked the more difficult this becomes and the more difficult to identify meaningful generic data and questions. In specific processes, such as the ones investigated as part of the operations refurbishment project, there is a tendency for the benchmarking team members not to be willing to look outside their own industry sector and to concentrate on the functionality of the process steps rather than thinking in terms of what they do (e.g. communicate positively, effectively and helpfully with their customers).

The experience of benchmarking at NWW indicates that it takes around six months to undertake and implement the findings of a benchmarking project. From the benchmarking projects undertaken a number of key lessons have been learnt. These have been distilled in the form of success factors and pitfalls to be avoided. It is hoped that these will serve as guidelines to other organizations which help to ensure that any benchmarking projects are effective. The key roles of a project sponsor, team leader and team member have been identified as crucial for success. The guidelines outlined in this chapter can prove helpful to other organizations in communicating to these three groups of people what is expected of them.

It is clear from study of the benchmarking literature that much of the material is very similar. The tendency is to focus on issues such as the history of benchmarking, the process steps and general discussion of benefits and potential problems. There appears to be a sparsity of written material based on actual benchmarking experiences. The study reported in this chapter goes some way towards extending knowledge of the benchmarking concept.

References

Anderson, B. and Patterson, P. G. (1996), *The Benchmarking Handbook*. London: Chapman & Hall.

Camp, R. C. (1989), *Benchmarking: The Search for Industry Best Practice that Leads to Superior Performance*. Milwaukee: ASQC Quality Press.

Camp, R. C. (1995), *Business Process Benchmarking: Finding and Implementing the Best Practices*. Milwaukee: ASQC Quality Press.

Codling, S. (1995), *Best Practice Benchmarking*. Hampshire: Gower Press.

Cook, S. (1993), *Practical Benchmarking: A Manager's Guide to Creating a Competitive Advantage*. London: Kogan Page.

Hanson, P. and Voss, C. (1995), Benchmarking best practice in European manufacturing sites. *Business Process Re-engineering and Management Journal*, 1(1), 60–74.

Leonard, K. J. (1996), Information systems and benchmarking in the credit scoring industry. *Benchmarking for Quality Management and Technology*, 3(1), 38–44.

Prasad, S., Tata, J. and Thorn, R. (1996), Benchmarking Maquiladora operations relative to those in the USA. *International Journal of Quality and Reliability Management*, 13(9), 8–17.

Zairi, M. (1995), The integration of benchmarking and BPR: a matter of choice or necessity? *Business Process Re-Engineering and Management Journal*, 1(3), 3–9.

Zairi, M. and Leonard, P. (1994), *Practical Benchmarking: A Complete Guide*. London: Chapman & Hall.

chapter twenty-two

Business Process Re-engineering

J. Macdonald and B. G. Dale

Introduction

Business process re-engineering (BPR) was popularized as a formal concept by the writings of Hammer (1990), Davenport and Short (1990) and Hammer and Champy (1993), but perhaps James Harrington (1987), with his emphasis on process improvement in action, was the real originator. The earlier work of Hammer and the later expanded version of Hammer and Champy tended to focus on corporate transformation while the other influential text of Davenport and Short has a focus on business process redesign, linking the concept specifically to developments in technology and industrial engineering. Many of the first cases of BPR had a heavy focus on information technology, to enable redesign implementation.

In recent times BPR has emerged as the concept which enables an organization to take a radical and revolutionary look at the way in which it operates and the way work is done, and references to it abound in management and technical publications with such words as 'radical', 'dramatic', 'rethinking', 'optimize', 'redesign'. It has become popular in a short period of time, promising amazing results very quickly in relation to corporate and technological change, transformation and competitive pressures. Some writers (e.g. Born 1994) regard it is a successor to TQM, making the point that, rather than continually improving a process, BPR challenges the need for a process. The protagonists of BPR argue that it, rather than TQM, is the concept which enables an organization to make the necessary step changes, originality and improvements to the business which will enable it to leapfrog the competition. On the other hand, writers such as Zairi (1996) and Harrington (1998) believe that BPR will soon fall out of favour with industrialists. There is an emerging view in the literature (e.g. Elzinga et al. 1995; De Toro and McCabe 1997; Zairi 1997) that business process management (BPM) is a better option. Martinsons and Revenaugh (1997) report that:

> Many managers now even avoid using the term whenever and wherever possible. Partly because its emergence coincided with a worldwide recession, BPR is now commonly associated with two things: (1) inflated consultancy bills and (2) slash and burn corporate 'downsizing'.

While TQM is based, in general, on continuous improvement in processes over a relatively long period of time, BPR emphasizes structural process redesign, process re-engineering and fundamental rethinking of the business by ignoring the status quo, leading to claims of producing faster returns in a relatively short period of time through its one-step solution to a problem. They are both philosophies to improve the performance of a business, but in the authors' view continuous improvement should come first and provide the base for the more radical change and improvements generated by BPR. It should also not be overlooked that TQM also drives breakthrough improvements.

The underlying issues in BPR are not necessarily new, albeit the language and approach is modern. The early material on the subject made little mention that the approach had its origins in other change initiatives and concepts. Its roots are to be found in scientific management (e.g. Taylor 1911); the system theories proposed by Beer (1981); the breakthrough concepts through a process approach advocated by Juran (1964); the benchmarking initiatives outlined by Camp (1989); the group technology concept pioneered by Burbidge (1963); work study concepts as typically outlined by Currie (1989); improvement initiatives in manufacturing systems proposed by Schonberger (1986), and modern information, communications and systems technology.

There is some confusion as to what constitutes BPR, what it covers, which initiatives it embraces, and its relationship with TQM. This is not helped by the variety of terms (e.g. business process improvement, business process redesign, business process re-engineering, core value-driven process re-engineering, process redesign, business restructuring, new industrial engineering, process simplification and value management) that authors use in their description of BPR, along with the associated imprecision with which the use them. However, most of the terms refer to roughly the same type of activity, pointing out that gains in performance can be achieved by taking a holistic and objective view of business processes.

The authors, along with writers such as Harrington (1995) and Kelada (1995), view TQM and BPR as complementary and integral approaches rather than ones that are in opposition to each other (see Macdonald 1995a). In fact many of the tools and techniques which have been proved and used in continuous improvement are employed in BPR projects, and a number of the principles and practices of BPR are very similar to those which underpin TQM. Our combined practical and research evidence points to the fact that those companies which have been successful in building continuous improvement principles into their business operation in an evolutionary manner have created the solid platform and environment on which to develop the concept of BPR. Those organizations starting with TQM will have a better understanding of processes, which is central to both TQM and BPR. Having learned how to change using the continuous improvement philosophy, they are more ready to deal with the more radical designing of new processes which is demanded by BPR. In general, it has been service industries and public sector organizations which have taken up the theme of BPR rather than manufacturing industry. It would be argued by managers in the former that, without BPR having been undertaken as part of the natural management process of running a business, they would simply not have survived. In general, service industries and the public sector have only relatively recently felt the winds of change.

As outlined in chapter 1, management have a tendency to be attracted to those initiatives which are easy to understand and can give them fast results. Attracted by consultants' promises of what BPR is about and what it can achieve, some manage-ments have been led to believe that it has superseded TQM. The justification for including the chapter on BPR in this book is to help managers identify the common-alities and differences. The aim is to present, in simple terms, what BPR means, its main approaches and methods, techniques employed and main principles and practices.

Approaches Used in BPR

The two main approaches employed in BPR are process redesign and process re-engineering, and these are examined below. The approaches are based on taking a holistic and objective view of the core processes that are needed to accomplish specific business objectives without being constrained by what already exists (i.e. 'clean slate'). BPR covers a range of activities that result in radical change, to either individual processes or to the total organization. The main differences between the two approaches are that the latter involves greater structural change and risk while the former is quicker and less costly to implement but with potentially fewer benefits and improvements.

Business Process Redesign

Hammer and Champy (1993) point out that every re-engineering measure usually starts with process redesign. Process redesign can be carried out in many different ways depending on the degree to which the process is to be changed; it usually takes the existing process(es) as the base. It concentrates on those core processes with cross-functional boundaries and is generally customer-focused, with a view to process simplification, streamlining, mistake-proofing the process, efficiency and adaptability. It tends to seek answers to questions such as:

- What is this process doing?
- What are the core competencies?
- What are the key elements?
- What are its key measurables?
- What are the main information flows?
- Is the process necessary?
- Is it adding value?
- Is it producing an output which fully meets customer requirements?
- How can it be improved?
- How can it be done differently?
- Who is the process owner?
- Can it be done by someone less skilled?
- Is the technology employed used to best advantage?
- Can new technology provide new solutions?
- Can activities be integrated?
- Can activities be done in parallel?

Process redesign has its roots in departmental purpose analysis (see chapter 16), which originated at IBM in 1984. It also uses many of the techniques used in organization and method (O&M) and work study, but employs modern methods of information technology to best advantage, in particular for integrating process activities. The emphasis has been on rationable databases, communication technology and networked personal computers to enable information to be shared and kept up to date, facilitating processes to be undertaken in simultaneous mode. Process redesign would be difficult to achieve without the formalized procedures arising from the application of a quality management system.

Business process re-engineering

Process re-engineering or new process design demands more imagination and inductive thinking and radical change than process redesign, with those charged with the implementation of a project encouraged to abandon their belief in the rules, procedures, practices, systems and values that have shaped the current organization. It raises and challenges assumptions such as make or buy decisions, structures, functional responsibilities and tasks, systems and documentation (e.g. supplier payment), elimination of specialist departments, etc. Hammer and Champy (1993) define re-engineering as:

> A fundamental rethink and radical redesign of business processes to achieve dramatic improvements in critical contemporary measures of performance, such as cost, quality, service and speed.

The approach is based on the view that continuous improvement is not sufficient to meet the organizational expectations for business development and change. Business process re-engineering seeks to make major fundamental, radical and dramatic breakthroughs in performance and is holistic in nature. The main focus is to ensure a 'clean slate' or 'greenfield' approach to processes, pinpointing that part of the organization on which to put the emphasis and highlighting the processes which add value. It is, however, not without the risks and demands on resources, time and costs which are associated with the efforts involved in a re-engineering project.

The concept is based on making best use of information technology (IT) in terms of communication and information-handling systems. It harnesses the enablers of technology and the release of the innovative potential of people to achieve breakthrough improvements, requiring a change from functional thinking to process thinking.

The Principles of BPR

The fundamental principles of BPR represent good management practice. Despite the difference in emphasis and terminology used by various authors the principles and values remain relatively common. From publications such as Hammer and Champy (1993), Macdonald (1995a, 1995b), Tinnila (1995) and Coulson-Thomas (1994), the main principles of BPR can be summarized as follows.

- Strategic in concept
- Customer-focused
- Output- rather than input-focused

- Focus on key business processes
- Process responsibility and decisions at the point where work is performed
- Cross-functional in nature
- Involve internal and external customer–supplier relationships
- Involve senior management commitment and involvement
- Involve networking people and their activities
- Involve integration of people and technical aspects
- Require clear communication and visibility
- Have a mindset of outrageous improvement
- People at all levels of the organization must be prepared to question the status quo in terms of technology, practices, procedures, approaches, strategies

A number of these principles are similar to those which are related to TQM as outlined in chapter 1.

Risks and Benefits of BPR

BPR projects tend to be across functional boundaries, eliminating functions and processes and changing their boundaries, and challenging the existing norms. Consequently, there are a number of risks associated with BPR and these need to be balanced against the potential rewards and benefits, including:

- The wrong processes are selected for BPR. If they are not core processes, the impact on the business will be of limited value.
- Inadequate analysis, planning and assessment, in particular, of current state analysis and process design.
- The upheaval and costs outweigh the savings, in particular, when the changes impact negatively on delivery schedules in terms of response and development times to customers.
- The long cycle time needed to complete a project and produce beneficial results to a business.
- Management and staff do not provide the necessary leadership and direction to the process (i.e. poor change management), and projects therefore fail to realize their potential.
- People fail to take ownership of the initiative.
- It excludes people from the lower levels of the organizational hierarchy in the design and building of new processes.
- Lack of attention to the so-called 'soft issues'.
- Misconceptions relating to downsizing and restructuring, creating resistance to change.
- Destruction of teams and teamwork.

There are a number of barriers that can inhibit radical change, including:

- Traditional management behaviour.
- Opposition based on fear of what the change might entail, in particular during downsizing, delayering and outsourcing.
- Lack of resources, time, commitment and 'belief'.
- The investment required in information technology and other systems.

A related issue to risks and barriers is the issue of how an organization's culture can adapt to empowerment. Empowerment within an organization's process will have a direct impact upon process expectations and system design. This impact may be within the re-engineered process and also at the point where that process affects others.

Useful discussion on the lack of success with BPR projects is provided by writers such as Deakins and Makgill (1997), King (1994), Hall et al. (1993), Kennedy (1994) and O'Brien (1995). Geisler (1997) has produced a book which not only identifies what went wrong with BPR but outlines how to recover from the effects of radical change.

The processes selected for BPR should be based on issues such as: critical success factors, significance to the business, degree of process failure, customer concerns, volume of paperwork, long lead-time, controls, degree of firefighting activities and financial cost to the organization.

The benefits of BPR include:

- Increased customer focus
- Improved profitability
- Improved quality and control
- Improved corporate flexibility
- Increases speed of service delivery and responsiveness
- Improved measurability within the processes operation and the management of that information

Implementation of BPR

Chan and Peel (1998) have carried out research which points to the fact that BPR results from external factors such as customers, competition and change, and from internal factors, including technology, efficiency, cost and strategic focus. In approaching implementation these motivational factors or drivers should be taken into consideration.

The implementation of BPR requires a greenfield approach along the lines of 'If we were to start this company now, with the knowledge we have, how would it be organized?' The focus is looking at completely new ways of accomplishing work, i.e. redesigning from scratch. However, there is no single methodology for BPR and an organization should adopt the appropriate practices which suit it best. The following are the key factors in the implementation of a successful BPR project:

Project champion

BPR will involve a number of cross-functional issues and strategic decisions; thus the sponsor of a BPR project must be a senior manager. The tendency to appoint the IT director or human resources director as the champion of a BPR project should be avoided because of the impact of technology on people. The champion should establish the vision and goals, allocate resources, empower employees, hold employees accountable for the activities allocated to them, resolve functional and departmental conflicts, and communicate and champion change.

Steering committee

As with all major projects it is recommended that a steering committee of appropriate personnel and representatives from major stakeholders is established. Its role will include:

- Develop policy.
- Define the improvement objectives and develop a vision statement for the process.
- Manage the project against the agreed time-scale.
- Provide resources and ensure that appropriate people are involved in the project.
- Ensure that the individuals involved have the right set of skills and techniques.
- Identify issues and resolve them.
- Challenge the status quo and continually ask the 5 whys.
- Resolve functional conflicts.

Process design team

Establish a process design team of six to eight members who have the appropriate skills, expertise and knowledge of processes and their analysis and measurement, facilitation and project management, IT and data-handling, innovation and creative thought, and team-building. Consultants and equipment suppliers often provide a useful supplement to the team. According to the project and the size of the organization, some members of the team may have to be full-time. This is justified on the basis that whole parts of the business may be subjected to re-engineering and by the length of time which is therefore needed to complete the project. The team must decide how to allocate tasks and whether or not to establish mini-teams to focus on sub-processes. It must also have regard for the potential effects that the processes redesign will have upon other existing processes.

The role of the team includes:

- Identify and map the current state of the existing processes involved in the project along with their related information flows.
- Define and understand the existing processes.
- Identify the critical processes.
- Challenge all assumptions surrounding the processes and how they have developed.
- Accept no boundaries or demarcations.
- Find breakthrough improvements.
- Design the new processes.
- Ensure that the people who will be affected are involved in the process.
- Decide how the changes will be measured and assessed.
- Pilot the changes and modify the design, as appropriate.
- Remain customer-focused throughout the whole of the redesign.
- Present the recommendations to the project sponsor and steering committee.
- Communicate on a regular basis with all those likely to be affected by the change.

Process owner

Once the process design team's recommendations have been accepted, the implementation phase can begin. This usually involves disbanding the team and the establishment of a process owner, responsible for the actual re-engineering and accountable for the process goals. This should be a senior manager selected from the process design team. The role includes:

- Ensuring that the plans are fully implemented.
- Obtaining and organizing the necessary resources.
- Selecting the implementation team.
- Overcoming any resistance to the changes.
- Encouraging people to follow the new ways of working.
- Managing the new process.
- Ensuring that the goals are achieved.

Implementation team

The team members are effectively the managers of the newly designed process. They will usually be drawn from the membership of the process design team.

BPR methodology

There are four main phases of a BPR project: preparation, innovation and design, implementation and assessment.

Preparation

The main activities in this phase are:

- Review the strategic objectives of the business as this will provide an indication of the need for BPR. From this review the decisions will be taken to redesign the key processes of the organization in line with the business objective. It also involves the setting of objectives for others.
- Choose the BPR project. This will include establishing the team and educating its members in the fundamentals of BPR.
- Map the strategic processes of the project as it is, concentrating on the big picture. The typical tools and techniques to assist with this are described in chapter 16.
- Identify and define customer needs and requirements, and pinpoint which of the key processes have the greatest influence on the customer. This will involve customer surveys and the like.
- Define strategies that can match business needs and characteristics with customer requirements.

- Through various activities identify the 'breakthrough' theme.
- Obtain steering committee approval for the ideas and develop clear objectives for the design team.

Innovation and design

This phase involves the following:

- Develop vision statements for the BPR project in order to represent an organization which has the following characteristics:

  - Based on a customer-orientated process
  - Customer needs and requirements determine products and services
  - IT services are designed to empower employees to serve customers
  - One point of contact and a unified face to the customer
  - All employees are clearly focused on the customer.

- Encourage the team to think outside of functions and processes and forget boundaries, hierarchies, authorities and limits of current systems and technology.
- The role of information technology in providing the radical change is important. The IT department should focus its efforts on the processes which have been redesigned or re-engineered.
- Be realistic about what BPR can achieve and ensure that the initiative is integrated with other improvement initiatives and infrastructures, in particular, existing processes and their expectations.
- Redesign or re-engineer the selected processes.
- The organization should be prepared for the change and address issues such as:

  - Restructuring the basic organization and reporting procedures
  - Redeployment planning
  - Payment and reward.

Implementation

This phase involves:

- Developing an implementation plan.
- Implementing the new process design in pilot mode.
- Agreeing the goals and objectives for the redesigned process and communicating them to all concerned.
- Developing rational metrics for the newly designed process.
- Addressing the cultural and people issues to support the smooth work of the re-engineered processes. This may require that the new process design be implemented in a number of phases. This will allow the people skills and other processes that affect the re-engineered process to develop at an effective speed and acceptable cost.

- Emphasizing teamwork, using the concept of the 'one-stop' shop and technology to share 'specialist' knowledge through 'generalist' team players.
- Developing education and training programmes to provide specific skills for employees to fulfil their new role.

Assessment

This involves:

- Deciding the methods of recording, monitoring and evaluating the effects of the changes.
- Managing the re-engineered business.
- Managing the people dimensions.
- Maintaining the change.
- Exploiting the gains.
- Reviewing and improving the methods for BPR.

Summary

The principles and practices of BPR have their base in other concepts such as TQM, work study, group technology, etc. The same applies to the tools and techniques used in BPR. The authors are of the view that BPR is complementary to TQM, rather than being an alternative or in opposition to it. For example, TQM can help to 'hold the gains' achieved through BPR and can create an environment that will help to ensure the success of BPR projects. The claims that BPR is a successor to TQM should be dismissed.

There has been considerable debate on the key differences between BPR and TQM. In short the former is based, in general, on radical and breakthrough change over a relatively short period, and the latter is based, in general, on incremental improvement over the longer term and on working within existing framework systems and procedures by improving them. This distinction is outlined in pictorial form by Imai (1986). In the authors' view, aiming for large step changes makes a project riskier and more complex, and also involves greater expense. Incremental change is safer and costs less. The simplicity of incremental improvement often overshadows the fact that in practice it requires effort and constant application to implement in an effective and efficient manner.

TQM and BPR do share common themes, such as a focus on customers, key processes, eliminating waste, and benchmarking. One of the key differences is that BPR places more emphasis on equipment and technology and TQM more emphasis on people. BPR tends to concentrate on one process at a time using a project-planning methodology, whereas TQM takes a more holistic view of the organization, building improvement into all its areas of operation. Total quality management acts as the foundation for an organization's day-to-day functioning and continual improvement that allows and supports the development of BPR as an effective business improvement tool. To get the best out of both concepts they should be combined and integrated to produce a comprehensive approach to business improvement. As mentioned in chapter 7, TQM can sometimes stall and plateau, and other initiatives, within the overall framework of the approach, can often provide the spark to revitalize it. BPR could provide this type of excitement, but to do so it needs to be positioned within the broader TQM approach.

BPR requires dedication, acceptance of risk and considerable upheaval. It is important that an organization is clear on this because it is so easy to find it in conflict with the potential cost savings. Not every organization is capable of accomplishing the level of change required, but any organization that has the ambition to be the best cannot ignore BPR but must accept the challenge. Some industries which operate in dynamic environments are more suited to taking on the risks associated with BPR than others, where the disturbance of processes could have severe consequences. It is also important for organizations to be clear on whether they need business process redesign or the more radical process re-engineering. Both are important to stimulate process innovation so that organizations can become more agile in responding to unpredictable changes and respond quickly to the needs and demands of customers.

Managers are central to the success of re-engineering projects and they must be prepared to change their role and power structures and provide the necessary leadership; see chapter 2.

References

Beer, S. (1981), *The Brain of the Firm*. Chichester: John Wiley.

Born, G. (1994), *Process Management to Quality Improvement*. Chichester: John Wiley.

Burbidge, J. L. (1963), Production flow analysis. *The Production Engineer*, 42(12), 742–52.

Camp, R. C. (1989), *Benchmarking: The Search for Industry Best Practices that Lead to Superior Performance*. Milwaukee: ASQC Quality Press.

Chan, P. S. and Peel, D. (1998), Causes and impact of re-engineering. *Business Process Management Journal*, 4(1), 44–5.

Coulson-Thomas, C. (1994), *Business Process Re-engineering: Myth and Reality*. London: Kogan Page.

Currie, R. M. (1989), *Work Study*. London: Pitman.

Davenport, T. H. and Short, J. E. (1990), The new industrial engineering: information technology and business process re-design. *Sloan Management Review*, 31(4), 11–27.

Deakins, E. and Makgill, H. H. (1997), What killed BPR? Some evidence from the literature. *Business Process Management Journal*, 3(1), 81–107.

De Toro, I. and McCabe, T. (1997), How to stay flexible and elude fads. *Quality Progress*, 30(3), 55–60.

Elzinga, D. J., Horok, T., Chung-Yee, L. and Bruner, C. (1995), Business process management: survey and methodology. *IEEE Transactions on Engineering Management*, 24(2), 119–28.

Geisler, E. (1997), *Managing the Aftermath of Radical Corporate Change: Re-engineering, Restructuring, and Re-invention*. Westport, Conn.: Quorum Books.

Hall, G., Rosenthal, J. and Wade, J. (1993), How does re-engineering really work? *Harvard Business Review*, November–December, 119–31.

Hammer, M. (1990), Re-engineering work: don't automate, obliterate. *Harvard Business Review*, 68(4), 104–12.

Hammer, M. and Champy, J. (1993), *Re-engineering the Corporation*. London: Nicholas Brealey.

Harrington, H. J. (1987), *The Improvement Process*. New York: McGraw Hill.

Harrington, H. J. (1995), *Total Improvement Management: The Next Generation in Performance Improvement*. New York: McGraw Hill.

Harrington, H. J. (1998), Performance improvement: the rise and fall of re-engineering. *The TQM Magazine*, 10(2), 69–71.

Imai, M. (1986), *Kaizen: The Key to Japan's Success*. New York: Random House.

Juran, J. M. (1964), *Managerial Breakthrough*. New York: McGraw Hill.

Kelada, J. N. (1995), *Integrating Re-engineering with Total Quality*. Milwaukee: ASQC Quality Press.

Kennedy, C. (1994), Re-engineering: the human costs and benefits. *Long-Range Planning*, 27(5), 64–72.

King, W. R. (1994), Process re-engineering: the strategic dimensions. *Information Systems Management*, 11(2), 71–3.

Macdonald, J. (1995a), *Understanding Business Process Re-engineering*. London: Hodder & Stoughton.

Macdonald, J. (1995b), Together TQM and BPR are winners. *The TQM Magazine*, 7(3), 21–5.

Martinsons, M. G. and Revenaugh, D. L. (1997), Re-engineering is dead: long live re-engineering. *International Journal of Information Management*, 17(2), 79–82.

O'Brien, B. (1995), *Decisions about Re-engineering: Briefings on Issues and Options*. London: Chapman & Hall.

Schonberger, R. J. (1986), *World-Class Manufacturing: The Principles of Simplicity Applied*. New York: Free Press.

Taylor, F. W. (1911), *The Principles of Scientific Management*. London: Harper & Row.

Tinnila, M. (1995), Strategic perspective to business process re-design. *Management Decision*, 33(3), 25–34.

Zairi, M. (1996), Uninspired by re-engineering. *Strategic Insights into Quality*, 4(1), 19–20.

Zairi, M. (1997), Business process management: a boundaryless approach to modern competitiveness. *Business Process Management*, 3(1), 674–80.

chapter twenty-three

Teams and Teamwork

B. G. Dale

Introduction

The development of people and their involvement in improvement activities both individually and through teamwork is a key feature in a company's approach to TQM. A key aspect of this is making full use of the skills and knowledge of all employees to the benefit of the individuals and the organization and to create a group culture. There are a number of different types of teams with different operating characteristics, all of which can act as a vehicle for getting people involved in improvement activities and improving organizational performance. Teams can be found everywhere and for almost everything, and most organizations have them. Some teams have a narrow focus, with members coming from one functional area; others are wider and cross-functional, dealing with the deep-rooted problems between internal customers and suppliers. Each type of team has its advantages. The names given to the teams are varied and include quality circles (QCs), yield improvement teams (YITs), quality improvement teams, continuous improvement teams, cost reduction teams, problem elimination teams, self-directed work teams, self-managing teams, process improvement groups, task groups, SPC teams, error cause removal teams, corrective action teams, kaizen teams and cross-functional teams, in areas such as design, quality assurance, costs, standardization, delivery and supply. There are groups of people already working together who are also involved in continuous improvement activity and form hybrids between two or more types of team. There is also interaction between different teams, and this form of team activity needs to be effective.

Japanese companies and their people are much more comfortable with the use of teams and teamwork as part of their continuous improvement efforts than is usually the case in European companies. This may be because of the divisive nature of Western industry: 'them and us', 'management and unions', 'staff and hourly paid', 'headquarters and operating locations', 'What's in it for me?', etc. It is often the case in European organizations that management will decide to launch some form of team activity as part of an improvement initiative, put the members together and expect the team to work in an effective manner without any form of training, coaching, direction, management attention, counselling or team-building. In such circumstances it is little wonder that the team starts to flounder within a few months of its inception.

This chapter, which is based on the UMIST research on teams (e.g. Dale and Lees 1986; Manson and Dale 1989; Briggs et al. 1993; Boaden et al. 1991; Dale and Huke 1996) and practical experience of working with teams in many different types of organization, examines the role of teamwork in a process of continuous improvement and outlines the operating characteristics of project teams, quality circles and quality improvement teams. The key constituents of teams in terms of sponsor, facilitator, leader and member are outlined. A method for evaluating the health of teams is described. Some guidelines are also given which should help to ensure that teams are both active and effective.

The Role of Teams in Continuous Improvement

Teams have a number of roles to play as a component in a process of continuous improvement. Teams can:

- Aid the commitment of people to the principles of TQM.
- Provide an additional means of communication between individuals, management and their direct reports, across functions and with customers and suppliers.
- Provide the means and opportunity for people to participate in decision-making about how the business operates.
- Improve relationships, and knowledge, develop trust, facilitate co-operative activity and adjust to change.
- Help to develop people and encourage leadership traits.
- Build collective responsibility and develop a sense of ownership.
- Aid personal development and build confidence.
- Develop problem-solving skills.
- Facilitate awareness of quality improvement potential, leading to behaviour and attitude change.
- Help to facilitate a change in management style and culture.
- Solve problems.
- Imbue a sense of accomplishment.
- Improve the adoption of new products to the production line.
- Improve morale.
- Improve operating effectiveness as people work in a common direction and through this generate interaction and synergy.

In 1993 the American Society for Quality Control (ASQC) commissioned the Gallup organization to assess employee attitudes on teamwork, empowerment and quality improvement. The survey of 1,293 adults, who were employed full-time, focused on a variety of topics, including extent of participation in quality teams, employee feelings of empowerment, and effects of technology and teamwork on empowerment. It was found that there was a high level of employee participation in quality improvement teamwork and there was considerable evidence which pointed to the positive effects of quality and teamwork on employee empowerment. It was also found that employees are very clear on the purpose of quality-related teamwork, under its multitude of names, and that those employees participating in such team-work are also more likely to receive training than those who do not participate.

Types of Teams

In the superior-performing organization teamwork is second nature. For example, the senior management work together as an effective team, managers of the various operating and functional units act as a team, people from different functions co-operate in the team activities which are needed in FMEA, SPC, simultaneous engin-eering, benchmarking, supplier development, ISO9000 quality management series registration and internal audits. In addition to teamwork within functions, it is common to find teams working together across the business. In some cases (see e.g. Crosby 1979) teams are hierarchical in nature – a corrective action team is formed on a directive from a quality improvement team. Unless effective teamworking and cohesion is seen at the top of an organization, it is unlikely that the managers will be able to encourage their employees to work effectively in teams. The superior-performing organizations use a variety of ways to facilitate team-building, improve relationships and reinforce the teamwork ethic. For example, Dale and Huke (1996), writing about their experiences in Hong Kong, give examples such as: carnivals, team competitions, social and recreational activities, and entry into the dragon boat race competition. Having made the case for teams it is important for the manage-ment of an organization to decide when and how to use teams, and what are the appropriate conditions that need to be in play.

There is a variety of types of teams with differing characteristics in terms of membership, mode of participation, autonomy, problem selection, scope of activity, decision-making authority, access to information, problem-solving potential, resources, and permanency which can be used in the improvement process. It is important that the right type of team is formed for the project, problem, or activity under con-sideration and that a working definition of the team is decided upon. Below are listed the most popular types of teams.

Project teams

As already discussed in chapter 1, the drive to improve quality originates at the top of an organization. If senior management identify the main problems facing the organization, key improvement issues can be developed which are then allocated amongst their membership for consideration as a one-off project. The project owner then selects employees to constitute a team which will consider the improvement issue. The owner can either lead the team themselves or act as 'foster-parent', 'sponsor' or 'guardian angel' to the team. Through participation in project teams, managers better understand the problem-solving process and become more sensitive to the problems faced by other types of teams. The senior management project team is one example of this type of team, but there are others. The typical characteristics of such teams are:

- The objective has been defined by senior management.
- The team is led by management.
- It is temporary in nature.
- The project is specific and significant, perhaps addressing issues of strategic change, and will have clear deliverables within a set time-scale.
- The team is organized in such a way to ensure that it employs the appropriate talents, skills, and functions which are suitable in resolution of the project.
- The scope of activity tends to be cross-functional.
- Participation is not usually voluntary – a person is requested by senior management to join the team and this is done on the basis of their expertise in areas related to the project being tackled.
- Team meetings tend to be of long rather than of short duration, although they occur on a regular basis.

Quality circles

Quality circles, when operated in the classical manner, have characteristics which are different from other methods of teamwork. They have been the subject of many books (e.g. Hutchins 1985; Mohr and Mohr 1983; Robson 1984) and the focus of much research (e.g. Bradley and Hill 1983; Hayward et al. 1985; Hill 1986), almost to the exclusion of research on other types of team activity. QCs, in the classical sense, have not been too 'successful' in Western organizations. They were short-lived and tended to fade out in the mid-1980s. In the author's opinion this is because they were introduced at a time in the West when organizations and their management did not fully understand and practise the principles of TQM and their experience of collaboration in the work environment was limited. A vast amount of experience was, however, acquired in the operation of QCs, much of which has been well documented. It is suggested that any organization wishing to develop effective teamwork and resolve some of the issues which arise in the operation of teams should consult the written wisdom on QCs, because they will find much good advice on facilitation, problem-solving skills, organization of meetings and maintaining the momentum.

A quality circle is a voluntary group of six to eight employees from the same work area. They meet, usually in company time, for one hour every week or fortnight, under the leadership of their work supervisor, to solve problems relating to improving their work activities and environment. The typical characteristics of QCs are:

- Membership is voluntary and people can opt out as and when they wish.
- Members are usually drawn from a single department and are doing similar work.
- All members are of equal status.
- They operate within the existing organizational structure.
- Members are free to select, from their own work area, the problems and projects which they wish to tackle – these tend to be the ones they have to live with every day; there is little or no interference from management.
- Members are trained in the use of the seven basic quality control tools, meeting skills, facilitation, team-building, project management and presentation techniques.

- Appropriate data-collection and problem-solving skills and decision-making methods are applied by QC members to the project under consideration.
- Meetings are generally short, but a large number are held.
- There is minimum pressure to solve the problem within a set time-frame.
- A facilitator is available to assist the QC with the project.
- The solutions are evaluated in terms of their cost-effectiveness.
- The findings, solutions and recommendations of the QC are shown to management for comment and approval, usually in a formal presentation.
- The QC implements the recommendations, where practicable.
- Once implemented, the QC monitors the effects of the solution and considers future improvements.
- The QC carries out a critical review of all its activities related to the completed project.

Fabi (1992) has carried out a wide-ranging analysis of the literature published between 1982 and 1989 on QCs and from this has analysed 40 empirical studies undertaken on QCs. From examination of this work, using contingency factors, he has identified the following factors which are critical to the success of QCs:

- Management commitment and support
- Involvement and support of employees and unions
- Training of members and leaders
- Organizational and financial stability
- Personal characteristics of the facilitator
- Individual characteristics of members
- External and organizational environments
- Organization readiness and implementation.

There have been a number of derivatives of QCs resulting in teams operating under a variety of names but with very similar characteristics to QCs. A case in point are the quality service action teams (QSATs) operated by the National Westminster Bank, in which small groups of staff consider specific topics and problems at local level. The intention is that every branch should have a QSAT (see Boaden et al. 1991).

Quality improvement teams

Teams of this type can comprise members of a single department, be cross-functional, and include representatives of either or both customers and suppliers. The objectives of such teams range across various topics but fall under the general headings of improving quality, eliminating waste and non-value-added activity, and improving productivity.

The characteristics of quality improvement teams are more varied than for any other type of team, but typically include:

- Membership can be voluntary or mandatory and can comprise line workers, staff or a mixture of both. Some teams involve a complete range of personnel from different levels in the organizational hierarchy.

- Projects can arise as a result of: a management initiative, a need to undertake some form of corrective action, a high incidence of defects, supplier/customer problems, or opportunities for improvement. It is usual to agree the project brief with management.
- The team is usually formed to meet a specific objective.
- In the first place, the team leader will have been appointed by management and briefed regarding objectives and time-scales.
- The team is more permanent than project teams but less so than QCs. In some cases teams disband after a project, in others they continue.
- Members are usually experienced personnel and well versed in problem-solving skills and methods.
- The team is self-contained and can take whatever action is required to resolve the problem and improve the process.
- The assistance of a facilitator is sometimes required to provide advice on problem-solving, use of specific quality management tools and techniques and keeping the team activity on course. In most cases a facilitator is assigned to a number of teams.

At Chesterfield Cylinders (a manufacturer of steel cylinders) the procedure and responsibilities for setting up a quality improvement team are as follows:

- The total quality steering group (TQSG) agrees the project for the team.
- The TQSG appoints one of its members to act as mentor for that team.
- The TQSG discusses possible candidates for team leader. The mentor then approaches the proposed team leader and invites him or her to lead the project.
- The mentor clearly identifies the problem to be addressed with the team leader.
- The mentor and the team leader agree the team.

From this point, the mentor's role is as follows:

- To guide the team leader when required.
- To monitor the team progress and ensure that the team is addressing the identified and agreed project.
- To give support to the team leader when problems arise that cannot be resolved by the team leader.
- To introduce outside expertise when required.
- To report back to the steering group on team progress.

Differences between Teams

Manson and Dale (1989) have carried out research on the differences between quality circles and yield improvement teams in one of the UK's largest printed circuit board manufacturers. Table 23.1 has been developed from their work.

It is recommended that when a company uses more than one type of team activity it clearly identifies the characteristics and operation of each type of team. For example, at Betz Dearborn Ltd. of Widnes (manufacturer of speciality chemicals

Table 23.1 Differences between quality circles and yield improvement teams

Feature	Quality circle	Yield improvement teams
Purpose	• Involve employees • Increase employee participation • Team-building • Develop people	• Improve process yields • Reduce scrap • Solve quality-related problems
Team-building	• Will only solve problems if an effective team has been developed • Members work together • Operate by consensus	• Formed around a problem • Members are given specific tasks • Onus is on the individual • Peer pressure to perform • Goals, targets and achievements are established and assessed • Team develops around its achievements
Leadership	• Section members/first-line supervisor • Members lack authority and power • Lack of access to functions, people, and information • Dependent on others for data and advice	• Production/section managers • Members are relatively senior • Independent
Problem-solving potential	• Limited • Minor problems • Limited skills	• Considerable • Major problems • Highly skilled
Project resolution rate	• Low	• High
Infrastructure	• Steering committee • Infrequent meetings • Lack of regular reporting of individual circle progress	• Steering committee • Monthly reports to managing director • Weekly reporting of leaders to steering committee

for water treatment), the following three factors are taken into account in deciding which improvement approach to adopt:

- Where the idea for the improvement originated.
- The strategic significance of the improvement.
- Whether the improvement affects more than one major area of the company's operation.

Commonalities between Teams

In relation to the operating characteristics of any type of team used in the quality improvement process the following two points should be noted.

1 The key issue is not the name of the team activity, but rather the structure of the team, its operating characteristics, remit, accountability, and ability to resolve problems.
2 If management initiate any form of team activity they have an implicit responsibility to investigate and evaluate all recommendations for improvement, implement all feasible solutions, demonstrate interest in the team's activities, recognize and celebrate success – otherwise there is demotivation of team members.

Any type of team is composed of a number of key constituents, and requires more than an enthusiastic membership if it is to be successful. The work of Belbin (1981) and his co-workers on the characteristics of successful and unsuccessful groups demonstrated that, for successful teamworking, a combination of types is required. Belbin identified nine types or roles within a team: company worker, chair, shaper, plant, resource investigator, monitor, evaluator, team worker, and completer/finisher. The following is adapted from guidelines developed by Betz Dearborn and Chesterfield Cylinders:

Team sponsor

- Quality steering group (QSG) member and a senior manager.
- Actively supports the team in its task, especially by contributing to the removal of road-blocks.
- Helps resolve priority conflicts.
- Mentor to the team leader.
- Ensures that the team leader has the skills and training required to lead the team.
- Communications link between the team and QSG and also with departments which are affected by the project.
- Ensures that the team's activities are accepted by the department in which it is working (e.g. holds meetings with the area management, staff and operator to help to generate a total understanding of the project and the reasons for it).
- The sponsor agrees a charter with the team. The charter should include:

- Objective
- Deliverables/outcomes
- Resources (team)
- Boundaries
- Time-frame.

- Ensures that other people and teams are not addressing the same project as the team.
- Ensures that the team and its leader are responsible for the processes which interface with the chosen project.
- Holds regular meetings with the team's facilitator.

Team facilitator

- Helps the team mentor and team leader in establishing the team.
- Ensures that the right balance of skills is on the team and available to the team.
- Acts as coach to the team leader and assists with tasks as requested by the leader.
- Responsible for team progress and direction.
- Ensures all team members contribute.
- Responsible for communication from the team to the world outside the team.
- Communicates team road-blocks to team sponsor and helps remove them.
- Identifies training needs of the team and provides and implements, as appropriate.
- Assists the team in preparing recommendations and presentations to management.
- Helps sponsor resolve external resource/priority conflicts.
- Celebrates success with the team.

Team leader

- The leader of a team can be chosen by management or be appointed by the team. Another issue to be considered is whether the role of team leader should be rotated amongst team members.
- Organizes and sends out agenda.
- Ensures the team members are familiar with the protocol of team meetings.
- Ensures the team has a convenient place to meet.
- Consults with line managers on suitable times for team meetings.
- Starts the meeting on time and adheres to the agenda.
- Takes minutes.
- Collates data.
- At the end of the meeting, agrees the date and agenda for the next meeting.
- Communicates minutes and follow-up actions.
- Needs to be an active contributor and listener.
- Ensures that team members know what is expected of them.
- Leads the definition and implementation of team processes.
- Prepares to commit time to the project.

- Responsible for team progress and direction.
- Understands and is sympathetic to the various stages of development that teams go through in the journey towards independence and accountability, i.e. the forming-storming-norming-performing cycle developed by Tuckman (1965). These steps in brief are:

  - *Forming*: getting to know each other
  - *Storming*: airing and resolving differences, building relationships and agreeing group goals
  - *Norming*: establishing group norms, working together, defining individual and team goals, and developing the meeting, communication and work processes
  - *Performing*: effective teamwork.

- Identifies any training needs of the team and its members.
- Provides regular verbal reports and copies of team minutes to the mentor about the progress of the team.

Team member

- Is clear on why they wish to become a member of a team (e.g. wish to solve problems and resolve concerns, improved access to information, increased involvement in decision-making).
- Needs to be enthusiastic about the project; its resolution must be of direct benefit to them.
- Must be a willing team member; not coerced into joining the team.
- Should contribute relevant experience.
- Is prepared to commit time outside team meetings to collect data and carry out agreed actions.
- Takes responsibility, as requested, for follow-up actions.
- Respects the role of team leader.
- Needs to be an active contributor.
- Needs to be an active listener.
- Is never afraid to say 'I don't understand'.
- Needs to be able to follow through actions.
- Should respect the ideas and views of other members.
- Takes minutes as and when requested by the team leaders.

Evaluation of Teams

It is not easy to evaluate the effectiveness of teamworking, other than by the effectiveness of the actual solutions produced and improvements made. It is, however, important that the 'health' of a team is regularly assessed. The observable characteristics of an effective team are:

- Everyone is participating, making a contribution and involved in actions and through this is achieving their personal potential.
- Relationships are open.

- Team members trust, respect and support each other and are prepared to adapt and be co-operative.
- Members listen closely to the views of other members of the team and have an open mind and maintain a positive attitude.
- Everyone expresses their views, ideas and problems and all available means are used to support ideas.
- Members respect the operating procedures and principles of the team and they own the team process.
- There is clarity of focus on the project being tackled and members know what is expected of them.
- The TQM team leader has the ability to translate ideas into action.

On the other hand, the usual characteristics of an ineffective team are:

- Poor leadership.
- Cliques, defensiveness, closed minds and blame culture within the team membership.
- Downright hostilities, conflict, competition and lack of tolerance between team members.
- Members are not all participating in the activities of the team.
- Limited communications between team members, and members have a tendency to act on their own.
- Insufficient attention to the team process.
- There is no pride displayed in the team activity.
- Members feel they are being taken advantage of and the higher performers reduce their efforts to those of the lowest performer.

Briggs et al. (1993) describe the aims of an audit, based on a semi-structured interviewing methodology, of the quality improvement teams operating at Staffordshire Tableware Ltd., in relation to:

- What teams were involved
- The members of the teams
- How teams were operating
- What projects were being tackled
- How participants felt about the programme

They go on to say that the information gathered 'was used to create a picture of team activity for use as: an historical record, prior to an expansion of the programme, a feedback tool to improve team effectiveness and to plot a course for future development of the team programme'.

UMIST have developed a 'team fitness check' which consists of a questionnaire completed by each member, the leader and the mentor of the team and then discussed and acted on by the team (and the management, if necessary). The 'team fitness check' is a diagnostic tool which helps a team to pinpoint strengths and areas for improvement of both the team and individual members to develop its effectiveness and efficiency. The idea came from a quality circle health assessment developed in the mid-1980s by Eric Barlow at Philips (Hazel Grove). The questionnaire considers the factors outlined in box 23.1.

BOX 23.1 TEAM FITNESS CHECK

1. Is your team meeting regularly?

Has not met for 6 months		Has not met for 3 months		Has not met for 6 weeks		Meets every 3 weeks
1	2	3	4	5	6	7

   If you have scored 5 or less:

   - Is it due to pressure of work?   Yes/No
   - Is it due to a lack of resources?   Yes/No
   - Is it due to company reorganization?   Yes/No
   - Is it due to the non-availability of the leader?   Yes/No
   - Is it due to the apathy of team members?   Yes/No
   - Is it due to the meeting time?   Yes/No
   - Is it due to shift patterns?   Yes/No
   - Is it due to the team comprising people from different shifts?   Yes/No
   - Is it due to lack of a convenient place to meet?   Yes/No
   - Is the project too large?   Yes/No
   - Is the project too difficult?   Yes/No
   - Is it due to some members of the team not identifying with the project?   Yes/No

2. Is the level of attendance at meetings satisfactory?

Less than 50% of members attend		Less than 60% of members attend		Less than 80% of members attend		All members attend
1	2	3	4	5	6	7

   If you have scored 5 or less:

   - Is it due to work pressure?   Yes/No
   - Is it due to members being off site?   Yes/No
   - Is it due to people being instructed not to attend?   Yes/No
   - Is it due to people having nothing to report?   Yes/No
   - Is it due to people being involved in other committees, projects and teams?   Yes/No
   - Is it due to a lack of interest in the project?   Yes/No

3. Are all members of the team involved in making decisions about the project and committed to resolving it successfully?

None committed		Less than 30% committed		Less than 50% committed		All committed
1	2	3	4	5	6	7

   If you have scored 5 or less:

   - Is it the nature of the project?   Yes/No
   - Is the project sufficiently challenging?   Yes/No
   - Is it the size of the project?   Yes/No
   - Is it due to all members of the team not being associated with some elements of the project?   Yes/No

- Is it due to a lack of innovation?   Yes/No
- Is it due to a lack of commitment?   Yes/No
- Is it due to members' unwillingness to talk openly about
  ideas?   Yes/No
- Is it due to members' unwillingness to talk openly about
  problems?   Yes/No
- Is it due to personality clashes within the team?   Yes/No
- Is it due to some team members believing they are more
  important than the team?   Yes/No
- Is it due to the size of the team?   Yes/No
- Is it due to lack of appreciation and recognition?   Yes/No

4. Is the team operating effectively?

Very ineffective   Very effective
1   2   3   4   5   6   7

If you have scored 3 or less:

- Is it due to the leader?   Yes/No
- Is it due to the team?   Yes/No
- Is it due to one member of the team?   Yes/No
- Is it due to one member of the team dominating the
  meeting?   Yes/No
- Is it due to a lack of information?   Yes/No
- Is it due to a clique?   Yes/No
- Is it due to a lack of trust and respect?   Yes/No
- Is it due to lack of communications?   Yes/No
- Is it due to personality clashes between the leader and
  members?   Yes/No
- Is it due to decisions based on opinion and not fact?   Yes/No
- Is it due to not all members of the team being involved
  in its activities and associated decision-making?   Yes/No
- Is it due to ideas and decisions not being properly
  evaluated?   Yes/No
- Is it due to members not feeling part of the team?   Yes/No
- Is it due to a lack of structure and procedure?   Yes/No
- Is it due to the size of the team?   Yes/No
- Is it due to lack of skills?   Yes/No
- Is it due to a lack of adherence to team rules; do these
  need to be revisited?   Yes/No
- Is it due to a lack of a periodic review?   Yes/No
- Is it due to a lack of mission and goals?   Yes/No

5. Are inter-meeting actions carried out satisfactorily?

Not at all   Very
satisfactory   satisfactory
1   2   3   4   5   6   7

If you have scored 3 or less:

- Is it due to a lack of leader co-ordination?   Yes/No
- Is it due to a failure to set priorities?   Yes/No

BOX 23.1   (cont'd)

- Is it due to workload priorities?   Yes/No
- Is it due to a lack of resources?   Yes/No
- Is it due to lack of member commitment?   Yes/No
- Is it due to poor definition of activities?   Yes/No
- Is it due to a lack of initiative?   Yes/No
- Is it due to lack of support from the mentor?   Yes/No
- Is it due to a lack of support from people outside
  the team?   Yes/No
- Is it due to a lack of empowerment?   Yes/No

6. Is the team receiving support from departments?

No support whatsoever						Complete co-operation
1	2	3	4	5	6	7

If you have scored 3 or less:

- Is it due to one or more departments?   Yes/No
- Is it due to management?   Yes/No
- Is it due to supervisors?   Yes/No
- Is it due to technical specialists?   Yes/No
- Is it due to lack of support from the mentor?   Yes/No
- Is it due to departments viewing the team as outside
  interference?   Yes/No
- Is it due to a lack of publicity about the team's activities?   Yes/No

7. Does the team require further training?

Yes   No

If YES, in which areas is training required?

8. Has the team received proper recognition of its activities?

No recognition whatsoever						Complete recognition
1	2	3	4	5	6	7

If you have scored 3 or less:

- Is it due to a lack of recognition from management for
  team efforts?   Yes/No
- Is it due to a lack of recognition from management for
  individual efforts?   Yes/No
- Is it due to a lack of recognition of individual
  contributions by the team?   Yes/No
- Are the current methods not sufficient?   Yes/No
- Are the current methods not suitable?   Yes/No

9. Do the members of the team regard the team as successful?

Not at all successful						Very successful
1	2	3	4	5	6	7

10. Summarize what actions you are going to take.

Dale and Agha's (2000) empirical research has identified the following measures for tracking the improvements to a business arising from teamwork:

- Achievement of service-level agreements
- Achievement of regulatory targets
- Customer satisfaction perception levels
- Recognition awards
- Employee motivation levels
- Employee satisfaction levels
- Level of team cohesion
- Level of training
- Unit cost (e.g. call-handling costs)
- Multi-skilling levels
- Error rates
- Willingness to become involved in terms of panel sessions, escorting visitors, and team presentations outside the plant

Team Competition

To formally recognize and celebrate team activity and encourage role-model behaviour a number of organizations hold an annual team competition/conference, usually held off-site, in which those team activities considered to be the best are presented. The judging committee of internal staff and external experts assesses the team projects in terms of theme selection, problem analysis and solution, members' participation and contribution, results and benefits, and presentation.

At the annual team competition of RHP Bearings (manufacturer of industrial, precision and aerospace bearings), each site holds its own internal competition to decide which team will represent it at the annual competition. At the formal event each team submits a project brief detailing issues such as team members, project objective and details, how the data were analysed, the problem-solving approach used, results and outcomes, and future opportunities. The team of judges assesses each team using the scoring guideline shown in box 23.2.

It is usual to award a commemorative certificate to each member of a team making a presentation and a small financial reward (e.g. vouchers), which is to be spent on a team activity such as a dinner, attendance at a sports event, theatre visit, a picnic, attendance at a training event, to improve the working environment, etc. The winning team gets a similar certificate and reward but, in addition, an annual trophy of some kind.

Paul Monk, managing director of RHP Bearings, writing in the company's Spring 1996 newsletter, which was devoted to the 1995 team competition, made the following comments:

> The standard of entries to the competition gets better each year. This year surpassed what has gone before.

> The Team Competition is symbolic. It is the crowning event in a year of good work and it represents the total quality ethic we embrace through involving all our people in order to improve the business results of our company and make it a better place to work.

> As a result of team working, scrap rates across the NSK-RHP group have halved in two years and productivity has increased by between 35 per cent and 40 per cent.

BOX 23.2   SCORING GUIDELINES

Teamwork   35 points

Did all the team members get involved?
Did they think and work outside the meeting time?
Did they share, care, support and develop?
Did they have regular meetings and reports?
Did they involve others when required?

Tackling the Problem   30 points

How was the project selected?
Did they consider people impact, complexity, company benefit?
Did they set clear and challenging objectives?
Were the objectives in line with company policy?
Did they use a systematic approach, e.g. PDCA?
Did they use appropriate tools and techniques?

Solution/Results   20 points

What was the degree of originality used?
Were all possible options considered?
Was an action plan shown for implementing the solution?
Are the objectives/plan being met?
Are results expressed in terms of objectives?
Are there other spin-off benefits?
Are the results relevant to the customer or internal customer?
Was the result verified as effective and permanent by monitoring
the implementation?

Presentation   15 points

Was it well planned and structured?
Did it emphasize the key points and justify the solution?

Guidelines for Developing Effective Teams

As outlined in chapter 1, a continuous improvement process will encounter periods of stagnation when nothing appears to be moving. This phenomenon is mirrored by teams whose members begin with high levels of energy but can quickly slump and suffer frequent troughs of inactivity.

To ensure that teams work effectively and efficiently the following factors should be taken into account:

- Management must commit themselves to nurturing and supporting teams. They need to release, on a gradual basis, authority, decision-making and accountability and put in place a suitable organizational support structure and connections between the team and the individuals and functions which it affects.

- Prior to launching any form of team activity in relation to the introduction and development of TQM, it must be ensured that the appropriate awareness training and education with regard to TQM have been undertaken.

- Each member must be clear about the aims and objectives of the team, the work to be accomplished by the team and its potential contribution to day-to-day operations. The team should have specific goals, and an action plan and milestone chart for the project in hand, with completion dates related to the objective. This not only assists in setting boundaries to the project but also helps the team to stay focused on it. All members of the team should benefit from the resolution of the project. The project must not be too large to discourage team members; an early success is vital.

- Team members must be trained in appropriate data-collection, problem-solving, experimental and decision-making methods and the team must ensure that it uses the taught skills and methods effectively. Members should be confident in the use of the tools they have been taught and also be aware of any relevant new tools. Training should include project-planning, team-building and team dynamics in order to provide an understanding of the behavioural needs which may determine team effectiveness and to help members to feel part of the team. They must also be aware of which type of tools and methods work best for specific problems or situations.

- Special coaching and counselling should be provided to the team leaders since they are critical to a team's success. They must have the appropriate leadership skills in relation to the team.

- The team mentors must be seen to be actively supporting and contributing to the team. This applies, in particular, to requests for resources and support from key organizational functions.

- The team should be disciplined and should have and utilize a set method of problem-solving based on fact and not opinion, along the lines of classic project management. Some companies have developed a process which it is recommended that its teams should follow. This process consists of a variety of steps covering the basic components of data analysis, problem definition, data-collection, solution generation, improvement actions, and monitoring the effectiveness of improvements. However, it is recognized that some teams prefer a less structured approach to retain flexibility.

- There should be a set of rules and operating procedures that guide the meetings of the team. A project-monitoring system also needs to be set up to ensure that the team is operating in an effective manner.

- Teams should meet on a regular basis and work to an agenda. Each meeting should be constructive, with a purpose, an aim and an achievable goal. The team must be led effectively in terms of direction, allocation of work, support, feedback encouragement, and participation, and must keep minutes and record actions. The team must never leave a meeting without agreeing future actions and the date and time of the next meeting.

- Once a team meeting has been agreed by its members, only in exceptional circumstances should the leader or any team member fail to attend the meeting.

- Periodic reports to management and the 'mentor' on team activities must be prepared. The results and decisions should be communicated accurately to the rest of the workforce. It is also important that management carry out a periodic review of each team's progress.

- People who are likely to be affected by the results of the project should be involved in the team activity.
- The team should receive appropriate recognition and celebration for successful improvements.
- The performance of the team on completion of a project should be evaluated and reviewed to see what worked, what did not and what could be done better, including the identification of training needs and pinpointing of barriers. This feedback should be constructive; it is recommended that team members are counselled on how to give and receive feedback in order to learn from each of their failures. It is sometimes useful to use someone from outside the company to evaluate team activity and provide added impetus to the team.

Summary

Teamwork is a key element of any TQM approach. There are a variety of teams with different operating characteristics which can be used in TQM. Superior-performing organizations employ a number of different types of teams. Different types of teams can be used at different stages of an organization's development of TQM. Some teams are drawn from one functional area of the business and have a narrow focus with perhaps limited problem-solving potential. Other types of teams are wider in focus and tend to be cross-functional. The type of team will depend on the nature of the problem and objectives and management must decide which type is needed. This chapter has concentrated on three types – project teams, quality circles and quality improvement teams – and described their operating characteristics.

It is surprising how many organizations make a number of fundamental mistakes in establishing teamwork as part of their TQM approach:

- Teams are not given any training.
- The wrong type of team is established for the project being tackled.
- The team is structured in such a way that members discuss their views on the cause of the problem and these ideas are then passed over to technical personnel and engineers for them to come up with a solution: the result is that team members feel they have achieved nothing and become disaffected with the team process.
- Too many teams are introduced at one time, which the infrastructure cannot support.
- The leader is unaware of the importance of their role to the success of the team.

The setting up of teams usually occurs within the first six months of introducing TQM. To help organizations avoid some of the common mistakes, guidelines have been outlined which should be considered prior to setting up any form of team activity. However, even if these are followed, teams are likely to encounter periods of stagnation when nothing appears to be happening. A means of assessing the health of teams has been proposed to help team members analyse strengths and areas for improvement and thereby overcome these periods of inertia and maintain performance and effectiveness. It is vital that teams learn from experience and make the necessary changes for the good of the team. It must be remembered that it takes hard work and commitment to develop effective teamworking.

Dale and Huke (1996) quote the director of materials of Maxtor (HK) Ltd., who likens teamwork to sport when he says:

> In our business, teamwork is of the essence, with product life cycles getting shorter and shorter; if any individual or department is not fully co-operating it is akin to a player in a sports team game dropping the ball.

Teams and groups are important, as has been outlined in this chapter, but their effects must not be over-emphasized in relation to individuals working alongside on organizational improvement initiatives.

References

American Society for Quality and Gallup Inc. (1993), *Employee Attributes on Teamwork, Empowerment and Quality Improvement*. Milwaukee: ASQ Quality Press.

Belbin, R. M. (1981), *Management Teams: Why they Succeed or Fail*. London: Heinemann.

Boaden, R. J., Dale, B. G. and Polding, M. E. (1991), *The NatWest Route to Quality Service*. Sheffield: Employment Department.

Bradley, K. and Hill, S. (1983), After Japan: the quality circle transplant and production efficiency. *British Journal of Industrial Relations*, 21(3), 291–311.

Briggs, R., Palmer, J. and Dale, B. G. (1993), Quality improvement teams: an examination. In *Proceedings of the Quality and its Applications Conference*, September, University of Newcastle upon Tyne, 101–5.

Crosby, P. B. (1979), *Quality is Free*. New York: McGraw Hill.

Dale, B. G. and Agha, T. (2000), Performance measures to identify teamwork. In *The Best of Quality*, vol. 10, 269–82. Milwaukee: ASQ Quality Press.

Dale, B. G. and Huke, I. (1996), *Quality Through Teamwork*. Hong Kong Government Industry Department, Booklet No. 7.

Dale, B. G. and Lees, J. (1986), *The Development of Quality Circle Programmes*. Sheffield: Manpower Services Commission.

Fabi, B. (1992), Contingency factors in quality circles: a review of empirical evidence. *International Journal of Quality and Reliability Management*, 9(2), 18–33.

Hayward, S. G., Dale, B. G. and Frazer, V. C. M. (1985), Quality circle failure and how to avoid it. *European Management Journal*, 3(2), 193–211.

Hill, F. M. (1986), Quality circles in the UK: a longitudinal study. *Personnel Review*, 15(3), 25–34.

Hutchins, D. (1985), *Quality Circles Handbook*. London: Pitman.

Manson, M. M. and Dale, B. G. (1989), The operating characteristics of quality circles and yield improvement teams: a case study comparison. *European Management Journal*, 7(3), 287–95.

Mohr, W. L. and Mohr, H. (1983), *Quality Circles: Changing Images of People at Work*. Massachusetts: Addison Wesley.

Monk, P. (1996), *RHP News* (Spring). Newark: RHP Bearings Ltd.

Robson, M. (1984), *Quality Circles in Action*. Aldershot: Gower Press.

Tuckman, B. W. (1965), Development sequence in small groups. *Psychological Bulletin*, 63(6), 384–99.

chapter twenty-four

Self-Assessment, Models and Quality Awards

B. G. Dale

Introduction

If a process of continuous improvement is to be sustained and its pace increased it is essential that organizations monitor on a regular basis what activities are going well, which have stagnated, what needs to be improved and what is missing. Self-assessment provides the framework for generating this type of feedback about an organization's approach to continuous improvement. It helps to satisfy the natural curiosity of management as to where their organization stands with respect to the development of TQM.[1] Self-assessment against the criteria of a quality award/ excellence model on which evaluation and diagnostics can be based is now being given a considerable amount of attention by organizations throughout the world. The main reason for this increasing interest is the MBNQA, introduced in America in 1987, and the EQA, introduced in Europe in 1991. The criteria of these awards encapsulate a comprehensive and holistic management model covering its various activities, practices and processes, and provide the mechanism for quantifying an organization's current state of TQM development by means of a points score. There are many definitions of self-assessment provided by writers such as Conti (1993, 1997) and Hillman (1994), but an all-embracing definition is provided by the EFQM (1999):

> Self-assessment is a comprehensive, systematic and regular review of an organization's activities and results referenced against the EFQM excellence model.
>
> The self-assessment process allows the organization to discern clearly its strengths and areas in which improvements can be made and culminates in planned improvement actions that are then monitored for progress.

There are a number of internationally recognized models, the main ones being the Deming Application Prize in Japan, the MBNQA in America and the EFQM

[1] Throughout this chapter TQM is used, rather than 'excellence or 'business excellence'. The rationale for this is explained in the section 'Quality, TQM and Excellence'.

excellence model in Europe. Although there are some differences between the models, they have a number of common elements and themes. In addition, there are many national quality/excellence awards (e.g. the UK Business Excellence Award, Hungarian National Quality Award, Irish Business Excellence Award, and the Australian Quality Award for Business Excellence) and regional quality awards (e.g. the North-West Excellence Award): see European Quality (2000). Most of the national and regional awards are more or less duplicates of the international models, with some modifications to suit issues which are of national or local interest. In America alone there are over 70 state and regional award schemes. Blodgett (1999) provides data from the National Institute of Standards and Technology (NIST) which shows interest in state and local awards in America is experiencing considerable growth (for example, in 1998 there were 830 applications, compared to 36 for the MBNQA.) Sometimes an organization will adjust the criteria and/or percentages of one of these models to cater for its own specific situation. Since the establishment of these awards there has been an explosion in published material describing them and comparing their characteristics (e.g. Brown 2000; Cole 1991; Conti 1993, 1997; Hakes 2000; Lascelles and Peacock 1996; Nakhai and Neves 1994; Porter and Tanner 1996; Steeples 1993; Vokurka et al. 2000).

The models on which the awards are based and the guidelines for application are helpful in defining TQM in a way which the management of all types of organizations – small, large, public, private, manufacturing and service – can easily understand. This is one of the reasons behind the distribution of thousands of booklets outlining the guidelines and award criteria. The majority of companies requesting them have no intention, in the short term, of applying for the respective awards; they are simply using the criteria of the chosen model to help them diagnose the state of health of their improvement process and provide indications of how to achieve business excellence. They help organizations to develop and manage their improvement activities in a number of ways. For example:

- They provide a definition and description of TQM, within a defined framework, which gives a better understanding of the concept, improves awareness and generates ownership of TQM amongst senior managers.
- They enable measurement of the progress with TQM to be made in a structured and systematic manner, along with its benefits and outcomes.
- Annual improvement is encouraged, and this provides the basis for assessing the rate of improvement.
- They force management to think about the basic elements of their business and how it operates, and about the relationship between actions and results, and how organizational change is facilitated: 'Where are we now and where do we need to be in the future?'
- The scoring criteria provide an objective, fact-based measurement system, and help gain consensus within the organization on the strengths and areas for improvement of the current approach, and pinpoint the key improvement opportunities.
- Sharing of best practices and organizational learning are facilitated.
- Education of management and employees on the basic principles of TQM is improved.
- They help develop a more cohesive company working environment.

Table 24.1   Benefits of the self-assessment process

Category	Benefits
Immediate	• Facilitates benchmarking • Drives continuous improvement • Encourages employee involvement and ownership • Provides visibility in direction • Raises understanding and awareness of quality-related issues • Develops a common approach to improvement across the company • Used as a marketing strategy, raising the profile of the organization • Produces 'people-friendly' business plans
Long-term	• Keeps costs down • Improves business results • Balances long- and short-term investments • Provides a disciplined approach to business planning • Develops a holistic approach to quality • Increases the ability to meet and exceed customers' expectations • Provides a link between customers and suppliers
Supporting TQM	• Helps to refocus employees' attention on quality • Provides a 'health check' of processes and operations • Encourages a focus on processes and not just the end-product • Encourages improvements in performance

Based on detailed research carried out in 10 companies Ritchie and Dale (2000) have summarized the benefits of self-assessment against a quality/excellence award model (see table 24.1). A full listing of the benefits which have been found to result from the self-assessment process is given in EFQM (1999).

To use any self-assessment method effectively as a business tool for continuous improvement, various elements and practices have got to be in place and management need to have had some experience with TQM to understand the questions underpinning the concept. What has not been implemented cannot be assessed. The decision to undertake self-assessment needs to be fully considered from all angles, and management must be fully committed to its use. In the author's view the use of self-assessment methods based on the quality/excellence award models is best suited to those organizations that have had a formal improvement process in place for at least three years, although there is a clear need to assess, in some way, progress before this time has elapsed. This is supported by Sherer (1995) the managing director of Rank Xerox (Germany), who, in explaining how the corporation won the EQA, says 'Do not use the award programme, your application for the EQA, as an entry point into your quality journey. It is something you should do after you have been on the road for a long time.' He goes on to comment: 'Do not try to run for the award too early.'

A similar point is made in the Deming *Prize Guide* for overseas companies (Deming Prize Committee 2000):

> It is advisable to apply for the prize after two to three years of company-wide TQM implementation efforts or after top management has become fully committed and has begun to assume a leadership role.

Having made this point, the models underpinning the quality/excellence awards are also helpful in demonstrating what is involved to managers in organizations that are not experienced in TQM. However, they must understand the potential gap that can exist between where they currently stand in relation to TQM and the model of the award being used in order to make comparisons.

This chapter opens by investigating the replacement of quality and TQM by excellence in the award models, and this is followed by a description of the Deming, MBNQA and EFQM models. It then examines the self-assessment process, and the associated success factors and difficulties.

Quality, TQM and Excellence

In recent times there has been a drive to change from quality and TQM to excellence in the criteria of the quality/excellence models. It is the author's perception that this originated with the EFQM and management consultancies, the former in response to the perceived tarnished image of TQM and the latter seeing a diminishing demand and/or increasing competition for their services. In response to the 'fallen star' image of TQM the EFQM, in their excellence model, have progressively stripped out reference to TQM and quality in both the criteria and the areas to address. In the 1999 version of the model, the members of the steering group responsible for the development of the revised model appear to be proud of this. Nabitz et al. (1999), in describing the move from quality management to organizational excellence, point out that 'The word quality does not appear in either the sub-criteria or the areas to address', and 'In the new model, the switch from total quality management to organizational excellence is a fact.'

However, de Dommartin (2000), who is the CEO of the EFQM, brackets TQM and business excellence together in describing the background to the revised model: 'Their objective became to provide a model that ideally represents the business excellence (TQM) philosophy . . .'.

This development in terminology has also been followed by national quality bodies such as the British Quality Foundation (BQF). However, it is noted that there is a lack of consistency in the use of 'quality', 'excellence' and 'business excellence' in the designations made by national bodies in their specific quality/excellence awards: see European Quality (2000).

The potential for confusion in terms of the language used in the description of what used to be termed TQM, but is now classed as business excellence or excellence is considerable. For example, at the November 1999 British Excellence Award ceremony the following terms were used during the course of the ceremony: business excellence; excellence; total quality; continuous improvement; quality improvement; continuous improvement programme; process of continuous improvement; and quality of service. The master of ceremonies punctuated and attenuated the first two terms at regular intervals during her announcements and introductions. Listening from the sidelines it was almost as though the words 'quality' and 'total quality management' had been struck out of her prompts and notes and replaced with 'excellence' and 'business excellence', with no clear rationale to the usage – if a word is mentioned a sufficient number of times and in a loud voice, then people will start to accept it.

This replacement terminology raises a number of issues, including:

1 If 'quality' is replaced by 'excellence' in the awards and models (e.g. UK Quality Awards to UK Business Excellence Awards and Irish Quality Association to Excellence Ireland), for the sake of consistency, should this not extend to 'quality' in the European Foundation for Quality Management and the British Quality Foundation? Another logical progression would be take out the word from the European Organization for Quality, American Society for Quality, International Academy for Quality, Institute for Quality Assurance, quality department, quality manager, quality policy, advanced quality planning, quality plans, quality assurance and quality control.

2 Many trees have been sacrificed in the cause of writing about quality issues in papers, conference proceedings, books, reports, etc. When the published material is studied, are readers expected to overwrite the word 'quality' with 'excellence'? This, as a logical development, would also involve some rebadging of tools, techniques and systems which are commonly associated with quality such as excellence function deployment, the seven excellence control tools, excellence management systems, excellence costing, acceptable excellence level, advanced excellence planning.

3 It also presents an interesting challenge for the writers and users of quality-related standards.

It has taken some considerable time to get across to employees within organizations and to the general public the importance of quality, its management and improvement. It can also be argued that this form of term replacement not only marginalizes quality but also reinforces the belief that TQM is a fad and that quality is no longer an important issue for business. Will a new set of terms undermine the undoubted progress which has been made in quality during the last two decades in the Western world? Whatever the sceptics think about TQM, continuous improvement, quality assurance, or whatever the approach is labelled, there has been considerable improvement in the products and services which are used in everyday life. The following comment by Cole (1999) encapsulates this view:

> It [the quality movement] left in its wake a greatly expanded infrastructure, a partial adaption of a variety of quality methodologies, and a renewed focus on how to serve customers better and how to use business processes to improve competitive performance.

The words 'business excellence' and, latterly, 'excellence' in terms of the EFQM model have been in regular use for at least three years, but it was only in the 1999 guidelines that a definition was put forward and the principles outlined. There is no rigorous definition of excellence and what, if any, is the distinction between this and business excellence. This leads to the view that it is just a play on words. In the EFQM (1999) guidelines, excellence is defined as:

> Outstanding practice in managing the organization and achieving results, all based on a set of 8 fundamental concepts.

These fundamental concepts of excellence are:

> Results orientation; customer focus; leadership and constancy of purpose; management by processes and facts; people development and involvement; continuous learning, innovation and improvement; partnership development; and public responsibility. (EFQM 1999)

In the 2000 revision of the ISO9000 series, the principles of quality management are defined in BS EN ISO9000 (2000) as:

Customer focus; leadership; involvement of people; process approach; system approach to management; continual improvement; factual approach to decision-making and mutually beneficial supplier relationship.

Allowing for interpretation of these individual principles it can be seen that there is little or no difference between quality management and excellence. This lack of clear water in definitions is confirmed when comparison is made with the 10- and 14-point cluster summaries of the teachings of Crosby, Deming, Feigenbaum and Juran and with what has been written about earlier in this book as the elements and practices of TQM.

Award Models

Deming Application Prize

The Deming Prize was set up in honour of Dr W. E. Deming back in 1951, in recognition of his friendship and achievements in the cause of industrial quality. Through the royalties received from the text of his 'eight-day course on quality control' Deming contributed to the initial funding of the prize. It was developed to ensure that good results are achieved through the implementation of company-wide control activities, and is based on the application of a set of principles and statistical techniques.

The author has led four missions of European manufacturing executives to Japan to study how they manage quality. It is clear from the evidence collected that the Deming Application Prize criteria have produced an almost standard method of managing quality (see Dale 1993). Compared to the West, there is much less company-to-company variation in the level of understanding of TQM and in the degree of attainment. This has helped to promote a deep understanding of TQM amongst all employees. Rather than argue about the merits of a particular approach, system, method or technique, the Japanese tend to discuss how to apply the TQM approach more vigorously through a common core level of understanding. JUSE (Deming Prize Committee 1998) outlines the following results which have been achieved in applying for the Deming Application Prize:

- Quality stabilization and improvement
- Production improvement/cost reduction
- Expanded sales
- Increased profits
- Thorough implementation of management plans/business results
- Realization of top management's vision
- Participation in and improvement of the organizational constitution
- Heightened motivation to manage and improve as well as to promote standardization
- Harnessing power from the bottom of the organization and enhanced morale
- Establishment of various management systems and the total management system

The original intention of the Deming Application Prize was to assess a company's use and application of statistical methods. Later, in 1964, it was broadened out to assess how TQM activities were being practised. The award is managed by the Deming Application Prize Committee and administered by the Union of Japanese Scientists and Engineers (JUSE). It recognizes outstanding achievements in quality strategy, management and execution. There are three separate divisions for the award: the Deming Application Prize, the Deming Prize for Individuals and the Quality Control Award for Factories. The Deming Application Prize is open to individual sites, a division of a company, small companies and overseas companies.

The Deming Prize was initially restricted to Japanese companies, but since 1984 has been open to companies outside Japan. It is awarded each year and there is no limit on the number of winners. On the other hand, the committee reserves the right not to award the prize in any year. It is made to those 'companies or divisions of companies that have achieved distinct performance improvement through the application of company-wide quality control' (Deming Prize Committee 1998). The data I have collected (Dale 1993) suggest that it has become customary in Japan for organizations wishing to improve their performance to apply for the Deming Application Prize. This arises from the continuous improvements which are necessary to qualify for the award, along with the considerable prestige associated with winning the prize.

The Deming Application Prize consists of 10 primary categories (see table 24.2) which are divided into a total of 66 sub-categories: each primary category has six sub-categories apart from quality assurance activities, which has twelve. There is no set number of points allocated to the individual sub-categories. It is claimed that the reason for this is to maintain flexibility. However, discussions with JUSE indicate that the maximum score for each sub-category is 10 points. This checklist is prescriptive in that it identifies factors, procedures, techniques and approaches that underpin TQM. The examiners for the Deming Application Prize are selected by JUSE from quality management experts from not-for-profit organizations. The applicants are required to submit a detailed document on each of the prize's criteria. The size of the report is dependent upon the number of employees in each of the applicant company's business units, including the head office. The Deming Prize Committee examines the application document and decides if the applicant is eligible for on-site examination. The committee chooses the two or more examiners to conduct this examination. Discussions by the author with JUSE suggest that considerable emphasis is placed on the on-site examination of the applicant organization's practices. It is also evident that the applicant organization relies a great deal on advice from the JUSE consultants. JUSE would also advise an organization when it should apply for the prize.

In 1996 the Japanese Quality Award was established. This is an annual award that recognizes the excellence of the management of quality. The concept of the award is similar to that of the EFQM model, with emphasis placed on the measurement of quality with respect to customer, employees and society. The eight criteria on which the award is based are similar to those for the MBNQA.

The Malcolm Baldrige National Quality Award

In a bid to improve the quality management practices and competitiveness of US firms, the Malcolm Baldrige National Quality Improvement Act 1987 – Public Law

Table 24.2   Quality award criteria

Deming Application Prize
Category
Policies
Organization
Information
Standardization
Human resources development and utilization
Quality assurance activities
Maintenance/control activities
Improvement
Effects
Future plans
Total

Malcolm Baldrige National Quality Award

Category	*Max.*
Leadership	120
Strategic planning	85
Customer and market focus	85
Information and analysis	90
Human resource focus	85
Process management	85
Business results	450
Total	1,000

European Quality Award

Category	*Max.*
Leadership	100
Policy and strategy	80
People management	90
Partnerships and resources	90
Processes	140
Customer results	200
People results	90
Society results	60
Key performance results	150
Total	1,000

100–107, signed by President Reagan on 20 August 1987, established this annual US quality award, some 37 years after the introduction of the Deming Prize. The award is named after a former American Secretary of Commerce in the Reagan administration, Malcolm Baldrige, who served from 1981 until his death in 1987. The Baldrige National Quality Programme is the result of the co-operative efforts of government leaders and American business. The purposes of the award are to promote an understanding of the requirements for performance excellence and competitiveness improvements and to promote the sharing of information on successful performance strategies. The Baldrige National Quality Programme guidelines contain detailed criteria that describe a world-class total quality organization. The criteria for performance excellence are available in business, education and health-care divisions.

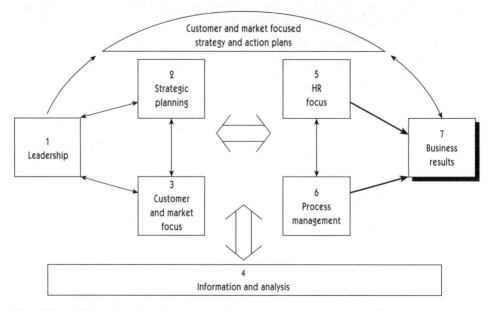

Figure 24.1   Baldrige criteria for performance excellence framework: a systems perspective
Source: US Department of Commerce (2001)

The programme and award are managed by NIST, an agency of the US Department of Commerce. The American Society for Quality (ASQ) administers the MBNQA under contract to NIST. It is claimed that each year up to 30,000 organizations request copies of the MBNQA criteria.

Up to two awards can be given each year, and there are an average of 60 applicants in each of five categories: manufacturing business units, service business units, small business (defined as independently owned, and with not more than 500 employees), education organizations and health-care organizations. The latter two categories were introduced in 1999; in that year half of the 52 applicants were from these two new categories, and, in 2000, 19 of the 49 applicants were from them. Since its inception in a single year there have never been fewer than two and no more than five awards; 48 companies have won the award from 1988 to 2001. Any for-profit, domestic or foreign organization and not-for-profit education and health-care organization located in the US that is incorporated or a partnership can apply. The applicant can be a whole firm or a legitimate business unit. The award is made by the President of the United States, with the recipients receiving a specially designed crystal trophy mounted with a gold-plated medallion. They may publicize and advertise their award provided they agree to share information and best practice about their successful quality management and improvement strategies with other American organizations.

Every Baldrige Award application is evaluated in seven major categories with a maximum total score of 1,000 (US Department of Commerce 2001). These are: leadership (120 points), strategic planning (85 points), customer and market focus (85 points), information and analysis (90 points), human resource focus (85 points), process management (85 points) and business results (450 points): see table 24.2 and figure 24.1. The seven categories are subdivided into 18 items and the items are further defined by 29 main areas to address. It is claimed that 'In the most competitive business sectors, organizations with world class business results are able to achieve a score above 700 on the 1000 point Baldrige scale' (US Department of Commerce 2001). The seven categories embody 11 core values and concepts – customer-driven excellence, visionary leadership, organizational and personal learning, valuing employees and partners, agility, focus on the future, managing for innovation, management by fact, public responsibility and citizenship, focus on results and creating value, and system perspective. The model in figure 24.1 is supported by information and analysis, with the remaining categories falling under customer- and market-focused strategy and action plans. The model includes the leadership triad (categories 1 to 3) and a results triad (categories 4 to 6).

The criteria and processes are reviewed each year to ensure that they remain relevant and reflect current thinking and, based on experience during the intervening period, their wording and relative scores are updated. It should be mentioned that like the EFQM model the MBNQA criteria were developed originally by the business fraternity, management consultants and academics.

The framework (see figure 24.1) has three basic elements: strategy and action plans, system, and information and analysis. Strategy and action plans are the set of customer- and market-focused company-level requirements, derived from short- and long-term strategic planning, that must be done well for the company's strategy to succeed. They guide overall resource decisions and drive the alignment of measures for all work units to ensure customer satisfaction and market success. The system consists of the six Baldrige categories in the centre of figure 24.1 that define the organization, its operations and its results. Information and analysis (category 4) are critical to the effective management of the company and to a fact-based system for improving company performance and competitiveness.

The evaluation by the Baldrige examiners is based on a written application (this summarizes the organization's practices and results in response to the criteria for performance excellence) of up to 50 pages and looks for three major indications of success:

- *Approach.* Appropriateness of the methods, effectiveness of the use of the methods with respect to the degree to which the approach is systematic, integrated and consistently applied, embodies evaluation/improvement/learning cycles and is based on reliable information, and evidence of innovation and/ or significant and effective adoptions of approaches used in other types of applications or businesses.
- *Deployment.* The extent to which the approach is applied to all requirements of the item, including use of the approach in addressing business and item requirements and use of the approach by all appropriate work units.
- *Results.* The outcomes in achieving the purposes given in the item, including current performance, performance relative to appropriate comparisons and/or benchmarks, rate, breadth, and importance of performance improvements, demonstration of sustained improvement and/or sustained high-level performance and linkage of results to key performance measures.

The assessors will use these three dimensions to score an applicant. Approach and deployment are scored together and both must be adequately described to get a good score. However, it is results that separate the real contenders from the rest.

High scoring in this category, which is heavily weighted towards customer satisfaction, requires convincing data that demonstrate steady improvement over time, both internally and externally, and that results are evaluated. Experience has shown that, even with a good internal approach and deployment strategy, it takes time for results to show.

Following a first-stage review of the application by quality management experts (i.e. leading management consultants, practitioners and academics), which it is claimed takes a minimum of 300 hours, a decision is made as to which organizations should receive a site visit. The site visits from a team of six to eight assessors take from two to five days. The visits are used to verify information provided in the application and clarify issues and questions raised in the assessment of the application. The assessors have to be fair, honest and impartial in their approach. A panel of judges reviews all the data both from the written applications and site visits and recommends the award recipients to NIST. Quantitative results weigh heavily in the judging process, so applicants must be able to prove that their quality efforts have resulted in sustained improvements. The thoroughness of the judging process means that applicants not selected as finalists get valuable written feedback on their strengths and areas for improvement. The detail of the report is related to a key themes and category summary, details of strengths and areas for improvement, individual category scoring range, and scoring distribution, and this independent feedback is considered by many organizations to be valuable consultancy advice. The awards are made by those organizations which are considered to best exemplifying the model criteria.

The European Quality Award

The European Quality Award (EQA) was launched in October 1991 and first awarded in 1992. The award is assessed using the criteria of the EFQM excellence model. This was created by Europe's leading senior managers, academics and consultants under the auspices of the EFQM and European Organization for Quality (EOQ) and supported by the European Commission. The EQA was broadened in 1996 to include public sector organizations, and in 1997 a special category for small and medium-sized enterprises (SMEs) (organizations with fewer than 150 employees) was introduced. According to the EFQM the EQA was intended to: 'focus attention on business excellence, provide a stimulus to companies and individuals to develop business improvement initiatives and demonstrate results achievable in all aspects of organizational activity'. While only one EQA is made each year from the finalists for the categories of: (1) large businesses and business units (2) operational units of companies (3) public sector organizations, and (4) SMEs, several European quality prizes are awarded to those companies who demonstrate excellence in the management of quality through a process of continuous improvement, providing they also meet the requirements set annually by the jury. The EQA is awarded to the best of the prizewinners in each of the four categories that is the most successful exponent of TQM in Europe. The winner of each of the four awards gets to retain the EQA trophy for a year and all prizewinners receive a framed holographic image of the trophy. The winners are expected to share their experiences at conferences and seminars organized by the EFQM. Introduced in 2001, applicants scoring 400 points or more but not award finalists were 'Recognized for Excellence'.

The EFQM excellence model is intended to help the management of European organizations to better understand best practices and to support them in their leadership role. The model provides a generic framework of criteria that can be applied to any organization or its component parts. The model is based on eight fundamental concepts – results orientation; customer focus; leadership and constancy of purpose; management by processes and facts; people development and involvement; continuous learning, improvement and innovation; partnership development; and public responsibility. The EQA is administered by the EFQM. In developing the model and the EQA, the EFQM drew on the experience in use and application of the MBNQA. The model (EFQM 2002) is structured on the following nine criteria which organizations can use to assess and measure their own performance:

1 *Leadership*: 100 points (10%)
   How leaders develop and facilitate the achievement of the mission and vision, develop values required for long-term success, and implement these via appropriate actions and behaviours, and are personally involved in ensuring that the organization's management system is developed and implemented.
2 *Policy and strategy*: 80 points (8%)
   How the organization implements its mission and vision via a clear stakeholder-focused strategy, supported by relevant policies, plans, objectives, targets and processes.
3 *People*: 90 points (9%)
   How the organization manages, develops and releases the knowledge and full potential of its people at an individual, team-based and organization-wide level, and plans these activities in order to support its policy and strategy and the effective operation of its processes.
4 *Partnerships and resources*: 90 points (9%)
   How the organization plans and manages its external partnerships and internal resources in order to support its policy and strategy and the effective operation of its processes.
5 *Processes*: 140 points (14%)
   How the organization designs, manages and improves its process in order to support its policy and strategy and fully satisfy and generate increasing value for its customers and other stakeholders.
6 *Customer results*: 200 points (20%)
   What the organization is achieving in relation to its external customers.
7 *People results*: 90 points (9%)
   What the organization is achieving in relation to its people.
8 *Society results*: 60 points (6%)
   What the organization is achieving in relation to local, national and international society as appropriate.
9 *Key performance results*: 150 points (15%)
   What the organization is achieving in relation to its planned performance.

The criteria, which are shown in table 24.2, are split into two groups: 'enablers' and 'results' (illustrated in figure 24.2). The feedback arrow indicates the importance of sharing knowledge, and encouraging learning and innovation; this improves the enablers which in turn leads to improved results. The scoring framework consists of 1,000 points, with 500 points each being allocated to enablers and results. The nine

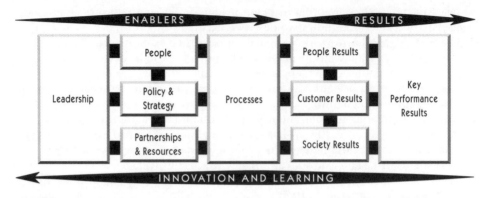

Figure 24.2   The EFQM excellence model
Source: EFQM (2002)

elements of the model are further divided into 32 criteria parts. For example, leadership is divided into four parts and people into five parts. The model is based on the principle that processes are the means by which the organization harnesses and releases the talents of its people to produce results. In other words, the processes and the people are the enablers which provide the results. The results aspects of the model are concerned with what the organization has achieved and is continuing to achieve, and the enablers aspects with how the organization undertakes key activities and how the results are being achieved. The rationale for this is that 'Excellent results with respect to Performance, Customers, People and Society are achieved through Leadership driving Policy and Strategy, People, Partnership and Resources, and Processes' (EFQM 2000). Each of these nine criteria can be used to assess the organization's progress to excellence.

The EFQM model is based on what is termed the RADAR logic: results, approach, deployment, assessment and review. The last four elements are used when assessing the enablers and the result element is obviously used to assess results.

- *Results* cover what an organization achieves and looks for: the existence of positive trends and sustained good performance, comparisons with previous, current and future targets, comparison of results with competitors and best-in-class organizations, understanding the cause-and-effect relationships that prompt improvements, and ensuring that the scope of the results category covers all relevant areas.
- *Approach* covers what an organization plans to do, along with its underlying reasons for this. It needs to be sound, systematic, appropriate, prevention-based, focused on relevant needs, and integrated with normal operations and support organizational strategy.
- *Deployment* is the extent to which the approach has been systematically deployed and implemented down and across the organization in all relevant areas.
- *Assessment and review* relate to both approach and deployment. Progress will be subject to regular review cycles analysis and measurement, with appropriate learning and improvements planned, prioritized and actioned.

The scoring is done on a sliding scale over five levels: 0 per cent range indicates no evidence, implementation or results; 25 per cent represents just getting started;

50 per cent indicates some progress being made; 75 per cent indicates considerable progress; 100 per cent is indicative of excellence.

The EFQM model does not stipulate any particular techniques, methods or procedures which should be in place. However, papers have been published by a range of researchers listing best practice in specific criteria. The organizations that put themselves forward for the award are expected to have undertaken at least one self-assessment cycle. Following this a 75-page report is written for large companies and public sector organizations and a 35-page one for SMEs. Once the application has been submitted to the EFQM headquarters, a team of four to eight fully trained independent assessors examines each application and decides whether or not to conduct a site visit. The assessors are mainly practising managers, but also include academics and quality professionals. The site visits provide the opportunity for the assessors to evaluate the application document, in particular deployment issues and check issues which are not clear from the document. Irrespective of whether or not the company is subject to a site visit, a feedback report is provided that gives a general assessment of the organization, a scoring profile for the different criteria and a comparison with the average scores of other applicants. For each part-criterion the key strengths and areas for improvement are listed. The feedback report for those organizations visited contains more detailed information. A jury with seven members from business and academia reviews the findings of the assessors to decide the European Quality prizewinners. The EQA is made to the organization judged to be the best of the prizewinners in each of the four categories.

The Self-Assessment Process

Self-assessment uses one of the models underpinning an award to pinpoint improvement opportunities and identify new ways in which to encourage the organization down the road of organizational excellence. On the other hand, audits (often confused with self-assessment by less advanced organizations with respect to their development of TQM) are carried out with respect to a quality system standard such as the ISO9000 series and are, in the main, looking for non-compliance and assessing to see if the system and underlying procedures are being followed. An in-depth comparison of audit and self-assessment approaches is provided by Karapetrovic and Willborn (2001). In BS EN ISO9000 (2000) audit is defined as a:

> Systematic, independent and documented process for obtaining audit evidence and evaluating it objectively to determine the extent to which audit criteria are fulfilled.

The first European survey on self-assessment was completed by a research team drawn from UMIST (UK), the Ecole Supérieure de Commerce de Paris (France), the University of Valencia (Spain), the Universität Kaiserslautern (Germany), the University of Limerick (Ireland) and Erasmus University Rotterdam (The Netherlands). The research, which was carried out by postal questionnaire, obtained data from 519 organizations and is reported by van der Wiele et al. (1995, 1996). The five most important reasons for organizations starting self-assessment were to:

- Find opportunities for improvement
- Create a focus on a TQM based on either the EFQM or MBNQA model criteria

- Direct the improvement process
- Provide new motivation for the improvement process
- Manage the business

This ranking provides a clear indication that internal issues are the most important motivation for organizations starting formal self-assessment. In some organizations a self-assessment process is introduced in response to changes in operating environment; company direction, and competitors. The need for improvement is now recognized in most cases, however well an organization may be doing. This is encapsulated by the comment 'Even if you are good now, you still have to get better.'

After gaining the commitment of management to the self-assessment process and carrying out the necessary education and training, the following are the main steps which an organization should follow in setting about self-assessment:

- Assess what the organization has done well.
- Identify what aspects could be improved upon.
- Pinpoint gaps and what elements are missing.
- Develop an action plan to pick up the pace of the improvement process.

A key aspect of the process is taking a good hard and honest look at the organization in order to identify its shortcomings, keeping in mind at all times a golfing analogy: 'You will never become a better golfer by cheating.' The process, on average, usually takes about three months.

There are several methods by which an organization may undertake self-assessment, varying in complexity, rigour and resources and the effort required. Each method has advantages and disadvantages and an organization must choose the one(s) most suited to its circumstances. Some organizations prefer to go for a full award simulation approach after using a matrix chart or questionnaire for educational purposes. Other organizations choose a more incremental approach. In general, organizations develop from using a simple approach to a more complex one, unless they have some external stimulus affecting the pace at which they address the process. These methods are outlined in detail in *Assessing for Excellence: A Practical Guide for Self-Assessment* (EFQM 1999). The broad approaches, which can be used separately or in combination, are:

- *Award simulation.* This approach, which can create a significant workload for an organization, involves the writing of a full submission document (up to 75 pages) using the criteria of the chosen quality award model and employing the complete assessment methodology including the involvement of a team of trained assessors (internal) and site visits. The scoring of the application, strengths, and areas for improvement are then reported back and used by the management team for developing action plans.

  Some organizations have modified and developed the criteria of the chosen award model to suit their own particular circumstances, provide more emphasis on areas which are critical to them, make the criteria easier to understand and use, and reduce some of the effort in preparing the application document. In some cases a corporation or holding company has set a minimum score which each of its facilities has to achieve within a set time-frame. Once an internal award has been achieved its continuation will require the successful completion of a subsequent assessment, usually within two years of the granting of the initial award.

- *Peer involvement.* This is similar to but less rigid than award simulation, in that there is no formal procedure for data-collection. It gives freedom to the organization undertaking the self-assessment to pull together all relevant documents, reports and factual evidence in whatever format it chooses against the appropriate model being used.
- *Pro forma.* In this approach the criterion is described and the person or persons carrying out the assessment outline the organization's strengths, areas for improvement, score and evidence which supports the assessment in the space provided on the form. It is usual to use one or two pages per assessment criterion.
- *Workshop.* This approach is one in which managers are responsible for gathering the data and presenting the evidence to colleagues at a workshop. The workshop aims to reach a consensus score on the criterion and details of strengths and areas for improvement are identified and agreed.
- *Matrix chart.* This requires the creation of an organization-specific matrix or using one of those produced by one of the award bodies (e.g. Excellent North-West). It involves rating a prepared series of statements, based on the appropriate award model on a scoring scale. The statements are usually contained within a workbook which contains the appropriate instructions. The person or persons carrying out the assessment find the statement which is most suited to the organization and notes the associated score. The assessment usually takes about 30 minutes.
- *Questionnaire.* This is usually used to carry out a quick assessment of a department's or organization's standing in relation to the award model being used. It is useful for gathering a view on employee perceptions with respect to the criteria of the model. It involves answering a series of questions and statements, which are based on the criteria of the award model used, using a yes/no format or on a graduated response scale. It is usual to ask for the appropriate evidence underlying the reply to the question. The workbook in which the questionnaire is contained usually encourages notes to be made on improvement actions. After the questionnaire has been completed a report is prepared identifying strengths and areas for improvement based on the numerical scores and written comments.

The choice of approach is dependent upon the level of TQM maturity. Organizations with less experience should use the simpler methods, while those that are more advanced should adopt the more searching and rigorous methods.

In recent times a number of self-assessment packages based on software have come onto the market; these claim to simplify the self-assessment process and provide a benchmark of progress against other organizations. Typical examples are the British Quality Foundation's Assess Rapid Score (this employs a questionnaire which is completed and compiled by a team – it is useful when starting out on self-assessment and requires little previous experience) and Assess Valid Score (this is similar to Rapid Score but is more sophisticated, with the ability to store strengths, opportunities for improvement and evidence). These approaches require input from one individual, although they can be rerun by others and the results compared to give a more comprehensive set of findings.

Assessment against a model, whether by internal or external assessors, has three discrete phases:

1 Gathering data for each criterion.
2 Assessing the data gathered.
3 Developing plans and actions arising from the assessment and monitoring the progress and effectiveness of the plan of action.

A number of flow diagrams have been produced which outline the self-assessment process; that reproduced in figure 24.3 is from *Assessing for Excellence* (EFQM 1999).

It is not the purpose of this chapter to regurgitate the details of a self-assessment process but simply to list the key issues which need to be considered by those organizations undertaking self-assessment for the first time:

- Reach agreement and be clear on the motivation for undertaking self-assessment and articulate the long-term expectations of the process.
- Senior management must be committed to the self-assessment process and be prepared to use the results to develop improvement plans.
- The people involved in the process need to be trained (i.e. training of assessors, training of employees who gather data, and the training of employees responsible for processes which are going to be assessed).
- Communicate within the business the reasons for and what is involved in self-assessment.
- Decide the self-assessment method(s) to be used.
- Plan the means of collecting the data.

    - Decide the team and allocate roles and responsibilities for each criterion of the model
    - Develop a data-collection methodology and identify data sources
    - Agree an activity schedule and manage as a project.

- Decide the best way of organizing the data which have been collected.
- Agree the means of co-ordinating the process.
- Present the data, reach agreement on strengths and areas for improvement and agree the scores for the criteria. If the assessment has been done on a departmental basis a decision needs to be made on whether or not to publicize the scores of individual departments.
- Feedback to facilitate organizational learning.
- Prioritize the improvements, develop an action plan and ensure that the ownership is with appropriate people.
- Regularly review progress against the plan.
- Ensure that self-assessment is linked with the business planning process. This is important to ensure that the areas for improvement are turned into actions which are implemented. In this way only if an organization has a business plan that is known to its various business units, and that business plan has specified within it items for improvement related to whatever model is being used will self-assessment be considered a success.
- Repeat the self-assessment.

Ritchie and Dale (2000) point out that organizations approaching self-assessment can experience difficulties in planning the process and allocating the appropriate

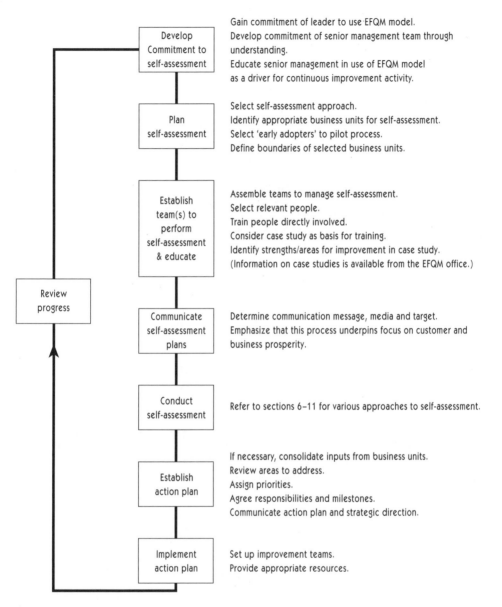

Figure 24.3 Self-assessment: general process
Source: EFQM (1999)

resources. They have developed a 'model', in the form of two matrices which show the characteristics and level of TQM understanding that an organization should demonstrate before employing any self-assessment approach. The prerequisite characteristics change depending on the technicality of the approach involved. The ones detailed are those that an organization needs to actively pursue and practise in order to successfully adopt self-assessment. This model is summarized in figures 24.4, 24.5 and 24.6.

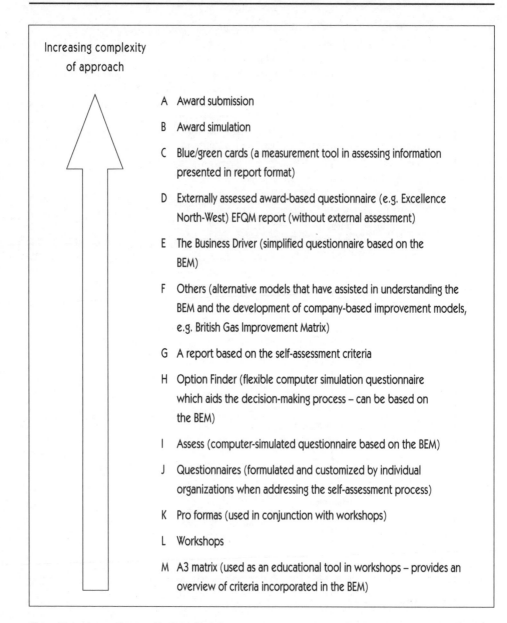

Figure 24.4   Approaches used in the self-assessment process

Prerequisite characteristics (of company/business unit)	Self-assessment approaches												
	A	B	C	D	E	F	G	H	I	J	K	L	M
● Long-term vision	✔	✔		✔									
● Ability to see the 'bigger picture'	✔	✔	✔	✔									✔
● Supportive directors	✔	✔		✔									
● Open-minded management	✔	✔	✔	✔			✔						
● Commitment and involvement at all levels in the process	✔	✔	✔	✔	✔	✔	✔						
● Knowledge of TQM tools and techniques	✔	✔	✔	✔	✔	✔							
● Ongoing continuous improvement strategies	✔	✔	✔	✔	✔	✔	✔						
● Ongoing performance monitoring processes	✔	✔	✔	✔	✔	✔	✔	✔	✔	✔	✔		
● Cross-functional integration	✔	✔	✔	✔	✔	✔	✔	✔	✔	✔	✔		
● Good communication networks	✔	✔	✔	✔	✔	✔							
● Possess an up-to-date working knowledge of all systems and processes	✔	✔	✔	✔		✔	✔	✔	✔	✔	✔	✔	
● Corporate culture that welcomes change	✔	✔	✔	✔	✔	✔	✔	✔	✔	✔	✔	✔	✔
● Identification of 'sponsors' for analysis	✔	✔	✔	✔			✔						
● Trained assessors	✔	✔	✔	✔	✔	✔		✔				✔	✔
● Educated staff regarding the self-assessment process	✔	✔	✔	✔	✔	✔	✔	✔	✔	✔	✔	✔	
● Welcome objective views on performance of business and processes	✔	✔	✔	✔			✔						
● Advocate the development of teams and quality groups	✔	✔	✔	✔									
● Computer literacy								✔	✔				
● Acknowledgement of the benefits of the self-assessment process	✔	✔	✔	✔	✔	✔	✔	✔	✔	✔	✔	✔	✔
● Ability to identify where self-assessment fits in with business strategy	✔	✔	✔	✔	✔	✔	✔	✔	✔	✔	✔	✔	✔
● Incorporation of self-assessment results into business plans	✔	✔	✔	✔	✔	✔	✔	✔	✔	✔	✔	✔	
● Co-ordinating self-assessment for the purpose of continuously improving the business processes	✔	✔	✔	✔	✔	✔	✔	✔	✔	✔	✔	✔	✔

Figure 24.5 The minimum characteristics that a company should exhibit, pre-adoption of prescribed approaches to self-assessment

Success Factors for Self-Assessment

A key to the success of self-assessments is that they have to be written down by the assessors. If they are purely verbal they will have far less power. Something written down has a life of its own and can be referred to again and again. It can also be related to a business plan and a subsequent improvement plan, and can be part of a PDCA cycle. Written assessments also mean they will be taken much more seriously by both assessors and the assessed.

Ritchie and Dale (2000) have identified the following criteria which are necessary for a successful self-assessment process:

- Gaining commitment and support from all levels of staff.
- Action being taken from previous self-assessments.
- Awareness of the use of the model as a measurement tool.
- Incorporation of self-assessment into the business planning process.

	Self-assessment approaches												
Prerequisite TQM-related characteristics (of company/business unit)	A	B	C	D	E	F	G	H	I	J	K	L	M
● Visibility of direction	✔	✔		✔									
● Specified aims/goals	✔	✔	✔	✔	✔	✔	✔	✔	✔	✔	✔	✔	✔
● Holistic approach to strategy, planning, processes and human resources	✔	✔	✔	✔	✔	✔	✔				✔	✔	✔
● Total acceptance of quality ethos	✔	✔	✔	✔	✔	✔	✔	✔	✔	✔	✔	✔	✔
● Top management leadership	✔	✔		✔									
● Top-down, bottom-up involvement	✔	✔											
● Multi-faceted, innovative management	✔	✔	✔	✔	✔	✔	✔	✔	✔	✔			
● Managers with the ability to lead and motivate	✔	✔		✔			✔	✔				✔	
● Enthusiastic managers and staff	✔	✔	✔	✔	✔	✔	✔	✔	✔	✔	✔	✔	✔
● Continuous development and training encouraged	✔	✔		✔	✔	✔	✔						
● Continuous improvement strategy active	✔	✔	✔	✔	✔	✔	✔	✔	✔	✔	✔	✔	✔
● Continuous review of processes and systems	✔	✔	✔	✔	✔	✔	✔	✔	✔	✔	✔	✔	✔
● Benchmarking processes	✔	✔	✔	✔			✔						
● Incremental approach to improvement	✔	✔		✔	✔	✔	✔	✔	✔				
● Cross-functional interaction	✔	✔	✔	✔	✔	✔	✔	✔	✔	✔	✔	✔	✔
● Integration of quality initiatives into routine activities	✔	✔		✔	✔	✔	✔						
● Direct and open channels of communication	✔	✔	✔	✔	✔	✔	✔	✔	✔	✔	✔	✔	✔
● Working partnerships with external organisations (formal and informal)	✔	✔					✔						
● Employee empowerment	✔	✔		✔									
● Increased focus on customer needs and expectations	✔	✔		✔	✔	✔	✔	✔					

Figure 24.6 TQM-related characteristics associated with individual self-assessment approaches

- Not allowing the process to be 'added on' to employees' existing workload.
- Developing a framework for performance monitoring.

Van der Wiele et al. (1996), in summarizing the findings of their survey, point out that self-assessment has a greater chance of success if the following conditions exist:

- Senior management are committed to the process and get involved.
- The business unit (BU) management team develops an improvement plan from the outcomes.
- The outcomes from the self-assessment are linked to the business planning process.
- Senior management monitor targets for the improvement plan developed.
- The management team of a BU presents its plan to the senior management.
- The people who undertake the self-assessment receive relevant training.

It is always difficult to clarify the impact of self-assessment on an organization's business results. However, those organizations with considerable experience of self-assessment do have a very positive perception of the impact of the techniques on their business performance.

BOX 24.1   DIFFICULTIES EXPERIENCED WITH THE SELF-ASSESSMENT PROCESS

- Lack of commitment and enthusiasm
- The time-consuming nature of the process
- Not knowing where to start
- Selling the concept to the staff as something other than an 'add-on' to their existing duties
- People not realizing the need for documented evidence
- Lack of resources; time, manpower, finance
- Maintaining the self-assessment skills of the assessors
- Lack of cross-functional integration between departments and units
- Getting the assessment done in time to link it into the business plans

Source: Ritchie and Dale (2000)

Difficulties with Self-Assessment

There are a number of problems that hinder the self-assessment process: these are nicely summarized in box 24.1. Research carried out by Coulambidou and Dale (1995) indicates that these types of problems are created by a lack of senior management support, an inability to plan self-assessment effectively and a low level of TQM maturity.

One set of problems relates to scoring against the criteria of the model; these are identified by Yang et al. (2001), who argue:

> The credibility and acceptance of the results from the self-assessment process against the EFQM model is dependent upon many factors, including the variability of scores obtained; the non-scientific method in which the scores are determined; the subjective judgements of the assessors and how they interpret criteria; and assessor's knowledge of TQM/excellence/continuous improvement. These problems are compounded if the assessors are inexperienced and there is a mix of experienced and inexperienced assessors in the same assessment team.

They have developed a model based on the evidential reasoning approach from multiple attribute decision-making which, it is argued, helps to reduce the variability of the scoring amongst the members of a team selected to an organization's EQA application document in award simulation mode.

Summary

Self-assessment on a systematic basis by an organization against one of the models described in this chapter can prove extremely useful in assisting it to improve its business performance. However, if used in an artless manner by organizations just starting out on the quality journey and without an adequate vision of TQM by the senior management team it will not provide the necessary results and may even push the organization down blind alleys. It can also lead to the risk of gathering a considerable amount of data which is then not able to be put to effective use. When used in such a naive way the emphasis tends to be on training staff as assessors, assembling data, preparing long reports, and assessment and annual point-scoring, without the development of the all-important action plans and the solving of the day-to-day quality problems. The focus tends to be on meeting a minimum set number of points for an internal award and which activities should be concentrated on to increase the score by a set number of points, rather than what are the priorities to increase the velocity of the improvement process. As a consequence the ongoing day-to-day quality problems which beset the organization will not be resolved. It is also observed that senior management become obsessive about gaining some form of award (regional or national) within a set time-frame.

In using self-assessment it is important that management attention is focused on the identification and implementation of planned and prioritized improvements and not on the mechanics and techniques of the assessment process or an obsession with scoring points. If this is not done they will run into the problem of self-deception.

The benefit of using self-assessment against one of the recognized models is not the winning of the award but its adoption as a methodology to assess progress, using appropriate diagnostics, and identify opportunities for improvement, not forgetting the need to satisfy and delight customers. This measurement of progress on a regular basis and comparison of scores from assessments is a confirmation to the management team that real improvement and achievement have taken place. The quantification of performance in terms of numbers is important for senior management. It is also important that the management team of the organization should buy in to the self-assessment process and be enthusiastic about its use. This applies, in particular, to developing action plans to address the outcomes of the self-assessment. They must also be clear on their objectives for self-assessment. When used in the correct manner, the challenge, effort and involvement help to generate an environment in which it is enjoyable to work.

It would appear that the MBNQA and EQA have generated an industry of its own in running training courses and advising organizations about how to understand the assessment process and the detailed requirements of the award criteria. In organizations this often creates an internal expert who, after intensive external training, applies the knowledge gained in providing advice to the local management team as to how each of the individual criteria can be interpreted and applied to their own particular area of activity. A danger inherent in this is that the 'expert' keen to demonstrate their knowledge ends up in detailed discussion on the mechanics of self-assessment and consequently the purpose of self-assessment is often lost. Another worrying trend is that some organizations seem to believe that using one of the models as the standard and almost as a checklist will automatically lead them to TQM. In such organizations people will continually use the terms 'excellence model' and 'quality award' almost as a talisman to guarantee that all will be right with their continuous improvement efforts. There is also the danger of treating self-assessment against one of the recognized models as a panacea, which is clearly not the case.

An organization has to be fairly advanced in TQM to be able to use self-assessment in an effective manner: what is not in place cannot be assessed. Registration to the requirements of ISO9001 can be a useful first step towards TQM; however, there is a large gap between these requirements and what is portrayed in the EFQM and MBNQA models. Those organizations which have recently acquired ISO9001 registration, and are not advanced in their quality management activity, would benefit from studying one of these models to gain an insight into what is necessary in order to develop a TQM approach to managing the business. Having identified the gap, they need to look at methods of introducing the basics of TQM, such as a consultancy package, the teachings of the quality management gurus, or a simple improvement framework. Once the basics are in place the organization should return to self-assessment to assess progress, and identify the next steps.

References

BS EN ISO9000 (2000) *Quality Management Systems: Fundamentals and Vocabulary.* London: British Standards Institution.

Blodgett, N. (1999), Service organisations increasingly adopt Baldrige model. *Quality Progress,* December, 74–6.

Brown, M. G. (2000), *Baldrige Award-Winning Quality: How to Interpret the Baldrige Criteria for Performance Excellence,* 3rd edn. Milwaukee: ASQ Quality Press.

Cole, R. E. (1991), Comparing the Baldrige and Deming awards. *Journal for Quality and Participation,* July–August, 94–104.

Cole, R. E. (1999), *Managing Quality Fads.* New York: Oxford University Press.

Conti, T. (1993), *Building Total Quality: A Guide to Management.* London: Chapman & Hall.

Conti, T. (1997), *Organisational Self-Assessment.* London: Chapman & Hall.

Coulambidou, L. and Dale, B. G. (1995), The use of quality management self-assessment in the UK: a state-of-the-art study. *Quality World Technical Supplement,* September, 110–18.

Dale, B. G. (1993), The key features of Japanese total quality control. *Quality and Reliability Engineering International,* 9(3), 169–78.

Deming Prize Committee (1998), *The Deming Prize Guide for Overseas Companies.* Tokyo: Union of Japanese Scientists and Engineers.

Deming Prize Committee (2000), *The Deming Prize Guide for Overseas Companies.* Tokyo: Union of Japanese Scientists and Engineers.

de Dommartin, A. (2000), Moving the excellence model. *Quality World,* May, 12–14.

EFQM (1999), *Assessing for Excellence: A Practical Guide for Self-Assessment.* Brussels: EFQM.

EFQM (2002),*The EFQM Excellence Model.* Brussels: EFQM.

European Quality (2000), National quality awards: annual review. *European Quality,* 7(1), 14–29.

Hakes, C. (2000), *The Business Excellence Assessment Handbook,* 5th edn. Bristol: British Quality Centre.

Hillman, P. G. (1994), Making self-assessment successful. *The TQM Magazine,* 6(3), 29–31.

Karapetrovic, S. and Willborn, W. (2001), Audit and self-assessment in quality management: comparison and compatibility. *Managerial Auditing Journal,* 16(6), 366–77.

Lascelles, D. M. and Peacock, R. (1996), *Self-Assessment for Business Excellence.* Berkshire: McGraw Hill.

Nabitz, U., Quaglia, G. and Wangen, P. (1999), EFQM's new excellence model. *Quality Progress,* October, 118–20.

Nakhai, B. and Neves, J. (1994), The Deming, Baldrige and European quality awards. *Quality Progress,* April, 33–7.

Porter, L. and Tanner, S. (1996), *Assessing Business Excellence.* London: Butterworth Heinemann.

Ritchie, L. and Dale, B. G. (2000), Self-assessment using the business excellence model: a study of practice and process. *International Journal of Production Economics,* 66(3), 241–54.

Sherer, F. (1995), Winning the European quality award: a Xerox perspective. *Managing Service Quality*, 5(2), 28–32.

Soin, S. (1992), *Total Quality Control Essentials: Key Elements, Methodologies, and Managing for Success*. New York: McGraw Hill.

Steeples, M. M. (1993), *The Corporate Guide to the Malcolm Baldrige National Quality Award*. Milwaukee: ASQC Quality Press.

US Department of Commerce (2001), *Baldrige National Quality Program 2001: Criteria for Performance Excellence*. Gaithersburg: US Department of Commerce, National Institute of Standards and Technology.

van der Wiele, T., Williams, R. T., Dale, B. G., Kolb, F., Luzon, D. M., Wallace, M. and Schmidt, A. (1995), Quality management self-assessment: an examination in European business. *Journal of General Management*, 22(1), 48–67.

van der Wiele, T., Williams, R. T., Dale, B. G., Kolb, F., Luzon, D. M., Wallace, M. and Schmidt, A. (1996), Self-assessment: a study of progress in Europe's leading organisations in quality management practices. *International Journal of Quality and Reliability Management*, 13(1), 84–104.

Vokurka, R. J., Stading, G. L. and Brazeal, J. (2000), A comparative analysis of national and regional quality awards. *Quality Progress*, August, 41–9.

Yang, J.-B., Dale, B. G. and Siow, C. H. R. (2001), Self-assessment of excellence: an application of the evidential reasoning approach. *International Journal of Production Research*, 39(6), 3789–3812.

part four

TQM through
Continuous Improvement

This epilogue chapter draws together some of the common themes which have emerged in the individual chapters. It covers a number of issues, including:

- The importance of quality
- TQM as a continuous process
- Measuring progress towards TQM

The chapter also identifies and describes a number of TQM issues to which organizations need to give attention if they are to achieve world-class quality status. These issues also present potential research challenges.

Chapter 25 – Managing Quality: Epilogue

chapter | twenty-five

Managing Quality: Epilogue

B. G. Dale

Introduction

This concluding chapter of *Managing Quality* pulls together the main themes and strands running through the book and identifies issues to which organizations will need to give particular attention in the future. It opens by examining what quality means to different people and its importance in business transactions. The case is made that improvement is a continuous process which is systematic, incremental and cyclic. It is argued that the senior management of an organization are always keen to know both where they are positioned in relation to the competition and also their perceived status within the industry and the marketplace. The means of carrying out such an assessment are explored. The chapter (and the book) is concluded by outlining a number of issues to which organizations will need to give more attention if they are to achieve world-class quality status.

The Importance of Quality

Most people now accept that quality is an important business issue. But what is quality? What do people mean when they speak of the quality of product, service, communications, or people? It is important for them to have a clear understanding of what they mean when the word is used in whatever context, so they know what to do to attain it and to continuously improve on it. It is unfortunate that there are so many different interpretations of quality. But by being amenable to wide and differing interpretations it remains appropriate in widely differing situations and circumstances. Thus it has a unifying effect, in that all genuine aspirations to improve are known to be going in the same direction, irrespective of the definitions of quality in individual cases. Indeed it may be that quality has become a common goal rather more readily than other desirable aims (e.g. productivity, profit, market share) simply because everyone understands its importance and can identify with it. It perhaps matters little that the designer, the human resources manager, the operations manager, the manufacturing engineer, the salesman, the installer, and the service engineer all have different interpretations of quality to assist them in developing their own contributions to the total quality image. The total quality image is the sum of a set of attributes, each of which has its own quality criteria. However, it is the responsibility of senior management to see to it that every contributor plays his or her part fully in fashioning the image (i.e. the image held by the customer) of the organization and its products and services.

Common threads running through all the contributions to this book are that customers are increasingly demanding improvements in the quality of products and services they receive and that the provision, improvement and maintenance of quality have become an important part of business policy in superior-performing enterprises. It is rare these days to find a thriving and successful organization where quality is not a basic business principle integrated with corporate objectives and strategies. Many businesses are experiencing massive changes in customer expectations (e.g. rapid changes in technology, pressure for instantaneous delivery, radical changes in distribution methods and an attitude of 'more value for less money'). An organization which does not continually satisfy its customers' needs and expectations will almost inevitably suffer a fall in market share and return on assets and, in certain sectors, could lose its 'licence to operate', to use a term from *Tomorrow's Company* (RSA 1995). Indeed it is significant that an increasing number of organizations are talking not just about satisfying customers but delighting them, by exceeding and going beyond their expectations (e.g. meeting latent requirements); selling value to the customer is a prime organizational theme. The enlightened executive knows that, while price and delivery are negotiable, quality in its widest sense is not.

There are also clear signs that the argument that ensuring products and services conform to customer requirements causes productivity to fall and costs to rise is now recognized by many executives as being fallacious; quality and productivity improvements and cost reduction should always be joint organizational objectives in striving for good business results.

TQM: A Continuous Process

From the contributions to this book the reader should have got the clear message that improvement is a process which, once started, should never end, with all employees getting to grips with changing the organization in a gradual manner. This process of improvement also concentrates on the elimination of waste and non-value-added activity through the creative involvement of all employees. The process is based on systematic, incremental and habitual improvement rather than, for example, relying on 'breakthrough' and 'innovative' advances as is the case with BPR. The argument advanced is that small-step improvements are cumulative in nature and can ultimately lead to a greater overall effect than a single large and radical change, which can lose its value with time (see Imai 1986 and chapter 1 above). It should be said that TQM can also deliver 'breakthrough' or 'outrageous' improvements through activities such as benchmarking.

A question commonly encountered is, 'How will an organization know when it has achieved total quality management?' The short answer is that it won't. Because TQM is based on a continuous process which is both proactive and reactive to changing needs, the marketplace, the environment, the business and to its customers and competitors, an organization will never arrive at TQM; it can only keep going further along the road. Phrases commonly used to describe this are 'a race without a finishing line', 'a road without an end' and 'attempting to get to the bottom of a rainbow'.

There are many ways of getting a TQM approach incorporated into an organization's day-to-day activities. There is no single route leading to success; different management styles and corporate cultures will need to take different paths. The introduction and subsequent development of TQM must be led by the company's senior managers and it must be accepted from the outset that it will be liable to setbacks, owing mainly to resistance to change (see chapter 7). There will be points in the process at which little headway will appear to be made, and only if the senior management team is monitoring the process proactively using a set of key metrics will it be able to act positively in order to maintain progress. Management's commitment to TQM must be demonstrated to all employees through, for example, the time they devote to the concept, their day-to-day leadership actions, behaviour and decision-making, and by proving to employees that they genuinely care about improvement.

It is also wise for an organization to understand that its competitors are making continual advances and that, to catch up or keep ahead, it is necessary to develop the process at a faster rate than that which the competition are achieving; today's state of the art, delight and latent features become tomorrow's standard performance. Because competitors' position can never be known with certainty, there is no prudent alternative other than to pursue perfection in all aspects of organizational activity.

Measuring Progress towards TQM

The evidence presented by the contributors to this book corroborates the case argued in chapter 1: that there are distinct stages or levels in the evolution of quality management, the stages being broadly characterized as inspection, quality control, quality assurance and TQM. It is evident that in some organizations, because of the type of business they are in, their cultures, systems, and procedures will be heavily biased towards inspection and quality-control-type activities. Clearly these organizations will have greater difficulty in progressing from one stage to the next than companies without such limitations and they will tend to display the characteristics of 'uncommitted', 'drifters' or 'tool-pushers' rather than 'improvers', as outlined in chapter 6.

The issues which seem to concern executives are where they stand in relation to their competitors, and their perceived status within the industry and the marketplace. There are many widely accepted business performance criteria which can be applied using readily available information. Examples are market share, sales turnover, volume of exports, profit, return on net assets, yield performance, share price, manufacturing output, complexity of the product or service and its prestige, and sophistication of technology and systems. However, a company's senior managers should be no less interested in issues such as the organization's progress towards TQM, the effectiveness of its quality assurance and improvement activities, and the efficacy of its expenditure on promoting TQM. This assessment of quality standing is not as straightforward as assessing other aspects of the organization. Scrap rates, process yield performances, process capability indices, quality costs, non-conformances found at product audit, customer complaints, warranty claims, service quality index, number of hours of defect-free operations recorded by employees and departments, numbers of quality-related incidents, and the number of product recall programmes are all measures which can provide some indication of a company's progress from an internal baseline, but it is unlikely that similar detailed data will be available from competitors, even though there is an increased sharing of data through the formation of benchmarking clubs and other types of networks. If no such comparative data are available, and there are no absolute measures, the question remains how to gauge a company's progress towards TQM.

This kind of assessment can be approached in a number of ways:

- By regular assessment of the progress being made by a company against internal benchmarks, including past performance and a 'perfect' situation. It is usual to quantify these key measurables and plot and monitor their performance over time.
- Self-assessment of internal performance using the EFQM and MBNQA models' criteria.
- By general comparison of the level of TQM activity against companies of high standing within and outside the particular industrial sector, for example, by benchmarking.
- Analysis of internal and external audit results and assessments by people external to the company.
- By attempting to understand how an outside independent observer might see the company.

These different approaches raise again the question of the definition of quality.

- The first measure, using internal benchmarks, will employ scrap costs, level of quality costs, customer complaints, quality levels as measured by the customer, number of line complaints raised at customer plants, defect reports, etc. as its measures, (i.e. quality can be expressed in numbers).
- The second measure is critical self-assessment of the organization's activities and results against a specific framework and set of criteria. For each of the EFQM model's nine criteria, data are available on the scores achieved by the 'best in class' per criterion for applicants.
- The third measure, comparison with companies of high standing, will use published information, visits to companies and discussions with managers, and will be concerned with advanced quality planning, improvement teams, SPC, mistake-proofing, quality skills and competencies, cycle time reduction, internal recognition, etc. Thus the measures of quality become subjective assessment of tools and techniques in use, systems in place, sophistication of TQM, and achievements and benefits.
- The fourth measure will mainly be concerned with reports and comments on systems, planning carried out, attitudes of management, training undertaken and customer awards based on such criteria.
- In the fifth measure, an outside observer, who is not necessarily knowledgeable about TQM, will have other criteria. This could very well be the end-user or customer, who may not be able to articulate their views and subsequently vote with their feet. Their judgement will probably be subjective, perhaps

based on superficial knowledge of the product or service, perhaps based on little experience, and influenced by hearsay and propaganda. Their measures of quality will include appearance, utility, cost, value for money, reported performance, reliability and serviceability. This type of qualitative assessment can extend beyond the product and/or service by making a judgement on the manner in which the producer, seller, or service-provider conducts their business (i.e. ethical, moral, economic and environmental issues).

Clearly these measures are so different it is not possible to reconcile them one with another, and managers must make the best judgements they can from them.

However, it is the in-house measures of quality and those based on customers' direct measures of product and service quality which are of the most immediate and direct use because they are the most visible, meaningful and motivational to the company's workforce. Among the in-house and active performance indicators which surface when attempting to assess an organization's standing with respect to TQM are:

- Scores attained using the EFQM or MBNQA models' criteria.
- Number of second- and third-party approvals and regional and national quality awards held.
- Number of preferred supplier-status awards held.
- Scores allocated by customers in their formal assessments of the organization's quality management system.
- Strengths and weaknesses of the quality management system indicated in a second- or third-party assessment.
- Frequency of quality management system failures.
- Internal and external quality levels per product, production line, and service.
- Lead time and schedule compliance.
- Number of defect-free hours of work registered by employees and departments.
- Total quality costs.
- Process capability indices.
- Number and type of tools and techniques employed, the order in which they were adopted, and how they are integrated one with another.
- Proportion of indirect personnel employed in the quality department.
- Number of invoice queries.
- Time taken to respond to customer problems.
- Number of people in the organization who recognize the difference between a quick fix and long-term corrective action, who get to the root cause of a problem rather than merely curing symptoms, and who react to the signal from a process rather than the noise.
- Resources allocated by management to long-term corrective actions, including budget and staff.
- Training budget as a percentage of annual sales and extent of staff training in TQM.
- Number of improvement teams in operation.
- Number of staff and areas involved in teamwork and improvement activities.
- Number of improvement projects being pursued and those which are successfully completed.
- Proportion of staff who have identified their internal customers and suppliers.

- Proportion of employees who practise continuous improvement.
- Proportion of employees who are satisfied that the company is customer-focused.
- Proportion of employees who are satisfied that the company is a 'quality' organization.
- Number of agreed departmental performance measures being used.
- Number of staff who speak the common language of improvement.
- Customer access to staff and attitudes of staff to customer complaints.
- Number of product recall programmes.
- Number of new products and services introduced and time to market.
- Staff turnover and absenteeism rate.
- Training days per person each year.

While in-house performance indicators are important, it is the customer assessment of the product and/or service which really counts, and it is important to have a set of measures which reflect the customer's viewpoint. There are a variety of means used to assess customer perceptions, obtain customer feedback and understand the marketplace, including surveys, interviews, customer-focus meetings, clinics, shows, product launches, mystery shoppers and field contacts (see chapters 5 and 11). It is helpful to combine the data collected in this way into a customer satisfaction index.

The measurement of progress in continuous improvement and TQM is now being written about in the literature. Burstein and Sedlock (1988), Saraph et al. (1989), Schaffer and Thomson (1992) and Wortham (1988), amongst others, touch on the subject. Crosby's (1979) quality management maturity grid and the spectrum of the quality management implementation grid of Dale and Smith (1997) detail some milestones on the journey of transformation and of course the criteria of the MBNQA and EFQM excellence models provide extremely useful route maps.

Measurement of performance and progress in meaningful terms is a difficult subject and one to which more research effort needs to be devoted. However, it is vital to review the performance trend of the key measurables to ensure that the improvement initiatives and projects are having the desired impact and that the organization is progressing towards world class.

TQM Issues which Need to be Considered in the Future

Chapter 1 was brought to a close by outlining a number of issues which need to be considered by an organization to help it develop TQM. Here I conclude *Managing Quality* by listing a number of issues to which organizations will need to give more attention if they are to achieve world-class quality status.

1   Tools and techniques such as self-assessment (chapter 24), statistical process control (chapter 20), failure mode and effects analysis (chapter 19), quality costing (chapter 9), design of experiments (chapter 18), quality function deployment (chapter 17), mistake-proofing (chapter 16), benchmarking (chapter 21), and the seven management tools (chapter 16) will continue to be seen as part of the core quantitative disciplines employed by an increasing number of organizations as important aids in facilitating and measuring

continuous improvement. More attention will focus on the less-used tools and techniques, such as policy deployment (chapter 8), quality function deployment and the seven management tools, in particular the latter for making the best use of qualitative data in relation to the application of QFD. The assessment of business process re-engineering (chapter 22) will continue with respect to its role in business improvement and its connection with TQM. The EFQM and MBNQA excellence models will become increasingly recognized by business as general management models useful as a starting point which individual business units then need to develop to fit their own situations. It is expected the misuse of such models will tend to decrease as managers become familiar with them, rely less on the use of management consultancies, the hype surrounding them dies away and management consultants switch their attention to the latest money-generating concept.

There is considerable scope for improving the use and exploitation of tools and techniques, and organizations need to give consideration to a number of issues, including a route map for their use and application, identifying which tools and techniques should be used together, the type of organizational changes which are needed to make the most effective use of tools and techniques, the role that particular tools and techniques play, ensuring that people make the best use of tools and techniques and, in particular, remembering the purpose of the tools they are applying, and the use of assessment methods to evaluate the use of tools and techniques (see Dale and McQuater 1998).

The importance of quality will come to the fore in e-commerce in the near future (chapter 13). One of the challenges will be to explore and adapt the quality tools and techniques to the e-commerce environment. For example as Duffy and Dale (2002) report, QFD can be used to capture the voice of the customer and the data used to build a website that the customer wants; SPC can be employed to monitor the voice of the process, to check if the processes are in control and provide guidance for improvement; and design of experiments can be used to find the optimum interaction of technical features in a site with marketing requirements.

There will be an increasing emphasis on the use of an evidential reasoning approach and multiple attribute decision methods by researchers to quality management issues. Yang et al. (2001) show how these methods have been used in the self-assessment process against the criteria of the EFQM model to help minimize scoring variation.

2 In relation to the collection and use of quality costs, activity-based costing and throughput accounting will grow in importance. Other issues which need to be evaluated include the different approaches and strategies that can be employed in the identification and collection of quality costs, development of quality cost models, justification of investment in prevention-type activities, development of quality cost performance indicators, and the best means of identifying and reporting 'bottom-line' and intangible benefits to demonstrate the effectiveness of TQM.

3 A considerable number of organizations have based their quality systems on the ISO9000 series of quality standards (chapter 14), or those of a major purchaser (e.g. QS9000). Looking forward, organizations without an ISO9001 certificate of registration will find it increasingly difficult to do business in

the world marketplace; this trend will be reinforced by the exponential interest of American industry in the series, driven by QS9000. However, this series of quality management system standards should be regarded by organizations as the minimum, and the objective should be to surpass the specified requirements. In particular, the challenge is to develop effective preventative disciplines and mechanisms and ensure that these drive continuous improvement and broaden the vision from being merely a paperwork system audit. It is predicted that the development of environmental management systems to meet the requirements of ISO14001 will help to make quality management systems which are based on the ISO9000 series more improvement-orientated.

4   Many SMEs have got ISO9001 registration and remain stuck on this quality management foundation stone. They require simple, effective and pragmatic advice on what are the next steps on the improvement journey. The TQM framework outlined in chapter 5 has proved an effective means of providing this guidance to aid development. The challenge is providing SMEs with practical and pragmatic advice, in appropriate and easily understandable stages, which can move them from ISO9000 series registration to EQA prizewinner status. However, the gap between the requirements of the ISO9000 series and the holistic nature of the EFQM excellence model cannot be bridged just by taking another list of criteria by which an organization can be measured. More of the basics need to be put in place before the EFQM model can be effectively used for assessing an organization; see van der Wiele et al. (1997).

5   There will be a development in the direction of integrating quality into the normal management procedures and operations of a business (chapter 15). This will be aided by the development of integrated management systems dealing with quality management, environment, occupational health and safety and data protection; see Wilkinson and Dale (1998).

6   Attention needs to be given to developing, in a continuous manner, the problem-solving skills, competencies and talents of all employees in the organization.

7   The impact of corporate culture on TQM and vice versa needs to be fully evaluated. Amongst the issues that need to be examined are:

   • How does an organization develop its culture so that everyone is committed to continuous improvement?
   • What is the best means of managing the change process?
   • Did those companies which are successful with TQM have a culture, prior to its introduction, different from that typified by traditionally managed companies?
   • What was the predominant management style?
   • What is the best means of facilitating such changes in traditionally managed organizations, in particular those in public ownership and monopoly/regulated supply situations and also in government departments?
   • How, when, where and at what pace does culture change take place?
   • What are the best means of measuring change?
   • How to change the attitudes of middle management?
   • How to ensure that production/operations personnel think quality as well as numbers and do not just value costs?

- What are the best means of empowering people to take ownership of their own quality and its improvement?
- What is the effect of national cultures on TQM?
- Are the impediments to progress common across different cultures?
- How can TQM be developed in a downsizing situation?

8   In this current age of privatization, contracting out of government services and pressure for value-for-money services, government departments, public services and service providers are coming under increasing pressure to pursue excellence. In these organizations the challenge is how to effectively apply the principles and mechanisms of continuous improvement and change the 'civil service' mentality which typically exists in such environments.

9   Continuous improvement initiatives must reach every part of an organization and every employee and every function needs to be involved if TQM is to become total. Quality needs to be seen and treated as an integral part of each department's activities. However, some functions and staff are more resistant to the concept of TQM than others. How to convert the cynics, 'blockers' and 'resisters' is a major problem in most organizations, and the same can be said for ensuring that improvement becomes a daily issue in situations when resources and people are already fully stretched and feel overworked. A related issue which needs attention is how to measure the 'conversion' of cynics – lip-service versus commitment.

There is a set of issues relating to employee relations including:

- What is the role of employee representation in TQM and will it have a diminishing or increasing influence?
- What are the effects of the democratizing process in TQM and the increasing values placed on the workforce and their skills on the traditional balance of power in the workplace?
- What, if any, effects will European labour laws have on TQM?

10   Quality will continue to permeate every function of an organization and become more integrated with business activities. More organizations will start to use policy deployment as the means to align all efforts in the organization towards its major goals. The role of the quality professional will need to change in response to this trend of increasing integration in both an operational and strategic sense. Bertsch et al. (1999a and 1999b) provide some details of the logic behind this and what will be required of quality managers/directors in the future. They argue that, when TQM is considered by an organization to be of strategic importance, fundamental changes will be needed not only in the role of the quality manager but in the type of skills they possess.

11   There will be a greater focus on process streams linked directly to customer groups and suppliers, replacing the traditional function-oriented structure. The challenge will be to integrate these process streams owned by different business organizations and align them to satisfy the requirements of a common end-user and to exploit specific market opportunities.

12   The best means of managing and organizing across a number of sites and locations is an issue being faced by many businesses with multi-site operations, in particular, when this embraces a number of countries. They typically seek answers to questions such as: What is the right type of organization,

structure and framework? What are the benefits of a controlled and managed development across sites compared with a 'do as they feel fit' approach? How to cater for site-to-site and country-to-country differences?

13   Revitalizing TQM after a period of stagnation is currently being faced by a number of organizations. Typical issues which organizations are wrestling with include: Why has stagnation occurred? Is it a natural phenomenon? What are the best means of revitalization? Chapters 5, 6 and 7 provide some guidance to identifying these problems and what can be done to overcome them. Most people in an organization will know why TQM has stagnated, but of more immediate concern is what is the best means of getting it going again and sustaining its momentum. This will continue in the future, with management coping with the effects of redundancy, recession, organizational restructuring, downsizing and changes in senior management, products, services and process and attempting to minimize the effects of these on TQM.

14   Many of the quality initiatives launched over the last 20 or so years have been cast aside and superseded by new ones. However, many initiatives have left positive deposits in the form of changes in organizational processes, systems and culture, which when built upon can potentially lead to an organization managing in a total quality manner: see Dale et al. (2002). The quality movement will continue to learn from these initiatives and integrate the lessons into the organizational memory. Further research needs to be done as to which combination of quality initiatives, taking into account different organizational environments, structures and culture, produces the greatest effect in embedding a TQM approach into an organization and thereby developing the necessary deep organizational changes, resulting in business performance improvement.

15   Some organizations are facing a situation which is much more difficult to deal with than TQM stagnation. This is when all improvement initiatives have collapsed and nothing more than ISO9001 registration remains. They require guidance on the best means of rekindling the process. This needs to take into account the conditions which caused the current problem and whether they have changed, the views from different levels of the organizational hierarchy on the reasons for the failure, current attitudes, what initiatives to take up, etc. Chapters 5, 6 and 7 provide some clues.

16   A number of companies which have received considerable publicity because of their perceived success with TQM have built up myths supported by considerable and readily available documentation of how good they are. The rhetoric surrounding this is perpetuated both inside and outside the organization. At the operating level of these businesses the reality often does not live up to the communicated word and what senior and some middle management believe the situation to be, in particular, at corporate headquarters. For example:

- There is a detailed and fully documented policy deployment procedure but it is all top-down cascade with little 'catchball', bottom-up feedback and little audit of the agreed plans and targets.
- It is a requirement that every business unit carries out a self-assessment which is subject to peer review but the plans to address the chosen areas for improvement are only given serious attention Prior to such a review taking place.

A challenge facing the senior managers of these organizations is to have the courage to stop believing their own self-perpetuating story of success, understand why things have not happened at the grassroots of the business as was intended by the corporate headquarters, and address the deficiencies to ensure that the message gets through to the operation; this requires strong and committed leadership.

17   Organizations should have measures of performance based on hard measures of customer satisfaction. The measures should be regularly monitored and fed back to all internal suppliers and customers (chapters 5 and 11) and a system of planning put in place to close any gaps between actual performance and expectations. The relevance and value of these measures will continue to present a challenge to management.

18   Teamwork in all its forms should be encouraged and the different types of team activity need to be integrated to get the best influence of synergy (chapter 23). Attention needs to be paid to which teams work best in which situations and why, and the effects that teams have on the day-to-day operation of a section/department.

19   Winning the 'hearts and minds' of all employees and cultivating motivation and commitment amongst the workforce is and will remain a key issue. The senior management team must work harder at sharing the organization's vision, mission and values and ensuring that they become a reality, and also at fostering and promoting an environment where people feel secure, trusted, and respected. Selfishness and indifference to the problems of others works against continuous improvement.

20   Timely and accurate data are a prerequisite of effective, quality-related decision-making. Quality information systems and quality databases need to be developed further in order to facilitate this, feedback of data internally and externally being a key issue.

21   A high proportion of quality problems are caused by poor communications. Organizations need to develop effective methods and channels which encourage open and honest communication in terms everyone can understand between employees at all levels, and between themselves, their suppliers, and their customers; chapter 5 provides some good examples. In this way employees will be encouraged to question what is done and why things are done in a certain way. Many major purchasers are using electronic data interchange systems in order to communicate more effectively with their supplier communities (chapter 12).

22   A key concern of major organizations is how to develop effective working relationships with their supplier base and jointly pursue improvement initiatives (chapter 12). While there have been a number of attempts at these, doubts still remain among some major purchasers about their ability to convert all their suppliers to TQM and, where it is possible, the most effective means of achieving it and integrating them into the improvement process. One clear principle for success is that the purchaser must be a good role model. There is also evidence that some organizations talk partnership but, in practice, do not act it. There are also different kinds of partnerships, and organizations must decide which best suits them and their suppliers. These type of issues are explored in Burnes and Dale (1998); they will continue to dominate the partnership sourcing and supplier development literature

throughout this decade. In the 'Working in Partnership with Stakeholders' section of *Tomorrow's Company* (RSA 1995) the following very relevant point is made:

> Tomorrow's company views key suppliers as true extensions of the company. It sets *target costs* and pursues them jointly with suppliers, sharing information and new ideas to reduce waste and improve performance. *Yesterday's companies regard suppliers as interchangeable vendors. They see cost cutting as a zero-sum game by which profits are increased only at the expense of suppliers.*

23 Quality must start with education. Organizations must invest to train employees at all levels in improvement skills in order to facilitate changes in behaviour and attitude; they must decide what type of improvement training is required and how this training should be conducted and used. In spite of all the quality propaganda, many production/operations people still view their first priority as meeting the production schedule, quota and cost targets. Only after achieving these objectives will they give some consideration to quality performance; habits of a lifetime are slow in dying. Having said this, there is an increasing realization that, while meeting the schedule pays salaries, shipping product which does not conform to the customer's requirements is self-defeating. This change in view is more likely to take place in organizations where the CEO and members of the senior management team act as role models.

24 It is vital that members of the senior management team continue to develop their understanding of TQM (chapters 1, 2, 3 and 4). A key issue is how to keep management's attention focused on TQM and ensure that they devote sufficient time to improvement activities and initiatives. A similar issue is how to maintain a strategic focus on a small number of projects. It is not uncommon to find that management believe they need to justify their TQM endeavours along with the requisite improvement resources. Detailed examination of why profitable businesses fail may help to provide the right type of evidence on this matter. More detailed guidance is required on what type of activities senior management should be involved with and what they need to do about TQM. Senior management also need help on the best means of conveying their commitment throughout the organization. The efforts made by both senior and middle management are often not visible to junior members of staff, who will often comment on their lack of perceived commitment, when this is not the case.

25 In the late 1980s and the 1990s there was almost a clarion call (e.g. Wilkinson 1992) that the reason why some introductions of TQM had been unsuccessful was a lack of focus on the so-called 'soft' issues of TQM. The EFQM model, with people management and people satisfaction being the next largest elements after customer satisfaction in terms of the number of available points, should have changed this perception. A future challenge is to decide how much influence the model has had on these people and soft quality issues, in particular management style.

26 The subject of TQM is now being given more attention in the European higher educational system, and courses featuring the subject are on the increase (see van der Wiele and Dale 1996). This trend needs to be encouraged

because, until TQM is recognized as a subject in its own right, the brightest young people will be deterred from studying it and the best graduates will not be attracted into the quality profession. An issue currently under debate is whether TQM should be taught as a separate subject in relation to under-graduate and postgraduate degrees awarded in quality management or as an essential component of all courses, in particular, at postgraduate level. Another debate starting to surface is whether universities and business schools should be structuring their MBA courses around the EFQM model.

Organizations, in the main, have some difficulty in seeing the need for TQM research by the academic fraternity, its relevance to their immediate requirements, how they might use the findings and in identifying the start-ing point for collaboration. A challenge facing the worlds of business and academia is to develop a closer working relationship with each other.

Two important factors hindering the development of TQM in European business is the shortage of able people qualified to take up quality manage-ment positions and the lack of exposure to quality management principles and methods of recently recruited graduates. The more advanced organiza-tions now see the function of quality management as crucial to their corpor-ate success and are appointing suitably qualified people. With respect to the lack of quality management in the course curriculum of many undergraduate and postgraduate degree courses, this situation is now changing. An increasing number of universities and business schools are starting to teach TQM as part of their degree courses and, through such exposure, graduates start to recognize the potential of employment prospects in quality management (see van der Wiele and Dale 1996).

27 From a quality management perspective e-commerce is still relatively immat-ure. As it develops and starts to flatten the value chain it will be necessary to undertake quality management-related research using this environment as the focus. Preliminary work has already been undertaken in identifying the main quality issues involved in website design (Cox and Dale 2002) and exploring, using the service quality gap model, the key quality factors and determinants in satisfying customers when they interact with businesses over the internet (Cox and Dale 2001).

Summary

During the course of the UMIST research on TQM carried out over the last 20 or so years we have observed and been involved in a large number of TQM initiatives. A number of these have been successful, others not so. What are the reasons for this? The lack of success is certainly not related to the concept of TQM. Rather, it is the way in which TQM has been introduced. It is surprising how many fundamental mistakes are made by senior managers and their advisers (both internal and external) in relation to issues such as communication, training, infrastructure, teams and projects, involvement and measurement. In addition there is a fundamental failure to stick at the basics and a tendency to become distracted by in-vogue concepts, systems and techniques. These mistakes are avoidable through improved knowledge and understanding of the subject and better planning. I hope this book will assist on all three counts.

In drawing this book to a close I quote one of the reviewers of the manuscript, a senior production executive of a major British company:

I have found that reading the manuscript has helped me to reflect on:

1 The things that we could have done better.
2 Areas that have been well managed.
3 The topics that we need to concentrate on in the immediate future.
4 The longer-term issues.

With these thoughts in mind, happy reading!

References

Bertsch, B., Williams, A. R. T., van der Wiele, A. and Dale, B. G. (1999a), The right role for quality managers. *European Quality*, 6(2), 8–11.

Bertsch, B., Williams, A. R. T., van der Wiele, A. and Dale, B. G. (1999b), The quality manager as change agent. *European Quality*, 6(3), 50–4.

Burnes, B. and Dale, B. G. (eds) (1998), *Working in Partnerships: Best Practice in Customer–Supplier Relations*. Berkshire: McGraw Hill.

Burstein, C. and Sedlock, K. (1988), The federal quality and productivity improvement effort. *Quality Progress*, October, 38–41.

Cox, J. and Dale, B. G. (2001), Service quality and e-commerce: an explanatory analysis. *Managing Service Quality*, 11(2), 121–31.

Cox, J. and Dale, B. G. (2002), Key quality factors in website design and use: an examination. *International Journal of Quality and Reliability Management*, 19(7), 862–88.

Crosby, P. B. (1979), *Quality is Free*. New York: McGraw Hill.

Dale, B. G. and McQuater, R. E. (1998), *Managing Business Improvement and Quality: Implementing Key Tools and Techniques*. Oxford: Blackwell Business.

Dale, B. G. and Smith, M. (1997), Spectrum of quality management implementation grid: development and use. *Managing Service Quality*, 7(6), 307–11.

Dale, B. G., Williams, A. R. T., van der Wiele, A. and Greatbanks, R. W. (2002), Organisational change through quality deposits. *Quality Engineering*, 14(3), 381–9.

Duffy, G. and Dale, B. G. (2002), *E-Commerce Processes: A Study of Criticality, Industrial Management and Data Systems*, 102(8), 432–41.

European Foundation for Quality Management (1998), *Self-Assessment 1998: Guidelines for Companies*. Brussels: EFQM.

Imai, M. (1986), *Kaizen: the Key to Japan's Competitive Success*. New York: Random House.

RSA (1995), *Tomorrow's Company*. London: Royal Society for the Encouragement of Arts, Manufacturers and Commerce.

Saraph, J. V., Benson, P. G. and Schroeder, R. C. (1989), An instrument for measuring the critical factors of quality management. *Decision Sciences*, 20(6), 810–29.

Schaffer, R. H. and Thomson, H. A. (1992), Successful change programs begin with results. *Harvard Business Review*, January–February, 80–9.

US Department of Commerce (2001), *Baldrige National Quality Program 2001 Criteria for Performance Excellence*. Gaithersberg: US Department of Commerce, National Institute of Standards and Technology.

van der Wiele, A. and Dale, B. G. (1996), *Total Quality Management Directory 1996: TQM at European Universities and Business Schools*. Rotterdam: Rotterdam University Press.

van der Wiele, T., Dale, B. G. and Williams, A. R. T. (1997), ISO9000 series registration to total quality management: the transformation journey. *International Journal of Quality Science*, 2(4), 236–52.

Wilkinson, A. (1992), The other side of quality: soft issues and the human resources dimension. *Total Quality Management*, 3(3), 323–9.

Wilkinson, A. and Dale, B. (1998), Manufacturing companies' attitudes to system integration: a case study. *Quality Engineering*, 11(1), 249–56.

Wortham, A. W. (1988), Rating quality assurance programs. *Quality Progress*, September, 53–4.

Yang, J.-B., Dale, B. G. and Siow, C. H. R. (2001), Self-assessment of excellence: an application of the evidential reasoning approach. *International Journal of Production Research*, 39(6), 3789–3812.

Index